DRUGGING AMERICA

A Trojan Horse

Rodney Stich

Diablo Western Press

Library of Congress Catalog Card Number 99-94724

Stich, Rodney–Author

Drugging America–A Trojan Horse

1. Drugs–United States; 2. Drugs-Central Intelligence Agency; 3. Department of Justice; 4. Drug Enforcement Administration; 5. Federal Bureau of Investigation; 6. Immigration and Naturalization Services; 7. U.S. Customs Service; 8. Mexico; 9. Judges- corrupt; 10. Media; 11. Congress

Other related titles written by Rodney Stich:
  Unfriendly Skies–History of corruption and air disasters, 3rd ed. (ISBN-0-9648005-0-0)
  Defrauding America–Encyclopedia of Secret Operations by the CIA, DEA, and Other Covert Agencies, 3rd edition, hard cover (ISBN-0-932438-09-1)

Hard cover ISBN– 0-932438-10-5

Published and printed in the United States of America by Diablo Western Press, PO Box 5, Alamo, California 94507

Diablo Western Press, Inc., is a Nevada corporation.

Credit card orders (telephone): 1-800-247-7389; FAX 1-925-295-1203
Checks and credit card orders to Diablo Western Press, PO Box 5, Alamo, CA 94507

10 9 8 7 6 5 4 3 2 1

IN APPRECIATION

I have great appreciation for the many courageous people who contributed to the reporting of intrigue, arrogance, deception, and criminal misconduct of people in key positions in the three branches of the federal government that I personally discovered and documented. By their willingness to provide information and documentation to me, I have been motivated to continue my efforts to inform as many people as possible of the harm being inflicted by these government personnel upon all of America and particularly on thousands of individual men and women.

Without their assistance, this and my other books would be less complete and a smaller part of the bizarre story could be conveyed to the readers.

These people, numbering in the dozens, consist of present and past government agents and deep-cover operatives from such government agencies as the Central Intelligence Agency (CIA), Office of Naval Intelligence (ONI), Drug Enforcement Administration (DEA), Immigration and Naturalization Service (INS), U.S. Customs Service (USCS), Federal Bureau of Investigation (FBI), Federal Aviation Administration (FAA), Secret Service (SS), and state agencies. Also, prior drug traffickers and Mafia family members.

These sources either discovered the misconduct described within these pages as part of their official duties, or they were part of the activities, acting under orders.

In preparing this manuscript for the printer, appreciation is given to Glenda Guilinger for her proofreading. Having acquired her pilot's license at the age of 17, she is my "co-pilot" and partner who spent many hours going over the manuscript and helping with corrections and clarification.

DRUGGING AMERICA–A Trojan Horse

CONTENTS

Introduction   i

About the author   ii

INTRODUCTION

Drugging America is a documentary on arrogance and corruption in government, and the resulting harm inflicted upon innocent people. The purpose for writing this book is to inform as many people as possible of the dangers faced by men and women, and families, throughout the United States. The contents show that the so-called war-on-drugs is a cruel hoax upon the people of the United States by people holding key positions in the three branches of the federal government.

This book will alert the reader to many of the covert activities in government, including those that target innocent people, reducing the possibility that the reader and his or her family will become victimized.

The author and his many deep-cover sources provide the readers with hundreds of years of combined experience in the area of government corruption as it adversely affects everyone. The contents provide a fly-on-the-wall insight into covert activities that are being kept from the public through the complicity of many in the broadcast and print media, by members of Congress, and virtually every government and non-government check and balance.

Readers who become familiar with the contents of this book (and the author's third editions of *Unfriendly Skies* and *Defrauding America*) will acquire an unusual knowledge and an understanding of government activities that very few people understand.

Especially valuable to the reader will be an understanding of how innocent people are falsely charged with crimes through the actions of thousands of government agents and informants who must justify their position and pay by targeting people, such as you, and bring charges that can result in years of imprisonment and destruction of your family.

For those who have been sheltered from the inner workings of covert activities, many of the events described within these pages will be almost too bizarre to believe. The author, while he was an airline pilot in worldwide operations, probably was also in that category. It wasn't until he became an FAA inspector responsible for air safety at the most senior program at the world's largest airline that he started discovering corruption in government and how it was tragically affecting thousands of people.

i

ABOUT THE AUTHOR

The author spent much of his adult life in aviation, starting out as a Naval aviator in World War II. He was probably the youngest multiengine pilot instructor and four-engine patrol plane commander at that time, holding these positions before passing his 21st birthday.

For about 14 years after the war, he was an international airline captain, flying virtually every propeller aircraft operated by U.S. airlines. He was one of the first pilots licensed by Japan, holding pilot license number 170, which he obtained while flying captain for Japan Airlines in the 1950s.

His flying experiences covered flying Super Constellations and Boeing Stratocruisers in the high-density New York, Chicago, Washington area, and were often followed days later by flying monkeys from India (for the Salk polio vaccine program), flying Moslem pilgrims to Mecca from such places as Beirut, Jerusalem, Bagdad, Teheran and Abadan, while Middle East flying was in its primitive stage. He was trapped in an Iranian revolution in 1953 when Mossadeq was overthrown by the CIA's Shah.

In 1962 he joined the Federal Aviation Administration (FAA) as an air carrier operations inspector, and in time he was assigned responsibility for air safety at United Airlines on their most senior pilot program. It was here that he discovered the deadly politics of air safety with a culture of air safety and criminal violations that caused and made possible a series of fatal airline crashes.

Outraged by what he (and other) inspectors discovered, he conducted an unprecedented hearing similar to that of an independent counsel, bringing witnesses and their testimony, and hundreds of documents, into a four-month-long proceeding that confirmed his charges of corruption in management within the FAA and at United Airlines which was closely linked to a series of fatal airline crashes.

Upon leaving the FAA, he devoted years to investigating and exposing other forms of corruption involving government officials in all three branches of the federal government. In 1978, he published the first of three editions of *Unfriendly Skies*, seeking to inform people of the unpublicized corruption in government and hoping to motivate them into some kind of meaningful reaction.

He has appeared as guest and expert on more than 3,000 radio and television shows in the United States, Canada, and Europe. European television stations have sent crews to the United States for the sole purpose of filming him. His books have twice been considered for television series, the first time by producer Jackie Cooper.

His background as a pilot, and his efforts to expose government corruption, have caused more than three dozen present and former government agents to contact Rodney Stich since 1988. Since that time, he has been in almost daily contact with at least one or more of these sources which include agents and undercover operatives in the CIA, DIA, DEA, FBI, INS, Customs, Secret Service, as well as international drug traffickers, Mafia family members, and others. During hundreds of hours of conversations and hundreds of letters, they have provided him with little-known highly-sensitive information and hundreds of supporting documents, revealing a pattern of corruption that can be described as a "Trojan Horse" attack upon the United States and the American people.

ii

In his book *Unfriendly Skies*, he reveals the deadly politics of air safety, describing details behind many fatal airline crashes never before reported to the public. The book, *Defrauding America*, goes far beyond the aviation field, revealing and documenting corruption throughout government and in the media.

Stich has appeared as guest and expert on more than 3,000 radio and television shows since 1978 in the United States, Canada, and Europe. European television stations have sent crews to the United States to tape Stich for specific subjects, including aviation and the involvement in drugs by government personnel.

He holds an Airline Transport Pilot certificate issued in 1946, with type ratings in the following aircraft: DC-8 and Convair 880-990 jets; Boeing Stratocruisers; Lockheed Constellation; DC-3; DC-4; Martin 202-404; Convair 240-340-440; C-46. He has flown other aircraft including various Boeing jets, including the 707 and 720; Lockheed Electra; DC-6 and DC-7. He holds a flight engineer rating in piston and jet aircraft; aircraft dispatcher rating; ground instructor rating and formerly a flight instructor rating. His primary function as an FAA inspector was conducting competency and rating tests of airline pilots and issuing ratings enabling the pilots to legally fly the aircraft.

He has been a member, since its founding, of the International Society of Air Safety Investigators; the Lawyer-Pilots Bar Association; Association of Former Intelligence Officers, and others.

Stich has paid a terrible price for his attempts to make the public aware of the corrupt activities in government that have inflicted and will continue to inflict great personal and financial harm upon the men and women of the United States.

Twice he had been contacted for the purpose of a television series on his books, the first time by producer Jackie Cooper who wanted to do a three-part series on his first edition of *Unfriendly Skies*.

For more information about him, put "Rodney Stich" into Internet search engines. Also, look at the web sites:

www.druggingamerica.com   www.defraudingamerica.com
www.unfriendlyskies.com   www.ciadrugs.com

CHAPTER ONE

DECADES OF CIA DRUG TRAFFICKING

The CIA's role in drug trafficking into the United States has been the subject of investigative magazine and newspaper articles, books, congressional testimony, and television presentations, for decades. I first became aware of this practice in the 1950s while I was an airline pilot flying for Japan Airlines in Japan and while flying in the Middle East transporting Moslem pilgrims to Mecca. During casual conversations with other pilots, they talked about the drug loads they were transporting for CIA-related activities. At that time there was very little attention given to the drug trade and I was as indifferent to the problem as the remainder of the population.

Dozens of highly documented books have been written by people who investigated the subject or who were involved in some aspect of drug trafficking. One of the first highly detailed books linking the CIA to drug trafficking was Alfred McCoy's *The Politics of Heroin in Southeast Asia* published in 1972, and his heavily documented 1991 update *The Politics of Heroin, CIA – Complicity in the Global Drug Trade*. McCoy was a professor of Southeast Asian history at the University of Wisconsin in Madison and had made an exhaustive study of the CIA's involvement in drugs while living in various parts of the world. He started investigating the drug trafficking in the 1950s, questioning people in all phases of the drug culture from the growers to the end users. His books describe how CIA helicopters, supposedly fighting communists in Vietnam, were hauling drugs from the fields to distribution points, making possible the heavy drug sales to American GIs.

PepsiCo and Coca-Cola Involved in Drugs

McCoy described the role of the PepsiCo bottling plant in the drug processing. Adolfo Calero was an executive with the PepsiCo bottling plant in Nicaragua, and was identified in several congressional hearings as a known major drug trafficker. He worked with the National Security Council and the CIA in their war activities in Nicaragua. Statements given to me over the years by various deep-cover sources clearly show that the PepsiCo and Coca-Cola companies, or their agents in foreign countries were involved in the drug business. McCoy described the many people who testified in closed-door congressional hearings for the past twenty years, leaving no doubt that the CIA was involved and primarily responsible for the drug crisis in the United States. He described the pressure put upon the media by the CIA to halt his book.

Many other highly detailed books have been written about CIA drug trafficking by people who were part of the operation. These include, among others, *Dope, Inc.*; *The Big White Lie*; *Cocaine Politics*; *Out of Control*; *Bluegrass Conspiracy*; *The Cocaine Wars,* and *The Crimes of Patriots*. But only a fraction of one percent of the American people have read them, insuring that they remain ignorant about the criminal and subversive activities implicating their leaders in government.

Activist Colonel "Bo" Gritz

In his book, *Called to Serve*, former U.S. Army Colonel James "Bo" Gritz described his several meetings in May 1987 with Khun Sa, the head of the largest heroin-producing region in Southeast Asia. Gritz had been on a team mission called LAZARUS trying to locate missing prisoners of war when he found evidence of massive heroin production involving the CIA and the military.

Khun Sa and U.S. Drug Pipeline

Khun Sa described to Gritz how he sought U.S. help in replacing the heroin crop with another salable commodity and how this offer was refused. Gritz described how heroin production in the Golden Triangle area shot up from 40 tons in the early 1950s to 700 tons in the early 1960s. During the first set of meetings, Khun Sa said to Gritz that he might consider telling who were his largest prior U.S. customers for the heroin, but would not disclose the present customers.

During the second set of meetings in mid-1987, Khun Sa brought his aides together for a meeting with Gritz, at which time the group provided Gritz specific information on who in the United States were his main customers for heroin. Gritz wrote in his book that these U.S. customers included:

- Theodore Shackley (who was formerly deputy director for covert operations in the CIA). Shackley was identified to me by several of my deep-cover sources as being actively involved in drug trafficking.
- Richard Armitage, also CIA, later holding the key position of Assistant Secretary of Defense in the United States. (He also handled much of the drug-money laundering for Khan Sa through Armitage's connections with the Nugan Hand Bank.) In his defense department position, Armitage was responsible for locating missing POWs. But if these POWs were found and returned to the United States, they could be expected to describe the U.S. involvement in drug trafficking.
- Daniel Arnold, also CIA, handled the arms and drug sales formerly handled by Armitage. He served as CIA station chief in Thailand.
- Jerry Daniels, a CIA agent who replaced Armitage when Armitage returned to the United States.
- Santos Trafficante, head of one of the many criminal cartels with which the CIA had been doing business for decades.

Gritz's trip to visit Khun Sa was known to Justice Department officials, who sought to have him arrested on bogus passport charges before he went back to Indochina. Gritz left the United States before this could be accomplished.

Among the many articles on CIA drug trafficking was the April 1988 story in *The Progressive*. The article described the testimony given by Michael Toliver concerning his flights for the CIA hauling drugs from Central America into the United States, including landing with 25,000 pounds of marijuana at Homestead Air Force Base in Florida. The article stated that Federal Judge Patrick Kelly found the testimony compelling enough that he called it to the attention of President Ronald Reagan, as well as the CIA, the FBI, special prosecutor Lawrence Walsh, and Congress. Judge Kelly directed federal marshals to deliver the transcript of Toliver's deposition directly to President Reagan. Toliver's story was broadcast on CBS television's *West 57th Street*. According to the article, no one from the Justice Department questioned Toliver about his serious charges.

"George Bush is Up to His Neck in Illegal Drug Running."

Numerous CIA operatives, including Phillip Agee who had been with the CIA for many years, have written about the various criminal activities of the CIA. An *Associated Press* article (January 29, 1990) quoted from Agee's speech at Oregon State University in Corvallis: "Bush Is up to his neck in illegal drug running on behalf of the Contras."

Much of the heroin entering the United States came from Southeast Asia in the Golden Triangle area according to a *U.S. News & World Report* article (March 26, 1990):

> *For more than a decade, Khun Sa, the warlord of opium, has flooded Washington with offers to end the poppy production within his Golden Triangle fiefdom in exchange for financial aid. The U.S. has not responded, and this year the region's crop could double from the levels of just a few years ago. Attorney General Dick Thornburgh unsealed an indictment against the man considered responsible for 40 percent of the U.S. heroin supply. But Sa is not likely to be booked soon. In the remote hills of Burma, a private army of thousands protects him.*

U.S.-Initiated Wars, With Heavy Casualties, Provided Logistics
For Start of CIA Drug Smuggling into United States

For decades the British and the French controlled the huge drug operations in Southeast Asia, which were taken over by the United States through the CIA in the 1950s. Vietnam was a CIA operation that escalated, either intentionally or unintentionally, providing the logistics for the CIA to greatly expand the drug trafficking into the United States.

Many Americans, brainwashed to believe that the Vietnam war was in the interest of freedom and to fight communism, supported the war that sacrificed the lives of 58,000 Americans. Great numbers were painfully injured and crippled mentally and physically. The phony argument was that the United States could not allow the people of Indochina to decide what type of government they would have, and that if they chose leaders with communist leanings it would in some way harm the United States. Believing that baloney caused many families to lose sons, husbands, and fathers, just as it had several years earlier in Korea.

Killing Millions in the Process

The mindset within the CIA, including the Phoenix Program that assassinated a reported 40,000 Vietnam villagers, the Vietnam war that killed millions, and the CIA's massive drug trafficking into the United States, is such that deliberate infliction of harm against Americans, and people of other countries, cannot be questioned. What isn't well known is why and who master-minded these attacks.

Even in Death the GIs Were Misused as Pawns

The CIA drug trafficking required large numbers of drug addicts. The CIA drug trafficking in Indochina resulted in many American servicemen in that CIA war operation becoming drug addicts. In addition, the bodies and the caskets of dead soldiers often contained drugs being smuggled into the United States on military aircraft. Plastic-wrapped drugs were shipped into the United States in the bottom of caskets, in body bags, and even in body cavities. Upon arrival at Air Force bases, and especially Travis Air Force Base in California, the drugs would be removed from the caskets and bodies that were identified by secret codes.

Many articles have been written in the alternative press about this sordid practice but withheld by the mainstream media. In one instance, an officer from the army's Criminal Investigation Division uncovered a large-scale heroin smuggling scheme using the bodies of dead GIs who perished in the CIA's Vietnam War. His group filed reports with the Pentagon describing how the bodies were cut open, gutted, and filled with sacks of heroin. Approximately fifty pounds of heroin with multi-million-dollar street value were stuffed into each body.

Widespread Practice Known or Controlled From Washington

The coverups in the military, in the CIA, in the Justice Department, weren't isolated rogue acts; the practices were too widespread. Exposure was blocked by high-level officials. Any time an investigator reported the problem, he or she was ordered to remain quiet.

These aspects of the CIA's Vietnam War that used Americans as pawns are never brought up at Memorial Day ceremonies. The American public is led to believe that the hundreds of thousands of dead, maimed, or injured Americans suffered for an honorable cause. This is not to discredit those who endured the fighting, but to bring reality into the picture.

Code Names For CIA Far East Drug Smuggling

The CIA drug trafficking had grown so huge that it was handled like a major corporation, but secretly. Different geographical areas and different types or levels of operations are given code names. In the Golden Triangle area of Southeast Asia, the code names included Operation Short Flight, Operation Burma Road, Operation Morning Gold, and Operation Triangle.

Expanding the CIA's Drug Smuggling Empire

A similar pattern and excuse was used to develop the smuggling of drugs from Central and South America into the United States. Fabricating another excuse, the CIA and other covert government entities encouraged, trained, funded, and armed, groups to undermine the Nicaraguan government. This operation toward Nicaragua provided the logistics for bringing large quantities of drugs into the United States. Again, the American public was manipulated to believe that Nicaraguans did not have the right to choose their desired form of government, and the United States, through its CIA, would correct the situation!

The CIA transferred some of its operatives who developed the drug trafficking in the Golden Triangle area of Southeast Asia to Central and South America. They reportedly included Theodore Shackley, Edwin Wilson (who is in federal prison for selling arms to Libya—which was a CIA operation), and Frank Terpil. In Central and South America the code names for CIA drug trafficking included Operation Snow Cone, Operation Toilet Seat, and Operation Watchtower.

Massive amounts of arms were sent from the United States by planes and ships, returning with drugs that were payment for the military equipment. Prior to the CIA's development of the massive drug shipments, the drug problems in the United States were relatively minor and mostly unheard of by the general public.

CIA's Purpose for Drugging America can Only be Speculated

Prima facie evidence exists that the CIA engaged in drug trafficking against America for years. Why this was done can only be speculated. Anyone reading the third edition of *Defrauding America* with its many other crimes against Americans could reach the conclusion that people in control of the CIA have engaged in acts for the last half century to morally, physically, and financially undermine the United States.

The general thinking has been that the reason for the government's involvement in drugs was to fund "black" operations. (As if that justified inflicting the drug scourge upon the United States!)

"Black Operations" are set up by the CIA to carry out a secret operation. These could be subverting foreign governments, assassinating foreign leaders, supplying arms to a group or country, setting the ground work for wars such as in Indochina, and many others as described in *Defrauding America*.

My CIA sources indicate that the profits from drug sales far exceeded what was needed for these operations. They report that most of the profits are hidden in off-shore financial institutions, and much of these funds come back in well-disguised forms and corporations, acquiring properties and businesses of all types—including broadcast and print media.

White House Involvement in Drugging America

Evidence is overwhelming that while the United States was inflicting war through surrogates upon Nicaragua, the White House and the National Security Council were directing the drug smuggling operations. People working closely with George Bush were key participants in CIA drug trafficking from Central America into the United States. John Hull, a friend of Dan Quayle and George Bush, was involved in the drug trafficking by making a fuel stop available on property that he owned in Costa Rica. Another close friend of Bush was Felix Rodriguez, who played a key role in the illegal arms and drug trafficking that were key parts of the Contra scandal.

My friend, and a close friend of Hull, Hoot Gibson, confirmed that Hull was a CIA operative in Costa Rica. Gibson owned land in Costa Rica and lived there for the past 20 years, and his wife was an attorney and member of the Costa Rican government. Gibson was a highly publicized TWA pilot who in the 1960s experienced a high-altitude jet upset that almost ended in disaster. A television documentary showed Gibson's exciting and near-fatal ordeal.

CIA operative Gunther Russbacher, whom I have known for over ten years, and whose many deep cover operations are detailed in *Defrauding America*, told me of the frequent visits of Senator Dan Quayle to Hull's Costa Rica ranch. Russbacher stated that Quayle was deeply involved with the Contra operation and drugs, as well as being closely associated with noted drug trafficker Felix Rodriguez. Russbacher said, "Quayle was one of our bag boys."

Propaganda to Justify Hidden Agendas

CIA-fed media releases claimed that the United States had to fund the Contras for freedom purposes and to combat communism. The real reason appeared to be the profitable drug trafficking. My CIA contacts stated the CIA was shipping arms to *both sides*, defending this practice in a tongue-in-cheek comment, "How else can we keep the war going?" (So much for the U.S. idealism in Nicaragua!) The CIA sought support from Congress for its Contra operation by reporting that the Sandinistas were trafficking in drugs and claimed that the Contras were not doing the same. In reality, it was just the opposite!

To stimulate congressional and public support for continuing to aid the Contras, the CIA installed video cameras in an aircraft flown by CIA pilot Barry Seal and secretly video-recorded the placement of drugs on board the aircraft at a Central American arms and drugs transshipment point. The White House stated that the drugs were loaded by the Sandinistas, making the tapes available to Congress and the media. The White House sought to inflame public opinion against the Sandinistas so that Congress would vote for funding the Contras. The people represented as Sandinistas loading drugs in that video were actually Contras. The scheme worked: Congress voted money for the Contras and the public was oblivious to having been duped.

All types of aircraft were used for flying arms to Central and South America and returning with drugs. Some aircraft were large airline or military types, landing in the United States at military or general aviation airports.[1] Some were single and twin-engine general aviation aircraft and usually landed at private airports.[2]

---

[1] Almost all military bases became drug transshipment points, and especially Homestead (Florida); Davis-Monahan (Arizona); Luke (New Mexico); McGuire (New Jersey); McClellan and Travis (California).

[2] Frequently mentioned airports include Mena Airport and others in the vicinity (Arkansas); Angel Fire Airport (New Mexico); Marana Airport (Arizona); Spirit of St. Louis Airport (Missouri); McMinnville Airport (Oregon); Coolidge Airport (Phoenix); Midland-Odessa (Texas); Lakeside Airport (Chicago); Addison Airport (Denton, Texas); Shamrock Airport (Houston); Pietra Negro (Black Rock), northeast of El Paso; and Redbird Airport in Dallas, (where I had once taught aviation flight and ground training). The airport at Mena, Arkansas, was a well-known CIA arms and drug transshipment point, and was featured on two television shows, *Frontline* and *Now It Can Be Told*, and in numerous newspaper stories.

Infamous Mena Airport and Two Presidents

Mena Airport, which is described in various pages, became infamous during the 1980s for the arms and drugs shipping through this western Arkansas airport by the CIA and other government agencies. It involved Oliver North, Vice President and then President George Bush, Arkansas Governor Bill Clinton and others who became involved in the covert activities.

Another Infamous Name in Drug Trafficking

Among the well-known names operating out of Mena Airport was Barry Seal, who coordinated frequently with Oliver North and who used the drug profits to purchase arms that went to Central America. But Seal was becoming a threat to the CIA drug operations; he knew too much, and talked too much about government drug trafficking. He thought that the threat of exposing high-level CIA and DEA officials in drug trafficking to Congress was insurance for him. But if he had known that Congress already knew about the drug trafficking and kept the lid on the scandal by coverups, he surely would not have been so confident.

The Threat of Exposing High-Level Corruption Eliminated

Seal was killed on February 19, 1986. On the day he was killed the FBI seized his personal belongings, hiding evidence of his CIA-sanctioned drug operations. His death conveniently kept him from revealing the CIA and DEA involvement in drug trafficking activities that would have been revealed at an upcoming trial.

Costa Rica Report On CIA Arms and Drug Trafficking

An 80-page report by the Costa Rican government (July 20, 1989) officially detailed and documented the U.S. role in drug trafficking in Central and South America. The report, titled, "Special Select Commission Appointed To Investigate Drug Traffic Crimes," was the official legislative assembly report of Costa Rica. Excerpts from the 115-page report (in Spanish) revealed what the mainstream U.S. media kept from the public, and showed the movement of arms from the United States to Central America was associated with massive shipment of drugs on the return flights. That report and other Costa Rican documents showed that Oliver North and John Hull were among Americans charged with drug and other crimes and for whom extradition warrants were outstanding in Costa Rica.

Sham Basis for Invading A Foreign Country & Killing Its People

In 1990, President Bush ordered the U.S. military to invade Panama on the argument that Colonel Manuel Noriega was allegedly violating U.S. laws by allowing drug trafficking through Panama. Noriega did in fact aid drug trafficking, assisting the CIA, DEA, the U.S. military, and the Mossad. Noriega assisted Oliver North and his associates, including Vice President Bush, in the arms flow to Central America and the drug-laden aircraft returning to the United States.

Many CIA personnel believe that Noriega was taken out because he knew too much about the involvement of U.S. officials and that he was demanding too high a cut for his part in coordinating the U.S. drug trafficking through Panama. After the invasion of Panama, the United States saw that key banking positions were filled by people who would continue the drug money laundering.

The U.S. invasion killed hundreds of Panamanians and inflicted billions of dollars of damages as it invaded this sovereign country on the pretense of outrage that Noriega engaged in drug activities. Twenty-six U.S. servicemen died, and none of their families knew the real reason for the invasion.

Arguably, employees and people holding office in the United States, who were secretly involved in drug trafficking, were far more guilty than Noriega, based upon their position of trust.

Noriega, as head of a foreign country, had the right to legalize drug activities just as many in the United States have argued that U.S. law should do. (This isn't my position, but it is a defense.)

Replacing Noriega with Other Drug Players

The drug trafficking through Panama into the United States didn't stop with Noriega's kidnaping. The Bush Administration arranged for the new president of Panama to be Guillermo Endura, president of a Panamanian bank extensively used by Colombia's Medellin drug cartel. Picked for vice president was Guillermo Ford, part owner of the Dadeland Bank of Florida. He reportedly was heavily involved in drug-money laundering. He was also chairman of Panama's Banking Commission. Another official selected by the Bush administration to be attorney general of Panama was Rogello Cruz.

U.S. District Judge Covering Up for CIA Drug Trafficking

The federal judge presiding over the trial of Manuel Noriega barred attorneys defending Noriega from presenting any information on the CIA's role, or that of Vice President George Bush, in drug trafficking or anything of a political nature. The judge repeatedly refused to allow CIA documents that Noriega needed in his defense to be introduced. Noriega's U.S. attorneys limited their defense arguments so as not to expose the CIA involvement in drug trafficking.

Paying for Perjured Testimony

Justice Department prosecutors rewarded known drug smugglers who had long prison sentences by dropping charges, or releasing them from prison, for testifying against Noriega as the prosecutor wanted them, while simultaneously protecting perjurers against perjury charges. An *Arizona Republic* article (November 27, 1991) described the huge rewards paid to major drug traffickers who testified against Noriega. Three of them, facing life terms with no possibility of parole, and with a collective 546 years in prison, were released and given immunity from further prosecution (including immunity from perjured testimony). They were given large financial payments, and their families brought to the United States.

The star witness against Noriega was his former pilot, Floyd Carlton, who faced life imprisonment with no parole for having flown large quantities of cocaine into the United States. Justice Department prosecutors allowed Carlton to transfer his drug-related assets from Panama to the United States, with no risk of forfeiture or income taxes. Carlton was also given several hundred thousand dollars, along with permanent U.S. residency for himself, his wife and children, and nanny.

Another Panamanian paid for his testimony was Ricardo Bilonick, who reportedly earned $47 million during a three-year drug trafficking period. He faced 50 years in prison unless he testified as Justice Department prosecutors wanted him to testify. His prison sentence was greatly reduced; he was allowed to keep millions of his drug-related income, and relieved of income tax liabilities.

Colombian pilot Roberto Striedinger, considered by Justice Department personnel as one of the top drug traffickers, and who flew large quantities of cocaine into the United States, was given a greatly reduced prison sentence. Justice Department personnel returned to Striedinger his seized bank accounts, Mercedes-Benz automobile, a 40-foot yacht, an airplane, and guns, including AK-47 assault rifles, Uzi and MAC-10 submachine guns (*Arizona Republic*, November 27, 1991).

When someone other than the government is using felons to testify, their testimony is discredited on the basis they had committed some prior offense. Presumably, a witness—not used by the government—must be a sequestered nun or someone fitting that background. When it suits government prosecutors, the testimony of felons is not only considered reliable, but they deserve to be handsomely paid for it. Title 18 USC Section 201(c)(2), known as the anti-bribery statute, makes it a criminal offense to offer anyone compensation for their testimony. But this applies only to the public, not government officials! On July 10, 1992, a federal jury in Miami sentenced Manuel Noriega to 40 years in federal prison.

Senate Testimony by Noriega's Pilot, Floyd Carlton

Floyd Carlton testified to a senate subcommittee in 1986, while wearing a hood, hiding his identity. Carlton testified about large quantities of drugs shipped to the United States from Colombia and Panama on Eastern Airlines, a fact that Eastern Airlines Captain Gerald Loeb had described to me in detail. Carlton corroborated that the ranch John Hull ran in Costa Rica was used by drug trafficking aircraft and that Hull was a close associate to Dan Quayle and George Bush.

In 1999, I started communicating with John Hull, and there is another side to the various stories written about him, which will be described in detail in other books. Briefly, Hull had purchased ranches in Costa Rica and farmed the land, doing quite well. In the 1980s, CIA agents approached him to use his land for airstrips, and being patriotic, he gave them permission. He was eventually abandoned by the CIA—a common tactic by that agency—and Hull had to flee the country, losing his land and years of work and investments.

U.S. Ignoring Noriega's Drug Trafficking Years Earlier

Carleton testified that he offered to give information in July 1986 to the U.S. Drug Enforcement Administration office in Panama, and the DEA refused to take the information. Carlton's evidence was extremely valuable since he had frequent direct contacts with Noriega and the Medellin and Cali drug cartels. The evidence included taped telephone conversations, documents, personal information about "money laundering, drugs, weapons, corruption, assassinations." But to have allowed Carlton to give that information would expose the CIA, DEA, and Mossad involvement in drug trafficking. Carlton testified that one of the DEA agents in Panama, who refused to receive the information, was Thomas Tyre.

Standard Obstruction of Justice Tactic

Using a standard Justice Department tactic to silence or discredit whistleblowers, U.S. agents arrested Carlton in January 1987, charging him with drug trafficking. The charges were made in such a way that Carlton would not be allowed to testify about the CIA role, which he had earlier sought to expose. DOJ charges in 1987 may have been to silence and discredit what he knew about CIA, DEA and U.S. military involvement in drug trafficking.

CIA—Noriega Drug Trafficking Coalition

Senator Kerry stated what was already well known, that:

General Noriega had been on the payroll and an employee of the CIA for many, many, many years and, I have been given to understand, up until rather recently. It is not inconceivable, but it is most probable that this activity that the CIA had with this thug [Noriega] who was in their employ, and how proud they must have been that one of their own, that they nurtured for so many years, had risen to this power position.

Articulating the "Depravity Of" Americas' Drug Users

The Subcommittee on Terrorism, Narcotics and International Communications published a 1988 report stating:

The reason for believing the narco-trafficking is a matter for national security is that the Latin criminal cartels who have profited from the depravity of some Americans constitute an international underworld so extensive, so wealthy, and so powerful that it can literally buy governments and destabilize entire societies. This is a national security matter...Latin drug trafficking directly detracts from our ability to defend ourselves from military attack. Drug abuse has affected readiness within our Armed Forces...

Operation Toilet Seat—Caribbean Drug Smuggling

The CIA used Boeing 727 and C-130 type aircraft to haul drugs from Central and South America to locations in the United States, including military bases, as was well known to military personnel. The planes were leased or operated by CIA proprietary airlines and flown either by CIA/DIA/DEA crews or by pilots for private airlines acting as fronts for the CIA, or CIA proprietaries.

Operation Watchtower

Operation Watchtower[3] was one of many drug trafficking operations from Central America consisting of the placement and operation of low frequency radio beacons to guide low-flying pilots from Colombia to Panama. It also consisted of making available to the pilots the radio frequencies and schedules of drug interdiction aircraft so as to avoid detection. Because of the extremely low altitude these drug-laden aircraft flew, often less than five hundred feet, they could not receive the line-of-sight navigational signals available through-

---

[3] *Riders X-Change*, Oct 1991 Edition; *Called To Serve*, 1991 Author Colonel James Gritz; *Freedom*, Nov-Dec 1993; *Freedom*, Jan-Feb 1993; *Freedom*, Jan-Feb 1995, authored by U.S. Army Colonel William Wilson.

out the world (VOR). Radio transmission from a drug-carrying aircraft on a particular frequency actuated a relay at the radio beacon that started up the gasoline-engine-powered generators and the radio transmitters used for navigation.

Military Involvement for Drugging America

The CIA utilized the Army Intelligence Agency in Operation Watchtower, which began in the mid-1970s. U.S. Army Colonel A.J. Baker was ordered to oversee part of Operation Watchtower. It turned the operation over to Army Colonel Edward P. Cutolo, who also commanded the 10th Special Forces based at Ft. Devens, Massachusetts. Cutolo had supervised Operation Orwell for the intelligence agencies. This operation spied on political figures for the purpose of blackmail. Many of my deep-cover sources described the military's passive or active role in the drug trafficking into the United States.

Cutolo's Fear Of Death Was Prophetic

Army Colonel Edward P. Cutolo, who had been ordered by the CIA to supervise Operation Watchtower, grew increasingly concerned about its illegality. He conducted an investigation in an attempt to bring it to a halt. Fearing he might be killed because of his investigation, he prepared a fifteen-page single-spaced affidavit dated March 11, 1980, describing the CIA drug trafficking and related undercover activities. Cutolo gave copies of it to several trusted friends[4] with instructions to release the affidavit to government officials and the media if he was killed or died under suspicious circumstances. He was prophetic. Colonel Cutolo died in a one-car accident near Skullthorpe, England, in 1980, while on a military exercise near the Royal Air Force base at Skullthorpe. Cutolo's death was under strange circumstances, and occurred shortly before he was to meet Harari. Cutolo was killed, as were several other people working with him who sought to expose the drug trafficking operation.

The Cutolo affidavit, the drug operation, and deaths, were the subject of a one-hour television documentary on A&E Investigative Reports (March 22, 1999).

The affidavit described the installation and operation of the radio beacons and several of the drug flights in which he participated. The first one occurred in December 1975, headed by Colonel A.J. Baker, under whom Cutolo worked. Cutolo stated in his affidavit that, in the February operation, "30 high-performance aircraft landed safely at Albrook Air Station," and "the mission was 22 days long."

The affidavit listed key people meeting the aircraft, including Colonel Manuel Noriega, who was then Panama's Defense Force Officer assigned to U.S. Customs; CIA operatives Edwin Wilson and Frank Terpil, and Mossad operative Michael Harari. Harari worked closely with U.S. intelligence agencies in the drug trafficking operation, sharing the profits for Israel and sharing the blame for the U.S. drug epidemic and associated crime wave. Harari had authority from the U.S. Army Southern Command in Panama to operate on military bases. Israel's Mossad participation in drug trafficking made Israel

---

[4] Colonel A.J. Baker; Hugh B. Pearce; Paul Neri, and eventually to Colonel James Gritz and William Tyree.

a participant in undermining the welfare and security of the United States.

Operation Orwell

The Cutolo affidavit described another undercover mission, Operation Orwell,[5] which consisted of spying on politicians, judicial figures, state law enforcement agencies and religious figures. Compromising information was then distributed to certain members of the military-industrial complex. Colonel Cutolo stated in his affidavit that the compromising information was needed to silence these people if information on the criminal activities leaked out:

> *Mr. Edwin Wilson explained that it was considered that Operation Watchtower might be compromised and become known if politicians, judicial figures, police and religious entities were approached or received word that U.S. troops had aided in delivering narcotics from Colombia into Panama. Based on that possibility, intense surveillance was undertaken by my office to ensure that if Watchtower became known, the United States government and the Army would have advance warnings and could prepare a defense.*

The affidavit listed some of the people against whom the surveillance was directed:

> *I instituted surveillance against Ted Kennedy, John Kerry, Edward King, Michael Dukakis, Levin H. Campbell, Andrew A. Caffrey, Fred Johnson, Kenneth A. Chandler, Thomas P. O'Neill, to name a few of the targets. Surveillance at my orders was instituted at the Governors residences in Massachusetts, Maine, New York, and New Hampshire. The Catholic cathedrals of New York and Boston were placed under electronic surveillance also. In the area of Fort Devens, all local police and politicians were under some form of surveillance at various times.*
>
> *I specifically used individuals from the 441st Military Intelligence detachment and 402 Army Security Agency Detachment assigned to the 10th Special Forces Group to supplement the SATs tasked with carrying out Operation Orwell. I also recruited a number of local state employees who worked within the ranks of local police and, as court personnel, to assist in this Operation. They were veterans and had previous security clearances. They were told at the outset that if they were caught they were on their own.*

Deaths Associated With Military Drug Operation

The Cutolo affidavit continued: "I have seen other men involved in Operation Watchtower meet accidental deaths after they were also threatened." Cutolo's affidavit identified the people who died in strange fashion and who had posed a danger of exposing the drug trafficking.

Sgt. John Newby received threatening phone calls and then died in a parachuting accident when his chute failed to open. Colonel Robert Bayard was murdered in Atlanta, Georgia in 1977 as he went to meet Mossad agent Michael Harari.

---

[5] Authority for the Army to become involved in this CIA operation came directly from FORSCOM through CIA operative Edwin Wilson, under Army Regulation (AR) 340-18-5 (file number 503-05).

Colonel Baker died while trying to determine if Harari had killed Colonel Cutolo. Colonel James Rowe was assassinated on April 21, 1989, in the Philippines within three days after Mossad agent Harari arrived in that country. Rowe had been investigating Harari's links to Cutolo's murder and to CIA operatives Edwin Wilson and Thomas Clines. Pearce was killed in a helicopter accident in June 1989 under mysterious circumstances. Congressman Larkin Smith died in an airplane accident on August 13, 1989.

The affidavit stated that Mossad agents associated with Operation Watchtower were being protected by CIA Director Stansfield Turner and George Bush and that Washington military authorities had approved the drug trafficking operation:

Harari was a known middleman for matters involving the United States in Latin America [and] acted with the support of a network of Mossad personnel throughout Latin America and worked mainly in the import and export of arms and drug trafficking. Edwin Wilson explained that Operation Watchtower had to remain secret...There are similar operations being implemented elsewhere in the world. Wilson named the "Golden Triangle" of Southeast Asia and Pakistan ... Wilson named several recognized officials of Pakistan, Afghanistan, Burma, Korea, Thailand and Cambodia as being aware and consenting to these arrangements, similar to the ones in Panama.

Referring to the huge profits received by the CIA from the drug trafficking, the affidavit continued:

Edwin Wilson explained that the profit from the sale of narcotics was laundered through a series of banks. Wilson stated that over 70% of the profits were laundered through the banks in Panama. The remaining percentage was funneled through Swiss banks with a small remainder being handled by banks within the United States. I understood that some of the profits in Panamanian banks arrived through Israeli Couriers. I became aware of that fact from normal conversations with some of the embassy personnel assigned to the Embassy in Panama. Wilson also stated that an associate whom I don't know also aided in overseeing the laundering of funds...Wilson indicated that most of Operation Watchtower was implemented on the authority of [CIA Thomas] Clines.

Spying On Politicians

Referring to Operation Orwell, which spied upon politicians for subsequent blackmail:

I was notified by Edwin Wilson that the information forwarded to Washington, D.C., was disseminated to private corporations who were developing weapons systems for the Dept. of Defense. Those private corporations were encouraged to use the sensitive information gathered from surveillance of U.S. senators and representatives as leverage [blackmail] to manipulate those Congressmen into approving whatever costs the weapon systems incurred.

As of the date of this affidavit, 8,400 police departments, 1,370 churches, and approximately 17,900 citizens have been monitored under Operation Orwell. The major churches targeted have been Catholic and

Latter Day Saints. I have stored certain information gathered by Operation Orwell on Fort Devens, and pursuant to instructions from Edwin Wilson have forwarded additional information gathered to Washington, D.C....Certain information was collected on suspected members of the Trilateral Commission and the Bilderberg group. Among those that information was collected on were Gerald Ford and President Jimmy Carter. Edwin Wilson indicated that additional surveillance was implemented against former CIA Director George Bush, whom Wilson named as a member of the Trilateral Commission.

Congressional Cowardice and Resulting Obstruction Of Justice

It is easy to understand how members of Congress can be blackmailed into covering up for criminal activities involving personnel of intelligence agencies or the Justice Department when information on their personal lives is secretly collected by the FBI and U.S. intelligence agencies for blackmail purposes.

Implementing Secret Political Surveillance Nationwide

The affidavit described some of the weapon manufacturers who received this CIA information:

Edwin Wilson named three weapons systems when he spoke of private corporations receiving information from Operation Orwell. (1) An armored vehicle. (2) An aircraft that is invisible to radar. (3) A weapons system that utilizes kinetic energy. Edwin Wilson indicated to me during our conversation, which entailed the dissemination of Operation Orwell information and the identification of the three weapons systems, that Operation Orwell would be implemented nationwide by 4 July 1980.

The affidavit made reference to classified information and "the activities of the CIA in the United States and in Latin America." Referring to people working with Edwin Wilson, the affidavit continued:

Each operation had basically the same characters involved...with Edwin Wilson...Robert Gates and William J. Casey...

Continuing Murders

Before leaving on his trip, Cutolo wrote a note to Colonel Rowe, informing him that he had arranged to meet with Michael Harari (in Manila). Why would a U.S. military intelligence officer meet secretly with a Mossad operative if the two intelligence agencies routinely met with each other? Cutolo died on May 26, 1980, his death caused by multiple fractures to the skull, other fractures, and punctured organs. These were out of the ordinary for the type of auto accident in which he was involved.

Master Sergeant Mark Larochelle, also involved in Operation Orwell, was killed during a helicopter training mission at Fort Chaffee, Arkansas in July 1990.

Colonel William Wilson, a Green Beret, described the drug trafficking in Operation Watchtower. After retirement he authored two articles appearing in *Freedom* (Nov-Dec 1993 and Jan-Feb 1995) describing his knowledge and role in the operation. Wilson served with the Army's Office of Inspector General, and assisted in uncovering and documenting the massacre of hundreds of Vietnamese civilians by American troops at My Lai on March 16, 1968.

Colonel Neri—Killed By Israel's Mossad?

As Colonel Cutolo suspected, Neri was killed, apparently to silence him. Paul Neri was one of the people who Cutolo entrusted with the affidavit and who had been requested to make the affidavit public upon his death. In distributing the affidavit to members of Congress and the media, Neri wrote:

Both Col. Rowe and Mr. Pearce agreed to go public after the meeting with Larkin Smith, to call for a full investigation into the events described in Col. Cutolo's affidavit. But both men died prior to the meeting with Smith.

Killing Of U.S. Personnel By Israel's Mossad

Referring to the Mossad, Neri's cover letter stated:

With the deaths of Col. Cutolo, Col. Baker, Col. Rowe (and Col. Robert Bayard named in Col. Cutolo's affidavit) it is hard to believe the deaths of these men are not the work of the Israeli Mossad. It is equally easy to attribute the death of Col. Cutolo directly to Operation Watchtower inquiries.

Meeting the same coverup response that I received for the past thirty years from the establishment media, Neri's letter stated:

For your information a copy of the affidavit will be sent to the New York Times, the Washington Post and the Boston Globe. The men who died so far...were good men. They attempted to let the public know what really occurred in Latin America, and in the never ending drug flow.

In 1980 Col. Cutolo died in an accident while on a military exercise. Just prior to his death he notified me that he was to meet with Michael Harari, an Israeli Mossad agent. It is my belief, though unsubstantiated, that Harari murdered Col. Cutolo because of the information Col. Cutolo possessed. I believe that Col. Cutolo died in his attempt to [expose] Operation Watchtower...

Colonel Baker enlisted the aid of Colonel James N. Rowe, and between Col. Baker, Col. Rowe and myself, we set out to prove that Harari murdered Col. Cutolo, and that Operation Watchtower...netted Edwin Wilson and Frank Terpil of the CIA a large sum of tax free dollars.

Prior to getting very far into the investigation, Col. Baker died. We had no doubt as to the guilt of Thomas Clines, whom we suspect was the master mind behind Operation Watchtower.

Neri went on to describe how Harari and Col. James Rowe[6] were in the Philippines when Rowe was assassinated. Neri's letter continued: "I believe Harari's motive for murdering Col. Rowe was due to Col. Rowe's inquiries about Harari's movements and relationships to Edwin Wilson, Thomas Clines and Manuel Noriega."

Referring to another death in those seeking to expose Operation Watchtower, Neri wrote:

In June 1989, Mr. Pearce was killed in a helicopter accident. The accident has a story of its own I am told. Both Col. Rowe and Mr. Pearce agreed to go public, after the meeting with Larkin Smith, to call for a full investigation into the events described in Col. Cutolo's affidavit. But both men

---

[6] Rowe was in the Philippines serving as chief of the Army Advisory Group.

died prior to the meeting with Smith.

Mossad Arms and Drug Trafficking

Paul Neri continued:

Since the Israeli Mossad openly traffics in arms and drugs in Latin America, a theory that Clines, Wilson, Terpil, Harari and Noriega engaged in Operation Watchtower is very easy to believe at this time, especially following the Libyan situation and the Iran-Contra affair. It all fits, this entire scenario carried over from Operation Watchtower directly into the Iran-Contra affair with the same characters.

"This Is Now Your Pandora's Box"

Referring to the deaths associated with the attempted exposure of Operation Watchtower and the Mossad's involvement, Neri wrote, "I'm sorry that I am unable to carry the work any further. This is now your Pandora's Box."

60-Minutes Coverup

Before he was murdered, Colonel Rowe also tried to get CBS's *60 Minutes* interested in the contents of the Cutolo affidavit, the murders, and the CIA-U.S. military-Mossad drug trafficking. CBS replied (July 13, 1987), refusing to proceed with the matter. Despite the responsibility of the media to expose government corruption, CBS chose to cover up. Coverup of a federal crime is a crime by itself under Title 18 USC Section 4.

This CBS coverup made possible the continuation of the drug trafficking and more murders. Over the years I encountered many deep-cover operatives who offered and provided evidence of the CIA drug trafficking to television and radio networks, and experienced the same coverups that I experienced the past 30 years.

Finally They Got Neri

On April 29, 1990, Paul Neri died. An unknown person wrote a short letter that was sent with the Cutolo affidavit and Paul Neri's accounting of what had happened, writing:

Mr. Paul Neri, of the National Security Agency, died on April 29, 1990. Before his death, he requested that I mail the enclosed affidavit to you. Paul Neri was concerned that he would be killed or lose his security clearance if he revealed the affidavit before he died. According to him, these facts are true. If you investigate and interview the parties named within the affidavit, you will find the information is true. I am simply carrying out the wishes of a good friend, but do not want to get involved any further; therefore, I shall remain anonymous.

Another Killing To Hide U.S. Involvement in Drugs

The Cutolo affidavit described the killing of an Army servicewoman, Elaine Tyree, who had knowledge of Operation Watchtower which she described in her diary. To shift attention from the actual killer and his connection to the ongoing drug operation, the military charged Tyree's husband with the killing. The Cutolo affidavit continued:

It was too risky to allow a military court to review the charges against Pvt. Tyree with Operation Orwell still ongoing and Senator Garn's office requesting a full investigation. Pvt. Tyree therefore had to stand before a civilian court of law on the criminal charges.

Found Innocent at First Hearing

At the first military hearing, the presiding judge found no reason to bind Pvt. Tyree's husband over for trial for the murder of his wife. This decision risked further investigation and possible exposure of the corrupt operation. Army pressure caused the county prosecutor to indict the husband for murdering his wife, even though the army knew the actual killer was someone else. The Cutolo affidavit stated:

> On 29 February 1980, Pvt. Tyree was convicted of murder and will spend the duration of his life incarcerated. I could not disseminate intelligence gathered under Operation Orwell to notify civilian authorities who actually killed Elaine Tyree.

Military Deep Cover

I made initial contact with William Tyree in 1994 and this contact continued for many years, during which time Tyree furnished me with considerable details and documents on Operation Watchtower, Operation Orwell, and other covert operations in which the military was involved. I am convinced that Tyree was framed by military officers and prosecutors in Massachusetts for the murder of his wife. Tyree prepared several highly detailed affidavits describing what he himself had observed of Operation Watchtower, describing it as a secret Army Special Forces operation.

Tyree was crew chief on a "sterile"[7] helicopter used in Operation Watchtower. The Special Forces Teams were used to install and maintain the radio beacons that were part of Operation Watchtower. Tyree described an incident in which a group of Green Berets[8] identified as Special Action Team Number 1 were ambushed in Colombia near the village of Turbo by four dozen soldiers from a Colombian Army Unit who mistook the SAT members for local bandits. Two of the SAT team members were shot before their radio request for air evacuation was carried out.

Drug Experiments on American Servicemen

In his February 10, 1992, affidavit, Tyree described reports of drug experiments on American GIs in Europe during the early 1950s by Doctor James P. Cattell. This information was given to Panama Defense Force (PDF) personnel (PF-8) by Edwin Wilson for the purpose of interrogations. Tyree's affidavit at a later date described how his wife started receiving threatening phone calls and notes left on parked vehicles in October 1978, warning her to stop writing and reporting the secret activities, including Operation Watchtower and Operation Orwell. Tyree identified the military superiors and members of Congress[9] to whom he reported the threats.

Colonel Rowe took command of Operation Orwell following Colonel Cutolo's death. Rowe advised Tyree of the continued surveillance activities, including that of Harvard Law School Professor Lawrence H. Tribe. The surveillance activities were initiated by Special Forces personnel because of the

---

[7] Special forces used the term "sterile" to indicate the aircraft was stripped of all identification, the purpose of which was to deny the role of the United States in the operation.

[8] The Green Berets were divided into three Special Action Teams, each one consisting of approximately seven men.

[9] Including U.S. Senator E.J. Garn (R-Utah)

people's opposition to Washington policies. Rowe told Tyree that he had substantial evidence showing that Colonel Edward Cutolo, Colonel James Baker, and Colonel Robert Bayard, were all victims of foul play, and that Mossad operative Michael Harari was involved in the deaths.

Tyree wrote that the last message he received from Colonel Rowe was just prior to Rowe's departure for Manila, where Rowe was assassinated in April 1989. Rowe told Tyree that if he remembered any more details on what Tyree had earlier told him, to call a certain phone number and leave a message.[10] After Rowe was assassinated, Tyree called the number and reached a Colonel Richard Malvesti,[11] who stated that he was in possession of the material on which Colonel Rowe was working. From time to time Tyree received newsclippings in the mail relating to personnel involved in Operations Watchtower or Orwell, without the name or address of the sender. Tyree stated that he thought the mailings were from Colonel Malvesti or Paul Neri of the U.S. National Security Agency.

Malvesti's activities on behalf of exposing Operation Watchtower and Orwell probably played a role in his subsequent death[12] on July 26, 1990. During a routine parachute jump in 1990, his parachute failed to open. This failure could easily be brought about by someone tampering with the chute.

General Carl W. Stiner, a four-star general who was commander in chief of the U.S. Special Operations Command, spoke at Malvesti's funeral, stating, "The Ranger experience is not for the weak or the faint-hearted." Excellent rhetoric, but it didn't address the criminal activities associated with Malvesti's death or the many others, or of the subversive and criminal activities by people allegedly representing and protecting the interests of the United States.

Tyree said that on July 23, 1990, he received the affidavit of Colonel Cutolo that was sent on behalf of Paul Neri, and that the information that pertained to Tyree and his personal observation was correct.

Tyree overheard several of the Panamanian military officers give credit to a Colombian armed forces officer named Eber Villegas for assisting the success of Operation Watchtower.

Tyree explained how he gave Secret and Top Secret U.S. documents to PDF and Israeli agents, possibly explaining how the drug-laden aircraft obtained the radio frequencies and flight schedules of drug-interdiction aircraft.

Pan American Defense Forces
Assisted the CIA-Military Drug Trafficking

Tyree told how members of the Panamanian Defense Forces (PDF) assisted in unloading the cocaine at Albrook Air Station. In one of his affidavits Tyree said:

I personally witnessed members of the Panamanian Defense Force (PDF) help unload the bales of cocaine from the aircraft onto the tarmac of Albrook Air Station. Among the PDF officers were Colonel Manuel Noriega, Major Roberto Diaz-Herrera, Major Lis del CID, and Major Ramirez.

---

[10] Phone number for Colonel Rowe was 919-396-3832.
[11] Malvesti was director for operations of the Joint Special Operations Command.
[12] Malvesti is buried in the Massachusetts National Cemetery in Bourne.

These men were always in the company of an American civilian identified to me by other personnel involved in the operation as Edwin Wilson of the CIA. Another civilian in the company of Wilson, I have since learned, was Israeli Mossad Agent Michael Harari.

Israel's Mossad Agents Killing Americans

Tyree wrote, "It is not uncommon for Israeli Mossad agents to kill Americans who the Israeli's deem a threat to the security of Israel." This belief has been stated to me numerous times by CIA contacts. The Israelis didn't hesitate to kill 34 U.S. sailors when it attacked the U.S. navy ship U.S.S. *Liberty* (June 8, 1967).

Tyree described seeing Wilson provide PDF officers with manila folders containing the following addresses: CIA, Office of Naval Intelligence, and Defense Intelligence Agency. The contents appeared to be photographs taken by satellites or SR-71 high-altitude spy aircraft.

Colonel Cutolo, who commanded the second and third Watchtower missions, and Tyree were transferred to the 10th Special Forces Group at Fort Devens, Massachusetts, along with another participant, Sergeant John Newby. As stated earlier, Newby started receiving threats upon his life, and his life ended in October 1978.

During the 1976 Watchtower operation, Tyree said that the pilots appeared to be mercenaries who spoke several foreign languages and had German, French, and English accents. The pilots and lead personnel in the first 1975 operations appeared younger and acted as if they were U.S. Army or U.S. Navy personnel. He thought that British Special Air Service (S.A.S.) pilots were on some of the flights.

Tyree said that Ted Shackley, a former high-ranking CIA operative, was deeply involved in Operation Watchtower and other CIA-related drug operations. He believed that the Navy's Task Force 157 participated in Operation Watchtower. He said that "Colonel. Baker, Col. Rowe and I believe Thomas Clines, with the aid of Edwin Wilson and Frank Terpil orchestrated Operation Watchtower...with full CIA auspices."

Describing Details Of His Wife's Death

Tyree described details of his wife's death. On January 30, 1979, Elaine Tyree was stabbed to death at the Tyree's off-post residence. Subsequently, Erik Y. Aarhus (U.S. Army SP4) and Earl Michael Peters were charged with her murder. Prior to his wife's death, Tyree had repeatedly contacted members of Congress[13] about his findings of drug trafficking from Central America; of the drugs and arms trafficking at Fort Devens, and the threats to him and his wife.

Sergeant Kenneth Garcy stated in an affidavit dated September 29, 1990, that Elaine Tyree was keeping a record of what she had learned about the drug operation. He said she intended to turn the diary-style book over to the Criminal Investigation Division (CID), and that Tyree was concerned about the safety of his wife. She started receiving threats and made these threats known to Colonel Cutolo, First Sergeant Frederick Henry, and Garcy.

---

[13] Including Senator J. Garn of Utah.

Francis M. Gardner, the manager of the apartments where the Tyrees lived at the time of Elaine Tyree's death, signed a statement before a notary public stating that he observed a person identified as Earl Michael Peters leaving the Tyree's apartment carrying a box (which the Tyrees had stored for him). Police arrived shortly thereafter and Elaine Tyree was found stabbed to death. According to Tyree the police never interviewed Gardner. Gardner stated to investigators that he saw the police remove the diary kept by Elaine Tyree and other papers. The police denied this.

Initial Decision Exonerated Tyree

Those charges ended with a decision[14] by Special Justice James W. Killam, III exonerating Tyree (May 15, 1979), and holding that Erik Aarhus and Earl Michael Peters should be tried for the murder of Elaine Tyree.

Prosecutor Protecting the Real Killer?

The district attorney refused to accept this decision. Instead, he moved to prosecute Tyree and blocked all prosecution of Peters. Local district attorney John Droney obtained an unusual ruling from the Massachusetts Supreme Judicial Court (SJC), dismissing the murder charges against Peters, even though he was seen leaving the murder scene.

Pentagon Coverup of CIA-Mossad-U.S. Military Drug Trafficking

Prior to Tyree's February 1980 trial, he sent a certified letter to the Pentagon detailing the criminal activities involving U.S. personnel in Operations Watchtower and Orwell. He received no response.

To prevent further investigation into the murder, Army officials conspired with Lieutenant J. Dwyer of the Middlesex District Attorney's Office and the county district attorney. They went to the Massachusetts Supreme Court and obtained a ruling prohibiting any court but the Massachusetts Supreme Court from ordering the arrest of suspects in the Tyree murder. This was without precedent, as any court in Massachusetts had authority to issue arrest warrants for murder suspects. But the ruling protected the real murderer, Michael Peters, who, if charged, would have exposed Operation Watchtower and Operation Orwell.

Massachusetts Judge James F. McHugh[15] refused to accept testimony from active duty personnel of the U.S. Army Special Forces who came forward to corroborate the existence of Operation Watchtower. The judge even threatened to charge Tyree with perjury if *he* decided that the statements were false. Army attorneys warned Tyree he would be prosecuted for divulging classified information, the military-CIA drug trafficking being considered "classified information." Judge McHugh refused to accept live testimony from active duty U.S. Army Special Forces personnel, who could expose the truth.

After Tyree was held guilty in the murder of his wife the military at Fort Devens, Massachusetts gave Tyree an honorable discharge. If Tyree had actually murdered his wife, the Army would undoubtedly have given him a dishonorable discharge. Even Elaine Tyree's father felt, and wrote, that he did not believe Tyree to be the murderer.

---

[14] Trial Court, First Northern Middlesex Division, Cases No. 271-272-273 of 1979 308 & 367.

[15] Middlesex Superior Court, Middlesex County, Massachusetts.

Destroying Evidence

In a December 5, 1979 letter on official letterhead of the Commonwealth of Massachusetts, District Attorney John J. Droney wrote to Colonel Cutolo:

I recommend that you destroy the surveillance material collected at the Tyree residence on January 30, 1979, if you have not already done so.

Droney was using, as the primary witness against Tyree in the murder of Elaine Tyree, the same person seen leaving the Tyree residence at the time of the murder.

Coverup by Chairman of Joint Chiefs of Staff

In 1994, President Clinton appointed Army General John Shalikashvili Chairman of the Joint Chiefs of Staff. Shalikashvili was the commander of the army unit that carried out Operation Watchtower. Colonel Cutolo succeeded Shalikashvili as the group commander of the 10th Special Forces Group, Airborne (SFG (A)). Since Colonel Cutolo was disturbed by the drug trafficking in Operation Watchtower, it can be assumed that the operation was originated by higher authority.

Jonestown Tragedy

Tyree had been part of a team operating in Surinam and French Guiana, and had insider information about Jim Jones and Jonestown in Guayana. Tyree wrote about former personnel from Army Special Forces groups training some of the enforcers at Jonestown prior to the mass murders and suicides. Tyree wrote that Congressman Leo Ryan who had traveled to Jonestown to investigate allegations of wrongdoing was to have been protected by an Army Special Forces team but that the team did not appear until after the congressman had been assassinated. Tyree wrote:

[The congressman] was hated by many different factions in the United States...the perfect place to assassinate him would be outside the U.S., where the law enforcement authorities are not as apt to control the evidence, crime scene, etc. This fact was known to [the state department], and they acted on it as a precaution. The Special Forces team assigned to guard the U.S. Representative didn't arrive on the ground in Jonestown until minutes after the U.S. Representative was dead. Several facts in dispute are:

- *Did the Special Forces team deliberately delay in reaching Jonestown? If so, why did they delay, and on whose orders did they delay?*
- *That the Special Forces team were the people that actually killed the U.S. Representative. This is possible, as the person who told me that version is a person who has always proved to be a creditable source.*
- *A number of Special Forces were training the ranchers in and around the Jonestown complex in security measures.*

Legal Action Seeking To Bring About Tyree's Release

In 1999, Attorney Ray Kohlman of Attleboro, Massachusetts filed a federal action in the U.S. District Court at Boston seeking to have a court receive evidence of government drug trafficking and also seeking Tyree's release.

As stated earlier, A&E Investigative Reports aired a one-hour television documentary that included the murder of Elaine Tyree (March 22, 1999).

Gunther Russbacher: High-Level CIA-ONI Operative

In the third edition of *Defrauding America* I write extensively upon the remarkable career of Gunther Russbacher, involved for decades in many high-level undercover activities for the CIA and Office of Naval Intelligence (ONI). His roles in some of the CIA's most bizarre events dwarf anything found in most fiction novels (some of which I have never described in any of my books).

Russbacher was my initial gateway into the blurry world of undercover activities in the late 1980s and this continued to the end of the twentieth century, at which time he became a key member of Austrian intelligence. He was very detailed in his description of undercover activities, and I feel he was very truthful in what he conveyed to me through thousands of hours of oftentimes deposition-like questioning covering a ten-year period.

Enlargement on Earlier Discoveries

When we first met, Russbacher refused to divulge any undercover activities to me. However, since he and I were both former Naval aviators, we had a certain bond that increased over time. At first he described his role in the Iran-Contra affair, and then in October Surprise, which are described in great detail in *Defrauding America*, along with other covert CIA activities.

Revealing CIA Drug Trafficking Activities

Russbacher described the different ways the drugs are shipped into the United States, including being shipped in sealed containers leased from Phillips Electronics and other companies. He described ways of circumventing Customs inspections in the United States and those incidents in which Customs and the DEA protected the drug shipments. He described the swapping of sealed containers at bonded warehouses in Hoboken, New Jersey and other locations, and the secret unloading of drugs at airfields throughout the United States, including Boeing Field in Seattle.

Deep-Cover Operative Trenton Parker

Another of the many confidential sources with whom I had contact was Trenton Parker who played a key role in CIA activities in the Caribbean.

Crossing Of Paths

Parker described the purpose of a flight from Dobbins Air Force Base near Marietta, Georgia in January or February of 1982, and included a description of the pilot. He said the pilot was a Navy Lt. Commander with the nickname of "Gunsel." Russbacher had told me several years earlier that Gunsel and Gunslinger were nicknames he used. Parker stated that the pilot was very articulate, which fit Russbacher's description. Russbacher confirmed that he did fly such a flight, and that the route of flight and the name of one of the passengers coincided with Parker's description.

It was ironical that Parker had crossed paths with Russbacher. It added still more corroboration of Russbacher's status. Parker provided me information on CIA activities that Russbacher had failed to mention. Once Parker gave me preliminary information about the activities, Russbacher then enlarged upon them when I asked. One such activity was called Operation Indigo which he described in court filings.[16]

Operation Indigo

Russbacher enlarged upon Operation Indigo. He said the full name was Operation Indigo Sky, and confirmed that it had been in operation since approximately 1976. Russbacher said that the operation consists of producing heroin in poppy fields in Nigeria and processing in the capital city of Lagos, along with transportation to Europe and the United States.

Russbacher stated that the intent of Operation Indigo Sky was to get an alternate supply for heroin coming from the Golden Triangle area and the Indian subcontinent. The operation began with the 1976 purchase of the Star Brewery in Lagos and its subsequent multi-million-dollar upgrade into a heroin processing facility. The brewery's name was changed to Star of Nigeria and then to Red Star. The transportation of the drugs from Lagos was initially by the CIA and DEA and then changed to contract operators. Most of the processed drugs in Operation Indigo Sky went from Lagos to Amsterdam, where it was further packaged and then shipped to European and United States destinations.

Parker provided me with a confidential employee status report showing his CIA status from December 23, 1964 to May 24, 1992. His last rank was shown as Colonel in the United States Marine Corp. The report showed that he had a top secret clearance, and that he was attached to Marine-Naval intelligence and to the CIA. His MSID identification number was 2072458. The reports identified Parker as a member of the ultra-secret Pegasus group, with headquarters in the U.S. Department of Labor offices in Fairfax, Virginia. The status report listed his alias, Pegasus 222.

Vice President George Bush and Colombian Drug Lords

Parker told me that the CIA, with Vice President Bush's approval, set up a sham drug bust in Miami during March 1980 using 4,000 pounds of cocaine, the biggest drug bust at that time. The purpose of the scheme was to generate support in the United States for the newly appointed drug czar, Vice President George Bush, justifying the use of the U.S. military in the so-called war against drugs.

CIA and Colombian Drug Lord

In carrying out the scheme, the CIA reportedly coordinated with Jorge Ochoa, a Colombian drug dealer. Ochoa organized many of Colombia's drug dealers to contribute cocaine for a large shipment into the United States, advising that there was safety in numbers. Most of the dealers didn't know that this was a planned drug bust and that they would lose whatever cocaine they contributed to the shipment. After the drug dealers contributed their cocaine into Ochoa's warehouse, Ochoa switched large quantities of bad cocaine that he had accumulated with good cocaine contributed by other dealers. Later, Ochoa sold the cocaine obtained in the switch for about fifty million dollars.

The 4,000 pounds of cocaine, including the bad cocaine that Ochoa had switched, was then shipped to Miami and seized by U.S. Customs, as planned. Bush got good publicity for his role as drug czar and Ochoa and his insiders

---

[16] U.S. District Court, Denver, United States of America vs. Trenton H. Parker, No. CR 93-43.

made over fifty million dollars by replacing good cocaine with bad cocaine.

The sting operation in which Parker participated used an informant to notify DEA agent Phelps in Bogota that the drugs were arriving at Miami International Airport on a particular flight at a given time. Phelps then notified DEA and Customs at Miami so they could be present at the aircraft's arrival.

DEA "Sophisticated" Drug Bust

There were comical elements to this planned drug bust. Parker described what he observed when the 4,000 pounds of cocaine arrived on board TAMPA Airlines at Miami International Airport. Watching the scene from an unobserved distance via binoculars, Parker said that the airplane with the two tons of cocaine arrived at the parking area, but there were no Customs agents there to seize the drugs, despite the considerable planning that went into the operation.

Several people working with Parker were at the aircraft, presenting the appearance of being there to unload the cargo. However, they intended to run off as the DEA and Customs agents appeared. But no agents arrived. The pilots wanted the drugs unloaded fast and wanted to leave. To avoid losing the drugs intended for the planned seizure, Parker's people unloaded the crates containing the drugs onto the tarmac.

The cocaine was hidden in boxes of Levi jeans, with yellow bands on the boxes containing the real Levi's, and white bands on the boxes containing the cocaine. Parker's people sprayed the boxes containing the cocaine with ether, used in the preparation of cocaine, insuring the cocaine would not be missed.

The absence of the expected DEA and Customs agents presented Parker with a problem. He advised his men by radio to stand by. An hour later, Parker saw through his binoculars a couple of Customs agents, engaging in frivolity, walking slowly toward the boxes, obviously unaware of the presence of drugs. Parker then radioed his men to stay clear of the area.

Parker watched through his binoculars as the agents poked holes in the boxes to check for possible drugs. The third box that they poked caused white cocaine powder to escape. Parker then radioed his people to immediately leave the area.

Parker boarded a commercial airline for return to Denver. That night the U.S. media described the drug find as the largest discovery in the nation's history. DEA and Customs officials described the drug-find as the result of an intensive coordinated effort between the DEA and Customs.

CIA Role in Establishing the Medellin Cartel

Parker told how the CIA set up the meetings in which various Colombian drug dealers organized into a drug trafficking cartel. Parker mentioned two preliminary meetings in late 1981 arranged by the CIA in which individual Colombian drug dealers organized into a cartel to facilitate the sale and shipment of drugs to the United States. He stated that the first meeting occurred with twenty of the biggest cocaine dealers in Colombia present; that the second and final meeting was held at the Hotel International in Medellin attended by about two hundred drug dealers, pushers, and smugglers. The Medellin Cartel was established in December 1981, and each of the members paid an initial $35,000 fee to fund a security force for the cartel members to protect their drug operation.

Further Confirmation of These Meetings and Their Purpose

Several years earlier Russbacher described these meetings to me, and then reconfirmed the meetings after I told him what Parker had told me. Russbacher stated there had been a preliminary meeting in September 1981 in Buenaventura, Colombia which established the format for the subsequent meetings. Russbacher attended the September 1981 meeting which was initiated by the CIA to facilitate drug trafficking into the United States, permitting the CIA to deal with a group rather than many independent drug dealers.

CIA Planning and Funding the Kidnap of Ochoa's Sister

Prior to organizing the Medellin cartel, the CIA created a crisis situation, providing an impetus for the Colombian drug dealers to consolidate their splintered members into the Medellin Cartel. Parker described the CIA operation in early December 1981 that led to the kidnapping of Jorge Ochoa's sister, Leona, from a University outside of Bogota. Parker said that, acting in his CIA capacity, he paid a group known as M-19 to carry out the kidnapping and to also kidnap Carlos Lehder. (Lehder escaped after he was captured.) The CIA paid the M-19 group three million dollars, of which two million dollars was in guns and one million in cash.

ORIGINAL TRANSMISSION DATE: 3/3/93 - RETRANSMISSION DATE 3/10/93

DOCUMENT CLASSIFICATION STATUS: T O P   S E C R E T

TO: MONA B. ALDERSON,
    LITIGATION DIVISION, OGC,   **CONFIDENTIAL**
    CIA/WASHINGTON D.C.
    PHO: 703-874-3107
    FAX: 703-874-3208

RE: INQUIRY OF 3/3/93   —   Defense Exhibit No. G-47-P-222
    MR. JOSEPH MACKEY,
    ASST. U.S. ATTORNEY,
    DENVER, COL.
    PHO: 303-844-2081
    FAX: 303-874-3208

NOTICE: PURSUANT TO THE NATIONAL SECURITY ACT OF 1947, 50 USC 401
& 402, ET. SQ. - THE FOLLOWING INFORMATION IS CONSIDERED
INFORMATION OF A CLASSIFIED NATURE INVOLVING NATIONAL SECURITY AND
SHOULD BE TREATED BY YOU AND YOUR DEPARTMENT/OFFICE ACCORDINGLY.

RE: BACKGROUND INFORMATION AND CURRENT OPPS-STAT ON SUBJECT:
    TRENTON H. PARKER AKA PEGASUS-222 - 2/2/45-COL.USMC/GS18
    ATTACHED MARINE-NAVEL ITLG-SEC/TAD-CIA-12/23/64 TO 5/24/92.
    SECURITY LVL/TOP SECRET/EXP 5/24/92. MSID NO. 2072458.
    SS NO. 553-60-1458. NSA/SPL-DDO/SEC-CHIEF-SP/AG PEGASUS UNIT.
    CONFIRM/REG/CIA/DENVER,CO. SBS/CUR/RES - DENVER, CO.
    ALL OPPS/ASSIGS CLASSIFIED TOP SECRET/UAVAILABLE.
    CUR/SEC/STAT: HIGH RISK. FED/CR/IDC/DENVER-1/27/93.

NO ADDITIONAL RECORDS OR BACKGROUND INFORMATION AVAILABLE FOR
RELEASE TO YOUR OFFICE AT THIS TIME ON SUBJECT DUE TO MATTERS OF
NATIONAL SECURITY AND PRESIDENTIAL DIRECTIVE/G-BUSH 5/24/92.

DO/DA RECOMMENDATION: - STANDARD DENIAL

ANSWER BACK/REF/P-222,
DO/COMM-CTR/3/3/93,
FOR/ITL/SEC - DDO/DDA,   **CONFIDENTIAL**
DRC/CIA/LANG/VA.

Copy of the CIA confidential document showing Parker's ONI and CIA status. Its use of the term Standard Denial, shows the CIA practice of lying.

"We made arrangements with Colonel Noriega, and this was the point where Noriega became involved with the CIA and the drugs," Parker said. He continued: "The deal was that the meeting between M-19 and Ochoa and Escobar would be held in a neutral point, namely Panama. During the second week of January 1982, everything was set up."

Pilot Friend Involved in Kidnaping Ochoa's Sister

Another one of my CIA sources, Russell Bowen, played a role in the kidnapping of Ochoa's sister. He piloted the DC-3 aircraft that flew Leona to a remote location where she was held until her release.

Paying Bribe Money to Nassau Prime Minister

Parker said he first landed at Grand Cayman Island, where he picked up five million dollars in cash from a CIA source. The next landing was at Nassau, where Parker paid Prime Minister Lynden Pindling one million dollars to get rid of a drug trafficker at Norman's Cay. Parker explained that Norman's Cay was a main drug transshipment point operated by Colombian drug dealer Carlos Lehder, who he described as one of the five keys of the Medellin Cartel. Parker stated:

Lehder was getting way out of line; he was shooting at people and when he finally shot at Walter Cronkite who happened to be sailing around in the area. Walter broke the news and a lot of people were saying how can this guy be operating out of Norman's Cay just off the shores of the United States?

Parker stated that Lehder was then forced to leave Norman's Cay and return to Colombia, where he joined the Medellin Cartel. Parker said that before leaving Nassau he was joined by Robert Vesco (wanted in the United States for money fraud), and then a CIA aircraft flew them to Havana, where they were met at the airport by security guards and Fidel Castro. Parker said:

I personally delivered two million dollars to Fidel Castro. And for those two million dollars he was to see that a shipment of arms was to go to M-19, which was a right-wing revolutionary force that we wanted to keep active so that we could have pressure on the government to bring about certain things that we wanted to do. And we needed pressure from below and pressure from above. He agreed to do that and he did do that.

Parker continued: "I took the remaining two million dollars and flew into Panama City, Panama and there I checked into Holiday Inn." where he met with the head of Colombia's M-19. Parker added: "I delivered my one million dollars to him and then I met with Colonel Noriega and delivered one million dollars to him. That one million dollars was to pay Noriega to act as the neutral party to help bring about the release of Ochoa's sister. Sure enough, Ochoa's sister was released." Parker continued:

And then he was also supposed to make an offer that he could and would provide protection for the drugs coming into the United States through the back door to the midway. And what that was, is that we had already made a move on the cartel to close down some of the small operations. At that time Noriega offered a connection into the Sandinistas, the drug operations. Refinery plants were set up there. And that's what we wanted, as we wanted to show the Sandinistas as being the bad guys and justify U.S. in-

volvement.

What we were doing was also financing operations because a certain group in the CIA was going ahead and flying guns down into Nicaragua, dropping them off by parachutes to the Contras. They then went over to the Sandinistas, picked up drugs and flew them into the United States, after which the money would be returned to the Sandinistas. In effect we were taking over some of the flying services for the Medellin Cartel. The money from the drugs produced the money for the guns and that is how the operation worked, and Bush knew the whole god-damn thing.

Parker explained that after completing that trip, he flew back to Denver where he was to go to trial on charges relating to a CIA operation called Operation Gold Bug. He explained that he was on a one-million-dollar self-recognizance bond, which was rather bizarre since any offense requiring that large a bond would be too serious to permit release on one's own recognizance.

Parker thought that charging him was a mistake unless it was to silence or discredit him. Parker said, "First, my trial was to start on February 2, 1982. Second, when it came up it came up by a pure fluke." He explained how the CIA was to protect him from prosecution. Prior to trial his CIA handlers instructed him to remain silent about the CIA operation as it was ongoing and that any exposure of it would have serious consequences. His handlers stated that he would receive a very light prison sentence or probation and would soon be free.

CIA Involved in JFK Assassination?

Parker said that after President Kennedy decided to pull U.S. troops out of the CIA's Vietnam operation, which would cause the loss of billions of dollars from the CIA drug trafficking, certain CIA factions decided to assassinate Kennedy. Pegasus people learned of the plot and told Kennedy two weeks before he was assassinated.

These statements added further fuel to the charges that the CIA was involved in Kennedy's assassination. In light of other CIA criminal activities, there should be little doubt that the CIA has the mindset to assassinate a president of the United States.

President Reagan More of A Puppet Head

Parker stated that after Kennedy's death, the Pegasus unit was not able to function as intended because of activities by U.S. presidents after the Kennedy assassination. He named Johnson, Nixon and Bush as knowing of the planned assassination, and that the Pegasus group had taped telephone conversations making reference to the operation. He stated that Reagan was not implicated like the others; he was more of a figurehead for powerful factions controlled by former CIA Director Bush.

Parker described the necessity of Pegasus going underground within the CIA because of the inability to report to a president, and that the files on corrupt CIA operations gathered by the Pegasus group were moved to various secret locations. Denver was one of the sites.

Parker said that his Pegasus group secretly gave files on the CIA criminal activities from 1976 to1982 to a member of the Joint Armed Services Committee, Congressman Larry McDonald. These files revealed corrupt activities by several U.S. presidents, federal officials, the CIA, and other members of government.

Parker said that McDonald let it be known to the press that he was going to reveal startling evidence upon his return from the Far East showing that the CIA and certain high-ranking public officials were part of an operation responsible for drug trafficking since 1963 from Southeast Asia. McDonald boarded KAL Flight 007, which was shot down by the Russians.

Operation Mother Goose

Parker described his various assignments in the CIA from when he first joined the Office of Naval Intelligence. He was involved during 1964 in the CIA scheme called Operation Mother Goose dealing with joint military selection, recruitment, and training of qualified enlisted men with security ratings. These people were educated and trained in basic covert and undercover activities. After training they were released from active military duty to enroll in colleges and universities under the GI Bill. While under CIA supervision, they infiltrated student activities and student movements as they related to the Vietnam War and other political areas. Parker trained at the United States Marine Corps base at Camp Pendleton, California.

Operation Back Draft

Parker's next CIA assignment was an enlargement upon Operation Mother Goose called Operation Back Draft. This operation provided financial assistance to students while attending college and trained them to infiltrate and disrupt student activities. Parker participated in this program while attending college and university programs in Southern California.

Another CIA contract agent, Ron Rewald, was used in a similar operation and was later recruited by the CIA to operate a proprietary in Hawaii known as Bishop, Baldwin, Rewald, Dillingham and Wong (BBRDW). This operation is described in detail in the third edition of *Defrauding America.*

To qualify Parker for use in financial operations, the CIA obtained employment for him with New York Stock Exchange brokerage firms from 1971 until 1974 in California and Colorado. While in those positions, he supplied confidential information to the CIA on customers' accounts and transactions. Eventually he opened his own brokerage firm as a front for the CIA through the SEC and NASD.

This is similar to the operation described to me by CIA operative Gunther Russbacher in which Russbacher received training at Mutual Life Insurance Company and then incorporated and operated a number of CIA financial institutions headquartered in Missouri. These institutions had offices throughout the United States including Denver, Dallas, Houston, Atlanta, and Traverse City, Michigan.

Operation Anaconda

Another CIA assignment held by Parker was participation in Operation Anaconda in the mid-1970s, through which CIA personnel ran for state and federal political office. Another purpose of the operation was to swing key elections to a particular candidate, away from one whose interest may be detrimental to the CIA or other covert government unit. This was used against Senator Church and Representative Pike after their committees exposed CIA misconduct.

Parker elaborated upon other CIA operations in which he was involved, including infiltration of U.S. financial institutions, drug operations in Central and South America, and the Nigerian operation known as Indigo Sky.

Operation Interlink

Parker appeared as guest on several talk shows with Tom Valentine of *Radio Free America*.[17] During one appearance on July 29, 1993, he shared the two-hour program with former CIA employee and author Fletcher Prouty,[18] describing the mechanics of the CIA's Operation Interlink. Prouty stated during the show that Parker's revelations "make this one of the most important shows on the CIA that has ever occurred."

Operation Snow Cone

Parker stated that the CIA and Justice Department had sacrificed him in 1982 to protect an ongoing secret scheme called Operation Snow Cone. He had been charged by the Security Exchange Commission (SEC) with a money laundering operation which was part of a CIA operation under Operation Interlink and Operation Gold Bug. This CIA operation was accidentally exposed by the SEC, which was unaware of the CIA's role in the ongoing operation. Usually Justice Department officials in Washington quickly step in and the charges are dropped. But in this case, the SEC charges were filed and publicized by the media so it was too late to retract the charges.

There was another possible reason for filing charges against Parker. He stated that his handlers had asked him to be part of an expanding drug operation in Nigeria called Operation Indigo Sky and that he refused. He didn't care to get involved in drug trafficking, and further, living conditions in Nigeria were deplorable.

Justice Department prosecutors and CIA personnel encouraged Parker to plead guilty, assuring him that he would be released as soon as attention to his case no longer existed. Parker pled guilty in 1982 and he refused all newspaper interviews. He was promptly hidden in the federal prison system, including months of diesel therapy which kept him from a law library and telephone.

The opportunity to seek legal relief arose while Parker was in an Arizona prison where he could prepare and file a post-conviction motion, which was heard by U.S. District Judge Marquez in Tucson on February 12, 1986. The judge ordered the prison warden and the U.S. Attorney to release Parker immediately. In 1992, U.S. Attorney Michael Norton in Denver charged Parker with money laundering charges that had been part of his CIA operations. At his arraignment, the judge ordered him released pending trial that was set for April 1993. Before his release, Parker occupied a cell with Stewart Webb, a private investigator whom I had met earlier, and who was trying to expose the HUD and savings and loan corruption in the Denver area. Webb showed Parker some of my writings, causing Parker to contact me upon his release.

---

[17] A syndicated show of Sun Radio Network, heard throughout the United States, and on short wave five nights a week.

[18] Prouty authored *The Secret Team*, and other CIA books.

Parker said that he had been with the CIA for approximately 30 years and was part of faction "B" and with a unit called Pegasus 222. The CIA reportedly has three factions. Faction One or sometimes referred to as Faction "A," appears to be under the control of the Justice Department: Faction Two or B-faction is supposedly under the control of the Office of Naval Intelligence. Faction. And Faction Three is small, including former OSS operatives and reportedly a loose-knit group of rogues.

While waiting for trial, Parker filed papers with the court listing the secret CIA operations that he would reveal. He also filed a list of documents that he would submit, including the confidential status report showing him to be a Colonel in the U.S. Marines assigned to the Office of Naval Intelligence and to the Central Intelligence Agency.

Once Parker filed the list of documents with the court, an assistant U.S. attorney in Denver complained to the judge that Parker should have filed the documents under seal because they revealed secret CIA activities. Because of those revealing documents, U.S. Attorney Norton dismissed all charges against Parker, which avoided revealing the Agency's dirty linen. Parker called me on March 23, 1993, stating: "All charges have been dropped. I'm going underground. Don't ask any questions." He then hung up.

A year later, in June 1994, the State of Arizona again sought to extradite Parker from Colorado. Colorado attorney Dennis L. Blewitt said to me that almost twenty law-enforcement personnel surrounded Parker's home and arrested him, based upon the Arizona extradition papers.

Parker then sought to have the papers filed in the previous extradition attempt, in the possession of another judge, sent to the court where the new extradition request was to be heard. Blewitt and several friends went to the clerk of the court where the case was pending, requesting help in getting from the other judge the necessary documents. When the clerk heard the name of the book *Defrauding America* she reached under the counter and pulled out a copy. When she realized that Parker was in the book she told the group not to worry, that she would get the records for Parker.

Reportedly, the clerk and the two judges had a copy of the book with Parker's activities described in detail. Arizona requested that a $500,000 cash bond be required for Parker's release pending a hearing on the extradition request. The judge settled for $3,500. After Parker was released he called me, describing the events, and said that even the Thornton city police, who arrested him, had a copy of *Defrauding America* in the police station, and it was being read by the people on duty. Several times Parker credited the book with bringing about his release. The way he described the events caused me to chuckle.

Prison Release Brought About by *Defrauding America* Book

After federal charges were dropped against Parker the State of Arizona filed money-laundering charges against him, arising from Parker's earlier CIA activities. Extradition papers were filed with Colorado authorities where Parker was residing, seeking to have him extradited to Arizona. Parker felt that this charge arose from activities of the United States Department of Justice.

Fighting extradition, Parker filed into court records the Expanded Second Edition of *Defrauding America*, referring to the sections explaining Parker's CIA activities and telling how Justice Department officials sought to silence or discredit CIA assets by filing sham charges and incarceration. The judge refused to honor the extradition papers from Arizona, ordering Parker released from custody. Parker felt that the book played a role in his release.

Meeting Foster at Mena

Before I would eventually lose contact with Parker, he described to me during a June 1994 telephone call a meeting he had at Mena, Arkansas at which there were present CIA asset Terry Reed and Rose Law Firm partner Vincent Foster. Parker said that CIA money laundering was the primary topic of discussion. This meeting provided extra support for the fact that the law firm was involved in the CIA-related activities.

Another source that I describe in *Defrauding America*, Leo Wanta, who played a role in destabilizing the Russian currency, described meetings he had in Europe with Vincent Foster.

During the years following these events Parker told me he wanted nothing else to do with any of the corruption in government. He felt that the nation's checks and balances were too corrupt, the public too illiterate about government misconduct, and too indifferent, for anyone to show any meaningful concern.

OSS-CIA Veteran Russell Bowen

Former OSS-CIA veteran, Russell Bowen, revealed considerable undercover activities to me when we first met in the early 1990s. Our somewhat similar backgrounds caused him to confide things in me that he ordinarily would not have done. Both of us were World War II pilots. We had flown in international operations and especially in the Middle East. And we had both flown the Curtis C-46 airplane which appears to bond into a group those pilots who have flown it. It was huge for the time, and when one of the two engines failed, it was like hanging onto a raging tiger to keep the plane under control. (This broad aviation background, and my crusader activities, gave me a camaraderie relationship with many deep-cover sources that I acquired over the years.)

Bowen gave me many hours of information concerning his activities for the OSS and CIA. Much of what Bowen told me was confirmed by other deep-cover operatives. The amount of information he provided was nothing near what Russbacher provided, but it still was valuable to understand the actions of the CIA and its predecessor during World War II, the Office of Strategic Services.

Bowen was a pilot in World War II flying P-38's with the rank of Lieutenant Colonel. He received the Distinguished Flying Cross, the Distinguished Service Medal, and other decorations for meritorious service. He said he was the youngest P-38 fighter pilot at that time.

Bowen in OSS and Then CIA Faction Three

During World War II, Bowen was brought into the OSS by General William Donovan, who was selected by President Franklin Roosevelt to form this intelligence unit. When President Truman disbanded the OSS in 1947, several dozen OSS members secretly maintained their organization under the cover of the CIA and were known as "Faction Three" in the Central Intelligence Agency. Bowen was part of a group of about seventy-five people from the former Office of Strategic Services (OSS).

In his OSS/CIA role, Bowen was the pilot for United Nations Secretary General Dag Hammerskjold, the Shah of Iran, and eventually Fulgencio Batista, the former dictator of Cuba. My flight paths and Bowen's had crossed when my piloting duties took me to the Middle East on temporary assignment from my base at Oakland, California. I flew Moslem pilgrims to Mecca during the summer months in the mid-1950s, and also flew through Middle East countries flying planes containing over 1600 monkeys from New Delhi, India to the United States for the Salk polio vaccine program. Bowen often flew DC-3 and C-46 aircraft from Kabul, Afghanistan to Beirut via Teheran, the route that I frequently flew in the same type of aircraft. Bowen was flying material for the CIA.

Bowen surprised me when he said that two employees of the airline that I worked for, Transocean Airlines, were CIA operatives: Allan A. Barrie, General Manager for Iranian Airways in Teheran, and Henry F. "Hank" Maierhoffer. I had flown for Transocean Airlines and had known them when I flew in the Middle East during the early 1950s but had no idea they were engaged in such activities. Bowen started up several airlines in South America after the war that served as covers for the CIA.

Casey's Undercover CIA Operations

Bowen said that he reported directly to William Casey in the CIA during the 1960s and 1970s. He indicated that Casey was with the CIA in a covert capacity after World War II and long before becoming its director in 1981. Bowen said that he flew dozens of covert CIA operations in the Middle East and Latin America, under Casey's direction. Bowen also mentioned meeting Casey and other handlers on his trips to Washington at secret places and receiving verbal instructions and suitcases filled with money.

Casey was part of the OSS during World War II until it was disbanded by President Truman in 1947. He then became a covert operative for the CIA with no publicized connection to the Agency until 1981, when President Reagan appointed him Director of the CIA.

Bowen elaborated upon his dealings with the Medellin and Cali drug cartels as a CIA operative and the role played by the Mossad in these dealings. Bowen was a friend of Theodore Shackley, a CIA kingpin in CIA drug activities, working closely with the cartels. Bowen said that the CIA provided Theodore Shackley the alias of Robert Haynes. Bowen worked with Shackley from the early 1950s to 1984.

Crashing in the Andes

In 1959, Shackley was on board a C-46 aircraft flown by Bowen when an engine failure forced them to crash-land on the eastern slopes of the Andes in Bolivia. I've also flown C-46 aircraft, and know that with an engine out, it is very difficult to maintain level flight, and especially at the high altitude being flown over the Andes. The plane crashed, but everyone survived.

I had an opportunity to question Shackley on this crash while I was a guest at the national convention for the Association of Former Intelligence Officers (AFIO) held at San Francisco in November 1995. While eating lunch at the convention I suddenly spotted Shackley and his wife sitting immediately across from me. Since I did not know if he had read my earlier books in which I made reference to him, and since I wanted to be low-key at this convention, I didn't introduce myself to him. However, I wanted to get Shackle's reaction to the plane crash described by Bowen, and asked former National Security Agency (NSA) agent Joe T. Jordan, who sponsored my appearance at the convention, to ask.

Crash Landing with CIA and Drugs on Board

Jordan said that Shackley "stated unequivocally that it was untrue." I didn't think that Bowen would lie to me on a matter like that so I called Bowen at his Florida residence, advising him of Shackle's reply. I asked, "Was there something going on with that flight that Shackley would not want anyone to know that he was on it?"

"Of course! It was loaded with drugs!" Bowen responded. Bowen enlarged upon the purpose of that trip. He stated that this trip occurred several years before Shackley was made CIA station chief in Miami, and that Shackley was instrumental in setting up the CIA drug trafficking into the United States from South America. Bowen said that the series of flights went from Miami, to Colombia, to Quayaqui, to Lima, and then to Arequita. After the plane left Arequita going eastbound over the Andes, one of the two engines failed, causing the aircraft to lose altitude. Bowen was able to maneuver the aircraft into one of the few available flat areas, and crash-landed the plane.

Bowen said that Shackley had arranged for cocaine to be loaded on board the aircraft, where it was hidden in the tail section. Bowen, Shackley, and the others then abandoned the crashed aircraft. Eventually the Bolivian authorities discovered the drugs, but the pilots and passengers were long gone. This would explain why Shackley wanted to distance himself from that crash.

Key CIA Official Setting up Drug Suppliers and Routes

Bowen said that Shackley went to Ascension, Paraguay to arrange for drugs to be shipped to Miami, meeting with the head chief of one of the Indian groups and a Lieutenant Colonel in Paraguay's military. Bowen said that these people were the backbone of Strainer's intelligence and drug dealing activities.

Bowen described the conflict between different CIA factions. "At that time," Bowen said, "Shackley was the leader of the CIA faction bringing the drugs in. The CIA team I worked for did not want the drugs in."

CIA Mastermind of Drug Route from South America

I asked who set up that initial drug operation. Bowen, referring to Shackley, said, "He was the mastermind of the drug operation. He had full authority to set it up."

Referring to the CIA headquarters that was first in Washington and then in McLean, Virginia, I asked, "Would you have any knowledge of whether McLean or Washington was aware of this drug operation?"

"They ordered him to do it."

Money Laundering Proprietaries

Bowen described one of the CIA proprietaries operated by Shackley, INTERKREDIT, with offices in Medellin, Amsterdam, and Ft. Lauderdale. During the Vietnam War Shackley helped manage the extensive CIA drug operations in the Golden Triangle Area, and was the executive director of the CIA Phoenix Program (that murdered over 40,000 Vietnamese civilians). Shackley directed the CIA's secret war against Laos in the mid-1960s, and later became chief of station in Saigon. He directed the transfer of tens of millions if not billions of dollars received from the CIA-promoted heroin trade in the Golden Triangle of Burma, Thailand, and Laos.

When Shackley was chief of station for the CIA in charge of Central and South American operations, he reportedly directed the massive drug trafficking into the United States that subsequently blossomed. He directed the operation known as "TRACK II," which led to the overthrow of the Salvador Allende government in Chile in 1973. He was just the man to coordinate the CIA's development of the burgeoning drug trafficking from Central and South America into the United States.

Bowen gave me details of the CIA ties to the Medellin drug cartel that Russbacher and Parker had described to me earlier. Each gave me details of the formation of the Medellin cartel from another perspective.

Unusual Attempt to Expose CIA Drug Trafficking

Bowen, like many other CIA operatives, became disenchanted with the CIA drug trafficking. In 1981, he wrote anonymous letters to U.S. Customs in Miami, reporting the details of the drug operation in the hope that it would be stopped. Nothing happened. During a flight in 1982, he tried another method to get publicity; as should have been expected, it backfired on him.

Bowen said that he was requested by CIA operative Henry Meierhoffer[19] to fly a trip to Medellin, Colombia carrying a government undercover agent and to return with another agent. But when Bowen arrived in Medellin, Shackley placed eight hundred pounds of cocaine on board the return flight, including two hundred pounds belonging to the Mossad.

On the return flight to the United States with the cocaine, he decided to land at an airport that had intensive surveillance for drug trafficking, Sylvania Airport in Georgia. His intent was to alert the authorities to the cocaine load and, in his way of thinking, cause the local police to take action against the CIA. This was rather naive, but his heart was in the right place. Bowen was blowing the whistle on the huge international drug operation involving some of the highest officials in the U.S. government. The plan backfired. Bowen was arrested for drug trafficking.

Standard Silencing Tactic

Bowen said that at his trial in 1985, the U.S. District Judge refused to allow him to have his CIA handlers, including Meierhoffer, appear as witnesses. The Judge refused to allow Bowen to produce records and testimony showing that he was carrying out CIA activities. Refusing to allow evidence to be pre-

---

[19] On March 2, 1984. Interestingly, Meierhoffer had been an employee of Transocean Airlines in Beirut during the time I was a captain for the airline.

sented that is necessary to a person's defense, when covert government activities are involved, is a standard pattern by federal judges. Almost every CIA and DEA person with whom I have talked, and who had been imprisoned, experienced this pattern, including Russbacher, Rewald, Riconosciuto, Wilson, and others.

Bowen's court-appointed defender displayed the usual lack of aggressiveness, with no desire to raise a defense that would expose covert government activities. It is probable that the naive jury felt that Justice Department prosecutors surely would not lie or bring false charges against an innocent person. They convicted Bowen, and he was sentenced to ten years in prison.

DEA-CIA Drugs-Arms-Trafficker, Basil Abbott

Another pilot with whom I had been in frequent contact was Basil "Bo" Abbott, who operated in the lower levels of undercover operations as a pilot for the Drug Enforcement Administration (DEA). His experiences provided another insight into the bizarre world of CIA and DEA drug trafficking. Abbott flew arms from the United States to Central and South America from 1973 to 1983 in small general aviation planes that were provided to him by the DEA. Over a period of several years Abbott provided me with details and maps relating to these arms and drug activities for the DEA and CIA.

DEA Drug Pilot Training at FAA Center, Oklahoma City

Abbott described receiving specialized pilot training from DEA Air Wing Commander, William Coller, at the FAA Academy in Oklahoma City, preparing him to fly drugs in and out of short dirt strips in Central and South America, how to ditch in the water, and other emergencies. Classroom training was given on how to avoid radar detection, the routes to fly and the hours to fly them so as to avoid detection by drug interdiction aircraft. Coller trained Abbott in numerous aircraft, including the Cessna 180, 185, 206, 210, and 310, and Piper Aztec, Aerostar and Navajo. (In 1999, Coller confirmed to me that he coordinated the Air Wing operation and that he did give Abbott flight training.)

During Abbott's DEA employment, he worked out of DEA offices in Denver, Charleston, and in 1978 the DEA facility at Addison Airport, north of Dallas. Abbott named other DEA pilots who, acting under DEA orders, flew drug flights from Central America to the United States. These pilots included Cesar Rodriguez, Daniel Miranda, and George Phillips.

Flying Arms For the DEA to Central America and Drugs Back

Abbott was ordered by the DEA to fly arms to numerous Central America locations. One of these flights, occurring in 1982, flew arms into a dirt strip near Bluefields, Nicaragua for the Miskito Indians. From there, Abbot flew to a strip known as B2E, where drugs were loaded for the return flight to the United States. Some of these flights landed at a small airfield near Memphis, Tennessee.

These flights were profitable for everyone involved, including the pilots. In addition to being paid in cash for each flight, pilots flying for the DEA were sometimes given part of the drug loads, which they later sold. Abbott received $60,000 and fifty pounds of pot for this flight to the Miskito Indians and return with drugs.

Abbott described flying drug loads out of small landing strips in Nicaragua, Antigua, Honduras, Costa Rica, Salvador, Guatemala, Belize, and Mexico. He arranged for fuel supplies and ground facilities at these locations, and regularly bribed local politicians to cooperate and protect the arms and drug flights. These flights were hazardous in many ways. Abbott described DEA pilots flying arms to the M-19 group in Colombia, during which some of the pilots were assassinated. Abbott's fluency in several languages besides English—Spanish, Swedish, Norwegian, and Danish—was helpful in covert activities. During his DEA-associated activities, he circulated in prominent Central America society, socializing with well-known political figures, including Alfredo Stroessner in Paraguay.

Abbott described a Bolivian 707 that regularly hauled drugs into Panama with the DEA's knowledge. When Abbott asked his DEA handlers about it, they told him to forget it.

Drug Planes Like Grand Central Station

"It was like Grand Central Station at some airstrips in Belize and Nicaragua," was how Abbott described the number of planes flying drugs. Abbott told how he and other DEA personnel flew to Santa Cruz, Bolivia, in a Convair 340 to set a trap for the son of the Israeli Ambassador, Sam Weisgal, involving a large shipment of cocaine to the United States. When the drug bust occurred, several people were killed. The DEA seized the drugs and then reshipped them as if they were DEA loads. Weisgal escaped the drug bust, but was later captured. However, Israeli pressure brought about his release.

Danger Of Knowing Too Much about CIA-DEA Drug Trafficking

On a flight to Cancun, Mexico (June 1983), DEA agents acting with Mexican police arrested Abbott. While in jail, he was interrogated by DEA agents Richard Braziel, Torry Schutz, Jerry Carter, and Assistant U.S. Attorney (AUSA) John Murphy. When Abbott wouldn't answer the questions, Mexican police, at Brazil's request, tortured him. U.S. agents then transported Abbott to a county jail in San Antonio, Texas, where he was visited by CIA agents who assured him that he would be released shortly. Instead, Abbott was sentenced to eight years in prison by Judge Fred Shannon. DEA agent Richard Braziel then told Abbott the sentence was only for show, and that they would get him released if he did not say anything about the DEA and CIA drug operations.

Abbott was eventually released. After his release on probation, Abbott tried to obtain media interest in DEA drug trafficking, including the Larry King Show. He had no more success than I had during 30 years of attempting to expose government corruption. Abbott even tried to give his evidence to Manuel Noriega's attorneys to show how Noriega was simply a part of the CIA, DEA, and Mossad drug trafficking into the United States.

One source did respond to Abbott's publicity efforts: the DEA, FBI, and Department of Justice. They fabricated a reason for arresting Abbott while on probation, stating that he had left the geographical limits of his parole at Dallas by flying a private plane to nearby Austin. Upon readying his plane for the return flight to Dallas, government agents arrested him, charging him with violating parole conditions.

Death to DEA Chief Pilot Exposing
Government DEA-CIA Drug Trafficking

Abbott described his frequent contacts with the DEA's Central America Bureau Chief, Sante Bario, and how the DEA silenced Bario to keep the CIA and DEA drug smuggling operations from the public. Bario was supervising agent in Mexico City for Central and South American affairs.

According to Coller, Bario became involved in drug trafficking on the side and was set up by a government informant in Chicago, where he was arrested. Another source had it that Bario knew too much about Mexican and U.S. government involvement in drugs, and that either or both governments wanted him out of the way.

DEA and Justice Department attorneys charged Bario with drug offenses, causing his imprisonment. When Bario was brought before U.S. District Judge Fred Shannon in San Antonio, Bario reportedly tried to describe his DEA duties and the DEA and CIA drug trafficking, but Justice Department attorneys and the judge blocked him from proceeding. After being returned to his jail cell in the Bexar County Jail in San Antonio, a prison guard gave Bario a strychnine-laced peanut-butter sandwich, causing immediate painful convulsions and subsequent death. The official autopsy report covered up for this murder, reporting that Bario died of asphyxiation.

Abbott described acquiring a common-law wife in Norway who later bore their child. She moved to the United States and started an import business bringing sweaters into the United States from Norway and Iceland. Abbott feared for the safety of his wife and daughter after the DEA targeted him, and he sent them back to Sweden.

Assassinating Abbott's Wife

After he was arrested and in federal prison at Bastrop (near San Antonio, Texas) his wife, living in Sweden, tried to get media attention on the DEA drug trafficking by talking to newspapers in Germany, hoping that this attention would force the DEA and Justice Department to release Abbott. Instead, she joined the long list of those who posed a threat to U.S. officials and their criminal activities; she was assassinated.

Abbott's grief over his wife's assassination, and the constant attempts by government agents to silence him, made him determined to expose the drug trafficking by the DEA, CIA and Justice Department. He sent me many letters describing in great detail the DEA and CIA drug operations, including maps of landing sites, people he contacted, and the names of other DEA pilots.

Abbott was released from prison on November 14, 1994, and became one of several former prisoners who credit my letters (such as to the parole board in Abbott's case), along with a copy of the second edition of *Defrauding America*, with bringing about their release.

Operation Buy Back—CIA-DEA Drug Smuggling Operation

Abbott told of an operation, which CIA-ONI agent Gunther Russbacher enlarged upon, involving smuggling drugs in frozen shrimp, using a CIA front company, Pacific Seafood Transportation Company. Russbacher and other CIA operatives confirmed the drug trafficking by Pacific Seafood. Russbacher said that shrimp containers "were filled with ice and everything but shrimp."

He said it was part of a joint DEA-CIA operation called Operation Buy Back.

Abbott described many of the people with whom he came in contact who were also heavily involved in drug-related activities. He described his close contacts with Eric Arturo Del-Valle, a member of Panama's Jewish community, and who was president of Panama. Arthur's family was in the sugar export business, which Abbott said was a subterfuge for cocaine exports to the United States by the Mossad.

Using Export Companies as Fronts to Ship Drugs

Abbott described the relationship between the major Bolivian drug traffickers, Sonia and Walter Atala, and the Roberto Suarez cocaine gang and the CIA. The Atalas leased a Boeing 727 in 1980 and 1981, painted the name Lloyd Aero Boliviano on the side, and used it to haul cocaine into Tocumen Airport from Bolivia and Paraguay. At Tocumen Airport the cocaine was off-loaded to a warehouse owned by the Atalas, which was a front for exporting Hitachi radios and television sets back to Bolivia and Paraguay. (Abbott also picked up cocaine numerous times at Tocumen Airport.)

From Tocumen Airport the cocaine was loaded onto small planes, or onto TACA Airlines, flying to the United States. Every morning at 6 a.m. TACA departed Tocumen for El Salvador, Belize, Costa Rica, Nicaragua, and eventually to New Orleans, Miami, and Houston. Cocaine was off-loaded at one or all of these stops in the United States. The cocaine would sometimes be driven from Atoll's warehouse at Tocumen to the Colon Free Trade Zone, placed into another of Atoll's front companies, and eventually put on ships going to the United States. Abbott described the frequent presence of Manuel Noriega at CIA and DEA drug transshipment points. He said that Noriega's CIA code name was "Nelson."

Belize as A Major Drug Transshipment Point

Abbott described the heavy drug trafficking occurring in Belize and how that country was used by the CIA for training Contras, similar to what was occurring in Arkansas at Mena Airport. Abbott described Operation Bushmaster in Belize, which was intended to take over the drug business from the many independent drug smugglers, being taken over by the CIA for greater profit and greater security. Busting independent drug traffickers was one of the joint CIA-Justice Department tactics to control the drug business into the United States. So powerful was the CIA's presence in Belize that it literally took over the government.

Helping Former Savings & Loan Kingpin with Drug Trafficking

He described a Mexican cocaine processing lab that he discovered north of Cuatrocienegas in the state of Chihuahua. Abbott stated that he helped Robert Corson, well known in the savings and loan scandals of the 1980s, set up that lab, after which DEA agents arrested Abbott. Abbott stated that cocaine processed at that lab was transported by land, and sometimes by air, to a small airstrip at Lajitas in West Texas, on land controlled by Walt Mischer. From there it was then flown to other points in the United States.

The Arkansas Connection

One of the Arkansas airstrips into which Abbott was directed to deliver drugs was south of Interstate 30 just southwest of W. Memphis, Tennessee, called Marianna. Several of my other deep-cover contacts described drugs going into that same airport, and the role played by state police in protecting the drug and arms operations.

DEA Agent Received Drug Load in Arkansas
While Arkansas State Police Provided Protection

Abbott described how Arkansas State Police protected drug loads by blocking off roads leading to small airstrips when drug flights arrived. He described one such instance occurring in the spring of 1982. Abbott flew a Cessna 210 containing 300 kilos of cocaine from one of several warehouses at Tocumen owned by drug traffickers Walter and Sonia Atala, to the crop-duster landing strip at Marianna, Arkansas. He made a fuel stop in Belize, famous for transition of drug-loaded aircraft, and then proceeded to his Marianna destination. A Memphis-based DEA agent took the cocaine from Abbott, while an Arkansas state trooper blocked the road leading to the landing strip. A week later, Abbott took off from that strip with six suitcases of money, delivering it to Cesar Rodriguez at Isla Contadora. Abbott said the plane was provided by Robert Corson through Jim Bath of Houston.

Further Confirmation of CIA-DEA Theft of Planes

Abbott described the CIA stealing of general aviation planes within the United States for use in the CIA's arms and drug shipments. This coincided with what several of my CIA contacts had stated to me for several years, and as described by former CIA asset Terry Reed in his book, *Compromised*. The stolen aircraft were repainted and new serial numbers applied, after which they were flown to Central and South America with loads of arms, and then drugs on the return flights.

Mexican Airliners and Drugs

It was in the early 1990s that Abbott described how he arranged the unloading of drugs from Mexican airliners in the Mexican desert near Texas. At the time this sounded rather bizarre, but his detailed description of the events over a period of several years convinced me that he was telling the truth. Further, an article (November 30, 1995) in the *New York Times* (and earlier in the *Los Angeles Times*) was headlined, "Drug Plane Unloaded in Mexico, Maybe by Police." The article described a Caravelle passenger jet being landed on a dry lake bed near Todos Santos, Mexico. The Caravelle was a French-built airliner that was flown by United Airlines during the 1960s.

Mexican Federal Police Protecting Drug Operation

Normally this operation would have gone unreported, as many others had occurred. But this drug operation was reported because of the unusual events surrounding its occurrence. The aircraft's nosewheel was damaged upon landing, preventing a subsequent takeoff. The article described how heavily-armed federal police unloaded the plane after it landed and then proceeded to destroy the aircraft. All identifying documents and avionics equipment were removed from the plane, the wings cut off, and an attempt made to blow up the plane. A large hole was bulldozed in the ground and the plane was buried.

Confrontation Between Mexican State and Federal Police

Complications developed while the plane was being destroyed. The state police commander and several deputies arrived to investigate, and were confronted in a tense standoff with the federal police, who advised that the army had been notified and the situation was under control. The 30 federal policemen involved in the drug operation were suddenly transferred and unavailable for questioning by the federal prosecutor in the Baja California jurisdiction.

Making reference to the use of large jets in similar situations, Mexican Foreign Minister Jose Angel Gurria said in a recent interview that drug traffickers had stopped using large passenger jets.

CIA Cable Analyst Michael Maholy

For several years, starting in 1993, I was in contact with deep-cover operative Michael Maholy whose primary duty was monitoring cable traffic at different CIA locations. Maholy started giving me information and a different slant on the role of federal officials in drug trafficking from Central and South America into the United States. Maholy said he was a liaison officer for the U.S. Embassy in Panama and worked for the U.S. State Department and CIA for over two decades. Maholy wrote in one of his letters about his role at a U.S. Embassy. In one of his many letters he wrote:

I have spent time in South American countries providing photos, documents, maps, and all intelligence for the U.S. Embassies in Central and South America. I first became acquainted with agent [Robert] Hunt in 1985 in Panama where I was the liaison officer for the U.S. Embassy. He was always accompanied by [Oliver] North and his team. This went on for several years. I recall reading cable traffic where his name came up repeatedly.

During my contacts with [CIA Director] William Casey, I was drafted into the Southern Zone (Central and South American countries) so that we could start operations on spying on Panama, Colombia, and other countries that were making huge amounts of money from drugs. They needed weapons and fire power. We, the CIA, provided them. They in turn sold us drugs ... many instances of cover-up conspiracies that continue to multiply as we are talking.

On one tour to South America I worked on a CIA-owned oil rig operated by a company called Rowan International, based in Houston, Texas. Rowan is a world-wide drilling exploration company with very friendly liaisons in Central America and South America, as well as Africa and Middle East.

While in Balboa Harbor off the coast of Panama, on the rig Rowan Houston, at approximately 2:00 a.m., a helicopter landed on the heliport. I was monitoring cables and traffic when our radar detected a small support group which turned out to be patrol boats, four in all. At this point I thought the rig was going to be taken over by hostile forces. But instead I could not believe who was getting out of the chopper: it was Noriega and another man. I contacted the "company man" and he informed me that this meeting was not to be documented and to go back and resume the task of cable and traffic. I found out later that this man with Noriega was [Mossad agent] Michael Harari. I found out later that they were trying to raise money for the CIA by selling drugs to plan the destruction of a hydroelectric power plant on the Orinoco River in Venezuela.

Over a period of many months, Maholy gave me details of CIA and Mossad drug trafficking. He named the companies owning the oil rigs off the coast of the United States, Central and South America, Nigeria, and Angola: Santa Fe, Zapata, and Rowan. He physically saw Evergreen International Airlines and Southern Air Transport hauling drugs, confirmed by cable traffic he handled.

I had repeatedly heard from investigators and CIA contacts that various divisions of the Zapata Corporation,[20] such as Zapata Petroleum, Zapata Off-Shore, Zapata Cattle Company, were heavily involved in drug trafficking. The oil rigs were used to carry out the drug operations. Drugs would be off-loaded from ships onto the drilling platforms and then taken into the nearby coastal areas in helicopters that were constantly carrying supplies and personnel. Maholy confirmed that this practice existed, having learned about it from CIA cable traffic and his own observations while on the rigs.

In another letter, Maholy wrote in part:

The real mission [of these oil and gas drilling platforms] was to funnel weapons and money to the Nicaraguans, and also to bring illegal drugs into the United States. Being a CIA-funded mission, the rig had Naval SEAL teams diverted through its location....Rowan International was a cover for a branch of Zapata Oil. Zapata Oil and Exploration had many land-based operations in Central and South America as well as offshore rigs.

We had access to military cryptographics such as the kW 135, the KL 16, KL 10 and the CW 4 to decode and sifter out any cable traffic from transmissions from Guatemala, El Salvador, Costa Rica, and Panama.

Maholy confirmed what other CIA sources had told me about the CIA drug trafficking through Pacific Seafood. He wrote:

This company [Pacific Seafood] used a number of vessels to carry out covert missions to run weapons, drugs and cash from country to country. Not only would their "shrimp" trawlers use the oil rigs for loading, unloading and refueling, and also to deliver large sums of money for aid to the Contras. The shrimpers would constantly converge on our rig to convert, store and transport all of the above. The crews were all seasoned paramilitary experts in their abilities to search and destroy, CIA trained and specialists in their fields.

It was from one of the shrimp boat captains that I would come to meet Barry Seal's main right-wing contact from Morgan City, La. His name was Russell Hebert, and the name on his shrimp boat was Southern Crossing. This boat had state-of-the-art radar, hi-tech navigation systems, extra fuel tanks, and a crew consisting only of "special forces or [Navy] Seals."

Maholy wrote that he remembers Russell Bowen flying onto the rig and then flying two DEA agents to Colombia. I called Bowen, who lived in Winter Haven, Florida at the time, and asked him about this flight. Bowen confirmed

---

[20] Zapata Corporation, based in Houston, was a CIA asset, and the stock partly owned by George Bush. Zapata Petroleum was organized by George Bush, who reportedly had major interests in various Zapata divisions

that it was him. I said to Bowen that Maholy mentioned having seen him at the oil rig, and Bowen then confirmed it, stating it was part of the operation that extracted CIA agent Sam Cummings from Costa Rica.

Offshore Oil Rigs and Drugs

Maholy described the drugs that he had seen on the oil platforms operated by the CIA and Zapata Corporation. In one letter he wrote, "A shrimp boat arrived with a load of cocaine with the markings of the Mossad's famous two triangles that resembled the Star of David."

Flying Slow to Avoid Suspicion

Maholy described how the drug planes would fly low and proceed from the off-shore oil rigs to the United States at very slow speeds of approximately 120 knots, so that they would appear on radar as helicopters servicing the rigs. Maholy described how the Ochoa drug cartel used the coastal oil rigs for drug transshipments. He described the role of a Venezuelan naval officer by the name of Lizardo Marquez Perez, who was in charge of this drug operation, and frequently seen on the oil rigs by Maholy.

Maholy described the coverup of the drug operation by such people as the Chief of the DEA cocaine operations in Washington, Ron Caffrey, Oliver North, CIA's Duane (Dewey) Clarridge, Army Lieutenant General Paul Gorman (commander of the Panama-based U.S. Southern Command), and others. Excerpts from some of Manhole's letters:

A person I've met on several occasions was in the Colombia Cartel, Carlos Lehder. During Operation Back Door he and several of his soldiers were planning to use CIA oil rigs and the shrimp industries to import drugs into America. Carlos had DEA personnel assigned to work with him. I myself have been to his home on Norman's Cay in the Bahamas. He had a stash of drugs shipped back and forth to Everglade City in the Ten Thousands Islands area of Southern Florida. When the rig Rowan Midland was in Venezuela, Carlos had a regular agent of his as a tool-pusher to oversee all shipments coming and going. The CIA would buy drugs and supply friends of the Colombian government with money and weapons.

They used the remote mangrove swamps to unload huge loads of pot and cocaine to get it to Miami to distribute. With help from CIA and DEA agents, Carlos would set up a few loads as decoy to make it look good so he could get major shipments into the United States. Operation Back Door had a priority of great importance. I was to monitor some of the cable and equipment, also scramble transmissions made from his boats and planes, so he could go undetected.

Also to make sure his money would be on the rig when he wanted it. Carlos got to be "mouthy." The government set him up and double crossed him. The rig was then moved to Aruba and once again set up as a relay station and command center. The M-19 group was also involved in several covert missions. Operation Back Door simply meant the drugs would come to America via the back door.

Maholy described his dealings with drug trafficker Barry Seal (aka Ellis McKenzie and a former pilot for TWA Airlines). Maholy said that Seal was involved with the Noriega Cartel in a top-secret operation. Seal's Miami contact was a person using the name of "Lit." They flew through airspace "windows" when the military radar would ignore the targets. As the planes approached the oilrigs off the coast of the United States the planes flew close to the water, avoiding radar detection.

Getting rid of the Drug Competition

Maholy elaborated upon his role in Operation Screamer which was a mammoth sting operation aimed at penetrating the network of mercenary pilots that were flying drugs in competition with the CIA. On this operation Maholy worked under DEA agent-in-charge Randy Beasley. Maholy told how Seal offered to turn informant, allegedly implicating high federal officials, including former Watergate prosecutor Richard Ben-Veniste. Maholy stated that "this made Beasley and others uneasy. Why? Because they themselves were dirty."

Largest Heroin Seizure in U.S. History: Another CIA Drug Operation

Much of what is written in the media is not what it seems. In May 1991, federal agents seized over 1,000 pounds of heroin in an Oakland, California warehouse, reportedly the largest heroin seizure in the nation's history at that time. Due to the compartmentalization common to intelligence agencies, the arresting agents were unaware that they interrupted a large-scale drug smuggling operation involving the CIA.

Five people were charged with importing heroin, possession with intent to distribute heroin, and conspiracy. A subtitle to a *San Francisco Examiner* article describing the case stated it was the "largest-ever seizure." Over 1,000 pounds of high-grade "China White" heroin was smuggled into the Port of Oakland from Taiwan.

The 1991 seizure of the largest quantity of China White heroin involved the arrest of two families from Thailand who lived in nearby Danville, California. The case was assigned to Judge Vaughn Walker.[21] His actions, and those of the Justice Department attorneys, showed evidence of covering up the CIA drug operation. Apparently, they learned that the drug seizure involved an ongoing CIA drug smuggling operation, and they now had to keep the lid on the drug seizure and avoid a publicity-generating trial.

Standard Practice of Judicial And
Justice Department Obstruction of Justice

Despite this being the biggest heroin seizure in the nation's history, Justice Department prosecutors and District Judge Vaughn Walker approved a lenient sentence for most of the defendants. Through a plea agreement reached in July 1993, the defendants pled guilty in exchange for probation or a short prison sentence. Several of the defendants pled guilty to knowing a federal crime had been committed and failing to promptly report it to federal authorities. By failing to promptly report a federal crime to a federal judge or other federal officer, the failure becomes a crime by itself (Title 18 U.S.C. Section 4). The plea agreement with its lenient terms eliminated a trial that could have exposed high-level government connections to the heroin operation.

---

[21] *USA vs Chen, et al.*, CR 91-2096 VRW.

Operation New Wave and Operation Backlash

CIA agent Gunther Russbacher first told me about that operation on August 23, 1993. He said it was a major heroin trafficking operation into the United States, and that the code name for the parent operation was Operation New Wave. The drug trafficking operation was coded as NW 688-01-B-NSC and called Operation New Wave. One segment was named Operation Backlash and coded BL421-D-06.

Russbacher stated that the operation, sanctioned on September 21, 1987, originated in San Francisco, and operated out of the offices of Levi International Imports-Pier 51. He then gave me the names of many key participants in the operation. He said that key personnel from the CIA included David Fuller from Los Angeles; John Beardsley from Mississippi, and Patrick O'Riley from New York City.

He said that those involved from the U.S. Department of Justice included Russ Taylor out of Lincoln, Nebraska; Saul Trattafiore out of Williamsport, and Sandy Weingarten out of St. Louis. Russbacher stated that they were all attorneys and, he believed, also Assistant U.S. Attorneys.

Drug Enforcement Administration participants in the drug operation, according to Russbacher, included Michael Cobb out of Orlando, and John David Pigg out of Oklahoma City. Pigg was killed in July 1993 in Anadarko, Oklahoma, reportedly for expressing disenchantment with the operation.

Russbacher described Navy Task Force liaison personnel as himself, using his navy alias of Robert Andrew Walker; John A. Woodruff (CIA person using that alias, and who is now deceased), and CIA operative Oswald LeWinter (with whom I had been in contact for many years).

Referring to Customs, Russbacher identified key participants as David Cohen out of the El Paso office; Precilla Montemajor and Taulyn Weber out of the San Francisco office, and Brett Sanderson out of the Seattle office.

Naming Mossad Agents

During a telephone conversation (September 6, 1993) Russbacher gave me the names of the Mossad personnel implicated in this drug trafficking operation who handled drug distribution in the San Francisco area.

First name is Robert Silberman, out of Chicago. Second name is Marta Bleiblatt, also out of Chicago. Third name, Simon, last name Goldblatt, he is out of Haifa and attached to New York. Fourth name, Ariel Colderman, San Francisco. Fifth one is Kasam Merchant, out of Los Angeles. Sixth one is David Turner, San Jose. Silberman and Bleiberg work for a company called Edeco. Goldblatt is a field supervisor on Operation White Elephant. The next one, the last three, are attached to Operation Lemgolem.

I told him that I would list their names in the next edition of *Defrauding America*, and he warned me about the viciousness of the Mossad and their killing of people in various countries whose statements or conduct displeased them. "I have no use for the Mossad and the harm they've inflicted upon the United States, and I'll take my chances," was my reply.

Mossad's Drug Trafficking

Several of my CIA and DEA sources who were directly involved in the drug trafficking described the Mossad's role in Central and South American drug trafficking. These sources described how the Mossad marked their drug packages, how the Mossad shared space on CIA aircraft flying drugs into the United States, and about the vast network of Mossad operatives throughout Central and South America engaging in drug smuggling.

Mossad operatives connected with the drug operations included Michael "Freddy" Harari and David Kimche. Both worked hand-in-hand with the CIA and the drug traffickers, including the Medellin and Cali Cartels. When U.S. forces invaded Panama to arrest Noriega, Harari was caught in the fighting. Despite the fact that the Mossad's role in drug trafficking was serious and that he was a co-conspirator with Noriega, the U.S. intelligence agencies allowed Harari to escape in an Israeli jet. If Harari had been captured and questioned, Israel's involvement in the drug trafficking could have come out, as well as that of U.S. intelligence agencies.

Former OSS and CIA operative Russell Bowen had told me he worked alongside the Mossad and Harari for many years. He told me that Harari had started his vast Central and South American operations by smuggling cigarettes and then branching out into drugs.

Mossad Agent Describing CIA Drug Trafficking

Ben-Menashe writes in his book, *Profits of War*, that "Whenever U.S. officials were caught red-handed doing something illegal, they usually lied like crazy and accused everyone else." Ben-Menashe's book tells about the drug trafficking into the United States by the CIA and the Israeli intelligence community, and how the profits went into the coffers of these intelligence agencies and into private companies controlled by them.

British Investigation

An investigation into drug trafficking was conducted by a British law commission headed by Lord Louis Blom-Cooper, which then conducted a year of hearings. The *London Times* referred to the commission's report as "a scorcher," which found:

- The use of Antigua by the Mossad for drug trafficking and for training and arming the private armies of Colombia's drug barons.
- Lying by CIA officials to the White House, claiming that the Israeli operations in Antigua were to train rebel forces to oust Panama's Manuel Noriega.
- Mossad's training of hundreds of Colombians into killers for assassination purposes.
- A long-standing practice by U.S. authorities to cover for the crimes of the Mossad group, which supported my findings and as described by my CIA and DEA sources.
- The role played by Israeli Major General Pinchas Shachar in the arms and drug operations. Shachar was the official representative for Israel Military Industries in the United States, with special access to the Pentagon and other guarded U.S. military installations. According to reports, CIA Director William Sessions wanted the British report entered into Shachar's file and to suspend his special privileges. Attorney General William Barr rejected the recommendation, keeping the American public in the dark

about this part of the drug trafficking. The article described how the Bush White House sought to ignore the report, just as the many other reports have been hidden from the American public.

Justice Department officials referred inquiries to the State Department, claiming it was a foreign affair matter, and the State Department referred inquiries to the Justice Department, claiming it was a criminal matter.

Implications of Israel's Mossad Involvement in Drugging America

The repeated discovery that the intelligence agency of a foreign country, Israel, was heavily involved in several of the drug operations conducted against the American people was disturbing. Throughout my discoveries I learned of the involvement of Mossad agents in the smuggling of drugs into the United States and other crimes, including the October Surprise scheme, the theft of the Inslaw software, and the looting of Chapter 11 assets.

Referring to the drug-smuggling projects, Operation New Wave and Operation Backlash, Russbacher said that the intent of the operations were bring heroin into the United States from the Far East using freighters, cruise-line transports, and other international lines. The ships would bring heroin from Far East ports through Central America, sometimes through northern South America, and then into the United States. Some of the intermediate points included Acapulco, Mazatlan, Sewantenego, Cabo San Lucas, and Ensenada.

United States ports included San Diego, Los Angeles, San Francisco, and Seattle. At San Diego, a transshipment point, non-military vessels went to the federal port known as O-1, District 00.01. In Los Angeles they used the Long Beach basin.

Also used were tankers, including the Greek tanker line Orion, which docked at Manhattan Beach, California. The oldest freighters would normally be Pan American or Iberian registry.

Drugs were also transshipped from Colombia, many times in ships of Norwegian registry, until 1989, and these were mostly cruise ships. Russbacher elaborated on the method of packing drugs on ships:

> On the cruise liners it was generally in the freezers, brought on board inside carcasses of beef. Also in the flour bags, 100 pound bags. They are referred to as flower barrels. On other types of ships it was either stored in the paint lockers, or there was a separate compartment built.

I asked, "What is the remuneration or rewards for the different agencies that are involved in this operation?" Russbacher stated that there is a "split profit sharing" where the profits are divided among various proprietaries or front companies used by the different agencies.

New York Times Article Describes Drugs on Cruise Ships

A *New York Times* article (September 6, 1998) described the arrest of cruise ship employees with Celebrity and Norwegian cruise lines. Crewmembers on the ships, involved in the drug trafficking, had code names such as Fidel, Ratty, 007, Puny. The drugs went from Jamaica to New York City and then to Bermuda. Speaking for the U.S. Attorney's office, Jodi Avergun said:

> You never think that while you're on vacation, you're in the midst of serious drug smuggling. You think you're safe and secure on a cruise to Bermuda but, in fact, there are drug smugglers serving you lunch or making

your meal.

Drug Smuggling Operations Still Active

Russbacher said the operations were active, but limited to DEA and Customs involvement. He said the CIA and Department of Justice dropped from active participation in March 1993, except for the criminal prosecutions in San Diego and San Francisco that had to be completed.

Uncoordinated Government Agency Drug Smuggling Operations

I asked Russbacher why the Department of Justice occasionally files criminal charges against people involved in drug smuggling operations tied in with the CIA or some other government agency. He said that the many individual fiefdoms in the CIA, Justice Department, and other agencies, and the compartmentalizing of information, result in charges being filed by one office against a person or operation that may be sanctioned by another office. Or, there may be turf battles between different agencies or between different offices of the same agency.

Thailand Drug Smuggling Operation

Since the defendants in the San Francisco action were from Thailand, I asked Russbacher how that country fits into the operation. He said the drug shipper in Thailand was a CIA front called Van Der Bergen International Shippers in Bangkok. "They're the ones that are responsible for gathering [the drugs] out of Southeast Asia," adding that Hong Kong was sought as a drug shipment point:

> But they [CIA] couldn't get an agreement going with the British out of Hong Kong. The problem was, they wanted a higher percentile participation than our government was prepared to give. Instead of using Hong Kong, we used Macao. Eighty percent of the morphine block, we are not talking about the liquid, comes out of Macao, before it becomes morphine sulphate.

Explaining the Mossad's Role in Drugging America

Russbacher described the role played by the Mossad in the drug trafficking into the United States in Operation New Wave and Operation Back Lash. He said the Mossad's role was to guard the shipments until they reached the United States. He said that one of his Mossad contacts was Delilah Kaufman, a paralegal with an Italian law firm in the San Francisco area.

Increased Budgets Threatened the Drug Shipments

Part of the operations was suspended in 1991 due to increased awareness at the southern transshipment ports. More federal funds were allocated for DEA and Customs agents, causing smuggling by certain DEA and Customs factions to be compromised. Even though the drug trafficking involved personnel from almost every federal agency responsible to prevent such trafficking, the smuggling was compartmentalized.

Eastern Airline Whistleblower

A former Eastern Airlines captain (EAL), Gerald K. Loeb, called me in 1994 and conveyed information about drug trafficking that he discovered while a pilot for the airline. He discovered a pattern of drug shipments going from Central and South America into the United States on EAL aircraft and shipment of pallets of money from Miami to Panama and Colombia.

Eastern Airlines as Drug-Related Carrier

Loeb frequently noticed, in departures from Miami for Central America, containers placed on board the aircraft, which followed a pattern of usually arriving at the last few minutes before departure. This was followed by same containers being off-loaded in Panama or Colombia in the presence of armed guards. The activity indicated drug and drug-money trafficking.

Loeb described how he gave detailed information of the drug trafficking to the Federal Bureau of Investigation, the Airline Pilots Association, to EAL President Frank Borman, and to *Time* magazine's Jonathan Beaty, all of whom kept the lid on the criminal activities.

Dozens of times Customs agents discovered drugs hidden behind aircraft inspection plates as the Eastern Airlines aircraft arrived in Miami. Eastern pilots were concerned over the drug trafficking, as they themselves could be charged with drug-related offenses. As ALPA Chairman of Legislative Affairs for the Eastern pilots group in Miami, Loeb received many complaints from pilots about drugs being found on their aircraft as it arrived in Miami. Loeb testified to Congress that there were over sixty cases reported to him where this happened.

FBI Retaliation Against People who Expose Drug Shipments

Loeb developed a friendship with a young Eastern Airlines station agent in Panama City, Panama, who revealed to him that cocaine was being shipped on Eastern Airlines planes from Colombia and Panama into the United States. Loeb contacted a friend, Governor Thompson of New Hampshire, and described the massive drug smuggling and drug-money shipments that he had discovered. The governor then contacted Justice Department officials, who arranged for Loeb and two other Eastern Airlines employees to give information to the FBI in Miami.

Loeb identified these FBI agents as Special Agent in Charge F. Corliss, Assistant Special agent (ASAC) William Perry, and Special Agent Rod Beverley. The Eastern Airlines employee from Panama was threatened by FBI personnel and warned that he himself would be charged with a federal crime if he reported the drug and drug-money trafficking. Under federal criminal statutes these threats constituted federal crimes.[22]

Other Eastern Airlines employees contacted FBI agents seeking to report drug trafficking that they had observed, including, among others, an Eastern Airlines flight attendant and a ground service agent. Instead of receiving the information from these people, FBI agents threatened to file criminal charges against them for not reporting the criminal activities earlier (Misprision of a felony). The FBI traumatized witnesses to keep them from reporting the criminal acts involving federal personnel, and is a practice that I had seen for years. The FBI threats caused the witnesses to remain silent, which is apparently what the FBI agents wanted and which the agents knew would insure that the drug trafficking continued! Some of these witnesses then blamed Loeb for what had happened, and then went under cover.

---

[22] Title 18 USC §§ 1512, 1513.

**Numerous Appearances Before Congressional Committees,
Followed by Congressional Coverup (and Misprision of Felonies)**

Loeb testified before numerous congressional committees, including Senator John Kerry's (D-MA) Subcommittee on Terrorism, Narcotics and International Communications. Referring to the meeting in Miami with the FBI, Loeb testified[23] that the FBI reported to Eastern Airlines president Frank Borman what Loeb and the other witnesses had said, and that the FBI said something had to be done to silence him and the other witnesses. Referring to his testimony, Loeb wrote in part:

The officials at Eastern Airlines and the corporate officers deemed [my reporting of the drug trafficking to the FBI] to be outrageous conduct. Having learned from the FBI within hours of my giving that information, they hired two private detectives and [then the harassment against me commenced] ....[Drugs aboard Eastern Airlines aircraft] was an ongoing scenario, particularly from Panama, the hub operation, and Colombia. Our crews were very aware that they were unwittingly being duped and flying cargo, as [the drugs and drug-money were] called, that was un-listed in their aircraft, un-manifested, into ports of call in the United States of America.

Hiring Private Detective Agency to Discredit Airline Captain

Loeb testified that a private detective agency hired by Eastern management, Intercontinent Detective Agency of Miami, offered bribes of $2,500 and $5,000 to people to discredit Loeb and the Air Line Pilots Association which was representing the pilots on whose plane drugs were found. The airline's president fired Loeb for being "disloyal" to the company, after which Loeb fought the dismissal. Eventually, Loeb took a financial settlement and left the airline. Two weeks after Eastern fired Loeb, the airline fired another pilot, Ramon Valdez, who had hired an investigator to obtain additional evidence on the drug and drug-money shipments on Eastern Airlines aircraft.

Coverup by Eastern Airlines' President

Loeb told me that when he first reported the drug trafficking on Eastern Airlines aircraft to Eastern president, Frank Borman, that Borman told him to mind his own business. Instead of responding to the serious problem, Borman and other Eastern management proceeded to harass Loeb.

Sudden Amnesia by Cowards

Initially, many Eastern Airlines pilots wanted to testify about the drug trafficking and drug-money laundering. But after they saw what happened to Loeb, they all developed "amnesia." Loeb reported the drug trafficking to the president of the Airline Pilots Association, Henry A. Duffy, and explained that over two dozen Eastern Airlines' pilots were actively involved in drug trafficking. Loeb said the ALPA president told him that drug trafficking was none of the union's business. (I encountered a similar attitude when I brought to Duffy's attention major air safety misconduct that was playing a key role in

---

[23] Testimony given on February 8, 1988 to the Subcommittee on Terrorism, Narcotics and International Communications, and as published under Drugs, Law Enforcement, and Foreign Policy: Panama, S. Hrg. 100-773, Pr. 2.

a series of fatal airline crashes, as explained in *Unfriendly Skies.*)

Bush, Noriega, And Drugs

Loeb told how, during the criminal proceedings against Noriega, that Noriega's attorneys told Loeb that they had audio and video tapes of Noriega and Bush, and would release the tapes if the charges were not dropped against Noriega. One of the attorneys asked Loeb to pass the information to the Justice Department prosecutors, warning that if the charges were not dropped, the tapes would be released. The judge in the Noriega trial refused to permit any evidence entered into Noriega's trial relating to the CIA or any other U.S. agency's involvement in drug trafficking.

American Airlines and Braniff Airlines had Similar Drug Problems

I asked Loeb if the airlines that took over the Central and South America air traffic after Eastern Airlines went out of business became involved in the drug trafficking. He stated that American Airlines encountered similar problems. He also described how Braniff Airlines was heavily used by drug traffickers before it went out of business.

The House Committee on Government Operations issued a report after its hearings (March 1992) titled "Serious Mismanagement and Misconduct in the Treasury Department, Customs Service, and Other Federal Agencies and the Adequacy of Efforts To Hold Agency Officials Accountable." The report stated in part:

This is the third in a series of hearings looking into allegations of mismanagement and misconduct by the U.S. Customs Service. Witnesses have testified about attempts by both Customs and Internal Affairs to prevent investigations from going forward. These are serious allegations. [Criminal would be more fitting!]

This hearing...focuses on the implementation of the Customs reorganization plan, and the accountability of the Inspector General. But what is really at issue here is the overall effectiveness of counter-narcotics law enforcement efforts along the U.S.-Mexico border. The credibility of the Customs Service is at stake. Allegations of improper associations between law enforcement agents and drug traffickers are bad enough, but the inability and unwillingness to properly investigate such allegations cause the public to lose faith in the ability of the United States government to fight the war on drugs.

The report revealed that government officials sought to block the testimony of witnesses, showing the existence of obstruction of justice, which by itself is a crime. Included in the report was a letter to the committee signed by anonymous field agents of U.S. Customs, stating in part:

We are writing to you to advise you of the continuing systemic corruption at the U.S. Customs Service. The "reorganization" of the Office of Enforcement has only removed necessary checks and balances. Integrity is virtually a non-existent commodity in Customs management.

Former DEA agent Michael Levine wrote in *The Big White Lie* how the Drug Enforcement Administration destroyed evidence that resulted in high-level drug traffickers escaping prosecution.

CHAPTER TWO

ARKANSAS DRUG ACTIVITIES

Arkansas, CIA, Mafia, NSC, and
White House Involvement in Drug Crimes

For years, a selected number of newspapers and magazines carried stories of the CIA arms and drug trafficking at the Mena Airport in Arkansas. Prosecution had been repeatedly blocked by Arkansas and federal officials. A May 21, 1992, *Arkansas Times* article carried a front page story of the drug trafficking, including three pictures of CIA contract agent and drug pilot Barry Seal, drug trafficker Jorge Luis Ochoa, and George Bush. Below their picture was the title, "BAD COMPANY." A subheading read "Arkansas's most notorious drug smuggler testified about his links to Colombia. His ties to Washington have yet to be explained." The article brought together the CIA's Mena operations, the drug smuggling, the shooting down of a CIA C-123 over Nicaragua, Lt. Col. Oliver North's arms shipments to Central America, and drug shipments back to the United States.

Drug Coverups by Governor Bill Clinton

The criminal activities surrounding the CIA arms and drug trafficking at Mena Airport were well known to local residents, the local police, the Arkansas State Police, and the media. The local *Arkansas Gazette* published numerous investigative articles describing the criminal activities and the coverup by the State Attorney General and Governor Bill Clinton.

Charles Black, assistant deputy prosecutor for Polk County, told Governor Clinton in 1988 about the drug trafficking, and asked that Clinton provide a million dollars to coordinate the evidence and prosecute. Clinton said he would get back to Black, and then never did. In 1991, the Arkansas Citizens Committee demonstrated in Little Rock, complaining about Clinton's refusal to investigate and prosecute the complaints concerning massive drug trafficking in Arkansas.

During a White House press conference, senior White House correspondent Sarah McClendon asked President Clinton about his knowledge of the drug trafficking at Mena Airport. Clinton replied that this was a federal problem. Responsibilities under law for these criminal activities involve state as well as federal authorities. As governor of Arkansas, Clinton had a legal responsibility to have the charges investigated. Instead, he obstructed justice by keeping Arkansas law enforcement personnel from meeting its investigative responsibilities.

Testimony Showing CIA Drug Trafficking and Joint
Drug Trafficking and Money Laundering with Organized Crime

Much testimony has been given by hundreds of insiders to congressional committees over the years depicting the involvement of U.S. government personnel in drug trafficking, drug-money laundering, and joint operations with organized crime. An example of this is found in several congressional transcripts marked Confidential, consisting of depositions taken in June 1991. One of the witnesses was a long-time CIA operative, Richard Brenneke, who testified in closed-door hearings conducted by members of the United States Congress and the Arkansas State Attorney General's office.[24] Brenneke's testimony described the CIA drug trafficking, CIA ties to organized crime, and CIA money laundering. The transcript stated that the testimony would be made available to the Special Prosecutor (Lawrence Walsh) in the Iran-Contra case, and for other purposes.

Joint Money Laundering for CIA and Mafia

In the transcript of that testimony, Brenneke described his activities on behalf of the Central Intelligence Agency, about his expertise in handling financial transfers worldwide, including money transfers for the Central Intelligence Agency, commencing in 1968 and continuing until 1985. Brenneke testified to "handling money for them [and] handling East Bloc weapons purchases primarily made in Yugoslavia and Czechoslovakia." He described flying as pilot for the CIA, including C-130 aircraft from Mena, Arkansas to various airports in Panama, including Tucuman Airport at Panama City, and into Colon. Brenneke produced pilot logbooks showing the flights that he made for the CIA into Mena and other locations.

Brenneke testified that the weapon shipments were met by "members of the Panamanian Defense Forces" and "by Michael Harari." He identified Harari in congressional testimony as a Mossad agent and "Manuel Noriega's partner in a number of business deals in Panama. I know that first hand because I had to deal with him."

He described carrying weapons and military personnel trained in Arkansas from Mena to Panama. He testified that the weapons frequently came either from government stores or through the Tamiami Gun Shop in Miami, Florida and that his co-pilot on many of these flights was another CIA operative, Harry Rupp.

Brenneke described drug-trafficking flights from Medellin to Mena and to Iron Mountain Ranch in Texas. He identified Rich Mountain Aviation at Mena Airport (Inter-Mountain Regional Airport) and Fred Hampton as own-

---

[24] Investigators conducting the questioning included William Alexander, United States Congress, 233 Cannon House Office Building, Washington, D.C.; Winston Bryant, Attorney General, State of Arkansas; Chad Farris, Chief Attorney General, State of Arkansas; Lawrence Graves, attorney in the office of Attorney General, State of Arkansas.

ing and operating the CIA-front operation.

CIA Cocaine Trafficking With Panamanians

When asked by congressional investigators about the nature of the cargo flown back to the United States, including into Mena, Brenneke testified, "I found the cargo to be cocaine; in some cases marijuana." He testified that on each return flight he carried 400 to 500 pounds of cocaine, which was loaded by Panamanian Defense Force soldiers onto the CIA aircraft.

Sale Of Drugs by CIA to Gotti's Organized Crime Family

When asked about the disposition of the drugs, Brenneke testified that upon landing at Mena Airport the drugs would be either off-loaded onto other aircraft, or stored in Rich Mountain Aviation's hangar. Brenneke testified that in some instances the drugs were received by Freddie Hampton of Rich Mountain Aviation, and in some cases "members of John Gotti's family in New York. One of them was an individual known to me by the name of Salvatore Reale." Brenneke testified:

Reale was Director of Security for Kennedy International Airport in New York City... Mr. Reale was one of Mr. Gotti's lieutenants. I watched the two of them interact. Mr. Gotti would provide directions, Mr. Reale would carry them out. It was his job to make sure that cargo being shipped through Kennedy was not lost, but properly located, and in some cases avoiding Customs.

This testimony linking organized crime with the CIA in drug trafficking, caused the Congressional investigators to ask, "Are you saying that you saw Mr. John Gotti, the famous head of the organized crime syndicate, in New York, together with Mr. Reale?" Brenneke replied, "Yes, sir, I did."

CIA Laundering Mafia's Drug Money to Overseas Accounts

In response to another question as to whether Mr. Gotti and Mr. Reale were connected with the Central Intelligence Agency, Brenneke replied:

Yes. As far back as 1968 and early 1969, we [CIA] had begun to launder money from organized crime families in New York. At that time, Mr. Gotti was an up and coming member of one of the families. I got to know them at that time. We used to wash their money overseas and put it in Switzerland in nice, safe places for them.

"So you worked for Mr. Gotti as well as for the CIA?"

Actually the CIA told me to do that on his behalf.

"So the CIA was in partnership or association with Mr. Gotti?"

Yes, sir, I would say a partnership.

"Can you describe the nature of the partnership?"

Sure. The organized crime members had a need for two things; they needed drugs brought into the country on a reliable, safe basis; they needed people taken out of the country or people brought into the country without alerting Customs or INS to the fact that they were being brought into the country. They also needed their money taken offshore so that it would not be subject to United States tax where they might have to declare its source. And so we [CIA] performed these kinds of functions for them.

CIA in Business of Drugging America for Decades

"Mr. Brenneke, are you saying that the CIA was in the business of bringing drugs into the United States?"

Yes sir. That's exactly what I'm saying.

"And that they were in partnership with John Gotti in this operation?"

I would say that they worked with Mr. Gotti and his organization very closely. Whether it was a formal partnership, I don't know. But there certainly was a close alliance between the two.

Brenneke testified that the Gotti people told him the drugs would be taken to "the New York City area, specifically Kennedy International Airport." He testified that the CIA handler he was working for was Robert Kerritt, and that Kerritt paid the various CIA assets in the Mena area. Brenneke continued:

Mr. Kerritt is a full-time employee of the Central Intelligence Agency...I and the CIA have dealt with the Gotti mob since 1968.

Organized Crime Family Paying CIA $50 Million for Drugs

"Did the Gotti organization, through Reale, pay money to the CIA for the drugs?"

Yes, they did, somewhere in the $50,000,000 bracket.

"How do you know how much money?"

Because I banked that money for them in Panama City, and ultimately transferred it to other locations in Europe.

"What would be the procedure for you to receive the payment from the Gotti organization for the drugs?"

Generally the money was given to us in cash.

"Us, you mean the CIA?"

Us, meaning the people I worked with, who were also associated with the Central Intelligence Agency. We would transfer the money to banks in Central and South America. And from there transfer it via accounts that I had established back in 1970.

Describing In Detail CIA-Organized Crime Drug Money Laundering

Brenneke was asked: "Let's take a payment from Mr. Reale in cash, and follow the procedure step-by-step as you know it for the transmittal of that money from the Gotti organization to the Central Intelligence Agency."

Okay. That money was delivered to us in cash. There were occasions where there were wire transfers, but the generally followed method was cash. That would be stored in the aircraft on its return trip to Panama. Once it reached Panama, we would put it into a bank account, which at that time was in the Banquo de Panama. And the account name was the initials, IFMA, which was a company that I set up in Panama City in 1970. The money would be subsequently and almost immediately transferred to Spain or Liechtenstein. From there it went to Monte Carlo, and the ultimate destination was Zurich or Geneva. But in any case, Switzerland.

"The money was given to you by the agent for the Gotti Organization?"

Yes sir. And there were other people besides the man that I've named.

Providing Detailed Records

Brenneke supplied the investigators with telephone records of that and other calls, providing further credibility to his statements. He identified the names of the CIA accounts that he had set up, offering the incorporation papers that were filed "in the late sixties and early seventies." Brenneke testified that he personally transferred money out of one account and into others. He testified that he discussed the money transfers with CIA employees Robert Kerritt and Robert Ellis.

Returning to questions about how the drug money from the Gotti crime family went into the CIA accounts, Brenneke explained:

I set up, in 1969 or 1970, a number of corporations in Panama City. Those corporations in turn opened bank accounts. Those bank accounts were accounts that I would normally use in the course of my business with the CIA to transfer money into the accounts, and from there to transfer them into specific accounts in Spain or, as I say, in some cases other countries in Europe. The ultimate destination was Switzerland, where those funds were. I knew where they went, because I'm the person who went in and gave the order to the banker to move them.

Secret CIA Bank Accounts Overseas

"And you had an arrangement with the CIA to organize those banks for the CIA, to open the account?"

That was what I specialized in doing. I laundered money there. When I was first recruited by the CIA, which was in 1968, 1969, all we were doing was selling mutual fund stock offshore.

"Name the banks [in which accounts were] opened for the CIA."

Panama City, Banquo DeMexico. At one point we were using a Citibank correspondent down there whose name escapes me. We had a man on-site who worked for us, as well as worked for Ron Martin, a man named Johnny Mollina. John would spend a lot of his time in Panama City and worked in one of the banks that we used. I set up more than one account in Madrid that was used. I set up an account in Brussels at Bank Lambert that was regularly used. I set up accounts at Credit Suisse, a Swiss bank. And Bank of Credit & Commerce, commonly referred to as BCCI. Also, a bank that no longer exists called Bank Hoffman. I set up a bank in Panama City on behalf of the mutual fund company I worked for so that I could ultimately control how the transfers were handled.

"And you organized a bank in Panama for the CIA?"

I organized it for the company I worked for. It was subsequently used by the CIA, and it was used by members of the organized crime families. The bank was called U.S. Investment Bank. It really existed in Panama City. You could actually go in and open a check account there.

Crime Family Money Laundered By CIA Operative

"And the money that you got from the Gotti organization that you put on the airplane [in Arkansas] and returned to Panama on the next trip, you personally took to a bank in Panama City?"

Yes, I did. Let's take Banquo DePanama, the Panamanian National Bank down there, as an example. I would go in and meet with, for instance, Johnny Mollina. John worked for one of the banks down there. I think it was Citibank that he worked for at one time. In any case, I would go in.

*I knew the bank officers by name. And I would provide them with direc-
tions as to how the money was to be transferred and where to transfer.
That is, it was to be transferred by cashier's check and courier to Madrid
in a specific account there, or it was just wire transferred to Madrid as a
transfer of funds from IFMA, a Panamanian corporation, to IFMA's af-
filiates in Madrid or Brussels at Bank Lambert. They needed to know that.
And then I would have to tell them at the other bank that money was
coming into that account.*

"So you would notify the CIA bank, or the bank having the CIA account in
Spain or in Switzerland?"

Yes, that the deposit had been made in Panama.

"How would you notify them?"

*Generally by telephone. And they would be told that...there were a variety
of codes that were used, but the message was very simple. You're going
to receive money in this account. The money will probably stay in the account anywhere from 24 to 72 hours, at which time it will be transferred
out of that account.*

Bearer Bonds To Launder Drug Money

"Did you ever utilize bearer bonds for the purpose of laundering money?"

*Sure. It was handled in two ways. When U.S. Investment Bank was active
in Panama it would issue bonds, no names on them, which was common.
It's common in Europe. It's common in Central and South America. And
those bonds actually belong to the individual that is carrying them, as, for
instance, the stock in IFMA belongs only to the person who happens to
have it in his hand at that moment. You lose it, you lose your money.*

"And what would you do with the bearer bonds?"

*The bearer bonds would be taken generally by courier, in some cases to
Banquo DeMexico in Mexico City and transferred from there or sent from
there by their couriers. By 1986, it was getting uncomfortable in Panama,
and so some of the Venezuelan banks in Caracas were used. The same
procedure was followed, though. The money would be deposited into an
account; you would walk into the bank, for example, and sit down with the
Vice President or Managing Director of the bank. You were clearly a
large depositor and a large customer of that bank. And you just simply explained that you wanted to deposit the money in this bag, and he would
just kindly go ahead and do so for you.*

Drug Trafficking Controlled from Washington

"Mr. Brenneke, under whose direction were you working in order to carry
out the function of depositing the money from the sale of the drugs to the New
York crime family?"

*"Bob Kerritt, an officer of the Central Intelligence Agency in Washington,
D.C."*

Protesting the CIA Drug Involvement

Brenneke described his adverse reaction to discovering the CIA involvement in drug smuggling into the United States and the CIA's involvement with
drug money laundering. In answer to a question, Brenneke testified:

When I found that we were bringing drugs into the United States, and that we were receiving money which was being put into accounts which I knew to belong to the United States government, as I'd set them up specifically for that purpose, I called Mr. Don Gregg, who was a CIA officer with whom I was acquainted, and complained about the nature of what we were doing.

Office of Vice President and President, and CIA, In Drug Trafficking and Drug-Money Laundering

Donald Gregg worked closely with George Bush when Bush was director of the CIA, and became his national security advisor when Bush was vice president of the United States. Bush later nominated Gregg to be Ambassador to South Korea. When asked about Gregg's response to Brenneke's concern about the drug trafficking, Brenneke testified:

I was told that it was not my business what I was flying in and out of the country. That I was hired to do specific things, and if I would do those things and not pay any attention to anything else, we would all be very, very happy. I didn't like that. He said shut up and do your job. I subsequently talked to Mr. Gregg on a number of occasions as well as to other people in the vice-president's office to voice my concern over the use of drugs, importing drugs into the United States.

CIA Role in Looting Banks

Brenneke testified about the criminal charges made against Heinrich Rupp concerning looting the Aurora Bank in the Denver area, saying "that was common in our line of work with the CIA."

When asked if Brenneke ever complained to CIA director William Casey about these activities, Brenneke replied:

Yes, I did on a number of occasions. And Mr. Casey's telephone logs would reflect phone calls to me, made to me in Lake Oswego, which was at that time the location of my office.

Testifying About Israel's Role in Drugging America

Brenneke testified about Israel's involvement in the drug smuggling operations, and that he had gone to Israel "because I tried everybody in the U.S. Government first, and they sure as hell weren't going to help" shut down the operations.

"Do you have any knowledge of the money coming from the Gotti organization being used for any other purposes, other than depositing in the bank accounts for the CIA?"

Sure. We had to run the operations at Nella, for instance. The training facilities at Nella had to be paid for. Nella was a training base for military and paramilitary folks from south of the border; Mexico, Panama.[25] The base was operated by the Central Intelligence Agency.

Brenneke identified CIA agent Terry Reed as one of the flight instructors at Nella. Reed co-authored the book *Compromised* with John Cummings, describing the drug trafficking and money laundering in Arkansas and Mexico, and involving Arkansas personnel, including Governor Bill Clinton and some

---

[25] Nella consisted of a small airstrip north of Mena that was used by the CIA for paramilitary and military training of personnel from Mexico and Central America, and used for training Contra pilots.

of his staff.

Moving CIA and Organized Crime
Drug Money Back into the United States

"Did you establish an account in the United States to get that money back into this country?"

Yes, I did. I established an account at Brown Brothers Harriman in New York City around 1980. That's a bank in New York City.

"How do you know that the money you picked up and that you received in Mena from the Gotti organization, and took to Panama, wired to bank accounts in Europe, came back to the United States?"

I ordered the transfer of funds.

"And to whom did you report these actions?"

I reported them to Don Gregg, Bob Kerritt, Bob Ellis and from time-to-time other people. I not only have notes, I have letters that I wrote to some of these people. Copies of these letters were submitted to congressional investigators.

Arkansas Attorney General's Attempt to Discredit Evidence

Chad Farris, Chief Deputy attorney General for the State of Arkansas, tried to discredit Brenneke:

Why would you care about the use of drugs as part of this CIA plan? If you were so concerned about the use of drugs in the operation because of the reasons you've described, why did you continue to take part in the operation; what do you hope to achieve by testifying here today; what's the purpose of your testimony, to you personally?

These were rather stupid questions. Brenneke had repeatedly objected to the CIA drug trafficking and working with organized crime. Quitting an uncover operation of this nature gets people killed! Brenneke was testifying because he was asked to testify, something that other members of Congress had avoided doing earlier.

Bank Records and Documentation Corroborating His Testimony

Brenneke clearly testified, without hesitation, times, dates, places, and either telephone logs or notes that he made of conversations with his CIA handlers in Washington. Brenneke testified to, and provided the Congressional investigators with writings that he sent to his CIA bosses in Washington complaining about the CIA role in drug trafficking and drug-money laundering and its operation with major crime families in the United States. He provided the investigators with copies of bank records, corporation papers, and detailed testimony, wherein there could be little doubt that his testimony was true.

No Perjury Charges Filed Against Brenneke by DOJ

No perjury charges were ever filed against Brenneke for this testimony about the CIA drug crimes. If his testimony was perjured, Justice Department prosecutors would have immediately filed criminal perjury charges against him, as they did once before when DOJ employees tried to cover up for George Bush's involvement in the scheme known as October Surprise. It would have also been a responsibility for congressional questioners to charge him with perjury if they felt his testimony was not true.

DOJ's Prior Sham Perjury Charges To Discredit October Surprise

Brenneke testified about the Justice Department's sham perjury charges against him for testifying in a 1988 federal court trial in Denver concerning CIA operative Heinrich Rupp. Brenneke testified that he saw George Bush and Donald Gregg in Paris during the period of October 18, 19, and 20, 1980, which was a key point in the "October Surprise" operation (which is detailed in *Defrauding America*).

Brenneke stated that in the Denver proceedings Justice Department attorneys offered him a plea agreement; plead guilty to perjury charges concerning his testimony about seeing Bush and Gregg in Paris and he would not receive any prison time or fine. Brenneke refused to commit perjury for DOJ personnel and refused to cover up for Bush's role in October Surprise. Brenneke went to trial and fortunately for him, the jury was smart enough to recognize the sham charges by the DOJ prosecutor. The jury found Brenneke not guilty.

Brenneke was involved in many other CIA activities. Tape recordings made of telephone conversations between Brenneke and Russbacher, in my possession, described their role in other CIA operations, including Operation Gladio, which sought to destabilize the Italian government in the 1950s.

Brenneke had given a speech at the University of Arkansas in 1991, which was videotaped, further describing the involvement of government personnel in drug smuggling into the United States.

Testimony by IRS Investigator Bill Duncan

William Duncan was an investigator for the Internal Revenue Service and spent several years investigating drug-related activities in Arkansas and the role played in these activities by Governor Bill Clinton, the Arkansas Development Finance Authority, Dan Lasater's brokerage business, and the Stephens' financial powerhouse. Duncan had functioned in the capacity of congressional investigator for the Subcommittee on Crime, and discovered the involvement of Arkansas officials and the CIA in drug trafficking and drug-money laundering. Duncan was a criminal investigator for the U.S. Treasury Department from 1973 through 1989.

In addition to what Duncan stated to me, I received a transcript of his congressional testimony, marked Confidential, given to a Joint Investigation by the United States Congress and the Arkansas State Attorney General's Office in June 1991. Duncan testified that one of his assignments was to "investigate allegations of money laundering in connection with the Barry Seal organization, which was based at the Mena, Arkansas airport." Duncan testified in detail about the drug-money laundering he uncovered, involving the CIA, and how attorneys with the Department of Justice repeatedly blocked investigations and prosecutions.

Pattern of Justice Department Obstruction of Justice

Duncan found, as I had in the past, that Justice Department attorneys routinely covered up for major corruption involving high-level government personnel. Duncan testified about the tactics used by Justice Department employees to protect the CIA and the people working with the CIA in drug trafficking and drug-money laundering.

DOJ Blocking Testimony About CIA Drug Smuggling in Arkansas

Duncan testified that important witnesses were not called by the U.S. Attorney to testify before the Grand Jury; that important witnesses with valuable information were not allowed to present it, being limited literally to giving their name, address, phone number, and type of employment. Duncan testified that the vice-president of Union Bank in Mena, Gary Gardner, wanted to testify about the CIA money-laundering and how Justice Department prosecutors blocked his testimony.

Duncan testified that he gave U.S. Attorney Asa Hutchinson in Fort Smith, Arkansas, the names of 20 witnesses for the grand jury investigation, all of whom had direct knowledge and evidence of drug-money laundering. Of the three witnesses called by the U.S. Attorney, Duncan testified that two of them were angry because the U.S. Attorney refused to allow them to give meaningful evidence to the grand jury.

Circumventing the DOJ Block by Going Direct to Grand Jury

I encountered DOJ coverups while I was a federal investigator for the Federal Aviation Administration and sought to report a pattern of criminal activities that I and other federal inspectors discovered as part of our official duties that were directly involved in a series of fatal airline crashes. I circumvented the DOJ blocking actions by sending a letter directly to a federal grand jury at Denver. As an FAA inspector-investigator, I appeared before a grand jury in the mid-1960s to give testimony as a federal investigator about the corruption at United Airlines and within the Federal Aviation Administration relating to a series of air disasters.

Back to Mena. One of the witnesses not allowed to present any of her meaningful testimony was Kathy Corrigan Gann. Duncan testified:

She was the secretary for Rich Mountain Aviation, who participated in the money laundering operation upon the instructions of Hampton and Evans. She basically said that she was allowed to give her name, address, position, and not much else. I talked to another witness. His name was Jim Nugent, a vice-president at Union Bank of Mena, who had conducted a search of their records and provided a significant amount of evidence relating to the money laundering transaction. He was also furious that he was not allowed to provide the evidence that he wanted to provide to the grand jury.

Duncan continued:

At a later date, I came in contact with the deputy foreman of the grand jury, who had previously given testimony to an investigator for the House Judiciary Subcommittee on Crime, concerning her frustrations as the deputy foreman of the grand jury. Her name was P.J. Pitts. She was perpetually involved in the grand jury as it heard evidence concerning the Barry Seal matter, and she related to me the frustrations of herself and the entire grand jury because they were not allowed to hear of money laundering. [The primary purpose of the grand jury was to obtain evidence about money laundering.]

She stated to me that they specifically asked to hear the money laundering evidence, specifically asked that I be subpoenaed, and they were not allowed to have me subpoenaed. She said the whole grand jury was frustrated. She indicated that Mr. Fitzhugh, who at that time was the U.S. Attorney, explained to them that I was in Washington at the time and unavailable as a witness, which was not the truth.

When asked how Duncan's superiors responded to the coverup, Duncan testified that he complained to his superior, Paul Whitmore, Chief of Criminal Investigation, and to the group managers, Tim Lee, Charles Huckaby and Max Gray:

They were very frustrated. Mr. Whitmore made several trips to Fort Smith, Arkansas to complain to the U.S. Attorney's office. He related to me on several occasions that the U.S. Attorney wrote him a letter telling him not to come to his office anymore complaining, that was unprofessional behavior. Mr. Whitmore felt there was a coverup.

"Do you agree with Mr. Whitmore's conclusion?"

Absolutely. We experienced a variety of frustrations from 1985 on, not being able to obtain subpoenas for witnesses we felt were necessary. I had some direct interference by Mr. Fitzhugh in the investigative process. Specifically he would call me and interrupt interviews, tell me not to interview people that he had previously told me were necessary to be interviewed.

IRS Covering Up For CIA Drug Trafficking

"Did you have any interference or interruptions from anyone within the U.S. Treasury Department?" Duncan was asked.

They interfered with my testimony before the House Judiciary Subcommittee on Crime. The Internal Revenue Service assigned to me disclosure litigation attorneys who gave me instructions which would have caused me to withhold information from Congress during my testimony, and to also perjure myself.

Drug-Money Bribe To U.S. Attorney General Ed Meese

"How did you respond to the Treasury Department?"

I told them that I was going to tell the truth in my testimony. And the perjury, subornation of perjury resulted because of an allegation that I had received, that Attorney General Edwin Meese received a several hundred thousand dollar bribe from Barry Seal directly. I received that information from Russell Welch, the [Arkansas] State Police investigator. And they told me to tell the Subcommittee on Crime that I had no information about that.

Duncan testified about other aspects of upper management acting to prevent exposure of the drug trafficking and drug-money laundering:

I received a subpoena from Deputy Prosecutor Chuck Black from Mt. Ida, to present evidence to the grand jury for the purposes of seeking indictments against the individuals at Mena. The Internal Revenue Service told me I would have to go back and deal with the same disclosure litigation attorneys who attempted to get me to withhold information from Congress and perjure myself, and I refused to do that. They withdrew support for the operations and basically kept me in the regional office in Atlanta and did not allow me to fulfill my responsibilities. This ultimately resulted in my resignation in June of 1989.

DOJ Prosecutor Covering Up For CIA Drug Trafficking

Addressing questions concerning the obstruction of justice, Duncan testified:

My superiors and I had continuing discussions because none of us, my managers nor myself, had ever experienced anything remotely akin to this type of interference. We couldn't understand why there was this different attitude. I had found Asa Hutchinson to be a very aggressive U.S. Attorney in connection with my cases. Then all of a sudden, with respect to Mena, it was just like the information was going in but nothing was happening over a long period of time. As soon as Mr. Fitzhugh got involved, he was more aggressive in not allowing the subpoenas and in interfering in the investigative process. He was reluctant to have the State Police around, even though they were an integral part of the investigation.

For instance, when the money laundering specialist was up from Miami, Mr. Fitzhugh left Mr. Welch in the hall all day until late in the afternoon and refused to allow him to come in. We were astonished that we couldn't get subpoenas. We were astonished that Barry Seal was never brought to the grand jury because he was on the subpoena list for a long time. And there were a lot of investigative developments that made no sense to us.

More IRS Requests For Perjured Testimony

Duncan testified that the IRS briefing attorney from Washington wanted him to cover up during the grand jury testimony (i.e., commit perjury). "Did you get the impression that she was ordering you to cover up the investigation?"

Absolutely. I would have thought a complete disclosure to Congress about the problems that we encountered was in order, but quite the opposite was true. They obviously did not want any negative testimony coming from me concerning the U.S. Attorney's office.

Attorney Bryan Sloan, a personal assistant to the Commissioner of Internal Revenue, Larry Gibbs, said, "Bill [Duncan] is just going to have to get the big picture."

Conspicuously Absent From Drug Investigations: DEA, FBI, Customs

Duncan testified that even though "allegations of narcotics smuggling, massive amounts of drug-money laundering" were involved, "conspicuously absent during most of that time were the DEA, FBI, and Customs." Among the state agencies not appearing, who had hard evidence of the CIA drug trafficking, were the Arkansas State Police, Polk County Sheriff's office, and the Louisiana State Police. Duncan testified that none of the law-enforcement personnel, who had knowledge and evidence of the drug trafficking and drug-money laundering, were called by the Justice Department to present their overwhelming evidence to the grand jury.

Miami U.S. Attorney Ordered Shutdown of All Mena Investigations

Duncan testified that the U.S. Attorney's Office at Fort Smith received instructions from the Miami U.S. Attorney's Office to "shut down the Mena Investigations at a point in time when they were ready to indict and present information to a grand jury." During another congressional deposition on July 24, 1994, Duncan testified:

By the end of 1987...thousands of law enforcement man-hours and an enormous amount of evidence of drug smuggling, aiding and abetting drug smugglers, conspiracy, perjury, money laundering...had gone to waste. Not only were no indictments ever returned on any of the individuals under investigation for their role in the Mena Operation, there was a complete breakdown in the judicial system. The United States Attorney, Western Judicial District of Arkansas ... refused to issue subpoenas for critical witnesses, interfered in the investigations, misled grand juries about evidence and availability of witnesses, refused to allow investigators to present evidence to the grand jury, and in general made a mockery of the entire investigative and judicial process.

Actions of IRS officials were purely and simply designed to impede the Congress of the United States in their investigation of issues which impact on the very heart of our judicial system, and ultimately the security of this country. Evidence...indicates that...the Mena, Arkansas Airport was an important hub-waypoint for transshipment of drugs, weapons. The evidence details a bizarre mixture of drug smuggling, gun running, money laundering and covert operations by Barry Seal, his associates, and both employees and contract operatives of the United States Intelligence Services. The testimony reveals a scheme whereby massive amounts of cocaine were smuggled into the State of Arkansas. Two witnesses testified that one of the Western District of Arkansas Assistant U.S. Attorneys told them that the U.S. Attorney's Office received a call to shut down the investigations involving the drug operation.

Similar Testimony by Arkansas State Investigator Welch

Another transcript sent to me, marked Confidential, was the testimony given by Russell Welch to the congressional committee in June 1991. Welch was an investigator for the Arkansas State Police for sixteen years. His testimony corroborated that of IRS investigator William Duncan. Welch added that U.S. Attorney Michael Fitzhugh of Miami blocked an investigation into the CIA drug trafficking and money laundering as Asa Hutchinson had done. Welch testified to the refusal by the Justice Department to issue subpoenas for those who had knowledge of the drug-related crimes. Welch testified that despite the fact that he had considerable evidence of the drug crimes, Justice Department personnel blocked his appearance before the grand jury.

Welch testified that one of the lady members of the grand jury had seen him in the hall outside the jury room and demanded of Fitzhugh to have Welch testify. Angrily, Fitzhugh told Welch the grand jury wanted to hear from him, but Fitzhugh refused to allow this.

Coverup by DEA

Asked how other federal agencies blocked investigation and prosecution of the drug trafficking and drug-money laundering, Welch testified that the cooperation from "the Drug Enforcement Administration in Florida was absolutely zero. Also, we didn't get any support from the Arkansas Drug Enforcement Administration."

Famous Drug Trafficker Working For CIA

Referring to drug trafficker Barry Seal, Welch testified "there was obvious government involvement [protection] with him." Seal was heavily involved in drug trafficking and drug-money laundering with the CIA and also with Arkansas officials and power-brokers, including members of Governor Bill Clinton's administration.

Welch described, as did others, the practice of aircraft flying into Arkansas from Central America and air dropping drugs at selected sites in Western Arkansas, which was often followed by helicopters picking up the drugs. He described Barry Seal smuggling "billions of dollars of cocaine and drugs into Arkansas over an eight to ten year period of time." Welch testified about the feelings of the grand jury and particularly the deputy foreman, Patty Pitts:

She expressed concern that they weren't being allowed to investigate the Mena Airport; that Mike Fitzhugh wasn't giving them the evidence that they needed to have; and wasn't giving them the witnesses they needed to have. She felt like they were being hindered.

Judicial Assistance in Obstructing Justice

Referring to the practice of certain federal judges aiding DOJ coverup of government-related drug offenses, he said U.S. Attorney Fitzhugh told him that "A federal judge would never let it get to court, and we would be wasting our time."

Attempt To Physically Disable Welch—Or Kill Him

Welch told me that while he was presenting evidence of the drug trafficking to Arkansas officials in Little Rock, he suddenly became deathly sick and was rushed to the hospital. Fortunately for him, the doctors discovered the problem. They told Welch that he had been sprayed with military-grade Anthrax (similar to what Saddam Hussein had threatened to use in the Persian Gulf War).

Obstruction Of Justice by National Security Council

The General Accounting Office started a probe of the Arkansas drug operation in 1988, but was shut down within four months by the National Security Council.[26] Several Congressional committees started similar investigations and then shut down. Pressure and coverup tactics came from President George Bush's administration at the federal level and from Governor Bill Clinton's administration at the state level.

DOJ Obstruction Of Justice Relating To Major Drug Crimes

In a prepared statement to a *Mena Star* reporter in 1988, Polk County Prosecutor Joe Hardegree said that the prosecution of drug-related crimes had come to a grinding halt because of links between drug traffickers and the White House.[27] Hardegree added, "I have good reason to believe that all federal law enforcement agencies from the Justice Department down through the FBI to the Drug Enforcement Administration received encouragement to downplay and de-emphasize any investigation or prosecution that might expose Seal's activities and the National Security Council's involvement in them."

---

[26] *Wall Street Journal* June 29, 1994.
[27] *Freedom*, May June 1989.

Volumes of Evidence, But No Prosecution

By 1983, the Arkansas State Police had almost three dozen volumes including several thousand pages of reports that provided overwhelming evidence of CIA drug smuggling activities and massive coverups by state and federal personnel and agencies. Since 1983, the drug trafficking and money laundering in Arkansas were investigated by and known to exist by virtually every federal and Arkansas agency responsible for bringing these crimes to justice.

Despite massive evidence of the criminal activities, officials in the U.S. Department of Justice and Arkansas police blocked prosecutions. Every attempt by individual investigators to appear before a grand jury to present evidence was blocked by Arkansas and federal officials.

DOJ Personnel Prosecuting Americans for Peanut-Size Drug Possession While Protecting CIA Truck Loads of Cocaine into U.S.

Paradoxically, tragically, while DOJ and other government agents were using government agencies to obstruct justice relating to CIA drug trafficking, they were relentlessly prosecuting Americans with peanut-size quantities of drugs in their possession and prosecuting Americans for being present while someone was *talking* about drugs.

The May and June 1989 edition of *Freedom* magazine said that "Two congressional subcommittees and the U.S. Customs Service are investigating secret activities around the quiet mountain town of Mena, Arkansas, including alleged drug running and arms smuggling." But these were only two out of many "investigations" by members of Congress into CIA drug smuggling, many of which received testimony from CIA insiders. Each of these investigations was followed by a coverup.

Mainstream Media Coverups of Major CIA Drug Crimes

The February-March 1992 issue of *Unclassified* described the large amount of evidence proving the existence of drug trafficking and drug-money laundering at Mena Airport, and the coverup by the media. It stated in part: "UNCLASSIFIED is genuinely puzzled about the absence of major media attention to Mena, especially given Clinton's prominence in the presidential race."

Arkansas Citizens Committee

A group of concerned citizens, known as the Arkansas Committee, had accumulated large quantities of evidence showing the CIA drug trafficking at Mena. Key people in this group were Charles Reed,[28] Mark Swaney, and Tom Brown of Springdale, Arkansas. In 1989, the group sent a petition to Governor Bill Clinton asking that the state exercise its responsibilities to convene a grand jury to receive their evidence relating to the CIA drug trafficking. Clinton sidestepped that request, stating it was a federal matter. (Before the head of that committee died of cancer, he turned over the group's records to

---

[28] Charles Reed furnished me with considerable data concerning the drug activities going on in Arkansas, expecting me to use it to help awaken the American public. He was a crusader seeking to make the public aware of the government corruption. He died on November 15, 1995, in his hometown of Salem, Massachusetts, shortly after sending me his total accumulation of data on government-associated drug trafficking in Arkansas.

me.)

Get-Out-Of-Jail Passes for CIA Drug Traffickers

The group discovered the drug trafficking activities involving the CIA , DEA, and Barry Seal. Seal was considered to be the biggest known drug trafficker at that time, working closely with the CIA and DEA. Every time Seal was accidentally arrested by law enforcement officers, he was subsequently released after intervention by CIA or Justice Department people. This get-out-of-jail pass was typical for many deep-cover operatives. In 1972, for instance, Seal was arrested in New Orleans with 14,000 pounds of explosives intended for Cubans working with the CIA, and promptly released.

Governor Bill Clinton Coverup of Major Drug Trafficking

Governor Bill Clinton was advised of the drug activities and it was requested that he order state law enforcement personnel to investigate. (As governor of Arkansas, he had a duty to investigate without being prodded by a citizen group.) Despite the gravity of the reported drug activities, Clinton and the U.S. Attorney[29] refused to conduct an investigation. At best, this was dereliction of duty; and more to the point, criminal obstruction of justice.

Separate Drug Laws for the Public and Government Personnel

Tom Brown, the pastor of a small church in Arkansas, helped expose the CIA and DEA arms and drug trafficking in Arkansas. To silence and discredit him, the same Justice Department personnel retaliated against Brown by filing drug charges against him. The church grew and used peyote and pot in their services as part of their religious beliefs. No payment was received with this practice. Justice Department prosecutors charged Brown with a criminal offense and U.S. District Judge H. Franklin Waters of Fayetteville, Arkansas, sentenced him to ten years in prison. One less trouble-maker for the CIA and Justice Department!

Drug Trafficking and DOJ Coverup at Angel Fire Resort

Several of my CIA sources described the CIA-related drug trafficking and drug-money laundering at Angel Fire, New Mexico, including that occurring at Angel Fire Ski Resort which was owned and operated by Bill Clinton's friend, Dan Lasater. An investigation into Angel Fire Resort was triggered in 1985 when former Angel Fire employees reported drug trafficking and drug-money laundering. This resulted in investigations by local and federal law enforcement officials.[30] Lasater owned Angle Fire Resort from 1984 to 1987, and sold it after he was sentenced in 1986 to two and a half years in prison for distributing drugs in Arkansas. (He was pardoned within six months by Governor Clinton.)

Coverup by DEA of Angel Fire
Drug Trafficking and Ties to Key People in Arkansas

A sequestered U.S. Customs report included a January 1991 memo written by Customs Air Interdiction Officer Lawrence E. Frost, which referred to the drug trafficking at Angel Fire and said in part:

During 1988, significant information was developed by Special Agent Norm Scott of the FBI and I regarding a large controlled substance

---

[29] Asa Hutchinson and later Michael Fitzhugh.
[30] *Sunday Journal*, New Mexico, May 8, 1994; *Albuquerque Journal*, May 8, 1994.

smuggling operation, as well as a large scale money laundering activity being carried out in the Angel Fire, New Mexico area.

The memo described how Frost and Scott requested information about Lasater from the Drug Enforcement Administration, which was in the DEA's possession because of charges against Lasater in Arkansas:

At no time did I ever receive any information from...DEA regarding any of the alleged conspirators in this case, although I knew that DEA had previously arrested and convicted the primary target of the investigation, Dan Lasater.

If the DEA had cooperated and furnished information, it is possible that Frost and Scott would have discovered Lasater's links to Governor Bill Clinton, the CIA's drug trafficking and money laundering.

CIA Asset Terry Reed Blows the Whistle on CIA Drug Trafficking

Terry Reed, a former CIA asset, and co-author John Cummings, authored a 1994 book describing what Reed discovered as a CIA asset in Arkansas: *Compromised: Clinton, Bush and the CIA.*[31] Reed, a former U.S. Air Force intelligence officer, was recruited by the CIA to train Contra pilots in Arkansas and later to start up a CIA proprietary in Guadalajara, Mexico. Reed's activities in the Mena, Arkansas area brought him into contact with the CIA and National Security Council's arms and drug trafficking, and the coverup by Governor Bill Clinton and members of his staff.

Reed's first employment with the CIA was as a flight instructor for Contra pilots at Arkansas' Mena and Nella airports. He worked with Barry Seal who told Reed about the involvement of Arkansas government officials in CIA drug trafficking and drug-money laundering. Reed was in frequent contact with people who later became front-page news.

Seal told Reed that millions of dollars of drug money was being laundered through the Arkansas Development Finance Authority and through Dan Lasater' brokerage company, and involved people close to Governor Bill Clinton. Seal told Reed that bags containing large amounts of drug-money were dropped into remote locations near Nella, and then picked up by helicopters or surface vehicles.

After Seal was killed, Lasater's bond business suddenly dropped, suggesting that Seal was indeed laundering money through Lasater's business.

Air Dropping Drugs onto Arkansas Clearings

Seal told Reed about dropping bags of money from aircraft into isolated clearings in Arkansas, including on property owned by Little Rock industrialist Seth Ward, upon which resided Ward's son-in-law, Fins Shellnut. Shellnut worked for bond broker Dan Lasater. Reed described how the bags of money, sometimes millions of dollars at a time, were dropped onto Ward's property, picked up by Shellnut, and then laundered through Lasater's bond brokerage business.

Lasater's bond brokerage business reportedly handled much of the drug money laundering in Arkansas until Dan Lasater was convicted of drug trafficking and sent to prison. Testifying against Lasater was Bill Clinton's

---

[31] Authored by Terry Reed and John Cummings.

brother, Roger, who was also charged with drug trafficking but given a reduced sentence in exchange for his testimony.

Secret Drug Meeting With Key People from Both Political Parties

Reed described a late-night meeting that he attended in a World War II
ammunition bunker outside of Little Rock, Arkansas, during which the siphoning of drug money was brought up. Reed stated that the people at the
meeting included Governor Bill Clinton; Clinton's Chief of Security, Arkansas
State Police Lieutenant Raymond Young; Clinton's aide in charge of the Arkansas Development Finance Authority (ADFA), Bob Nash; Attorney Robert
Johnson of the CIA proprietary, Southern Air Transport; Reed's handler, John
Cathey, andMax Gomez (alias for Felix Rodriguez, with close working relationship to Vice-President and then President George Bush).

Clinton's chief of security, Lieutenant Raymond Young, waited outside
the bunker while the meeting was in progress. (Young was the same Arkansas
State Police officer who filed and carried out fraudulent criminal charges
against Reed at a later date.)

Attorney for Covert CIA Airline and Later, U.S. Attorney General

Reed had been in frequent telephone contact with the man he knew as
Robert Johnson. Johnson directed the drug trafficking and drug-money laundering, the training in Arkansas of Contra pilots and fighters, and authorized
Reed to set up the CIA proprietary in Mexico. At a later date, Reed learned
that Robert Johnson was really William Barr, appointed by President George
Bush to be Attorney General of the United States, the nation's top law-
enforcement position.

Damage Control

Reed's CIA contact, William Barr, known at that time by his alias Robert
Johnson, told Reed that Attorney General Edwin Meese had appointed Michael Fitzhugh to be U.S. Attorney in Western Arkansas, and that he would
stonewall any investigation into the Mena, Arkansas drug-related activities.
This obstruction of justice by Justice Department officials did occur.

Federal Officials Protesting Siphoning
Off Of Drug Money By Clinton's Group

The purpose of this meeting was to protest Arkansas officials taking too
great a percentage of the drug money laundered by Missouri officials, and the
attention caused by the drug conviction of Bill Clinton's brother, Roger
Clinton.

NSC Oliver North and Future Attorney General into Drugs

Reed described how Oliver North and William Barr authorized him to
start a CIA proprietary in Mexico posing as a high technology trading and
consulting firm. Reed moved his family to Mexico, thinking the operation was
legitimate and of long duration. Reed worked closely with Oliver North, Felix
Rodriguez, and Barry Seal. Before long, Reed discovered that the CIA front
company he operated was being used by the CIA for gun-running and drug
smuggling and this was confirmed in July 1987. He advised his CIA handler
that he wanted out of the operation, and under cover of darkness, Reed moved
his family back to Arkansas where he went into hiding. He then became targeted for retaliation by one of Arkansas's state police officers who was on

Governor Bill Clinton's staff.

Attacking A Potential Whistleblower

With the knowledge that Reed acquired during his CIA connections in Arkansas, he posed a threat to the drug operations implicating CIA, DOJ, and Arkansas personnel—including Governor Bill Clinton. This danger was addressed by Arkansas State Police fraudulently charging Reed and his wife with fraud, conspiracy, and mail fraud relating to the theft several years earlier of Reed's aircraft, and allegedly making a false claim to the insurance company.

For three years the Reeds had to fight Arkansas State Police agencies, which included Governor Bill Clinton's chief of security, Raymond Young. Reed reported that Young forged documents, used perjured testimony, and falsified evidence, seeking to put Reed and his wife in prison.

Reed describes how U.S. District Judge Frank Theis blocked their defenses, and dismissed evidence showing the sham nature of the charges, claiming the evidence was irrelevant.

Time Magazine Coverup of CIA and High-Level Corruption

During their attempts to defend themselves against the false charges *Time* magazine sought to discredit the Reeds and what they were exposing. A *Time* article (April 20, 1992) was entitled, "Anatomy of a Smear" with a subtitle, "Terry Reed loves to tell reporters scandalous tales about Bill Clinton and the Contras. The trouble is the stories are false."

Time falsely stated that Reed had no connections to the CIA or Barry Seal, despite considerable proof given to *Time* reporter Richard Behar. The article stated that "The only trouble with Reed's sensational tale is that, not a word of it is true."

Time had repeatedly, over the years, engaged in attacks on people exposing government corruption and CIA drug trafficking. Throughout this and my other books are examples of this coverup, disinformation, and ridiculing of those who courageously expose the criminal and subversive acts of high government personnel. *Time* magazine was one of the publications that I repeatedly notified of the criminal activities, beginning while I was a federal investigator. Never once did the magazine report the evidence I offered.

Freedom Magazine Confirming Reed's CIA Connections

In response to the *Time* coverup and discrediting article, *Freedom* magazine, which had been exposing the CIA drug trafficking in Arkansas, published an article (May 1993) titled, *The Drugging of America*, expanding on the criminal activities by exposing the *Time* coverup. *Freedom* magazine wrote: "According to knowledgeable sources interviewed by *FREEDOM*, Terry Reed was one of the players in CIA covert operations based at Mena."

Clinton's CIA Drug Smuggling Coverup As Governor and President

Governor Bill Clinton's protection of CIA drug activities and DOJ coverups while governor of Arkansas could be expected to be followed with similar actions after he became president of the United States. The California legal newspaper, *Daily Journal*, wrote in its July 21, 1994 issue that "The Clinton administration has been undermining existing anti-drug efforts on all fronts." The article charged President Clinton with dismantling almost the entire White House Office created to lead the fight:

Surgeon General Joycelyn Elders repeated calls for drug legaliza-
tion...government-led domestic marijuana eradication has been substan-
tially curtailed...The president has ordered a massive reduction in De-
fense Department support for drug interdiction...proposed that Congress
cut $100 million in drug-treatment funding and $130 million in drug-
prevention education... For 1995, the president wants to cut 625 positions
from federal drug enforcement agencies, the DEA, FBI, Border Patrol,
U.S. Customs Service and others, and reduce federal drug-prosecution
personnel by more than 100 positions.

CIA-MILITARY DEEP COVER PILOT GENE TATUM

Another one of my many deep-cover sources who was ordered to fly drugs while he was a U.S. Army helicopter pilot was Gene "Chip" Tatum. He was ordered to fly drugs from Fort Campbell, Kentucky to the airport at Mena and Little Rock in Arkansas. Tatum started providing me with information and documentation that support his statements, including affidavits, letters, and copies of military flight plans showing the names of well-known individuals and records of drug shipments.

In 1998, after revealing many secrets relating to CIA and military drug trafficking, he was forced to go underground, reportedly under threats from the Department of Justice.

Drugs, Vice President, Attorney General, Noriega, and Mossad

Tatum joined the U.S. Army in 1971 and was initially assigned to Vietnam, after which he was trained as a helicopter pilot. He also became commander of a unit in the ultra-secret operation known as Pegasus. He was assigned to fly helicopter flights in Honduras and Nicaragua, working CIA missions, and working with the National Security Council's Oliver North and CIA operations with Amiram Nir and Felix Rodriguez. In carrying out these missions, he associated with such key people in government as William Barr, George Bush, General Manuel Noriega, and Mossad agent Michael Harari. Tatum had frequent contact with Oliver North while North was assigned to the White House's National Security Council, and William Barr who later became attorney general of the United States.

Tatum said his Pegasus missions were secretly embedded in an Army medical unit (3/498th Medical Company from Fort Riley, Kansas) and that CIA agent Henry Hyde was responsible for the finances of the unit, including arranging lines of credit. While under orders of the National Security Council (NSC) and the CIA, and working under cover as a U.S. Army helicopter pilot, Tatum was instructed to infiltrate the 3/498th Medical Company and pose as a medevac pilot. In this capacity he flew wounded personnel to medical stations. But priority was given to CIA and NSC assignments over the carrying of wounded personnel.

Operating Pegasus Missions

In the 1980s he flew helicopters in Central and South America, flying "Medevac" helicopters taking Contras and civilians to emergency care centers. Tatum was command pilot of one of two helicopter flight crews from the 3/498th Medical Company based at Fort Stewart, Georgia that were sent in 1985 to Palmerola Air Base in Honduras. Each crew consisted of a pilot, co-pilot, medic, and the crew chief. Tatum was part of the medevac mission for Joint Task Force Bravo.

On one flight out of Palmerola (MCHG), he carried as passengers the pilots of the C-123 that was shot down in Nicaragua, Bill Cooper and Buzz Sawyer. This was the incident that forced media exposure of the CIA and White House's role in Nicaragua. The plane had been hit by a surface to air missile. The only survivor of that flight, Eugene Hasenfus, was the person responsible for kicking military cargo out of the back of the aircraft. He survived because he carried a parachute, and jumped out of the aircraft before it crashed. His subsequent capture and interrogation precipitated the exposure of the Iran-Contra affair.

Transporting "Medical Supplies" From Remote Jungle Sites

While at Palmerola Air Base in Honduras, Tatum flew helicopter flights to Illopango, El Salvador, where Corporate Air Service, a CIA-owned aviation company was based, and to various Contra camps in Honduras and Nicaragua. Although the reason for his assignment to the Medevac unit was to move wounded personnel to treatment centers, he discovered that he was frequently ordered to transport large white coolers marked "Medical Supplies" and fly them to landing strips for pickup by fixed-wing aircraft, usually C-123 and C-13s. These aircraft were flown either by military or private pilots, who took the "medical supplies" to Panama and then the United States.

Using U.S. Military to Fly Drugs into the United States

Once, during a hard landing resulting from an engine failure, one of the coolers broke open, and while taping the coolers shut he discovered that instead of the contents being medical supplies they were filled with bags containing cocaine. Tatum would discover many more flights carrying similar "medical supplies."

Describing One of His Flights

On one of his flights to El Ocotal in Costa Rica, Tatum carried Felix Rodriguez (also known as Max Gomes), a close associate of Vice President George Bush, in the Contra operation; General Gustavo Alverez of Honduras, and Joseph Fernandez, another CIA agent. Upon landing at Ojo de Agua-El Tamborcita, they were joined by Michael Harari, a Mossad agent and security advisor to General Manuel Noriega of Panama; by William Barr (attorney at the CIA's Southern Air Transport located at Miami at that time and before he became attorney general of the United States), and Barry Seal. Seal had flown Noriega and Harari to the meeting in Seal's Learjet aircraft (tail number N13SN).

In the past, Tatum reached Barr by phone at the CIA's Southern Air Transport in Miami, and under the name, Robert Johnson.

Purpose Of Meeting: Discover Where Drug-Money Is Being Stolen

The purpose of the meeting was to determine who was responsible for stealing over $100 million in drug money on the three routes from Panama to Colorado, Ohio, and Arkansas. This theft was financially draining the operation known as the "Enterprise." By comparing computerized records, Tatum said that it was determined that the theft was occurring on the route from Panama to Arkansas.

Seal, Clinton, Or Noriega Stealing Drug Money
From White House Drug Operation

Tatum said that at the end of the meeting he went with Fernandez to the helicopter where a portable secure phone was set up to communicate with Washington by satellite link. The first call was made by Fernandez to Oliver North, informing North that the theft was occurring on the Panama to Arkansas route, and "that means either Seal, Clinton or Noriega."

VP George Bush and William Barr Discussing Drug Money Theft

Fifteen minutes later, the portable phone rang, and Vice President George Bush was on the line, talking to William Barr. Barr said at one point, referring to the missing funds, "I would propose that no one source would be bold enough to siphon out that much money, but it is more plausible that each are siphoning a portion, causing a drastic loss."

Barr told Bush that he and Fernandez were staying in Costa Rica until the following day after first visiting John Hull's ranch. Barr then handed the phone to Tatum, who was instructed by Bush to be sure that Noriega and Harari boarded Seal's plane and departed, and for Tatum to get the tail number of Seal's plane.

Tatum said that Barr then dialed another number, immediately reaching then governor Bill Clinton. Barr explained the missing money problem to Clinton, explaining that over $100 million of the "Enterprise" monies had disappeared along the Panama to Arkansas connection. Barr suggested that Clinton investigate at the Arkansas end of the Panama to Arkansas route, and that he and Oliver North would continue investigating the Panama end of the connection, warning that the matter must be resolved or it could lead to "big problems."

(This description of missing drug money provided further support to a subsequent meeting in Little Rock, described earlier by Terry Reed, during which William Barr accused Clinton of siphoning drug money and that this had to stop.)

Missing Money Notation on Military Flight Plan

The SATCOM phone equipment was then stowed on the helicopter, and Tatum waited for Noriega and Harari to leave in Seal's Learjet. Tatum then flew his passengers to Tegucigalpa, and turned into military operations a copy of the flight plan (dated March 25, 1985). Tatum wrote on the back of the flight plan:

Meeting with Gen Noriega/SATCOM with North and Gov of AK concerning missing monies. Dropped off Noriega at airport in S.D. Met Barry Seal in 13SN. Seal took Gen Noriega & Harari.

Several days later, Tatum flew from Tela, Honduras to La Cieba, picking up Oliver North, Felix Rodriguez, General Alverez of Honduras, and Amiram Nir. They then flew into several villages on the Nicaragua-Honduras border to determine their suitability for cargo drops by CH-47s the following month.

"One More Year of This and We Can All Retire"

Tatum then flew the group to Santa Anna, Honduras, meeting with Enrique Bermudez and other Contra leaders, and visited a cocaine processing facility. Tatum described the strong smell of jet fuel and acetone, and the large fuel pods that had the tops stripped off of them and in which were fuel and leaves. Tatum repeated what North said: "One more year of this and we'll all retire." adding, "If we can keep those Arkansas hicks in line, that is," referring to Barry Seal and Governor Clinton.

Vice President George Bush Concerned About Drug Money Theft

While General Alvaraz went with the Contra leader to discuss logistics, North, Rodriguez, and Nir continued through the wooden building inspecting the cocaine. Tatum repeated what North said: "Bush is very concerned about those missing monies. I think he's going to have Jeb arrange something out of Colombia." (Would "Jeb" be Jeb Bush?)

"No One Big Enough To Stop It"

As Tatum listened to these conversations, he remembered the army officers' remarks in Ojo de Agua when Tatum complained about transporting drugs during military operations: "Tell no one. There's no one big enough in your chain of command to stop it." Having heard North discuss the involvement of Vice President Bush and Governor Clinton, Tatum understood that earlier statement.

Tatum then flew back to La Cieba and then to Tela, returning the following day to home base at Palmarola, where Tatum put a few notes on the back of the flight plan filed with base operations:

ROM ACM/Rodriguez for night. USN to WASPAM/Santa Anna/Lemez—No problems recon successful—Rodriguez, North, Nir, Dr. Gus. Others (4).

Recipient Of Drugs, Mossad Operative "Dr. Harari"

During another trip, Tatum picked up at Dustoff Operations six coolers mislabeled "medical supplies," and flew them to an airstrip at Trijillo, where they were given to a C-130 crew bound for Panama. Tatum asked the pilot, "Who gets these?" The pilot looked at the manifest and said that a Dr. Harari would be called on arrival. The alleged doctor was none other than Mossad operator Michael Harari, and the phony Doctor title went along with the phony medical supply labels on the coolers.

Another military flight plan showed Tatum making a flight on April 9, 1985, into a small village forty kilometers east north east of Ocotal in Nicaragua. Tatum met Felix Rodriguez and Contra leader Enrique Bermudez, and the three of them inspected a cocaine processing facility located in a large tent, containing all American equipment. Inside were several women packaging cocaine.

Four 110-quart white coolers, marked "medical supplies," were then put on Tatum's helicopter for delivery to a C-123 aircraft at San Lorenzo. Tatum then flew back to his home base, at which time he wrote on the back of the flight plan that he filed with military base operations the details of the cocaine lab inspection.

White House and CIA Cocaine Operation

During a flight from Palmerola to El Paraiso, Honduras, his passengers told Tatum they worked for Corporate Air Services out of Ilopango Air Base in El Salvador and that they were meeting with Contra leaders to coordinate air drops to various Contra camps. When the meeting was over, Tatum was given a white cooler marked "vaccine" weighing over 200 pounds and instructed to deliver the cooler to a C-130 at Las Mesa airport in San Pedro Sula, Honduras. The cooler was dropped while being taken from the helicopter, and Tatum used aviation tape to reseal it. After removing the old tape and looking inside the cooler, he discovered that the contents consisted of what appeared to be over 100 bags containing a white powdery substance: cocaine. The resealed cooler containing the cocaine was then put on a C-130 that was departing for Panama.

Cocaine Bound For World Court as Evidence—Said Oliver North

At one time, upon returning to Palmerola Air Base—thinking that Oliver North did not know about the cocaine trafficking—Tatum called Washington and advised North of the cocaine discovery. North told him a wild story: "The Sandinistas are manufacturing cocaine and selling it to fund the military. It was bound for the world courts as evidence."

One of the many military flight plans filed by Tatum, dated March 1, 1985 described delivering two white coolers marked "medical supplies" to Dustoff (MEDEVAC) Operations. Felix Rodriguez than ordered Tatum to deliver the coolers to him at Tela, Honduras (LYA). Tatum checked the contents, and found them filled with about 100 kilos of cocaine. As ordered, he delivered the coolers to Rodriguez, who was waiting in front of an old DC-3. Tatum then returned to his home base at Palmerola, and made the following notation on the back of the military flight plan that he had filed with base operations:

Q/U Two coolers "med supplies" Checked contents—white powder—appr 100 sacks each.

Stealing Secret Frequencies from U.S. Military Communications Site

Rodriguez instructed Tatum to obtain the secret frequencies used by the military at a tactical communications site (TAC) called Skywatch, which was the focal telemetry point of several military satellites in this hemisphere. The military had refused to release this information to the CIA, causing the CIA to carry out a plan to steal the secret codes. The Agency contaminated the water supply with an unusually high concentration of chlorine, causing widespread stomach cramps and diarrhea among the soldiers. This required calling for medical personnel to fly to the site and treat the sickened personnel. While the personnel were being treated, Tatum went into a communication van and copied the frequencies from the equipment in use.

Reports To Washington about Military Drug Shipments

Upon his return to Palmerola that afternoon, Tatum called CIA agent Donald Gregg on a secure telephone line, passing along the frequencies that he had copied. Gregg then instructed Tatum to pass the frequencies to CIA agent Clair George at Langley. Before having the call transferred, Tatum told Gregg of his discovery of cocaine in the coolers. Gregg repeated the false excuse that the coolers were bound for the world courts as evidence against the Sandinistas. Tatum was then transferred to Clair George, who took the information and was advised that he would pass the information to Dewey "Duane" (Dewey) Clarridge of the CIA).

Tatum then went to Base Operations and noted this information on the back of the on-file flight plan and the mission briefing sheet. Copies of some of these forms are on following pages. On this particular flight Tatum wrote:

North arranged for water contamination at TAC site—I flew medevac to site and while medic attended—I collected TAC FQCYS for North. Upon departure forced to auto-rotate. Declared emergency-bad torque and cracked tail boom.

One of many military flight plans filed by Tatum was a March 5, 1985, flight that carried CIA and Mossad asset and agent, Amiram Nir; General Gustavo Alverez, a Honduran Army Chief of Staff who often used the alias, Dr. Gus, and a Honduran Colonel who was the General's aide. On this mission, Tatum flew into six villages listed on the flight plan, picked up soldiers, and took them to El Paraiso, Honduras.

At El Paraiso, as they prepared to leave, four large white coolers were put on board the helicopter. Pointing to the coolers, Tatum asked Rodriguez, "Evidence?" Rodriguez responded by patting the cooler with his hands, saying, "You catch on fast." Tatum landed at San Lorenzo (SNL), Honduras, dropping off Rodriguez and the coolers. Upon return to home base at Palmerola. Tatum wrote on the back of the operation's flight plan, "4 coolers similar to cocaine cooler."

Public Funded CIA-Military Drug Deliveries to Arkansas

Tatum told about the flights in military helicopters carrying the white coolers to the Arkansas airports at Mena and Little Rock while he was assigned to Special Operations at Ft. Campbell in Kentucky during 1983 and 1984. The medevac unit at Ft. Campbell, 324th Medical Battalion, was a supporting unit for Task Force 160, a Special Operations Unit under CIA control. Flight crews of the 324th Medical Battalion rotated in and out of Honduras on tours that lasted four months.

Governor Bill Clinton's Associates Received Cocaine Deliveries

Tatum described several of the people who met his helicopter's arrival at Mena and Little Rock: Governor Bill Clinton's friend, Dan Lasater, who was usually accompanied by a plain-clothes policeman who produced a badge and identification showing him to be Raymond "Buddy" Young. Tatum said that Young showed up in Honduras posing as a member of the Arkansas National Guard. Occasionally, Lasater was accompanied at the Mena Airport by Jerry Parks, who helped in the off-loading of the coolers. Jerry Parks operated a security company that had close ties to the Clinton administration in Arkansas.

Danger to Threaten Exposing Clinton and CIA Drug Ties

Some years later, Parks had a falling out with Clinton and had threatened to expose information about Clinton and the drug activities. This caused him to be added to the list of people in Arkansas who were either killed or died under mysterious circumstances.

Drug Meeting with CIA's William Barr,
Mossad's Harari, Governor Clinton's Buddy Young

During one flight to Tegucigalpa on March 15, 1985, Tatum met with William Barr, Michael Harari, and Buddy Young (head of Governor Bill Clinton's security detail). Barr represented himself as an emissary of Vice President George Bush, who would be arriving soon. The purpose of the meeting was to arrange for Vice President Bush's arrival.

The following morning, Young and Harari flew back to Palmerola with Tatum. Because of the high noise level in the helicopter, the passengers, Young and Harari, wore headsets and spoke over the aircraft intercom system to each other, possibly unaware that Tatum could hear their conversation. Tatum was copying this conversation on his knee pad until he ran out of paper. Tatum recorded the conversation:

Young: Arkansas has the capability to manufacture anything in the area of weapons, and if we don't have it, we'll get it.

Harari: How about the government controls?

Young: The governor's on top of it. And if the feds get nosey, we hear about it and make a call. Then they're called off. [As he looked down at the countryside] Why the hell would anyone want to fight for a shit-hole like this?

Harari: [Shaking his head] What we do has nothing to do with preserving a country's integrity. It's just business, and Third World countries see their destiny as defeating borders and expanding. The more of this mentality we can produce, the greater our wealth. We train and we arm; that's our job. And in return, we get a product far more valuable than the money for a gun. We're paid with product. And we credit top dollar for product. [i.e. drugs]

Young: [Still looking confused.]

Harari: Look, one gun and 3,000 rounds of ammo is $1,200. A kilo of product [cocaine] is about $1,000. We credit the Contras $1,500 for every kilo. That's top dollar for a kilo of cocaine. It's equivalent to the America K-Mart special; buy four, get one free. On our side, we spend $1,200 for a kilo and sell it for $12,000 to $15,000. Now, that's a profit center. And the market is much greater for the product [cocaine] than for weapons. It's just good business sense. Understand?

Young: Damn! So you guys promote wars and revolutions to provide weapons for drugs. We provide the non-numbered parts to change out and we all win. Damn, that's good!

Harari: It's good when it works. But someone is, how do you say, has his hand in the coffer.

Young: Well, we get our ten percent right off the top and that's plenty. Gofus can make it go a long way.

Harari: Who is Gofus?

Young: Governor Clinton. That's our pet word for him. You know they call the President "Potus" for president of the United States. Well, we call Clinton "Gofus" for governor of the United States. He thinks he is anyhow.

Harari: That's your problem in America. You have no respect for your elected officials. They are more powerful than you think, and have ears everywhere. You should heed my words and be loyal to your leaders. Especially when speaking to persons like me. Your remarks indicate a weakness, something our intelligence analysts look for.

Young: Oh hell, Mike. Everybody knows the Clintons want the White House and will do anything to get it. We know about the cocaine. Hell, we've picked it up before with Lasater when he was worried about going on Little Rock Air Base to get it.

Harari: [Changing the topic, Harari questioned Young about his knowledge of who the players were.]

Young: Clinton thinks he's in charge, but he'll only go as far as Casey [CIA director] allows. Me and my staff, we keep the lid on things, you know: complaints about night flying, Arkansas people are private folks, they don't like a lot of commotion, and Mena just isn't the right place for the operation. It keeps us busy at the shredder, if you know what I mean. Dan's the man [Lasater]. He does magic with the money. Between him and Jack Stevens we don't have to worry a bit. Then we got Parks. If there's a problem, he 's the man. We call him the Archer. That's the code name that Casey and Colby told us to assign to that position. Finis oversees our drop zone. Nash, he's just the boss' yes man. Personally, I think he's a mistake.
            Seal and his guys, I like his attitude "and leave the driving to us."

Harari: You like Seal?

Young: Hell, he's the only one I trust; respect is the word.

Harari: Do you see him much?

Young: Hell, yes. We test drive Clinton's rides [cocaine] before we send 'em on, you know. [Laughing and grinding his hips.] Say, how much coke can you can make in a week?

Harari: One camp can produce 400 keys [kilos] a week. The others are about half that. But that's just our operation here. We have other sources in various parts of the world. Why do you ask?

Young: The Governor wanted to know our capacity.

Harari: Who else is on the team?

Young: Well, hell, I forgot who I told you about.

Harari: [Harari repeated the list from memory.]

Young: OK, there's the manufacturers; hell, these two. [At this point Tatum ran out of paper on his knee board, and didn't recognize the names; but they sounded like Johnson and Johnson.]

Upon landing at his base, Tatum made a notation on the back of the previously filed flight plan:

This was a mission to Tegucigalpa. Bush visit/met with Barr & had dinner at German restaurant.

Oliver North Passing Out

On another day, Tatum was alerted for a flight at 5 a.m. to pick up three wounded soldiers at a Contra camp near Choloteca, Nicaragua, and pick up two observers on the way back from Choloteca: Oliver North and Lt. Col. Navarro. As the casualties were loaded into the helicopter at the Contra camp, the medic had to remove a piece of wood sticking out of a bad wound in the chest area. As the medic cleaned the area a hole the size of a softball appeared. North saw it and fainted. Tatum caught him and popped an ammonia capsule under his nose to revive him. The flight then departed for San Lorenzo, Honduras, where the casualties were unloaded. Back at the Palmerola base, Tatum completed the Mission Brief Back report, writing in part:

> *Arrived at SLN—Arrival at the helipad the emergency vehicles were not waiting. There was no answer on Medevac FQCY FM 45.10 or on ..... 49.10. Confusion on ground causing ground time delay of 15 min. Medics' duties were compounded when Mr. North fainted.*

As I looked over the many copies of flight plans that Tatum gave me, they provided still more evidence of the following:

- Mossad agent Michael Harari was on many of the flights associated with the CIA and military drug shipments, providing still further indication that Israel's Mossad is helping the CIA inflict drugs upon the United States.
- William Barr, who Bush appointed to be the top law enforcement officer in the United States—U.S. Attorney General—played a key role in the smuggling of drugs into the United States. Tatum's statements about reaching Barr at Southern Air Transport in Miami through the name of Robert Johnson confirmed what Terry Reed, author of the book *Compromise*, had told me and had written. Nothing like having members of felony drug operations hold the position of U.S. Attorney General—in control of the United States Department of Justice—and a vice president of the United States. With this type of influence no one needs fear being arrested. And don't forget the Mafia groups working with the CIA who also receive Justice Department protection that is not available to U.S. citizens.
- The drugging of America involved the CIA, the military, National Security Council, the White House, George Bush, and Governor Bill Clinton, among many others.
- That Mena, Arkansas was a key CIA transshipment point for cocaine coming into the United States on return flights from Central America.
- The existence of a two-tier code of criminal justice, in which people holding key positions of trust in the U.S. government go unpunished for their role in moving tens of thousands of pounds of hard-drugs into the United States, while the average "Joe" or "Jane" is given years in prison for possession of drugs the size of an M&M. That even beats Mexican "justice!"

Attachment 5

REQUEST AND AUTHORIZATION FOR TEMPORARY DUTY

TO: CC AFCS, RICHARD GEBAUR AFB, MO — FROM: CC 3 MCCP, TINKER AFB, OK — TELEPHONE 4441

THE FOLLOWING INDIVIDUAL(S) WILL PROCEED ON TDY:

1. NAME (Last + First + M. I.), GRADE, SSAN	2. UNIT, FUNCTIONAL ADDRESS, SYMBOL, MAJOR COMMAND	3. SECURITY CLEARANCE
XXXXXXXXXXXXXXXXXXXXXXXXXXXXXXXXXXXXXXXXXXX TATUM, DOIS G. JR., SGT., XXXXXXXXXXXXXXXXXXXXXXXXXXXXXXXXXXXXXXXXXXX	3MCCP DOR TINKER AFB, OK. AFCS	TS-SSIR ATOMAL

4. EFFECTIVE ON OR ABOUT	5. APPR NO DAYS INCLUDING TRAVEL TIME	6. DDALV	7. LEAVE ADDRESS
2JAN74	89	N/A	NONE

8. PURPOSE	9. ITINERARY VARIATIONS AUTHORIZED
MILITARY ADVISOR COMMUNICATION SPECIALIST/AIR AMERICA INC.	FROM: TINKER AFB, OKLA TO: CLASSIFIED LOCATION RETURN TO: TINKER AFB, OKLA

10. EXCESS BAGGAGE AUTH PER PERSON UNLIMITED POUNDS PIECES	12. ADVANCE AUTHORIZED (Civilians only) $ NONE	15. IAW AFR 30-9 (Military) OR JTR, VOL 2 (Civilian) FOR ALL NECESSARY TRAVEL EXPENSES INCLUDING $ FOR REGISTRATION AND ADMISSION FEES. THE FEE COVERS COST OF MEALS AND LODGING FOR NIGHTS.
11. NAME OF DESIGNATED OFFICIAL COURIER	13. SUB RATE (Airmen only) $ N/A 14. PROPER AREA CLEARANCES HAVE BEEN OBTAINED	

16. MODES OF TRANSPORTATION

A. [ ] TRAVEL BY PRIVATELY-OWNED CONVEYANCE HAS BEEN DETERMINED AS MORE ADVANTAGEOUS TO THE GOVERNMENT
B. [X] TRAVEL BY GOVERNMENT (Vehicle) (Aircraft) DIRECTED.
C. [ ] TRAVEL BY COMMERCIAL AIRCRAFT (First Class Accommodation) APPROVED BY PER AFM 75-6.
D. [X] OTHER (Identify in item 18)

17. SPECIAL INSTRUCTIONS

A. Submit Travel Voucher within 5 workdays after completion of travel; for confirmatory orders, within 5 days of receipt of orders.
B. Attach receipts showing cost of all lodgings used during the period of this claim.
C. If TDY is for 30 or more days duration at one location, then: Pursuant to AFR 30-15, you will report to the base housing referral office servicing your TDY station before entering into any rental, lease, or purchase agreement for off-base housing.
D. Prior to travel overseas comply with the Foreign Clearance Guide for passport, immunization, and clearance requirements.
E. Return air movement designator will be obtained from the local area priority issuing agency.

18. REMARKS

AIR CODE #23759006B
ABOVE LISTED INDIVIDUALS TO BE AFFORDED ALL ITEMS REQUESTED ON PRIORITY 1 AVAIL.
ALL ITEMS TO BE CHARGED AGAINST FUNDING CITATION AUTHORIZING TDY

19. DATE	20. ORDERS ISSUING/APPROVING OFFICIAL (Type Name, Grade and Title)	
2 JAN 74	LT GEN, USAF CHIEF MILITARY INTELL ADV TO JCS	

22. AUTHORITY	23. SPECIAL ORDER NUMBER	24. DATE
CIA FILE REGULATION	TB-569	1JAN 77

25. DESIGNATION AND LOCATION OF HEADQUARTERS DEPARTMENT OF THE AIR FORCE	26. EXPENSES CHARGEABLE TO ACCOUNTING CLASSIFICATION
CLASSIFIED FILE	ADV CIC 27. TDN N/A

28. DISTRIBUTION	29. SIGNATURE ELEMENT OF ORDERS AUTHENTICATING ELEMENT
RT #1,5,8	CLASSIFIED FILE

Travel Authorization for Gene "Chip" Tatum

3. DUE TO THESE POTENTIALLY LIFE-THREATENING SITUATIONS, AND WITH THE IMPENDING DEPLOYMENT OF UT 85 MEDICAL ASSETS INTO THIS THEATER. [U. ALL MEDEVAC A/C AND CREWS DEPLOYING TO HONDURAS IN SUPPORT OF COMBINED/JOINT TRAINING EXERCISES WILL BE PLACED UNDER THE [OPERATIONAL CONTROL OF] JTF BRAVO MEDICAL ELEMENT. THIS WILL ENSURE THAT THE EXERCISE IS ADEQUATELY COVERED AND THAT AIR CREWS IN SUPPORT OF OTHER THAN JTF BRAVO MED ELEMENT'S MEDEVAC SECTION ARE KNOWLEDGEABLE OF TH AOR. HOST NATION FLIGHT REQUIREMENTS AND HEALTH FACILITIES, AND US MEDICAL CAPABILITIES/LOCATIONS IN-THEATER.
4. POC AT SCSG MAJ LEDFORD (A) 282-5803

Back of Travel Authorization

Gene "Chip" Tatum

DECLARATION

I, Dois Gene Tatum, declare:

I was a helicopter pilot for the United States Army from 1982 to 1986, during which time I flew missions in Central America and also from Ft Campbell, Kentucky.

From 1986 to 1992 I was an agent for the Central Intelligence Agency, operating under a deep-cover assignment.

During this time I witnessed activities involving high-level U.S. personnel that I felt were unlawful, and I reported these activities to my superiors in the U.S. Army and to my handlers in the Central Intelligence Agency, to the National Security Council, and to various individuals, including William Barr, Oliver North, George Bush.

Among these activities were rampant drug smuggling into the United States involving people in control of the Central Intelligence Agency, the Drug Enforcement Administration, the armed forces of the United States, among others.

I have documented some of these activities on military flight plans, showing as passengers on certain flights, the following: William Barr; Buddy Young; Felix Rodriguez; Oliver North; Joe Fernandez; Manuel Noriega, and Mike Harari.

I have visited cocaine laboratories with the above people, who were inspecting the drug smuggling operations in Central America.

I have documented on some of these military flight plans the nature of the cargo being carried in white coolers that were fraudulently marked as "medical supplies," which I accidentally discovered to be cocaine.

During one flight and related meeting, I was present while there were discussions as to where drug money was being siphoned on the Panama to Arkansas run. Present at this meeting were Manuel Noriega; William Barr (associated with CIA proprietary Southern Air Transport and later attorney general of the United States); Joe Fernandez; Mike Harari; General Gustavo Alverez. Participating in this meeting via satellite telephone was Vice President George bush, Oliver North, and William Jefferson Clinton, then governor of Arkansas.

I had reported these illegal operations to my superiors, including William Barr; Oliver North; George Bush; Felix Rodriguez; Joe Fernandez; Don Gregg; Dewey Clarridge.

After I refused to perform a mission that I felt were beyond my willingness to execute, I notified my handlers that I wanted out of the operation, which at that time was known as Operation Pegasus. Their response was to warn me that no one leaves the operation.

I declare under penalty of perjury that the above facts are true and correct to the best of my knowledge and belief. Executed this _____15TH_____ day of August 1996 in the County of Hillsborough, State of Florida.

Dois Gene Tatum
aka Gene D. Tatum

Declaration by Gene Tatum concerning CIA Drug Trafficking

DEEP-COVER CIA ASSET TOSH PLUMLEE

Another of the many sources providing me confidential insider information about the role of U.S. government operations in drug smuggling, and involving many of the same people as already described, was William "Tosh" Plumlee. After joining the army in Dallas, he worked under several case officers with OSS and CIA ties, including Captain Edward G. Seiwell. Plumlee received pilot training under the GI Bill at White Rock Airport in Dallas, after which he worked at Red Bird Airport south of Dallas, becoming involved with several CIA-front companies. (I was a flight and ground instructor at Redbird Airport in 1949 and 1950, teaching the instrument and airline transport pilot courses, before I started flying as pilot for various airlines. Plumlee and I had also worked for the same airline, Pioneer Airlines at Love Field in Dallas.)

Plumlee was a former deep-cover military and CIA asset from 1956 to 1987 with a long history of CIA activities.

Fighting Alongside Fidel Castro as CIA Operative

He was sent to the Miami area where he became involved in covert operations in Cuba, the Caribbean and Central America. Most of this time he flew guns and ammunition for various factions in half a dozen countries. Plumlee said he was driven by the adventure and the paychecks. He explained that in his covert operations he had to keep other federal agencies from knowing about the clandestine and usually illegal operations.

Covert Operations Have Ring of Unreality for the Public

He was one of a handful of North Americans fighting to overthrow Batista and install Fidel Castro. He described how covert activities have the ring of unreality to the public because of their lack of knowledge about the activities. Those who work the 8 to 5 shift cannot comprehend what goes on in covert operations.

CIA Arming Castro while White House Sought To Assassinate Him

He was involved, while connected to military and CIA intelligence, fighting alongside Fidel Castro's rebel forces in Cuba; he flew aircraft in Southeast Asia for Air America, and flew arms to Central America and drugs on the return trips. All under orders from his government handlers. There were many other similar reports, indicating that the CIA armed Castro to overthrow the Batista government, and then after Castro took over in Cuba, the White House sought for the next several decades to overthrow him. This would suggest that the CIA was continuing its practice of undermining governments all over the world, or, that the CIA's activities were contrary to those established by the White House. Either scenario has happened many times before.

In the 1960s, Plumlee flew missions evacuating defecting Russian missile technicians out of Cuba and trained Cuban pilots in Nicaragua and Happy Valley, prior to the Bay of Pigs fiasco. He flew in Southeast Asia, in Laos and Cambodia, about the time of the Tet offensive.

CIA and Military Personnel Involved in Drug Operations

Plumlee tried to leave covert operations after a tour in Vietnam, but his handlers kept calling him for other deep-cover or "black" projects. He wrote:

It was in Mexico where I saw the widespread government corruption on both sides of the border. Someone in Washington was turning a blind eye toward drug shipments from Colombia being smuggled through Mexico and into the United States. It was obvious, our intelligence information was being tampered with at the highest level. Millions of dollars, dirty drug money, was being routed through Panama by the cartel, some of it to be used to influence the upcoming presidential election. Some of the illegal cargoes were flown and transported by other CIA operatives and military personnel holding civilian status, thus covering their CIA-Military affiliations from public view.

Plumlee had flown and had contacts with key people in the Contra and drug operations, including Bill Cooper (captain of the C-123 plane shot down over Nicaragua). He worked for various CIA proprietary or front companies, including Riddle Airlines, the Dodge Corporation, Inter-Mountain Aviation, Evergreen Helicopters, Act Technology, Air America, CDG American Services, In-Air, and other companies that he couldn't remember. (Ironically, Evergreen helicopter crews would occasionally land one of their large helicopters on my motel property in Yuba City, California, and stay at the motel.)

Given Many CIA Aliases

As a standard CIA procedure, the agency gave Plumlee different aliases when working in different undercover operations, including Buck Pierson, James Plumlee, James H. Rawlings, William H. Pierson, Juan Carbello, and some that he couldn't remember anymore.

In the early 1970s Plumlee was attached to an operation in Miami, Florida called Jay Emway, which involved assassination attempts upon Fidel Castro. Plumlee was involved in black operations with the Pentagon while also working with the CIA. He became a CIA contract pilot, taking orders from the Pentagon and worked through the National Security Council staff. Plumlee worked in the CIA's Jim Wave operation, which was another CIA scheme to assassinate Castro

U.S. Military Working With Mafia People

Plumlee flew many black operations, including flying arms to Central America and drugs into the United States, being advised that these activities were in the national interest. He described the heavy involvement of the military, the Pentagon, the staff of the National Security Council, in these drug activities. He described how the military and intelligence groups worked with Mafia people and casino-associated crime groups. He described assassination attempts on Dominican dictator Rafael Trujillo, and Fidel Castro, and kidnapping people in foreign countries. He described how these illegal operations were given the pious-sounding name of national security, the same label used to support secrecy on subversive and criminal activities against the United States.

CIA's Attempt To Assassinate Eden Pastora

Plumlee described how one of the Contra commanders on the Southern Front, Eden Pastora, also known as Commander Zero, refused to engage in drug trafficking as the other Contras did. The CIA then tried to assassinate Pastora during a media conference held at La Penca, Costa Rica, during which Pastora was expected to expose the CIA-DEA drug trafficking. The conference started in chaos as a bomb exploded and killed several people.

Operation Whale Watch and Operation Watchtower

Plumlee confirmed the existence of Operation Whale Watch and Operation Watchtower, drug smuggling operations involving the CIA, U.S. military, National Security Council, and others, that others had described to me. He told me about his drug flights from Central America to the United States for the CIA, with stops at places he marked on maps that he provided.

U.S. and Mexico Cooperation in Drug Smuggling!

Evidence of some of the most bizarre and contradictory deep-cover operations has periodically surfaced during my many years of obtaining information from my dozens of insiders. Plumlee talked about the close cooperation between Mexican and U.S. government personnel in drug smuggling, for which there is other evidence in later pages. This defies comprehension, but remember there are many factions working under the umbrella of the U.S. government and they often have contradictory agendas. Plumlee described the practice of Mexican police and military protecting drug traffickers, something that will be described in considerably more detail in later pages.

CIA's Drug Corridors Through Mexico

Plumlee described one of the drug corridors used by the CIA that ran the length of Baja California with a refueling stop at an airstrip north of Cabo San Lucas. He described another common drug route that he flew, starting in Panama, with stops at Santa Helene in Costa Rica, Puerto Escondido in Southern Mexico, and then up through Baja California to Mexicali.

He delivered drugs to airfields throughout the Southwest, including Borrego Desert airstrips, one near Humboldt Mountain in Arizona where drugs would be pushed out of the aircraft, an airstrip near Buckskin Mountain close to the Colorado River, and at abandoned mine sites between Parker and Havasu City, Arizona.

Apples, Pears, And Bananas

Plumlee described some of the code words used in radio and other communications. "Apples" was the code word for small arms and ammunition. "Oranges" referred to C-4 explosives and primer cords. "Pears" referred to electronics. "Bananas" referred to personnel. For instance, if he was to deliver a government agent, he would say on the radio, "Bananas are delivered."

"Code 6" referred to the flyway through Central Mexico and crossing the U.S. border at Piedres Negras, and then into the Big Bend region of Texas. "Code 7" referred to the air route along the Baja Peninsula, through San Felipe and Mexicali, to drop points in the Anza-Borrego Desert, Twenty Nine Palms, or the former Patton bombing range east of the Salton Sea.

Plumlee sent me a map containing data on a major drug trafficker at the Delgado Ranch near San Felipe: Luis Carlos Quintero Cruz. Plumlee was part of a major drug deal in 1986 involving Quintero that involved the Contras.

Some of the data Plumlee conveyed to me corroborated what several of my other sources who flew the drugs told me.

Plumlee provided me with various documents relating to the drug trafficking by U.S. forces, one of which was marked Secret, dated February 13, 1990, which stated in part:

Apparently one month ago (January 1990) ━━━━━ *and AVINA-Batiz were engaged in conversation when AVINA-Batiz told* ━━━━━ *that the flow of drugs into the United States is the best solution to Latin America's problems. The poisoning of American youth is the best answer to the down-trodden Latin American masses in retaliation against the imperialistic actions of the United States....has learned that the reporter from Vera Cruz (FNU) Valasco, before his death (1985) was allegedly developing information that, using the DFS as cover, the CIA established and maintained clandestine airfields to refuel aircraft loaded with weapons which were destined for Honduras and Nicaragua. Pilots of these aircraft would load up with cocaine in Barranquilla, Colombia and enroute to Miami, Florida, refuel in Mexico at narcotic-trafficker-operated and CIA-maintained airstrips .... Cubans were working a similar type of refuel operations, picking up cocaine in Medellin, Colombia and flying it thru Cuba into Miami.*

Smuggling Arms Into Mexico and Destroying FBI Report

An August 10, 1976 FBI report from the special agent in charge of the Phoenix office (62-2116) to the FBI director confirmed that Plumlee had flown a large shipment of arms to Albuquerque for later flight to San Diego, that there was a 1963 government report on the matter in Phoenix file 26-20103, and that the "file has been destroyed." The FBI report further stated, "This would fit into the time frame PLUMLEE alleged on 8-10-76 wherein he was instructed to leave a plane loaded with arms in New Mexico." The 1976 date suggests that the United States was clandestinely shipping arms to Mexico. A CIA attempt to destabilize or overthrow another government?

FBI Report of Plumlee's Covert Activities

In a FBI report (000037) it was stated that Plumlee had advised special agents of the Cincinnati Division that under authority of a government cover agent, Larry Allen of Miami, Plumlee arranged to fly munitions to the Castro forces in Cuba. On or about July 5, 1958, he flew a DC-3 airplane from Miami International Airport to an abandoned military airport on Marathon Island in the Florida Keys, where the plane was loaded with arms and ammunition and flown to Cuba. Allen paid Plumlee $900.00 for this flight.

The FBI report stated that "it was [Plumlee's] desire to establish his credibility concerning his past activities [working for government agencies and] in establishing contact with the FBI in Arizona in the event he should ever become involved in border-line activities." The report stated that Plumlee agreed to provide a written report to the Phoenix FBI office. The report stated that Plumlee was also flying for Regina Airlines and Riddle Airlines. Among the various CIA agents mentioned in the reports were Larry Allen, Johnny Smith, Frank Sutter, John Roselli, and John Martino. The FBI's reports showed the Federal Bureau of Investigation knew of the various covert and surely illegal activities by the CIA and the military.

I asked Plumlee if he knew why the CIA and the White House's position changed from supporting Castro into suddenly calling him an enemy of the United States. He said that President Ike Isenhauer was supportive of Castro but the moment that President Kennedy took office, the support reversed.

Castro then sought help from Russia and suddenly became an "enemy" of the United States.

Plumleee provided me with a picture of him seated in the pilot's seat of a C-130, which was taken of him by pilot William Cooper who was shortly thereafter shot down over Nicaragua in a C-123, exposing the U.S.'s role in undermining the Nicaraguan government. As I looked at notations that Plumlee made on the back of the picture, I saw the name, Crittenden Air Transport, one of my sources who headed a CIA proprietary airline that I describe in great detail in Defrauding America. Plumlee explained that he personally delivered that C-130 to Crittenden of Crittenden Air Transport, which provided still more support for Crittenden's CIA connections.

Operation Grasshopper: Another Government Drug Operation

Plumlee described the operation known as Operation Grasshopper and using government contract pilots to fly drugs, including Barry Seal. Plumlee described the protection given to the CIA drug trafficking by other government agencies.

Murder Of Drug Pilot by Mexicans and Murder of Witness

Plumlee described the brutal murder of a former Air America pilot, Maurice Louis Gonzales, in Quedo Loco Lobo, near Oaxaca in Southwestern Mexico, by Pepe Suequez. Plumlee described how an informant sought to report the killing to American authorities, who then allowed a Mexico police officer to be present. Later, Mexican police retaliated against the informant for reporting the killing to American authorities by horribly mutilating him and leaving him to slowly die in a Mexican prison yard.

Hundreds Of "Drug Stings" That Never Happened

Plumlee said that his government handlers tried to cover up for the government's drug shipments into the United States with the explanation that the drugs were used in sting operations. Plumlee said, "We were documenting the loads and the routes and waiting for the big busts. But the busts never seemed to add up to the amount of cocaine we were bringing in." He said that many of the men in the "black ops" with whom he worked felt extremely uneasy about the illegality of the drug shipments. They occasionally talked of exposing the drug trafficking as a group, and complained to their DEA and CIA contacts. The questioning pilots were told, "You've got to keep the big picture in mind, or you might blow a major sting operation."

One Agency Arresting Another Agency's Drug-Hauling Pilots

Plumlee said that he knew of about 125 pilots flying drugs for the CIA, the DEA, and the FBI, some of whom would infiltrate other government groups to determine what they were doing. Occasionally, one government agency would arrest a pilot flying for another government agency or even another office of the same agency. The agency authorizing the operation might either call and obtain the pilot's release, or simply sacrifice the pilot and disavow any relationship. The pilot then goes to prison, sometimes for life. Plumlee brought out that different agencies would file charges on people working for other agencies, so that they could show greater results and support their request for higher funding.

Plumlee said that the DEA, CIA and FBI were spying on each other's covert deals. He described landing a DC-3 loaded with over 1200 pounds of cocaine in Scottsdale, Arizona, where he was to meet an FBI contact who failed to meet the plane. Plumlee then called the FBI, trying to contact the agent. Plumlee said, "The FBI thought I was some kind of nut." That trip had started from an airfield called "The Farm," near McAllen, Texas. His instructions were to deliver the arms to the Contras, and then return with a load of drugs.

Arkansas Drug Drops

Plumlee described the air drops of cocaine-filled bags in the areas around Russellville and Mena in Arkansas, mostly in national forest areas, and the subsequent pickup by helicopters. He described how he was involved in several of the helicopter pickups. He said aircraft would go north from the Bayou Buff area to Mena and up to Antlers, Oklahoma. Most of these drops would be at night, with daytime pickups by helicopters. (This same operation was described by Tatum and other pilots.)

He described how helicopters would pick up the drug drops in daylight, with one group authorized to pick up blue colored drug-laden bags, and another group authorized to pick up bags of another color. One of the helicopter companies that he mentioned was American Services.

Method of Paying Pilots

Plumlee explained, pilots were paid either by check from the CIA proprietary or front companies to which they were attached, or by cash. He said that his checks or money usually came from military intelligence sources, including Sitco, and sometimes regular military pay. He said to this day he still had not received a military discharge.

At the request of his military handlers, in 1988, Plumlee started a pilot recruitment agency in Southern California called Pilot's Aviation Network for the purpose of recruiting pilots to continue flying drugs for the various U.S. agencies.

Reason For Government to Arrange for Seal's Assassination

Plumlee described his role in Operation Grasshopper, a top secret military operation in which Barry Seal was a part. Another operation in which he was involved was code named "AMSOG." Seal was also a part of that operation. Plumlee described the government's double-cross of Seal which led to Seal's assassination. The intent was to keep Seal from testifying about the government's drug and money laundering activities at a trial that was to shortly start. Plumlee said Seal was a military operative in the early days of AMSOG, a joint operation involving Mexican and American government personnel.

Plumlee described an incident in Mexico where a prisoner, seeking to give him and his DEA agents information about the killing of an American pilot by a Mexican drug lord, was then killed by Mexican guards.

Lijitas, Texas Drug Transshipment Point

Plumlee described the heavy amount of arms trafficking from the United States into Mexico and then to El Salvador, and the drug trafficking on return flights. He described what another deep-cover source, Basil Abbott had told me, that arms and drugs were flown from Mexico into a small airstrip at Lijitas, Texas, just across the Mexican border.

Secret Codes To Prevent Interdiction of Government Drug Pilots

Plumlee confirmed what other pilots had told me, about military personnel giving him contact codes to get back into the country without being intercepted. Referring to the secret codes given to him that halted drug interdiction flights, Plumlee said, "I have seen interdiction planes turn away after we squawked our transponders, and let us into the country, not molested, and not have Customs waiting for us when we land."

Plumlee described another procedure to avoid interdiction. At a certain geographical point upon entering U.S. airspace, the pilot would call a particular ground station from the air and say, for instance, "Bravo One, Bravo One," after which the ground station would answer, "Okay Bravo One, we have a lock." The pilot would then hit the "Ident" button on the transponder. If the code was correct, there would be no interdiction and Customs would not be waiting the plane's arrival.

Stealing Arms from U.S. Armories to Arm Chiapus Mexicans

Plumlee described the stealing of guns and ammunition from National Guard arsenals throughout the United States, which were then used to supply the Cuban rebels, the Contras, the Mexicans in Chiapus, Mexico, and various third world countries. The purpose was to destabilize other countries or overthrow a particular government. Private arms merchants, working with the CIA, Department of Defense and other Pentagon operations, obtained the documentation necessary to move the arms out of the United States.

In *Defrauding America*, CIA operative Gunther Russbacher described the looting of U.S. arsenals in other covert operations. In one instance, the arms were taken out of National Guard armories and sent to Iran–via Israel–as part of the bribe used in the October Surprise operation to delay the release of the American hostages seized in Teheran (as described in *Defrauding America*).

National Security Staff Operating Secretly from NSC Council

Plumlee discovered that the unlawful arms shipments and drug trafficking involved the CIA and other government entities, and even the National Security Council and the White House. Plumlee said the National Security Council often did not know about the arms and drug trafficking activities conducted by the staff of the council.

Tactics to Hide Criminal Activities from the Public

Speaking about how people in control of government agencies keep the government drug trafficking from the American people, Plumlee said:

We've lost a lot of people that's been killed or assassinated or discredited because for whatever reasons, they were going to blow the whistle on current operations they were involved with. Elements within the agencies that are involved would definitely put hit men out, if it was going to jeopardize their on-going operation. Independent operatives within the agency sometimes take it upon themselves to protect the operation, and also to protect their profit margins.

Presidential Spin-Doctors

The Reagan and Bush administrations were accusing the Sandinistas of drug trafficking, seeking public and congressional support for the war against this third world country. But Plumlee described (as others have done) how he discovered that it was the Contras, supported by the United States, who were heavily involved in drug trafficking. Actually, other sources who flew arms to Central America said they delivered arms to both the Contras and Sandinistas, and that both sides paid for the arms with drugs.

Drug Cartels Penetrating U.S. Data Bases

Plumlee described how the drug cartels had sophisticated decoding devices that decoded DEA and CIA messages, and that the cartel decoded a message showing that one of the traffickers, named Rodriguez, had given testimony to the DEA. The cartel then beheaded the informer.

Congress' Decades Of Complicity in Crimes Against Americans

After Plumlee decided that the drug operations were not lawful undercover operations, but rather criminal in nature, he contacted members of Congress and the media, expecting as I did years ago that they would exercise their responsibilities, receive the information, and use it in such a way that the criminal activities would be exposed, prosecuted, and halted. Plumlee testified to several House and Senate committees, including the Senate Foreign Relations Committee, as an insider who had the evidence of CIA and DEA drug trafficking. He testified to the close cooperation between Mexican and U.S. officials in the drug smuggling operation. He described how witnesses who were suspected of exposing the U.S. involvement in drug smuggling were assassinated. As other insiders have discovered for many decades, the members of Congress covered up for the criminal activities that he—at great risk to himself—revealed. (As I sometimes say, I believed in Santa Claus, the Easter Bunny, government integrity, and congressional responsibility, but not any more.)

Repeated Depositions with Members of Congress

In 1983, several years before the lid of secrecy on the Contra scandal was slightly lifted by the U.S. media—forced into doing so by the shooting down of the "Hasenfus" flight—Plumlee met several times with Senator Gary Hart's aide, Bill Holden. Plumlee gave precise details, documents, CIA and other maps, field maps, coded flyways, names, military codes, that left no doubt that these activities did exist. This information was passed on to various congressional committees, none of whom allowed the American public to know about it. Remember, coverups like this are federal crimes.

Senator Hart conveyed the information to Senator John Kerry (D-MA), chairman of the Subcommittee on Terrorism, Narcotics and International Communications. Several of my other informants who were an active part of the arms and drug trafficking also contacted Senator Kerry. In a February 14, 1991, letter to Senator John Kerry, Senator Hart stated:

> *Mr. Plumlee raised several issues including that covert U.S. intelligence agencies were directly involved in the smuggling and distribution of drugs. He provided my staff with detailed maps and names of alleged covert landing strips in Mexico, Costa Rica, Louisiana, Arizona, Florida, and California where he alleged aircraft cargoes of drugs were off-loaded and replaced with Contra military supplies. He also stated that these operations were not CIA operations but rather under the direction of the White*

House, Pentagon and NSC personnel. My staff brought these allegations to the attention of the Senate Armed Services Committee and the Senate Intelligence Committee at the time, but no action was initiated by either committee.

In 1991, journalist Art Goodtimes of the *Telluride Times-Journal* wrote a letter (January 13, 1991) to Senator John Kerry offering to provide maps, data, and testimony of former CIA agent Tosh Plumlee. The letter advised that Plumlee was involved in flying in Central America and had evidence of the U.S. government's involvement in illegal drug trafficking through Mexico, El Salvador and Panama. The letter stated in part:

Government's involvement with illegal drug operations, infiltrated by military undercover operatives...Plumlee's intent to get a federal investigation into the illegal covert activities instigated by various agencies of our government in Central America.

A DEA report dated February 13, 1990, marked SECRET, stated in part:
BUENDIA had allegedly gathered information on...the relationship the CIA had with known narcotic traffickers in Vera Cruz area....the CIA narcotic trafficker situation was very delicate (not to be spoken about)....information on CIA arms smuggling and the connection the CIA had to narcotic traffickers....Shortly thereafter, Eden Pastora, aka Commander ZERO, who had given BUENDIA information on CIA arms smuggling allegedly suffered a CIA sponsored bomb attack while traveling in Costa Rica....It was later learned that BUENIDA had allegedly obtained information that would expose high ranking members of the PRI political party who were assisting the CIA with arms smuggling and knew of the CIA link to narcotics traffickers. [Buenida, who was exposing drug trafficking by the CIA and high officials of Mexico's PRI party was killed by elements of the Mexican DFS security detail.]

Plumlee was only one of many people having direct knowledge of these criminal activities and who gave this information to members of Congress. The sheer number of insiders risking their lives by coming forward should have had some effect upon members of Congress. You guessed it: none.

Hiding From Retaliation by U.S. Authorities

Plumlee eventually went underground, hiding from his prior handlers, and settled in a small town near Denver. In a book Plumlee was writing, he described the government corruption that he saw in Mexico involving both Mexican and U.S. officials and how both either participated in or did nothing to halt the drug trafficking. To the best of my knowledge, Plumlee gave up writing the book because of the widespread public indifference.

Another of Many Hoaxes upon the American People

Seeking to get public support for the U.S. attempts to undermine the Nicaraguan government, President Ronald Reagan appeared on television holding up a picture allegedly showing Nicaraguan Sandinistas loading drugs onto a plane in Nicaragua that was piloted by Barry Seal. Plumlee, a friend of Seal, said that the picture was not taken in Nicaragua, but in Panama, and misrepresented to the public what was actually taking place. Plumlee said that the C-123 aircraft from which the picture was taken had on it a global positioning instrument wherein a satellite could identify the location of the aircraft, and the record shows that the plane never went to Nicaragua.

Plumlee said the camera in the C-123 aircraft was rigged up by the CIA at Rickenboch Field and that he helped rig the switching arrangement. The idea was to fraudulently indicate to the American public that the Sandinistas were engaging in drug trafficking, when in fact, as Plumlee stated, it was the Contras—and U.S. agents—who were most active in drug trafficking. The American public was, again, duped by their own leaders.

Seal's Ace-In-The-Hole Protection Was Valueless

Plumlee described how Barry Seal told him he had an ace-in-the-hole against federal prosecution. This ace-in-the-hole was Seal's threat to report the CIA-DEA-White House involvement in drug trafficking to the media and to Congress. Like Tatum, Plumlee, and many others, each of these checks and balances would have ignored his charges and even ridiculed him. Eventually, government personnel set him up to be assassinated by Colombians.

Evidence of Government Corruption Withheld on National Security Excuse—The Law Calls It, Obstruction Of Justice

During a taped interview for Jeremiah Films in 1995, Plumlee stated:

The result of that testimony [to various congressional committees] was that the testimony was sealed. The committee censored it, calling it national security and top secret. A lot of the pilots that flew and testified to the committees had the same problem. Their testimony was not released. Pilots and other ground crew personnel, who made these allegations in 1982 and 1983, were systematically purged from those operations. There was systematic character assassinations of a lot of good people that had done a lot of black operations, one in particular was Barry Seal, who was a personal friend of mine. ... they discredited people with fake documents.

Military Bases as Drug Transshipment Points

We flew some of the drugs into Air Force bases along the southeast coast, and some in the West and the Southwest...including Homestead Air Force Base. DEA has a very good handle on [the drug trafficking] around Arkansas and Louisiana, but their investigations were completely shut down, stopped in their tracks...and the people who had the information about this operation were suddenly transferred and can't be found now.

Starting about 1981, the [CIA-DEA] drug smuggling problem was just really starting to escalate. It didn't really start until the latter part of 1981 and 1982, about the same time that Reagan said we're fighting a drug war, and a lot of money was appropriated for that....From the time that the money was appropriated to start [the drug war] we saw a 400 percent increase in the illegal drugs that were coming into this country.

High Level Government Block-Obstruction of Justice

Someone had the power to intercept that information, to destroy the information and the operatives that had gathered the information. Even to the point of putting them in jail, discrediting their character, by assassinations, assassinating their character by labeling them as "cartel drug runners."

Drug Cartels could have been Shut Down 20 Years Ago

Plumlee felt that it would have been easy to shut down the drug cartels 20 years ago:

What I'm saying is the cartel could have been shut down in 1981. The information was there from the informants that had infiltrated the cartel.

Heavy Military Involvement in Drugging America

Plumlee said that he flew over 6600 pounds of cocaine into the United States in government-sanctioned operations. He said many of his flights were for the military, a fact little known, as most of the blame goes to the CIA. He said that his military handler was out of a military base in Arizona.

CBS's Reversal of What Plumlee Said

Plumlee appeared on CBS Television (November 15, 1996) as CBS televised CIA Director John Deutsch's appearance before a high school in the Watts area of Los Angeles. After Deutsch was filmed—denying any CIA involvement in drugs—CBS showed Plumlee stating in a 30-second clip that he flew drugs; that he did so under orders of individuals, and that the CIA was not involved. After I saw that segment, I contacted Plumlee, since he had earlier gone into great detail describing the CIA involvement in drug smuggling. Plumlee had clearly stated this fact to CBS over the last few years and had provided the TV network with documentation. Plumlee was outraged that CBS took his statements out of context as Plumlee was referring to another drug smuggling operation that was controlled by the National Security Council, the Pentagon, and the White House.

In response, I wrote a letter (November 22, 1996) to Bruce Rheins, *CBS News* producer in Los Angeles, complaining about that coverup and others I experienced for the past 30 years. I advised him that I also had considerable evidence of covert agencies and the military smuggling drugs into the United States, and had over two dozen former agents of the FBI, CIA, DEA ready to testify to these activities.

Rheins responded (November 25, 1996): "Your name has surfaced quite frequently in my research surrounding the allegations of the CIA's involvement with the distribution of crack cocaine in South Central Los Angeles." He made no attempt to obtain any information from me. On the contrary, I was canceled from two subsequent CBS television productions.

Tosh Plumlee In C-130 Aircraft

DOD INTERNATIONAL FLIGHT PLAN   31/1997

PRIORITY INDICATOR	FF ADDRESSEE(S) INDICATOR(S)	

FILING DATE/TIME 26 FEB 85   ORIGINATOR INDICATOR

SPECIFIC IDENTIFICATION OF ADDRESSEE(S) AND/OR ORIGINATOR

8 DESCRIPTION	7 AIRCRAFT IDENTIFICATION AND SSR DATA	8 FLT RULES AND TYPE OF FLIGHT
FPL	Dustoff 213 C3313	VM
9 NO. AND TYPE ACFT AND TURBULENCE CATEGORY	10 COM/NAV/APP EQUIP SSR	
UH-1	FGUV / C	

13 AERODROME OF DEPARTURE AND TIME   FIR BOUNDARIES AND ESTIMATED TIMES

MHCG 1630Z →

18 SPEED AND LEVEL   ROUTE

090 VFR → MHCG → EP → HLM INT → MHCG

17 AERODROME OF DESTINATION AND ETA   ALTERNATE AERODROME(S)

MHCG 2165 →

18 OTHER INFORMATION

OPNS US Mil TAT 70-15213
Refuel at HLM

)

///// NOT FOR TRANSMISSION /////
SUPPLEMENTARY INFORMATION

19 ENDURANCE	PERSONS ON BOARD	EMERGENCY AND SURVIVAL EQUIPMENT	
FUEL 3+20 -08/ 4 RDO/		12 → 243 → 160 →	
TYPE OF EQUIPMENT		LIFE JACKETS	RADIO FREQ.
POLAR → DESERT → MARITIME → JUNGLE → GLOBAL →	JACKETS → LIGHT → FLUORESCEIN →	2828	
DINGHIES COLOR NUMBER	TOTAL CAPACITY	OTHER EQUIPMENT	
DINGHIES → COVER	RMK/ PRC 90		)

REMARKS		AIRCRAFT SERIAL NUMBERS AND TYPE OF AIRCRAFT IN FLIGHT
TATUM BRAMINTR Rodriguez WATKINS	PAX Sut Fm Wally Loxcid COOPER SAWYER	

CREW LIST [✓] ATTACHED [ ] LOCATED AT: Dustoff OPNS
PASSENGER MANIFEST [ ] ATTACHED [ ] LOCATED AT: 477th Field

COPIA CERTIFICADA

AIRCRAFT NAME STATION OR ORGANIZATION	NAME OF PILOT IN COMMAND; INSTRUMENT RATING	SIGNATURE OF PILOT IN COMMAND OR DESIGNATED REPRESENTATIVE
3/149th MED CO / MCHW	TATUM, CW2	

PILOT'S PREFLIGHT CHECK	BASE OPERATIONS USE		APPROVAL
			REQUEST CLEARANCE AFTER (8)
NOTAMS	CURRENT P/FCIC CARD	P P L	B
AIR SPACE RESTRICTIONS	SPECIAL BRIEFINGS		
AIRCRAFT/DEST NAV AIDS	DIP CLNC/US CODE /PPR		MISSION/CONTROL AUTHORITY
WEATHER AND WINDS	SZ FLT/GAT/OAT	T A T W R	
SIDS FLIPS AND CHARTS	VIP CODE/BLOCK TIME		
FLIGHT PLAN LOG	PAX MANIFEST		
POPPY SEED REPORTS	CUSTOMS FORM		
FOREIGN CLNC GUIDE	FLT ORDERS OR CREW LIST		SIGNATURE OF APPROVING AUTHORITY
COMMAND LOCAL DIRECTIVES	FUEL REQUIREMENTS		

FORM

Sample copy of Chip Tatum's military flight plan with notation on back that cooler marker "vaccine" broke open and cocaine discovered inside.

CHAPTER THREE

SECRET CIA FINANCIAL INSTITUTIONS

A primary CIA drug-money laundering operation was Nugan Hand Bank with headquarters in Sydney, Australia and branch offices in Far East countries. Drug money laundering was the primary function of this CIA operation, with offices conveniently located in the Golden Triangle drug producing area. Nugan Hand Bank was incorporated in 1976 in the Cayman Islands, a popular money-laundering location, and believed to be a replacement for Castle Bank & Trust that had been incorporated in Nassau, Bahamas. Secondary functions for Nugan Hand were arms sales and funding covert activities.

Staffed By the CIA

Most of the management personnel of Nugan Hand Bank were intelligence community personnel. The most visible partners were Francis Nugan, Michael Hand, and Maurice Bernard Houghton. When Nugan Hand shut down, most of the staff moved to other CIA operations, including Bishop, Baldwin, Rewald, Dillingham and Wong in Hawaii. These players, with a long CIA and military intelligence background, included, for instance, Admiral Earl Yates, General Leroy Manor, and General Edwin Black.

Nugan Hand had vast amounts of money hidden in assets and financial holdings throughout the world. Either to appear as a legitimate international investment operation, or to defraud people out of millions of dollars, Nugan Hand took deposits from individuals throughout the world. When the cover for this CIA operation was blown, these funds were quickly moved to other CIA proprietaries, inflicting financial losses upon the investors and depositors. Many of the individuals putting money into the CIA's Nugan Hand Bank were military personnel, who eventually lost everything they deposited.

Exposing Nugan Hand Fraud

Nugan Hand's cover was blown on April 11, 1980, by a reporter for *Target*, a Hong Kong financial newsletter. This exposure required Nugan Hand to immediately shut down the operation, destroy evidence of its CIA links, and for the key players to leave town.

Francis Nugan was one of the most visible players in the Nugan Hand operation. He was an alcoholic with a reputation for talking too much, a trait that threatened to expose the CIA's role in the operation. Assassins killed Nugan (January 27, 1980), leaving his body in a car alongside a lonely road outside of Sydney, Australia. A bolt-action rifle was found alongside the body, and the scene was made to look like a suicide.

An unspent bullet remained in the firing chamber of the bolt action rifle. For an unspent bullet to be in the chamber after firing the shot that was instantly fatal, someone—other than Nugan—had to manually operate the bolt handle. Nugan obviously did not do this. The bullet had killed Nugan instantly, blowing away much of his skull and scattering it throughout the car. There were no fingerprints on the gun, indicating that whoever fired the fatal bullet wiped the fingerprints from the rifle.

Calling Card of CIA Director on Nugan's Body

The only identification on Nugan's body was a calling card apparently overlooked by the killers: William Colby, former Director of the Central Intelligence Agency, with a meeting date written on the back. Colby was legal counsel for Nugan Hand and had connections to the Wall Street law firm of Reid & Priest, suggesting that this firm was a front for the CIA or a CIA proprietary.

Hand Surfaced in CIA activities in Iran and Caribbean

Before Australian authorities started an investigation, Michael Hand disappeared, along with most of the Nugan Hand records. Although the media reported that Hand had disappeared, leaving no trace, one of my CIA sources, Trenton Parker, told how he and Hand had worked together in the early 1980s. Hand had first gone to Iran, working with the CIA, and then to the Caribbean. Parker stated that he and Hand took over one of the drug trafficking operations for the CIA in Central and South America. He said that Hand's experience in developing the Golden Triangle drug operations for the CIA made him useful in expanding the drug operations from Central and South America into the United States.

Most U.S. Media Kept Nugan Hand Affair Out Of the News

The CIA's Nugan Hand affair received considerable media attention in Australia, but the mainstream media in the United States said virtually nothing about this CIA operation. Australian authorities conducted numerous investigations, but in their final report they white-washed the Nugan Hand affair.

Major Efforts to Destroy CIA Links

After Nugan's body was found, intense activities were initiated to destroy evidence linking Nugan Hand Bank to the CIA. Retired three-star U.S. General Leroy J. Manor (formerly chief of staff for all U.S. forces in Asia and the Pacific), who had been head of Nugan Hand's Philippine office, tried to have the wire services block the reporting of Nugan's death. Recently retired Rear Admiral Earl P. Yates (formerly chief of staff for strategic planning for U.S. forces in the Pacific and Asia) flew to Australia to direct the shredding of documents. Yates was president of Nugan Hand, and lived near CIA headquarters at Langley, Virginia. Michael Hand joined in the shredding. Maurice

Houghton and his attorney, Michael Moloney, also arrived. Hand threatened lower-level employees, stating if Maloney's orders to sanitize the files before the law arrived weren't followed, "terrible things would happen; your wives would be cut up and returned to you in bits and pieces." (*Wall Street Journal*, August 24, 1982)

Two *Wall Street Journal* articles (August 25 and 26, 1982) described Nugan Hand Bank as a drug and arms-related operation, staffed by CIA and military personnel. The articles stated in part:

Nugan Hand bank was deeply involved in moving funds about the world for big international heroin dealers...U.S. servicemen are big losers in failure of Nugan Hand Bank.

Australia's Royal Commission on Drugs found so much evidence of drug and drug-money trafficking by this CIA operation that it recommended a separate Royal Commission be appointed just for the bank's operations. But Australia's intelligence agency, ASIO, blocked an investigation, reflecting the common practice of intelligence agencies to protect each other rather than their own country. U.S. officials stymied every attempt by Australian authorities to obtain information about Nugan Hand Bank.

During its investigation, the Royal Commission found that drugs were flown into a landing strip by former Air America pilot K.L. "Bud" King and Michael Hand. The strip was on a real estate development promoted by U.S. singer Pat Boone and financed by wealthy shipping magnate D.K. Ludwig. King, who also worked for the Boone-Ludwig project, whose testimony could have been very damaging to Nugan Hand and U.S. officials, died mysteriously in a fall.

Australian authorities connected Nugan Hand not only to drug and arms transactions, but also to contract murders, of which there were several associated with Nugan Hand's demise. Australian attorney John Aston and his law firm were found to represent Nugan Hand and various drug traffickers, and the law office was used as a drop point for money to be secretly deposited and moved by Nugan Hand.

Disappearance of One Billion Dollars

Hand disappeared as Australian authorities sought to question him about Nugan's death, the Nugan Hand Bank operation, and the disappearance of approximately one billion dollars from the bank.

Bishop, Baldwin, Rewald, Dillingham & Wong

After Nugan Hand's cover was blown and the operation abandoned, the CIA brought into existence another financial institution based in Hawaii: Bishop, Baldwin, Rewald, Dillingham and Wong (BBRDW). This CIA proprietary was started, operated, and funded by the CIA in 1979, using many of the same high-level people that had staffed Nugan Hand Bank. By the end of 1980, BBRDW began setting up offices in Hong Kong, Taiwan, Indonesia, Singapore, and Australia, all former Nugan Hand locations, staffing the offices with over 30 CIA agents. Some of these agents were the same high-level people that operated Nugan Hand Bank (General Edwin Black, General Leroy Manor, Admiral Lloyd Vassey, Admiral Earl Yates, Walter McDonald, and Maurice Houghton). As in most CIA-related proprietaries, its key management was comprised of CIA-related personnel.

The CIA used BBRDW as a international investment company cover, with 120 employees staffing offices in sixteen countries, including Hong Kong, India, Indonesia, Taiwan, New Zealand, Singapore, London, Paris, Stockholm, Brazil and Chile. CIA personnel opened and operated these far-flung offices.

For appearances, the CIA placed in charge of its BBRDW proprietary a Honolulu businessman, Ronald Rewald, who had worked for the CIA years earlier while attending Milwaukee Institute of Technology. That CIA college project was called Operation MH Chaos, and consisted of spying on student groups during the mid-1960s. The CIA gave Rewald the alias WINTERDOG. Other CIA divisions had parallel programs called Operation Mother Goose and Operation Back Draft.

Rewald's first CIA station chief and handler was Eugene J. Welch, who was later replaced by Jack Kindschi, followed by Jack W. Rardin, all of whom coached Rewald on CIA operations. Several years later, Rewald would be the fall-guy when the cover was blown on BBRDW.

Because this book focuses more on drug trafficking, the full story of BBRDW can be found in the third or latest edition of *Defrauding America*. Ron Rewald and I became good friends and over several years he provided me a great amount of information on all forms of CIA activities, some of it corrupt operations.

Funding Secret Bank Accounts for U.S. Officials

In March 1996, Rewald gave me several boxes containing hundreds of CIA documents generated from the CIA's secret operation in Hawaii. Within these boxes I found highly sensitive material, including notes that Rewald had made while the titular head of BBRDW. Certain notes and information provided to me by Rewald divulged CIA drug related activities, including drug money laundering. As I gathered from looking over the material and by talking with Rewald, he was unaware of many of the CIA activities originating out of BBRDW.

Deeply imbedded in these documents was an envelope labeled "Attorney-Client information." The information was dynamite, divulging secret bank accounts set up for well-known politicians and covert agency operatives. The notes in the envelope listed high-level people with secret CIA-funded accounts. The names on the left side of the notes were the aliases Rewald used to identify the people on the right for which there were secret bank accounts opened and funded by the CIA through DDRDW.

Irwin M. Peach	*George Bush*
Mr. Bramble	*George Bush*
Commander Quinstar	*General Hunter Harris*
Mr. Apan	*Robert W. Jinks*
Mr. Grey	*Robert Allen*
Farrah Fawn	*Jackie Vos*
General Shake	*Arnold Braswell*
Mr. Branch	*Richard Armitage*
Mr. Denile	*William Casey*
Slimey Affirm	*Stanley Sporkin*

Captain Perjury   *Ned Avary*
Attorney Doright   *Robert Smith*

Arnold Braswell was commander-in-chief of U.S. Pacific Air Force (CINCPAC). Rewald's notes also indicated that fictitious names were used to hide money for B.K. Kim, Philippines President Ferdinand and Imelda Marcos, among others. Richard Armitage was U.S. Assistant Secretary of Defense and reportedly heavily involved with drug trafficking while in Vietnam. William Casey was Director of the Central Intelligence Agency. Stanley Sporkin was legal counsel for the CIA, and then a federal judge in Washington, D.C. In this capacity, he unlawfully dismissed one of my federal actions seeking to expose the government corruption in which he was involved.

These notes, written by Rewald over ten years earlier when he was head of BBRDW, provided additional evidence of U.S. officials hiding their money in secret bank accounts overseas. The accounts were in financial institutions in Hong Kong, Switzerland, and the Caymans.

Information on another sheet that I found in Rewald's papers revealed activities engaged in by CIA agents embedded into BBRDW and its various subsidiaries. These are the activities in which Rewald refused to get involved, including CIA drug trafficking.

These notes revealed other activities that I hadn't known about earlier. While Rewald was hospitalized in Honolulu, sources kept him informed of some activities being taken to remove and hide the funds from BBRDW and subsidiary accounts. General Hunter Harris called President George Bush to alert him that the cover on BBRDW had been blown, and wanted instructions as to how to proceed. CIA head, William Casey, then called Robert W. Jinks, and told him to work with Robert Allen. Jinks was then ordered to proceed to Texas to get bank account numbers and then go to the Cayman Islands where the accounts were located.

Rewald's notes indicated that someone from CIA headquarters at Langley, or an associate of Robert Allen, eventually went to the Cayman Islands and moved BBRDW's funds to another offshore country. Robert Smith, who wasn't directly involved in the money transfer but aware something was going on, learned that a General in Texas was to give Robert Jinks bank account information and that he, Robert Smith, was to go to the Caymans to retrieve the hidden money. General Arnold Braswell was to assist in this removal, but because of stress and his drinking problem, he was too unreliable and was not used.

Similar efforts were being taken to remove funds from BBRDW and subsidiary accounts in Hong Kong and Switzerland. About this time, funds were being received from secret arms sales and Rewald said that Ned Avary diverted these funds away from BBRDW.

While these events were taking place, Robert Allen sought to force Jackie Vos to disclose the whereabouts of the Green Book that listed these accounts so as to destroy the records.

Forbes Magazine Editor Reported Similar Financial Irregularities
Former senior editor of *Forbes* magazine, James Norman, had reports

(*Media Bypass*, February 1996) that a secret group in the intelligence community, outraged at what was going on, infiltrated bank money transfer systems and discovered large quantities of money sequestered in overseas bank accounts for government figures. One of these people was allegedly Vincent Foster, who made a number of one-day trips to Switzerland to conduct bank activities.

Rewald Invited To Washington by President George Bush

Rewald wrote in his notes that he had met President George Bush twice in Hawaii, and had been invited to meet with the president in Washington for lunch or dinner, along with someone that Rewald identified as "Brady." All of these people were described in Rewald's notes by their code names, but a separate sheet of paper identified who they were, except for "Brady."

I asked Rewald about these, and he stated that he made the list of names with secret offshore bank account numbers. I asked Rewald, "Referring to the fictitious names for offshore bank accounts, do I correctly understand that you made up the alias names yourself?"

You mean, Peach for Bush? That was done well after the collapse [of BBRDW] and was done to disguise my reference to the accounts so that someone picking it up wouldn't know what I was talking about. These people certainly had these accounts.

Ronald Rewald

SECRET AGREEMENT

1. I acknowledge the fact that because of the confidential relationship between myself and the U.S. Government, I will be the recipient of information which, in itself, or by the implications to be drawn therefrom, will be such that its unlawful disclosure or loose handling may adversely affect the interest and the security of the United States. I realize that the methods of collecting and of using this information, as well as the identity of persons involved, are as secret as the substantive information itself and, therefore, must be treated by me with an equal degree of secrecy.

2. I shall always recognize that the U.S. Government has the sole interest in all information which I or my organization may possess, compile or acquire pursuant to this understanding. No advantage or gain will be sought by me as a result of the added significance or value such information may have, due to the Government's interest in it.

3. I solemnly pledge my word that I will never divulge, publish, nor reveal either by word, conduct, or by any other means such information or knowledge, as indicated above, unless specifically authorized to do so, by the U.S. Government.

4. Nothing in this understanding is to be taken as imposing any restriction upon the normal business practices of myself or my organization: i.e., information normally possessed by us or gathered in the regular course of business will continue to be utilized in accordance with our normal practices.

Declassified By _13+025_

date _8/25/85_

SIGNATURE:

Signature of John H. Mason

REPRESENTATIVE OF U.S. GOVERNMENT

SIGNATURE:

Ronald R. Rewald

CMI Investment Corporation

ORGANIZATION

DATE

Handwritten date 25 June 1979

DATE

CIA secrecy form for Ronald Rewald, under CIA cover of Consolidated Mutual Investment Corporation.

CHAPTER FOUR

ANATOMY OF A
SECRET CIA AIRLINE

In mid-1995, I started a friendship with a 15-year veteran of deep-cover CIA activities who provided me with detailed information on highly-secret covert activities. Stephen Crittenden operated a CIA proprietary airline, Crittenden Air Transport (CAT), based in Bangkok, Thailand, with a small office at the Miami International Airport, and several subsidiaries. He described how the CIA starts up a secret proprietary airline and puts a figurehead in position as the titular head of the operation.

Years earlier, CIA operative Gunther Russbacher had told me about Crittenden Air Transport, describing it as a CIA operation, and I listed it as such in the second edition of *Defrauding America*. But it wasn't until after that second edition was published that Crittenden contacted me. We spent dozens of hours in frequent deposition-like sessions and exchanged dozens of long detailed fact-filled letters during which I learned more about the secret operation of that airline. Some CIA operatives referred to that airline as the "ghost" airline because it was often seen in covert operations but little was known of it, including where it was based.

Start Of A CIA Proprietary

Crittenden joined the Army at 17, and was in the Army Special Forces program. He did four 9-month tours of duty in Vietnam from 1969 to 1973 and was with Air America from January 1974 to December 1975.Crittenden's conduct in Vietnam drew the attention of the CIA, and he was selected to be the head of a new airline. At 24 years of age, Crittenden had much to learn about operating an airline, but the CIA provided management personnel and did most of the scheduling from CIA headquarters at McLean, Virginia. He was provided a mentor to organize and operate the airline that was given the name, Crittenden Air Transport (CAT).

In January 1976, Crittenden Air Transport commenced operations with five C-123 aircraft, an office building in Bangkok (with offices in Sydney, Australia and Miami) and $20 million in start-up operating cash provided by the CIA. This high-level CIA involvement permitted Crittenden to fly many of the flights. It was a business person's dream. He had no mortgage payments to make, and engine replacements and aircraft upgrading were provided by the CIA at no charge. Most of the aircraft loads consisted of arms and drugs, with payment for full loads even when flying partial loads or empty.

First Flight To China

In January 1976, Crittenden Air Transport (CAT) made its first flight in a two-engine C-123, which was to Beijing, China, delivering a load of small arms and picking up a load of heroin. CAT received a $100,000 check from the CIA's Shamrock Corporation in Ireland for that flight. Crittenden, a young man given an airline by the CIA, thought he had really hit the big time. Far bigger payments would be made in the future. (CAT should not be confused with an earlier CIA airline, Civil Air Transport out of Taiwan, that also used the initials, CAT.)

The drugs from that flight were unloaded at Bangkok, Thailand, where another CIA proprietary (or front) airline, Southern Air Transport (SAT), transported the drugs in its four-engine C-130 to Los Angeles. At that time, Crittenden Air Transport was only flying twin-engine short-range military C-123s, and Southern Air Transport was flying long-range four-engine C-130s.The C-123s flying from Bangkok to Clark Air Force Base near Manila carried approximately 10 to 12,000 pounds of heroin.

CIA Provided CAT Additional Aircraft

Several years after the formation of Crittenden Air Transport, the CIA provided Crittenden Air Transport with seven military C-130s and one Boeing 707, which came from Evergreen International Airline's operation at Pinal Airport near Marana, Arizona, a small town north of Tucson. No money was paid for the aircraft, and no money was owed on them. Eventually, Crittenden Air Transport had over 15 large aircraft.

After receiving the long-range C-130 aircraft, Crittenden Air Transport then handled much of the Pacific Rim cargo for the CIA that was formerly handled by Southern Air Transport. These flights usually flew from Hong Kong to the United States via Honolulu. After this change, Southern Air Transport confined its operations mostly to Central and South America (until it returned to the Pacific rim in approximately 1987).

With the additional and longer-range aircraft, the CIA had Crittenden flying into additional countries, including the United States, Mexico, France, Germany, Great Britain, Egypt, Italy, Colombia, Bolivia, and Panama. Payments for these flights came through the CIA's Shamrock Corporation, with checks written on various bank accounts, including the Bank of Credit and Commerce International (BCCI), Valley Bank in Phoenix (a reported CIA proprietary), Bank One, and Barclays Bank in Miami. (Barclays is a major British bank headquartered in London, with offices throughout the world.)

Common destinations in the Pacific were Sydney, Manila, and Singapore. Out of Miami, common destinations included San Salvador in El Salvador, Guatemala City in Guatemala, Managua in Nicaragua, San Jose in Costa Rica, and Panama City in Panama. A typical flight from Manila or Bangkok to the United States would make several fuel stops and proceed to various destinations in the United States, including Miami (where Crittenden had a small office) or Mena, Arkansas. Special codes were used during air traffic control procedures that advised Customs not to inspect that aircraft.

Loads of Arms and Drugs for the CIA

Crittenden went into detail describing the types of cargo he carried, the people he dealt with, and many specifics concerning logistics, fueling, billing, payments, and other data that could only be known by someone in a position held by Crittenden. Most of the loads were either arms or drugs, including heroin from Southeast Asia or cocaine and marijuana from Central and South America. Crittenden explained that other covert proprietary airlines, such as Southern Air Transport and Evergreen, also carried similar loads for the Drug Enforcement Administration.

Further Description of Drug Trafficking

Crittenden described numerous CIA flights transporting drugs into the United States. He described his contacts with Fernando Canles, then head of the Bolivian Air Force, who transported cocoa paste in their own aircraft to Medellin, where it was then off-loaded for further processing into cocaine. Crittenden described flying Canles to La Paz in 1984 in a newly overhauled Lodestar 500 (a converted piston-powered Lockheed Lodestar). Crittenden said that he gave Canles flying lessons in the Lodestar, and that Canles had an expensive condo in Key Colony in Key Biscayne, Florida.

Meeting With Colombian Drug Trafficker Pablo Escobar

Crittenden described the many drug loads that he flew for the CIA out of Southeast Asia and Central and South America. He described various contacts that he had with known high-level drug traffickers. He described his Miami meeting with Pablo Escobar in 1990 to arrange payment for a CIA drug flight out of Colombia.

Paymaster for Drug Cartels?

Crittenden described Colombian and Bolivian drug cartel people landing their Cessna Citations and Lear jets at Marana Airport, arriving to obtain payments for prior drug shipments. These were usually flights from Colombia and Bolivia, and which usually took off from an airport outside of Mexico City and then on to Marana, 50 miles into the United States from the Mexican border. Stephen said these planes never cleared Customs.

State Police Protecting Drug Loads

Crittenden went into detail about drug loads that he flew for the CIA into Mena Airport in Arkansas. He described the practice of Arkansas State Police guarding the unloading operations, closing off the airport access roads during unloading, which coincided with what other pilots had told me who had flown drugs into Mena.

Shamrock Corporation, CIA Paymaster

Other CIA assets, including Gunther Russbacher, had described the role played by the CIA's Shamrock Corporation in Ireland, disbursing money for various CIA operations, including bribe money to federal judges and other covert agency assets. Crittenden described his relationship with Shamrock that focused on other areas of Shamrock's activities. He said that the Shamrock Corporation paid his airline for the flights flown, which he said totaled over $500 million for flights from 1976 to 1988.

Orders From CIA Headquarters

Crittenden described how he received his instructions from the CIA for his various missions. In some cases, he called his handler, Ross Lipscomb, at CIA headquarters in McLean, Virginia. Crittenden remembered the confidential phone number as 202-357-1100, and when the switchboard operator answered, Crittenden would respond, "Access code 4613," after which he would be switched to his CIA contact. Stephen said that the "3" in the code signified that he was Level Three.

Instructions for Avoiding Radar Detection

In some cases his instructions came on computer floppy disks which he would put into his computer. He described receiving floppy disks on some occasions around 1978 from CIA asset G. Gordon Liddy, sometimes receiving the disks in the garden area of the DuPont Center in Miami. Included in the floppy-disk data was information about avoiding radar detection while flying drugs into the United States from Central and South America.

CIA Stolen Aircraft Operation

Crittenden described another facet of how the CIA (and the National Security Council under Oliver North) used stolen aircraft in the Contra arms and drug-smuggling operation. CIA assets Gunther Russbacher and Terry Reed described this practice. Crittenden described how twin-engine Beech D-18s were stolen and then sent to Volpar Aviation at Van Nuys Airport in California for a Volpar conversion to nose-wheel from tail-wheel configuration. Crittenden stated that a Sam Virse from Memphis, Tennessee, took many of these aircraft to Volpar.

Elaborating more on this operation, Crittenden stated that Aviation Materials on Sweeny Road in Memphis, Tennessee, was an aircraft salvage yard containing wrecked Beech 18s, Queenairs, Kingairs, Barons and Cessna 366 and 377s. Reportedly, the owner, Graham Lotts, would give the aircraft manufacturer's data plates that were riveted onto the fuselages of the wrecked aircraft to Virse, who owned an airport at Bud Island in Memphis. Virse reportedly had a couple of assistants who would steal identical aircraft. The manufacturer's identification plates would be removed from the stolen aircraft and replaced with the data plates from the wrecked aircraft. The aircraft would then be flown to Volpar in Van Nuys to be repainted and modified.

Crittenden stated that Volpar knew the CIA was picking up the aircraft after modification, but was probably unaware that the aircraft were stolen. He said that this practice continued from 1976 to 1988, during the time of the CIA, State Department, and National Security Council's arms and drug trafficking in the Contra operation.

Requiring FAA Assistance

Crittenden described how someone within the FAA at its Oklahoma City registration division cooperated in this scheme by furnishing Sam Virse presigned aircraft Airworthiness Certificates to be used in the stolen aircraft having the substituted manufacturer's identification plates.

Companies Cooperating with the CIA

Crittenden described several airlines which were involved with the CIA in a cooperating relationship, including Eastern and Braniff when they were still operating, and Continental. These cooperating airlines received various benefits for their covert role with the CIA, including fuel allotments and fuel discounts, mail contracts, hidden subsidies or payments.

Another Side of CIA-Evergreen Operations

Crittenden described the practice of stealing jet engines and other valuable equipment and avionics from Eastern Airlines aircraft that were stored at Marana Airport after Eastern went into Chapter 7 bankruptcy. He described how low-time jet engines were removed from Eastern Airlines' Lockheed 1011s and other aircraft and then replaced with high-time nearly run-out engines, and the records altered to cover up for these activities.

This mindset could be expected to be accompanied by similar conduct in other aircraft maintenance practices, such as placing worn parts on aircraft and counting on averages that they would not be discovered. A former Evergreen mechanic, Andy Anderson, based in Australia, filed a lawsuit against Evergreen Airlines (*Portland Free Press*) charging that he was fired for objecting to the practice of installing worn-out parts on Boeing 747s and other aircraft and falsely showing them as meeting replacement specifications.

One of Evergreen's government contracts involved the "Logair" contract, flying military equipment and supplies from one air force base to another. (In my earlier flying days I also flew this contract operation as a pilot for Transocean Airlines in the 1950s.)

A video was produced about Evergreen's covert activities and CIA connections that was titled, "Welcome to Evergreen." The video caused the Air Force Office of Special Investigations (AFOSI) to conduct a secret investigation of Evergreen in 1995.

Revolving Door: Congressional CIA Oversight to CIA Employee

Former Congressman Denny Smith, who had oversight responsibilities for the CIA, later became a member of Evergreen's board of directors.

Sending Military Equipment to Central America

Another CIA operator in Houston, Ted Smith, sold and traded military equipment throughout the world. When a deal was made, Crittenden Air Transport would load the military equipment at Fort Hood, Texas, and at that time the list was given to a Major Robert Cooper. Often, the goods were unloaded in San Salvador, El Salvador. Crittenden said the CIA people responsible for subsequent distribution were James Pennington and John Forsyth.

Ports-Of-Call Airline

Crittenden said his airline did business with Ports-of-Call Airline that flew passengers to vacation destinations and also had cargo flights for hauling arms and various cargo, such as food to Ethiopia. He said the airline hauled drugs for the CIA. The airline was based in Denver and had a fleet of Boeing 707 and Convair 880 and 990 jets. After Congress conducted closed-door hearings into the Iran-Contra affair, and after Denver papers carried stories of its questionable operation, the CIA shut down the operation.

Crittenden said his C-130 aircraft hauled four loads of cocaine during 1983 and 1984 to Guatemala City, where the loads were transferred to Ports-of-Call Convair 990 jets. Each C-130 carried approximately 20,000 pounds of drugs that were distributed into two Convair 990s. Ports of Call operated in close liaison with Evergreen International.

Contact With CIA's Evergreen Airline

Evergreen International Airlines was known to be a CIA proprietary or front, and was first told to me in the early 1990s by CIA operative Gunther Russbacher. Crittenden had frequent contacts with top management people at Evergreen's McMinnville, Oregon, headquarters, and Evergreen's more secretive operation at the Marana Airport. Crittenden thought that the McMinnville operation was relatively clean as far as drug trafficking was concerned and that the drug shipments went through Marana.

Crittenden described how CIA money was flown from CIA headquarters at McLean, Virginia to Marana, sometimes using a Boeing 707 with NASA markings, flown by CIA pilots, including himself. Part of this money was reportedly used to pay for drug shipments arriving from Central and South America.

Crittenden had dealt personally many times with Evergreen's president, Dale Smith. Stephen said that Smith was more of a figurehead and that for many years the main person was Mike Irwin who provided Stephen with a card authorizing his presence at the heavily guarded Marana operation. Crittenden said Don Doss was head of aircraft scheduling, and was a level-two CIA asset. Doss's immediate boss was Walt Burnett.

Listening To CIA Conversations

A practice that I had with Gunther Russbacher was repeated several times with Crittenden. While I had either of them on the phone I would use my telephone conference-call capabilities to call CIA assets and CIA companies that they knew, and I would then listen to the conversations, which provided further support of Crittenden's CIA status. During a June 1995 telephone conversation between Crittenden and Evergreen's Walt Burnett, the conversation clearly established that they knew each other and had engaged in CIA-related activities. During another call that I placed to Evergreen's Walt Vernon in June 1995, it was equally obvious that they had both engaged in CIA activities.

The same was done with other CIA proprietaries and assets. Calls were made to Southern Air Transport (SAT) headquarters in Miami, during which he talked CIA business with a key management person whom he had known for the past 12 years. It was obvious they knew each other, that they worked and had worked for the CIA. Other secret conference calls were made to other CIA proprietaries and to present and former CIA assets, each of which discussed prior or present CIA activities. Similar calls were made to other CIA assets with whom Crittenden was familiar.

Phone Contacts with China's Chung Family

Several calls were made to the Los Angeles representatives of China's powerful Michael Chung family with whom Crittenden's CIA airlines did considerable drug hauling in the past. Crittenden described how the Chung family flew drugs from China to Hong Kong, and then his C-123s would fly the drugs to Clark Air Force Base in Manila, where Southern Air Transport's long-range aircraft would fly the drugs into the United States.

During the phone calls that I listened to, Crittenden was dealing with representatives of the Chung family in Los Angeles, who were seeking to have Crittenden obtain for them a fleet of Boeing 727 aircraft to start an airline in China. One of the loads that would be carried by the airline would be drugs. During a series of telephone conversations, Crittenden arranged for a Cesar Resurreccion to inspect 727s in Tucson at Hamilton Aircraft Sales.

The Same Chung Family Bribing Clinton and Democratic Party

Several years later, Johnny Chung was implicated in funding large amounts of political campaign funds to President Clinton and the Democratic Party, which many people claimed was bribe money.

Describing A Crittenden Air Transport Subsidiary

Crittenden described another subsidiary of Crittenden Air Transport, Saarkes Air Cargo, based in Abai Dabai, whose main cargo was drugs. The CIA furnished the proprietary with three Boeing 707s, which were used to fly drugs to Bangkok, Shanghai, Miami, and Mena Airport in Arkansas. Even though Saarkes was listed as a Crittenden Air Transport subsidiary, Crittenden, who was the titular head of the airline, had no control over it. (Russbacher had told me years earlier about this covert CIA airline.)

During various telephone conversations, Crittenden stated names of people with whom he had contact. These included Captain Jack, the alias for the CIA pilot flying for Rowan Drilling out of Houston, and who was reportedly a SR-71 pilot for the CIA. Crittenden said his real name was Sonny Knoles.

CIA Smuggling Guns To the IRA

Crittenden told me of a 1988 C-130 flight to Ireland carrying CIA arms and a stinger missile for the Irish Republican Army. The flight originated at Fort Hood and then flew to Dublin, where it cleared Customs. The C-130 then took off and landed in a field south of Dublin, where the arms were off-loaded.

During one of several phone calls I made connecting Crittenden to a secret IRA location in Ireland, we had a prisoner, Michael Martin, place a call to the IRA location (which was in a bar in Ireland). A special security code was used to get the phone operator to connect to the secret IRA location. When the call was over, Crittenden asked me what I thought. I said that I couldn't understand a single word Martin or the person in Ireland said because of their heavy Irish brogue. (At that time, Crittenden was in prison. An interesting story as to how he was released—following my filing of an amicus brief in court—is found in the third or later edition of *Defrauding America*.)

Martin had introduced himself to Crittenden while at the federal prison at Phoenix, asking if he was Stephen Crittenden. Martin had helped in the unloading of the arms in Southern Ireland on the flight flown to Ireland.

Crittenden explained that the Evergreen Shipping Lines based in Taiwan was part of the Evergreen Group, which included the CIA's Evergreen International Airlines. He described people who worked with him, including Robert Newbould, who was chief pilot for Crittenden Air Transport and after its shutdown, flew for Rowan Drilling out of Houston, Texas.

Crittenden Described Some Of the People He Dealt With

Crittenden described people with whom he worked, and their activities. These included, for example, Randy Cotheran, a marijuana distributor in Tennessee; Louis Reyes Heradia, Mafia in East St. Louis; husband of Michelle Stockdale of Springfield, who owned a fleet of trucks that moves marijuana; Mark Goiter of Great Falls, Montana, a mercenary and major drug runner; David Hadley, a cult leader; Robert Brashes of College Park, Georgia, a mercenary and assassin, who worked for the Agency, who he described as level three, a CIA sanction group, and Coletta Flying Service, Ypsilanti, Michigan, hauling material for the Cali cartel.

Crittenden's Organized Crime and Drug Cartel Business Contacts

He described his friendship, through the CIA, with various drug cartel people, including Hernando Villarell, Cardehana, Colombia. Crittenden described his Mafia contacts made through the CIA, especially in the St. Louis area. When I asked what the CIA did for the Mafia, he said, "We haul weapons and drugs to them." He described being given by the CIA the names of judges and Mafia people, especially in Missouri and Illinois, to contact if he encountered trouble. He gave me the names and phone numbers of many Italian and Mexican Mafia people who worked routinely with the CIA, including assassins that did sanctions (murders) for the Agency.

Checking His Credibility

I checked Crittenden's credibility in several ways. I had already been advised by other deep-cover people of the existence of Crittenden Air Transport. I had listened to telephone conversations that I placed to known CIA proprietaries. I quizzed Crittenden repeatedly about minute details of his operations, the aircraft specifications, the type of navigation systems installed on the aircraft, and other specifics that covered intricate areas of CIA activities during the 15 years that Crittenden operated the CIA proprietaries. No one could have been so well informed, and so quick with the answers, if that person hadn't been directly involved. When Crittenden didn't know about a particular area that I asked, and which he had no reason to have known, he quickly admitted it, rather than fabricate, which could have easily been done. I had Crittenden's address book containing the names and phone numbers of his many contacts, including drug kingpins with whom he and the CIA did business. More is stated about Crittenden in the third edition of *Defrauding America*.

CERTIFICATE OF TRANSFER

Lockheed/USAF ("Seller"), Tucson, Arizona, does hereby sell, assign and transfer to Crittenden Air Transport ("Buyer"), of 625-627 Pra Sumain Road, Bangkok, Thailand ,10200, the following property:

PROPERTY: Lockheed C-130 H/J
       IDENTIFICATION NUMBER: 4288

The Seller warrants that the property is being transferred to the Buyer is under U.S Department of Defense restriction and maynot be sold and/or transfered outside of the United States witout prior approval of the Secratary of Defense.
The above property is sold on an "AS IS" basis. The Seller makes no warranties, express or implied (except as specifically stated above).

This transfer is effective as of August 9, 1980.

The property is now located at Davis - Motham A.F.B., Tucson, Arizona, and all of such property is in the possession of the Seller.

Lockheed/USAF

By: _____
      Lockheed/USAF   Gen. Wayman Nutt

Crittenden Air Transport

By: _____
      Crittenden Air Transport

Bill of sale from Lockheed to Crittenden Air Transport for C-130

Two of Crittenden's C-130s in Cambodia

CHAPTER FIVE

DOJ–PROTECTED DOMINICAN DRUG TRAFFICKERS

T his chapter focuses on Dominican drug cartels along the northeastern seaboard, the funding of U.S. political parties by these cartels, Justice Department protection of the cartels, and Department of Justice retaliation against government agents who report these matters. Much of the material for this chapter came from insiders in the U.S. Immigration and Naturalization Service (INS), the DEA, the Pennsylvania attorney general's office, and other law enforcement groups in the New York area.

One of the Heroes—and Victims—In the Sham War-On-Drugs

Former INS agent Joseph Occhipinti was a key figure in fighting drug traffickers and drug cartels. He spent over 20 years with the U.S. Immigration and Naturalization Service, primarily in drug-related investigations. During that time he earned over 70 commendations and awards, including three from the U.S. Attorney General. Because of his outstanding work, he was promoted to chief of the Anti-Smuggling unit for the New York City area, and in that position he gained considerable knowledge about the operation of Dominican crime groups operating in the northeastern section of the United States.

Testimonial To Corrupt Politicians, Criminals, and DOJ Personnel

As Occhipinti brought about the arrest of many politically-connected criminal elements, politicians and Justice Department personnel blocked further investigations and prosecutions. In addition, and working in unison, all three groups retaliated against him and brought an end to his long and outstanding government career.

His family suffered severe hardships, and Occhipinti ended up in prison for allegedly violating the civil rights of drug traffickers—something that had never happened before. His plight is another endless testimonial to the deeply entrenched corruption in U.S. politics and the Department of Justice.

Project Intercept

One of several multi-agency task forces Occhipinti coordinated was the 1987 operation called Project Intercept, and included personnel from the Drug

Enforcement Administration (DEA), Port Authority Police Department (PAPD), and the Immigration and Naturalization Service (INS). The purpose of bringing agents from the various agencies into one group was to coordinate their investigations, evidence, and prosecution of criminal activities

That operation was credited with identifying how Dominican drug lords and other ethnic organized crime groups were involved in drug trafficking, money laundering, and alien smuggling activities at major New York airports. It had a high arrest and conviction rate for drug traffickers and was so successful that Project Intercept became the subject of congressional hearings.

It was so successful that—after the politically powerful Dominicans and drug traffickers complained—the INS District Director terminated it within a year of its startup. Occhipinti was then ordered to concentrate instead upon filing reports against employers who hired illegal aliens. This group did not have the political clout of the drug traffickers and the large Dominican population.

Project Resurrect

Starting in 1988, Occhipinti coordinated another multi-agency undercover operation called Project Resurrect, involving agents from the New York City District Attorney's office, Postal Inspection Service, and the U.S. Department of State. This project resulted in the successful prosecution and conviction of over two dozen Dominican organized crime figures in the New York City area.

The project exposed the role of a group known as the Federation of Dominican Merchants and Industrialists of New York, otherwise known as the Federation. This group operated bodegas, money transfer businesses, travel agencies, boutiques, loan companies, and an assortment of other businesses. (Bodegas is the term used by people in the Spanish community for grocery stores.) Project Resurrect exposed the role and control by the Dominican Federation in drug trafficking, drug money laundering, and alien smuggling activities. One of the people arrested and convicted was a key member of the federation, Executive Board member Martha Lozano.

Discovering Theft Ring at JFK Airport

One of Occhipinti's investigations focused on a high-level smuggling operation at New York's John F. Kennedy Airport. Due to a shortage of government agents, the Immigration and Naturalization Service hired private agencies to do some of its routine tasks. Wells Fargo was one of the companies hired, being responsible for placing illegal aliens caught by INS agents—on board aircraft to be sent back to their country of origin. The company engaged in a "shell game" that protected illegal immigrants from being deported.

Corrupt employees of Wells Fargo developed a profitable scheme. When an illegal alien was arrested, his or her relatives would be contacted, and for a price, the illegal alien would be replaced by an impostor. The impostor—who was legally in the United States—would be placed on board the aircraft and flown out of the United States. He or she would then fly back as a legal or documented alien. The illegal alien would meld into the community and most likely succeed in remaining in the United States.

Operation Red Eye

In 1989, Occhipinti was involved in another multi-agency task force called Operation Red Eye. It was composed of agents from the DEA, Port Authority, Amtrak Police Department, and INS, whose goal was to interdict at major New York City transportation centers illegal aliens smuggled into the United States via Mexico and the Canadian border.

The project was very successful in apprehending illegal alien drug couriers employed by the Dominican drug cartels and other ethnic crime groups. The operation was shut down when the U.S. Attorney's office in New York (SDNY) complained that the interdiction stops were based on racial profiling.

Of course, if Dominican crime groups were using Dominicans in large numbers to smuggle drugs into the United States, it would be somewhat ludicrous not to focus on Dominicans. That charge would be like complaining about focusing on Colombians coming out of high drug trafficking areas in Colombia when they constituted the primary people engaged in the illegal activities.

Over a period of time, Occhipinti felt that the U.S. Attorney's office was not cooperating with the multi-agency task force and instead, actually sabotaging their lawful operation. In this way, large quantities of drugs entered the United States with the help of Justice Department employees.

Investigating Drug-Related Murder Exposed Other Crimes

The murders (October 18, 1988) of two NYPD officers, Michael Buczek and Christopher Hoban, in the Washington Heights section of New York City caused the police department to ask for Occhipinti's assistance because of his expertise in Dominican organized crime activities. (Washington Heights had turned into a major Dominican neighborhood, where Dominican organized crime base much of their operations, and which has one of the highest homicide records. When I was growing up many years ago on the New Jersey side of the Hudson River across from Washington Heights, it was considered a desirable middle-class neighborhood.) As a result of this investigation, the murderer was reported to be Dominican drug lord Daniel Mirabeaux.

During this investigation, Occhipinti discovered a major Dominican drug operation controlled by Freddy Antonio Then, who established training camps in the Dominican Republic teaching people how to traffic in drugs. He reportedly smuggled these people illegally into the United States from Mexico. Then arranged for these smuggled aliens to be married to a U.S. citizen and thereby obtain permanent resident status with the arranged marriage.

Occhipinti learned that Then was buying local grocery stores, bodegas, which were often used for various illegal activities, such as drug trafficking and drug money laundering. Occhipinti arrested Then several times on various charges, including illegal gun possession. Then's prominence in the Dominican population and as a key member of the Federation would shortly be used against Occhipinti.

Project Bodega

Another multi-agency task force in which Occhipinti was involved, in 1989, was called Project Bodega, and composed of agents from the DEA, Customs service, FBI, New York Police Department, Manhattan District Attorney's office, and INS. It investigated activities at the many bodegas in the New York City area where certain known criminal activities were prevalent.

Manhattan District Attorney Supported the Task Force

Because of its successful discovery of criminal activities, the Manhattan District Attorney's office was so pleased with the group's work that it assigned several of its prosecutors, including John F. Kennedy, Jr., full time to prosecute the cases that were generated.

The task force discovered a widespread pattern of criminal activities involving Middle East and Dominican groups in the New York-New Jersey area, some of them associated with bodega grocery stores operated mostly by Dominicans, Cubans, and Middle East people. In the New York-New Jersey area, bodegas were often a front for unlawful activities. During consensual searches of bodegas, the task force discovered evidence of drug trafficking, drug money laundering, food stamp fraud, food coupon fraud, loan sharking, and smuggling of illegal aliens.

Involvement of CIA-Front Company: Sea Crest Trading Company

Investigators discovered that many bodega activities involved Sea Crest Trading Company, incorporated in Connecticut, with its main office in Greenwich, and another office in New York City. Closely tied in with Sea Crest was Capital National Bank in New York. Involved in the Sea Crest group were CIA operatives from the Cuban Bay of Pigs fiasco. Sea Crest started operations in 1984, and during the 1980s and 1990s was extensively used by the CIA in various activities.

Years earlier, several of my CIA sources, primarily Gunther Russbacher, described Sea Crest and Capital National Bank as CIA-front companies and recipients of DOJ protections. The president of Capital National Bank, Carlos Cordoba, a Cuban national, was convicted in 1992 of bank fraud. Despite the importance of the offense, he received only a token probation sentence—which would be routine if the bank was in fact a front for the CIA.

A confidential source in the New York Police Department (NYPD) Special Investigations Unit reportedly uncovered evidence of arson and other criminal activities by Sea Crest, and that Sea Crest had key political connections that were protecting it against prosecution. As with other city, state and federal agents, he was intimidated and harassed by higher-ups. During the investigation, he discovered a conflict of interest between attorney Christopher Lynn, a member of the NYPD Civilian Complaint Review Board and his defense of those involved in Sea Crest's illicit activities. The confidential source reported the disappearance of critical evidence on Sea Crest's drug activities.

An affidavit, executed on March 1, 1994, by Domingo Antonio Lovera, described the growth of Sea Crest over the years in usurious loans, using Dominicans and Cubans to obtain and collect loans from bodega operators. Lovera described how Sea Crest used Capital National Bank to launder the money obtained from various illegal operations. Investigations showed that this CIA-front company made a practice of putting Dominicans into bodegas and then forcing them into various unlawful activities. Because of the high-interest and usurious loans (permitted where Sea Crest was incorporated Connecticut), and high monthly payments, bodega operators found they *had* to engage in criminal activities to keep from losing their businesses.

Sea Crest and Bodegas in Connecticut

In a two-part series (August 1998), the *Hartford Courant* described the activities of Sea Crest Trading Company, the Dominican-run bodegas, and various criminal activities. The article described drug dealers ducking into bodegas immediately after making drug sales and giving the cash to the bodega operators, and drugs being purchased from the operators. Quoting Hartford police Detective Robert Lawlor. "The bodegas provided a meeting place and the cover of a legitimate business. It hasn't reached the point here that it has in New York, but it's only a matter of time."

The newspaper made reference to a 1997 classified report by the U.S. Department of Justice on Dominican drug trafficking and said dealers "move proceeds by disguising them in the financial records of travel agencies, boutiques, grocery stores and other Dominican-run businesses." Despite the Justice Department's knowledge of Sea Crest's activities, the CIA-connected company appeared to have a get-out-of-jail card that kept them from being prosecuted.

Dominican Revolutionary Party (PRD)

According to an article in Puerto Rico's *El Vocero* newspaper, Dominican Revolutionary Party (PRD) members, including Simon Diaz and Pablo Espinal, contributed money to President Clinton's reelection campaign during a fund-raiser at Coogan's Irish Pub in New York's Washington Heights. The article stated that this drug-tainted money was linked to the Dominican Revolutionary party. Vice President Al Gore posed for pictures with Diaz and Espinal. The article identified Simon Diaz as vice president of a New York City chapter of the PRD and that he was currently under investigation by the Drug Enforcement Administration (DEA) and anti-narcotic agencies concerning PRD's "alleged nexus with international drug cartels."

Private Investigator Uncovers Similar Criminal Activities

A concurrent investigation by a private investigator uncovered considerable evidence of criminal activities at bodegas that the multi-agency task forces were discovering, especially as it related to food coupon fraud. Private investigator Ben Jacobsen, a retired New York detective, was working as chief investigator for the A.C. Nielson Corporation which administered the food coupon program for many large companies selling to grocery stores. Corporations estimated that they were losing over $200 million a year in fraudulent coupon redemptions.

Jacobsen's investigation uncovered canceled checks and other evidence showing Sea Crest Trading Company and one of its associate companies, Control Book Keeping, to be behind this practice.

The food coupon fraud worked like this: People involved in the fraud brought into a central location newspapers and magazines containing food coupons that were intended to be used to purchase a particular food item. The coupons were clipped, put into a barrel or some other device that dirtied them to look like they had been handled by Customers. The coupons were then distributed to different bodegas who then sent them to coupon redemption centers. When the checks were sent to the grocers for these coupons, the checks were either endorsed over to Sea Crest Trading Company or cashed, and the money sent to Sea Crest. Sea Crest reportedly was at the center of this scam.

FBI Coverup

FBI Special Agent Lionel Baron of the FBI's New York City terrorist unit obtained from Ben Jacobsen the names of his informants with the expressed intention of infiltrating Sea Crest. Despite receiving considerable evidence showing the criminal activities *did* exist, Baron and the FBI never went forward with any prosecution.

When *New York Post* reporter Al Guart requested access to Baron's investigative notes under the Freedom of Information Act, the FBI replied there were no notes and no investigation. This false statement by the FBI was made despite the fact that Baron had interviewed a number of witnesses, including Cesar Cabral, Hector Rodriguez, Alma Camarana, Peter Navaro, Luis Rodriguez, and Detective Raul Anglada, proving that an investigation had been made. Rodriguez had even given a sworn affidavit to the FBI relating to a usurious loan from Sea Crest. Guart discovered many of the alias corporations used by Sea Crest.

Investigation of Sea Crest Blocked at State and Federal Levels

Guart's continuing investigation into Sea Crest's activities, including interviews with law enforcement agents, confirmed to him that in every case, investigations and prosecutions were blocked by high-level state and federal personnel. This is further evidence of DOJ obstruction of justice when criminal activities involving the CIA or other covert agency, and covert illegal operation, is involved. In every one of my books, I give details of how state personnel–law enforcement and judges—cooperate with federal DOJ personnel to block investigations of highly sensitive, and usually corrupt, activities by federal agencies. And this includes state and local "law-enforcement" and judicial personnel in retaliating against anyone threatening to expose these activities.

Guart interviewed Bronx Borough President Fernando Ferier regarding Sea Crest's operations in the Bronx with the intent of getting the Bronx District Attorney to investigate the company. Ferier denied knowing anything about Sea Crest, but said he would set up an appointment with the Bronx District Attorney. When Guart conducted a Lexus check, he discovered a *New York Times* article (August 13, 1993) in which Ferier assisted Sea Crest in procuring a special ordinance to rebuild their building which had mysteriously burned in the Bronx. In the article, Ferier was quoted as referring to the president of Sea Crest, Mr. Berkovitz, as "my good friend Bernie."

New York Post Coverup of Covert Criminal Activities

Guart prepared four news articles on Sea Crest which were to be published, but weren't. His editor told Guart that they were afraid to publish the articles. Earlier, when the *New York Post* ran a series of articles, "The Framing of a Cop," which made reference to bodegas and Sea Crest, the newspaper received bomb threats and threats from the Dominican Federation that they would boycott the *New York Post* in the Washington Heights section of New York.

A DEA report (October 16, 1992) provided by Occhipinti alleged that Sea Crest was reportedly responsible for over $500 million in money laundering operations from the Washington Heights section of New York City.

The Federation

The multi-agency task force discovered that members of the Federation were frequently involved in criminal activities, that major drug groups were using the federation businesses as fronts, and that the Federation's influence extended into political offices, including New York City Mayor David Dinkins. The Federation started putting pressure on political figures, seeking to disband the task forces led by Occhipinti.

Customs Investigation Halted By CIA Pressure

A confidential source in the New York Police Department Intelligence Unit knew about the Dominican Federation's involvement in criminal activities following a prior joint investigation with U.S. Customs (Customs Case # NY 02AR8NY003). Targets in that investigation included Pedro Allegria and Federation Vice President Erasmo Taveras who had been indicted in 1989 and later convicted of a $70 million money laundering and loan sharking scheme. According to the confidential source, the CIA ordered Customs to drop the pending indictments against several of the Dominican drug traffickers, who then continued to engage in money laundering activities—with the protection of the DOJ—despite evidence presented to the U.S. Attorney by Staten Island Borough President Guy Molinari in 1992.

Bergen County Investigation Halted

Under-sheriff Jay Albert of the Bergen County, New Jersey, Sheriff Department authorized a criminal investigation into Sea Crest and the Federation's infiltration into that county. The investigation was turned over to detectives Juan Lopez and Wayne Yahn, who gathered evidence substantiating the involvement of Sea Crest and the Federation. Their investigation was terminated on the basis of an alleged jurisdictional dispute with the Bergen County prosecutor's office.

Project Esquire: Investigating U.S. Attorney's Office

During the Project Bodega investigations the group discovered from a police informant, Alma Camerena, that a former assistant U.S. Attorney and his law partner were allegedly part of Then's drug cartel operations and also involved in political corruption. According to Camerena, the former U.S. attorney was attending sex and drug parties with his former colleagues in the U.S. Attorney's office and receiving favored treatment in criminal cases involving his clients. Occhipinti said, "I found the allegations to be credible for a variety of reasons."

Occhipinti reported these allegations to Assistant U.S. Attorney David Lawrence, who was the Deputy Chief of the Criminal Division, with whom Occhipinti had previously worked. Lawrence then arranged to debrief Camerena. After questioning Camerena, and determining that the charges were true, showing depravity in the U.S. Attorney's office, instead of addressing the matter, Project Esquire was terminated.

Search of Dominican Bodegas

Occhipinti's task force had multiple investigations going simultaneously. Focusing on the criminal activities in the bodegas, the task force sought additional court-admissible evidence by conducting consensual searches of several dozen bodegas in the Washington Heights section of New York during the last half of 1989 and early1990. In conducting consensual searches, the owner or operator is asked to sign a consent form agreeing to having their properties searched. Otherwise, a search warrant must be obtained.

In one search of the Then's Brothers Grocery Store, the task force discovered $131,000 in cash bundles destined for Sea Crest. This money was later judicially forfeited as drug proceeds by the U.S. District Court in Manhattan. In another bodega owned by Richard Knipping in the Bronx, the task force discovered hundreds of newly-issued government food stamp books for which Knipping could provide no explanation. These seizures and related criminal charges started major retaliation efforts against Occhipinti by various members of the Federation, Dominican criminal cartels, the black Mayor, David Dinkins, and the U.S. Attorney's office in New York City.

Drug Traffickers and Immigrants Reacted With Demonstrations

The politically powerful Dominican drug traffickers, the Federation, and Mayor David Dinkins orchestrated demonstrations against Occhipinti in the drug-infested Washington Heights area of Manhattan. Rather than support the head of the multi-agency task force, Project Bodega was terminated, despite the heavy concentration of drug and other criminal activities discovered during the bodega searches. Drug trafficking then escalated.

Using Clinton's Tactics--Blaming The Republicans

Mayor Dinkins issued a statement claiming the search of the bodegas was a "Republican Conspiracy" intended to sabotage the 1990 census and intimidate immigrant voters from going to the polls. Dinkins was referring to the large numbers of illegal aliens in the area, many of whom voted for him in the prior election which resulted in the slim majority that won him the election.

Dinkins didn't tell the people the investigators were looking for criminal activities, and found many, and were not conducting a dragnet. What Dinkins was probably afraid of was that the increased police activities would keep illegal aliens from the voting booths where he had a large following in the Dominican community. Dominicans constitute a large voting block in the New York and other urban areas in the Northeast. Figures indicate there were over half a million Dominicans in New York City alone, and that they will outnumber all other Hispanic groups within a few years. Dinkins had been receiving large contributions from the Federation and the Dominican crime figures, being another reason for wanting to shut down the investigation of criminal activities involving mostly Dominicans.

Consensual Searches Violated Their Civil Rights?

The Federation, the immigrants, the drug traffickers, and Mayor Dinkins claimed that the searches violated the civil rights of the bodega operators, and focused their charges against Occhipinti, even though he was only one member of the task force. It was necessary to focus the attacks on one individual in order for the protest to succeed. The group pressured the U.S. Attorney to file criminal charges against Occhipinti for violating their civil rights. This had never been done before against a government agent on the basis of an alleged technical violation. The group charged Occhipinti with violating their civil rights on the basis of the consensual searches—despite the fact that the bodega operators had signed consent forms before the search.

Several members of the multi-agency task force told the U.S. attorney that there were no violations of anyone's civil rights during the task force's search of the bodegas. IRS Special Agent Ronald Nowicki was present during the search of Knipping's bodega and stated there were no violations of search procedures. DEA Agent John Dowd was also present during the search of Knipping's bodega and stated that the search was legal. But this wasn't what the DOJ prosecutors wanted to hear.

Reporting Threats Against Occhipinti to U.S. Attorney

Alma Camarena, the legal secretary in the law offices of former AUSA Jorge Guttlein, and Andres Aranda, overheard the attorneys discussing ways to eliminate the threat that Occhipinti posed to their Dominican and drug trafficking clients. Upon hearing these threats, Camarena went to the U.S. Attorney's office to report what she heard, and was interviewed by Assistant U.S. Attorney Jeh Johnson. "Mr. Aranda told Mr. Guttlein that he would like to have Mr. Occhipinti eliminated." Camarena said, adding that Guttlein didn't like that idea and said he would think up another plan.

After she gave this information to the U.S. Attorney's office, Johnson, or someone else in the U.S. Attorney's office, gave this confidential information, and the name of the confidential witness, to Camerena's boss who was the target of the charges!

U.S. Attorney Protecting Drug Cartels

Instead of protecting a respected government agent, the U.S. Attorney filed criminal charges against Occhipinti. These charges were based upon the perjured statements of the bodega operators—most of whom were engaging in criminal activities and who were continuing their unlawful activities—to justify obtaining an indictment against Occhipinti from a grand jury.

The indictment charged Occhipinti with failure to obtain written consent of the bodega operators before searching the premises. He relied on their verbal consent. Also, that he kept for his own use money seized by the task force group (During trial, the jury held him not guilty of that charge, and at a later date some of the bodega operators who made that charge admitted that they lied.)

This was the same U.S. Attorney's office that had been covering up for the criminal activities that Occhipinti and his task force had been exposing. It was the same office that had covered up for the CIA-Mafia drug trafficking reported by one of their own agents, Richard Taus, during this same period, which is described in other pages.

Peculiar Comparisons

Compare these civil rights "violations" with the common practice of DEA and ATF agents breaking down the doors to peoples' homes, throwing the residents to the floor, shoving loaded pistols in their faces, and occasionally shooting and killing innocent people. These agents have the full support of the Department of Justice and federal judges. There was a difference; Occhipinti was exposing powerful drug traffickers, who had connections with CIA operations, and who had political connections.

Usual Withholding Of Exculpatory Evidence by DOJ Prosecutors

Transcripts of the grand jury proceedings showed DOJ witnesses lying when they testified they did not have prior criminal records. DOJ prosecutors withheld this perjury from the grand jury members and from the defense during the jury trial. Also withheld from the grand jury and trial jury was the fact that the task force had discovered contraband and illegal activity at each of the locations that they searched

Black Activist Federal Judge with Strong Ties to
Democratic Mayor Dinkins and the Federation

Selected to be the judge for Occhipinti's trial was U.S. District Judge Constance Baker Motley, the first black woman appointed to the federal bench and who had a radical and biased reputation. Federal court procedures require assignment of judges to a particular criminal trial be done on a normal rotation process, and is normally done by the court clerk. Judge Motley was *pre-selected* instead of chosen at *random*. Occhipinti said U.S. Attorney Jeh Johnson's face reflected joy and he gave a "thumbs-up" sign when Judge Motley's name was announced as being the trial judge.

Motley had close political ties to black mayor of New York City, David Dinkins. She was a protégé of Raymond Jones, a powerful black leader of Tammany Hall who was also an associate of David Dinkins in the Harlem Carver Democratic Club.

A Mafia Don Would Have Been Pleased With This Lineup

A *New American* article (February 21, 1994) stated that during Motley's senate confirmation hearings, evidence was presented showing Motley to be an ardent Young Communist League organizer who established student cells at New York University. The records showed that Constance Baker, her maiden name, was training for the Red Underground. Despite this record, Senator Edward Kennedy nominated Motley to become America's first black female federal judge, and other senators, wanting to get as many of the black votes as possible, quickly endorsed her.

The prosecutor, Jeh Johnson, was a former law clerk for the judge, and it was said that he was her "Godson." The article raised another problem that should have been the basis for changes in the trial setting:

There was bad blood between [Johnson] and Occhipinti as a result of the Project Esquire investigation or corruption within [Johnson's] office. Further, some of Johnson's associates alleged that he had boasted that an Occhipinti conviction would land him a high-paying private sector job-a prediction that has been fulfilled. Today, Johnson's office walls at the prestigious New York law firm of Paul, Weiss, Rifkin, Wharton and Garrison are adorned with artists' renderings of the Occhipinti trial, which Johnson regards as "trophies."

Record of Overturned Decisions

Judge Motley had more decisions overturned on appeal than any other judge in that circuit, indicating she was either legally ignorant, contemptuous of the law, or rendering decisions based on personal interests or money under the table.

Pre-Trial Problems For Occhipinti

Making matters worse for Occhipinti, his attorney, Norman Mordkofsky, was suffering a nervous breakdown. The heavy media publicity and street demonstrations, and the loss of his legal practice, caused Occhipinti's trial attorney to suffer severe stress before the trial, causing Occhipinti to seek substitution with another legal counsel. The attorney explained his serious problems to Judge Motley and filed a motion to be excused so that Occhipinti could obtain another attorney. Judge Motley denied the request, calling the attorney a liar. Occhipinti ended up with incompetent legal representation.

A week earlier, New York Supreme Court Judge Anthony Scarpino removed Mordkofsky from a murder case because of his bizarre behavior. The judge publicly admitted that there was no question that Mordkofsky was suffering some kind of psychological problem. After Occhipinti's trial, the attorney was admitted to the hospital for psychiatric care.

In one letter to me, Occhipinti wrote:

During my trial, he talked about committing suicide on several occasions. Judge Motley demanded that he go to trial. On the trial records, Mordkofsky demonstrates before the jury bizarre behavior as well as his failure to call very much needed defense witnesses or go through the counts of the indictment. It was also determined that his breakdown was attributed to the termination of his law practice.

His two partners were criminal defense lawyers who represented many Dominican organized crime figures I was investigating, including some of Freddy Then's drug associates. Clearly, I had won several crucial criminal cases which made Mordkofsky's two partners look bad. Another important fact I later learned that Mordkofsky's next door neighbor was an attorney who incorporated many of the Dominican Bodegas with suspected ties to the Federation and Sea Crest. In fact, it was this very same attorney who represented the Then Brothers grocery store on the $131,000 forfeiture case. I truly believe that there was immense pressure on Mordkofsky, which resulted in his nervous breakdown. There are medical and hospitalization records to document this breakdown.

DOJ Prosecutor Threatening Witnesses

The Justice Department's prosecutor threatened witnesses who wanted to testify on Occhipinti's behalf. Occhipinti explained:

The Manhattan District Attorney's office, who provided the staff for the multi-agency task force, included three Assistant District Attorneys and a team of investigators. They wanted to testify on my behalf. They knew the project was lawful and had proper predication. In fact, Ann Rudman, chief of the Asset Forfeiture Program, tried to convince INS not to close down the project.

Yet, these District Attorney officials never came forward. According to Jacobson and others, the Manhattan District Attorney's office was threatened by SDNY prosecutors that if they came to my aid, they might subject themselves to federal prosecution since they jointly worked on the task force with me.

Also, in the documented setup of another NYPD police officer, Louis Dellapizzi, on fabricated civil rights charges, Attorney Andres Aranda was never indicted for the setup because of reported influence by SDNY prosecutors. If Aranda had been indicted, many suspect that as part of a plea-bargain deal, he would have confirmed my setup and exposed the official corruption at the US Attorney's office.

Typical Judicial Chicanery

During the trial, Judge Motley refused to allow the defense to introduce information about the criminal background of the Dominicans witnesses who claimed Occhipinti violated their civil rights, despite the fact that this information was relevant to assess the witnesses' credibility. Motley made numerous rulings that kept any information about CIA and criminal activities from being heard by the jurors.

DOJ Withholding Exculpatory Evidence

Most of the bodega operators who filed civil rights complaints against Occhipinti had prior criminal records, and continued to be charged with criminal violations after the trial had ended. This information was known to the prosecutor who unlawfully withheld the information throughout the trial proceedings. Federal law requires that the prosecutor provides the defense with all exculpatory evidence known to the prosecutor; this requirement is routinely violated by the Justice Department attorneys, who never suffer any retaliation for it.

Prosecutorial Deception

There were numerous prosecutorial errors before and during trial, all intended to insure that the jury decide Occhipinti guilty. To obtain the indictment from the federal grand jury, U.S. attorney Johnson withheld exculpatory evidence and made inflammatory statements against Occhipinti. The prosecutor threatened and intimidated witnesses who would be testifying in Occhipinti's defense. One official with the NYPD admitted to Jacobsen that NYPD officers involved in Project Bodega were being threatened with indictment if they came to Occhipinti's defense.

Outraged Attorney Files Court Affidavit

During the trial, attorney Angel Nunez, who had been observing the proceedings and becoming outraged by the prosecutorial and judicial misconduct, submitted an affidavit into court records detailing the numerous trial irregularities. Nunez interviewed those who filed the complaint against Occhipinti, and in 55 undercover taped conversations they admitted the searches were legal in their estimation, contradicting their grand jury and trial testimony.

Nunez tried to submit an affidavit into the trial relating to these findings, showing a conspiracy against Occhipinti and the witnesses lying. Judge Motley refused to allow the affidavit admitted into the trial. When Nunez tried to admit the tapes and transcripts into the hearing, she again refused, compounding her refusal by seizing the tapes, preventing them from being used elsewhere. When the judge heard that Occhipinti reported these irregularities to the media, she put a "gag order" on Occhipinti, preventing him from speaking out, surely an unconstitutional order.

Guilty, Said the Jury

The jurors, from a heavy drug-trafficking area that Occhipinti's group had targeted, handed down a guilty verdict against Occhipinti (June 12, 1992) on the charge of conspiracy to violate the civil rights of the bodega operators.

First Law Enforcement Officer
Sentenced To Prison for Alleged Technical Error

Never before in American history had a federal law enforcement officer been criminally prosecuted in a case where there was no violence involved and where the officer had done a routine consensual search, and merely involved an "alleged" technical violation. Even if, for argument, Occhipinti, a key agent in U.S. Customs, had actually violated some technical search procedure, that would not subject the officer to prison. Instead, the evidence obtained in a faulty manner would be excluded and administrative action possibly taken against the officer. It had always been, and still is, government policy to conduct an administrative hearing, and certainly not file criminal charges. The FBI never conducted any hearing. The question is, Why did the Department of Justice file the sham charges?

Ending A Successful Drug-Fighting Career

Judge Motley sentenced Occhipinti to 37 months in a maximum security prison where Occhipinti would be surrounded by convicted drug dealers that he helped put in prison. This same tactic was used to eliminate other witnesses against government corruption. Read on.

Justice Department Retaliating Against FBI Supervisor

FBI Special Agent in Charge (SAC) of the New York office, Jim Fox, had replied to media questions, stating the FBI had evidence showing Occhipinti was innocent of the charges and that the government was withholding the evidence. In retaliation, the FBI suspended him—two months prior to his planned retirement.

Occhipinti filed a motion for a new trial, based upon Fox's statements, but Judge Motley denied the motion. Fox died of cancer in 1998.

Fallout From Justice Department's Conduct

There were several expected consequences to the Justice Department's charges against Occhipinti:

- Government agents were put on notice not to go after politically-connected criminal elements in the Dominican community.
- Caused other government agents to ignore politically connected criminal activities.
- Established an "acceptable" procedure for retaliating against government agents who threaten politically-connected criminals.
- Emboldened larger and well-connected drug traffickers to continue or escalate their criminal activities, knowing they would be protected by DOJ personnel. Small-time drug traffickers, with no political or CIA connections, would receive DOJ attention.
- Made possible continued crimes, some of it violent, against Americans and against America.

Another of Many DOJ Contributions to Increased Crime Activities

A 1993 report by the president of the New Jersey Police Benevolent Association said that in the year before Occhipinti's conviction the local Drug Enforcement Agency conducted 2,700 investigations, and that the year after Occhipinti's conviction, that number dropped to 500. The reason given was that agents feared being sent to prison for carrying out their drug investigations.

The president of the New York-New Jersey Port Authority Police Union said that their officers had ceased all consensual searches and drug interdiction activities in the ports of New York and New Jersey, out of fear of being charged with civil rights violations (of politically-connected criminal groups).

Sgt. Lenny Lemer of the NYPD-DEA drug task force gave testimony to Congress revealing that during a 1992 criminal investigation they discovered at Sea Crest evidence of the conspiracy against Occhipinti. The U.S. Attorney's office in New York ordered Lemer to remain silent about this information, giving the sham excuse that there was an ongoing investigation. The Justice Department prosecutors chose to use the obviously biased statements from major drug traffickers over the statements of any of the government agents.

Appeal Process on Heels of Watts Riots and Local Demonstrations

With a new attorney, Stephen Frankel, Occhipinti appealed his conviction. Oral arguments were scheduled (June 1992) at the Second Circuit Court of Appeals. The appeal was based on ineffective assistance of counsel, prosecutorial misconduct, and judicial errors. The appeal brief and appendix exceeded 750 pages.

Trying to intimidate the judges, the Dominican Federation staged a noisy demonstration in front of the court house. The noisy group carried warning signs warning of riots in Washington Heights if Occhipinti's trial decision was overturned, and then packed an overflowing court room where oral arguments were to be heard.

Apparently intimidated—and fearing a Watts-type riot—the judges suddenly refused to allow oral arguments, despite the fact that was the reason for the hearing. Normally, an appellate court takes weeks or even months before it issues a decision after an oral hearing, taking time to digest the written and oral arguments. In Occhipinti's case, the decision was rendered within one hour of the "hearing," apparently to placate the near riots of Dominican immigrants, drug traffickers and bodega operators.

Risks In Prison

His appeal rejected, Occhipinti was ordered to turn himself in on June 12, 1992. The day before he was to turn himself in, Occhipinti appeared on a New York television show, the *Jackie Mason Show*, and explained what really happened. Judge Motley retaliated, ordering the U.S. Marshal to immediately arrest Occhipinti. The marshal ignored her order and told Occhipinti to surrender the next morning. As is customary, Occhipinti was placed in leg irons and body chains and sent by prison plane to El Reno, Oklahoma. The greater distance from New York insured he would have difficulty getting publicity or using other legal remedies.

Recognized By Prisoners He Previously Arrested

As Occhipinti entered the general prison population at El Reno, Oklahoma, he was recognized by some of the prisoners from New York whose incarceration came about as a result of Occhipinti's task force. Fortunately, sympathetic prison guards, made aware of the risk, put Occhipinti into solitary confinement. While this protected him from physical harm, the isolation resulted in a breakdown. DOJ prison officials blocked every attempt by Occhipinti to be transferred closer to his family, realizing that he and his supporters would be working to bring about his release.

Many People Protested the Outrage and
DOJ Protection of Politically-Connected Criminals

Many courageous people expressed outrage at sentencing a key government drug agent to prison for having reported the criminal activities in the New York area. Staten Island Borough President, Guy V. Molinari heard about Occhipinti's plight, and even though Occhipinti was not one of his constituents, Molinari started an investigation, acquiring several affidavits from key people that proved Occhipinti's innocence.

FBI Trying To Set Up Borough President Molinari

Molinari's actions seeking to reveal the truth behind the DOJ's prosecution of Occhipinti started an all-too-common DOJ retaliation. Assistant U.S. Attorney Valerie Capone and FBI Special Agent Jarrett investigated Molinari's staff on the excuse the evidence the staff had uncovered relating to the drug cartel conspiracy was fabricated. Capone also threatened NYPD Detective Lemmer with potential prosecution for providing Molinari with exculpatory evidence relating to the Occhipinti setup and coverup of criminal activities in the New York area.

The DOJ, through its FBI agents, then tried to entrap Molinari, using a woman wearing a wire-recorder seeking to trap him with sham charges. They also charged Molinari with compensating a person for giving testimony. (More about this law and this practice in later pages.)

Media Reference To FBI Setup of Molinari

An article in the *New York Post* (April 26, 1995) made reference to the misuse of the FBI's powers against Molinari: "Guy Molinari Fumes: FBI tried to set me up." The article stated in part:

Staten Island Borough President Guy Molinari angrily charged yesterday that two FBI agents sought to entrap him in a criminal scheme with the help of a "wired" government informant. "It's outrageous," Molinari said. "If they will do this to me, an elected official, I hate to think what they might do to a member of the general public." Molinari came under FBI scrutiny during his relentless efforts to prove the innocence of Joseph Occhipinti, the Immigration and Naturalization officer who was convicted and imprisoned on charges of conducting illegal searches of drug locations in upper Manhattan. Occhipinti, the most decorated officer in INS history, served seven months of a 37-month prison term before President Bush commuted the sentence, principally at Molinari's behest.

Molinari, who had never heard of Occhipinti, became involved only two days before the agent was sentenced. He was so appalled at what he saw at the sentencing that he and his staff launched an independent probe. Molinari concluded that Occhipinti had been framed and convicted on the perjured testimony of drug dealers. Molinari's efforts on behalf of the beleaguered agent—who is not even a constituent—are among his finest hours in a long career of public service. But those efforts started his problem with the FBI.

"When a small team of FBI agents working out of Queens arrived at my office, it became clear to me that the focus of their investigation was not the evidence we had produced but the involvement of me and my office in the matter," Molinari told me yesterday. "Here was I, a law-abiding citizen, seeking to redress what I believed to be a miscarriage of justice, and finding that I had become the target of the FBI probe. They tried to get me to commit a crime. It's outrageous."

Molinari's evidence against the FBI includes a sworn affidavit from Alma Camarena, a former law clerk who first informed the government that Dominican drug lords were planning to frame Occhipinti. [With Justice Department assistance!]

In the affidavit, Camarena swears: "On or about January or February of 1993, I was contacted by [an FBI] agent to come to their office in Queens. I agreed. At that interview, they said that they wanted me to set

*up Mr. Molinari by my wearing a wire against him. I said "Yes only be-
cause I was afraid." The trap was to get Molinari to admit he offered
Camarena a job in exchange for tainted testimony.*

*Camarena said she overheard the agents planning the operation.
"They were bragging how they would get a helicopter to circle Mr. Molinari's office to overhear my conversation with him." she swore. "They
said when Mr. Molinari agreed to get me a job on the wire, they would arrest him."*

*Camarena said she called Molinari, but "I never said what the FBI
wanted me to say. The FBI agents appeared upset because I didn't repeat
everything they wanted."*

*Molinari told the FBI's Office of Professional Responsibility that the
agents seemed more interested in investigating him than in the criminal
conspiracy or the perjury against Occhipinti.*

Drug Dealers, Immigrants, and DOJ Personnel
In Conspiracy Against Law Enforcement Officers

Molinari articulated this fact from looking at the Occhipinti case as he
said, *The Occhipinti case is very significant. It is part of a new phenomenon in which law-enforcement officers are being convicted on the perjured testimony of drug dealers.*

Complaining To FBI's Lapdog Office of Professional Responsibility

Molinari complained to the FBI's "lapdog" Office of Professional Responsibility (OPR) about the scheme to file false charges against him. Almost
a year later, the FBI responded:

*There is insufficient evidence to find that the allegations made by you and
supported by Alma Camarena are substantiated. While it appears that on
August 28, 1992, the agents discussed with Camarena the possibility of
her wearing a wire in some type of cover action against you, and that she
agreed to do so, the idea was not endorsed by the agents' supervisor and
was flatly rejected by Department of Justice attorneys.*

President George Bush Pardons Occhipinti

After acquiring considerable evidence and affidavits clearly showing how
drug traffickers and DOJ personnel set up Occhipinti, Molinari requested
President George Bush to commute Occhipinti's sentence. Other concerned
people also contacted Bush. On January 15, 1993, shortly before Bush left
office, he signed a commutation for Occhipinti. However, he refused to give
Occhipinti a full pardon, which left Occhipinti with a felony conviction. During the 1980s, Bush was heavily involved in CIA activities in which Sea Crest
played an important role and he was also in the loop with the heavy drug trafficking associated with the Contra affair.

Continuing To Expose Criminal Activities Upon Release

After Occhipinti was released from prison, as a private citizen, he presented evidence he had concerning the many criminal activities to various law
enforcement agencies that had jurisdiction and responsibilities in those areas.
During a meeting (February 2, 1993) in the office of the Bronx district attorney to discuss Sea Crest and Dominican crime activities, attended by district
attorney personnel, Occhipinti described the evidence that the task force group
had acquired. Before leaving, an unnamed investigator privately told Oc-

chipinti that no investigation would be conducted because of the high political links to the CIA and Dominican organized crime operations.

Brooklyn District Attorney Drops Investigation

Brooklyn District Attorney Charles J. Hines had meetings with Occhipinti (1993) concerning the evidence Occhipinti's group had acquired, which was in his jurisdiction and area of responsibility. Hines stated he would authorize an investigation into Sea Crest. That interest suddenly cooled and the investigation was dropped.

Bronx DA Halts Investigation

During a meeting with Assistant District Attorney Edward Friedenthal in the Bronx (January 12, 1994), Friedenthal told Occhipinti that an investigation would be conducted into Sea Crest, based upon information provided by Occhipinti's task force. An unnamed Bronx investigator from the district attorney's office told Occhipinti that no investigation would be conducted due to political concerns, alluding to the political connection between Mayor Dinkins and the Bronx district attorney. He was correct; no investigation was conducted.

New Jersey Investigation Halted

A conference took place (July 21, 1994) with Sgt. Jim Mullholland of the New Jersey Police intelligence unit, Occhipinti, and several high ranking deputy attorney generals from New Jersey, which was arranged by former New Jersey Attorney General Robert Del Tufo. A week earlier (July 13, 1994), Occhipinti and several New York City law enforcement agents testified before the New Jersey Senate about Dominican organized crime operations in New Jersey. New Jersey law enforcement personnel then planned to act upon the information. That is, until they were contacted by Justice Department personnel. The investigation was then halted.

Postal Service and ATF Coverup

Federal agents from the U.S. Postal Inspection Service and the Alcohol Tobacco and Firearms Bureau interviewed Occhipinti (December 1994) concerning these criminal activities. According to a confidential source, Postal inspectors and the Organized Crime Strike Force for Newark, New Jersey, had indicated an interest in Sea Crest Trading Company. That investigation was stopped.

Congressman Traficant Seeking Congressional Hearing

Complaints of the criminal activities and government coverups were brought to Representative James Traficant's attention. He obtained a confidential June 1992 DEA report that corroborated there was a special interest group protecting Sea Crest corrupt activities. The DEA report said that Sea Crest laundered over $500 million dollars a year from Washington Heights. Traficant placed into the Congressional Record (September 27, 1996–E1734) affidavits and other evidence showing the existence of the CIA and Dominican drug offenses in the United States. He also referenced Justice Department's actions blocking the exposure of these activities.

Dominican Diplomat Confirming Dominican Criminal Activities

Ramon Antonio Grullon, a former Dominican diplomat, prepared two affidavits (March 10, 1994) that were entered into the Congressional Record by Traficant. In the affidavits, Grullon said he had been recruited by Federation members Pedro Allegria and others to participate in a conspiracy against Occhipinti and that the motive for these acts against Occhipinti was Occhipinti's investigation of Sea Crest and the Federation's bodegas. Grullon described the criminal activities of Sea Crest and the involvement of Richard Knipping and Jose Liberato in the illicit operations.

Drug Money to U.S. Politicians

Grullon also described being present when drug money was given to certain elected officials. Throughout these pages are reports of U.S. politicians and the two political parties knowingly receiving drug money.

Congressional Resolution That Went Nowhere

A resolution was entered into the Congressional Record (April 28, 1993) by Representative Dick Zimmer seeking the appointment of a special or independent prosecutor to investigate the matters that Occhipinti discovered. The resolution stated in part:

Whereas, there is voluminous evidence that in 1991 and 1992 Mr. Occhipinti may have been the target of a well orchestrated conspiracy by Dominican drug dealers, leading to his prosecution on civil rights charges under 18 U.S.C.A. 241 and 242; (1) This House memorializes the President and Congress of the United States to appoint a special or independent prosecutor to investigate the case of Mr. Joseph Occhipinti, including an investigation of the alleged drug cartel conspiracy against Mr. Occhipinti, and, further, of the alleged Justice Department coverup in the handling and prosecution of the Occhipinti case. The President is memorialized further to grant, if the investigation warrants, a full pardon so Mr. Occhipinti can clear his name.

This House further memorializes the President and Congress of the United States to seek a congressional investigation examining the extent of Dominican crime operations in the United States especially in New Jersey.

Congress Did Nothing to Offend the Dominican Constituency

Despite the gravity of the criminal activities in the New York area uncovered by the various law enforcement agencies, and despite the obstruction of justice activities by DOJ personnel, no one in Congress wanted to investigate the problems. Some were covering up for the Justice Department and others were too scared and cowardly. There were many other links to the Occhipinti matter that would be revealed by any thorough investigation. An investigation would alienate a large political constituency in the Dominican groups.

A full investigation would reveal, for instance, the decades of CIA drug trafficking; drug money going to *both* political parties; the most recent examples of drug money going to the Democratic party and President Bill Clinton.

Seeking Congressional Relief for Occhipinti

Further information supporting Occhipinti's innocence and the DOJ-organized crime coalition against him was provided by an affidavit placed into the Congressional Record (E1734) on September 27, 1996, by William Acosta, which stated in part:

(2) I am a former thirteen year law enforcement official who successfully infiltrated the Medellin and Cali Colombian drug cartels. I am considered an expert on the Colombian and Dominican drug and money

laundering operations in the New York City area.

Political Corruption Involving John F. Kennedy Airport

(3) In 1987, I was previously employed as an undercover operative for the United States Customs Service, wherein I was assigned to route out corruption at John F. Kennedy International Airport. In 1987, I was the principle undercover agent on "Operation Airport 88," which resulted in the prosecution and conviction of seventeen government officials for bribery corruption and related criminal charges. I was then promoted to Special Agent and reassigned to the Los Angeles District Office.

Evidence Of New York Police Corruption

(4) In 1990, I was appointed to the New York City Police Department as a Police officer. In view of my Colombian heritage and confidential sources close to the Colombian cartel, I was eventually assigned to the Internal Affairs Unit. During my undercover activity, I generated evidence of police corruption for the Deputy Commissioner of Internal Affairs which was later corroborated by the "Mollen Commission" hearings which investigated police corruption.

Drug Cartel Conspiracy Against Occhipinti

(5) On January 14, 1992, Manuel De Dios, a close personal friend and world renown journalist executed the attached notarized affidavit, wherein, Mr. Dios corroborated the existence of a drug cartel conspiracy against Mr. Occhipinti. The orchestrators of the conspiracy were major Dominican organized crime figures connected with the "Dominican Federation" which is the front for the Dominican drug cartel. The Federation are the principle drug distributors in the United States for the Colombian cartel. Unfortunately, Mr. De Dios was assassinated before he could bring forward his sources who could prove the drug cartel conspiracy against Mr. Occhipinti. After Mr. De Dios' assassination, I too became fearful of my personal safety and never made public the evidence on the Occhipinti case.

Corroborating the Federal Conspiracy

(6) It should be noted that I personally assisted Mr. De Dios in this investigation of the Occhipinti case which corroborated the Federation conspiracy. In fact, I personally accompanied Mr. De Dios to the Washington Heights area where we secretly taped recorded Federation members who confirmed the drug cartel conspiracy. Those tapes still exist and can exonerate Mr. Occhipinti. In essence, Mr. Occhipinti was set up because of his increased enforcement efforts on Project Bodega which was exposing and hurting the Dominican Federation's criminal operations in New York City, which included illegal wire transfers, drug distribution, gambling operations, food stamp fraud, food coupon fraud, among other organized crime activity.

Criminals Protected By High-Level Government Officials

(7) My investigation also determined that Mr. Occhipinti was exposing a major money laundering and loan sharking operation relating to the Federation which was controlled by the Sea Crest Trading Company, of Greenwich, Connecticut. Sea Crest also maintains an office at 4750 Bronx River Parkway in the Bronx, New York.

Sea Crest was using the Capital National Bank in order to facilitate their money laundering operations. In 1993, Carlos Cordoba, the President of Capital National Bank was convicted in Federal Court at Brooklyn, New York for millions of dollars in money laundering and he received a token sentence of probation. My investigation confirmed that Sea Crest, as well as the Dominican Federation, are being politically protected by high ranking public officials who have received illegal political contributions which were drug proceeds. In addition, the operatives in Sea Crest were former CIA Cuban operatives who were involved in the "Bay of Pigs." This is one of the reasons why the intelligence community has consistently protected and insulated Sea Crest and the Dominican Federation from criminal prosecution.

Dominicans and Colombians Partners in Drugging America

(8) At present, there are nine major Colombian drug families which control drug operations in the New York City area. These drug families often referred to as the "Nine Kings." The Dominican Federation are part of their drug trafficking and money laundering operations. I possess documentary evidence, as well as video surveillance tapes of their drug operations. In addition, the New York City Police has investigative files to corroborate this fact. I have also uncovered substantial evidence of political and police corruption which has been intentionally ignored. In fact, it is my belief that former New York City Police Internal Affairs Commissioner Walter Mack, who I directly worked for, was intentionally fired because of his efforts to expose police corruption. I plan to make public this evidence to the United States Congress, as well as key members of the media in order to preserve this evidence in the event I am assassinated like Mr. De Dios.

Usual Department Of Justice Obstruction Of Justice

(9) It should also be noted that criminal Investigators Benjamin Saurino and Ronald Gardello of the U.S. Attorney's Office in Manhattan similarly ignored the evidence I brought forward to them on the Nine Kings and Dominican Federation. These two investigators were credited for convicting Mr. Occhipinti and they made it clear to me they didn't want to hear the evidence I had on the Federation which could have exonerated Mr. Occhipinti. They were only interested in corruption cases I had brought to their office. In fact, I recall a conversation, wherein, Investigator Saurino asked me about my involvement with Manuel De Dios and if I knew anything about the Occhipinti case. He then stopped and referred to Occhipinti in a derogatory manner, by saying "He's no *** good." Realizing his bias and lack of interest in investigating the Federation and Nine Kings, I changed the subject of conversation.

Rampant Corruption in New York Police Department

(10) In April 1995, I resigned from the New York City Police Department, Internal Affairs Unit after it became evident that my efforts to expose police corruption were being hampered. The same reason why I believe Commissioner Walter Mack was fired. It became evident to me that my life was in eminent danger and I could be easily set up on fabricated misconduct charges like Mr. Occhipinti. In fact, they brought departmen-

tal charges against me in 1995 and I won the case. The trial judge also admonished the department on the record for perjury. Often, I found myself isolated and in constant danger working alone in the worst neighborhoods of the city without a backup. Today, I possess substantial evidence to prove that the NYC Police Department media campaign to demonstrate that they could independently police themselves and route out corruption was simply a media ploy to avoid having an independent counsel to oversee their internal affairs unit. In reality, corruption is still rampant in the department and high ranking police brass are intentionally terminating viable corruption investigations in order to avoid future scandals exposed by the Mollen Commission. I also possess a consensually monitored tape conversation which implicates a high ranking police official who received bribes from the Dominican Federation.

Drug Cartels and U.S. Politicians

(11) I am willing to testify before Congress as to the allegations set forth in this affidavit. In addition, I am willing to turn over to Borough President Molinari and Congressman Traficant the documentary evidence I possess on the Dominican Federation, the Nine Kings and the Occhipinti drug cartel conspiracy. There are other important pieces of information relating to drug cartel operations and political corruption that I have not made public in this affidavit in order to protect my sources as well as ongoing media investigations that I am involved with. In addition, I am willing to submit to a polygraph examination to prove the veracity of my allegations.

William Acosta

Another Witness Came Forward—And Paid A Deadly Price

In the same Congressional record, Manuel De Dios, former editor of *El Diario/La Prensa* Newspaper and editor of a weekly newspaper known as *Canbyo*, gave an affidavit that was published several years later in the Congressional Record (September 27, 1996). The affidavit stated:

During the course of my work for Canbyo I understood to write an expose concerning criminal complaints brought against an Immigration and Naturalization Service Supervisory Special Agent named Joseph Occhipinti by various members of the Federation of Dominican Merchants and Industrialists of New York. During the course of my investigatory work in researching the article, I interviewed numerous individuals who are members of the Federation of Dominican Merchants and Industrialists of New York. These individuals confided to me that Mr. Occhipinti had been set up by the Federation and that the complaints against him were fraudulent. These individuals have indicated to me that they are in fear of their safety and as a result would not go public with this information. I would be more than willing to share my information with any law en-

forcement agencies or Courts concerned with these matters and would co-operate fully in any further investigations.

Expose DOJ-Protected Corruption: Pay the Consequences

In an all-too-common scenario befalling people who expose DOJ corruption, De Dios paid the price. He was gunned down and killed on March 11, 1992. His death would not have happened but for the DOJ conspiracy of coverups and obstruction of justice, an all-too-common consequence of their misconduct.

John F. Kennedy, Jr: Profile in Cowardice

An article in *The New American* had the title, "Profile In Cowardice." It described a prominent New York socialite who contacted Congressman James Traficant (December 2, 1993) and provided information on one of the DOJ's steps taken to frame Occhipinti. The witness was identified in the article as "A.R.," and identified as a friend of AUSA John F. Kennedy, Jr. That witness stated that during a June 11, 1991, conversation with Kennedy, and the night before Kennedy was to testify against Occhipinti, that Kennedy was concerned that he was being forced to testify for political reasons. He added that he was being used to prejudice the jury, and that he had never heard of the Occhipinti case. Occhipinti's defense team had the witness undergo a polygraph examination, which he passed for his truthfulness. The article stated in part:

He testified that Kennedy bemoaned the fact that the next day he would have to testify against an innocent man. According to J.R., Kennedy stated that he was being "forced" to testify for political reasons and that he was being "used" to prejudice the jury.

Dominican Republic Diplomat Supported Occhipinti

A *New American* article (February 21, 1994) described a witness, identified as "R.A.G," who held several diplomatic positions for the Dominican Republic, including that of Consul General and Ambassador to Jamaica, who gave two highly sensitive affidavits (August 19, 1993) that provided more details about the conspiracy against Occhipinti. One affidavit stated in part:

On or about the end of 1989, I was personally told by Dominican businessmen Jose Delio Marte, Silvio Sanchez, Pedro Allegria, and Ernesto Farbege that they needed my political assistance in eliminating former Immigration officer Joseph Occhipinti. They explained to me that Occhipinti was a threat to their illegal businesses, which included loan sharking, gambling, drug distribution, and the employment of illegal aliens.

In his second affidavit, he stated in part:

I have confirmed why government witness Jose Liberato, a complainant against Mr. Occhipinti at trial, had falsely testified against Mr. Occhipinti and participated in the conspiracy. Mr. Liberato, a bodega owner, is a major participant of Sea Crest Trading Company and its illegal activities.

In his affidavit he also named the person who delivered drug-related money from the Federation and Sea Crest to the Dinkins political campaign.

DOJ Witnesses Arrested Again

Most of the witnesses used by DOJ prosecutors against Occhipinti had criminal records. After the trial, they continued to engage in criminal activities and continued to be arrested. An example: *New York Daily News* headline

(June 17, 1993) read:

Vice Cops Bag 3 in Bribes. Two of the people named were brothers, Jose and Joaquin Checo, who had filed charges against Occhipinti and had been arrested by the New York Police Department for gambling and bribery offenses at their bodega. In the same article, New York Police Department spokesman, Raymond O'Donnell, referred to the two brothers as members of a Dominican organized crime organization known as The Federation.

"We're going to do to you like we did Occhipinti!"

The immigrants learn fast. As the brothers were being handcuffed, one of the police officers, Sgt. Frank Perez, heard an employee holler, "You can't get away with this. We're going to do to you like we did to Occhipinti!"

Occhipinti Describes What Happened

Occhipinti described during an October 11, 1997, telephone conversation the findings of his multi-agency task force while investigating criminal activities in New York while working with AUSA Louis Freeh:

Let me explain to you why things happened, in connection with my case. I had the connections, and why I think they prematurely fired Jim Fox, the FBI Director. There is a company called Sea Crest Trading Company in Greenwich, Connecticut. Now we know, and its been established that they've been the target of as many as ten federal and local investigations. And in each and every case, the investigations were ordered terminated by the Justice Department.

CIA, Capitol National Bank, and Dominican Organized Crime

The company was being run by certain Cubans who were involved in the Bay of Pigs. And they had, as part of their money laundering operations, they were dealing with Capitol National Bank in New York, being run by Carlos Cordoba, another CIA operative. I understand that, in Dominican organized crime, it's probably one of the most vicious ethnic crime groups in the United States.

Sea Crest, Dominican Federation, and Organized Crime

And what they do is, they basically intermingle and usually work hand in hand with the Cuban organized crime network, particularly in the gambling operations. So what happens, without realizing it, I stumbled into this Operation Bodega, never realizing that the Dominican bodegas that I was hurting was part of this Dominican Federation which is actually the front of an established Dominican cartel and that the fact that they were using in their money laundering operation, the Sea Crest Trading Company.

Top Expert on Dominican Organized Crime

I was the Chief of Immigration and Naturalization Service. I was working mostly drug cases, and I was probably the most expert on Dominican organized crime. Nevertheless, all in all, I thought that I was being set up simply because I was hurting Dominican organized crime and that I knew the federation was a very politically powerful organization. And I just believed the time that they went to Mayor David Dinkins, convinced him that I was a racist and that I was hurting their operations, and Dinkins, who attributed his win in the 1988 election due to the Dominican

Federation which is a front, called for a federal civil rights investigation.

Attorney For Organized Crime Network Former AUSA

Now what happened, I uncovered evidence into this cartel that I was investigating, that their chief legal counsel was a former Assistant United States Attorney in the southern district of New York, and that according to my source who is a credible informant and who was willing to wear a wire, she alleged that this former Assistant U.S. Attorney was the legal counsel for the Dominican Federation.

And he said to me, this guy's name was David Lawrence, who was chief of the criminal division. David Lawrence said to me, 'I want to interview this woman." So I brought her in. Not only was she credible, she actually had documents in her possession that could put this guy, this former Assistant U.S. Attorney and his partner, away in jail for a variety of drug trafficking, money laundering violations.

Prosecutor Leaking Evidence To Organized Crime

What happened is, a week after I brought her in, her information was leaked to this former assistant for whom she worked in that law firm saying, "I know what you did; my people told me, and the U.S. Attorney is trying to set me up, and he said he put a contract on Camarena." It's clear I went to the U.S. Attorney with viable evidence and he refused to work on it.

What they actually told me was, "Leave the investigation alone; leave it alone." Now at the time I simply said, well, you know what it is; the U.S. Attorney is very much concerned about their prestige. What happened was, in the southern district a year earlier, FBI had arrested an assistant U.S. Attorney for drug possession, and his name was Pearlmuttan.

DOJ Blocking Exposure of Crime Activities in New York

What I thought at the time was, well, they're blowing New York simply because they had a scandal two years earlier and they're trying to avoid a potential scandal, and they're only concerned about their image. But when David Lawrence told me to leave this investigation alone, I was angry. A New York City police officer was murdered and I'm on the trail of a major Dominican cartel. That's when I started my Operation Bodega, knowing that I wasn't going to get any support from the Justice Department.

NYC Prosecutor Circumventing DOJ Obstruction Of Justice

So I went over to Morgenthau's office and he was convinced that Operation Bodega not only would net the cartel but expose the money laundering operations as well as the alleged corruption. He assigned three assistant district attorneys to my case and within a ten-month period we began to develop substantial evidence not only on the Dominican federation but Sea Crest Trading Company.

Receiving Bribery Offers

And I knew I was getting close to the operation because two, actually three bribery offers were made to me and immediately I went back to the FBI, the supervisor in the corruption unit. And I told him everything I uncovered on Sea Crest and on this former federal prosecutor. And he was convinced; he wanted to do an undercover investigation. He was so con-

vinced that he actually assigned a case agent. And the goal was for me to accept bribes, set them up and take them down and squeeze them and find out who's corrupt.

What happened is, when we get to my meeting in the southern district of New York, which is the criminal division, I get told by them that the southern district would not go with the undercover operation. He said to me specifically, he said, "Something smells."

So I realized that several months before that they told me they didn't want to do Operation Esquire.

Drug Cartels Demanding Shutdown Of Drug Investigating Unit

I had worked previously in the corruption unit and I had some confidence in them, so when the Dominican Federation held their press conference on the steps of City Hall demanding that my operation be closed down and that I be investigated for federal civil rights investigation, at the time I didn't have knowledge of all the facts; I just simply thought I was hurting a drug cartel; they needed to try to make it into a racial issue with politicians, with the Republican thing, and that's what happened. So at that the pieces to the puzzle weren't being put together. What happened was, they simply thought that I would be prosecuted and convicted and be taken away. And no one would even listen to me. But what would ultimately happen was that I was a credible person, and every time the media investigated my case, they found out that I was innocent and that I had been set up by drug lords.

Drug Lords Controlling U.S. Attorney's Office

And that the drug lords influenced the U.S. Attorney's office to selectively prosecute me. Now we know that because several PD undercover operations were done where they went actually into the same bodegas who testified I conducted unlawful searches and capture them on national TV involved in criminal activity. What happened was, I was in prison, and the pressure was so much on the White House that they had to do something. My case was getting a lot of notoriety.

I asked, "What charges did they make?"

They charged me for federal civil rights violations. The first officer in American history to be charged under the federal civil rights with illegal consent search. The claim was, yes his signature was on the consent, but they claimed they didn't sign the consent form until after the search. The first officer to be caught; it's an administrative violation under the exclusionary rule. If a judge thought a search was illegal, they'd just throw the case out of court. I was the first one to ever be prosecuted. The bottom line was, President George Bush, under intense pressure and because of his relationship with Staten Island president Molinari told him there was so much evidence for my innocence, he gave me clemency—he didn't give me a full pardon but he gave me clemency and got me out of jail.

What happened was, in January I get my retirement because I had 22 years in the government, and I'm a credible witness. Very credible, and what everyone basically puts it up to is, this is an illustration of how powerful the struggles are in our United States, and secondly how they're able to manipulate the civil rights to their advantage. At that point I became not only hero to American law enforcement but even some of the civil rights groups have been convinced that my case was a clear case of how the drug cartel was using civil rights laws to their advantage. Right now I have a lot of friends, a lot of credibility. What I thought I could put together was the following.

Occhipinti Supported by FBI SAC Jim Fox

I started to realize when witnesses came forward that Jim Fox was one of my biggest supporters. While I was in jail, Jim Fox publicly stated that there was evidence of my innocence despite the fact that the FBI was refusing to release the evidence. What we believe happened was the following:

We believe, while I was in jail, the Justice Department conducted an investigation. And they cut Jim Fox out of the loop for one reason or another. We believe Jim Fox realized that I was being framed and he asked one of the agents who conducted the investigation what happened. We believe when he saw what happened he publicly announced he was to retire in a couple of months.

Motion for New Trial

Now when these public statements were made, we made an application for a new trial based on newly discovered evidence from the drug cartel. We specifically made mention that Jim Fox made public statements, and I know that the U.S. Attorney was very upset with him. Cause they called him down and they asked him to give a deposition saying that his public statements were taken out of context. He refused to do it, and he was fired; he was terminated about three months before his retirement.

"What's the status of that? Has he taken any legal action?"

Basically he left and became one of the heads of security for a major bank; he passed away about 3-4 months ago. Let me tell you what we uncovered. A major investigator for a clearing house that deals in food coupons; you know those coupons when you go shopping. He brought to my attention that terrorist groups were using coupons as a way to front international terrorism. He explained that it was a 200 million-dollar-a-year operation. And they were using bodega supermarkets. Sea Crest Trade company was to do the money laundering.

Bodegas as Clearing House for Criminal Activities

Most of your Middle East terrorist groups were using several ways to raise money for terrorism. One was food stamp fraud, the second was food coupons, and the third was pirating of films that was sold out of supermarket bodegas that was controlled by the Federation. And they were using the bodegas as a clearinghouse for Sea Crest Trading Company, which explains why I was getting them a little nervous. But he said to me, "Joe, you're missing the picture here. The Dominicans are involved with the Cubans, but don't you realize what really happened here?" And this is what he explained.

Bodega Money to Terrorist Groups

When Ben Jacobson began his investigation into the food stamp fraud and coupon fraud, he was the chief investigator for E. C. Nielson Company that administers food stamps in the coupon program. In his investi-

gation he said that what really was happening was that much of the coupon redemption would be concentrated at a little grocery store. And when he became suspicious that the monies were going to terrorist groups, he reported his findings to the FBI.

But what happened was, the President had given me clemency, and I knew that I had been set up. The evidence clearly showed it. We believed I had been set up solely by the Dominican drug lords and that I was easily prosecuted because I wasn't perceived as a team player because I was attempting to expose corruption. So what happened was, Ben Jacobson opened my eyes and he explained to me what happened. And he's a credible guy. Not only is Ben Jacobson a retired New York City detective; he's also a college professor that teaches at Rutgers University. He is also the chief investigator for E. C. Nielson Company. And this is what he proceeded to explain:

IRS Retaliation for Exposing CIA and Dominican Crime Activities

Ever since he started his investigation at Sea Crest, he became the focus for retaliation by the IRS and others; he was basically told to leave the investigation alone. He couldn't understand why. What he was able to connect was that Sea Crest, based on documents he obtained, they're called UCC's; Universal Commercial Code. Let me explain; if I lend you a thousand dollars I fill out a promissory note that you registered with the county clerk on a form that's called the CC. With this investigation he started to notice that many of the people who were tied into Sea Crest were from the Middle East, managing stores that he suspected, supermarkets, mini-markets, that he suspected had ties to terrorism. And he reported his findings to the FBI. He provided them evidence of the funding for terrorism. What happened was, the FBI, just like the other investigations by the IRS, were ordered by the Justice Department to terminate it. And this is why he believed that happened.

They needed a way, a mechanism to launder the money. So it was decided that they would bring in the Mujahedeen principals into the United States, set them up in mini-markets and supermarkets and utilize Sea Crest Trading Company as a way to funnel money to the Dominican Republic, and then back. And the money was earmarked for arms.

Coalition of Sea Crest, CIA, and Terrorist Groups

What happened, he thinks, is while the government may have had a legitimate reason for using Sea Crest Trading Company, which was being run by former CIA operatives, Cuban Nationals, they never realized that the terrorist groups were using the money. And when Ben Jacobson provides them with that intelligence and they closed it down because they were told to, we believe, the bombing of the World Trade Center resulted.

World Trade Center Bombing Funded By DOJ-Protected Groups

Now if you look at the convicted people on the World Trade Center Bombing, one fellow is Salan Abdel-Rahman. He owned a mini-market in Jersey City. If you pull the UCC [report], it comes back "Crest Trading Company." So what happened was, the Justice Department and the CIA were afraid that if this information was ever exposed, it would show that the FBI was alerted that these monies through the food and coupon fraud actually funded the bombing of the World Trade Center, and that the FBI failed to take any action. There would be a major scandal. Now we believe this is one of the reasons why Jim Fox knew what was happening. He was the one who spearheaded the entire FBI investigation into the bombing of the World Trade Center. So listen to this very carefully.

DOJ Shuts Down Congressional Investigation

Congressman Traficant begins a series of inquiries into Sea Crest under the Freedom of Information Act, and almost immediately they close it down. They refuse to give any information, quoting national security. So what I think we have here, the real scandal is, the CIA realized the federal agency was being set up in order to protect their operation, they allowed me to go to jail.

CIA Funding World Trade Center Terrorists

But the real story was that the CIA used Sea Crest Trading in order to facilitate money for Mujahedeen during which time it inadvertently got into the hands of suspected terrorists. They were alerted of that fact; they failed to take any action; the bombing occurred, and they've got to do damage control. They were afraid if the American public learned about this it would be a major scandal.

Drug Cartels Funded Clinton's Election Campaign

To further compound this now, what's been happening with the White House? We've now learned that the Dominican Federation is a front for cartels and Sea Crest Trading Company was behind many, many fund raisers for the Clinton-Gore campaign. Now this is published in the New American magazine. What I'm saying here is published also in the Congressional Record. I think this guy Richard Taus, and what he says, was accurate and what was happening in the New York FBI office.

CIA Influence Over the Media

Now the guy who broke the story, the guy who came up with the evidence, is a reporter for the New York Post by the name of Al Guart. But the paper refused to print it; apparently the CIA must have a lot of influence in the media. The Post refused to allow him to break the story. There's another guy, Karl Ross. He does investigative reports for some of the largest magazines and newspapers, and also the Washington Post. And they're refusing to allow him to break his story on Sea Crest. The point I'm trying to make here is, this is what was happening. This is what we could prove. That viable local and federal Investigations into the Sea Crest Trading Company have been suspiciously terminated by the Justice Department. Why?

I just wanted to let you know that the Sea Crest Trading Company appears to have been a CIA operation, it was being run by the Cuban mob that was involved in the Bay of Pigs. We know their connection with the Colombian and Dominican cartels. But as I said, apparently that was used as a front to money launder the money for the Mujahedeen when, during that process, monies were actually diverted to actual terrorist groups and the FBI knew about it, was told not to do anything and then, when the bombing occurred, there was a big scandal there.

Occhipinti Today

And how did Occhipinti fare after his many years of dedicated government service? After 22 years of federal service, after receiving many awards, he was forced to retire on a disability pension. He suffered from post-stress trauma, hypertension, heart disease, gastro-intestinal disorders, surely brought on or worsened by his years of fighting crime and government coverups. Occhipinti wrote:

I will always cherish my many law enforcement accomplishments and my efforts to protect our borders from drugs. Unfortunately, I realize now that my dedication to duty was in vain. I was very naive. I believed in the criminal justice system and the alleged war against drugs. I realize now that we have lost the war against drugs.

Moreover, how politically powerful foreign drug lords are in the United States. I was getting too close to the major players in the drug world and had to be eliminated. Fortunately, I wasn't murdered like journalist Manuel De Dios. Instead, the drug lords sent a more powerful threat to law enforcement; they can now manipulate and misuse to their advantage, important civil rights laws that can imprison and intimidate dedicated law enforcement officers.

At present, due to my landmark civil rights prosecution, which never involved police brutality, racial bias or corruption, drug interdiction in many jurisdictions has been terminated. The police assigned to drug interdiction often rely upon consent searches and will not subject themselves to possible imprisonment and loss of a career due to an allegation of an unlawful search and seizure. My only regret is that I took away precious time from my family and subjected my loved ones to tremendous hardships simply because I wanted to do my sworn duty.

Nostalgia Writing Of Occhipinti's Tragic Downfall

It has been sad to write about what powerful and corrupt people have inflicted upon Occhipinti and his family. It reminded me of what I went through, first as a highly qualified FAA inspector assigned to the most senior program at United Airlines while it experienced a series of major air disasters, and then later what I experienced as I sought to expose other forms of government corruption. It is very probable that Occhipinti and I, and others like us, were fools, trying to protect a public who didn't care to get informed or show any responsibility.

IRS After Those Who Wrote Stories About Occhipinti's Case

During a discussion with Occhipinti in March 1999, he said that almost every reporter who exposed the DOJ corruption has had the IRS after him.

Radio and Television Appearances to Inform the People

Upon being released from prison, Occhipinti appeared as guest on several hundred radio and television shows, exposing the crime and drug cartels and their political influence. His grueling schedule caused him to collapse on board an airliner (November 21, 1993) followed by four days of hospitalization. Since 1978, I had appeared as guest on over 3000 radio and television shows and it can be especially tiring, especially when on a tour and doing seven or more shows a day. Worse, discovering that no one does anything with the information. Like talking to sheep.

Protection of Ethnic Crime Groups

In one of his writings, Occhipinti explained some of the problems associated with the United States' attempts to fights powerful ethnic crime groups:

I have seen dozens of viable federal and local investigations into Dominican organized crime groups prematurely terminated by federal authorities. Why? In July 1997, the FBI published a confidential intelligence report on Dominican organized crime operations in the United States, which confirm what I have known for the past twenty years. There has been much speculation that many of these investigations were prematurely terminated due to possible national security reasons, or maybe, the principals were government informants that had to be protected.

It is important to note that the biggest crime threat facing the American public is the growth of international drug syndicates in the United States. Foreign drug lords and organized crime have adapted very well in setting up criminal operations in the United States for a variety of reasons. Foreign drug lords and ethnic organized crime groups have learned the essence of American politics and know how to manipulate the political and criminal justice systems.

Dominican Cartels Principal Distributor of Colombian Drugs

For instance, U.S. law enforcement sources have developed convincing evidence that the Dominican drug cartel is the principal distributors of narcotics in the United States on behalf of the Colombian drug cartel. In addition, they are credited for laundering billions of dollars in drug proceeds both here and abroad. Yet, we rarely see media reports that publicize Dominican organized crime. Why?

Dominican Drug Cartels Politically Powerful

Many ask me why the Dominican cartel has become so politically powerful in the United States. I explain that they will often operate as a legitimate political action group, often making unlawful political contributions to elected officials and having become successful in conducting widespread election fraud. Clearly, the ability to deliver campaign contributions and needed votes to win an election can understandably influence most political candidates.

Organized Ethnic Crime Groups

Hopefully, you can better understand why foreign drug cartels have become politically powerful in the United States. It also explains that when ethnic organized crime groups become the targets of law enforcement scrutiny, they seek immediate political intervention in hopes of terminating a criminal investigation or inquiry. In many cases, elected officials are successful in influencing authorities to terminate a criminal investigation by often alleging officer misconduct, or that the investigation was racially motivated.

Most Drug Crimes Committed By Organized Ethnic Crime Groups

In the United States, statistics will show that the majority of organized crime activity in the United States is being committed by organized ethnic crime groups: have seen dozens of viable federal and local investigations into Dominican organized crime groups prematurely terminated by federal authorities. Why? In July 1997, the FBI published a confidential in-

telligence report on Dominican organized crime operations in the United States, which confirm what I have known for the past twenty years. There has been much speculation that many of these investigations were prematurely terminated due to possible national security reasons, or maybe, the principals were government informants that had to be protected.

It is important to note that the biggest crime threat facing the American public is the growth of international drug syndicates in the United States. Foreign drug lords and organized crime have adapted very well in setting up criminal operations in the United States for a variety of reasons. Foreign drug lords and ethnic organized crime groups have learned the essence of American politics and know how to manipulate the political and criminal justice systems.

Most Drug Crimes Committed by Ethnic Crime Groups

In the United States, statistics will show that the majority of organized crime activity in the United States is being committed by organized ethnic crime groups. Yet, the Justice Department's "Organized Crime Strike Forces" continues to target and prosecute traditional Italian organized crime groups, which represent less than one percent of organized crime activity in the United States. Why? Is it because it has become "politically" incorrect to target these other ethnic crime groups? Or, are these foreign drug lords being protected by elected officials or the intelligence community?

Ethnic Groups Taking Over Drug and Other Criminal Activities

Partly because of naïveté, partly because of American's gullibility, partly because of Americans who are willing to sabotage America's interest for money from special groups, ethnic groups are taking over all types of criminal activities that make all of America suffer. Even the Japanese version of the U.S. Mafia: "yakuza." has taken advantage of America's love affair with drugs. Many Colombian and Mexican drug traffickers, and the yakuza, set up businesses along the Mexican-U.S. border after NAFTA came into being. Little is known in the United States about yakuza activities, or even its existence. Years ago, CIA agent Gunther Russbacher described his dealings in the Midwest with the yakuza, most of which I left out of my books for another day. It was reported to me that a company with packing houses in Mexico along the U.S. border, Fruitiko, is associated with the Japanese yakuza.

CIA-DOJ Funding, Training, Arming, and Protecting Terrorists

Evidence not publicized by the Justice Department, Congress, or the mainstream media shows a relationship between the World Trade Center bombing and the criminal activities government agents sought to report, which DOJ employees blocked.

Money to fund the terrorist bombing of the World Trade Center came from the very same criminal activities that Occhipinti and other government agents sought to halt: and DOJ employees protected! This conduct by the people and culture in the Department of Justice made possible the bombing of the Center, and these acts included the shutdown of various investigations, the sham charges against Occhipinti, the aiding and abetting of crime groups that I have documented in all of my books.

Financing World Trade Center Bombing
With Bodega Food Coupon Fraud and Drug Money

A New Jersey news service, *Golden State News Service*, distributed to newspapers (October 1995) the following in-depth interview with several key New York area law enforcement officers relating to the bombing of the World Trade Center:

The terrorist bombing of the World Trade Center was financed with drug and other racket money laundered and leveraged through small ethnic grocery stores. What's more, terrorists even now are siphoning off more such funds. The real leader in the World Trade Center bombing has been allowed to flee capture, and all this is happening under the apparent protection of the Center Intelligence Agency...

According to Jacobson, it was the monies generated from the Sea Crest food coupon redemption fraud scheme that financed the bombing of the World Trade Center according to Jacobson, Sea Crest is suspected of being the source of a two hundred-million-dollar a year food coupon redemption scheme ... Jacobson alleges that Sea Crest has been protected by the Justice Department because of an alleged CIA operation that utilized that firm....

Occhipinti says he and Jacobson, acting independently of each other, have tried repeatedly to interest various federal state and even local law enforcement authorities to follow through on investigations of Sea Crest. "But always the investigations go nowhere." Lenny Lemmer, a detective sergeant with the New York City Police Department, said recently in a sworn statement that he has encountered similar dead-ends in probing Sea Crest and its alleged drug cartel connections...

Lemmer said he was called to meet several times with FBI agents and federal prosecutors, who tried to intimidate him into abandoning any leads he might uncover about Sea Crest or anything exculpatory about Occhipinti. Lemmer said he was aware of "concrete evidence" about alleged Sea Crest money laundering activities in Bogota, Colombia, and conveyed this information to an FBI agent.

In a recent interview, Jacobson confirmed that proceeds from coupon fraud paid for the World Trade Center bombing, and that Sea Crest had received redemption checks signed over by Middle Eastern and Dominican grocers suspected of participating in such fraud. The conspiracy is so loose that money may be siphoned off to terrorists without all parties involved in the original loan-shark-coupon scams being aware of it, according to investigators.

History of Funding Terrorists and Paying the Price Afterwards

The United States funneled over three *billion* dollars to the Mujahedeen in the 1980s, and provided training in the use of weapons and terrorist activities. This was done despite the known hatred of the Mujahedeen for the United States due to its one-sided support for Israel. The knowledge that these acquired terrorist tactics and weapons would eventually be used against the United States was ignored.

CIA Fronts In the United States Funneled Money to Terrorists

Since 1990, my CIA sources explained how Sea Crest—a CIA front—laundered money to obtain military equipment and provide training for the dered money to obtain military equipment and provide training for the Muja-hedeen in Afghanistan during the 1980s. Occhipinti's task force discovered that the funding of terrorists existed in the 1990s, and that some of the money was going to terrorists in the United States.

A key figure in one of the terrorist groups was Sheik Omar Abdel-Rahman, who was convicted by a New York jury for his role in planning the bombing of the World Trade Center building. He was sentenced to life in prison and nine co-conspirators were sentenced to long prison terms.

CIA Granting Visa to Known Terrorist

Despite his known terrorist activities, including his involvement in the plot to assassinate Egypt's Anwar Sadat, a CIA agent in the U.S. Consulate office in Khartoum, Sudan, issued a one-year visa for Sheik Omar to enter the United States in May 1990. He arrived in New York in July, and a few months later the State Department revoked the visa, advising the U.S. Immigration and Naturalization Service (INS) of this fact. However, high-level pressure caused the INS to issue a green card to Sheik Omar several months later.

The people who funded Sheik Omar's entry into the United States included Mustafa Shalabi (Director of Alkifah, a support fund for Mujahedeen fighters based in Brooklyn); Muslim Brotherhood member and CIA asset from Afghanistan, Mahmud Abouhalima, and El Sayyid Nosair, an Egyptian. They had received training, funding, and arms from the CIA.

Besides receiving CIA training, Nosair and Abouhalima had been earlier trained by the terrorist, Abu Nidal. The U.S. Army in 1989 sent Sergeant Ali A. Mohammed to Jersey City to give training to recruits for the Mujahedeen. Among those receiving this training were Abouhalima and Nosair. Nosair, Abouhalima, and Omar were later convicted of waging terrorist warfare in the United States.

FBI Coverup of Terrorist Activities

Nosair was suspected of the 1990 murder of Rabbi Meir Kahane, a Jewish militant in New York City. Following this murder, the FBI obtained a search warrant and seized terrorist material from his Jersey City apartment. Included in this material were bomb-making material, a list of people marked for death, which included Rabbi Kahane, bomb-making instructions, and pictures of targeted buildings, including, would you believe, the World Trade Center!

The FBI made no arrests, and withheld this information from New York City prosecutors seeking to arrest those responsible for Kahane's murder. This withholding of evidence played a key role in his December 20, 1991 acquittal.

DOJ Coverup Helped Plan Airliner Bombings

Funding Nosair's defense were funds from criminal activities associated with Sea Crest Trading Company, the same CIA-related operation that funded the bomb components and their assembly. Many of these activities were under the supervision of Ramzi Yousef, an Afghan terrorist who came to the United States into Sheik Omar's group in 1992.

Yousef was convicted in late 1996 of involvement in a number of attempted bombings of U.S. aircraft in the Far East. The plan was to place bombs on over a dozen commercial airliners which would have killed, if successful several thousand people. Also assisting in protecting the terrorists was New York judge William Schlesinger, who granted the terrorist's attorney

William Kunstler extraordinary latitude while hamstringing the prosecution.

World Trade Center Bombing Made Possible by DOJ Coverups

Without funding from Sea Crest Trading Company, and without Justice Department personnel blocking prosecution of Dominicans drug traffickers and Sea Crest, it is very probable there would not have been the money to fund the terrorists. The bomb blast killed six people, injured over a thousand others, and did over $500 million in damage in the February 26, 1993, World Trade Center bombing.

The imprisonment of Sheik Omar, following the World Trade Center bombing, did not destroy the group's ability to conduct further terrorist acts in the United States.

"Dominican Drug Money May Have Helped Elect Our President"

Reports indicated that U.S. and Dominican Republic politicians were receiving substantial money from Capital National Bank, Sea Crest Trading Company, and the Dominican Federation. An in-depth *The New American* article (April 28, 1997) was titled: "Dominican drug money may have helped elect our President," and said in part:

A report from Puerto Rico suggests that the Clinton White House has accepted drug-tainted contributions linked to the Dominican Republic's radical Dominican Revolutionary Party (PRD). PRD members ... made campaign donations last September during a Democratic National Committee fund-raiser at Coogan's Irish Pub in Washington Heights [in New York City]. PRD members Simon Diaz and Pablo Espinal supported the campaign of U.S. President Clinton....

Both Diaz and Espinal reportedly posed for pictures with Vice President Al Gore, according to PRD leaders. Diaz is vice president of a New York City chapter of the PRD and president of a group of party-affiliated businesses. He is also currently under investigation by the Drug Enforcement Administration (DEA) and various other anti-narcotics agencies with regard to the PRD's "alleged nexus with international drug cartels" as El Vocero reported....

Furthermore, although U.S. federal officials were aware of the links between PRD and the drug cartels, "for reasons that remain unclear, these officials exerted pressure to derail active investigations in the matter."

Despite his known drug and crime connections, Jose Francisco Pena-Gomez, the PRD's leader and Dominican Republic presidential candidate was President Bill Clinton's choice in the Dominican elections held in 1994 and 1996. This recommendation followed the campaign contributions received by Clinton and Gore.

Luck Of President Bill Clinton and Al Gore

On May 10, 1998, another potential witness and threat against President Bill Clinton and Vice President Al Gore died. Former Dominican Republic presidential candidate Jose Pena-Gomez was a potential threat to them because of the drug money Gomez and his drug-related groups gave to the Clinton-Gore campaign and because of the Clinton administration's protection of Dominican drug trafficking and other crimes. Pena-Gomez died from pulmonary edema.

PARALLEL DISCOVERIES IN PENNSYLVANIA

Four agents from the Pennsylvania Bureau of Narcotics Investigation office (BNI) were experiencing similar problems with Dominican drug traffickers, high-level coverups, and retaliation. Agents John R. McLaughlin, Charles A. Micewski, Dennis J. McKeefery, and Edward Eggles, working as a team, discovered evidence of widespread criminal activities by the Dominican Revolutionary Party and Dominican crime figures. They also suffered retaliation that insured the continuation of the drugs and related crimes.

The BNI narcotic agents discovered that drug money was gathered and distributed at fund raisers held in Pennsylvania and that various government agencies were actively aware of these facts. They also discovered drug money funneled to U.S. politicians and to the U.S.-backed candidate for the presidency of the Dominican Republic, Jose Francisco Pena Gomez, who was being supported by the Clinton Administration.

Ties To Colombian Drug Traffickers

McLaughlin described what he found about Colombian connections:

While at intelligence meeting, I received a document from Interpol that described an organization of Dominican drug traffickers with ties to the Cali cartel in Colombia dating back to at least 1991 and also documents hundreds of kilos of cocaine seized as well as approximately 100 people either arrested or having outstanding arrest warrants. This organization has ties to the Dominican Revolutionary Party headed by Jose Francisco Pena-Gomez who was being backed by the U.S. Department of State in the last election.

Pennsylvania Attorney General Protecting Drug Traffickers

On May 10, 1996, McLaughlin notified the Deputy Attorney General of a major heroin shipment due to arrive from New York and a large amount of drug-money being laundered. Harrisburg Attorney General's office refused to allow a bust to occur. The surveillance team was called off and the heroin sale occurred that evening at 7:45 p.m., with Dominicans taking back to New York over $100,000. Shortly thereafter, over 116 overdoses from heroin were reported from using the heroin brand, "Dead Presidents." Numerous drug overdoses and deaths were reported from using another form of Dominican heroin called "Super Buck." BNI agents were ordered not to interfere with these sales which were occurring at various Philadelphia street corners.

Dropping Charges Against 85 Drug Traffickers

McLaughlin was told that from April 16 to November 19, 1996, the Philadelphia district attorney's office dismissed 85 defendants who were caught with $879,000 worth of heroin, $47,000 worth of crack, $148,000 worth of cocaine, and the confiscation of large sums of money, vehicles and weapons.

In addition to protecting the major drug trafficking, this sent a message to other government agents that they should not investigate any of the Dominican drug traffickers, drug-money launderers, or drug-money-related political contributions.

Retaliatory Removal That Protected Drug Crimes

Shortly thereafter (April 16, 1996), Arnold Gordon, First Deputy District Attorney for Philadelphia, met with the Attorney General and charged that there was a problem with the BNI agents in the Philadelphia office. This was followed by a series of adverse actions against the four agents that halted their drug investigations into the politically-connected drug traffickers.

The Pennsylvania attorney general's office took McLaughlin off drug cases on the sham excuse that McLaughlin made a grammatical error on an affidavit. McLaughlin referred in an affidavit to "the" informant instead of "an" informant, an error that was meaningless in light of the details in the report, and could be made by anyone without any unfavorable results. It was clear; the Pennsylvania attorney general's office was protecting drug traffickers from arrest by state police officers!

Another Example of Legal Fraternity Misconduct

On January 13, 1997, a confidential informant (CI 902-96) told BNI agents that a prominent defense attorney, Guy Sciolla, was telling his Dominican clients to falsely report that BNI narcotic agents skimmed money from them when they were arrested. This was the same as one of the two charges Dominican drug traffickers made against Occhipinti. They must have learned from that to use the same tactic against other government agents. McLaughlin reported this to the District Attorney's office. Again, the Pennsylvania prosecutor refused to act against the attorney.

Fearing For the Life of an Informant

During a BNI meeting at Philadelphia headquarters (March 27, 1996) attended by CIA Agent Dave Lawrence, McLaughlin and Regional Director John Sunderhauf, Lawrence wanted the name of one of BNI's key inside informants who was disclosing highly sensitive information about Dominican drug trafficking. Recognizing that the state attorney general's office was blocking the investigation and prosecution of known drug traffickers, McLaughlin, fearing for the life of the informant, refused to reveal the informant's identity.

FBI Pressuring Informant To File False Affidavit

McLaughlin reported (July 8, 1997) that a Confidential Informant (Nr. 910-95) called BNI agents about FBI agents from the Federal Corruption Probe Task Force pressuring him to sign an affidavit containing derogatory statements about BNI agents that weren't true.

Retaliatory Reassignment—Oh How I Know the Problem!

In May 1996, State Attorney General Tom Corbett announced that McLaughlin and the three other BNI agents working on Dominican-related cases would be reassigned and would not get their regular jobs back. Despite the agents' request for information as to what they had done wrong, no reason was given. They were reassigned and given menial and often degrading tasks. I know the tactic; while I was with the FAA, reporting very serious air safety and criminal violations and a culture of corruption among its mid-management personnel, related to a series of fatal airline crashes, I was transferred to an undesirable assignment. My predecessor on that same problem, who reported similar air safety and criminal violations associated with crashes at United Airlines—one of which was the world's worst—was also transferred. His destination was Puerto Rico, a not very desirable location. In both cases, United Airlines management personnel bragged that they were responsible for our transfers.

On June 3, 1996, the BNI agents were told that they could no longer get information from the New York DEA office, thereby depriving the BNI of important drug-related information. (And also vice versa.) On July 18, 1996, the Pennsylvania district attorney's office advised the narcotic agents that the office would accept no more cases from them. On August 21, 1997, U.S. Customs agent John Malandros told McLaughlin that he was ordered to drop the investigation into the Revolutionary Dominican Party.

Media Aiding and Abetting Drug Traffickers and Coverups

Within a few days, the media started printing and airing a series of stories critical of the narcotic agents and protective of the drug traffickers and government retaliation and coverups. On April 23, 1996, Philadelphia's *Channel 3 News* did a lead story comparing the BNI agents to a group of Philadelphia police officers who created false crimes and wrongfully accused people in the 39th Precinct. That misleading television story was followed by others, including derogatory stories in the *Philadelphia Inquirer* and the *Philadelphia Daily News*.

For reasons unknown to the agents, Supervisor Lou Gentile in the Pennsylvania attorney general's headquarters in Philadelphia, ordered the narcotic agents not to correct the false media stories. These media sources had enough access to insiders to know the true story. They chose to mouth the official government line. Former Attorney General Tom Corbett told agents to "take it on the chin," and that he wouldn't correct the false media stories.

ACLU Protecting the Criminals

ACLU attorneys stated that they intended to seek monetary damages for the Dominicans arrested by the BNI agents. A liberal Democrat, State Senator Vince Fumo from Philadelphia, urged convicted Dominican drug dealer Felix Torres to seek vengeance against the BNI agents: "Sue them, bankrupt them, take their houses from them. That's the only time they're going to get the message."

Reporting the Problems to Senate Investigators

McLaughlin described these activities to investigators from the Senate Intelligence Committee, including chief counsel John Bellinger, Janice Kephart, and Al Cummings. He informed Randy Scheunemann on the staff of the National Security Advisor. Year after year, the same malfeasance, nonfeasance, coverups, obstruction of justice, you name it!

McLaughlin called Senator Arlen Specter's office (October 15, 1996) concerning the Dominican Republic drug trafficking and the Justice Department's protection of their drug activities. The Senate Select Committee on Intelligence asked McLaughlin to testify (behind closed doors) about the drug trafficking and other criminal activities, and the obstruction of justice at the state and federal levels.

Obstructing Congressional Investigation into Drug Trafficking

Seeking to prevent McLaughlin from testifying about the criminal activities and their coverups to Congress, the Pennsylvania attorney general's office sent him a memo barring him from testifying (November 7, 1996). The attorney general also sent a fax to Senator Specter that McLaughlin was not to appear before the Senate Intelligence Committee. No reaction from Specter.

Threats if He Testified Before Congress

John Kelly, Regional Director for the Pennsylvania Attorney General office, threatened McLaughlin with termination if he testified before Congress. Under federal law, this threat was a criminal act. (Title 18 USC Section 1505, 1512, 1513 and the related obstruction of justice statutes)

McLaughlin *did testify* in executive session (secret from the public) to the U.S. Senate Select Committee on Intelligence (January 29, 1997). No action was taken, despite the serious implications of the testimony.

No actions were taken by Congress when Occhipinti and his group described the serious problems, or the Pennsylvania agents, or the many others described within these pages and my other books. Members of Congress had years earlier become criminally implicated in the underlying crimes, including drug trafficking, by their pattern of coverups.

Earlier Reports Of Drug-Related Corruption
In Pennsylvania Attorney General's Office

Corruption and obstruction of justice in Pennsylvania's top law enforcement agency existed for years. Reference is made to a friend of many years, Darlene Novinger, who is described elsewhere within these pages. She was an undercover operative working with several government agencies investigating drug-related crimes in the Pennsylvania and Florida areas.

Filing A Civil Rights Complaint Against
Government Officials and Drug Traffickers

In response to the obstruction of justice and retaliatory actions by Pennsylvania and federal officials, the four agents filed a lawsuit in late 1997 in the U.S. District Court for the Middle District of Pennsylvania under the Civil Rights Act and as a *Bivens* complaint. The complaints, filed by Pennsylvania attorneys Don Bailey from Harrisburg and Samuel Stretton from West Chester, charged the defendants with conduct that was criminal, subversive, and related to aiding and abetting the smuggling of drugs into the United States. The introductory statement in the Complaint stated in part:

This is a civil rights complaint brought to redress, inter alia, the deprivation of the plaintiffs' federally guaranteed interests in free speech and property. This is also a Bivens' complaint, the gravamen of which is that a Dominican drug organization, through the protection of certain persons in the State Department and the CIA, was effective in having the plaintiffs' law enforcement efforts stopped and their careers destroyed.

The plaintiffs ... began gathering evidence on the PRD, a Dominican political party supported by the United States, which indicated that illegal drugs were being prolifically sold at will in the United States to our Black and Hispanic populations. This money was being put into American elections .... Plaintiffs contend that they discovered a highly organized Dominican group organized as the Revolutionary Dominican Party (PRD), a political party seeking power in the Dominican Republic, that was, and is, protected and sanctioned, unlawfully, by agencies of the United States government, to include the CIA and the State Department, enabling the Dominicans to distribute illegal drugs at will to the Black and Hispanic populations of the Eastern Seaboard.

Plaintiffs also allege that in furtherance of the unlawful policy of protecting the large-scale distributors of illegal narcotics to largely captive center city populations, the defendants have utilized the offices of the United States Attorney for the Eastern District of Pennsylvania, and the FBI, to pursue an oppressive threatening investigation of the plaintiffs in an effort to destroy their Credibility and silence them.

These tactics include the ferreting out of plaintiffs' information sources so that they may be silenced [killed] through the mechanism of a federal grand jury. They ask this Court to appoint, or urgently request, a special prosecutor, independent of the Justice Department and either political party, to investigate the coverup they allege in order that they and some of their sources can be saved from more abuses ... ask this court to issue an order forcing federal authorities to protect Confidential Informant "P-Man," 902-96, who is now known to them, immediately.

General Allegations

In the Complaint, the four narcotic agents charged that the defendants in various combinations engaged in conspiracies to:

* Block government agents from halting the flow of illegal drugs into the United States.

* Allow the flow of illegally procured money from the sale and distribution of drugs in the United States into the political coffers of Francisco Pena Gomez of the PDR in the Dominican.

* Prevent disclosure and/or further discovery by the plaintiffs of the flow of illegally procured money from the sale and distribution of drugs by the PRD to black and Hispanic Americans.

* Discredit the plaintiffs in order to destroy their credibility and thus their ability to participate in the prosecution of drug traffickers.

* Protect the proceeds (money) of Dominican drug dealers and traffickers from exposure and prosecution.

* Protect the government conspirators, both named and unnamed, from criminal prosecution for their role in aiding and abetting the illegal sale and distribution of drugs in the United States.

"Dominicans Now Dominant in East Coast Drug Trade"

A mid-1998 *New York Times* article was titled, "Dominicans Now Dominant in East Coast Drug Trade." Department of Justice personnel have played a major role in bringing this about.

Undercover Agent Speaks Out

On December 12, 1994, James Ridgway de Szigethy executed an affidavit admitting that Sea Crest had been a CIA operation, a fact that he had learned from his activities as an informant for the Naval Intelligence Service, as well as from his CIA associates.

De Szigethy also revealed that the assassination of Prince Chitresh "Teddy" Khedker in New York City was committed by CIA operative George Cobo. According to De Siegethy, the prince was a CIA operative involved in the Sea Crest operation in Canada. Cobo was a Cuban national trained by the CIA. De Szigethy provided Congressman Traficant with other affidavits and documents regarding Sea Crest and the Occhipinti conspiracy. DeSzigethy was previously polygraphed with respect to another affidavit he executed and found to be truthful.

DOJ Drops Criminal Investigation of Drug Fighters

U.S. Attorney Michael R. Stiles issued a statement (February 18, 1999) announcing the closing of its investigation into suspected criminal activities against—would you believe—the four Pennsylvania narcotic agents! No mention of any investigation into the drug traffickers and the evidence accumulated against them.

Gravity of the Implications

The Occhipinti and McLaughlin cases provide prima facie evidence of widespread drug and other criminal activities involving a segment of the population largely composed of immigrants to the United States. Key people in this group had connections to the CIA. There were repeated coverups and obstruction of justice by almost every level of the state and federal criminal justice system, and a pattern of retaliation against those few government agents with the courage and integrity to carry out the responsibilities of their jobs.

Government Agents Form Group to Protect Against High-Level Retaliation and Right to Perform Their Legal Responsibilities

A group was formed to bring together government agents who suffered the type of retaliation suffered by Occhipinti, McLaughlin and others, called the National Police Defense Foundation, with its home office in Washington, D.C., and incorporated in New Jersey. The purpose of the association was to protect the rights of law-enforcement personnel and the public; to provide assistance, services, and counseling for law-enforcement personnel. Occhipinti is the executive director of the foundation. (National Police Defense Foundation, 1422 K Street NW, Washington, DC 20005. Web site: www.umm.com/npdf)

CHAPTER SIX

DEA COMPLICITY

Federal control of drugs goes back many years. The Federal Bureau of Narcotics (FBN) was established in 1930. Another agency to fight drugs was established in 1966, the Bureau of Drug Abuse Control (BDAC) within the Food and Drug Administration. In 1968, the FBN and BDAC were consolidated into the Bureau of Narcotics and Dangerous Drugs (BNDD) in the Department of Justice. In 1970 Congress passed the Drug Abuse Prevention and Control Act which consolidated various drug-control legislation. Title II of the Act was known as the Controlled Substance Act (CSA) and this gave Congress the authority to regulate interstate commerce relating to drugs.

This act also placed drugs into various categories based upon the dangers, the potential for abuse, and also a category for legitimate medical use. Other government agencies had drug-related responsibilities, including the U.S. Customs Service, which had a drug investigations unit and so did the FBI.

In 1973, the various government agencies with drug responsibilities were consolidated in the Department of Justice division known as the Drug Enforcement Administration (DEA). The DEA is the only government agency whose sole function is to fight drugs. U.S. Customs still has this function, but it is combined with other responsibilities and is primarily focused on drugs crossing the borders. Under its dual responsibilities, the FBI retains responsibility for investigating drug-related offenses. The responsibilities of the DEA can be listed as follows:

* Investigation and initiation of prosecution of drug law violators.
* Coordination of a national drug intelligence system in cooperation with federal, state, local and foreign officials.
*Enforcement of the Controlled Substances Act.

DEA Air Wing

The DEA has an air wing which started in 1971 under the DEA's predecessor agency, the Bureau of Narcotics and Dangerous Drugs. The Office of Aviation Operations has over 100 aircraft of all sizes. The Air Wing headquarters had been at Addison Airport, north of Dallas, and then moved to Alliance Airport at Fort Worth.

60–Minutes TV Show On Government-Protected Drug Trafficking

During a *60-Minutes* television program (November 21, 1993) several DEA officials and agents revealed serious problems within the Drug Enforcement Administration. They described the CIA's smuggling of large quantities of cocaine into the United States, the CIA's "contacts" with Colombian drug traffickers, and the obstruction of justice by U.S. officials. Robert Bonner, a former head of the Drug Enforcement Administration, and Annabelle Grimm, a DEA agent in Caracas, Venezuela, revealed drug trafficking that was protected against prosecution by Justice Department and DEA officials.

In one instance described by Bonner and Grimm, over 2,200 pounds of cocaine were brought into the United States with the help of the CIA's station chief, James Campbell and CIA agent Mark McFarlin. Bonner and Grimm explained how CIA agents blocked DEA agents from stopping the shipment by going directly to the CIA's top command in Washington.

Appearing on the show with Bonner and Grimm was General Ramon Guillen Davila of the Venezuelan National Guard, explaining that drugs were regularly shipped into the United States by the CIA. He described a 3,300-pound load that was so huge it would not fit into the Boeing 707 cargo door. He stated that the drug trafficking was approved by the CIA. He also stated that he had immunity and therefore was able to appear on the *60 Minutes* program without being arrested.

Ooops—Sorry, A Mistake

The CIA, made aware of the *60-Minutes* show ahead of time, quickly issued a statement (November 19) implying that the drug shipment was an accident rather than an intentional act (*New York Times*, November 20, 1993). Many people, and much planning, were required to smuggle this huge quantity of nearly pure cocaine into the United States and bring about its sale; it was no accident! My CIA contacts laughed at the CIA's excuse. They recognized that the 3,300 pounds of cocaine was only a small part of the drugs the CIA smuggles into the United States every year.

Grimm described the huge warehouse in Caracas used by the CIA to store the drugs before shipment to the United States. Guillen explained how the CIA conspired with Venezuelan officials, including himself, to bring drugs into the United States in CIA-controlled aircraft. At that time, Guillen was head of a joint CIA-Venezuelan task force responsible for *preventing* drug trafficking.

The State Department chief responsible for overseeing international narcotics matters, Melvin Levitsky, explained that an indictment against General Guillen would require the United States to cut off aid to Venezuela, and therefore no charges would be filed. Much of the world's coca, from which cocaine is obtained, is grown in Bolivia, Peru, and Venezuela, and constitutes a major part of their income. This fact is no secret to the CIA, and the CIA relies upon these countries for much of the cocaine that *it* smuggles into the United States.

Mainstream Media Blackout on the Serious Charges

Very few newspapers reported anything about the serious charges made on the *60 Minutes* show despite the national impact and the grave implications of high-level government involvement in a practice responsible for a major share of the crime and murders in the United States.

Standard Excuses Used For Obstructing Justice

The standard CIA excuse, when questioned about its drug smuggling, is that it is a sting operation, or the actions of a rogue agent, or to obtain information about drug smugglers. DEA agent Grimm said that these explanations were "ludicrous." When Justice Department officials were questioned, they replied that there was "no evidence of criminal wrongdoing." Justice Department officials said their investigation "Revealed instances of poor judgment and management, leading to disciplinary actions for several CIA officers."

The CIA tried to show that it took corrective action when this multi-million-dollar drug shipment was discovered, stating that one CIA officer resigned, and a second had been disciplined. Surely they should face something other than a resignation or forced retirement! The CIA station chief involved in the massive drug trafficking, James Campbell, was promoted and then retired. Not a single government employee responsible for bringing this huge quantity of drugs into the United States was punished.

Many people implicated in a drug sale, even as little as the size of an M&M, or who were present when others were talking about drug sales, have been sentenced to many years in federal prison. Surely, a government official, in a position of trust, who commits a similar offense should receive a greater sentence. A government official, responsible for several million times the amount of drugs ordinary drug traffickers deal with, *under the law*, should receive a similar life sentence.

"I Think They Made A Mistake," Lapdog DeConcini Said

When asked by Mike Wallace of *60 Minutes* about the CIA drug smuggling, Senator Dennis DeConcini, replied, "I think they made a mistake." DeConcini helped protect the massive looting of the savings and loans, and covered up the criminal activities that I reported to him over a period of many years. DeConcini did admit that the "mistake" leading to over a ton of cocaine reaching the United States "can kill people, and probably did." The senator, a former prosecutor, excused the failure to prosecute any of the CIA people responsible for bringing in the 3,300 pounds of cocaine that probably exceeded—a billion times over—the quantity that would cause an ordinary citizen to be imprisoned for life.

"Biggest, Whitest, and Deadliest Lie Ever
Perpetrated On U.S. Citizens by Their Government."

Michael Levine, a twenty-five-year veteran of the Drug Enforcement Administration (and prior drug agencies), authored the 1993 book *The Big White Lie,* exposing the drug trafficking sanctioned by federal officials. The former DEA agent wrote that the so-called war on drugs is the "biggest, whitest, and deadliest lie ever perpetrated on U.S. citizens by their government." He described how the CIA, the DEA, and other intelligence agencies blocked investigations and prosecution of high-level drug traffickers. Levine described how the CIA was primarily responsible for the drug epidemic as seen from his perspective.

Levine repeatedly uncovered CIA links to drug trafficking while he was a DEA agent. He discovered the CIA was primarily responsible for the burgeoning drug activity from Central and South America into the United States, and that the biggest drug dealers were CIA assets. He found that federal judges and Justice Department prosecutors dropped the amount of bail for high-level drug traffickers who were CIA assets.

CIA–Supported Drug Traffickers Seizure of Bolivian Government

Levine said the CIA supported drug traffickers who then seized control of the government of Bolivia. He went into detail concerning how the top people involved in drug trafficking, such as the Bolivian government officials, were protected against exposure and prosecution by DOJ personnel and that many of these protected individuals were CIA assets. He wrote that U.S. officials are "afraid the world would find out there wouldn't be a cocaine government in Bolivia if it wasn't for the CIA." He described how high DEA and Justice Department officials "intentionally destroy drug cases" and put conscientious DEA agents at risk, even causing their deaths. Levine explained how major drug cases involving CIA assets receive little or no media publicity, thereby protecting the CIA's criminal activities. Levine stated in his book the problem with raiding suspected drug labs. He said that when the site was raided there was evidence of a prior drug lab, but it no longer existed; the drug cartel having been warned of the planned raid.

Failed Drug Raids

One of my contacts who worked for the DEA told me why this occurred. Basil Abbott, a DEA contract pilot, would be told about the raid by DEA personnel and instructed to pass this information to his contacts in the foreign government, who would then warn the drug cartels. Abbott said that among the people he warned of impending drug raids were Sonia Atala and her husband, Walter. Levine described the huge drug trafficking by Sonia and Walter Atala and how the CIA, DEA, and the Justice Department protected them.

Abbott spoke Spanish and had become friends with key government officials throughout South America. During several years of frequent contacts with Abbott, he described the guns that he and other government contract agents flew to Central and South America for the DEA, and the return flights loaded with drugs, often unloading them at the DEA facility north of Dallas at Addison Airport.

Justice Department Obstruction of Justice

Levine wrote about the situation that I encountered over a 30-year period, commencing while I was a federal investigator. When Levine sought to expose drug trafficking by CIA and DEA assets, Justice Department personnel harassed him and even threatened to put him in prison on bogus charges.

DEA And State Department Protecting Burma's Drug Lords

DEA Agent In Charge, Richard A. Horn, based in Myanmar (formerly Burma), reported the involvement of U.S. officials in drug trafficking and sued former State Department and CIA officials in that Asian nation for subverting his official drug fighting activities (*Wall Street Journal*, October 27, 1994). Horn's lawsuit charged that State Department and CIA officials retaliated against him because his exposure of drug traffickers interfered with their protection of the lucrative Burma drug output. Myanmar reportedly produces over half the heroin on the world market.

Horn charged that the State Department's chief of mission in Myanmar, Franklin Huddle, Jr., worked with the CIA station chief to sabotage Horn's anti-drug efforts, and tried to bring about the death of an informant who had been assisting Horn in his activities.

Wall Street Journal Article Reported Similar Conflicts

Clashes between conscientious government agents and corrupt government personnel are common. A *Wall Street Journal* report (October 27, 1994) made reference to various DEA agents whose efforts have been blocked by CIA officials:

Drug-enforcement agents and CIA officers have clashed in Venezuela, Colombia, Haiti and other countries where military and government officials have been accused of complicity in the drug trade.

National Security Council, Vice President George Bush, and Drugs

DEA Supervising Agent In Charge, Celerino (Cele) Castillo, had repeatedly reported the large amount of cocaine being smuggled into Florida, Texas, and California by mercenary pilots used by Oliver North. In an interview with *The Texas Observer* (Associated Press, June 17, 1994), and as written in Castillo's 1994 book on drugs, Castillo stated that he observed large quantities of drugs shipped to the United States through Ilopango Air Force Base in El Salvador. He said that in 1986 he reported these findings to his superiors in the DEA and to the U.S. ambassador to El Salvador, Edwin Corr, with no reaction. Castillo stated that he told Vice President George Bush about the drug trafficking during a cocktail party in Guatemala City (1986) and that Bush "just smiled and walked away from me."

Castillo said that when the drugs were unloaded at drug transshipment points, CIA-affiliated trucking companies transported the drugs throughout the United States,[32] and that organized crime took most of the drugs upon arrival in the United States.

Supervisor Of DEA's Air Wing Describes DEA Corruption

For several years I had been communicating with William Coller, formerly a supervisor at the DEA's Air Wing based at the Addison Airport north of Dallas, Texas. (It has since been moved to Ross Perot's Alliance Airport at Fort Worth.) Coller wrote the DEA's flight manual, "Flying in Latin America," and was among the first DEA pilots to fly DEA aircraft into Latin America on undercover operations.

"If the People Only Knew..."

Coller brought out another side to the drugs secretly flown into the United States by government agencies and people who seized control of them. In one letter, Coller wrote, "If Congress and the people had any idea of just how rampant the corruption was inside the agency they would be shocked. The corruption is widespread and its extent is known only to those at the highest level of the internal affairs division in DEA headquarters." He said that despite international law to the contrary, DEA planes were constantly flying without permission into the airspace of other countries. He described how DEA planes

---

[32] CIA contacts identify some of the CIA-related drug haulers: MNX Trucking; Jayes' Truck Driver Training School; Jiffey Truck Driver Training School; and Zapata Trucking Company, a division of the Zapata Corporation in Houston.

flew hundreds of miles into Mexican airspace chasing drug planes and working on undercover operations. Coller described the routine overflying of Colombian airspace by DEA aircraft, stating he did it himself. He described how DEA planes flew at night in and around major airports with their lights off, creating danger of a midair collision.

He described one flight into Mexico in a DEA Convair 240, landing at an airport when suddenly the plane was surrounded by armed Mexican units. All the DEA agents on the plane had guns, which was strictly illegal under Mexican law. The heavy airport security was due to the president of Mexico arriving. The heavily armed DEA agents remained hidden in the plane, avoiding a confrontation. Making this an especially difficult situation, the DEA flight had not received approval from Mexican authorities to fly into Mexico. Mexicans are very conscious of the sovereignty of their nation.

Bribing Foreign Police to Kidnap Local Citizens

Coller described flying a DEA DC-3 to Haiti to pick up seven people who had been arrested by Haitian police at the request of the DEA, and then flying the kidnapped Haitians to the United States in the middle of the night. The Haitian police were bribed to carry out this illegal international kidnaping. Coller continued:

I was fed up with the mission, the lies, and the politics. It is an easy jump to go from a government sanctioned illegal operative (who is doing so many things illegal under the auspices of the government) to one who is operating outside the law—only, this time for himself.

US government agencies do many illegal things. They illegally enter other countries. They conduct illegal overflights. They spy. They subvert. They lie; they cover up; they plant dope and false information; they install illegal listening devices and illegal beepers; they threaten, and they plot to involve other family members in crimes so that they can convince the main person to plead guilty rather than take the case to court, so that the government will release his wife and children.

Fabricating Evidence

Agents fabricate and exaggerate evidence. They talk to each other during court when they know they should not. That is, when they were to have been sequestered and ordered by the court not to compare or share testimony with one another. They kill when they shouldn't. Waco, Ruby Ridge, etc. They beat people and lie about it. They use illegal weapons. They lie on their travel vouchers. They fly illegally-equipped aircraft and violate many of the FAA's rules which others would go to jail for if caught. They ruin lives. I have seen the deliberate destruction of property during the execution of search warrants, and the theft of property during search warrants. I have seen it all.

They will let one smuggler go to catch another one. Or they will ignore, excuse, or pay, one drug smuggling group in exchange for favors concerning spying, terrorist acts, fighting communism, etc. Examples: Sammy the Bull Gravano was excused for 19 murders in exchange for his testimony against Gotti. Revolutionaries in some countries are permitted to harvest and sell their opium in exchange for their cooperation in com-

bating an incumbent government considered hostile to the U.S. interests. Bottom line is that an agency such as the CIA often finds itself pitted against other enforcement agencies with a completely different agenda.

DEA Personnel Paid by Drug Cartels to Ignore Drug Activities

Coller said he was surprised to learn that many DEA resident agents assigned to foreign offices (attaches) would find all types of reasons for *not* cooperating or assisting with a drug case in their area of responsibility. He said that some of these agents were paid by drug cartels to look the other way, not to make any arrests, and not to make any damaging reports. Coller said that, as in the United States, "Token busts of small people were arranged to make things look good. Cocaine labs, little more than a hole in the ground filled with coca leaves, were discovered and reported so as to make things look good. Staged events."

DEA Role in Torture

Coller said that the DEA agents did not have to commit torture, "The locals did it for us. They used stun guns against Americans. We watched them brutally torture others—usually their own citizens. We often violated U.S. laws barring torture, just by being present, by condoning, and encouraging the practice."

Camarena and Coller Witness Mexican Torture

Coller described a torture incident that he and Enrique "Kiki" Camarena witnessed in Mexico. Coller had flown two Mexican federal police officers to an area near Mazatlan looking for a marijuana distribution ring. In a small village they broke into a home and started torturing the father. Coller explained:

The Mex-feds grabbed the homeowner, stripped him and threw him onto the floor, on his back, naked. One fed held his head, another his feet, while another sat on his chest and began to interrogate him. Another went into the kitchen and mixed up a concoction of soda and peppers in what appeared to be a wine bottle with a long neck. A wet T-shirt was placed over the man's face and his mouth was stuffed full of some form of cloth. The interrogation continued.

When the man refused to answer correctly, the Commandante sitting on his check began to slap his face while another poured the liquid mix down his nostrils. He held his breath for a while. That is, until the fed holding his feet gave him a strong charge of electric current to his testicles with his cattle prod. The subject gasped, drew the lethal mix into his lungs and began to choke violently. A few more slaps and punches. A couple more charges from the prod.

The man talked. Kiki Camarena was with me when this occurred. I was tempted to write the people who produced "The Camarena Story" to let them know the "other side of the story." Kiki routinely witnessed such atrocities and eventually died at the hands of another torturer, from the other side. Kiki was one heck of a good agent. A handsome, intelligent, and charismatic man whom I admired. But I'll never understand why he tried to take on the Mexican traffickers alone. He, better than anyone else, understood the Mexican mentality about such matters and had to know he couldn't win. They killed him.

Coller said that Camarena, with whom Coller had worked, often made illegal surveillance flights into Mexico. Coller was told that the United States paid $50,000 to Mexican police to kidnap and turn over to U.S. agents the doctor who participated in Camarena's murder.

During another conversation with Coller he went into more details about Camarena's torture and murder.

Kiki knew too much about everything. The main story is that he hired a Mexican pilot that flew him around in Mexico locating all the opium, poppy, and marijuana fields. He put the heat on certain people, the big guy, Caro Kintero (sp). He's the guy that was controlling those fields. And he was right next to top ranking Mexicans politicians and officials. And so, Caro Kintero got together with some other people and they hired some acting and past members of the Mexican federal judicial police to kidnap Kiki. Then they took Kiki and his pilot and tortured them both. And that stopped the investigation into a major major big time smuggling operation.

Coller described how the bodies were dumped on a road and then the excruciating nature of the torture was discovered. Wood sticks had been jammed up into his rectum and internal organs punctured, parts of his skin was ripped off, and other tortures that Latin American police, military and crime groups routinely perpetrate. (Including that which is taught by the CIA's School of the Americas.)

Spraying Dangerous Chemicals on Foreign Citizens

Coller described the complaints that people in foreign countries made to him about U.S. spraying of dangerous chemicals on the crops:

I have been asked, "How would you like it if a group of Bolivian agents came to your town with noisy helicopters and began spraying poisonous chemicals on your crops, in your backyard, on your children? You'd be furious. Well, so are we. You have no business coming to our country spraying us with poison." To survive those many years in government work meant I had to get my act right. In so doing, I unwittingly poisoned my own mind, lost all I had, and must spend many years locked up. Am I solely to blame? Did the government share in this process of warping my perception of right and wrong? I think so. We were made to believe we were above the law.

"Drugs were brought into the DEA Air Wing headquarters."

Contract pilot Basil Abbott told me about flying drugs from Central and South America to the DEA hangar at Addison field. I asked Coller about Abbott's statements and other information that I had received about DEA agents smuggling drugs into the United States. Coller admitted, "Yes, drugs were brought directly into the DEA Air Wing headquarters in Addison, Texas."

Government Agents Stealing Part Of Seized Loads For Themselves

Coller described how government agents diverted some of the drugs they seized to their own use, knowing that those who had been caught with the drugs would not complain since the smaller amount of drugs often lessened the prison sentence. He described how government agents and confidential informants would set up a crime operation and then induce people to be part of it. In other words, government agents would induce people to commit some type of drug-related offense that they would otherwise not do except for the coaxing and pressure of the agents or their informants.

Drug Trafficking Through Waco Airport—Bigger than Mena

Referring to the infamous Mena, Arkansas airport, where a great amount of CIA drugs passed during the 1980s, Coller said:

I can tell you that Mena in no way compares with what's happening in Waco. Waco is a big, major, heavy-duty, paramilitary operation. They take up one whole side of the Waco operation. Major operations run out of there with big aircraft to all parts of the world. It is no secret that the spook shop uses Waco. Everyone on the field knows it and speaks about it in hushed voices.

Coller Explained How the End of his DEA Career Occurred

Coller said that he was arrested while he was a DEA supervisor, doing something that he knew was wrong. He described flying a load of marijuana into a small landing strip on a ranch several miles west of Corpus Christi. Customs undercover agents induced him to fly the marijuana and provided the landing strip for him to use. Customs allowed the first load to hit the street with plans to induce Coller to fly a cocaine load in on the second flight, which would permit them to file more serious charges against him with a life-in-prison sentence.

Coller refused to fly the cocaine load that the undercover agent sought to have him do; Coller felt marijuana was satisfactory, but not hard drugs. Customs even offered to provide their own plane and a pilot to go with him. Again, Coller refused. Satisfied that they could not induce Coller to commit a greater offense, they charged him with trafficking in marijuana.

In trying to capture him, the government had Coller on their "Top-Ten" list, offering $10,000 reward for information leading to his arrest. He said prosecutors don't give a second thought to the families that are destroyed when they charge an innocent person or greatly enlarge the charges over what actually existed.

Using Private Sources Permits Committing Unlawful Acts

Coller explained why the government offered $10,000 reward for his capture, which got bounty hunters into the act. Government agents are more restricted to lawful means to bring about a person's arrest, but bounty hunters usually violate these protections. Since government personnel are not directly involved in bringing about a person's capture, they can also say that they did not know or approve of the methods used. This is the same philosophy used by the CIA and other covert operations. By having cutouts, contract agents, or fronts doing the dirty work, the government can always deny any knowledge or authorization in failed or exposed covert operations. Deniability or disavow are the terms used. Coller admitted he did wrong. But he also revealed much of what is wrong elsewhere:

I can state with certainty that spending many years violating the law in order to enforce the law altered my behavior, changed my perception of right and wrong, all of which led to my violating the law. There are lots

*of dirty agents for one reason or another. I regret with all my heart that
I ever worked for DEA; it is a stupid job. We were vastly overpaid for
what little we did.*

*It ruins families, it poisons minds, it is a meaningless, misguided en-
terprise, and when I look back over my life I see nothing that I'm proud
of. I did nothing constructive or positive. What I did was put many people
in jail for victimless crimes. Realizing now what they all went through,
and how many families I destroyed, gives me no satisfaction whatsoever.
Like a child, I played cops and robbers at taxpayers' expense and wasted
a good part of my life. We changed nothing. And I sold my soul to the government for nothing.*

Making A Study of Role Reversal

While in prison, Coller made an intensive study of role reversal among
government agents, and studied the work of Professor Albert Bandura of Stanford University, believed to be the world's leading authority in the field of
cognitive psychology. Coller wrote a 23-page treatise on how a government
agent's behavior is affected by the type of undercover work he does. Coller
wrote about the many years of undercover work he did for the DEA, including
the lying, perjury, unlawful and corrupt activities requested by government
prosecutors.

Transfer Of Values

He wrote of the transfer of values when, as a DEA agent, he acted like a
smuggler to catch smugglers. He associated with Mexican police while they
tortured their own citizens. He led a life of deception. He cited studies showing how government agents in these positions take on the identity of the
groups they are infiltrating. He described the problems that "develop when
agents with the CIA or DEA for example are trained and programmed to perform anti-social, subversive or illegal acts," and how this changes their behavior and thinking.

Witness the Donny Brasco affair in which the FBI's deep-cover agent began to identify with his Mafia targets. He lost his identity, committed many
crimes, and was protected from the legal consequences so that the FBI could
continue using him as a witness rather than be charged with them.

Executioners for the Government

They become desensitized to "behavior that is dangerous, repugnant, even
illegal." His treatise compared the changes to the psychological treatment the
CIA had conducted years ago to alter the behavior of certain individuals. It is
a form of brainwashing. He cited studies showing how behavioral changes
take place in such people as Navy Seals, Army Rangers, Special Forces soldiers, CIA operatives, and DEA agents who become "executioners for the
government." He described how outrageous behavior is justified under such
high-sounding terms as "freedom, democracy, police action, or the war on
drugs."

Role Reversal for Government Agents: Acting Like Criminals

Coller described how undercover agents of various agencies become so
involved in their work that they unwittingly poison their minds and become
like the people they are working against. Dr. Michel Girodo, psychologist for

the FBI, has written about this extensively. Coller explained and repeated some of Dr. Girodo's writings:

Our government has trained thousands of undercover operatives. Many of them, particularly those on the front line with DEA and CIA; those who specialize in undercover operations, do change. They destroy their own minds in the process. Right and wrong get mixed up. Black and white are replaced with various shades of gray.

The street always rubs off on the agent; it is never the other way around. The wrongfulness of certain acts no longer registers because many of these agents have been living a "lie" and violating the law in order to enforce the law. They become desensitized to their own misconduct and sometimes lose their identity. Few people realize how bad it is. The bottom line is that our government is steadily creating hundreds of rogue cops by teaching them the tradecraft of lies and then paying and rewarding them for such illegal behavior.

These agents will never be the same. They will never look at life normally. Under a very thin veneer of civility lies a rogue warrior in all of us who have been subjected to the big government school of smugglers, liars, subversives, and cheats. One simply cannot play that kind of game, live that kind of lie, behave as a criminal, and not be affected. Their families see the changes.

Unlawfully Seizing Aircraft and Other Assets

Illegal aircraft seizure happens when agencies fabricate evidence. A case I am familiar with went like this: The agent looked through the aircraft window and could see nothing [to justify searching the aircraft]. He broke into the plane anyhow, making an illegal search without a warrant, looking for evidence. He saw what appeared to be a marihuana seed. The seed was repositioned so that it could be seen from outside the window. Other agents were brought to look at it. All seemed to think that it looked like a **seed***.*

A warrant to search the plane was obtained and a search ensued. Nothing could be found, so a vacuum was brought in and the carpet of the plane was vacuumed. Three seeds were found. (One turned out to be a small stone which looked like a seed.) The two seeds and a spoon full of dust were sent to the DEA lab and they determined through sophisticated testing that, indeed, there must have been marijuana in the plane at one time.

The plane was a twin-engine Piper Seneca. It was seized. The owner went to court and contested the seizure. Agents testified that they saw the seed through the window. It never came out that the seed had been positioned to be seen before other agents arrived. 51/1000ths of a gram of so-called marihuana residue was found.

The law does not specify how much dope must be found; only that drugs were found in the plane. The seizure was upheld by the court and the person lost the plane. The entire affair was bogus. That is often how it works. The courts in their mistaken belief that agents tell the truth, believed them. The law itself is horrible in that it allows such abuse of power. One must always remember that agents believe that "the end justifies the means."

Turning These Creatures Loose Upon Society

The government trains and employs thousands of undercover operatives in a wide variety of its agencies. DEA, ATF and CIA are among the worst offenders. But all the other agencies suffer from the same problem: FBI, IRS, Customs, and agents of the various military intelligence agencies. The government creates these undercover creatures and turns them loose on society. Our own citizenry becomes victim to these often ruthless operatives, whose minds have been poisoned and whose tactics are bound only by their imagination.

Fearful of Being Rearrested

As with most released prisoners, it is very easy to be rearrested. Many rights enjoyed by other people do not exist for released prisoners, and any minor "infraction" gives government agents the opportunity to put someone back in prison, which it appears they enjoy doing. Coller wrote:

I'll be out of here in six weeks. The cops are already expecting me and will probably try to set me up. I told you that back in 1990 Customs agents tried to entice me into flying a load of cocaine for them, which would have resulted in a life sentence for me! It was their idea; their dope; their plan. All I had to do was agree to fly it and I would have been hit for life. In fact, I would not have needed to even make the flight; just agree to do it. It was that close. [The same southwest Customs region had Richard Pitt and Rodney Matthews flying drugs for them, as described in other pages.]

Coller was released from prison on March 1, 1999. Coller had been arrested and convicted in 1992 and spent seven years in prison. He vowed to never again get near drugs.

****

DEA Drug Trafficking and Murder In Mexico?

Another bizarre side to the DEA's involvement in drugs was explained to me in 1998 by Rumaldo Solis, who was a 15-year veteran of the U.S. Immigration and Naturalization Services (INS) until he discovered a very serious matter involving DEA drug trafficking and murder in Mexico. His attempts to have that investigated caused him to lose his job and to be falsely charged with a drug offense and sentenced to prison.

Solis was on duty at Port Hidalgo, Texas, when a series of events started unfolding that had profound international implications and would disrupt, if not destroy forever, his family. The events started one night while on duty when several Mexican nationals came to his office and reported events that exposed other angles about the corrupt involvement of U.S. government personnel in drugs.

The spokesman for the group was a Mexican national by the name of Juan Garcia Abrego. Because Solis was himself formerly a Mexican citizen, Abrego felt confident revealing what he did. Speaking in Spanish, Abrego described in great detail a drug trafficking operation and murder at a mountainous airstrip near Los Mochis, Mexico involving a DEA agent. (Los Mochis is located along the Eastern Shore of the Gulf of California.)

Hired In Los Mochis

Abrego described how he, his brother, and several other Mexicans were hired in Los Mochis by a Mexican national who identified himself as the "capataz" (foreman or supervisor). The capataz was hiring men to transfer cargo between aircraft at a remote mountain airstrip about two hours drive from Los Mochis.

At the airstrip, the cargo handlers off-loaded cocaine and marijuana from aircraft arriving from Colombia and other South American locations onto aircraft and 18-wheeler trucks going to the United States. They also off-loaded from aircraft arriving from the United States pallets of money and 55-gallon drums of chemicals for processing cocaine.

DEA Drug Smuggling Operation in Mexico

Abrego described the day that transfer of drugs between planes was delayed until the arrival of an aircraft from the United States. When that plane arrived, three people jumped from it and headed to a nearby warehouse. As one of them jumped, his wallet fell from his pocket, without being noticed. This wallet was picked up by Abrego's brother, who then went into a nearby storage area and looked at the contents. He and several other cargo handlers saw a government identification card stating, "Drug Enforcement Administration" on one side and on the other side a picture and name of a DEA agent: George Cons.

Missing Wallet Discovered

Abrego said, when the DEA agent discovered his wallet missing, the foreman ordered the cargo handlers to stand facing a wall, after which they were searched. It was found in the pocket of Abrego's brother. At that point, Abrego said, sobbing, the DEA agent pulled out a pistol and shot Abrego's brother in the back of the head, killing him instantly. The foreman than ordered the cargo handlers to bury the body.

Making Their Escape

The laborers were heavily guarded to keep them from escaping, possibly to prevent information being revealed about the drug trafficking operation or the murder. About three months later, Abrego and several of the laborers escaped, making their way to the INS station at Port Hidalgo, near Brownsville, Texas, where Solis was on duty. The distraught and crying Abrego described in detail the drug smuggling operation and the killing of his brother.

Mexican Drugs Going to United States via Planes and Trucks

Abrego described what happened the day his brother was killed. He described how the cargo handlers overheard conversations indicating the destination of some of the drugs going to the United States via U.S.-based aircraft and 18-wheeler trucks. They overheard truck drivers referring to a company known as "FRUTIKO," which Solis understood to be a Japanese company with plants along the Mexican border that processed frozen fruit and shipped it in 55-gallon drums. These products were then shipped into the United States via various border crossings, including Reynosa Tamaulipas where Solis was on duty.

After listening to Abrego's description of the drug-smuggling operation, Solis called DEA Special Agent Gary Morrison in nearby McAllen, Texas, explaining what he was being told. Morrison then advised he would be there within an hour.

Acting as translator during the interview, Solis made notes of Abrego's explosive statements. Abrego stated that various types and sizes of aircraft went through this remote airstrip, including corporate and airline types. Solis said that Abrego told him the planes arriving from South America had registration numbers on the side starting with the letters HK and XA, among others. Abrego said some of the planes were painted green and the pilots of the planes coming from the south were Hispanic and Anglo American.

EPIC Inquiry

During the interview, Morrison contacted the central record office at El Paso, Texas, called the El Paso Intelligence Center (EPIC)[33] and made an "Epics" inquiry. This confirmed that a George Cons was a DEA agent assigned to the Arizona area.

Start Of DEA and Multi Agency Coverup

Despite the enormous sensitivity of the information provided, Morrison instructed Solis to tell Abrego to go back to Mexico and that Abrego would be called if needed. As a trained and highly experienced investigator, Solis recognized this was the beginning of a coverup. An investigator doesn't tell such an important witness in such an important matter of national magnitude to leave the country, where the witness would most probably not be available again, and where he would probably be murdered to silence him.

Solis made notes during the interview, writing down the names and addresses of the witnesses. Before leaving his office that night, Solis made a copy of his notes on the office copy machine, leaving the original in his office mail box, in the presence of DEA agent Gary Morrison, and put a copy in the glove compartment of his car.

Missing Report

Upon returning to his office the next morning, Solis discovered his report had been removed and in its place was a copy of a drug trafficker's Mexican birth certificate from the State of Tamaulipas, Mexico. Solis felt whoever took his notes was leaving him a message: back off!

Using his copy of the notes, Solis typed a report which he then took to the port director, Hilda Trevino. In the office with Trevino was recently-retired port director Herb Best. Solis described to them the contents of the report and his interview the night before.

Keeping the Issue Alive

When Solis did not hear anything further on his highly explosive report, he made several inquiries of his supervisors about the status of any investigation. He started receiving warnings from INS and DEA personnel that it would be in his best interest to forget about it, which he refused to do. He continued

---

[33] EPIC, or the El Paso Intelligence Center, is a center located in El Paso that houses members of most of the large law enforcement agencies, including the DEA, FBI, Customs, FAA, Coast Guard, ATF. It is designed so that a government agent can make one call and find information pertaining to a particular individual or group, or any other matter relating to law enforcement.

to question the lack of activity on the matter.

FBI Agent Warning Solis to Forget the Matter

When Solis refused to remain quiet, he started receiving anonymous telephone threats. Government personnel warned him to remain quiet. (Reminds me of old times in the Federal Aviation Administration!) FBI Special Agent Orlando Munoz from the McAllen office visited Solis in early 1993, warning Solis that he had been told "too many times to shut up and forget the whole affair." Threatening a government agent to prevent him from reporting a federal crime is a criminal act under Title 18 USC Sections 1905, 1912, 1913.

Start Of FBI Retaliation Against Solis

Munoz, acting under U.S. Attorney Melissa Annis, obtained court authorization to put a recording device on Solis' home phone, giving false information to Chief District Judge Norman Black to justify the court order. Munoz claimed that Solis was a nephew to major drug trafficker Juan Garcia Abrego.

In December 1994, FBI Special Agent William Vanderland obtained a search warrant for Solis residence and carried out a typical blunderbuss attack on his home, breaking down the door to carry out the search rather than knock. Solis' son, clad only in his underwear, had a large-caliber gun put to his head by FBI Special Agent Lamar Pruit, who then ordered the young boy outside the house.

Three FBI agents in the paramilitary force from the McAllen office, Orlando Munoz, William Vanderland and Charles C. Gregorski, searched Solis' residence and seized his records, including his copy of the report about the DEA drug smuggling operation and murder in Mexico.

FBI and U.S. Attorney Team Fabricated Charges

Acting in typical unison, FBI agents and the U.S. Attorney fabricated charges, accusing Solis of drug-related offenses and using a government computer to facilitate drug smuggling. The DEA stayed out of the prosecution, preventing Solis from claiming retaliation for having reported the DEA drug smuggling operation.

Attorneys Protecting Their Government Relationship

Trying to obtain competent and trustworthy legal counsel against the charges, Solis went through three attorneys, each of whom sought to protect his relationship with government attorneys by urging Solis to plead guilty. One attorney even threatened Solis' family when Solis objected to pleading guilty. However, one of Solis' attorneys requested from the DEA a copy of the report that Solis had written, that had been sent by Gary Morrison to the DEA internal affairs in Washington. The response came back that the report was lost.

Caving in to Government Corruption

During the jury trial with a lackadaisical public defender, the federal judge refused to allow Solis to present government witnesses. After the prosecutor threatened to charge Solis' wife with criminal offenses, Solis caved in and pled guilty to one count.

Family Breakup Following Attempts to Report Drug Offenses

Solis described how his family suffered following his arrest and incarceration. Their "friends" no longer wanted anything to do with them. Government threats and harassment caused his daughter to have a miscarriage. His son was forced to drop out of college. Solis' insurance company canceled his auto and home insurance because he was convicted of a felony. Financial chaos followed.

Useless Appeals to Congressional and Media Checks & Balances

Solis sent many letters to members of Congress and to the media, describing the DEA drug smuggling and the killing of a Mexican in Mexico by a DEA agent. No response. He sent a May 4, 1998 letter to Congresswoman Maxine Waters and got back a form letter thanking him for his information. (I had first contacted Waters in the mid-1980s while she was a California state representative. Except for her loud rhetoric, her coverup of hard-core government corruption hasn't changed to this day.) Solis wrote to his Washington representative from Texas, Solomon Ortiz, and received no response. The congressional indifference and coverups that Solis encountered were the same reaction encountered by countless other government agents who at risk to themselves sought to bring high-level government corruption to the attention of those having a responsibility to act.

Notifying Mexican Officials of U.S. Drug Trafficking and Murder

The criminal activities Solis reported had serious international ramifications that should have been of major interest to the Mexican government. Solis wrote letters to Mexican officials describing the DEA's drug operation in Mexico and the killing of one of their own citizens in Mexico by a U.S. agent. None responded.

Mexican Journalist Responded—Followed by His Death

In March 1997, Solis reported the DEA's crimes to Mexican journalist Benjamin Flores Gonzales, a reporter for *La Prensa* in the Sonora area of San Juan Rio Colorado. Flores started investigating the Solis matter, trying to find Abrego and the other Mexicans who had accompanied him to the Port Hidalgo station. Flores' activities constituted a threat to the DEA's drug smuggling operation, to the DEA agent allegedly involved, to the Justice Department hierarchy involved in the cover up, and threatened to expose U.S. involvement in drug trafficking.

The fatal bullets came on July 15, 1997. Flores was gunned down outside his office in San Juan Rio Colorado, killed by nearly two dozen bullets from an AK-47 into his back and face. That ended the investigation into the DEA drug smuggling operation. Ironically, when I received a Mexican newspaper article describing his death, the same article described the killing of another person described within these pages, Esteban Borges Figeroa, whose death was brought about by Justice Department sabotage.

Mexican Governor Accused DEA of Protecting Drug Cartels

Solis called the governor of the Mexican state of Sonora, Manlo Flavio Beltrones, at Hermosillo, and spoke to his secretary, Rosie. Solis said that an explanatory letter was on its way. Beltrones never acted on Solis' information. A few days later, Beltrones accused the DEA of protecting a major Mexican drug smuggling group, the Amado Carrillo Fuentes organization, and furnishing them with information to protect their drug operations.

Similar To Colombian Government Drug
Operation and Murder in the United States

A comparison to what reportedly occurred in Mexico would be a Colombian government drug operation and murder occurring within the United States and Justice Department officials and the president of the United States covering up. However, after thinking that one over, what is occurring in the United States is not much different from that scenario.

Joint Mexican-U.S. Drug Involvement?

One explanation for Mexican officials not responding to the report of a DEA drug trafficking operation in Mexico and the murder of a Mexican national by a DEA agent could be that both Mexico and U.S. officials were involved in the drug trafficking, and protecting each other. Nothing is too bizarre after 30 years of insider information.

Solis Still In Prison

In 1999, when this edition was printed, Solis was still in prison and nothing had been done about the DEA drug smuggling operation in Mexico or the murder of the Mexican national by either government.

Putting Government Officials on Notice

Despite encountering 30 years of government coverups, I decided to put U.S. officials on notice, I sent a May 24, 1998, certified letter to Attorney General Janet Reno describing what INS agent Solis had discovered and reported as part of his official duties. I also included a copy of Solis' affidavit and a near duplicate of Solis' original report. Despite the gravity of the information, no response.

Seeking to circumvent the coverup by U.S. officials, I put Mexican officials on notice of the reported DEA crimes committed on Mexican territory, thinking they would *have* to respond because of the gravity of the matter.

Requesting Solis to Prepare A Duplicate of the Report

Because the INS, DEA, and FBI had hidden Solis' explosive report and seized his copy during the search of his home, I asked Solis to prepare another one based upon his memory. Although many particulars could not be remembered, such as Abrego's home address and phone number, Solis prepared the report, a copy of which follows:

DECLARATION/AFFIDAVIT

I, Rumaldo Solis, under penalty of perjury, declare:

The intent of this declaration/affidavit is to:

* Expose a major drug smuggling operation directly involving an agent of the U.S. Drug Enforcement Administration.

* The deliberate murder of a Mexican national by an agent of the U.S. Drug Enforcement Administration, perpetrated in Mexico, to cover up for the involvement in a major drug smuggling operation with international implications and that agent's involvement or control of the criminal enterprise.

* The felony coverup of these activities by agents of other agencies of the U.S. government, including various divisions of the U.S. Department of Justice, including the Federal Bureau of Investigation, U.S. attorneys, Drug Enforcement Administration, and the Immigration and Naturalization Service.

* It is my belief, that for the good of the United States and Mexico, and in the interest of justice, that I make these facts known, and for these facts and this declaration-affidavit to be used by investigator and activist Rodney Stich to accomplish these goals.

I was an agent for the Immigration and Naturalization Service from 1981 To 1995, having 15 years of experience as a government agent. My relationship with the INS during this time was entirely satisfactory, until I discovered a major drug smuggling operation involving a DEA agent by the name of George Cons. When I made an official written report of what I discovered, and pursued the matter after encountering a cover up by INS and Drug Enforcement Administration officials, I was threatened with retaliation and job action by various people, including agents of the Federal Bureau of Investigation. They warned me that if I continued to report and inquire about the official drug-smuggling report I had previously prepared that I and my family would suffer the consequences.

That official government report not only included a major drug smuggling operation into the United States, involving an agent of the U.S. Drug Enforcement Administration, but also the killing of a Mexican national by a DEA agent. In addition to that report, the matter subsequently involved official coverup and obstruction of justice by agents of the Federal Bureau of Investigation, Immigration and Naturalization Service, the Drug Enforcement Administration, followed by further coverups involving a U.S. attorney and other officials in the U.S. Department of Justice.

When I continued trying to meet my federal responsibilities as a federal agent and sought to have the drug smuggling operation and murder investigated, false charges were filed against me by the FBI and U.S. Attorney.

Because of threats upon me and my family, and the refusal of my attorneys to raise a meaningful defense, I pleaded guilty to one charge.

The following is a brief description of the official report that I prepared exposing a major drug smuggling operation, the murder of a Mexican national, implicating a DEA agent:

At some time in 1989, the exact date I cannot recall, while I was on duty in the INS office at the Hidalgo Port of Entry station near McAllen, Texas, a Mexican national came into the office and provided me detailed information about a major drug smuggling operation and the killing of his brother by a DEA agent. I prepared a written report of what this witness stated.

The witness said that he, his brother, and a group of Mexican nationals, were working at a remote mountain airstrip in Mexico, at which large aircraft arrived from South America loaded with drugs, and large aircraft arrived from the United States carrying 55-gallon drums of chemicals, and money to pay for the drugs. Their job was to unload and load drugs, chemicals, and money between aircraft arriving from Central and South America and the United States.

This witness described how the drug transfer between several aircraft were waiting the arrival of the person apparently in charge of the operation. When that plane arrived, and that individual got off

Solis's initials: *R. S.*   1

Reduced size of Solis' Affidavit

the aircraft, his wallet fell out of his pocket. That wallet contained a government-issued photo and identification of George Cons, an agent for the Drug Enforcement Administration.

When DEA agent George Cons later discovered that his wallet was missing, he ordered the Mexican laborers lined up and searched. When the wallet was discovered in the possession of the witness' brother, DEA agent Cons reportedly pulled out his gun and shot, point-blank, the witness' brother. Cons then ordered the Mexican laborers to bury the body.

Several days later, the witness managed to escape from the heavily guarded remote airstrip, and made his way to the INS office near McAllen, Texas, where he gave me a detailed information. This information was made into an official government report as part of my official duties.

The laborers were guarded day and night to prevent their escape, but several days after the killing of the witness' brother, several of them, including the witness, managed to escape from the heavily guarded remote airstrip. The witness made his way to the in the INS's Hidalgo Port of Entry office near McAllen, Texas, while I was on duty.

The distraught and crying witness described to me in detail the drug smuggling operation and how DEA agent Cons killed his brother.

While listening to the witness' description of the drug smuggling operation and murder, I called DEA Special Agent Gary Morrison in the nearby McAllen, Texas, office, explaining what I was being told. Morrison then advised that he would be there within an hour, meeting us at the bridge between McAllen, Texas and Reynosa, Mexico. During the interview, I acted as translator, and recorded the witness' statements.

During the interview, Morrison contacted by phone the central record office at El Paso, Texas (EPIC) and made an "Epics" inquiry, which confirmed that a George Cons did in fact work for the DEA, assigned to the Yuma, Arizona office. NCIC is the El Paso Intelligence Center that centralizes information about drug offenses.

Despite the enormous national and international implications of the information being provided by this witness, Morrison instructed me to tell the witness to go back to Mexico, which I conveyed to the witness in Spanish. Before leaving the office that night, I obtained the witness' address in Mexico, that of other witnesses names and addresses, and included these in my official report. I then put that report into my office files, while Morrison was present.

As a trained and highly experienced INS investigator, I recognized that this was the beginning of a coverup. An investigator doesn't tell such an important witness in such an important matter of national and international implications, to return to Mexico, where the witness would most probably not be available again, and where he could very probably be murdered to keep him from testifying.

When I arrived back at my office the following morning, I discovered that my official report had been removed, and in its place was a Mexican birth certificate for drug trafficker Juan Garcia Abrego. It is my belief that the placement of a personal document relating to a drug trafficker was to associate me with a criminal enterprise and in that way silence me and my knowledge of the DEA-related drug operation.

I raised the mater with various DEA officials, threatening to expose a major drug operation organized and protected by government personnel in control of key government offices. It was apparent that I was "not on the team." When I persisted in trying to meet my federal job responsibilities, anonymous phone calls to me at my home and at work warned me that dire things were going to happen if I did not drop the matter, and that my job as an Immigration and Naturalization officer would come to a halt. I reported these threats to INS officials, and they did nothing about it.

In addition to the anonymous threats made by telephone, I started getting threats from government officials. FBI Special Agent Orlando Munoz out of the McAllen office visited me in early 1993 at the Hidalgo Port of Entry office, warning me that I had been told "too many times to shut up and forget the whole affair." The FBI was threatening a government agent against reporting what was clearly criminal and subversive activities against the United States! As I sought to have the matter reported and investigated, I was warned by INS and DEA personnel that it would be in my own best interest to forget about it.

I reported the drug smuggling operation and the threats against me to various members of Congress, including Congressman Solomon P. Ortiz of the 27th congressional district, describing the murder of the Mexican national by the DEA agent, the drug smuggling operation involving large numbers of U.S. aircraft and personnel, the coverups and obstruction of justice by officials at the DEA, Immigration and Naturalization Service, the FBI, U.S. attorney, and Department of Justice in Washington. None responded to my letters.

When I continued to keep the issues alive, employees of the DEA, INS, FBI, and office of the U.S. attorney participated in falsely charging me with using government computers in drug smuggling activities. The FBI charged me with using a government computer to facilitate drug smuggling. It appears that the DEA stayed out of the prosecution so that I couldn't raise the defense of retaliation for having reported the DEA drug smuggling operation.

FBI Special Agent Munoz traveled to Houston, obtaining a court authorization to wire tap my home phone. Munoz gave Chief District Judge Norman Black false information as Munoz tried to justify the telephone tap. Munoz said that I was a nephew to major drug trafficker Juan Garcia Abrego. This scheme, making false statements against a government agent, in a scheme to obstruct justice, was approved by U.S. attorney Melissa Annis before it was presented to Judge Black.

The Justice Department's FBI and U.S. attorney then misstated that drug matter discussions normally undertaken by me as part of my job, taken out of context, indicated that I was engaging in drug trafficking.

In December 1994, FBI Special Agent William Vanderland obtained a search warrant for my residence, using a large number of state and federal agents to carry out the search. When my son answered the door, he was ordered by FBI Special Agent Lamarr Pruit into the front yard to be searched, holding a large caliber gun to the boy's head. Copies of my records pertaining to the drug smuggling operation and the murder of the Mexican national were seized during this raid.

Trying to defend myself against the sham charges filed by Justice Department employees, I went through three attorneys, discovering that they all wanted me to plead guilty.

These statements are true and correct to the best of my belief. Executed this ___28___ day of June 1998, at the federal prison in Pekins, Illinois.

Rumaldo Solis
Rumaldo Solis

From-memory duplication of original sequestered report

UNITED STATES GOVERNMENT
MEMORANDUM
UNITED STATES IMMIGRATION &
NATURALIZATION SERVICE

DEA SEAL

Date: November 12, 1988. [This date is approximate]

To: Hilda B. Trevino, Port Director
Subject: Information relating to DEA agent involved in drug smuggling and murder in Mexico.
From: Rumaldo Solis II

A Mexican national came to the INS office at Port Hidalgo yesterday evening around 8:30 P.M. He stated that he wanted help from American authorities concerning the murder of his brother by a DEA agent that he identified as George Cons. Shortly after he provided me with preliminary information, I contacted by phone the DEA office at McAllen, Texas, requesting the assistance of DEA internal affairs since a DEA agent was involved.

DEA agent Gary Morrison arrived within an hour to continue the questioning of the witness, while I acted as translator.

The witness presented to us his Mexican identification to prove his identity. He stated that he, his brother, and several others was hired at Los Mochis, Mexico, to work at a ranch about two hours driving time from Los Mochis, Sinaloa, in Mexico. The Mexican who hired them, and whose name he did not remember, transported them in a pickup truck to a mountainous area ranch. The witness stated that during the two-hour trip his ears started to pop as the truck climbed to higher altitude.

When they arrived at the ranch, they were greeted by another Mexican who introduced himself as the foreman of the ranch. This foreman took them on a tour of the ranch, which consisted of a landing strip, warehouses, airplanes, armed guards, and various types of vehicles.

The foreman explained to them that the job consisted of loading and unloading airplanes and large vehicles, and to pack and unpack bundles. They later learned that the material being loaded and unloaded, and the packaging, consisted mostly of cocaine and marijuana. They also unloaded stacks of money, and chemicals used for drug processing from planes and vehicles coming from the United States.

The cocaine and marijuana loads were loaded onto aircraft and trucks going to the United States. The chemicals and money were unloaded from airplanes and trucks coming from the United States and then placed on board airplanes and vehicles going to Central and South America. The witness stated that he and his group started working immediately thereafter.

The witness stated that some of the planes had aircraft markings on the side that began with letters, including HK, XA and N.

The witness described an event that occurred approximately two months ago, associated with the arrival from the United States of an airplane with three occupants on board. As one of these occupants got out of the aircraft and walked to one of the storage buildings, his wallet fell to the ground, without him noticing it. The brother to the witness picked up the wallet and went inside a nearby building to examine it. As they looked in the wallet they found a photo of the person who dropped the wallet, George Cons, and identification as an agent for the United States Drug Enforcement Administration.

The witness said that a few minutes later, the foreman called everybody outside and lined them against a wall. The person who dropped the wallet then search them and found the wallet in the possession of the witness' brother. The DEA agent then pulled out a gun and shot the witness' brother in the back of the head, killing him instantly.

Signature: *Rumaldo Solis*   1

The other workers were then instructed to dig a hole and bury the body. After the body was buried, the workers were ordered to resume loading and unloading various aircraft.

The witness stated that the DEA agent's identify was known to the foreman, who had stated that the agent was in charge of the entire operation and that nothing could be either loaded or unloaded until his arrival.

Several days after the DEA agent murdered the witness' brother, the witness and several other workers managed to escape. The witness made his way to the INS office at Port Hidalgo.

During the questioning of the witness in the presence of DEA agent Gary Morrison, and after the witness revealed the name of DEA agent George Cons, Morrison telephoned EPICS to verify that the DEA had an agent by that name. It was confirmed that George Cons was an active agent for the DEA in Arizona.

The witness gave me his name and address in Los Mochis as [this information cannot be remembered but is in the original report]. The witness also gave me the names of the others who were hired at the same time in Los Mochis. These were [this information cannot be remembered].

At the end of the interview, I was instructed by Morrison to order the witness to return to Mexico and if his presence was needed he would be contacted. I advised Morrison that because of the seriousness of the matters described by the witness that he be given permission to remain in the United States until the investigation was completed. Morrison refused to allow this.

Without Morrison present, the witness expressed concern about this lack of interest and that he would not return to Mexico, fearing for his life if he did return.

Rumuldo Solis
Rumuldo Solis

****

I, Rumuldo Solis, declare that the above writing is close to the original that I prepared and filed as an official government report while I was an long-time agent for the U.S. Immigration and Naturalization Service. This writing is now prepared from memory. There may be some specifics that could not be remembered, and the date of the report is only approximate. The report that I prepared at the time contained the names of the witness and the others who were hired in Los Mochis, along with some of their addresses. I cannot remember this information and it is omitted from the report. But the other details are accurate, having been given considerable thought after the event occurred, because of the gravity of the matters reported.

I declare that the other facts stated herein are true and correct, to the best of my knowledge and belief. I make this declaration under penalty of perjury.

I prepared this report after the witness left the INS office at Port Hidalgo where I was on duty, and placed the report in my desk, in Morrison's presence. The following morning, the report was missing. In its place, someone put the birth certificate for Mexican drug trafficker, Juan Garcia Abrego.

After finding this birth certificate, I gave it to INS special agent Ramiro Salinas.

Rumuldo Solis
Rumuldo Solis

Signature: *Rumuldo Solis*   2

Registered Letter Notification to President of Mexico

I sent certified-mail letters to Cesar Lajud, Consul General of Mexico at San Francisco (April 20, 1998); Jesus Reyes Heroles, Mexican Ambassador in Washington (May 11, 1998); Mexican President Ernesto Zedillo (May 11, 1998). No responses. A copy of the letter sent to President Zedillo follows:

From the desk of Rodney Stich   (lettervmazpres.m11)

P.O. Box 5, Alamo, CA 94507; phone: 925-944-1930; FAX 925-295-1203
Author of *DEFRAUDING AMERICA–Dirty Secrets of the CIA & other Government Operations*
DISAVOW–A CIA Saga of CIA Betrayal
UNFRIENDLY SKIES–History of Corruption and Air Tragedies
Member
Association Former Intelligence Officers (AFIO)   *Association of National Security Alumni*
International Society of Air Safety Investigators (ISASI) *Lawyers Pilots Bar Association (LPBA)*
Former FAA air safety investigator   *Former airline captain and Navy pilot*
E-mail: stich@defraudingamerica.com   *Web sites: www.defraudingamerica.com; www.unfriendlyskies.com*
Internet search engine: "Rodney Stich"

May 11, 1998

Ernesto Zedillo, President of Mexico
Los Tinos
Puerta # 1, 11109
Mexico, D.F.   Registered mail

Reference: Reporting crimes against the Mexican government and the Mexican people.

Dear Mr. Zedillo:

This letter puts the Mexican government on notice of major crimes against the government and the people of Mexico by agents of the U.S. government. During my many years of investigations, starting as a federal investigator for the United States government, I acquired a great amount of evidence concerning criminal activities by these agents against the people of the United States. Recently, a former agent of the U.S. Immigration and Naturalization Service (INS), holding U.S. and Mexican citizenship, disclosed to me the contents of a report that he made which had major international implications, particularly for the government and the people of Mexico. The following is a brief description of the crimes against your country:

* An agent of the U.S. government (Drug Enforcement Administration) was reported in an official report of the Immigration and Naturalization Service (INS) to be coordinating, in Mexico, a large drug smuggling operation at a remote mountainous airstrip a couple of hours driving time from Los Mochis.

* That agent of the U.S. government reportedly murdered a Mexican national at that airstrip when that Mexican national, working as a cargo loader loading drugs onto aircraft destined for the United States, discovered the identify of the U.S. government agent.

* The murder of a Mexican journalist in Mexico, shortly after he started investigating these matters, was probably due to an attempt to cover up for the involvement of U.S. agents in these crimes against Mexico.

* That agents of several U.S. government agencies aided and abetted these crimes against Mexico, covered up for them, and then retaliated against the INS agent who filed the report that was then criminally destroyed or hidden. These agents were from the U.S. Department of Justice, Immigration and Naturalization Service, Drug Enforcement Administration, and U.S. attorney.

* The drug smuggling operation involving major segments of the U.S. government were also directed against the people of the United States, a fact that has been proven by the evidence I have been provided by several dozen former federal agents and operatives.

* The murder and drug trafficking, implicating agents of the U.S. government were also directed against the people of the United States. These facts have been discovered by me and a coalition of several dozen present and former government agents and deep-cover operatives. The coverups, the

1

obstruction of justice, the continuation of the criminal activities, are documented standard operating procedures by people holding key positions in the government of the United States.

PRIOR COVERUP BY MEXICAN OFFICIALS

Part of this information had been sent by the INS agent to various Mexican agencies, including the Mexican consul in Texas. I also sent information to the Mexican consul in San Francisco. We never received a response, indicating that these Mexican officials are covering up for crimes against Mexico and its people by agents of the U.S. government. Obviously, this has monumental implications.

My Credibility:

I am a former inspector and investigator in the government of the United States, who discovered during the past 30 years patterns of documented corrupt practices involving federal officials in all three branches of government. Over two dozen government agents have provided me with additional court-admissible evidence during the past ten years.

Part of this government corruption, and the well-orchestrated coverup and obstruction of justice, is detailed and documented in the books, *Defrauding America* and *Unfriendly Skies*, and referred to in the Internet web sites, http://www.defraudingamerica.com; http://www.ciadrugs.com; and http://www.unfriendlyskies.com.

A Major Scandal Against Mexico and Its People

The murder of a Mexican national, on Mexican territory, by an agent of the U.S. government, to cover up for a criminal drug trafficking operation conducted by a U.S. agent on Mexican soil, has serious implications for Mexico, its people, and produces additional evidence of interference in the operation of other government by certain people in control of the United States.

My primary interest in providing this information to Mexican officials is to expose the corruption by U.S. government officials that are inflicting great harm upon many innocent people.

I am making copies of this letter available to others. Obviously, if you continue the coverup of these crimes against your own people, the scandal takes on even greater importance.

Sincerely,

Rodney Stich

Registry number: 823791139

On April 27, 1999, I received a telephone call from the Mexican consul at San Francisco, Arturo Balderas, stating that he received a request from President Zedillo's office to interview me concerning the material that I had sent to him June 5, 1998—almost a year earlier. He wanted me to come to the Mexican consulate and I told him I couldn't make it for at least two weeks as I was completing the final editing on my book. I did ask him to fax me the request. His fax stated in part: "In regard to the letter that you sent to the President of Mexico, Ernesto Zedillo, reporting crimes against the Mexican government. "I will appreciate that you call me, in order to set up an appointment to talk about your concern."

DEA ROLE IN THE LOCKERBIE BOMBING
Within a year of the December 21, 1988 downing of Pan Am Flight 103 over Lockerbie, Scotland, I started receiving information from CIA, DIA (Defense Intelligence Agency), and other sources as to what actually happened. The information from these sources revealed why and how the bomb was placed on the aircraft, again showing the consequences of government involvement in drugs. The following information is contrary to the line being given out by U.S. officials.

Reason For the Bombing
On July 3, 1988, the U.S.S. *Vincennes* shot down an Iranian airliner, killing 290 people. The airliner was on a scheduled flight, on a heavily traveled civil airway, climbing through 12,000 feet, when the U.S.S. Vincennes launched a missile at it. The missile, hitting the airliner, broke it into many pieces, causing the eventual death of 290 people, some of whom fell over two miles before they were killed upon impact.

Iran was obviously furious, and Iran's Ayatollah was reported to have issued a "fatwa," a Muslim proclamation that several U.S. airliners would be downed in retaliation. Iran then contracted with a terrorist group headed by Ahmed Jibril to bring about the downing of U.S. aircraft. The downing of Pan Am Flight 103 over Lockerbie would be facilitated by a drug smuggling operation controlled out of the DEA office in Nicosia and involving DEA and CIA personnel and drug traffickers from Lebanon and Syria.

One Of Many CIA-DEA Drug Smuggling Operations
The ongoing drug-smuggling operation used Pan Am aircraft out of Frankfurt that were departing for the United States. It was this drug smuggling operation that made possible the placement of the bomb on Pan Am Flight 103.

This is how the drug smuggling operation worked: A courier would check his bags at Pan American in Frankfurt, and the bags would pass inspection. However, before the bags were placed on the aircraft, baggage handlers replaced one of the previously inspected bags with another bag containing approximately 200 pounds of heroin.

Jibril, paid to bomb one or more U.S. airliners, had no trouble using the CIA's own illegal operation to put the bomb on Pan Am Flight 103. The Jibril group reportedly bribed the Turkish baggage handlers to place an additional bag on the aircraft, which contained the bomb. Because of a flight delay, the bomb that was set to explode over the North Atlantic exploded over Lockerbie.

At first, the United States recognized Jibril as the main suspect. But then the United States needed Syria's cooperation in attacking Iraq after Iraq invaded Kuwait. Since Syria was the home to one part of the CIA-DEA drug smuggling operation and also the home of the Jibril group, the United States could not charge Syria with harboring them. Further, revealing how the bomb was put on the aircraft risked exposing the CIA-DEA drug smuggling operation.

Justice Department officials then fabricated far-fetched theories as to how two Libyans placed the bomb on board Pan Am Flight 103—contradicted by the evidence. Many articles in the European press showed the U.S. charges against the Libyans as false. German police, for instance, who knew about the CIA-DEA drug pipeline, gave no credence to the Justice Department's fabricated evidence and false charges. A more thorough description of the Pan Am Lockerbie disaster, the evidence, and the usual Justice Department retaliation of those who reveal the truth, can be found in the third edition of *Defrauding America*.

CHAPTER SEVEN

CUSTOMS COMPLICITY

The U.S. Customs Service is a division of the Treasury Department and charged with protecting the borders of the United States. It is the primary agency for drug interdiction into the United States. Customs has an air wing with over 100 aircraft. Experienced pilots are hired and then trained to be law-enforcement officers, flying various fixed-wing and rotary wing aircraft. These pilots are not required to be street agents as in the case of DEA pilots. It has airborne and ground-based radar detection sites to spot drug smuggling aircraft.

As a comparison, pilots for the Drug Enforcement Administration Air Wing are taken from the ranks of street agents who have a commercial pilots license. DEA pilots do primarily surveillance and logistical support, while Customs Service pilots interdict and chase suspected drug traffickers to the point of landing, at which time the pilot being chased would be apprehended.

In 1985, the U.S. Customs Service abolished the U.S. Customs Patrol (CPO) along the border and placed it into the Office of Investigations, which was later renamed the Office of Enforcement (OE). The Customs Patrol was created upon the abolishment of the Customs Security Officer (CSO) and the creation of the Drug Enforcement Administration in 1973. The DEA was created by the transfer from U.S. Customs of a large number of Special Agents, leaving the remaining Customs Special Agents without any authority to conduct narcotics investigations because of the "White Paper" negotiated between DEA and Customs.

The Customs Patrol was initiated as a non-investigatory uniformed law enforcement agency responsible for interdicting narcotics and other illegal goods smuggled into the United States by land, sea, and air. All narcotics interdictions were referred to DEA for investigation.

Written memorandums of understanding between the DEA and Customs in the mid-1990s gave the DEA responsibility for all domestic and foreign smuggling investigations, leaving Customs with drug investigations directly related to their work at the border.

Veteran Customs Agent Whistleblower

John Carman, a 20-year veteran of the U.S. Customs Service, started his government service with the U.S. Secret Service in Washington. This was followed by several years as an agent for U.S. Customs at the Calexico Port of Entry and then at the San Diego port of entry at San Ysidro. His primary duties were to detect and interdict narcotics, for which he received many commendations. His last position was as Senior Customs inspector in the San Diego office. Carman said his drug-interdiction work was repeatedly blocked by Customs supervisors, who allowed large quantities of drugs to enter the United States, and allowed interdicted drug traffickers to go back to Mexico.

Definite Practice to Protect Powerful Drug Traffickers

Carman repeatedly reported that his superiors were allowing major drug loads to go through border check points at San Diego. Carman provided me with considerable information showing repeated actions by Customs personnel to protect large drug shipments crossing the border from Mexico. He filed a suit in U.S. District Court (September 1997) alleging that he was fired in June 1997 because he reported drug-related corruption within the Customs service.

Carmen witnessed gross violations of government regulations, widespread drug smuggling by government employees, and aiding and abetting of drug trafficking by Customs agents and supervisors. He observed Customs personnel protecting and passing through major drug traffickers and drug loads. He repeatedly reported these violations in writing to Customs Office of Special Counsel and the Internal Affairs Division. No corrective actions were taken. The problems were ignored, the reports dismissed, and the perpetrators allowed to continue their criminal acts. The only "corrective" action taken was to retaliate against Carman. Here are a few examples of what Carman discovered and reported:

- On October 29, 1985, he seized 400 grams of Mexican brown tar heroin and was then ordered by his supervisors to give the heroin back to the Mexican drug trafficker and release the person. This happened several times and Carman said the supervisors who ordered him to release the heroin were Charlie Gastellum and Honorio Garia. Carman reported this violation to Customs' Office of Internal Affairs. No action was taken.
- In June 1988, while working at the Commercial Export Gate at San Ysidro, a suspicious looking sealed container arrived from the Long Beach holding area. Before Carman could inspect the container, his supervisor, Filenon Fuentes, cleared it without conducting any examination.
- He was ordered to remove data from Customs data base that he had inserted earlier, that required a suspected Mexican drug trafficker, Jorge Hank Rhon, to be checked for drugs whenever he crossed the border check point. Rhon had powerful political connections on both sides of the border; he had a private zoo near his Caliente racetrack in Tijuana, and was the son of one of Mexico's top drug lords, Carlos Hank Gonzalez, a former Agriculture Minister. The senior Rhon was manager of the Grupo Hank Business empire based in Tijuana, which had controlling interests in many businesses. These included banks on both sides of the border, and an interest in Taesa Airline, which had a drug-hauling reputation. Hank

Gonzalez's son, Carlos Hank Rohn, was reportedly the one who used Citibank to hide the drug money of Raul Salinas, whose brother was the president of Mexico. Despite this history, Customs supervisors removed the red tag from the computer data base.

Customs Protecting Powerful Drug Lords

Carman said, "Jorge Hank Rohn is a person they don't want to touch. They don't *want* us to check him. They don't *want* us to search him. They don't *want* us to put his name in the computer." Carman said the supervisor who told him this was John "Jack" Maryon.

Protecting A Major Mexican Drug Trafficker

The Zaragosa family that reportedly was heavy into drug shipments regularly sent trucks into the United States, often with large drug shipments inside. In one instance in 1990, a Zaragosa family propane truck, whose ownership was hidden in the company Hidrogas de Juarez, was stopped as it was crossing the border at San Ysidro. Drug-sniffing dogs were madly barking at the truck, indicating they detected drugs. The supervisor, Arthur Gilbert, tried to dissuade Customs agents from inspecting the truck, claiming the dogs were reacting to another smell.

Release Of Cartel Driver Caught with 8500 Pounds of Cocaine

One of the agents threatened to report the matter to Customs Internal Affairs if the supervisor refused to allow the truck to be inspected. A search then revealed 8500 pounds of cocaine. Despite finding cocaine that would net an American citizen several life sentences, Customs Supervisor Art Gilbert allowed the Mexican truck driver to return to Mexico. Carman felt that the supervisor was there to be sure the truck was *not* detained by the Customs agents.

Despite this and similar incidents, Gilbert was protected by U.S. attorney Alan Bersin in San Diego. Carman said a check of the phone records showed Gilbert making over 200 phone calls, as many as five a day, to a major drug trafficker in Mexico. Bersin was a former classmate to Bill Clinton, who appointed him U.S. attorney after the unprecedented firing of all U.S. attorneys upon taking the office of President of the United States. This action halted many ongoing criminal investigations, blocked obtaining indictments, and permitted placing in this key position people protective of the President and his croonies.

Line Release Program Helped Drug Traffickers

U.S. Customs inaugurated a program called "line release." a plan to drastically reduce the number of inspections as trucks cross the border from Mexico into the United States. Under this program, large 18-wheeler trucks are routinely waved through without being inspected, permitting thousands of pounds of drugs to enter the United States.

Non-Inspection List

Customs had a non-inspection list, allowing Mexican companies and Mexican drivers to cross the border without being inspected. The commissioner of U.S. Customs Service said (October 1, 1995) that "drivers hauling goods into the United States from Mexico would have to undergo intensive background investigations before they would be approved for programs that allow importers to skirt routine cargo inspections." Customs agents laughed at this statement, saying "The Mexicans don't track people the way we do, and if they did, they wouldn't share the information with us."

Fabulous Profits For Customs Agents

Carman said that Customs inspectors make huge hidden incomes by waving vehicles through inspection points without stopping. In one instance at El Paso, Customs Inspector Jose de Jesus Ramos was arrested trying to wave a truck through without inspection that contained 2,000 pounds of cocaine. In that instance, the Customs agent notified the drug trafficker by beeper that he was on duty and the lane number that he would be checking. When the vehicle carrying the drugs got to the Customs agent, it would be waved through without being inspected. The Customs agent was to have been paid $1 million for that simple and hard-to-prove act.

A *U.S. News and World Report* article described the actions of Customs Agent Ricardo Felix who received hundreds of thousands of dollars in bribes for waiving vehicles through without inspection.

Carman cited an incident where he apprehended a Mexican female crossing the border with $16,000 cash stuffed into her clothing, bra, and handbag. Supervisor Filemon Fuentes, contrary to Customs regulations, gave the money back to her, allowed her to enter the United States, and suppressed the report. Carman reported this violation to Customs Internal Affairs, who cleared the supervisor of any wrongdoing, despite the fact it violated Customs rules and smelled of wrongdoing.

Customs kept a "Red Book" file on these incidents, and when Carman viewed the reference to the matter, he found the facts were falsified by the supervisor. Carman brought this alteration-of-records to the attention of Assistant District Director Gurdit Dillon who, instead of investigating the matter, started retaliating against Carman.

Carman was quoted in a *North County Times* newspaper (September 13, 1997), "I hope to inform people about what's going on down at the border. These people are involved in illegal activities." The article continued:

In the lawsuit and an interview, Carman accused Customs agents, including supervisors, of allowing people with drug connections to waltz across the border without being checked, as well as accepting bribes, falsifying reports and deleting information about certain people from intelligence files. "They don't want you to do your duty," he said.

"They want you to look the other way. They don't want you to search certain people. It's obvious that they are trying to show preferential treatment for certain people. The drugs that are caught at the border are usually small amounts being carried by "non-professionals," he said. "The type of stuff that we're getting at the lower level is a mere pittance compared to what's actually coming through, and when we do focus on a big one it's by accident," Carman said.

"Customs agents' anger borders on revolt," read the headline on a *San Diego Union-Tribune* (October 1, 1995) article with the subtitle, "Many accuse bosses of corruption, indifference." The article stated in part:

Across the country, men and women on the front lines of the U.S. Customs Service are at war with their own superiors. They have alleged corruption at the highest levels, and many say that in doing their jobs they feel more like clerks than cops these days. Employees of the federal government's oldest law enforcement agency laments that their very mission, collecting trade revenue, arresting import smugglers and inspecting everything from baby clothes to contraband, is being eroded from within. Nowhere has this criticism been more vocal than in San Diego County.

Here, current and former Customs inspectors have made so much noise about what they feel is poor management and corruption that their complaints have prompted questions by politicians in Washington and several government investigations, including one by the FBI into Customs corruption all along the Southwest border. The agency, [U.S. Customs Service Commissioner George Weise], Weise said recently, is in the midst of a major reorganization and downsizing as a result of Vice President Al Gore's program for reinventing government. [President Clinton promptly slashed personnel involved in drug interdiction upon becoming president.]

One San Ysidro inspector said it has been made clear to him that the major responsibility of Customs is to facilitate trade and keep importers happy. Drugs, he said, "Just don't seem to be a priority."

Ties Between Customs Officials and Mexican Drug Traffickers

Carman told me about the ties between Customs supervisors and Mexican drug traffickers and drug money launderers, and the socializing between the two diverse groups. He described the ties between Jorge Hank, a former Mexican Minister of Agriculture, and Customs officials in San Diego, including the former District Director, Allan J. Rappoport. Customs officials in Washington refused to take any action. A Customs report (March 21, 1991) referring to Rappoport stated in part:

The purpose of this memorandum is to provide a synopsis of the findings of this investigation. This investigation was predicated on allegations that Rappoport allegedly consorted with known criminals. It was also alleged that Rappoport was implicated in a conspiracy to smuggle illegal aliens and/or illicit drugs into the United States across the Mexican border. During the investigation it was determined that Rappoport retired and is no longer an employee of the U.S. Customs Service. Based on the above, this investigation has been closed administratively.

Associate of Major Drug Kingpin on Crime Commission

Making matters worse, Rappoport maintained a position on the San Diego Crime Commission. Wouldn't the thousands of imprisoned people like to receive the same leniency shown to this DOJ-protected government official!

Carman said that when Rappoport was advised that he was under investigation, Rappoport resigned within 24 hours. Despite considerable evidence against him, the U.S. Attorney did not pursue any prosecution as they would have done if he was an ordinary citizen. To have prosecuted him would have reflected upon drug trafficking by U.S. Customs—and much more.

Carman described an incident where a car passing through the San Ysidro border crossing was stopped, inspected, and after a check in the National

Crime Information Center's (NCIC) data computer, discovered the car was reported as stolen in the United States. Instead of seizing the car, Customs supervisor Filemon Fuentes and Customs liaison agent Sonny Manzano allowed the driver to return to Mexico—with the stolen car belonging to an American citizen.

Entering False Information into Government Data Bases

Carman reported that Customs officials were entering altered intelligence reports into the TECS computer database. (TECS: Treasury Enforcement Computer System, and MOIR) is Memorandum Of Information Received) For instance, Carman entered data on a murder suspect that Carman and another Customs agent found driving a stolen car. The information was later altered by Supervisor Arthur Gilbert.

Forged Release Authorization by Bogus Customs Inspector

Carman reported alteration of an inspection record relating to a shipment in the commercial holding area at Long Beach by a Customs agent signing his or her name as Inspector Bluitt. Carman checked the TECS computer system database and found there was no Inspector Bluitt listed.

Mexicans Caught with Drugs and Drug Money Protected

Carman reported Mexicans, some of them Mexican law enforcement personnel, found with drugs and drug money in their possession, were allowed to proceed, and then the records falsified to omit the law violations. This benevolent attitude by Customs officials did not apply to Americans caught with drugs.

Ordered To Remove Prominent Mexican
Drug Traffickers from Computer Data Base

In 1994, Supervisor and Branch Chief John "Jack" Maryon and another supervisor ordered Carman to remove from the TECS computer files the names of key Mexican drug traffickers and drug-related government officials who were the subject of Carman's earlier reports. One was Roberto de la Madrid, a former governor of Baja, Mexico. Carman said one of the Mexicans was known for his violence and serious violations.

DEA Drug-Carrying Aircraft

Carman told me of one instance where a Beech Kingair arrived at Browns Field in San Diego from Mexico, carrying DEA agents. Customs agents were instructed by supervisors not to go near the plane. Another Customs supervisor later told him the plane was carrying cocaine. Carman said he had heard from other agents about many DEA planes arriving from Mexico carrying cocaine.

Overflights for Mexican Aircraft

Regional Director John Heinrich in the Long Beach Customs office signed a directive authorizing 167 specifically-named Mexicans flying in private planes from Mexico into the United States to over-fly border inspection points. Since Mexico is truly a narco-state, with endemic involvement in drug trafficking by local and national police, its politicians, and its military, this blanket over-flight authority was obviously prone to drug smuggling into the United States. Making this list even more preposterous, as long as any *one* of the Mexicans on the Customs list was on board the flight, *everyone else* on the aircraft was free to avoid the border check points—including drug kingpins.

One of the conditions that the Customs authorization said had to be met was that the pilots could not carry on board the aircraft any aviation charts from Mexico or Central and South America. This restriction was bizarre. No pilot would fly from Mexico without Mexican aeronautical charts.

That U.S. Customs Service authorization was dated October 2, 1993, identified by the code, AIR-5-LA:I;LAX:0, and addressed to Mr. Jorge Alva Hernandez, Director of Operations, Jets Ejecutivos, Hangar 4 Plataforma Aviacion General, Delegacion Venustiano Curarra, Mexico City, D.F. Mexico 15620. The authorization, addressed to Mr. Alva Hernandez, said in part:

Your application for...over-flight exemption has been approved. Your exemption expires on October 4, 1994. To continue your over-flight exemption in the future, you must file an application at least thirty (30) days prior to expiration. The aircraft listed below are approved for this over-flight exemption: [List omitted]

Carman said in April 1999 that Heinrich had been recently promoted and transferred to Washington, responsible for over 100 border inspection stations.

Consequences Suffered by Honest Government Agents

In 1995 after the media, including the San Diego *Union Tribune,* published Carman's allegations, Customs supervisors fired Carman. As if this wasn't enough, he was rushed to the hospital when a large pickup truck came crashing into his car on a side street, making no effort to stop or apply brakes. Carman received multiple broken ribs. The Filipino driver tried to flee but witnesses caught him. Carman had received death threats on the phone, his tires slashed, wheel lugs removed from his car, and items stolen from his property.

Politically-Correct Head of Customs Indifferent to Problems

The pattern of corruption in Customs was repeatedly reported to politically-correct Customs Commissioner Carol Hallett. Politicians recognized the vote-getter value of politically-correct appoints, such as the starry-eyed head of the FAA, Jane Garvey, and in this case, U.S. Customs. They simply do not know the ropes, or are too scared to fight the system, so problems go uncorrected.

In response to questions, Customs spokesman George Weise made a standard off-the-shelf response, as stated in the San Diego *Union-Tribune* (October 1, 1995):

Jobs and budget have been slashed, and that tends to make some of Customs' 15,000 employees uneasy." Weise ... defended the integrity of the service, saying it always has policed itself and prosecuted wrongdoing within its ranks. Weise added that he has given personal assurances that no employee with information about corruption would be penalized for coming forward.

Meaningless Whistleblower Posters on Government Walls

Carman, and many other government employees—including myself—have been misled into thinking that the walls of posters encouraging employees to report government misconduct meant what they said. The Whistleblower Protection Act is mostly meaningless and intended for show. Carman discovered this too late. And so did I.

A fairly standard reaction to government agents' reports of criminal activities is to discredit the agent and then fire him or her. This happened to Carman. This tactic is standard in the FAA, the FBI, and virtually every government agency. Carman was fired on June 19, 1997, after almost 20 years of service with various government agencies. He exercised his Civil Service remedies and found, as many other government inspectors had found, that this "remedy" is meaningless. He then filed a civil complaint for damages, including a *Bivens* claim, in the US District Court at San Diego (June 19, 1995).

Poor Media Reporting

Despite the enormous implications of a major government agency aiding and abetting the drug smuggling into the United States, the mainstream media kept the lid on years of reports by government insiders, except for a few brief watered-down television spots or short articles. Mike Wallace taped a three hour and thirty minute interview with Carman, but it was never aired. "Dateline" taped Carman, but made only a brief reference to the problems.

Carman didn't do any better with members of Congress. He contacted many of them, including Representatives Maxine Waters, Jim Kolbe and Charles Rangel, and Senators Diane Feinstein and Fred Thompson. None responded

The local *San Diego Union-Tribune* did provide some coverage of the more minor problems, omitting reference to the serious corruption matters. In one article (October 1, 1995) the paper said:

Agents contend that turf wars, red tape and pressure to produce have prompted some in their ranks to cut corners. "We are not only in a drug war. We are at war with the DEA (Drug Enforcement Administration)," one agent said. The two agencies have been locked in a battle for drug-fighting supremacy ever since the DEA was literally cut from a rib of the Customs Service in the 1970s and given primary responsibility for fighting the drug war.

Customs-Arranged Murder of Horner's Informants?

Customs agent Mike Horner was another Customs agent who "foolishly" tried to carry out his federal responsibilities by reporting the internal government corruption. One of Horner's supervisors asked Horner to provide him the names of two of his informants who had provided information about a large drug shipment. Horner provided this information, and within days one informant was killed and the other nearly killed with multiple stab wounds. Eventually, Horner had enough and took a medical retirement.

Chaos in Customs Revealed by Congressional Investigation

The hundreds of complaints by government agents throughout the southwestern part of the United States finally forced an investigation (1992) by a subcommittee of the House Committee on Government Operations: Commerce, Consumer, and Monetary Affairs. This hearing was conducted by Representative Doug Barnard, Jr. Although its report was startling, nothing came of it. The criminal activities against the United States by people in key government positions continued, despite the gravity and consequences of such conduct.

Serious Mismanagement and Misconduct in Customs

The committee issued a 1553-page report titled "Serious Mismanagement and Misconduct In the Treasury Department, Customs Service, and Other Federal Agencies and the Adequacy of Efforts To Hold Officials Accountable." The committee report stated that its function was to "investigate thoroughly allegations of mismanagement and misconduct, to hold accountable individuals at all levels who are responsible or otherwise culpable, who had information of misconduct and did not report it." Excellent rhetoric!—absolutely devoid of any corrective actions.

Throughout the huge House report were detailed incidents in which Justice Department employees, U.S. Attorneys (such as USA Linda Akers), blocked federal investigators from obtaining information, from pursuing evidence of corruption by federal agents, and aiding and abetting the retaliation of those agents who sought to report such corruption.

Texas Customs Supervisor Constantly Blocking Investigations

One section of the report dealt with the Customs problems encountered by AUSA David Hall who headed a multi-agency task force in the southwestern part of the United States. The Justice Department in Washington decided in 1987 to set up several field offices for the Narcotics and Dangerous Drugs Section (NDDS) of the Department of Justice Criminal Division, and one was in San Antonio, which Hall headed. In that position, Hall encountered repeated problems with Customs supervisors blocking the prosecution of major drug traffickers.

Hall testified to the House committee that Customs was the lead agency in the task force and that Special Agent in Charge (SAC) Neil Lageman in the San Antonio office was the lead agent. Hall testified that Lageman repeatedly blocked finalizing investigations by transferring agents whenever their investigations were about to lead to indictments against major drug traffickers. Over 12 agents were taken off the project in this way, without any reason.

Many Investigations Shut Down Short Of Indictments

When AUSA Hall protested these obstructionist tactics to Lageman, Hall was told, "It is none of your business what Customs did with its personnel." Replacements caused many investigations to be shut down. In addition, there were six different supervisors over these agents in a two year period, creating further chaos in the San Antonio Customs office. Hall testified about these unexplained removals of Customs agents from the task force:

Several of the reassignments were made even after I protested to Mr. Lageman that due to the agent he was removing I would lose an indispensable part of a particular investigation .... They were disruptive of the operations of the task force .... The overall effect of the Customs turnovers was to wreak havoc on the operation of the task force.

One of our biggest problems was the constant change in the Customs hierarchy. [Referring to the major drug traffickers that escaped arrest, Hall testified] There were at least 12 investigations that died. Three or four of these, I considered to be very significant. One of the investigations hinged on a proposal to operate a money laundering store front for targeted and known heroin smugglers from Asia. Customs refused to approve this proposal.... Another investigation of a large-scale cocaine distributor failed when the undercover agent who was working with the violator was reassigned. The agent believed that the target dealt in 100-pound quantities of cocaine....

A third investigation was of a major cocaine smuggler and money launderer, and it was not pursued after reassignment of all three agents who had been working on the case. The agents had information that the target had imported over 1,000 kilograms of cocaine and was living on what was reported to be a $1 million ranch....[Because of Customs blocking action] I closed the task force in June 1990....abysmal mismanagement of the Customs cooperation in the task force....

The other agencies did not trust their information with the Customs Service and as a consequence did not share information freely....One particular individual with an exorbitant amount of cocaine dealing, living on a very big ranch in real luxury, and that was easily identifiable by our task force. And yet, that investigation ceased when the task force was stopped [due to internal sabotage by Customs, the FBI, and U.S. attorney].

Sabotage of Imminent Arrest of Major Drug Lord

Neil Lageman, by AUSA David Hall's own testimony, did everything possible to block the arrest of major drug traffickers. In another chapter, contract undercover pilot Rodney Matthews, working out of the San Antonio office, was about to cause the arrest of a major international drug lord when Customs and DOJ sabotaged the operation, permitting the drug trafficking to continue.

Customs Employees and Mexican Drug Traffickers

A Report of Investigation (August 2, 199), included in the House report, contained the following statements:

A Customs official was seen at the racetrack in Mexico in the private box of a drug dealer...A former inspector was seen at the house of a target of the La Esperanza investigation....A target of the La Esperanza investigation stated, "Don't worry, my friends in Customs will take care of the problem." [Habiniak-La Esperanza Mining Company]

One report of an interview with FBI Special Agent Claudio De La O, included in the House report, stated:

De La O said that the FBI had considered opening a corruption investigation on Customs Employees, but it was never opened.... De La O referred to the Abrego drug organization as the "mob." He explained that the mob would search out law enforcement officers who would provide information concerning potential search warrants, law enforcement aircraft coordinates, law enforcement scrutiny pointed toward members of their organization, information on border stops, NCIC lookouts, TECS lookouts, information on currency investigations and most of all, the ability for the officer to keep other officers away from members of the organization....

As another example, [Customs agent whose name was blacked out] was seen at many parties given by the mob. De La O stated that the agent was closer to the mob than anyone he knew....De La O stated that he also had problems working with the Cameron County Sheriff's office due to similar allegations [of drug involvement and harassment of federal agents].

An April 21, 1990 letter to Customs Regional Commissioner James C. Piatt, included in the House report, stated:

Customs agent Solomon Rodriguez was passing loads and making big bank deposits....All the files were missing....I continued to gather information about ties between the Inspectors and different off-shots of the Guerras organization.

Testimony of Many Agents Proved
Widespread Criminal Obstruction of Justice

The testimony of the government witnesses revealed chaos and mismanagement throughout the federal agencies responsible for fighting the so-called war-on-drugs. For instance, Customs Agent Jim Dukes, assigned to the Criminal Division of U.S. Customs in San Antonio, Texas, said in his opening statement to the House committee (March 27, 1992):

We are what is commonly referred to as Whistleblowers and appear before you to testify honestly about serious breaches of integrity within the Customs Service by management officials, which are violations of criminal laws as proscribed under Title 18 of the United States Code and the Department of Treasury's Minimum Standards of Conduct.... We all have, individually and separately, previously reported and made sworn statements about these matters to Customs Office of Internal Affairs, Treasury Inspector General's Investigators, the Government Accounting Office, the FBI, and other government agencies [with no corrective action taken]....We had spoken to nine other investigative bodies, including Internal Affairs, and all we had done was ruin our career and our health practically.

Dukes testified, as did other Customs agents, that after he started reporting corruption in Customs, including reports of Customs supervisors and other agents protecting drug traffickers, that the standard government reaction took place: supervisors started attacking his veracity and credibility.

Three Internal Customs Investigations and Coverups!

Dukes made reference to three recent investigations of Customs corruption and mismanagement, all of which described the problems in general terms. The investigations included the September 16, 1991, report prepared by the Treasury Office of Inspector General, U.S. Customs Service, titled "Greater Management Attention Needed for Southwest Region Problems," the Customs Commissioner's Blue Ribbon Panel titled "Review of Integrity and Management Issues of the United States Customs Service" (August 1991), and the report by the Inspector General of the Treasury Office titled "Management of Customs Southwest Region." Dukes called them "just short of being a whitewash."

He added: "I will testify on serious matters of misconduct by Customs management officials. Everything that I will state here has been reported to Customs Internal Affairs and the Treasury OIG (Office Inspector General)."

Special agent Thomas Grieve, San Antonio

Testifying before the House committee was Special Agent Thomas Grieve with U.S. Customs Service. Prior to joining the Customs Service he had been a criminal investigator with the IRS, and prior to that, a Special Agent with the Drug Enforcement Administration. Grieve testified:

The mismanagement, misconduct, and criminal acts that we will discuss here today are real. The Customs Service in San Antonio has been primarily concerned with the perception of fighting drugs, rather than actually doing it. It didn't matter if high-quality criminal cases were being made. What really mattered were statistics, no matter how obtained. It is easier to assign agents to task forces and pirate their statistics than it is to develop investigations from information gathered from outside sources. Upper management is more concerned with the perks of the job than they are with any real accomplishments.

Grieve described how Customs supervisors, including Neil Lageman, repeatedly protected major drug traffickers by barring agents from performing their jobs or by transferring them when their investigations were about to bring arrests. He said:

I had the opportunity to deal with a confidential informant (CI) who had been a major heroin smuggler. His knowledge of heroin trafficking was excellent. It was extraordinary. He had access to the highest levels of BCCI (Bank of Credit and Commerce International). The same CI gave me information that would have enabled us to tap into major smuggling rings. We would have used some pretty unique methods to tap into these organizations to both launder their money and monitor their couriers.

Grieve described a conversation between Deputy SAC Jay Silvestro and SAC Neil Lageman, when Lageman said, "Drug cases are nothing but problems and I don't want problems." (This was the same attitude I and other inspectors encountered in the FAA, as managers didn't want inspector reports of accident-causing air safety problems.)

Refusal To Take Action Caused Drugs To Enter the United States

Grieve testified: "It is my opinion that since we took no action, we were responsible for unknown quantities of heroin being smuggled into and made available on the streets of this country. We had everything set up to accomplish our mission. When it came to actually doing the job, we were told we couldn't do it." This was similar to the FAA culture, where office Supervising Inspectors don't want reports of air safety problems or violations because they cause problems for the office.

Special Agent David Ruiz, San Antonio

David Ruiz was a criminal investigator for Customs. His testimony and prepared statement, appearing in the House report, stated in part:

Customs is an agency run amuck with leaders who hold their personal objectives above policies, procedures, and even the law. The Office of Enforcement is plagued with an incompetent and ill-trained management core. On this very core OE builds its policy and makes decisions from which to run the war on drugs. Resident Agent in Charge (RAC) Louis Dracoulis made it clear on one occasion when he told me that if he ever gave me an order he expected it to be followed, even though it was illegal.

This [internal conduct] failure in the very core of OE takes a fatal turn in enforcement of law when management cannot be trusted even to be truthful and honest in its normal course of daily activity. Management has no regard for the truth, and is willingly lying both officially and unofficially.

Lying To Confidential Informants

Ruiz described the practice of lying to confidential informants and the deception played upon them by Customs Service supervisors. Sophisticated CIs or documented undercover agents Richard Pitt and Rodney Matthews, described elsewhere in these pages, did not know of this practice when they carried out highly sensitive and dangerous undercover operations on the basis of instructions and authorizations given to them by Customs agents in Texas.

Threats to Kill Government Agent Exposing Narcotic Traffickers

Ruiz testified about threats to his life for having arrested key drug traffickers:

In September 1976, my former supervisor threatened to kill me or have me killed for arresting certain narcotic traffickers. This threat was witnessed by the then assistant U.S. Attorney and chief of the criminal section of the western judicial district of Texas. The assault was witnessed by two DEA special agents. On May 18, 1984, management chastised me for reporting Customs pilot Gerald Weatherman for smuggling endangered species, sea turtle-skins, into Kelly Air Force Base from the Grand Cayman Islands, utilizing a Customs Service aircraft.

Special Agent Herbert P. Hailes

Part of the testimony and prepared statement by Special Agent Herbert Hailes appeared in the House report:

It is an "old-boy management network" Lageman's style of management was autocratic, Machiavellian, and dictatorial, resulting in general office chaos, disruption of major investigations, and set into motion a never-ending feeling of fear, confusion, frustration, and burnout. He personally took the severest disciplinary action available on any agent who was not a sycophant. Intimidation, threats, and micro-management ultimately affected every phrase of investigative work in the district. A case in point was Lageman's posture on national priority investigations. He said that "perception is above all what matters!...it does not matter whether we make arrests or seizures ... what matters is the perception Region and headquarters has of what we tell them."

The Commissioner wants to portray the Service as a benevolent and well-controlled organization operating according to law, and directive, and doing nothing wrong; when the record declares resoundingly otherwise. Those of us who protest the serious mismanagement and misconduct spend more time and energy fighting the retaliation and the relentless petty harassment than fight the "war on drugs." Agents are constantly bogged down in the strife and political power plays with inept and unscrupulous managers. I firmly believe that people in this agency who are a part of the twisted system will attempt the removal of myself and my

*colleagues. It will be cleverly tried through some fabricated issue and os-
tensibly "for the good of the service," while the renegade managers wave
good-by with their "sweetheart" deals.*

SAC John H. Juhasz

Special Agent in Charge (SAC) John Juhasz testified and submitted a prepared statement. Juhasz had been selected to head a task force to conduct investigations into misconduct and corruption by state and federal officials in
Arizona that was given the code name "Firestorm." He testified that the FBI
refused to become a part of the task force. Rather strange, since that is one of
the key areas of their responsibilities. The House report included a copy of a
letter that Juhasz sent to Customs Commissioner Carol Hallett, which said in
part:

*I am writing to inform you of the continuing tragedy of Customs and other
law enforcement corruption in Arizona.....corruption of Customs employees....trying to deal with the drug related corruption of law enforcement
officers on the Arizona-Mexico border.... the Customs Office of Enforcement (OE) is out of control....Despite the glaring mismanagement that was
rampant in [Thomas McDermott's] office, he was promoted to Headquarters last year....I found out that the DEA was deliberately withholding
valuable intelligence from my office concerning corrupt border inspectors, and I suspected that Javier Dibene, the SAC of the Justice Department Office of the Inspector General for Arizona (OIG, formerly Immigration OPR), was deliberately quashing corruption investigations of immigration inspectors and Border Patrol Officers on the border.... There
was a major coverup [by the FBI and U.S. attorney] This was at least
partly due to a strong "good old boy" network and due in another large
part to the fear of what such a well orchestrated investigation would in-
evitably uncover.*

Loads Of Cocaine Passed by Arizona Customs Inspectors

The House report described audio tapes transcribing the conversations
between two rival drug dealers describing in detail the corruption of Customs
and INS border inspectors. Part of the House report addressed this matter:

*The tapes contained the unequivocal identification and implication of
Customs border inspectors by name in corruption that involved the deliberate "passing" of large (600 pound) and numerous periodic (alleged to
be weekly) loads of cocaine by the inspectors, and the involvement of their
family members in the importation of cocaine. The report showed the
coverup of the tapes and their implications by local FBI Supervisor Joe
Reyes.*

*Also covering up for the tapes was Customs SAC Javier Dibene, who
then destroyed what he thought was the only copies. These decisions were
made despite the fact that the tapes contained the obvious, straight forward naming of the inspectors...The Customs inspectors referred to by
name in the tapes had been under investigation for over one year....Di-
bene asserted that if the inspectors were involved in corruption, he could
understand (condone) their activity because they came from poor, humble
beginnings and needed to provide for their families....Javier Dibene's ac-*

tions concerning the audio tapes serves to confirm...that he was actively suppressing corruption investigations. Equally as puzzling is the internal storm of controversy in DEA that followed the delivery of the tapes by S/A Vasquez.

ASAC Gerald Murphy of the DEA in Tucson refused to allow our IA agents to meet with or even speak to S/A Vasquez to arrange further debriefing of their confidential informant. In fact, ASAC Murphy reprimanded Vasquez for giving Customs IA the tapes and informed all of his agents that they were not to generate any reports addressing law enforcement corruption, and no information concerning such corruption was to go out of his office without his prior approval.

What this really meant, since ASAC Murphy refused to pass along corruption intelligence, was that no allegations of corruption would be turned over to the proper agencies for investigation. Thus, the drug dealers could continue to smuggle large (tons) quantities of drugs into Arizona from Mexico through corrupt border inspectors without fear of being investigated....The entire matter was ignored and the DEA and the FBI continued to disregard our requests for cooperation....began discovering the extent of the efforts taken by Javier Dibene to cover up corruption and quash investigations. This was quickly realized to be potentially a major embarrassment to the DOJ OIG. [Office of Inspector General.]

It is now apparent that in order to avoid large scale embarrassment to these agencies, the Task Force and Juhasz had to be stopped....nearly daily allegations of corruption made by DEA informants to the Special Agents....Critical records, reports, and intelligence data have disappeared from Dibene's office and the DEA' Nogales, Arizona office.... as the FBI, DOJ OIG, and DEA embarrassed at being caught covering up drug related law enforcement corruption in Arizona ... Who can exert so much political pressure in Washington, D.C? It is undisputed that a large portion of the drugs reaching our streets and injuring and killing our youth are allowed to enter the country through unscrupulous and corrupt law enforcement officials....Law enforcement officers on the Arizona-Mexico border, at all levels, have been corrupted. It does not matter whether this is due to bribes, sexual favors, real or threatened blackmail, or just plain fear of standing up and being counted.

Further Evidence of Government Drug Shipments into The U.S.

On Page 1206 of the House report are the following statements:

- In July 1990, FBI and Customs Albuquerque executed a controlled delivery of 1,646 kilograms of cocaine from Colombia to New Mexico.
- Unknown to the FBI, the Customs SAC had arranged for media coverage of the arrests and seizures. (This sabotaged the obtaining of evidence against a major drug shipper.)

Customs Furnished the Plane, the Pilot, and the Drugs

- At the news conference, Customs led the media to believe that the delivery of cocaine into the State of New Mexico was planned and executed by the drug traffickers, when, in fact, Customs had supplied a pilot, an aircraft, a vessel, and took delivery from the Colombians. (This is similar to many drug runs by Rodney Matthews and Richard Pitt described within these pages.)

The House report described how all, or almost all, of the Customs employees in the Yuma, Arizona office were guilty of embezzlement.

Routine CIA Drug Shipments Through Los Angeles Airport

Twenty-year veteran Customs agent Frank C. Newman submitted a report dated August 14, 1990, to the House committee (pgs 971-979) revealing CIA drug shipments through Los Angeles International Airport. This was dynamite testimony, and further corroborated the years of information provided to me by my many CIA and other inside sources who either flew the drugs, arranged for the shipments, or discovered the practice. Portions of Newman's testimony and report were entered in part into the Hearing report:

I have been a Customs Inspector at Los Angeles International Airport for thirteen years. I have seen a number of questionable events related to narcotics laws over the years. The most shocking event occurred about a month ago. I found out by accident that **agents of the Drug Enforcement Administration were escorting a large shipping container loaded with cocaine into the country.** *I called our Internal Affairs people within minutes. Approx two weeks later another shipping container loaded with cocaine arrived.*

Controlled Drug Smuggling By CIA

I have seen "controlled deliveries" before, but these most **recent incidents make the ones that I have worked on before look minuscule.** *Someone at your level should be asking, "How can we justify importing large loads of cocaine in hopes of stamping out cocaine in the U.S.? At what levels of government are these deliveries authorized? Do members of Congress such as yourself know about these controlled deliveries, especially such large loads? Are these loads coming into just Los Angeles, or other major cities in the United States as well?"*

With such large loads coming in, how much has been allowed to get to the street? What would the citizens of the U.S. say if they found out about such large loads? It seems reprehensible that officers of the Border Patrol and Customs Inspectors can risk their lives, and get killed, on the Mexican border looking for this stuff, and we then find that our own officers in another unit are bringing large loads of cocaine by us on a routine basis.

Bombshell Disclosures: No Response

Although CIA and other government insiders had testified for years about CIA drug smuggling into the United States, this testimony from a Customs agent, put into a congressional report, should have caused major repercussions. Instead, nothing followed except the usual coverup by the media, Congress, the Department of Justice, and virtually every other government and non-government check and balance. Newman's prepared statement, which also appeared in the House report, stated in part:

On 7-5-90 I was working baggage at terminal Two at LAX. A man who identified himself as the security chief for Pan American Airlines approached me and gave me information as follows: A shipping container

with 32 boxes of diplomatic material weighting 804 kgms (net) was being
escorted into the country by **three U.S. drug enforcement agents**. *I made*
a photocopy of his information, thanked him and went directly to SCI Dan
Vigna. I asked if he knew anything about a load of dope coming into the
country and he replied, "Yes, there is a shipment of coke coming." I in-
formed him that I was going to call Internal Affairs and did so immedi-
ately. After all the crosses and double-crosses associated with narcotics,
it is always best to cover oneself by calling Internal Affairs, and I did this.

Several years ago, Customs inspectors in the Carolinas were ordered
by agents of the CIA to clear a shipload of goods from Poland as part of
the Iran-Contra affair with no questions asked. A few years later, even
though these inspectors had acted in good faith, the Commissioner of
Customs, William von Raab, wanted their heads on a platter. It had
proven politically embarrassing to him when the Iran-Contra investiga-
tors found out that the shipment of goods on the freighter were really ille-
gal guns and ammo. A situation like this also occurred in New Orleans.
The inspectors were made into scapegoats.

Implying Routine Shipments of Cocaine by CIA-DEA-Customs

Newman made reference to ten large shipping containers of fish that had
arrived from South America on Air Canada under suspicious circumstances
that he wanted to inspect. His supervisor ordered him not to inspect it. Newman described the incident to the House Committee:

A Customs House broker told me that he had heard about a large load of
cocaine being brought in one month earlier. He then described exactly the
date, the airline, the commodity, and the country of origin. I immediately
contacted Internal Affairs. The agent told me that both **DEA and Customs**
agents had told him that they hadn't brought any loads of cocaine into
the country on that day. *I was left with two theories: corrupt members of*
Customs management arranged the load and set me up to sign it off; or
DEA or Customs agents arranged the load and wanted to keep it quiet,
so they lied to the Internal Affairs agent. I have asked myself a number of
times, How many other inspectors have also been set up to sign off loads?

Newman described another incident of drugs arriving on a Pan Am flight:

I had found out about a **load of cocaine arriving on Pan Am Flight 416**.
I was certain that a "dirty" load had arrived. Agents from both Internal
Affairs and Office of Investigations had both denied knowledge of a load
of cocaine, but voiced a willingness to check it out. Approximately ½ hour
later another agent from Office of Investigations called to demand where
I had received the information about the load of cocaine [apparently try-
ing to silence the informant].

CIA Cocaine Load into Los Angeles Was Normal and Proper

Two weeks after the prior shipment of cocaine, Newman heard of another
large cocaine shipment. He contacted Customs Airport Director Eileen Colon,
who assured Newman that "She had double checked and could assure me that
all of these **large controlled deliveries of cocaine were proper**. She also
stated that I would still receive a letter of reprimand." The reprimand was for
Newman calling Internal Affairs when he heard about the prior cocaine ship-

ment, which Colon called a technical error.

Grave Implications and Further Support Showing Drug Smuggling by Government Agencies

What these statements were admitting was that large shipments of cocaine were regularly being shipped into the United States by government personnel and agencies. This information supported the years and years of similar statements made to me by my government undercover sources. Think of the significance of this! In a March 27, 1992, letter to Representative Doug Barnard, Newman wrote:

Smuggling, corruption, and graft are, and have been an integral component of border culture and society for the last two hundred years. Individuals growing up in the border environment are going to be loyal to their families first, friends second, and their employer, the United States of America, third. Presently, huge numbers of Texas law enforcement officers who grew up on the border are involved in varying degrees in smuggling activity. The list includes sheriffs, deputies, city, state and federal law officers. The Texas border is rapidly becoming a "little Colombia," with no end in sight.

Dynamite Discoveries Followed by Letters of Reprimand

Despite uncovering these criminal and even subversive activities by government personnel, Customs supervisors made no attempt to address the serious matters. Instead, they placed a letter of reprimand in Newman's file alleging that he made a technical violation by reporting the major criminal offenses to Customs Internal Affairs: bypassing the SAC who would have covered up the matters. In effect, the major drug traffickers went scot-free, but the agent reporting the crimes was reprimanded.

Protecting Informant from DEA Agent

Newman described the incident where one of his informants told him about a shipment of jewelry that was arriving which was shown as a $200,000 value when in fact it was a $600,000 value. His investigation caught the deception and the shipment was seized. Several days later, DEA agent Darnelle Garcia asked Newman the name of his informant. Newman refused to provide this information, fearing for the informant's life. Newman wrote:

This was so preposterous that I told him that I didn't give out the names of my informants. A few days later another inspector told me that Garcia's informant had owned part of the large shipment of jewelry that I had seized. I can only presume that my informant would have been badly beaten or killed if I would have given out his name. For the record, Darnelle Garcia is presently awaiting trial in federal court in Los Angeles for acts of corruption on the job.

Perilous Position of Customs Contract Agents or Informants

Under these conditions, it is obvious that any contract agent carrying out undercover assignments for U.S. Customs would be easily disavowed if the authorized operation became a political liability.

Operation Polar Cap

Newman described how Customs covered up for what would become the largest money laundering operation ever busted by the government involving jewelry stores in the Los Angeles area.

Brinks Money Laundering Operation in Los Angeles

In reporting a large money-laundering operation in Los Angeles at Brinks, Newman wrote:

In 1985, I found that Brinks, the armored car company, was importing gold bullion and coins for sale by their company. People were bringing paper sacks full of cash and trading it for gold shot and coins.

Newman checked with Gary Cunitz, their cargo coordinator, asking him if he ever had the feeling that Brinks had been laundering drug money by selling gold? Cunitz replied, "Yes, and that's why we stopped selling gold." After Brinks stopped the practice, a Brinks vice president "quit" the company and set up a separate operation selling gold.

Newman filed a report on this money laundering operation. Instead of filing charges, Customs supervisors merely required Brinks to file government forms known as CF 4790. Newman was furious; it was a huge money laundering scheme that had gone on for years and the company's crimes were ignored.

Felony Retaliation Against Government Agents

The House report devoted considerable space to government retaliation against agents who reported corruption by management personnel, including drug trafficking offenses, or who discovered government-protected drug smuggling operations. Appendix 9 in the report, for instance, was titled: "Material Concerning Continuing Retaliation By Customs Officials Against Whistleblowers In San Antonio and Chicago." This retaliation violated numerous federal criminal statutes, including Title 18 USC Section 1505 relating to obstructing proceedings before government departments, agencies and committees, and Title 18 USC Sections 1512 and 1513 which pertain to threatening witnesses. The congressional committee did nothing about these criminal acts that undermined the responsibility and the functions of that government agency.

Smoking Hallucinogenic Substance?

Despite all the internal reports of corruption and coverups in the Customs Service, Customs Commissioner Carol Hallett, wrote in a February 15, 1992, letter to FBI Director William Sessions: "In the past several years, as a direct result of the FBI and Customs working together [i.e., coverups of internal corruption], notable accomplishments have been achieved in the area of dismantling large drug trafficking organizations."

The smoke and mirrors went both ways. Sessions, in a February 26, 1991, reply, wrote: "The importance of the January 22nd meeting was to reaffirm the long-standing spirit of cooperation between the FBI and the United States Customs Service (USCS) and strengthen the lines of communication between our agencies. Your assistance and positive support in resolving these issues is indicative of the spirit of cooperation that has been the benchmark of FBI and USCS relations. I look forward to a continuation of that tradition."

These letters appear to be written by people on another planet, or surely, under the spell of some strong hallucinogenic substance. No matter, the public takes it all in as gospel, and that is what counts!

Duplicity of Congressional Obstruction Of Justice

For over 30 years I have encountered and documented congressional obstruction of justice. Many deep-cover insiders, FBI agents, and others have provided prima facie proof of the corruption to members of Congress—who then covered up. These were major criminal acts that made possible great harm upon the United States and many of its people. The 1553-page report, one of many revealing reports, received the same coverup by members of Congress and most of the media. None of the committee members, or any other congressional committee members who knew about the findings in that report, made any effort to bring about the cessation of the drug smuggling into the United States by federal employees and agencies. This type of coverup violated many federal criminal statutes for which an ordinary person would end up in prison.

Customs Service Drug Smuggling Report: Disappearance

An *Associated Press* (AP) story (May 3, 1993) described an explosive eight-volume file prepared in December 1990 that disappeared from a final Washington report in 1991. The missing files described "Customs Service drug smuggling" and reported a pattern of drug trafficking by Customs inspectors. This report was sent to Washington and then removed from government files. Most newspapers refused to print the AP story, but I found it in the *Oakland Tribune*.

Are Mexico's Cartels Buying U.S. Cops?

The title on a *U.S. News & World Report* article (March 8, 1999) was "The Corrupting Allure of dirty drug money." with the subtitle, "Are Mexico's cartels buying U.S. cops?" The article described INS inspector Rafael Landa, with a salary of $35,000 a year, having $300,000 cash stored in his Nogales, Arizona home. It was believed that two Mexican drug gangs paid Landa and two other INS inspectors almost a million dollars for allowing over 4000 pounds of cocaine to cross the border. That quantity of cocaine had a street value of over $1.5 *billion*.

Customs Agent Taking Kickback from Government Informant
Customs Agents Taking Kickbacks From Informants

An article in the *San Francisco Daily Journal* (July 24, 1998), referring to U.S. Customs Service agents, said: "A number of incidents brought strong criticism to the [Justice Department], among them the government's failure to disclose that a U.S. Customs agent took a $4,000 kickback from an informant in a major drug-smuggling trial." Former Customs Agent Frank Gervacio received a $4,000 kickback in a drug case from government informant Michael Woods in a major international marijuana case. The kickback tainted a major drug case involving a former member of the Thai parliament, Thanong Sirprechapong, in which over 90,000 pounds of marijuana were smuggled into the United States during the 1970s and 1980s. The attorney for the Thai defendant moved to have the case dismissed on the basis of the misconduct between the informant and the U.S. Customs agent. The kickback resulted in criminal charges filed against the Customs agent in U.S. District Court, San Francisco (*U.S. v. Gervacio*, CR97-0275MHJP N.D. Cal).

Federal Judge Marilyn Patel Orders Leniency
For the Agent Whose Conduct Undermined Major Drug Case

Despite the seriousness of the matter, the position of trust which the government agent occupies, and the fact that a multi-year investigation of a major drug operation was legally undermined, U.S. District Judge Marilyn Patel sentenced Gervacio on March 1, 1999, to only 100 hours of community service and ordered him to pay a fine in the amount of the kickback (March 1, 1999). Not much more than a person receives for a traffic offense. In the third editions of *Unfriendly Skies* and *Defrauding America*, I describe in detail the corruption by this federal judge that covered up for major high-level crimes against the public.

There can be several reasons why a government agent receives a kickback from a government informant. The government agent and an informant may have engaged in a conspiracy to set up an innocent person, which results in the informant receiving compensation based upon the recommendation of the government agent, and the government agent builds up a favorable record for job actions. The informant than kicks back part of the government compensation to the agent.

Another reason could be that the informant is alerted to a major drug ring by the government agent and given insider information that the informant can then claim in a notice of criminal activities made to the government agency. After being paid for "his" tip, the informant kicks back part of the government money to the government agent who provided him the initial information.

"A National Disgrace"

FBI agent in charge Steve McCraw in Tucson described the bribing of U.S. agents along the border as "a national disgrace." Drug Enforcement Administration Chief Thomas Constantine estimated that drug cartels pay over $1 million every week in bribes to government agents.

A February 1999 Treasury Department report stated that the Customs Service had repeatedly failed to fight internal corruption, and continues to be affected by a "long history of strife and infighting" involving its two internal investigative units.

How Corrupt Government Agents Increase Their Income

There are many ways for government agents responsible for drug-related matters to increase their income. For instance:

- Notify drug traffickers when the inspector will be on duty at a border check point so that the trafficker can be waved through without an inspection.
- Pass along knowledge of an arrest warrant about to be served.
- Pass along knowledge relating to the trafficker, or an informant, existing in one of the government databases.
- Make a bogus inspection of a drug-laden vehicle and allow it to pass inspection.
- Wave a vehicle on through the inspection station without being inspected, knowing that it contains drugs.
- Destroy evidence in the files pertaining to a targeted drug trafficker.

How Other Government Agents Protect Major Drug Traffickers

- Refuse to initiate investigations, or close down investigations, using the excuse there is no evidence of a crime—when the evidence of such crime does in fact exist.
- Transfer or reprimand agents who develop evidence sufficient to indict.
- Order agents not to conduct an investigation of a particular person or company known to be involved in drug trafficking.
- FBI agents or U.S. Attorney refusing to act on evidence of criminal activities.
- FBI agents or U.S. attorneys falsely stating the evidence is not sufficient to convict.
- FBI and/or U.S. attorney filing sham criminal charges against government agent who reports crimes being protected by higher officials.
- Government supervisors filing unfavorable reports about an inspector, or transferring him or her into an assignment away from the scene of the corrupt activities.
- Charge investigator with technical violations and take disciplinary action against him or her, when the investigator is reporting politically-sensitive or government-protected corruption.

Instructed To Commit Fraud and Perjury by DOJ and Customs

Mark Conrad was a veteran in the Customs Service, who was resident agent in charge (RAC) in Customs Internal Affairs at Houston, responsible for a nine-state area. He retired from U.S. Customs Service in December 1998. He was very vocal in articulating the misconduct he had seen over the years. He provided me with information about corruption in Customs and the Department of Justice. In one letter he said:

I can give you explicit details of my being asked to lie in Federal Court in Ft. Lauderdale; to ignore blatantly false representations to a Federal judge in San Diego, to lie in an internal investigation, etc. I can provide you with actual documents that prove the government altered computer records (Internal Affairs reports) to reflect what management wanted— not what the facts were and I can provide you with specific sources and outside independent government agents that can confirm what I say.

Customs Admits Internal Corruption

"U.S. Customs Admits Its Own Drug Corruption," was the title to a New York Times article (February 17, 1999) as it referred to an Office of Professional Responsibility (OPR) report which stated in part:

The officials said the number of (internal corruption) cases might be higher because the corruption often required little involvement by an officer whose only overt activity was to turn away when a car carrying drugs pulled up at an inspection lane. Such cases are extremely difficult to detect, given the volume of cross-border traffic.

One of the most serious issues to emerge in the report was the animosity between the agency's internal affairs unit and the Office of Investigations, which conducts criminal inquiries into violations of Customs laws. The report found what it called a "long history of strife and infighting" between the two units, an animosity based on investigations agents' belief that agents assigned to internal affairs "are incompetent, overzealous and spend too much time investigating matters that are unrelated to corruption."

Two Internal Affairs agents interviewed in the course of the review said the hostility had "a debilitating effect on their ability to perform their jobs diligently" and "diminished the importance of their work."

Some agents cited instances in which investigations agents interfered with or compromised investigations. The report did not cite specifics but said that two Federal prosecutors had considered excluding Customs agents from corruption cases because of the conflict that the report said had reached "critical proportions."

Where is the Outrage?

Despite all the evidence of widespread culture of corruption in government, despite the effect that this corruption has on government institutions, upon national morality, and upon the drug-related violence, no outrage is heard.

Picking on the Average Joe or Jane
While Protecting Those Paying for Protection

The corrupt culture that permeates U.S. Customs protects the major drug traffickers who can and do pay bribes or kickbacks. To offset those drug traffickers that are allowed to pass through Customs, some agents pick on those who aren't in a position to pay for protection: the average Joe or Jane passing through Customs. Agents receive extra money for catching people smuggling small quantities of drugs, and this extra compensation leads to harassing abuses against many people who have not committed any smuggling offenses.

Personal Outrages Resulting from Personal Searches

The television show "Frontline" (April 29, 1999) documented the cases of people, including women, who were subjected to body cavity searches, who were detained for hours at a time, made to take laxatives while detained and endured people watching them defecate, looking for ingested drugs. This can happen to you, your wife, your mother, and you must accept it. This is all a part of the deteriorating constitutional rights that younger people don't realize are now lost, but rights that had previously existed, before they were born.

CHAPTER EIGHT

FBI VETERAN REVEALS
CIA-MAFIA-DRUG TIES

A veteran FBI agent and highly-decorated Vietnam veteran provided still further corroboration to the fact that the CIA has been smuggling drugs for the past 40 years, that the CIA has been engaging in drug trafficking with Mafia segments, and that the FBI and other Justice Department divisions have covered up for these interrelated crimes.

Richard M. Taus had been a Special Agent for the FBI from 1978 to 1988, during which time he was assigned to organized crime and foreign counterintelligence operations. He held the responsible position of relief Supervisory Special Agent (SSA) in the New York City area. In addition to his FBI duties, Taus was a Pilot-In-Command (PIC) flying missions for the FBI's New York Field Office. The *New York Times Reference Book For the Year 1988* lists Taus under "FBI Events." In the 1980s he conducted an undercover operation as part of a group consisting of 17 special agents. He also held the rank of Lieutenant Colonel in the aviation branch, U.S. Army Reserve.

A Brief History Of Richard Taus

Taus had two tours of duty flying combat missions in Vietnam during which he received three Bronze Star Medals and seven Air Medals, as well as several decorations for meritorious service. In 1967-68, as an Armed Forces Courier officer, Taus fought in the Tet Offensive and flew in the siege of Khe Sanh. In 1970-71, as a Helicopter Unit Commander for the First Cavalry Division, Taus, then Captain, flew Boeing CH-47 Chinook helicopters directing rescue-and-recovery operations.

On that last Vietnam tour, Taus adopted a Vietnamese orphan he brought back to the United States and who now bears the name, David Taus. This adoption was historic and received national media attention. It required obtaining specific approval and assistance from President Thieu and President Johnson, and amending U.S. Immigration and Naturalization laws. David Taus would later work for the FBI in the mid-1980s as a personnel analyst in the New York Field Office.

Taus Reporting CIA Drug Trafficking in Vietnam

While he was a helicopter unit commander in Vietnam, Taus discovered and reported to his supervisors widespread drug trafficking by the Central Intelligence Agency. Taus described how the CIA transported drugs that were sold to American GIs in Vietnam and Laos, causing over a third of the armed forces in Vietnam to become drug addicts. These GIs were often too drugged out to either fight or defend themselves. In addition, in that condition, they often killed their own officers, a practice known as "fragging."

Hesitant About Revealing Government Corruption

I first made contact with Taus in 1997, and he was hesitant about revealing government corruption that he discovered while an FBI agent. I explained to Taus that there was a U.S. Supreme Court decision rendered about 15 years earlier stating that a federal employee had a greater duty to report criminal activities by his superiors than a duty to cover up for such crimes because of any employee secrecy agreement. I also explained that in my opinion, the statutory requirement to report federal crimes, such as required by federal criminal statute Title 18 USC Section 4, superseded any secrecy agreement required to be signed by government employees or agents. *Failure* to take unusual actions to circumvent the massive government and non-government coverups, and expose these criminal activities, would make *us* culpable of aiding and abetting the activities that were inflicting such great harm upon the people of the United States.

It wasn't as if we were endangering lawful secret operations or deep-cover operatives. We were making known very serious criminal and even subversive activities which required circumventing the coverups by government and non-government checks and balances. If we did not do that, we would be joining the complicity of coverups and obstruction of justice responsible for the continuation of these corrupt conditions. Government retaliation upon Taus had silenced his ability to report these matters, but exposing them in a book would at least make some of the people aware of what was occurring behind the scenes in government.

Internal FBI Coverups Too Pervasive

Taus said he did all he could to report these criminal activities, but the coverup was too pervasive. The coverup included senior FBI officials such as Oliver "Buck" Revell, who had earlier stalled and stopped legitimate FBI investigations concerning both the Irangate and Iraqgate scandals, similar to his boss, J. Edgar Hoover, protecting organized crime for many years.

Discovering Criminal Activities in CIA, White House

He stated in general terms about discovering evidence of major criminal activities involving the CIA, the White House, and other government operations. Over a period of several years, Taus provided me with sufficient data to write a book solely on his discoveries as a military pilot and then an FBI agent. This chapter covers a small part of what Taus conveyed to me.

CIA Hauling Drugs

While Taus was piloting a helicopter in Vietnam he heard over the aircraft radio a distress call from the pilot of an Air America C-46 aircraft about to make a crash landing. Taus proceeded to the crash site and landed, offering to fly the unharmed pilots to their base of operations. But the crew refused to leave the aircraft, saying they would wait for Air America people to arrive. The reason for refusing to leave the aircraft was suggested by the nature of the cargo; it consisted of heroin, estimated at about 4000 pounds. (Air America and its predecessor airline, Civil Air Transport, among others, was one of many CIA airlines. While I was flying captain for Japan Airlines out of Tokyo, where many of these CIA-associated pilots went for recreation, I learned from them that the CIA was hauling drugs.)

Military And Congressional Coverup Of CIA Drug Trafficking

Upon return to base, Taus made a written report to his military unit commander describing the heroin on the Air America aircraft. He also sent a letter to his New York congressman, reporting the CIA's drug smuggling operation. A congressional "investigation" followed, which covered up for the CIA's drug smuggling—a congressional coverup that has gone on for the past 40 years.

Air America Crew Heavy Drug Consumers?

The final congressional report stated that the heroin on the Air America aircraft was not for the CIA, but for the personal use of the crew. Four thousand pounds for the personal use of the crew?

Discovering CIA Drug Trafficking in Vietnam and In United States

Taus returned to the United States from Vietnam and became part of the New York National Guard, assigned to instructor duties for the U.S. Army Command and General Staff College courses. While on military duty with the National Guard, he was sent to Central and South America several times on special missions, during which he learned more about the global drug trafficking business and the involvement in it of the CIA, State Department, and U.S. military.

FBI Reports of CIA Involvement in Other Criminal Activities

After leaving the military, Taus joined the FBI as a Special Agent, and continued his ties to the military as a senior officer in the Army Reserve. During his FBI investigations, Taus discovered covert CIA operations in the United States, including looting the savings and loans, and other criminal activities. These were all undercover operations that had been described to me over the years by undercover agents who were part of the CIA activities. Hearing it from a veteran FBI agent provided more corroboration.

CIA Infiltrating the FBI

Taus explained how the CIA had infiltrated the FBI and discovered the names of FBI agents and informants, and investigations that could expose covert and criminal CIA operations. The CIA knowingly gave false information to FBI agents, seriously jeopardizing FBI missions and misleading top Justice Department and White House personnel. Most of this false information is still in FBI records.

20 Years of Reporting CIA Drug Trafficking

Taus was very concerned about the CIA drug smuggling that he observed over a 20-year period of time while an Army officer and then while an FBI Special Agent. This concern was increased by his discovery that the CIA was actively involved in drug trafficking with organized crime figures in the New

York area. And if this wasn't enough, his concern was further heightened by FBI supervisors ordering him to shut down his investigation.

Taus and other FBI agents discovered CIA drug trafficking as a result of their investigations into other organized crime activities, and aided by the Pennsylvania Crime Commission Report on drug trafficking among pizza outlets and cheese dealers. The Pennsylvania report described extensive inter-state and international drug-trafficking involving Mafia figures throughout the United States and Canada.

Pizza Connection Drug Cases

Taus, while heading an FBI investigative team, discovered CIA involvement with the *American* Mafia in drug trafficking during the time when Assistant U.S. Attorney (AUSA) Louis Freeh was prosecuting the *Italian* Mafia's drug trafficking activities in the Pizza Connection drug cases. Freeh's prosecution of these cases propelled him to prominence in the FBI and he eventually became the director of the bureau.

It was Taus' belief there was a conflict between the Sicilian Mafia drug activities and those of the American Mafia, and that the CIA's connections were with the American Mafia. He felt that the *selective* crackdown on the Sicilian Mafia was to eliminate competition to the CIA-backed American Mafia. Freeh was protecting the Mafia's American segments that had CIA drug ties. Taus explained, "Other known figures with connections or associations to the CIA escaped federal prosecution." Also, the Pizza Connection drug charges focused on low level Mafia figures while protecting high-level drug kingpins and their accomplices in government. Taus explained the obstacles blocking prosecution by well-placed political figures, judges, and others. He explained how AUSA Freeh blocked the issuance of subpoenas for such companies as Cremosa and Drexel-Castle, which had CIA connections.

Taus explained that the American Mafia was an entrenched third generation and that the Sicilian Mafia, which was more violent, was creating not only competition in the drug business but also causing too much friction.

Difference Between Street Mafia and Higher-Level Mafia

Taus explained the difference between the street Mafia represented by the five crime families in New York and the higher-level Mafia imbedded in blue-chip Fortune 500 corporations and in high government positions. He described the situation in which the Sicilian drug trafficking involved in the Pizza Connection cases was interfering with other government drug-routes and supplies from the Middle East through Turkey, Bulgaria, Syria, and Lebanon. He said it was this competition that caused Justice Department personnel to eliminate the Sicilian Mafia from the drug business.

The media gave Louis Freeh credit for developing the Pizza Connection cases but Taus explained that the credit belonged to the Pennsylvania Crime Commission.

Discovering Other CIA Drug Connections, Including the K-Team

During Taus' FBI investigations, he discovered that several of the people involved in the drug trafficking were members of a CIA group in Freeport, Long Island, known as the "K-Team." Several of the CIA K-team operators were associated with a CIA-related firm, Drexel Company, which later changed its name to Castle Securities after its CIA-controlled Cayman Island parent, Castle Bank. One of the key figures in the K-Team was Sal Imbergio, who ran for mayor in Freeport.

Drexel, Burnham, Lambert and Mafia Connections

Taus explained that Drexel was connected to the larger business firm of Drexel, Burnham, Lambert, a junk-bond securities company with Mafia associates and high-ranking political connections in New York State. He explained that he tried to show Louis Freeh the connections between the Drexel firm and the drug activities of the Pizza Connection, but Freeh refused to act on the information, concentrating instead upon the Sicilian Mafia members while protecting CIA-related operations.

Mafia, Drugs, Savings and Loans, and The CIA

Taus listed some of the Mafia figures involved in drug trafficking who he investigated. These included Carmine Persico, a member of the Colombo crime family; Salvatore Piga, a Luchese crime family member; Mario Renda, a Mafia untouchable heavily involved in looting of savings and loans during the 1980s; Angelo Ruggiero, a member of the Gambino crime family, and Giuseppe Lamberti and Salvatore Mazzurco, partners in the Mafia-controlled Pronto Demolition Company.

Piga went to First United Company in Garden City, Long Island, a brokerage house dealing in credit exchanges that was owned by Mario Renda. Renda had numerous foreign operations, some of which were shell companies to confuse investigators and for diverting funds. Taus explained that some of these were associated with Oliver North's Enterprise operation in Central America.

Ties With the CIA's Southern Air Transport

One of Renda's firms, Amalgamated Commercial Enterprise (ACE), played an important role in the weapons and drug shipments to and from Central and South America and Florida. ACE was also doing business with and supporting Southern Air Transport's missions involving arms and drug shipments that were part of the White House's National Security Council and CIA operations.

Southern Air Connection to Drugs and the CIA

Taus described how his investigations took him to Florida and discovery of Southern Air Transport's relationship to the CIA and drug trafficking, which provided more corroboration to what was revealed to me by my many CIA sources over the last decade. He discovered the involvement in drug trafficking by the National Security Council, Oliver North, and the White House.

More Evidence of CIA Looting of Savings and Loans

Taus described finding evidence of CIA connections in looting the savings and loans, adding: "The Freeport CIA station was involved in financial fraud with unsecured loans, unauthorized securities, dummy shell corporations, and the bilking of numerous savings and loans." He described the CIA's unlawful participation and meddling into areas handled by other government agencies, such as the State Department, Defense, and Commerce. He described how Irangate and Iraqgate were some of the consequences of the illegal CIA activities.

Details of most of what Taus found during his FBI investigations had been told to me for the past ten years by my CIA and other deep-cover sources, some of whom were carrying out these activities under orders of their superiors or handlers. Taus' separate discovery of these matters, while an FBI agent, provided further corroboration to what others had told me was true.

FBI Supervisor DeVecchio Refused To Act On Taus' Reports

Taus described how his immediate supervisor, R. Lindley DeVecchio, refused to act on his reports of CIA-related drug trafficking. The reason why his FBI supervisor did *not* act on the CIA and American Mafia drug trafficking surfaced several years later. In late 1996, DeVecchio was charged with aiding Gregory Scarpa, a member of the Colombo organized crime family. The relationship between organized crime and Taus' FBI supervisor came out during a hearing in federal district court in Brooklyn.

FBI Turncoat Responsible for Many New York Murders

Federal prosecutor Valerie Caproni charged DeVecchio with lying, claiming that the FBI agent had fed confidential information to Scarpa, and that this information fueled murderous warfare between two Mafia factions in 1991 and 1992 as they each sought control of the Colombo crime family. Ten mobsters and an innocent teenager were killed. Caproni said Scarpa was a battle commander in one faction and played a leading role in bringing about the murders.

CIA Assets in Congress

Taus wrote, "Our infamous congressional leaders are either former CIA agents, such as congressman Henry J. Hyde, or stooges for them, such as Arlen Specter, Charles Schumer (now a senator), Alfonse D'Amato and even my own representative, Peter King of Nassau County."

CIA Arming the IRA

He described discovering that the CIA provided arms to the IRA. In *Defrauding America* I mentioned Stephen Crittenden, the head of a covert CIA airline, who described to me flying a C-130 into Ireland with a load of arms for the IRA.

Based upon his vast FBI background, Taus wrote about the Mafia's infiltration of government:

There is a sanctioned Mafia organization that works within our government and industries. I know. I have discovered it under the veneer of the surface "street gangsters" such as Gotti, Scarpa, Bonanno, etal, who answer to an appointed Godfather (the late Paul Castellano). In turn, Paul takes orders from his first cousin Vito Castellano who works for the Governor of New York in Albany, N.Y. Incredible? I do not know who is boss now.

Taus told about his informant who had revealed the CIA drug route that was associated with the Pan Am Flight 103 disaster over Lockerbie.

Investigating the CIA-Front, The K-Team

In the 1970s, the FBI started receiving reports of criminal activities involving a group known as the "K-Team" operating out of Freeport, Long Island. Taus' FBI superiors ordered him in 1981 to start an undercover operation to investigate this group. The cover for this FBI investigation was the Freeport

Soccer Club, and enabled the FBI to infiltrate the K-Team operation. During that investigation, Taus discovered the K-Team operations included several CIA operatives.

The Enterprise, Iraqgate and Irangate

The K-Team had connections with the patriotic-sounding National Freedom Institute which conducted its operations under the name, "The Enterprise." Taus said that this was the same "Enterprise" that repeatedly surfaced in the Iran-Contra congressional hearings. During this FBI investigation, Taus' team discovered that the K-Team was a CIA operation and that it was engaging in drug trafficking, looting of savings and loans, and activities related to what later became known as Irangate and Iraqgate. Taus' team discovered in 1983 that K-Team members arranged for Iraq to obtain U.S.-backed loans for agricultural products and that the money was used to purchase war material. These loans for the purchase of war material continued until Iraq used the military weapons to invade Kuwait. The Reagan-Bush team knew of the diversion of U.S. funds for military use years before the 1989 Iraqi invasion of Kuwait. Their coverups, or active role in the funding and military buildup, made possible the Gulf War and the events that followed.

Discovering Scandals Several Years Before Media Exposure

Several years before the public heard about the National Security Council's "Enterprise" involving among others, Lt. Col. Oliver North, Navy Vice Admiral John M. Poindexter, and Air Force Major General Richard V. Secord, Taus was reporting their illegal activities in his FBI reports.

Taus' team discovered that one of the Iraqi players in the U.S. loans for commodities, was Fadhil Al-Marsoumi, Baghdad's largest weapons dealer, that the money for commodities was being diverted to military purchases, and that the Reagan White House knew this in 1983.

Terminating the FBI Investigation and Informants

Shortly before the 1988 presidential elections, Taus' supervisors instructed him to shut down the undercover FBI operation and terminate the informants working for him. Three of the FBI informants failed to remain silent and sought to give their stories to the media. In 1988 and 1989, they were *really* terminated. One was an electrician, Ritchie Roberts, acting like the "plumbers" in Nixon's Watergate, rigging electrical devices such as bugging equipment, and also deactivating security alarm systems. Another informant who refused to remain quiet was Thomas Ziegler (alias Charles Schering), a carpenter, who worked with Roberts. Both lived in Queens, New York. Roberts and Ziegler, working for the CIA's K-Team, broke into the Grenadian Mission at the United Nations building in New York, obtaining documents, and planting evidence to falsely discredit people. Taus said that they were assassinated by CIA agents.

"I never Thought the FBI Would Do Something Like This"

Taus said the third assassination, of Steve Lopez, was conducted by FBI agents, and received media attention in *The Staten Island Advance* and the *New York Post*. Taus said, "I never thought the FBI would do something like this."

Taus said that he reported these assassinations to his FBI supervisor, Manny Gonzalez, who replied he "could do nothing to assist me with these revelations." In 1993, Gonzalez was appointed by Louis Freeh to be an Assistant Director-In-Charge of the Federal Bureau of Investigation.

FBI's Assassins

For years I had been told by some of my CIA contacts that the FBI had assassins in their employ, and I found this hard to believe. Although CIA assassinations were admitted to me by my CIA contacts—at least two of whom participated in assassinations early in their CIA careers—I had difficulty accepting the fact that the FBI would stoop to this level. Hearing it from Taus, an FBI veteran, gave support to what other deep-cover operatives had told me in the past. One of the FBI names that was frequently repeated as a assassin for the FBI was Chuckie Peters.

Circumventing the FBI Obstruction Of Justice

Outraged at the FBI's coverup of the CIA drug trafficking, the corruption leading up to the arming of Iraq through sham agricultural loans, the coverup of assassinations, and other crimes, Taus wrote to FBI Director William Sessions, reporting the criminal activities that his group had discovered, and the coverup by his FBI supervisors. When Sessions did not respond, Taus wrote letters to members of Congress. None responded

"Desist or You Will Be In Great Trouble"

Foreign newspapers started exposing the Iran-Contra activities, circumventing the U.S. media coverup and forcing Congress to address the issues, at least the minor issues. Taus wrote:

When the revelations occurred in November 1986, the Team became increasingly desperate. The FBI files were being filled with misinformation about the "Enterprise" and its team members. There were assassinations. I was instructed by my FBI supervisor, Patrick Groves, to "eliminate" my informants and cooperatives who were no longer interested in cooperating with the K-Team's own investigation. The FBI case agent on the "K-Team" case, Carmine Rivera, told me that I would be seriously hurt by my continuing investigation into Oliver North's Enterprise. Finally, supervisory FBI officials warned me "to desist or you will be in great trouble."

The FBI was doing everything possible to cover up the criminal activities that independent prosecutor Lawrence Walsh was empowered to investigate. Taus wrote that the FBI coverup was in part unnecessary because Walsh covered up for the hard-core criminal aspects associated with the Iran-Contra affair, as did members of Congress.

Independent Counsel Coverup of CIA Drug Trafficking

Walsh had received boxes of hard evidence on the government involvement in drug trafficking associated with the Contra affair from state and federal investigators and from insiders sending him evidence, including the evidence that I sent to him. Taus identified this coverup as he wrote,

Walsh conducted his investigations into the Irangate affair using the same FBI agents who tried to cover up the matter at the direction of the CIA.

Taus wrote that a young staff attorney for Walsh, Jeffrey Toobin, was continually stifled by the FBI under the umbrella of the phony "national security" label. (Toobin wrote a book, *Opening Arguments,* about these coverup problems.)

Using A Standard Justice Department Tactic

On November 4, 1988, shortly before the presidential elections, the FBI took steps to silence Taus. He was arrested by his own FBI associates on sham charges. At first, the FBI charged Taus with using a government credit card to obtain ten dollars worth of fuel for his personal car. (Taus had used the credit card to fuel his personal car used on a government assignment when a government car was not available.) Then the FBI charged him with molesting young boys allegedly occurring almost a year earlier. (My FBI sources say that this would not be a federal offense.)

Using State Agencies in the Conspiracy

The quickly concocted federal charges were dropped as soon as New York state prosecutors filed charges alleging Taus had sexual conduct with several young boys who were members of the Freeport Soccer Club (the organizational structure used by the FBI for undercover cases). By transferring the charges to state courts, federal prosecutors prevented Taus from claiming the charges were retaliation for reporting government personnel involved in high-level criminal activities.

Bail was set by the Nassau County district attorney and cooperating state judge at an unprecedented $2,500,000, insuring that Taus would not be free to publicize the government corruption that he discovered. Prior to that time, Taus' FBI performance ratings were outstanding, as were his military records.

Judge Blocked Presentation of Exculpatory Evidence

Taus explained how New York state Judge Edward Baker refused to allow the jury to hear any testimony or disclosures about the government's motivation for arresting him. (This is a standard tactic by cooperating judges.) Judge Baker refused to allow evidence to be presented showing that the boys who made the charges had first denied that there were any sexual violations.

Prosecutors Threatening the Alleged Sexual Victims

Baker also refused to allow testimony showing that the families of the boys had been earlier charged with criminal offenses and that the charges were dropped after the boys had testified as the prosecutors wanted them to do. Also, that the boys were themselves threatened with incarceration if they did not testify as prosecutors wanted. There were other judicial violations that denied Taus a fair trial.

The trial record included sworn testimony by senior FBI supervisory agents stating that "Taus was involved in highly sensitive national security cases," and that "his arrest was ordered at the highest level in Washington."

32 to 90 Year Prison Sentence Insured Taus' Silence

Psychiatrists and psychologists hired by the prosecutor admitted that Taus told them that there was a major coverup and conspiracy involving the Iran-Contra scandal, told them of the CIA drug trafficking activities and that it reached into the highest office in the country, and included Vice President George Bush. They testified that Taus described the coverup of high-level criminal activities, adding that in their many years of experience they felt Taus was telling the truth. The jury, probably believing that surely the government would not be charging Taus with the offenses if he wasn't really guilty, held Taus guilty (November 1990), and Judge Baker sentenced Taus to prison for 32 to 90 years!

This sentence was outrageous even if, for argument, Taus *had* been guilty of relatively minor sexual encounters. Contrast this with the refusal to prosecute (or the relatively minor charges against) the hundreds of Catholic and other priests who actually preyed on boys. Over a period of years I discovered that sham child molestation charges are common tactics to silence or discredit state or federal agents who blow the whistle on high-level government corruption.

Limited Media Publicity

Taus' attempts to report the criminal activities did get some media publicity after his January 1991 sentencing. An article in the October 28, 1991, issue of *Time* was titled, "Reagan Knew Everything." An October 26, 1992, article in *US News & World Report* was titled, "Cover-Up." Other disclosures of what Taus discovered were later contained in an article by Ben Bradlee appearing in *Guts & Glory*.

The media reported the existence of the K-Team that Taus and other FBI agents discovered to be a CIA operation in Freeport, and that it was the home of the infamous "Enterprise" operated by the National Security Council's Oliver North. The K-Team met the requirement of CIA-Director William Casey and the NSC's Oliver North when the Reagan Administration fueled the war in Nicaragua, undermining the government that had replaced the brutal CIA-backed Somoza regime. An informative article on the K-Team activities was found in the December 4, 1992 issue of *Washington City Paper*.

The CIA reacted to this publicity with the standard practice of releasing a report with some truth to it and then building on it with false information, denying that it had any part in the K-Team operation.

Help From Old Friends

MIT Professor Norm Chomsky tried to help Taus by referring him to John Kelly, the former U.S. Assistant Secretary of State for Near Eastern and Asian Affairs. Kelly wanted to do a story about the FBI coverup on his 1994 Public Broadcasting Series (PBS-TV), *Inside the FBI*, but Taus declined, fearing possible violations of the Secrecy Agreement Act. Kelly later testified before Congress after Iraq invaded Kuwait, falsely explaining that the State Department was unaware of Iraq's intentions. The CIA and the White House knew what was coming; they made it possible for Iraq to build up its military might to conduct such an invasion.

Asked To Falsify Reports

Taus explained that one of the events that triggered retaliation against him was his refusal to falsely sign the FBI's yearly statement requiring FBI agents to certify that they know of no unreported criminal activities. His supervisor wanted him to sign that he knew of none, when in fact he knew of a great amount of high-level criminal activities which his supervisor wanted covered up. When Taus refused to falsely state on that yearly form that he knew of no criminal activities, his Supervisory Special Agent warned him that he wasn't on the team. That warning, and his reporting of the CIA's criminal activities and the FBI's coverup to FBI Director Sessions and Congress was followed by the false charges against him that resulted in a virtual life sentence in prison.

Removal of His Accusers for Sex and Other Offenses

After Taus was convicted and sentenced, nearly all of his opponents were fired or resigned. The prosecutor and Deputy Chief District Attorney J. Kenneth Littman, who prosecuted Taus for alleged sexual violations, was ousted by the District Attorney for soliciting sex with a minor in the Nassau County courthouse. A November 6, 1993, New York *Daily News* article addressed the matter with the title, "Prober A Heel: Long Island Teen." A November 5, 1993, article in *Newsday* was titled, "Prosecutor Ousted." Taus' trial judge, Edward Baker, retired under questionable circumstances while making front-page headlines in the August 13, 1993, issue of *Newsday*.

FBI Sessions and FBI ASIC Fox Were the Next Ones Fired

FBI Director William Sessions was later fired by President Clinton after Sessions stated he would make an investigation of government corruption. The Assistant Director-In-Charge of the FBI's New York office, James Fox, who was present when Taus was falsely arrested, was suspended shortly before he was to retire. He refused to retract a statement that he made to the media declaring the innocence of another government agent being falsely charged to silence his exposure of high-level drug activities and political bribery: Immigration and naturalization Agent Joseph Occhipinti. Occhipinti is described in other pages. Occhipinti had sought to expose Dominican drug trafficking and drug money bribes to U.S. politicians and ended up being charged by DOJ prosecutors with violating the civil rights of crime families. The stress on Fox may have contributed to his subsequent demise.

Confirmation of His FBI Reports on Criminal Activities

In seeking to obtain evidence revealing the probable retaliatory acts originating from within the Justice Department, Taus requested under the Freedom of Information Act files concerning him and his reports of criminal activities involving Iraq, Iran, and CIA drug trafficking. The FBI replied in an October 1995, letter that the FBI had over 2,400 pages containing both his name and matters relating to Irangate, but refused to give him copies. Taus had no copies of the records that he prepared as an FBI Special Agent, and as he said, if he *had* kept copies, they would have been seized when the FBI ransacked his home after the false charges were made.

Mysterious Death of FBI Assistant Director

Taus wrote about the mysterious death of William Sullivan, Assistant Director of the FBI who resigned from the FBI after more than 36 years of service. He quit because of the coverups by the FBI, including the coverup of Mafia activities by former FBI Director J. Edgar Hoover. Sullivan was responsible for Taus' entry into the FBI and the two of them had a close relationship. Sullivan's attempt to expose some of the FBI's coverup activities was halted by his suspicious death in a 1977 hunting accident.

Federal Bureau of Investigation

RICHARD M. TAUS
Special Agent

95-25 Queens Blvd.
Rego Park, NY 11374   (212) 459-3140

Taus's FBI Calling Card

THE UNITED STATES OF AMERICA
TO ALL WHO SHALL SEE THESE PRESENTS, GREETING:
THIS IS TO CERTIFY THAT
THE PRESIDENT OF THE UNITED STATES OF AMERICA
AUTHORIZED BY EXECUTIVE ORDER, MAY 11, 1942
HAS AWARDED

THE AIR MEDAL

TO

CAPTAIN RICHARD M. TAUS 107368987 ADJUTANT GENERALS CORPS UNITED STATES ARMY

FOR MERITORIOUS ACHIEVEMENT
WHILE PARTICIPATING IN AERIAL FLIGHT
DURING THE PERIOD AUGUST 1970 TO NOVEMBER 1970 IN THE REPUBLIC OF VIETNAM

GIVEN UNDER MY HAND IN THE CITY OF WASHINGTON
THIS   17TH   DAY OF   MARCH   19 71

GEORGE W. PUTNAM, JR.
Major General, USA
Commanding

SECRETARY OF THE ARMY

Captain Taus' Air Medal—Vietnam Operation

Helicopter Pilot Richard Taus in Vietnam

Affidavit of Richard M. Taus

I, Richard M. Taus, declare and state: I am a former Special Agent for the Federal Bureau of Investigation assigned to the New York Field Office and the Brooklyn-Queens Metropolitan Resident Agency from July 1978 to November 1988. I was assigned to both the Foreign Counter-Intelligence Division and the Criminal Division.

During this period of time, my investigations into these matters revealed criminal activities and operations which I reported and documented to my superiors in the FBI, as follows:

The involvement of official, agents and operatives of the Central Intelligence Agency (CIA) with organized crime members and drug-trafficking activities. And the participation by members of the CIA who engaged in the looting of the Savings & Loan (Thrift) Industries, financial scams and fraudulent securities transactions.

The involvement of people from the National Security Agency Staff and Council and the White House in criminal activities associated with funding the acquisition of military supplies and equipment, arms and ammunition which were referred to as the Iran-Contra Arms Initiative, known as Irangate, and the Iraqi Scandal, known as Iraqgate.

The associations between known and suspected members of the Mafia and CIA agents in conducting drug-trafficking activities and financial frauds.

I was ordered by my supervisors in the FBI to halt these investigations, destroy my written reports, terminate my informants and make no reference to these criminal and subversive activities implicating high-ranking government officials, politicians, Mafia and business leaders who controlled and manipulated government agencies and operations.

Without any support from my superiors at the FBI New York Field Office, I then sent a letter describing what I had discovered in my official status as an FBI Special Agent to the FBI Director, William Sessions, and this was ignored. I proceeded to write Congressional officials, among them Senators Arlan Spector, Alfonse D'Amato, John Kerry and Congressmen Norman Lent, Charles Schmur, and many others who were on both the Senate and House Intelligence Oversight Committees. None of the above officials or representatives provided any support or assistance in exposing the CIA-White House corruption and the obstruction of justice tactics by my FBI superiors.

My sole purpose in preparing this affidavit, to be used by the former FBI Special Agent-In-Charge of the Los Angeles Field office, SAC Ted Gunderson, is to bring to justice the criminal and subversive activities that I and other government agents and operatives have discovered during our official and government related duties.

I declare and affirm under penalty of perjury that these statements are true to the best of my knowledge and belief. Executed this 13th day of August 1997, in the County of Clinton, State of New York.

Richard M. Taus

LINDA O'CONNOR
Notary Public, State of New York
No. 01OC5019612
Qualified in Clinton County
Commission Expires

Former New York City Vice Squad Investigator

Two of my other sources had sensitive information on matters relating to Taus' activities. My friend of many years, Jim Rothstein, described what he discovered and reported while a vice squad detective on the New York City Police Department (NYPD) in the 1960s and 1970s. During his many years as a vice squad detective he frequently reported CIA involvement with organized crime and drug trafficking. He described the reports that he had filed of CIA drug sales to the blacks in New York City, naming some of those who were involved. His reports described how CIA operatives sold drugs direct to black distributors from about 1967 to 1972, after which time organized crime groups took over the distribution. The CIA then concentrated on supplying drugs to the crime groups. Rothstein described his contacts with a key black who acted as an intermediary between the CIA and minor drug dealers.

"Take A Disability Retirement or Suffer The Consequences"

Rothstein's supervisors didn't want Rothstein's reports of CIA activities. His reports also threatened to expose high level people in the New York Police Department (NYPD) and local politicians. His NYPD supervisors gave him a choice: take a disability retirement or suffer the consequences. He took the disability retirement in 1981.

Rothstein described how a package of evidence exposing the CIA drug and Mafia links was put into the safe of New York district attorney Robert Morgenthau, and how the evidence disappeared by the following morning. He described how New York City and county authorities refused to prosecute high-level drug bosses while concentrating on low-level street vendors.

Military Involvement with Organized Crime

Referring to Army Colonel Edward Cutolo, referred to in earlier pages, Rothstein said that he had seen Cutolo's involvement with the Mafia in drug trafficking. He explained that Cutolo, like other military people involved in the drug trafficking, would often have second thoughts and seek to extricate themselves from the operation. That desire may have ended deadly for Cutolo.

Daughter of Mafia-CIA Insider

Another source whose information dovetailed with Taus' information was the daughter of a Mafia-CIA figure. She provided me additional information about some of the crime figures Taus described. Dee Ferdinand, the daughter of Albert Carone, described the bizarre and complex relationships between her farther, the Mafia, and the CIA. Al Carone was a member of the Gambino family and had connections to other crime groups in the eastern part of the United States. He was also a detective on the New York City vice squad, a member of the military, and a CIA operative.

Dee said that her father was in the OSS during World War II (the predecessor to the CIA), working in military intelligence (CIC). After the war, he returned to New York, continuing his relationship with the Mafia families, and also became a member of the New York Air National Guard, 27th brigade and the 42nd Infantry division. His earlier army rank was Sergeant, which eventually was raised to the rank of Colonel when he died in 1991. He is buried in the national cemetery at Santa Fe, New Mexico.

Carone was a white-shield detective in the 42nd and 81st precincts while working with the New York City police department. He took frequent leaves of three or four months at a time to carry out operations for the CIA, using military cover. His connections with the NYPD ended in 1966, after which he concentrated on Mafia related activities with the CIA.

Activities with Sicilian and American Mafia

Dee described some of the Mafia's meeting places and front-operations. She referred to a restaurant and catering place in New Jersey called "The Tides" and the "Riviera Club" in the Bronx. She said Cosmo Fish and Shrimp Company in Nevada had connections to organized crime.

She described some of the drug trafficking names that she heard in her home, including Shavey Lee's in Chinatown, New York, where her father frequently visited. Dee said that Shavey Lee had drug connections in Hong Kong. She described the relationship between the Sicilian and American Mafia, and how the Sicilian Mafia first got started working with the CIA during World War II. She said that it was the Sicilian Mafia in Italy that controlled the American Mafia. She describe how Vito Genovese kind of adopted her father when her father was growing up in Brooklyn, and that relationship eventually got him into key positions within the Mafia families. Her father called Genovese, Uncle Vito.

JFK Assassination Ties

Referring to what her father and Marita Lorenz had told her (Marita Lorenz worked for the CIA. She was a girl friend to Fidel Castro and bore a son from their romantic relationship. She played a little-publicized role in the JFK assassination):

My father knew Frank Fiorini, the alias for Frank Sturgis. One and the same person. Frank Fiorini was there also [Dallas]. Jack Ruby was the payoff man involved with the JFK assassination. Marita had given me information about traveling by car with three Mafia-CIA figures from New Orleans to Dallas, arriving in Dallas the day before the assassination, and facts that strongly implicate this group with the assassination of President John F. Kennedy.

Dual CIA-Mafia Ties

Dee described her father's concurrent relationship with the Mafia, the New York City police department, and the CIA. Key points that she described were confirmed by independent sources, including Jim Rothstein of the New York Police Department and CIA operatives Gunther Russbacher and Oswald LeWinter. She often filled in missing Mafia and CIA links that FBI Special Agent Richard Taus had suspected during his FBI investigations.

Having grown up in a Mafia family and being friends with top Mafia bosses, Dee was very helpful in explaining the complex relationship between the Mafia and the CIA. She explained details of her father's activities as a CIA paymaster, moving money to and from the Mafia families in New York, New Jersey, and Pennsylvania, the CIA, the Mossad's involvement, and payoffs to the New York City police department.

Comparing Notes Between FBI and Mafia Families

Taus had given me a list of some of the Mafia figures that he investigated, and I asked Dee what she knew about them. She said that some of the people were her family. For example, she said, "Angelo Ruggiero was my father's cousin." Neil Dellacroce was related to her father. Referring to Joe Percillia by his alias, Joe Pickle, Dee said that he was with the Genovese family and the Gambino family as they merged. He was also with the Colombo family.

Dee said that her father's primary connections were originally with the Genovese and then with the Gambino family, and also the Colombo family through Joe Percillia. She said her father also had lesser connections to other Mafia groups.

Growing Up in A Mafia Family

Dee described life growing up in a Mafia family, explaining:

You have to understand when I was growing up, there was no such thing as organized crime being spoken. It was a way of life with certain people in your home, or you were in their home, or whatever. You didn't know what these people did. Everybody's dad was like everybody else. They went to work every day and that's it. Would they talk about killing people? No. Nothing seemed dysfunctional. It was just a family. You didn't think anything odd. What you saw in your home and how you were treated by these people was not how they were on the outside. You didn't think about it. You didn't know what these people did. It came out after a while as you got older. You wouldn't talk about something like that. What is spoken in the home never goes beyond the home.

Referring to Santos Trafficante, Dee said, "He was a good friend of my dad. He was at my wedding. Uncle Sonny. That's what I called him." Referring to Sam Giancana, she said, "Giancana was a good friend of my dad."

Drugs and the New York Police Department

Dee said her father was a detective and "bag man" in the New York City police department, collecting money that was distributed to captains and inspectors as payoffs for "looking the other way" where drugs were involved. Dee explained that her father, while a plain clothes detective in the New York City police vice squad, paid money to the captains and inspectors of different precincts, and paid off mob figures. Referring to Inspectors Jack Lustig and Vince Nardiello, Dee said, "They were involved in the payoffs, and these are the people my father worked with."

CIA Paymaster

"My father was not only part of organized crime, but also a CIA paymaster." When I asked where that money came from, she replied, "The monies always came from the agency or the mob, in cash." When I asked what crime families were paid off, she said, "All the families."

Mob Boss Castellano as Breakfast Guest

She described how Paul Castellano, the boss of the New York crime families, was a frequent breakfast visitor at her home, and how she knew him as Uncle Paul. (Castellano was later murdered on orders of John Gotti.) Dee explained that Castellano was a brother-in-law to the former mob boss, Paul Gambino, and got the job because his wife was Gambino's sister.

Assassins for the CIA

Dee described how the Mafia handled assassinations in the United States that were requested by CIA personnel, explaining, "When the Agency needed people assassinated in the United States, the mob was used." (The CIA does its own assassinations overseas. Deep-cover operatives Gunther Russbacher and Russell Bowen had reluctantly described their role in assassinations many years earlier.)

Drug Deals Between the Mafia, CIA, and Mossad

Dee said that her father started in drug trafficking in the Vietnam days, for the CIA and the Mafia. Explaining other aspects of the Mafia's drug dealings, Dee said, "Sam Giancana did a lot of drug deals with the Agency." She added that organized crime and the CIA had regular drug dealings with Noriega and the Mossad, and that former Mossad operative Michael Harari was routinely involved. "A lot of this money was split with the Mossad and the Agency. They had to use the mob; there isn't too much difference between the CIA and the mob. They worked together."

Frequent Contacts with CIA Agent Shackley

Dee described the frequent contacts that her father had with CIA agent Theodore Shackley relating to drug trafficking. (Shackley's drug involvement was described to me by several CIA operatives over the past ten years.) Dee described how she called Shackley several years ago, demanding that her father's grave marker be changed, showing him as colonel instead of staff sergeant. (Sergeant was Carone's permanent military status and colonel was his temporary commission status.) Within two weeks, the marker was replaced, showing his rank as Colonel.

Operation Amadeus: Joint CIA-Mafia Drug Smuggling Operation

Referring to the CIA-Mafia drug trafficking, she said she knew from what her father said that the drugs coming from South America went to the Colombo, Genovese, and Gambino families, and that it was a joint CIA-Mafia drug operation under the code name Operation Amadeus. She said that during World War II, Operation Amadeus was involved in transporting Nazi officers from Germany into South American countries. According to her father's notes, Operation Amadeus split into several other operations, including Operation Sunrise and Operation Watchtower.

CIA-Mafia Drug Money Trail

Repeating what she learned from her father, Dee said part of the money trail went through a bank in England, to the Bahamas, Bank of Zurich in Switzerland, among others. She said her father carried cash between Mafia figures and the CIA.

Targeting the Blacks in Harlem

I told Dee what Rothstein had told me about CIA drug sales to the blacks in Harlem, and Dee gave me another side of that operation. She confirmed that the CIA and the Mafia did target the blacks in Harlem for drug consumption, adding:

In Harlem, the blacks, definitely. It was their [CIA-Mafia] mainstay. That's how their money came, but it backfired on them. They really didn't think it would get into the white communities as much as it did. They targeted blacks and Puerto Ricans. My father was always saying, "Who gives a shit about the niggers!"

Dee told me about calling Congresswoman Maxine Waters' office and explaining who she was and about the drug trafficking, including the targeting of the blacks, and the lack of interest shown by Waters' staff. That reflects similar lack of interest shown by Waters' office when some of my drug trafficking sources also volunteered information about their CIA-DEA drug trafficking knowledge.

False Sexual Charges

Dee explained how internal politics within the NYPD resulted in her father being falsely charged with child-molestation offenses, causing him to be sent to the psychiatric unit of South Oaks Hospital. He was then given a choice of retiring or being prosecuted. "My father wound up with a full pension. Charges were dropped. This is how they set them up." Other CIA operatives, including long-time CIA veteran Gunther Russbacher, had told me years earlier about the CIA's use of pornographic and prostitution services used to get incriminating evidence on key political figures for blackmail purposes.

"I'm not long for this world; it's over."

After being ousted from the New York City police department, Carone moved his family to New Mexico (August 1980). He continued his military and CIA connections, traveling frequently to various military bases, including Kirkland Air Force Base, Fort Bliss (El Paso), and others. Eventually Carone fell out of favor with the CIA. Following a trip made to Mexico in 1984, Carone told Dee that he "wasn't long for this world; it's over." Dee said her father felt the CIA had poisoned him, which prompted him to start revealing other CIA-Mafia secrets to her, asking that she eventually make the information known. Before his death, Carone was diagnosed with chemical toxicity of unknown ideology by doctors who sought to determine the cause of his medical symptoms.

Oliver North's Involvement with CIA-Mafia Activities

Dee described how her father made frequent reference to a John Cathey and his contacts with Cathey involving drug trafficking activities in the Contra operation. Cathey was the alias frequently used by Oliver North.

Input from CIA Operative Gunther Russbacher

Because of Gunther Russbacher's varied CIA background and dealings with organized crime families, I called him in England and asked if he knew Al Carone. He did, and started giving me additional information, including the fact that Carone was known as "Big Al," and that one of his aliases with the Chicago mob was "Pincheron." Russbacher said that Carone was working with the Delente and Bufalino crime groups.

Input from CIA Operative Oswald LeWinter

Oswald LeWinter, another long-time CIA operative with whom I had been in contact for years, said he also knew Carone. During that conversation, LeWinter told me that in the Pizza Connection cases, Justice Department prosecutors filed charges against certain Mafia figures such as Gaetano "Don Tanino" Badalamenti, while protecting higher figures in the drug trafficking organization. This coincided with what Taus had told me. LeWinter described how Tomasso Buscetta, the mob witness used by Justice Department prosecutors in the Pizza Connection cases, was a CIA operative who would testify, and who would cover up, as desired by government prosecutors. LeWinter said that New York Senator Alfonse D'Amato was heavily involved with the Mafia.

CHAPTER NINE

INTRIGUE OF UNDERCOVER CONTRACT PILOT

This chapter focuses on an unusual tool occasionally used by government agencies to infiltrate drug operations as they seek evidence to bring about arrests and termination of the operation: contract undercover agents. Very few of them exist. They provide their own airplanes, they fund the undercover operations, they take enormous risks, and they are paid on the basis of missions accomplished.

They carry out undercover operations that require they act as drug traffickers so as to infiltrate the targeted drug operation. They rely upon the integrity and trustworthiness of the government agents who direct and authorize their undercover activities, most of the authorizations given verbally.

This chapter focuses on the bizarre and convoluted activities of Rodney Matthews, one of those contract pilots who infiltrated the inner workings of some of the top and most dangerous of all drug kingpins. He initially worked undercover for the Texas Department of Public Safety (DPS) and then for U.S. Customs Service in San Antonio, Texas, with occasional work for the Drug Enforcement Administration (DEA).

Matthews did not know about the problems within U.S. Customs that were identified in a 1992 House report which revealed massive integrity problems within that government agency, and which exist today. If he had known of the internal problems, he would have realized that reliance upon the verbal authority given by Customs agents had grave consequences. At any time, for any number of reasons, the government agents giving him authority to haul drugs as part of undercover operations could deny having given the authorization. In a case like this, a long prison term can follow, even life in prison.

Targeting America's Number One Drug Target: Pablo Escobar

Under his government authority, Matthews targeted top drug lords, including America's most-wanted and dangerous drug trafficker at that time, Pablo Escobar. Just as he was about to succeed in this endeavor, Department of Justice personnel blocked that operation, and through perjury and corruption, caused Matthews to receive a life-in-prison sentence, while simultaneously rewarding part of the Escobar group.

Brief View of the Matthews Family History

First, a brief history of the Matthews family that goes back to George Washington's time. One of Matthews' relatives on his father's side was a General under President James Madison in 1812: General George Matthews. An article about General Matthews appeared in the *Miami Herald,* written by noted Florida historian, Joe Crankshaw:

> *Things were looking bad for the Spanish governor of East Florida, Juan de Estrada, in 1812. Fernandina had fallen to a ragtag army of American Adventurers who proclaimed themselves to be the Republic of Florida. They had captured Fort San Nicolas near the St. Johns River and were now besieging St. Augustine.*
>
> *On March 26, 1812, John Houston McIntosh, leader of the "Patriots," as the ragtag army was known, sent a message to Estrada demanding the surrender of St. Augustine and the Castillo de San Marcos. He offered liberal terms, promised protection for Catholics, and assured the Spaniards that Florida would be quickly annexed to the United States.*
>
> *On April 4, 1812, General George Matthews, an agent for President James Madison, left Fernandina promising to capture St. Augustine and then go on to liberate all of South America from Spain. It was brave talk. Matthews, McIntosh and others had also been working on the Indians. They had told the Indians that this was a white man's war and to stay out of it. They rejected Indian offers of assistance in fighting the Spanish.*
>
> *The besieging force numbered 300 militia and, due to the intrigues of the times, 100 regular soldiers from the supposedly neutral United States. Off shore, American privateers, private vessels licensed to capture foreign shipping, bottled up the port. Estrada had about 300 men, mostly untried blacks trained as colonial troops, with which to defend the town and fort. He was determined he would not surrender, and he sent to Havana for help. He also sent an agent, Sebastian Kindelan, out into the surrounding wilderness to seek help from the Seminole Indians who had moved onto the Peninsula.*

Matthews fought alongside Washington in the battles of Brandywine and Germantown where he was wounded and spent four years on a British prison ship in New York harbor. The National Archives shows Matthews was a colonel under Washington and a Brigadier General in the militia.

Before the 1812 attempt to annex East Florida, George Washington traveled to Georgia and supported Matthews in his successful bid for governor. But in 1812, Matthews fell victim to corrupt politics and was betrayed and disavowed by elements in his own government. He was branded a pirate and a criminal, and lost everything, including his life.

Love for Flying Motivated Matthews to Transport Marijuana

Rodney Matthews was addicted to flying, having learned to fly at the young age of 16, funding his flight lessons with odd jobs. To continue his love for flying, he started transporting low-tech electronics into Mexico in 1970, and eventually, this led to flying marijuana into the United States. This was before the drug culture took on the extreme violence with hard drugs that exists today.

In 1984, Matthews' luck ran out. His airplane, being flown by another pilot, had just landed at Matthews' private airstrip at Damon, Texas, with 600 pounds of marijuana when government agents showed up. That pilot was arrested by Texas Department of Public Safety (DPS) agent Robert Nestoroff and U.S. Customs agent Richard Nichols from the San Antonio Customs office. Matthews was subsequently charged with that marijuana offense when the pilot became a witness for the government and had charges dropped in exchange for testifying against Matthews. Matthews believes his brother-in-law provided government agents with information leading to the arrest at the Damon airstrip. That information was given in exchange for having charges against the brother-in-law dropped.

Matthews' Talents Wanted by the Government

Luckily for Matthews, he had talents wanted by the State of Texas and by the federal government. Needing the services of someone with Matthews' background to bring about the arrest of top drug traffickers, Nestoroff and Nichols offered to expunge Matthews' arrest record and allow him to keep his assets in exchange for help obtaining evidence against several suspected drug traffickers. They included Jimmy Norjay Ellard, John Phillips, Larry Manley, and John McFarland.

Working for Pay After Immunity was Granted

After working off the deal for immunity against prior charges, Texas DPS agents continued to use Matthews in other cases, paying him for his services. Some of these cases originated from information Matthews acquired on his own, and some targets or leads were given to him. As Matthews' value became known to other government agencies, they approached him to work for them as well. Matthews started working for Customs agents in San Antonio, Houston, and Miami, and occasionally for the Drug Enforcement Administration (DEA). At the government's request, Matthews started transporting cocaine, something that he had not done before.

Routine Granting Of Immunity for Prior Drug Trafficking

In a later trial, Charles S. Harrison from Customs headquarters in Washington, testified that government agents gave drug traffickers immunity for prior offenses if they cooperated in obtaining evidence on other drug traffickers.

The government has used undercover agents, sometimes called Confidential Informants (CI), for years in the so-called war-on-drugs. But Matthews fell into a different category. He was a contract agent or cut-out for the government, funding their investigations, providing his own expensive aircraft, incurring the high expenses, and assuming the risks of being tortured or killed by the targeted drug organizations.

In this capacity, Matthews was paid by the government only when his efforts proved successful. He was also paid by the trip when government agents instructed him to pick up drug loads in Colombia or other locations and deliver them to designated locations in the United States. For each of these trips, he was often paid $40,000 to $50,000. In many cases he was allowed to keep money obtained from the targeted drug lords to offset his expenses, and he kept records of these monies and the expenses incurred.

Government agents gave Matthews various aliases to keep his true identity from drug traffickers and also from other government agents and agencies. These aliases included such names as Bill Martin, Bill Miller, and "Shadow."

Shifting the Dangers—And Deniability—To Contract Agents

To carry out its policy of denying responsibility for operations it carries out throughout the world, including the United States, U.S. agencies use either proprietaries, fronts, or contract undercover agents. "Proprietaries" are secret corporations or companies in which government ownership is hidden, and are widely used by the Central Intelligence Agency. Examples would be Air America, Nugan Hand Bank, and others listed in the third edition of *Defrauding America*. "Fronts" are corporations or companies that allow the government to secretly use their facilities in carrying out clandestine activities. These would include law offices, public relations firms, banks, insurance companies, newspapers, magazines, publishers, and an endless list of other businesses. "Contract undercover agents" are individuals doing work for government agencies such as the DEA, Customs, FBI, or the CIA. They are sometimes called "cutouts."

If the operation fails and gains media attention, the authorizing agencies and agents simply deny any knowledge, authority, or responsibility. To add credibility to this lie, Justice Department prosecutors will usually file criminal charges against the contract agent, fraudulently stating the person did not have government authority to do what was done. Matthews, and another contract agent yet to appear in these pages, were acting as government-authorized undercover agents in such places as Mexico, Jamaica, Bahamas, Guatemala, and Colombia.

Confidential Informants (CI)

Another category of people who simply provide information and do not have the knowledge and do not provide the funding and equipment that contract agents provide are called "confidential informants" or CIs. They can be a very onerous group, who openly lie with full knowledge of Justice Department prosecutors, and are used as paid witnesses against people targeted by Justice Department prosecutors. None of the key individuals within these pages, including Richard Pitt, Rodney Matthews, Barry Seal, and others, were in this category, even though the government may have loosely referred to them as confidential informants.

Complex and Dangerous Operations

Great expense and complex planning are standard with the few contract undercover agents that various government agencies use. Sophisticated aircraft are often used that can cost a million dollars or more, and which are sometimes lost during undercover operations. Replacement engines can run into hundreds of thousands of dollars. An insurance claim for a lost aircraft often cannot be made due to the undercover nature of the operation.

Acting Like A Drug Smuggler to Succeed

In order to infiltrate high level drug organizations, Matthews obviously had to act like a drug trafficker. This was expected of him and verbally authorized by government agents. Even though drugs would occasionally hit the streets, the intent was to get evidence on top-level people and bring down the entire operation. Also, when drugs were allowed to reach their destination, arrests would often be made down the distribution chain so as not to focus suspicion on Matthews.

To be effective, an undercover operative must be resourceful, flexible, able to think quickly on his feet, take immediate advantage of any opportunity that arises, act the part of a drug trafficker, and try to avoid being a government undercover agent and subsequently killed. Because of the complex and ever-changing nature of undercover operations, and the lack of expertise in these areas by government bureaucrats, the undercover agent must have the freedom to function in various undercover roles outside of internal government guidelines.

Given Wide Latitude by Government Bureaucrats

Government bureaucrats, sitting safely in their offices and without the experience possessed by people such as Matthews, do not understand the complexities of infiltrating powerful drug organizations. This lack of knowledge and the constantly changing conditions required that Matthews and other contract agents in a similar capacity be given wide latitude and discretion in bringing about a successful infiltration of the targeted crime group.

Danger from All Directions

The combination of informal verbal authority and wide discretion to carry out the task of infiltrating powerful drug groups carries great risks for the contract agents who assume there is a uniform procedure and recognition among different government agents and agencies. They believe that an undercover agent working under authority given by one agent will be respected by agents of another agency or another office of the same agency. Many contract agents discovered after the fact that this situation did not exist.

Matthews Set Up Many Sting Operations

For over a year, Matthews described to me in hundreds of pages of factual information and documents undercover operations he carried out under the blanket authority given by various government agents from U.S. Customs, the Drug Enforcement Administration (DEA), and U.S. attorneys. In one of the letters he wrote:

I set up the 500 kilo load out of Cali to Panama in 1990. I set up the 600 kilo air-drop in the Gulf of Mexico in 1990 and I was on the Customs boat that received it. I set up the bust of the 300 kilos that caused Emmons to be busted in Florida in 1989. I flew in the cocaine and set up the 50 kilo bust in Ontario, California, where my $100,000 was seized in February of 1989. Between 1984 and 1986, I set up numerous grass [marijuana] loads, including a ship out of Colombia.

Matthews' Introduction into Mexican Presidential Drug Protection

The type of work Matthews was doing required that he initiate investigations that could lead to drug busts. One of these self-financed investigations took him, physically, into the presidential palace in Mexico City. In trying to infiltrate a suspected drug smuggling operation known as the "Emmons group," Emmons introduced Matthews to a Cuban National referred to as "Fernando," who worked out of a real estate office, Symms Realty, located west of Miami International Airport. Fernando was reportedly a middleman furnishing front companies, bogus loans to facilitate money laundering, and various drug-related activities. Fernando had good connections in Colombia and Mexico for moving drugs. Matthews explained:

Fernando put me in touch with staff in the presidential palace in Mexico City who were part of the Presidential Task Force on Drug Trafficking. This Presidential Task Force would have to be notified before any major drug bust could occur, to preclude embarrassment to the President. This would be my protection or guarantee against arrest or interference. I had several meetings with these officials which included a military officer. They furnished me with aerial photos of different airstrips I could use in the Pozo Rica area and offered to introduce me to the General who controlled the area. They also provided me with stacks of drawings and diagrams for an abandoned petroleum pipeline and associated landing strips on the Texas-Mexico border that they wanted to utilize for moving drugs. After meeting them at the Presidential Palace and going for lunch at a nearby restaurant several times, I became overwhelmed with the fact that the trail I had followed led to the Presidential Palace of Mexico.

U.S. Protecting High-Level Mexican Drug Traffickers

Before committing myself to any actual hands-on drug shipments using Mexico for transshipping I thought it prudent to advise Customs Agent Nichols, who was my contact for international-related operations at that time. Because it involved top level officials of the Mexican government, I phoned Nichols from Mexico City for instructions whether or not to proceed. To my surprise, Nichols' response was to back off, after I have invested several months of work, several hundred thousand dollars, and waited for almost two years to reach this point.

I had questions, but I figured who am I to question the wisdom of my government. I walked away from the whole deal in amazement of what was going on in the Presidential Palace, and after all my work and expense the U.S. government simply said—forget it.

Infiltrating the Victor Stadter Organization

In 1986, San Antonio Customs agent Richard Nichols recruited Matthews to target the Victor Stadter group suspected of drug smuggling activities ranging from California to Florida, with operations in Texas and an auto dealership in El Monte, California known as B and D Motors. It was suspected that the organization brought tons of cocaine into the United States. Matthews had first met Stadter in 1981 during an aircraft trade in which Matthews was trading a Cessna 210 for a Lake Buccaneer. When Stadter learned that Matthews was rated to fly a DC-3, he started opening up about his drug activities.

Part of Pablo Escobar's Operation, Top Target Of U.S. Agencies

The Stadter organization was reportedly tied in with the Colombian drug kingpin Pablo Escobar and his aide, Jimmy Ellard, bringing large quantities of drugs into the United States. At that time, Escobar was considered the greatest drug-smuggling threat to the United States, and guilty of hundreds of brutal murders. Obtaining evidence against the Stadter group would assist in getting to Escobar.

Escobar was credited, or blamed, for greatly expanding the drug trade by bringing together many individual drug shippers into a group. He terrorized the country, blowing up buildings, and was responsible for the bombing of an Avianca airliner killing 110 people, and many other murders. In November 1985, Escobar joined forces with heavily armed guerrillas and took over the Palace of Justice in Bogota, killing many of the Colombian Supreme Court judges. He was responsible for killing many journalists, politicians and police.

Matthews' activities were a threat to Escobar's organization, including Escobar himself and one of his key aides, Jimmy Ellard.

Between 1986 and 1988, Matthews made nearly two dozen trips to California in an attempt to infiltrate the Stadter organization—all funded by Matthews himself, taking all the physical risks. These attempts to infiltrate the group stalled, and it wasn't until two years later, in 1988, that his attempts to infiltrate the group started making progress. He started associating with two of Stadter's pilots, Greg Thompson and another pilot whose first name was Benjamin and known as "Crazy."

Matthews ingratiated himself with one of Stadter's underlings, Diane Borden, becoming intimate and buying her a new Mercedes. She told Matthews that she counted as much as 15 million dollars of drug money at a time. She told him about Greek fishermen on Florida's West Coast who brought ashore drugs that were air dropped into the Gulf of Mexico by the Escobar group working with Stadter. Matthews represented himself as a "player," a polite term for a drug trafficker.

Borden's husband, a pilot, was killed in a California plane crash while delivering a shipment of drugs for Stadter. Thompson had been waiting at the destination airstrip for Borden to arrive and had gone to the crash scene to remove the cocaine from the crashed aircraft.

Escobar Organization Air-Dropping Drugs to the Stadter Group

Matthews eventually became accepted by the Stadter group and discovered further evidence that the group was transporting drugs for Pablo Escobar and his close aide, Jimmy Ellard. The Stadter-Escobar group used Beech Kingair aircraft flying from San Andres Island, located north of Colombia between Jamaica and Honduras, flying to the drop-zone where one of Stadter's boats would be waiting.

When the Kingair arrived at the drop zone, and after making radio contact to confirm everything was in order, bundles of cocaine were dropped into the water near waiting boats, and then the planes returned to San Andres Island. Several tons of drugs entered the United States in this manner every week.

CIA Using San Andres Island as A Drug Transshipment Point

Matthews thought the CIA had a drug transshipment operation on San Andres Island. He explained that Escobar's Kingair would return to San Andres Island and that U.S. aircraft following it would turn away as it approached the island.

Matthews, Customs and DEA Agents, Retrieving the Drugs

As Matthews was slowly infiltrating the Stadter group he convinced Stadter to allow him to pick up the drugs during one of the airdrops. Matthews was in the receiving boat, along with Customs agent Peter Delsandro from the

Ft. Lauderdale office and another agent from the DEA, during one such pickup. After the drugs were picked up, government agents ordered Matthews to personally deliver the drugs to Cubans at Broward Mall in Ft. Lauderdale, where he then met Carlos Duque.

Duque was arrested on a drug charge and then released on bail pending trial, at which time he promptly fled. A year later, Duque was captured in Costa Rica. At his trial, Assistant U.S. Attorney (AUSA) Bill Shockly called Matthews to testify, which put Matthews at great risk since he was still infiltrating major drug operations in Colombia.

Matthews Responsible for Bringing About Ellard's Arrest

Several years earlier, in 1985, Matthews' undercover activities brought about the arrest of Pablo Escobar's partner, Jimmy Ellard. Ellard had flown a drug load into the United States from Belize in 1984 and was to have landed at San Marcus Airport in Texas where Matthews was waiting with government agents, who would then arrest Ellard. Instead of landing at San Marcus, Ellard landed at Eagle Lake, Texas, about 70 miles west of Houston, apparently to rip off the drug load. Despite this diversion, government agents accidentally discovered Ellard and his drug load, and arrested him. Shortly after his arrest, Ellard was released on bail and fled back to Colombia, rejoining the Escobar operation.

Ellard had been a former deputy sheriff in Fort Bend County, Texas. He was again arrested in 1990 while living under a false name in Florida. He pled guilty in 1991 to his leadership in a large smuggling operation that flew nearly 30 tons of cocaine from Columbia to Florida.

During questioning, Ellard told government agents how he was able to evade the government's radar interdiction system.

While living in Colombia in the late 1980s, he provided Dandy Munoz-Mosquera—Pablo Escobar's assassin—knowledge on how to put a bomb on board a Colombian airline, Avianca, that killed over 100 people, including the two police informants that were their targets.

Uncomfortable Working Sensitive Operations with New Agents

Matthews had been working with Customs agent Richard Nichols in the San Antonio office, relying upon his verbal authorization to fly drugs as part of government-authorized undercover operations. He felt uncomfortable about this verbal arrangement and his discomfort surfaced in June 1988 when Nichols told Matthews that he would be gone for several months attending job-related training at Marana, Arizona. Nichols told Matthews he would be working under Customs agents Tom Grieve and Jim Dukes during this time.

An Irresponsible Request of Matthews by A Customs Agent

Before Nichols left, Grieve asked Matthews to fly a drug load into the United States without being granted immunity, and take the chance of getting caught. This was an irresponsible suggestion. Grieve was playing it safe. If the operation backfired and received media attention, Grieve could easily lie. Unknown to Matthews, lying was part of the Customs' culture. The Customs agent could say he knew nothing about the drug flight, and Matthews could end up with a life-in-prison sentence.

Another possible reason for Grieve's request was that Customs was trying to set up Matthews for an arrest and get rid of an undercover agent who had learned too much about the involvement of government personnel in drug trafficking.

"I'm Getting In Too Deep"

Matthews refused Grieves' request: "I'm getting in too deep. I'm afraid some of this stuff will come back on me down the road." Matthews told Nichols that he needed authorization from higher authority. Matthews later explained:

Nichols assured me if I would continue my efforts he would arrange that I hear the authorization from someone higher up. We discussed the possibility that if I had authority to fly loads in myself, perhaps we could wrap up the case in a few loads. Otherwise, it could go on for years. The meetings were set up and I was assured by a special prosecutor out of Main Justice in Washington, AUSA David Hall, that I could fly loads in myself.

A second meeting was held on August 23, 1988, seeking to reach an agreement where Matthews would be willing to continue the undercover efforts to infiltrate the Stadter organization. This meeting, held at a San Antonio restaurant, was attended by Customs agents Richard Nichols, Tom Grieve and Jim Dukes; Texas Department of Public Safety (DPS) agents Robert Nestoroff and Kenneth Dismukes, and Justice Department AUSA David Hall. Dismukes advised Matthews that the authority to authorize such operations was with federal agencies, that Texas agents could not grant such authorization.

Carte Blanche Authority to Fly Drugs—But Don't Tell Us!

Hall stated that Matthews had carte blanche authority to fly drugs into the United States as part of his government-authorized undercover activities. Grieve then told Matthews, "You have carte blanche from the special prosecutor to do whatever it takes. You can't tell us everything, or we will have to interdict the load and the load will never reach the target." Matthews asked Grieve, "What if it takes more than one load?" to which Grieve replied, "Do whatever it takes." After Grieve said this, Dismukes' face turned beet-red and he walked out. (Matthews had been given specific authority to fly drugs into the United States as part of normal sting operations in 1986, 1987, and 1989.)

Drug Loads Picked up and Delivered for U.S. Customs

Although Grieve said they would have to interdict the drug load if they knew about it, Customs agents knew of many drug loads entering the United States without being interdicted. These included CIA drug loads being clandestinely shipped into the United States, and drug loads that Customs agents specifically directed Matthews to pick up and deliver to destinations in the United States. More about this in other pages. For flights like these, for which Matthews simply provided transportation for the drugs, the government paid him $40,000 to $50,000 per trip. (I received copies of some of the checks.)

Top-Level Justice Department Authority

Dave Hall, who had given Matthews authorization to fly drug loads, was a former trial attorney assigned to the Narcotic and Dangerous Drug Section, Criminal Division, Department of Justice, and head of a multi-agency task force based in San Antonio that consisted of agents from Customs, DEA, and

IRS. Being Washington-based in a key Justice Department position, his authorization to fly drugs came from the Justice Department's highest offices.

Unknown to Matthews, Hall was encountering a great amount of problems in the San Antonio Customs office, and particularly from SAC Neil Lageman. As stated in earlier pages, a 1553-page report prepared by the House Committee On Government Operations detailed mismanagement, internal bickering, corruption, and interference with major drug busts throughout U.S. Customs in the southwestern part of the United States. This was not the environment for a government undercover agent to put his faith in the verbal authority given by a Customs agent. But Matthews was unaware of these serious internal problems.

Prophetic warning, "In the end, they're gonna screw you."

After the meeting, Dismukes warned Matthews that *in every case that he personally knew of*, where a contract undercover agent participated in that type of operation, he would eventually be charged and prosecuted, despite the authority given him by government agents. Matthews wrote:

Dismukes approached me in the hall. He was visibly upset that the feds were allowing drugs to hit the street. His face was red and his eyes were also red and watery. He was having trouble restraining himself. He told me it was my choice, but if I "went along with the feds on this and got in any deeper, eventually they will hang you out to dry; it always happens like this. In the end, they're gonna screw you."

Matthews later wrote, "I should have listened."

Holiday Drug Loads Plan To Catch Escobar and Stadter

In mid-1988, Texas Department of Public Safety (DPS) and San Antonio Customs agents asked Matthews to again try to infiltrate the Stadter organization. Through his earlier connections with the Stadter group, Matthews managed to have the group allow him to fly two loads of cocaine into the United States before committing larger loads to him. Matthews advised Texas DPS and Customs agents of the two test loads and that he planned to fly one load on Christmas day, 1988, and the next load on January 1, 1989. No objection was raised.

"It's Gonna Be A White Christmas"

Nestoroff, acting as communication liaison, received a message from Matthews on his answering machine on Christmas Eve stating, "It's gonna be a white Christmas." That was the code indicating Matthews would be flying to Colombia and bringing in a load of cocaine the next day, as part of the previously discussed plan.

Matthews landed in Florida on Christmas day with 1,400 pounds of cocaine. A member of the Escobar-Stadter group, "Chicha," received the bulk of the load in Fort Lauderdale. One hundred ten pounds of the original cocaine shipment (50 kilos) were driven to California by Douglas "Dancer" Voet, a member of the Stadter organization. DEA agents in California, unaware of the undercover operation, seized the drugs.

The Second Load Went Badly

On December 30, 1988, Matthews left a message on Nestoroff's answering machine advising him that he would bring in a load of cocaine the next day. Nestoroff passed the word to Customs in San Antonio, and Customs assured Nestoroff that the information would be passed on. Either through bureaucratic carelessness, or deliberately, that wasn't done. On this flight, Matthews had one of Stadter's pilots with him, Greg Thompson. Matthews landed his Merlin turbo-prop plane at the remote Colombian airstrip and trouble started immediately. Matthews explained:

> As soon as the plane landed, another group or faction moved in and attempted to take the load, the plane, and anything else of value. A small-arms fire-fight ensued during the loading and fueling, about a half mile away on the only road leading to the strip. I left the engines running for the fueling and loading, with Greg Thompson, the copilot, holding the brakes. Special outboard fuel receptacles had been installed for this purpose.
>
> As I deplaned and stepped away from the plane, I heard the shooting start. Max jumped in the jeep with four or five others and headed down the road to lend support to those guarding the road. After about 25 minutes, the jeep returned. Max was sitting on the passenger side of the jeep, being held up in the sitting position by a person sitting behind him. Max's chest was covered with blood. Max had taken a high caliber round, probably from the back as the hole in his chest was near the size of my fist. Max and the guy holding him up were Italians who had lived in Colombia for many years. When I walked over to the jeep to talk to Max, the guy holding him up said, "Max finito," meaning Max is finished [dead].

Matthews finally was able to take off from the airstrip, but there were other problems. As he approached Florida, his radar-detection equipment showed his plane had been picked up on radar. Thompson wanted to dump the load into the ocean, but Matthews wanted to save the undercover operation. He changed heading for his home strip at Damon, Texas.

Arrested by the Same Agency That Authorized the Operation

Matthews hoped that if an interdiction plane had gotten close enough to get the registration number on the side of his aircraft, Customs would realize he was carrying out an undercover operation and cover for him. After landing at Damon, Matthews and Thompson moved the 700-kilo drug load onto a pickup truck and drove from the airstrip. About five miles away, on Farm Road 1462, they were stopped and arrested by Houston Customs agents. This arrest occurred despite the fact that San Antonio Customs agents had notified Houston that Matthews would be arriving with a load of drugs as part of the two test runs. Or was it planned that way? Matthews was getting a taste of how undercover operations authorized by agents in one office were not recognized by agents in another office of the same agency.

***Houston Chronicle* Protecting Drug Traffickers**

Greg Thompson contacted Stadter's attorney, who in turn contacted Stadter. Stadter then contacted his newspaper friend, Bob Sablatura who then wrote several *Houston Chronicle* articles favorable to Stadter that sought to shift blame to federal agents. Sablatura contacted the television program, *60-Minutes*, to play up the angle of corrupt state and federal officials attempting to entrap his friend, Victor Stadter.

Stadter's Interesting Background Shown By the Movie, "Breakout."

Stadter had purchased a ranch near Leakey, Texas in the 1980's where he controlled a small newspaper. Information given to me showed Stadter orchestrating a scheme to free someone falsely accused of a murder and incarcerated in a Mexican prison. A book was written about it, followed by a 1975 movie, *"Breakout,"* starring Charles Bronson. The movie was allegedly based upon Stadter orchestrating the 1971 rescue by helicopter of a prisoner (Kaplan) in a Mexican prison.

Stadter had allegedly been a thorn in the side of the CIA and State Department since he brought about Kaplan's escape. Kaplan was an heir to a vast fruit company in Latin America and he was at odds with the CIA. The agency then reportedly orchestrated the murder of his grandfather and with the cooperation of corrupt Mexicans, arrested and sentenced Kaplan to 28 years in prison. The other heirs to the fruit company operation were amenable to CIA activities, and it was felt that Kaplan's imprisonment would bring about a management change favorable to the CIA. Kaplan's wife paid to have a pilot free her husband from the Mexican prison.

Back to Matthews

After the arrest, Texas DPS and San Antonio Customs made it known that Matthews was conducting an undercover operation. AUSA Dave Hall also got involved, making it known that Matthews had carte blanche authority to engage in his undercover drug-related activities. Charges against Matthews and Thompson were eventually dropped. Matthews' Merlin prop-jet aircraft (N707PK), his truck, and his car, which had been seized, were returned. However, the publicity given to the arrest was an embarrassment to Customs officers in the southwestern division, and they sought to deny Matthews had authority to fly the drugs. Matthews explained the reason why certain Customs officials refused to provide him the support following the holiday drug bust:

> *I'm saying that after it hit the newspapers that cocaine was smuggled in and no one was charged, it was a terrible embarrassment to the government that they would have to admit the cocaine hit the street; that they allowed cocaine to hit the street; that they were allowing those kind of things in order to get convictions, to get people busted, or to get to certain targets.*

Secret San Antonio Customs Coverup Report

In an effort to make it appear in Customs records that the test runs were not known or authorized by Customs agents, and unknown to Matthews, an 18-page report (February 16, 1989) was prepared in the San Antonio Customs office by Agent James King. This was sent to the U.S. Customs Regional Enforcement Commissioner. That report was followed by a Customs coverup memorandum written by San Antonio Special Agent in Charge (SAC) Neil Lageman. These reports charged Mathews with unlawfully flying drugs into the United States, omitting all reference to the authority given by AUSA Dave Hall and Customs agents. The reports ended up in Washington and intended to protect U.S. Customs supervisors. That report remained hidden from Matthews for several years.

If Matthews had actually flown the drugs into the United States without authority and for his personal use, Customs would have been required to promptly charge Matthews with drug-related offenses and DOJ prosecutors to file charges against him. This was not done.

Another Problem

The person who took the 50-kilo drug load to California after the drugs were unloaded in Florida had $100,000 of Matthews' money on him when arrested, which was to be returned to Matthews. Matthews asked Texas DPS Captain Don Cohn to send a letter to Washington explaining that the drug seizure in California, and seizure of the $100,000, was part of an authorized undercover operation. Cohn instructed DPS Agent Robert Nestoroff to write the letter. This would justify releasing the $100,000 to Matthews. The letter created a major problem.

Igniting an Internal Customs Firestorm

The two Customs reports falsely implying that Matthews' test runs were not a Customs-authorized operation—which had gotten to Washington, were then contradicted by the letter sent by the Texas Department of Public Service. This contradiction created problems within U.S. Customs. It also created problems for Matthews.

Multiple Reasons to Put Matthews out of Commission

Matthews' later discoveries of high-level corruption, and his threat to a major Colombian drug lord with CIA connections, would generate other reasons for government officials to get rid of Matthews. It was necessary to also discredit—and possibly imprison—the Texas DPS agent who wrote the letter to Washington stating that Matthews had authority to fly the drug loads: Robert Nestoroff.

Seizure of New Year's Load Resulted in A Kidnapping

There was other fallout from the loss of this second load. The daughter of one of Matthews' friends in Colombia was kidnapped, and Matthews acted to bring about her release. Matthews explained the kidnaping:

The kidnaping was a result of the New Year's eve 700-kilo load being leaked to the Houston Chronicle. That newspaper article literally started a war in Colombia between those who believed I was furnishing valid AWACS schedules and those who believed I was an informant. The two owners of that load were Molina, who controlled the Colombian emerald industry and Gaucho Rodriguez, a.k.a. "The Mexican."

Matthews Helping to Rescue Kidnapped Girl

The girl was kidnapped and held until they were paid for the loss of the load. My girlfriend's brother worked with a military colonel in the Colombian army. I personally turned over several hundred thousand dollars to the colonel. I was asked to fly a group of about 25 men from the North Coast of Colombia to a ranch about 75 miles northwest of Bogota.

They furnished a Howard 500 [airplane] that was based at the Santa Marta airport. It was a motley crew that I picked up on the Guijira east of Rio Hacha at a clandestine airstrip. Some of the men were dressed in neat military uniforms with automatic weapons and others were shabbily dressed with old bolt action rifles and shot guns. They loaded some of the heavier weaponry in the forward cargo compartments. We landed on the ranch northwest of Bogota before dark, and I waited with the plane.

The following day the group returned. I was assured by my girlfriend's brother that the girl had been released and was in safe hands in Medellin, Colombia, where she had been held at a small farm outside of town. I flew the crew back to the strip on the Guijira and returned the plane to the Santa Marta airport, where I took an airliner back to Bogota.

Executing 18 People

It was not until the next morning, while I was drinking coffee and reading the newspapers in the Hotel Tacandama, that I saw where Molina and at least 17 of his leading security force members were handcuffed and removed from the house where a large party had been in progress with a Mexican and a Colombian band. Those 18 people were executed. No one else was harmed, according to the Colombian newspaper. The ranch was in the area northwest of Bogota where I had landed. I later learned that someone at the party was forced to call via high frequency radio the ranch where the girl was being held, and order her released. The people who were holding the girl in Medellin were all killed by the military, according to the newspapers. The girl was never mentioned in the newspapers. Gaucho, the Mexican, met his demise shortly thereafter, and the pressure was off of me in reference to the "Chronicle" article about the 700 kilos which only hinted I may be an informer.

DOJ Informing Colombians Matthews was U.S. Informant

It was when AUSA Thompson sent out a two-page fax to major media around the country, officially notifying the world that I was a U.S. government informant, after I refused to cooperate in the coverup and the prosecutor's request to falsely name other people, that really did me in. This was done while my case was still under seal and Thompson knew my wife and child were in Latin America, easily accessible to the cartels of drug traffickers I had burned. I'm sure Thompson, Customs and DOJ officials thought I would be killed or be begging to cooperate in their coverup that would protect them from embarrassment and censure. The 1998 ABC news documentary only opened the door to the coverup.

Government Agents Again Give Matthews A Clean Slate

Present at this meeting were Texas Department of Public Safety (DPS) agents Robert Nestoroff, Don Cohn, Jim Fields, and David Davis, and Customs Special Agent in Charge (SAC) John Farley, Agents Richard Cardwell and Tony Singleton. During this meeting, Farley offered Matthews a clean slate if he would agree to do undercover work for Houston Customs and the High Intensity Drug Trafficking Area (HIDTA) task force. It wasn't really necessary to be given a clean slate as the holiday drug loads were authorized by Customs personnel. The statement by Customs personnel that they were giving Matthews a clean slate appeared to be another attempt to show the holiday loads were *not* authorized.

Clean-Slate Meeting

The "clean-slate" immunity was for the holiday drug load arrest and all the previous operations connected to the Stadter group (that had already been authorized by Justice Department's Dave Hall and Customs agents from the San Antonio office), or any other drug load. Matthews had this to say about the meeting:

> *The gist of the meeting was 'Let's put this behind us and move on.' Houston Customs advised me they had some specific operations they wanted me to help them with. In return, I would be given a 'clean slate.' I accepted part of the responsibility of the holiday loads fiasco and agreed to assist them using my planes, assets, and skills. This came to be known as the 'clean slate meeting' I set up a load of cocaine out of Cali, Colombia, to be delivered to a military base in Panama using my wife's Aztec. Everything went like clockwork.*
>
> *While I was negotiating with the Colombians in New York to receive their load, I learned of a newspaper article in the Panama newspapers that fingered me as an informant. The Houston people I worked with said it was the Panamanians they worked with who had leaked the information to the press. I didn't suspect anything because I thought I was back in the good graces of Customs. I didn't know about the 18-page report yet that was just sitting there smoking, it was so hot, and they couldn't prosecute me for fear of embarrassment. I had been hearing about an official letter or memo from Customs, black-balling me from any further work for them. It didn't make sense because Customs kept using me over and over and over. I continued to do some operations for Houston "free-gratis". I eventually settled into flying contract smuggling flights for Houston HIDTA. On many of the flights as I previously indicated, it looked as though I was deliberately being set up to be killed. At that time, I didn't know of any reason why anybody in the government would be trying to kill me.*

Continuing to Work Undercover Operations

Matthews had several undercover operations going. He shifted his attention from the Stadter project, that had been undermined by Customs, to the Nelson Emmens group that he had been trying to infiltrate since 1986. Part of Matthews' tactics to infiltrate the group was to broker the purchase of two airplanes for Emmens through Matthews' front company, Rod Aero. Matthews, trying to have Emmens use him for drug transporting, told Emmens he had a safe route to the United States based upon his access to AWACS schedules (Airborne Warning and Control System). This was not true, but the ruse was used to gain Emmens' confidence. Matthews then had to confirm that the initial two loads were actual drug loads and not dummy runs, a tactic drug traffickers sometimes use to check the security of a run. If this was done, and a non-drug-load was busted, Matthews' usefulness would cease, and the target would be alerted and escape punishment. In November 1989, Matthews had accumulated enough evidence to bring about Emmens' arrest.

The seizure of the New Year' test run by Customs undermined the operation to get evidence against Stadter and indirectly, the Pablo Escobar organization, requiring that the focus be put on other targets. Houston Customs personnel met with Matthews at the Lakeside Airport conference room in Houston (November 1990), purporting to use him against other targets.

Furnishing Transportation for Government Cocaine Flights

As Matthews previously described to me, the contract drug flights were flights where he simply provided transportation requested by government agents, flying to remote Colombian airstrips designated by Customs agents and delivering the drugs in the United States to people designated by the same agents. At that time, Matthews didn't realize the flights were a small part of a much larger practice of government agents and agencies flying drugs into the United States, as explained to me for the past decade by a long list of undercover agents. I asked Matthews about these flights, and he confirmed that he did not know what was done with the cocaine for which he had provided transportation and which he delivered to Customs and DEA-designated parties in the United States.

Juan Carlos Facholos Operation

In another undercover operation Matthews carried out for Houston Customs (1990), it ultimately resulted in the seizure of 491 kilos of cocaine from the Juan Carlos Facholos operation. In that operation, Matthews used his wife's Piper Aztec to carry a drug load from Cali, Colombia to New York via Panama. However, the drugs were seized by U.S. agents in Panama. While Matthews was negotiating to get the drugs released and simultaneously negotiating with the Colombians in New York to bring about delivery, Panamanian newspapers printed information indicating Matthews was a U.S. government informant. Matthews suspected this information came from Customs personnel in the San Antonio office.

Flying Captured Drug Traffickers into the United States

Besides flying undercover operations to ensnare drug traffickers and flying drug loads arranged by government agents, Customs agents paid Matthews to provide personnel transportation. One such flight was flying government agents from his Damon, Texas airstrip to Aruba in his Merlin and then from Aruba, flying two Colombians who had been previously arrested with the cooperation of Aruban authorities to Hooks Airport near Houston, Texas. He received a $40,000 government check for this flight.

Suspicious Government-Ordered Drug Flights

Other flights for which Matthews merely provided transportation had serious overtones that Matthews did not recognize at the time. Matthews said several of his drug hauling flights were directed by government agents who directed him to specific airstrips to pick up the load and then deliver the load to various places in the United States to government agents. Government agents sometimes gave Matthews hand-drawn maps of airstrips showing the pickup location. Matthews was given government questionnaires to fill out after the flight. Matthews' only involvement in these flights was to provide transportation for which he was paid by the U.S. government, *with* government checks. There was no effort to infiltrate any drug group.

Far More Drugs Shipped Than Indicated for Sting Operations

The excuse given by government supervisors when Matthews asked about why drugs are being shipped into the United States was that the drugs were being used for sting operations. Unknown to Matthews at that time, those flights were part of an overall drug smuggling operation involving the Central

Intelligence Agency (CIA), the Drug Enforcement Administration (DEA) and the U.S. military. Matthews described several of these drug-hauling flights for which he provided transportation:

Of the five drug flights, three were to Guatemala and two were to Colombia. Jerry Garner and Mike McDaniels were the DEA lead agents for these flights. The first of these flights was to a hayfield type landing area in Central Guatemala from my hangar in Delray Beach, Florida to Guatemala, where I picked up the cocaine and delivered it to agents waiting at my Texas hangar. Jerry or Mike was always waiting, usually accompanied by other Customs or DEA agents. I made an inspection run in my MU-2 to identify the surrounding terrain, look the strip over and obtain the GPS coordinates. At that time I didn't even know Jerry or Mike. Tony Singleton with Houston Customs put me in touch with them and we made all the arrangements by phone and fax. They faxed me a hand-drawn map and other instructions one afternoon. On each of these cocaine flights the agents, Jerry and Mike, provided me with a hand-drawn map of the strip area. On a couple of occasions afterwards I was given a numbered government form to fill out concerning the clandestine airstrip and what transpired.

Government Agents at Both Ends of Drug Loads

In answer to one of my questions about drug load pickups ordered by government agents for which he provided transportation, Matthews replied:

After the holiday loads fiasco, it was almost always government agents on the receiving end here in the United States or at a military base outside the United States. After going to work for Houston HIDTA in 1990, most of the cocaine loads were handled by the government on both ends. I was just a contract pilot flying cocaine for the government. On the pickup end, the government made the arrangements.

Sham Excuses Given to Drug Cartels for Successful Drug Runs

Several times, drug cartels asked Matthews to explain his success at bringing drugs into the United States without being caught. To avoid suspicion that he was a government undercover agent, Matthews told them that he was obtaining AWACS schedules from his U.S. Customs connections. They offered to pay him for copies of these schedules, which he then fabricated. Escobar and Ellard paid Matthews $500,000 each time he provided the bogus schedules. Because of the large time slots when there were no AWACS planes covering the particular area, the success rate at not being interdicted—with or without AWACS schedules—provided Matthews a certain amount of credibility.

Drug Cartels Funding Part Of Matthews' Undercover Operations

By being recognized as a successful drug transporter, Matthews had his targeted drug traffickers provide him money to buy planes and other expensive equipment. In one case, a targeted drug lord gave Matthews $300,000 to improve his airstrip at Damon, Texas, in preparation for transporting 10,000 to 15,000 kilos of marijuana aboard a DC-6. DPS agents inspected the property at Damon, Texas and approved the plan.

Coca-Cola in the Drug Business?

A low-key contract undercover agent working for the DEA and CIA, who hauled arms to Central and South America during the Contra operation in the 1980s, Basil (Bo) Abbott, frequently talked about how he flew drugs for the DEA in DEA-provided aircraft. During one conversation, Abbott told me that the land owned by Coca Cola in Belize was heavily planted with marijuana. I asked Matthews if he knew anything about this. He wrote:

There are little patches of marijuana growing all over Belize with some larger fields in the south. I never flew over the Coca-Cola property specifically and looked. However, I can confirm that at one time one of the foremen or managers for the Coca-Cola plantations was heavily involved in loading airplanes with marijuana and facilitating smuggling flights.

Guantanamo Naval Air Station and Drugs

Customs agents frequently directed Matthews to fly drugs from Colombia into Guantanamo Naval Air Station in Cuba. During these flights into the naval base, the procedure was to radio to the Navy control tower using code names given to him by the DEA, including "Hot-Rod" and "Dark-Cloud."

Upon landing at the naval station, the drugs would be unloaded by military personnel or DEA agents. They would then be loaded onto a U.S. Customs Beechcraft Kingair and flown to Homestead Air Force Base by Customs pilots, one of whom Matthews knew by the name of Dornak.

Richard Pitt, another contract pilot whose exploits are described in the next chapter, also told me about the many drug flights that he flew into and out of this navy base. [I thought to myself, how things have changed; during World War II, when I was a Navy flight instructor in PBY seaplanes, I flew many training trips to that same naval base. At that time, the sinister activities that started with the formation of the CIA in 1947 did not exist.]

Placing Tracking Devices on Matthews' Aircraft

Matthews explained how DEA and Customs agents placed tracking devices on his aircraft, including flights from Guantanamo Naval Air Base to Colombia. Matthews said the devices were basically transponders that emitted a particular code displayed on the radar screens of air traffic controllers. He explained that one type of device emits the signal "suspect" on the controllers' screens.

On one flight in April 1992, Matthews noticed the technician entered into his records the number C-38, which stood for the 38th flight to Colombia that year. It seemed that Matthews was not the only pilot used by government agents to fly drugs from Colombia to the United States facilities.

Plan to Capture Pablo Escobar

In 1990, Matthews suggested a plan to Customs agents for him to capture Colombian drug lord Pablo Escobar and fly him into the United States. At that time, Escobar was America's Number One drug target. They approved the plan; it was Matthews' life at risk, using his own plane, and his own money, with no risk to U.S. government agents. In trying to carry it out, Matthews set up money laundering and electronic smuggling operations with the Escobar group. The plan to kidnap Escobar was based upon luring him to a place where he could be kidnapped and flown to the nearest U.S. military base.

Escobar was considered the biggest drug trafficker and the most brutal, and considerable efforts were exerted by the United States to bring about his capture.

Escobar Bombing Hilton Hotel in Cartagena

In an earlier attempt to bring about Escobar's arrest, Matthews met with Escobar and other cartel members in the Cartagena Hilton Hotel over a three-day period. Escobar had been on the "wanted" list for some time and Matthews thought this was a good time to bring about Escobar's arrest. He called Texas DPS agent Robert Nestoroff, advising that Escobar was at the hotel. Nestoroff then notified EPIC (El Paso Information Center) and this information was then given to Colombian authorities. Before they arrived at the hotel, someone alerted Escobar to the imminent arrival of Colombian police, allowing him to escape. Thinking that someone on the hotel staff had reported his presence, Escobar had the hotel bombed.

Matthews explained his plan to bring about Escobar's arrest:

The first attempt to capture Pablo Escobar was a quasi-sanctioned operation. The plan was to lure Escobar to a clandestine airstrip about a hundred miles from Colombia's border in Brazil. This would cut off his support in the Colombian military and reduce his cadre of personal body guards. My group out of Barranquilla, Colombia, had an HF [high frequency] radio setup near the strip and were in touch with my girlfriend in Barranquilla who would call me at my hotel in Boa Vista, Brazil, when Escobar was ready to be picked up.

The strip was 140 miles from Boa Vista. I notified Peter Delsandro in Miami Customs by fax the day before the Panama invasion that I would be bringing the fugitive into San Juan, Puerto Rico, less than 1000 miles from the strip. My phone call from Barranquilla did not come that day because the hotel phone lines were down. I assumed there was a delay and waited. I didn't know the lines were down. The plan had gone like clockwork. Pablo and his group arrived in a helicopter that carried only six people. My group easily got the drop on them. With me being more than a day late, the group under my Colombian partner began to panic. Pablo offered them more money than I was paying, a lot more. My partner hit the jungle with his hand-held aircraft radio. My delayed phone message caused me to arrive a day late in the middle of a situation that was not friendly. I was circling over the strip trying to make radio contact with my guy on the ground to get the OK-to-land signal.

Suddenly the left engine was ablaze [from ground fire]. It felt like someone hit the plane with a sledge hammer. The left engine began surging and the feathering control was jammed solid. I saw pieces of metal protruding through the cowling. We were loaded with fuel and loaded for bear. It was a slow descent to find the nearest clandestine gold mining/smuggling strip along the river. The strip was soft, the nose wheel sunk in and broke off. The left wing went down on the tip tank and we were sliding 10 degrees to 15 degrees to the left of the strip toward the trees. As we began to slide off the left side of the strip, I locked up the right brake and she changed direction enough that it came to rest slightly to the right of the strip, partly on the strip. The right main gear had partially collapsed and the left wing pointed upward at about a 30 to 40 degree angle. The tip tank had been ripped open and fuel was pouring down the leading edge of the left wing onto the burning engine.

We all got out of the plane and for about 20 minutes it was like the fourth of July. One of the passengers had a camera and was able to photograph the different stages of burning and the marks on the dirt strip to indicate what had occurred. When the fireworks began to die down, the Indians began slowly emerging from the jungle. These were real Indians with the tattoos on their faces and stretched bottom lips, wearing leather straps. There was a Colombian on the strip who had an HF radio in the jungle nearby. He knew the whole deal and tried to turn the Indians on me. He called me "Del Norte Americana agente." I had some friends standing by or working the gold fields nearby. They saw the smoke and came to rescue us in a Bell 205, just in time.

The next day, I faxed Delsandro of Miami Customs a photo of what was left of the plane and told him to disregard delivering the fugitive to San Juan Puerto Rico Customs.

Covert Publicity Resulted in Operation Shanghai

Since Escobar was the top drug lord targeted by the United States, Matthews' nearly successful plan to capture him caused U.S. officials to authorize Matthews to conduct another attempt. This plan was called Operation Shanghai. Key people involved in approving the plan included Congressman Charles B. Rangel, who headed at that time the Congressional committee on narcotics; Customs Commissioner Tom McDermott, who named the plan Operation Shanghai; Special Agent in Charge Charles Rosenblatt; six Miami Customs officials, and former U.S. Attorney Steven Rozan. At that time, Rozan was a nominee for the political U.S. Attorney position at Houston. Rosenblatt authorized Matthews to engage in money laundering and smuggling electronics to finance and facilitate the operation.

At the urging of Rozan, it was agreed that Matthews would be paid $5 million if he could bring about the successful kidnaping of Pablo Escobar. Secretly, Rozan demanded that Matthews give him half the reward money. That plan fizzled out for various reasons. At a later meeting, Matthews was represented by attorney F. Lee Bailey.

In 1999 I sent two letters to Congressman Rangel, one of them certified mail, asking Rangel for his comments on the plan. He refused to respond to either letter.

Loss of $700,000 Insurance on the Plane

In the first attempt to capture Escobar, Matthews lost his plane from gunfire, as previously mentioned. That plane, a Mitsubishi MU-2 Solitaire, registration number N25GM, was covered by a $700,000 insurance policy. Former AUSA Steven Rozan, then an attorney who worked with Matthews, suggested that Matthews have the Rozan-Berger law firm file a loss-claim with the insurance company, and this was done. But the insurance company refused to pay. Matthews could have filed a law suit, but this would require testifying in court and exposing his undercover status. This decision caused Matthews to lose $700,000, one of the down-sides to being a contract undercover agent for the government. Matthews filed an accident report with the Federal Aviation Administration at Ft. Lauderdale, which included the affidavits of two Brazilian pilots who were on board the aircraft. Matthews had taken the Brazilian pilots along because they were familiar with the area, the people, and their language. One pilot, Jorge Rogerio, was well known in the Brazilian media as "Marijuana George."

Government Plan to Kill Matthews?

Toward the end of his career as a government contract agent, there were a number of incidents where it appeared government agents were trying to bring about his death. One incident occurred when Customs agents directed Matthews to pick up a drug load at a short airstrip on the Colombian island of Provendencia in the Central Caribbean. This was one of many flights in which government agents directed Matthews to pick up a drug load in Colombia and then fly it to a designated destination either in the United States or to Guantanamo Bay Naval Air Station.

Before taking off from the naval base, a DEA agent instructed Matthews to arrive and land *after* dark, using the make-shift runway lighting provided. As a precautionary measure, Matthews left the base early so he would arrive while there was still light, permitting him to inspect the airstrip from the air. To his surprise, there were two high hills at each end of the dirt strip, requiring a much steeper approach to the short runway. If he had arrived at night and made a normal approach to the relatively short airstrip with the unlighted hill on the approach end, it is very possible he would have crashed.

Dissatisfied With his Safe Return

Upon his return to Guantanamo Bay Naval Air Station, and while taxiing with his drug load to a hangar near the coffee shop, an obviously angry Customs pilot Matthews knew by the name of Dornak rushed toward the plane, shouting, "Why did you go in before dark and land?" Matthews said that it appeared Dornak was surprised he had made it back. Matthews said that Dornak flew the cocaine from the naval station to Homestead Air Force Base on at least two occasions that he knew of. He said that Dornak followed him one evening as they landed at Matthew's airstrip, and that Dornak almost lost control of the Kingair as he landed. (Matthews said that Dornak often drank heavily while at Guantanamo Bay Naval Air Station and had been working closely with AUSA Terrence Thompson, who later filed sham charges against Matthews.)

European Undercover Operations

In 1991, Matthews expanded his undercover operations to Europe, flying his Merlin to carry out several operations. His Palm Beach, Florida company, Rod Aero, had a contract to provide pilot and aircraft services for a pending contract with Disney Corporation in France, which never materialized. Matthews wrote:

My last flight to Europe in the Merlin III-B was a far cry from earlier flights where every minute was a struggle for survival in the old round engine planes. With the Merlin cruising at 24 to 26 thousand, the cabin pressure was about 3000 feet. It was a very quiet and comfortable plane,

*kind of like sitting on your favorite chair in your living room watching TV.
I had enough fuel to go non-stop straight across the Atlantic from Gander
to Shannon with enough IFR reserve to go to Paris or London, which cut
the stress factor considerably. I had the same autopilot flight director
system as the space shuttle, coupled to Omega-Loran-GPS and all the
other good stuff. At a glance I could take my position with three different
nav systems and if all three agreed within a quarter mile, one could be
fairly confident that was where you were at. It was really a super low-
stress flight compared to some of the earlier flights with two and three
pilots, totally stressed out to the point where when you finally reached
your destination, you felt like you had rowed across the Atlantic.*

Matthews' description of flying the North Atlantic reminded me of the many
flights I flew as captain on the North Atlantic in Boeing Stratocruisers, Lockheed Constellations, DC-4, and even two-engine C-46 aircraft.

Secret Tracking Device Disrupted European Air Traffic Control

During one of his European flights, unknown to Matthews, Customs had
installed a secret tracking device on Matthews' plane. This tracking device
emitted a signal that appeared on the air traffic controller's radar screen as two
planes flying side by side, and this caused serious air traffic problems. From
Europe, Matthews telephoned Texas DPS agent Robert Nestoroff, asking him
to find out what government agency and what agent had put the tracking device on his aircraft, and for instructions and permission to disconnect the device. Nestoroff found out that Houston Customs agent Richard Cardwell had
installed the device, and with Cardwell's permission, Matthews had it discon-
nected.

Funding the Defection of an Iraqi Pilot and Iraqi Aircraft

Matthews initiated and carried out a complex plan that had significant international implications but received no publicity. Acting on his own, Matthews placed ads in two publications in 1991: *Trade-A-Plane*, a widely-read
aviation publication listing all types of aircraft, parts, and services for sale,
and *Aviation International News*.

The purpose of the ad was to bring about the defection of an Iraqi pilot
and an Iraqi aircraft by offering to pay $100,000 to any Iraqi pilot who de-
fected with an Iraqi aircraft. As a result of the ad, Houston television station
KHOU, a CBS affiliate, had Matthews appear, with his face blacked out, describing the purpose of the reward. The purpose of the operation was to de-
moralize Saddam Hussein and his military and provide an impetus for other
Iraqis to defect. It was a long shot by Matthews that he thought up on the spur
of the moment. An Iraqi pilot *did* respond. Matthews wrote:

*Nobody, including myself, believed it would work until I got the call. It
ended up that I paid the Iraqi pilot $100,000 out of my own pocket. It was
a crazy deal that changed as it developed. The Iraqi pilot's mother was
Jewish and was under investigation with her brother, who also lived in
Iraq. The pilot wanted the money to get his family out of Iraq to save their
lives. When the pilot was told the deal about the photo that would be in
the world news, he refused the money and threatened suicide right there
on the spot. He explained that he did this to save his family and now they*

*would be killed for sure. We had the highway blocked off with traffic
backed up for miles both ways, and the Iraqi pilot gets down on his knees
and starts praying to Allah in Muslim fashion.*

*Within minutes, during refueling, a new deal was cut right there on the
highway. The pilot was given asylum in Israel where he was debriefed.
The pilot's family also was given asylum in Israel after their successful
departure from Iraq. I believe the Brits ended up with the Mig-29. Everyone involved knew if the U.S. State Department were consulted, they
would have opted to go with the propaganda and let the pilot's Jewish
mother and her brother die in Iraq. Turns out the pilot's uncle in Iraq was
working for Israel and that's what started the investigation of his Jewish
mother.*

At first, Matthews didn't want me to write about this Iraqi operation for fear
of alienating those who helped the defecting Iraqi pilot. I managed to convince
him that we could keep certain names secret and still get the message out.

Matthews didn't have a copy of the ad that he placed in the tabloid-size
Trade-A-Plane. I took a chance and asked the people at *Trade-A-Plane* to
search for that ad and send me a copy, a monumental task. Very obligingly,
they found the issue, the second February issue in 1991. I also contacted *Aviation International News*, asking them to locate the ad, but they did not respond
to my request.

Matthews's Bright-Red Jet

Matthews in Casa Jet

Matthews in his Merlin

Reduced-Size Copy Of Half-Page Ad Appearing In Trade-A-Plane

Matthews' Description of Iraqi Pilot Defection

In response to my questions about the particulars involving the defecting Iraqi pilot, Matthews wrote:

It all started with a phone call from an Israeli, Abe, who saw my ad in Trade-A-Plane. He wanted to know if I was serious and mentioned that if the pilot's family could be resettled in another country with financial assistance and if I had a place to land, it might be possible. I felt it was my patriotic duty to do anything I could to help my country, and my government had been good to me. And these kind of operations were my specialty.

Subsequent to talking to Abe several times and after he furnished me with some pretty impressive travel documents, I delivered the first hundred thousand dollars in cash to show him I was serious. I sent my ex-wife Judith from New York City to Israel with money, and equipment purchased in Miami. On the first trip she carried battery operated fuel pumps, filters and two hand-held FM transmitters-communication receivers.

She also carried two transponders and a top of the line (T-CAD) Terminal Control Avoidance device. The small five watt trans-com's low power output could not be monitored more than five miles away and is used for close-in clandestine air-ground communications.

Abe and Colonel E.G. met her at the airport and assisted her through Israeli Customs. (Matthews wanted to avoid publicity for the Israeli General, "E.G." who assisted in the operation.)

The next trip she carried two small hand-held GPS units. One was modified with suction cups on the top side so that it could be quickly stuck to the top of the inside of the aircraft's plexiglass canopy for unobstructed satellite reception through the plexiglass.

This was state-of-the-art at the time and sometimes there were not enough satellites up and in position for it to function. The precise nav equipment was necessary to eliminate a situation where the pilot would be required to fly around searching for the landing area, creating unwanted attention. This was a non-export item at the time, but Customs had authorized me to smuggle electronics at the Operation Shanghai meeting so I reasoned that I could justify it if push came to shove.

Abe, a former Air Force mechanic, came up with Mig-29 flight and maintenance manuals that were partially translated into English. According to him, it was compliments of the British, who seemed to be amused at the effort. A London-based pro-coalition media group or propaganda group, financed to the hilt, was biting at the bit to jump on this issue if it came to fruition. The sudden change in plan could have caused sour grapes among some in the skullduggery community. The Israeli authorities Abe talked to would not consider allowing an armed Iraqi aircraft to enter their territory under any circumstances.

Kurds Assisted the Operation

A well-known Lebanese-Colombian family out of Barranquilla, Colombia provided me with the drug trafficking connection in Syria, to block off a road and refuel the plane. This group was originally led to believe it was a drug flight refueling stop from Afghanistan. The logistics were S.O.P. for Latin American clandestine flight operations. Fake auto-truck accidents were used to block off about 2- ½ miles of road. On each end of the landing area, a group of well-organized Kurds accomplished this with precision and persuasion. I doubt they ever made this much money before, even in drug smuggling operations.

It was necessary for me to obtain the coordinates in advance, using the G.P.S. for each end of the landing area, the magnetic direction of the landing area, and a waypoint aligned with the landing area 3 to 4 miles out, for the approach. I walked every foot of the landing area inspecting it carefully, measuring width, checking for obstructions, an area for fueling, and an area for turning around to take off. The night before the landing, we removed the necessary obstructions.

The landing was set up for first light of day while most people would still be sleeping. The plan was to make one low-level inspection pass at 100 to 150 meters and a back-to-basics wide race track pattern return for landing, using the waypoint. It was less than a 30 minute flight from his Iraq departure point. The refueling was necessary for a reduced landing weight on a questionable surface. Only the Colombians could have matched the speed and efficiency of the clandestine fueling operation.

Discharging the Ammunition Before Landing In Syria

The heavy ordnance was discharged before arrival. When he touched down at about 140 knots slightly off center, he had to shove the nose down as we had previously discussed in order to see to stay in the center of the narrow road. This lengthened his landing roll to more than 5000 feet. As soon as he shut her down we were on it before he cleared the cockpit, pumping in the mixture of kerosene and aviation gas.

Abe had his act together from talking to the pilot and studying the maintenance manual. We used both of the battery operated fuel pumps to reduce fueling time. Once fueling was in progress, Abe and one of his crew started removing live ordnance. Balahson, a young Israeli officer in levis manned the camera.

Military personnel were stationed in surrounding areas and the Syria-Iraq border was lined with military lookouts. Syria was a participant in the coalition against Iraq during the Desert Shield, Desert Storm campaigns. The AWACS were up on a regular basis, the whole flight was under 500 feet (150 meters), but the AWACS still could have tracked it to the landing site under the right conditions. The morning of the landing we told the Kurds we would be using a military plane for the drug flight so they wouldn't fire on it or abandon their posts.

The Mig Didn't Look Like A Drug Plane!

When the Kurdish spokesman or leader drove up during the fueling and saw the ominous looking Mig-29 straddled the road while Abe removed ordnance from under the wing, the look on his face was as if he were witnessing the second coming of the Lord. [They had earlier been led to believe that this was a drug plane from Afghanistan that needed to be refueled.] *Two fighters made a pass over our location. I looked at Abe for a reaction, it didn't bother him so it didn't bother me. The Kurd was stunned by the Mig-29, you didn't have to know about airplanes to see this was a weapon of mass destruction.*

The Iraqi pilot was attempting to explain in broken English that his mother and uncle were still in Iraq, contrary to the plan. One of Abe's crew was trying to get a photo of the Iraqi pilot standing by the plane with the suitcase of money and told him he would be on the world news that evening.

Iraqi Pilot Threatening to Commit Suicide

The Iraqi pilot threatened suicide saying his mother would be tortured and killed. He wanted to return the balance of the money. The Kurd leader was watching all this and went into a rage about how we were all going to be killed because of the CIA. The pilot got down on his knees in the Islam tradition and began to pray. It was at this time that I thought to myself, "Only when I get back to the U.S. will I be sure I made it out of this mess."

Little did I know at this very time a U.S. prosecutor in Fort Lauderdale was plotting my destruction. I would be betrayed and disavowed by elements in my own government! I took the camera and gave it to the pilot, explaining no pictures would be taken. Abe explained to the pilot, everything would be done that could be done to save his family and they would still receive the promised assistance. I promised the Kurds double the original amount, which helped to calm them down. They were about ready to go off on us. From start to finish the operation costs me close to a million and I was asked to return the travel documents. The Kurds had taken a couple of distant photos that were turned over after they were paid. The photos showed the tail section of the aircraft protruding beyond the rear-end of the fuel truck. One of these photos was in my house when it was seized. Balahson has the other.

The restart went OK for this particular plane had a small battery start APU [auxiliary power unit] for starting the big engines. There was no question it was a Mig-29. It matched the maintenance manual of another Mig-29 in detail with the large twin vertical stabilizers, conventional controls, 3,500 pounds of thrust, capable of MAC 3. The landing gear was or appeared to be much beefier than similar U.S. fighter aircraft. The flight manual specs were scary in that the U.S. had several different aircraft that can match it in a specific area but we don't have any one plane that can match it in all areas. Because of the rugged simplicity and conventional controls, it couldn't require much special flight training. The Iraqi pilot only had 450 hours of flight time total. It can also be operated in the bush without a specialized ground crew or ground power unit.

The aircraft departed and that's all I want to say about it. There were some unconfirmed news reports of an Iraqi fighter being shot down or missing. There was some talk the British ended up with it.

I traveled by airline with the bogus travel documents to avoid attracting attention when I went over to do the deal. Some of the cash went over on the Merlin trip in hundred dollar bills.

To God and My People

When it was all over, I asked Abe, "Who is it that you ultimately answer to?" He responded, "Ultimately, to God and my people."

Further Explanation on Iraqi Pilot and Iraqi Plane Defection

Over a period of time and after many back and forth letters, Matthews added more details. He explained that the Iraqi pilot in Iraq was contacted through the pilot's uncle, and the uncle worked closely with Abe, who provided the maps and Global Positioning System unit that enabled the pilot to accurately find the improvised landing strip.

Matthews said that Abe and an Israeli general, who Matthews would only identify as General E.G., handled the many complex arrangements, including arranging for a fuel truck at the landing site and paying the necessary bribes.

Changing Plan to Avoid Hostility Between Iraq and Israel

Matthews explained that almost one million dollars were expended to obtain the pilot's defection. His *Trade-A-Plane* advertisement offered $100,000 to the defecting pilot. To this amount, Abe managed to obtain additional money for the expenses incurred by the defection process made more complex to avoid political repercussions if the pilot landed in Israel. For political reasons, another plan was developed to avoid hostility between Israel and Iraq. It was also necessary to change the original plan to first get the pilot's mother and uncle out of Iraq when it was realized that their departure would focus attention on the Iraqi pilot. The plan was changed to have all of them leave at the same time.

Original Plan was to get Publicity from Pilot's Defection

Matthews said his original idea was to get maximum adverse publicity for Saddam Hussain by publicizing the pilot's defection. The plan was to get a picture of the defecting and the aircraft for publicity purposes. By changing the plan, Matthews said, "It appeared to me the greater impact for the U.S. had been lost, but there was the consolation of taking one more weapon away from Saddam Hussein."

I asked why there was so much secrecy at keeping Israel's role secret during the defection. Matthews explained:

This would give Saddam Hussein one more reason on a long list to attack Israel diplomatically and/or militarily. The publicity could have increased tension between the United States and Syria, a coveted coalition member at the time, if conflict had erupted between Syria and Israel due to the fallout. There was no coordination between Israel and the Alawite minority-controlled Syrian government. Despite coalition membership there was too much friction and distrust between the Syrian government and Israel to coordinate anything. Israel obviously still had people in Iraq that could be connected to that operation that could be jeopardized. I doubt they now want publicity.

I thought it was quite an accomplishment to take out one of Saddam's top-line fighters without a fight at a time when the United States was risking American lives to accomplish this objective. On a personal basis it didn't do anything but cost me money that I could certainly use now.

Matthews explained he made fueling arrangements through a Lebanese family in Colombia and Kurds in Syria. Matthews had to pay $75,000 for fuel and the use of a fuel truck to fuel the Mig-29when it landed in Syria. He said that the Lebanese family living in Barranquilla, Colombia cut the deal with elements in the Alawite minority-controlled Syrian government, which involved bribes so that no one interfered with the refueling flight which had been described as a drug flight from Afghanistan.

Drug Money Links to A Major Political Party

After the Iraqi pilot defection occurred, Matthews went back to his undercover activities. During these investigative activities he discovered money being paid to the Democratic Party in Texas to pay for a U.S. Attorney position. Matthews had received $500,000 from the Pablo Escobar group in return for bogus AWACS schedules, and placed the money for safe keeping with attorney Steven Rozan, a former AUSA in Houston and a nominee for U.S. Attorney in that office. The understanding was that Rozan would hold this money until Matthews needed it.

Matthews explained that money is occasionally needed for emergencies associated with government undercover operations such as an arrest in a foreign country, an aircraft accident, the need for a replacement engine, and anything else that requires money. Matthews said, instead of holding Matthews' money for safekeeping, Rozan used the money to pay off his own political friends and personal debts. Matthews had already paid him for legal services and Matthews considered this diversion of emergency funds to be theft.

Drug Money for Political and Judicial Appointments

Matthews said he discovered Rozan was sending briefcases of money to the chief financial officer of the Republican Party for political and judicial appointments and other favors. Matthews made this information known to Houston Customs agents who in turn notified U.S. Attorney Roberto Martinez in Miami, advising that Matthews was recording conversations supporting the bribe money. Matthews described how the bribe money worked:

The drug money went to political campaign chief financial officer Robert Holt, by way of Steven Rozan, who was a former Assistant U.S. Attorney vying for a U.S. Attorney appointment in Houston. I had flown Rozan to Midland on more than one occasion to deliver a briefcase to two gentlemen at the airport. Rozan explained to me how he visited Holt's office, described his secretary, etc.

Rozan had asked for additional funds of $500,000 from the same drug trafficking group to give to Holt. Rozan claimed this would buy him friends in high places and guarantee that he would be appointed the U.S. attorney's position in Houston or a position just as important.

I met the man in Midland, Texas who received the briefcases of money from Rozan when I flew Rozan to Midland, Texas. Rozan would not risk carrying the briefcases of money on the airlines.

I advised Customs agents Singleton and Farley what was going on, and they suggested I obtain incriminating tape recordings, which I did. I also set up a deal with Rozan to deliver the $500,000 in drug money he *requested in Houston, a sting operation targeting Rozan and his political friends. Houston proposed the operation to the Miami U.S. Attorney's office, and I was arrested after that.*

When the sting operation on Rozan and his incumbent political friends was proposed by Houston Customs agents to Miami U.S. Attorneys' office under Martinez, it set off an alarm. Martinez was a strong supporter in the Bush camp. He knew Holt had run the campaign for Bush and Quayle in '88 and '92. The sting operation was to deliver another $500 thousand of obvious drug money to Rozan in Houston and go from there to get Holt. Miami's U.S. Attorney's office not only squashed everything, but Thompson took it even further and scuttled the Montana trial against Rozan, which was the link to Holt. As it stands, there is only scant circumstantial evidence against Holt and the Republican finance committee, thanks to Miami U.S. Attorney's office and Thompson.

The whole thing came to a dead end when I was arrested. The thrust of the trial in Montana was to convict Rozan and then get him to set up and roll on Holt. When Rozan was acquitted through Thompson's maneuvers, the threat to Holt and the campaign finance committee was cut.

After I gave Greg Laughlin (Democrat) a copy of the Matthews papers indicating the Republican presidential campaign leadership may be involved in taking large amounts of drug money in return for political appointments, he switched over to the Republican party and gained the support of Haley Barbor, the head of the Republican campaign funding. I never heard a word back from him. He lost his seat in the following election. Robert Dornan out of Orange County, California, was the only one to lift a finger to help me, after I sent letters to over 140 U.S. representatives and senators. [Dornan also lost his seat after investigating Matthews' charges.]

Matthews explained he had originally flown Rozan and his law partner, Sid Berger, from Fort Lauderdale to Andrau Airpark in Houston with the $500,000 contained in two silver metal suitcases.

The Montana Property Known as Top Gun

Matthews acquired the Montana ranch known as Top Gun from Jimmy Ellard, the aide to Pablo Escobar, and then placed the documents for the property transfer with Rozan for safe keeping while Matthews advertised in a Costa Rican newspaper seeking to trade the Montana property for land in Costa Rica. The intent of seeking Costa Rica property was to entice Pablo Escobar to visit the property and then be arrested.

Forging Signatures to Montana Ranch

Matthews said Rozan then used the Montana ranch as if it was his own property, as Rozan reportedly had done with Matthews' $500,000, and placed the property into the name of his law partner, Side Berger.

Matthews said Rozan forged the signature of Ellard's girlfriend, Miriam Heins, who was on the title, and had his office secretary, Chris, notarize the forged signature. If this is correct, there is the possibility that whoever owns that ranch could lose it if a legal attack was made on the title based upon the forged signature. The Montana ranch was located near Kalispell on the west side of Glacier National Park. It was eventually divided into several parcels.

Analyzing Taped Conversations Between Matthews and Rozan

Matthews provided me with the transcript of a taped conversation (May 8, 1992) between himself and Rozan at Matthews' Cancun, Mexico, residence. Matthews explained that Rozan and his law partner, Sid Berger, visited him several times in Cancun and this taped conversation was made during one of those visits. The transcript was bits and pieces of the conversation and I asked Matthews to explain what was said. The transcript was explained by Matthews as follows:

* Conversation between Rozan and Matthews concerning the bribe money paid to the Democratic Party to purchase a U.S. Attorney's position in Houston.
* Funneling of drug money to the Republican party at Midland, Texas.
* Rozan encouraging Matthews to move to Brazil and not return to the United States so as to avoid a pending Justice Department prosecution of Matthews and keep Matthews away from a criminal trial in Montana in which Rozan was the defendant.
* Discussed the $240,000 the government owed Matthews for the last five trips that he made hauling government people and drugs.
* Discussed the Montana ranch which was formerly in title of Jimmy Ellard using the alias, Joe Cernoch, the name of the deceased husband of his girl friend, Miriam Hiens, who lived in Barranquilla, Colombia.

Retaliating Against "Uncooperative" Members of Congress

Matthews interested California Congressman Robert K. Dornan in the drug-money bribes. On February 2, 1996, Dornan notified Matthews that he was initiating a congressional inquiry with U.S. Customs Service. The possible consequence of this congressional "snooping" was that a large amount of money was funneled into the congressional election for Dornan's challenger, resulting in Dornan losing the election. Because of election irregularities, Dornan challenged the election results, but with a Democrat in the White House controlling the Justice Department, the challenge went nowhere.

The Prophetic Statement of the Texas DPS Agent

"In the end, they're gonna screw you," was the statement made to Matthews by Texas Department of Public Safety officer Kenneth Dismukes. And he was right! Matthews was learning too much. Discovering the bribing of government officials and politicians just made matters worse for Matthews. In Fort Lauderdale, AUSA Terrence J. Thompson obtained from a grand jury an indictment against Matthews for the two holiday drug runs that occurred almost three years earlier—and which were known to Justice Department prosecutors during that entire period. Something triggered the need to get Matthews out of the picture. Government agents even authorized Matthews to fly other government operations after the holiday drug loads, something that they would not have done if Matthews had really flown unauthorized drugs into the United States.

In obtaining the indictment against Matthews, the prosecutor had Pablo Escobar's aide, Jimmy Ellard—who played a key role in the death of 110 people in the bombing of the Avianca airline—provide testimony to the grand jury. Ellard was in prison and was promised his release and other benefits if he testified against Matthews as the prosecutor wanted him to testify.

Customs Arresting Matthews for Drug Loads They Authorized

Customs Internal Affairs agents—the same agency that authorized the flights—arrested Matthews on June 26, 1992, charging him with drug offenses related to the holiday drug loads.

During several telephone conversations with Texas DPS agents, and particularly Robert Nestoroff, Thompson learned that Texas DPS and federal agents would testify that Matthews had authorization to fly the two holiday runs. Thompson tried to get Nestoroff to deny Matthews had such authorization. Nestoroff replied that taped telephone conversations between himself and AUSA Dave Hall showed that Matthews had authority to fly the loads. Thompson said that Nestoroff should keep these tapes from Matthews' attorneys, a clear violation of the requirement that prosecutors provide the defense with any exculpatory information.

Nestoroff replied that it was required by law to provide such evidence to the defense. Thompson said he had no intention of making the tapes available. Nestoroff then said that Matthews' attorneys *already* had copies of the tapes.

Replacing the First Indictment

Realizing that these tapes undermined his charges against Matthews and that Texas DPS personnel would not commit perjury for the prosecutor, Thompson obtained from the grand jury (September 7, 1993) another indictment to replace the first one. The second indictment eliminated the charges that were in the first indictment and charged Matthews with conspiracy to bring drugs into the United States between 1985 and 1988, relying primarily upon the statements to be made by Jimmy Ellard—a former aide to Pablo Escobar—who was a prison inmate with years of imprisonment remaining on his sentence.

He was in prison because of Matthews' earlier undercover work for Texas DPS and Customs agents. Now, Justice Department prosecutors were offering the incarcerated convict the opportunity to get back at Matthews, and be released from his long prison sentence—by testifying as Justice Department prosecutors wanted him to testify. Further, he would be allowed to keep his drug-tainted assets, and as an extra bonus, would be protected against being charged with criminal perjury for his perjured testimony. Ellard couldn't lose.

The Public Would Not Do Too Well in This DOJ Scheme

The public would not do too well in this DOJ scheme. They would lose the drug catching efforts of Matthews, and have inserted into the community a major drug kingpin responsible for thousands of pounds of cocaine entering the United States!

Ellard's testimony consisted of unsupported statements that he had seen Matthews haul drugs into the United States from 1984 to 1988, and that Matthews had paid over five million dollars to Texas DPS agent Robert Nestoroff for protection and Customs agent Richard Cardwell for AWACS schedules. For this testimony, he would be handsomely rewarded.

Summary of Problems Using Ellard

There were a few not-so-minor problems using Ellard as the Justice Department's star witness against Matthews. For instance:

- Ellard had been a major drug trafficker who brought tons of cocaine into the United States.
- Ellard played a key role in the death of over 100 people.
- Ellard was also indirectly connected to the United States' Number-1 drug cartel target.
- Ellard was formerly a Texas police officer, making his violation of trust an even worse offense under federal criminal law.
- Department of Justice personnel were releasing into the general population an extremely dangerous criminal.
- Ordinary men and women were being arrested and imprisoned by the same Department of Justice attorneys for possession of M&M amounts of cocaine, destroying families at a wholesale clip. It is probable that almost the entire federal prison population sentenced collectively to hundreds of years in prison would have brought into the United States, or dealt in drugs, that were far less in quantity that Ellard had admittedly brought in.
- Government offices would be further corrupted by the culture in the Department of Justice, which spreads, cancer-like, throughout government and throughout society.

Possible Reasons for This Convoluted DOJ Conduct

Something smelled rotten here, and the answer might be found in why the Department of Justice would want Matthews taken down, silenced, and discredited. Something smells, when Department of Justice officials block the arrest of a major U.S. drug lord by sabotaging the contract agent hired by Customs to bring about his arrest. Something smells when a key aide to the drug lord, guilty of many murders and tons of cocaine smuggling, is given his freedom by Department of Justice officials in exchange for the imprisonment of a courageous contract pilot seeking to bring about the arrest of the drug kingpin!

Here are a few reasons why the Department of Justice officials might have wanted Matthews imprisoned. Matthews knew of:

- Drug loads flown into Guantanamo Bay Naval Air Station and into the United States on behalf of Customs and DEA agents, part of the widespread smuggling of drugs into the United States by government personnel and government agencies—a major scandal waiting for the public to recognize.
- Drug money going to purchase U.S. Attorney's positions.
- Drug money going to the Democratic party.
- Matthews was a threat to the Pablo Escobar organization—who had close ties to CIA drug smuggling operations.

Ellard's Plans to Blow Up Drug Planes

Matthews told me how Ellard designed the bomb that Escobar used to blow up the Avianca airliner and the reason for placing the bomb on the aircraft: kill two people Escobar wanted eliminated. Matthews knew this information from prior conversations with Escobar and Ellard. Matthews wrote:

Ellard had proposed a plan to Escobar, to rig his drug planes with explosives while the drug plane was parked on the strip in Colombia at night, and had asked me to detonate the charge with a remote control device from a surveillance airplane if the drug plane was being followed, in order that his drug pilots could not testify against him if caught. Escobar went behind Ellard's back and attempted to devise a plan to shoot down the interdiction plane instead of his drug plane in order to save his load. I was first compelled to see that neither of these plans were carried out. My next priority was connecting Stadter to the air-drop operation in the Gulf. I also wanted to maintain a bridge to Escobar after Stadter went down. Numerous loads of cocaine hit the street in the process.

Using Another Major Drug Trafficker Against Matthews

Another witness used by the prosecutor against Matthews was Nelson Emmons, the drug trafficker that Matthews had earlier targeted in a DEA-directed operation that resulted in Emmons receiving a 17-year prison sentence. Now, Justice Department prosecutors offered another major drug trafficker his release if he testified against Matthews, using the prosecutor's transcript.

Over 100 Cocaine Loads into the United States

The Justice Department prosecutor coached Ellard and Emmons on the testimony he wanted to hear. During cross-examination, Emmons was forced to admit to smuggling over 100 loads of cocaine by boat into the United States. It can be assumed that these huge drug loads played key roles in many drug overdoses, murders, and other crimes.

Emmons testified that Matthews profited by helping him make the transition from drug smuggling by boat to drug smuggling by plane by teaching him to fly twin-engine aircraft. In order for the government to have a basis for seizing Matthews' home, Emmons fabricated testimony stating that Matthews sold drugs from his home. With Emmons and Ellard, it was a case of "Tell me what you want me to say and I'll say it."

Chief of Texas Department Of Public Safety Supported Matthews

With credit to the Texas DPS and their agents, especially Nestoroff, they testified in Matthews' behalf, along with many other government agents. The Texas Department of Public Safety took the position they would not be part of any cover-up or perjury, and they provided evidence showing that Matthews' activities were authorized.

In August 1992, AUSA Terrence Thompson had visited Texas Department of Public Safety headquarters in Austin, Texas, meeting with DPS assistant chief of law enforcement, Mike Scott. Thompson advised Scott that he was investigating Matthews' role in the Christmas Day and New Year drug flights. This set off alarm bells with Scott. "We immediately laid out the whole story on the task force investigation for him." Scott later said. A *Dallas Morning News* article on January 29, 1995, said:

Thompson got mad when I confirmed that Bob Nestoroff, if subpoenaed, would testify truthfully that those two flights were sanctioned by the federal government. Thompson refused to receive copies of DPS records on the task force, including recordings Sgt. Nestoroff made of phone conver-

sations with federal authorities who acknowledged that Mr. Matthews' efforts were sanctioned by the government.

Texas DPS agents recorded conversations with AUSA David Hall showing that state and federal agents authorized Matthews to fly drugs into the United States. When Thompson learned that these tapes were made available to Matthews' attorneys, Thompson was furious. Scott testified to this reaction, and testified as to how he told Thompson that the tapes would have to be made available to the defense. Scott testified, substantiating the prosecutor's obstruction of justice tactics:

Thompson appeared upset on the telephone. I explained that they probably got the copies through Mr. Burton [Charlie Burton, Nestoroff's attorney from Austin, Texas]. But I said, "Mr. Thompson, it shouldn't have mattered anyway because under discovery you would have had to divulge the existence of the tapes." And he said, "I had no intention of telling them that I had the tapes."

Texas DPS Testified Matthews' Holiday Flights Were Authorized

Texas DPS Chief Michael Scott continued his testimony, revealing that much of the information contained in those tapes was inconsistent with the theory of the government in its prosecution of Matthews. He explained that the first indictment the Justice Department prosecutor filed against Matthews involved the December 25, 1988, and January 1, 1989, drug loads that had been authorized and were known by Texas DPS and Customs agents.

Government Immunity for Period Covered by Second Indictment

Testimony also brought out the fact that even if Matthews had brought drugs in during the period covered by the second indictment he had been given immunity twice for any private flights he might have conducted during the periods from 1985 to 1990. Matthews had been an undercover agent for the Texas DPS, DEA, and Customs offices for this entire period of time and had been given carte blanche authority and immunity.

Typical Justice Department Threat Against Witnesses

Scott further testified about the DOJ's prosecutor threatening DPS agent Nestoroff:

Suddenly, Bob [Nestoroff] got hit with subpoenas for bank accounts, phone records, everything. He had his security clearance with Customs jerked. We saw it as intimidation, a hint that Bob should not testify at Matthews' trial.

Scott testified that after DOJ prosecutor Thompson learned that Matthews' attorney had the tapes showing he had authority to fly drugs, Justice Department prosecutors dropped the charges. And then promptly fabricated new ones—offering a prisoner his freedom to testify against Matthews. The prisoner was to testify that Matthews had furnished AWACS schedules to Ellard and Emmons from 1986 to 1990 which Matthews had allegedly purchased from government agents.

Texas DPS Agent Robert Nestoroff Supported Matthews

Texas DPS agent Robert Nestoroff testified about a meeting held in November 1990 at Lakeside Airport in Houston. This was a meeting where government agents agreed that Matthews' prior flights—if they had been without authority—would be wiped clean from the slate if he helped with some specific operations for Customs and cooperated with the High Intensity Drug Trafficking Area task force (HIDTA). In response to a question asked by defense attorney Ronald Dresnick, Nestoroff testified:

> *Farley said that they wanted to clean the slate with Mr. Matthews and that they had some things that they wanted him to do and they would like him to come over and work for them.*[Referring to the "clean state" statement] *That everything that occurred with his past was forgotten and that they wanted to talk to him and get him to work for them for a group they had over in Houston, Houston HIDTA, High Intensity Drug Trafficking Area task force. I felt like, I told my captain that what Farley had wanted all along was coming to fruition, that he wanted to use Mr. Matthews as a CI [Confidential Informant] and that we would probably be cut out of the deal.*

Referring to efforts by U.S. Customs in Houston and San Antonio to use Matthews, Nestoroff testified that agent Richard Nichols called him and said that his agency would "like to bring Matthews into the organization." Responding to questions about whether Justice Department prosecutors wanted to prosecute Matthews, Nestoroff replied:

> *I thought it was pretty rotten that they told the man he could do one thing and then they tried to lie their way out of it. I felt that what they were doing, dropping the investigation [of Stadter] was at least in part a vindication to me.*

DPS Tape Recordings Showing DOJ Attempts to Suborn Perjury

Nestoroff provided tape recordings revealing Justice Department personnel trying to get him to lie and deny the fact that Matthews had been given authorization to fly the drug loads. The introduction of these tapes into the trial infuriated the Justice Department prosecutor. Nestoroff testified concerning a December 14, 1988 meeting, relating to the upcoming "holiday load" drug runs:

> *The gist of the December 14th (1988) meeting, which was attended by myself, Lieutenant Dismukes, Rodney Matthews, Tom Grieve, Jim Dukes, and Dave Hall, was the upcoming Christmas-New Year's trip and what in fact Mr. Matthews was supposed to do. He was told that if in fact he was placed in the position of having to run the load, that he should go ahead and do so. [Matthews was] an excellent informant. You see, this is an informant that didn't mind going and putting himself in danger and going into the lines of dangers several times for us, and he never questioned it. He was one of the best informants that I ever had.*

Nestoroff stated he reported his activities to his immediate supervisor, Kenneth Dismukes and that these meetings were made known to DPS Captain Don Cohn. Nestoroff added:

> *This didn't sound right, but we had a subsequent meeting with the Assistant U.S. Attorney [Dave Hall] assigned to the investigation, and I got the same story from him. He told Mr. Matthews that he had authority to do what Mr. Grieve wanted him to do, including flying to Colombia, if need be, to pick up a load of cocaine and bring that load of cocaine back into*

the United States. And as far as Grieve was concerned, he started out by saying that the load could get away, if necessary, if it had to.

Nestoroff testified that Customs was alternating between whether to prosecute Matthews or Stadter—the drug lord that Matthews and other government agents were trying to arrest. Nestoroff was asked, "Now, going back to late January 1989, there were these meetings and these meetings were to determine whether Mr. Matthews would be prosecuted or not. Whatever happened to the Stadter investigation?"

Nestoroff replied that charges were dropped against the Stadter drug organization, including Vic Stadter, his pilot Greg Thompson, and his associate Diane Borden. In effect, the Department of Justice tactics not only released from prison into the general population Ellard and Emmons, but also resulted in investigations being dropped against other suspected drug traffickers. The Department of Justice's conduct raises serious questions about what were the Department of Justice's real motives. Nestoroff continued, as he testified about the meeting where Matthews refused to fly drugs without authorization:

Then Mr. Grieve said that it was possible to get Customs authorization for Mr. Matthews to fly a load of cocaine if he was put in the position to do so, but that if it was necessary for him to be put in that position, that he should be vague in his response to what he was telling us, so that if they didn't have specific information, then they wouldn't have to interdict the load if it came in. They're telling Mr. Matthews to be vague and if he's going south (Central and South America for drugs), to use coded messages or be very vague about what he was doing. And just let us know that he was going south to do a trip.

DOJ Devoting Major Attention to Discrediting Matthews' Witnesses

Seeking to discredit this testimony, the DOJ prosecutor repeatedly sought to discredit Nestoroff by charging—without any evidence—that Matthews had bribed him to avoid arrest, and acted to discredit Customs agent Cardwell by stating that Matthews bribed him to provide AWACS schedules. Seeking to discredit Cardwell, the DOJ prosecutor sought to discredit his employment application by alleging, without evidence, that Cardwell had lied about the amount of piloting hours he had so as to get a pilot's job with Customs.

The prosecutor alleged that Matthews sold AWACS schedules to drug cartels, which helped to avoid interdiction and assisted in bringing 50,000 kilos of cocaine into the United States. In the mindset of Justice Department prosecutors, the drug traffickers bringing in the huge quantities of drugs were entitled to their freedom in exchange for life-in-prison of the person who allegedly sold them AWACS schedules!

25 Government Witnesses Versus Mass Murderer and Two Major Drug Traffickers—And Guess Who Wins!

Twenty-five government agents and two assistant United States attorneys testified in Matthews' defense. Contradicting their testimony were the two major drug kingpins and the mass murderer. It would be difficult to more clearly depict the arrogance and corrupt culture in the Department of Justice that permits such mentality to control the awesome power of the Department of Justice.

Strange Alliances: DOJ and Dangerous Narco Terrorist Against Government Contract Pilot Rodney Matthews

At that time, the United States considered Pablo Escobar Gaviria the most dangerous narco terrorist. He was responsible for many bombings that killed and maimed hundreds of innocent people, including the deaths of 110 people on the Avianca aircraft. He was one of the most brutal of all drug traffickers. Dozens of buildings were bombed as he brought a reign of terror upon Colombia.

Escobar converted drug trafficking into big business, responsible for shipping huge amounts of cocaine into the United States. Escobar, sometimes known as the "Godfather," had been listed by *Forbes* magazine in its list of the top 100 non-U.S. billionaires (July 1988). He brought individual drug traffickers into a cartel that increased the quantity of drugs coming into the United States. At that time Escobar was considered the most dangerous of all drug traffickers, surely Number One on the U.S. list of drug traffickers. The expenditure of vast U.S. efforts and funds were made to capture Escobar and his associates. Jimmy Ellard was a close associate or partner to Escobar, and now being handsomely rewarded for testifying against a government contract agent who had been responsible for his earlier imprisonment.

Pablo Escobar's Top Aide Sitting Alongside the DOJ Prosecutor

For the Department of Justice personnel to use Escobar's close aide to sabotage a contract government agent, to allow that aide, Jimmy Ellard, to sit alongside the U.S. Attorney in court as if he was an honorable person, reflects the sordid culture in the U.S. Department of Justice. And it coincides with what I have documented for the past 30 years about the arrogance and criminality in that misnamed government agency. With the help of the Department of Justice, in the Matthews case, the Escobar group proved that the bad guys really *do* win—with help like they received from DOJ personnel.

In Jest, DOJ Using Escobar as A DOJ Witness

In a moment of jest, Matthews wrote, "Thinking back on it all, it's probably a good thing for me that I didn't bring about Escobar's arrest; looking at [DOJ prosecutor] Thompson's way of doing things, Escobar would have been one more government witness against me." ☺

DPS Agent Kenneth Dismukes Confirmed Matthews' Authority

Testimony by DPS Kenneth Dismukes told how Matthews was brought to a Customs meeting at which Customs wanted to use Matthews in undercover operations, particularly into the Vic Stadter investigation. Referring to Customs agent Rich Nichols, Dismukes testified:

> *Rich Nichols informed us that they [U.S. Customs] were part of a task force, a financial task force and they wanted to use Mr. Matthews to fly a load of cocaine to the Vic Stadter organization, trying to infiltrate them in that manner.*

Referring to Matthews' statement during the meeting, Dismukes testified:

> *He would be willing to do it, but having known those people [drug traffickers] from the past, they would expect him to more or less fly a test load, and if that went through, then they would go for a bigger deal. He was told to fly a load of dope, if necessary, to get on the street for distri-*

bution. I had warned Mr. Matthews that he'd be taking a risk and I advised him not to do it. I told him if something happened and something went wrong [such as media publicity] he'd be left hanging out to dry.

DEA Agent McDaniel Supported Matthews' Authorization

DEA agent Frank Michael McDaniel from the Houston DEA office testified on behalf of Matthews. He testified that the DEA, U.S. Customs, the Justice Department, and the Texas Department of Public Safety had all given Matthews carte blanche authority to carry out drug interdiction operations. Referring to confidential informants and undercover agents, McDaniel said:

We have people that have been charged with another crime, particularly narcotics, that are working to reduce their sentencing in that particular case that they've been charged with. We have others that have specialized services that they can provide to help us in an undercover role, and then we have others that are there for other different type of motivation, for money, or to reduce the flow of narcotics in this country and various other things like that.

McDaniel was asked, "What was your understanding as to the capacity or the role that he was acting?"

Matthews was a pilot and could assist us in our undercover operation of taking one of his aircraft, flying to a clandestine airstrip or a rural strip in Central or South America and transporting the shipments back to the United States for us, where we could have the narcotics seized in the custody of the traffickers in the United States.

McDaniel explained, in response to a question as to how it was determined how much to pay Matthews:

We would discuss it with our supervisors and determine the amount of risk that was taken by him and the amount of overhead and different items, we would come up with a figure and then submit that request to Washington, D.C.

McDaniel testified about the $200,000 the government still owes Matthews. He testified about the great dangers faced by Matthews in his government directed and authorized activities. McDaniel testified that the work was "extremely dangerous for the pilot" and that when undercover pilots go to pick up a drug load at the destination, "sometimes people will kill the pilot and take the aircraft."

Confirming Non-Dipping

In response to questioning about whether Matthews ever diverted any of the drug loads to his own use, McDaniel testified:

In our undercover role [as drug buyers], the traffickers would inform us before [Matthews] even arrived in the United States how many kilograms of cocaine would be loaded on the plane, and then we would be accountable to those traffickers for delivering a certain quantity of that cocaine into the hands of their associates in the United States.

Washington Customs Supervisor Supported Matthews' Authority

Customs supervisor Charles S. Harrison from Washington, D.C., who was Agent In Charge of the Houston office from 1986 to 1992, testified that he knew that the Drug Enforcement Administration utilized Matthews in undercover drug flights, after the Houston and San Antonio offices intended to prosecute Matthews for the holiday drug loads. Harrison testified he knew AUSA Dave Hall and other government agents authorized Matthews to haul drugs into the United States, including the holiday drug loads.

Customs Agent Nichols Confirmed Matthews' Authority

Customs agent Rich Nichols was one of the agents who recruited Matthews to infiltrate the Stadter group. Nichols testified that Matthews had government authority to haul drugs as part of government directed undercover activities. He described the 1988 meeting that was attended by Customs personnel Tom Grieve and Jim Dukes, and DPS personnel Kenneth Dismukes, Robert Nestoroff, himself, and by Matthews, during which plans were made for Matthews to infiltrate the Stadter organization.

Government Instructions To Matthews Had To Be General

Nichols testified that the instructions to Matthews had to be general in nature, and that it was up to Matthews to infiltrate the organization in whatever way was necessary. Nichols testified about a second meeting in August 1988 attended by himself, Robert Nestoroff, Rodney Matthews, and Special Assistant United States Attorney Dave Hall who was heading the financial task force of which Nestoroff was a member at that time:

The purpose of that meeting was to acquaint Mr. Hall with Mr. Matthews, and we did discuss at the second meeting the flying in of contraband cocaine. Specifically Mr. Matthews said, "You realize in order for me to get close to Vic Stadter, I'm going to have to fly some [drug] loads," and I said that's not gonna be a problem.

Matthews Had Implied Government Authority
To Fly the Holiday Loads to Obtain Evidence

Under an important recognized doctrine of law, Matthews had implied authority to transport the two holiday loads as part of the plan to obtain evidence on a large drug-smuggling operation. Implied power is power to carry into effect the orders given to infiltrate a major drug cartel and includes all steps that are necessary to carry out that purpose. Ballentine's Law Dictionary describes "implied authority" as follows:

Implied authority is authority of an agent, circumstantially proved, which the principal is deemed to have actually intended the agent to possess. This is authority of an agent arising independently of any express grant of authority, as from some manifestation by the principal that the particular authority in question shall exist in the agent, or arising as a necessary or reasonable implication in order to effectuate other authority expressly conferred, embracing authority to do whatever acts are incidental to, or are necessary, usual, and proper to accomplish or perform the main authority expressly delegated to the agent. Annotation: 55 ALR2d 27, Section 4[a]; 3 AM J2d Agency Section 71. (19Am J2d Corp Section 953)

Assistant U.S. Attorney Testifying For Matthews

Assistant U.S. Attorney Thomas I. Meehan, Jr. from the Houston office testified that AUSA Dave Hall (out of the Washington office of the Department of Justice) on assignment to the San Antonio office, had told him that Matthews was authorized to fly drug loads. Matthews' attorney, F. Lee Bailey, asked Meehan during the trial: "In essence then, you, as a prosecutor, understood that what Rodney had done had been within his charter in Hall's opinion, and there would be no criminal case?" Meehan answered in the affirmative, that Matthews did have authority to carry the drugs that he carried.

Referring to a memorandum that Meehan wrote after talking to AUSA Hall, Meehan testified:

After Mr. Matthews and Greg Thompson had been arrested, Dave Hall and a fellow named Bob Nestoroff from the Department of Public Safety in Texas arrived in Houston to talk about whether those charges were going to be pursued by us. During that meeting, the understanding I had from Hall was that although Matthews was working on the Vic Stadter case that Hall considered the load of cocaine that had come in on the 31st as part of that, [even though] he had been unaware it was coming in at the time it came in. I had that same understanding from Bob Nestoroff, and that also applied to a different shipment, a considerably smaller shipment at Christmas time.

Carte Blanche Authority To Fly Drugs

Bailey handed Meehan a report that Meehan had earlier prepared and asked: "Did Dave Hall use any words that are perhaps unusual in the narcotics business when it comes to the operation of a confidential informant as respecting this case and Rodney Matthews?" Meehan responded:

Carte blanche, certainly. I know that Hall told me that in his opinion the shipment into Fort Bend County [Matthews' airstrip at Damon, Texas] was part of the Stadter investigation. As far as he was concerned, Matthews had carte blanche to do anything he had to do in connection with that case, and consequently that was the defense to the charge, and I dismissed the charges.

During this questioning, Meehan testified that he knew that the pilot arrested with Matthews on the New Year arrest "was a member of the Stadter organization and a fellow that Matthews was trying to deliver to the government."

DEA Agent Garner Confirmed Matthews' Authority

DEA agent Jerry Garner's testimony supported the testimony given by McDaniel. Garner testified to the government-authorized drug pickup by Matthews:

Mr. Matthews provided transportation of drugs. He provided a service for us. He was instructed to go to a specific location, pick up cocaine, and return to the United States, which he did, and he did very well.

Late Discovery of Perjured Testimony in Matthews' Trial

Although many government agents courageously came forth and gave truthful testimony, there were government agents who knew the path to advancement in government, and that included lying as Justice Department prosecutors wanted them to lie, or to give half-truths that had the same effect as lying. Customs agent Ken Cates gave testimony that fit into this category. This deception came out during a later trial when attorney Daniel Cogdell of Houston compared the transcript of testimony given by Cates to the grand jury that indicted Matthews with a memorandum that Cates had previously written. Cogdell read from the Customs report that Cates had written several years earlier:

During these meetings, these federal officers posed little, if any, restrictions on Matthews' proposed criminal activities which clearly were to include smuggling of narcotics into the United States which were destined for the Stadter criminal organization.

Cogdell then read from the transcripts of testimony Cates had given that led to the jury indicting Matthews. Cates testified to the grand jury that he had interviewed the agents at the meeting that authorized Matthews to fly drugs and that Matthews was not given authority to haul drugs into the United States. Cates omitted the fact that Nestoroff, Dismukes, Hall, all agreed during the meeting that Matthews had been given authority to fly drugs into the United States. By omitting key facts, Cates lied to the grand jury, permitting an indictment to be handed down.

Cates was next in line to San Antonio SAC Neil Lageman. By placing the blame on Matthews for the holiday loads, this would take the blame off San Antonio Customs and off Department of Justice officials who authorized the multiple loads of cocaine to hit the street. Neil Lageman issued the early 1989 memorandum charging Matthews with illegally flying drugs into the United States on Christmas and New Year's day.

Lageman Severely Criticized for Protecting Drug Traffickers

Lageman was severely and repeatedly criticized in a 1535-page House report for repeatedly blocking the prosecution of major drug traffickers. Cates later resigned from U.S. Customs Service and Lageman was transferred. (It is standard practice in government to transfer incompetent people to another location and often promote them in the process, especially in the Federal Aviation Administration where I had insider knowledge.)

Exculpatory Evidence Seized From Matthews by DOJ

While Matthews was in prison waiting for the trial to start, government agents and prison officials seized most of his documentary evidence, including government checks that constituted payment for flying drugs into the United States. One was a $40,000 check paid to Matthews by Houston HIDTA/DEA for one of several such flights.

AUSA Thompson kept many exculpatory documents from Matthews' defense team that had been seized from Matthews' home and his prison cell. These included a critical document involving AUSA Meehan's testimony concerning the carte blanche memo, fax correspondence with Houston DEA and Miami Customs, tape recordings and photos, and the Lageman memo that constituted a coverup. Also withheld from Matthews' defense, but not discovered until after the trial, were tapes made by Ellard on a small recorder that Ellard had sent to his wife which described the benefits he would receive in return for testifying against Matthews, and other papers.

Assassination Attempt Against Matthews by DOJ Witness

On January 13, 1992, before an indictment was handed down, an assassination attempt was made upon Matthews and his wife. He had received a call one evening from a person saying, "This is important, it's about Jimmy Ellard," and asked Matthews to meet him at a nearby 7-11 store. Only Ellard would know that Matthews would have been receptive to a person using Ellard's name. At that time, Matthews didn't think it was a hit team because they would not have used Ellard's name. Upon arriving at the 7-11 outlet in his pickup, a man opened the door on the passenger side, slid in and shouted, "Let's go to your house. Now!"

Matthews realized his wife was also an intended victim since she had heard Ellard's name from the caller and would be a witness against Ellard to Matthews' murder. Upon pulling out onto the street, Matthews swerved the pickup hard, throwing the gunman off-guard. He seized the gun and during the struggle three shots were fired, narrowly missing Matthews. The gunman then jumped out of the pickup and ran off.

The assassination attempt on Matthews occurred shortly after Ellard discovered from his attorney, Bill Norris, that Matthews was responsible for his 1985 arrest. Ellard's attorney had discovered this fact after Matthews had gone to another attorney in Miami seeking legal help in getting Miami Customs to release the twin-engine Merlin they had seized. During their discussions, Matthews had casually mentioned he was responsible for Ellard's arrest. It was by sheer chance that Matthews contacted that particular Miami attorney, who was a friend to Ellard's attorney, and who passed along the information that Matthews had given him. It is also believed that AUSA Thompson told Ellard about Matthews being responsible for his arrest. With Ellard's murderous background, the prosecutor surely knew that Matthews could be Ellard's assassination target.

DOJ Prosecutor Denied what the Evidence Proved

When Matthews' attorney tried to bring to the jury's attention the attempt to assassinate Matthews and that the attempt was probably directed by the prosecutor's chief witness, the prosecutor sought to discredit the assassination-attempt story. Otherwise, it would adversely affect the credibility of the prosecutor's main witness. Testimony by local law enforcement officers showed that an assassination attempt *did* occur. Judge Ursula Ungaro-Benages blocked presenting any evidence on the matter, assuring Matthews' attorney that "he would not need to bring that up to win this case." Either she misjudged the jury's reaction to the evidence, or she was helping to protect the Justice Department's sham action against Matthews. Her overall conduct indicates the latter.

Standard Problem with Defense Attorneys

Matthews encountered problems with his defense attorneys, something that appears throughout these pages, and throughout all of my books. His first attorney, Marty Raskin, wanted Matthews to "cooperate" with the prosecutor, saying at one time, "Only Thompson can help you." Matthews then hired Miami attorney Ronald Dresnick who in turn brought in F. Lee Bailey. (Dresnick became a state judge after the Matthews trial.) To be on the safe side, Matthews hired attorney Ralph Gonzales to sit during the trial and keep an eye on Dresnick and Bailey.

During the trial, Matthews asked Dresnik and Bailey to bring witnesses in who approved Matthews' role in Operation Shanghai—the plan to kidnap Escobar, which would show government officials authorizing him to violate the law for an undercover operation. Matthews said Bailey told him he didn't want to drag the government officials through the dirt. Through the dirt?

Dresnick opposed bringing in the government officials to testify about the plan to kidnap Escobar, saying it would weaken the defense. That made no sense; at that time, Escobar was the most publicized target of U.S. law enforcement, and showing Matthews' attempts to kidnap him would hardly weaken the defense; it could, however, weaken the prosecution. Who were they trying to protect? It is *very* common for attorneys to present a weak defense to avoid antagonizing government attorneys with whom they will be working throughout their careers.

Evidence Of Matthews' Innocence Ignored by Jurors

Strong evidence of Matthews' innocence was introduced during the trial. One document, an 18-page confidential Texas DPS document dated February 15, 1989, gave details of Matthews' government-approved undercover operations, stating in part:

12. Customs Special Agent Grieve advised Matthews that, if necessary, approval could be obtained for him to fly a load of Cocaine. Grieve advised Matthews that he should continue with his attempts to infiltrate the smuggling organization and, if placed in a position of flying a load of Cocaine, should make case agents aware of the situation but to keep details vague because if the agents had specific information, the agents would be required to interdict the load.

13. On or about August 1, 1988, at the request of Matthews, another meeting was held in San Antonio with Assistant United States Attorney Dave Hall to clarify the government's position regarding Matthews' culpability if in fact Matthews was required to fly a load of Cocaine for the Stadter organization. Hall advised Matthews that if in fact Matthews was placed in a position of flying a load of contraband, Matthews would not be prosecuted if the case agents were aware of the situation beforehand and would not be placed in a position where Matthews would have to testify in court. Hall instructed Matthews to do whatever was necessary to infiltrate the Stadter organization. Present at that meeting were Investigator Nestoroff, Matthews, Hall, and pilot Nichols.

26. Matthews advised that a Thanksgiving smuggling trip was possible and that he would be required to fly the trip with Thompson [Stadter's pilot]. Grieve again reminded Mathews to communicate with Investigator Nestoroff but not to be specific because if specific details were known, then Customs Service would be required to interdict the load.

31. Nestoroff advised Cardwell that Matthews was involved in an undercover capacity with a large smuggling organization and that Matthews felt that any obvious indication of surveillance on the airstrip might alert suspects of law enforcement presence. [Houston Customs agents were in the process of sabotaging the undercover operation approved by San Antonio Customs agents.]

47. Matthews advised that there was still a possibility of a test load which, if intercepted, would compromise any larger loads. Special Agent Grieve advised Matthews that, if necessary, a load would be allowed to get through to California but that if Matthews was intercepted by surveil-

lance or radar, then there was no way that Grieve could intervene and that the task force would "take care" of Matthews and keep him from being prosecuted.

49. Grieve again advised that a load would be allowed to reach California if necessary to remove Matthews from risk of exposure and to increase the possibility of identification and arrest of other members of the Stadter organization. Grieve emphasized that the ultimate objective of the investigation was the arrest of Stadter.

50. Grieve reminded Matthews that he was to be vague about specific details of any smuggling trip because if he provided specific information, then it would increase the risk of premature action by the Customs Service. Grieve advised Matthews to provide only cryptic information regarding the trip. In fact, if a load was to be brought in over Christmas, Matthews was jokingly advised to use the phrase, "It's going to be a white Christmas."

69. Nestoroff briefly explained to Farley the ongoing smuggling investigation on Stadter and the involvement of Matthews to Supervisor Farley, and requested that Farley either contact Assistant United States Attorney Hall or the Assistant United States Attorney in Houston and brief them regarding the participation of Matthews before placing Matthews in jail. Nestoroff also advised Farley that Matthews had stated that Thompson was using the alias name Kevin Cook and that Thompson was allegedly a fugitive out of the Los Angeles area.

73. Hall advised that as far as Hall was concerned, Matthews was operating within the guidelines that Matthews had been given and that the information would be provided to investigators at a meeting scheduled for Monday morning, January 2, 1989.

Customs Protecting the Stadter Drug Organization

The DPS memorandum, marked "DPS Sensitive," described how Customs Service Supervisor John Farley in Houston was advised of a highly sensitive undercover operation into the Stadter drug organization occurring at Matthews' airstrip at Damon, Texas, and not to undermine the operation by conducting an obvious surveillance. Despite being advised of an undercover flight about to arrive at the airstrip, Customs agents from Houston were there and arrested Matthews and Stadter's pilot, Thompson.

Customs Again Protecting A Major Drug Operation

This arrest was ordered by Houston Customs despite the fact that they knew it was an authorized undercover operation, and knew that by making the arrest, it would permanently destroy the ongoing multi-agency attempt to arrest Stadter and bring a halt to his organization's drug smuggling activities. The question arises as to whether government agents wanted to eliminate Matthews, or they wanted to protect a major drug operation.

The arrest made Stadter realize that Matthews was conducting a government undercover operation infiltrating his drug organization and that finished the carefully crafted multi-task force operation seeking evidence against Stadter's large drug smuggling operation. Stadter was never prosecuted. Was this what was wanted all along?

Sworn Affidavit Details Government Authority to Matthews
Other evidence surfaced. A confidential Texas DPS affidavit prepared by Nestoroff (October 23, 1991) stated in part:

> *Matthews has been actively working as a cooperating individual for the Texas Department of Public Safety Narcotics Division ("TDPS") since 1984. I have been his contact agent since that date....Matthews had been advised by an Assistant U.S. Attorney that he had "Carte Blanche" in this investigation and that he "would be taken care of" if problems developed....Matthews has provided information and assistance over a period of eight (8) years which has resulted in the seizure of large quantities of Cocaine and Marijuana by Texas DPS, US Customs, and DEA and to the conviction of numerous defendants for violation of both state and federal laws. He has also supplied valuable intelligence information regarding numerous large scale smuggling operations in the United States, Mexico, and Colombia.*

Approving Lie Detector Test Until it Supported Matthews' Innocence
To provide further proof that Matthews was testifying truthfully, Matthews' attorney motioned the court to allow Matthews to be polygraphed on the key issues. The court approved giving Matthews a polygraph test, and approved the person conducting the test. But after the test showed Matthews answered the questions honestly, and that he did not fly unauthorized drug loads, AUSA Thompson objected to the admissibility of the polygraph test based on lack of notice to the government.

The government surely couldn't be prejudiced by having evidence presented that would determine Matthews' innocence or guilt! Under law, the prosecutor's responsibility is to insure justice, not to put innocent people in prison. The test arose because of the prosecutor's questioning, and the prosecutor had plenty of time to address the test results. The polygraph operator had been used by the Justice Department in the past on its own cases and surely was considered competent and reliable to conduct the test. The prosecutor couldn't challenge the competency of the polygraph examiner, George Slattery, nor that the test was not performed correctly.

Under law in the Eleventh Circuit, polygraph tests are admissible, upon meeting six tests. The court concluded that the six issues that must be met were met, except possibly for prior notice. The only issue was notice to the government, whether the issue was collateral or central, and if prejudice outweighed the probative value. Matthews faced life in prison, and Judge Ungaro was willing to allow this to happen on a minor technicality.

Matthews' attorney argued that the polygraph issue did not arise until the prosecutor's chief witness, Jimmy Ellard, testified on cross-examination. Judge Ursula Ungaro-Benages, insuring that the prosecutor's case would not be undermined, refused to allow the exonerating key parts of the test results to be made known to the jurors.

Matthews' Target—Escobar—Killed on Day Matthews Testified
Ironically, the same day that Matthews was to testify during trial in November 1993 about the plan for Matthews to kidnap Escobar, Escobar was killed in Medellin, Colombia.

Pattern of Prosecutorial Misconduct and Inflammatory Lies

AUSA Thompson engaged in a pattern of lying, deceptive arguments, and inflammatory statements throughout the trial. During the final closing argument, Thompson held up a large photo of the military jet that Matthews purchased and he said to the jury, "This is what Mr. Matthews was going to use to shoot down U.S. Customs interdiction planes." There was never any evidence introduced to support that inflammatory statement. Because this statement was made during the prosecutor's final argument, there was no opportunity to contradict it.

Using A Bright Red Plane to Shoot Down U.S. Aircraft?

I saw a picture of the jet. Painted bright red. This is hardly the color Matthews would have used if the plane was intended to shoot down government aircraft.

Prosecutor Comparing Matthews to Saddam Hussein was Ironic

In his inflammatory statements to the jury, Thompson linked Matthews to Saddam Hussein and Muammar el Qaddafi, and appealed to the jury's patriotism, which required finding Matthews guilty:

When faced with an enemy, the United States doesn't blink when looking into the cold stare of a Muammar Qaddafi or Saddam Hussein, and they don't blink when they stare into the cold, greedy eyes of this defendant. And that's what this case is about, ladies and gentlemen.

Prosecutor's Reference to Iraq was Especially Ironic

The prosecutor's statements equating Matthews with Saddam Hussein was especially ironic since it was Matthews who had paid for and had arranged for the non-publicized defection of an Iraqi pilot and aircraft. Matthews had invested part of his assets and undertaken a complex plan to bring about the defection of an Iraqi pilot and Iraqi aircraft, contributing to what could have been a major public relations victory for the United States. Thompson—as corrupt a prosecutor as one would find anywhere—had the audacity to link Matthews to Saddam Hussein!

Misstatement of Drug-Related Assets

During the trial, the prosecutor referred to the expensive planes that Matthews owned, implying that he acquired them from non-authorized drug flights and that his Customs handlers knew nothing about them. He owned at various times several Mitsubishi turbo-prop aircraft, each with a value of almost $1 million. In reality, Customs did know about the aircraft, had even flown in them, and had contracted with Matthews to use the planes. On one flight from San Antonio to Tampa, Florida, Matthews carried Customs agents Tom Grieve and Jim Dukes and AUSA Dave Hall. The purpose of that flight was to have Miami Customs release a plane that had been earlier seized from Matthews by Miami Customs agent Gene Wilkinson.

Judge Revealed Key Exculpatory Facts Without the Jury Present

Without the jury present, Judge Ungaro-Benages admonished the prosecutor for the false statements made against Nestoroff and Cardwell that misled the jury into thinking Matthews was guilty. She said, "What was presented at trial certainly did not amount to criminal wrongdoing by any stretch of the imagination with respect to either Cardwell or Nestoroff."

"Sick, Symbiotic, Manipulative, and Exploitive Relationship"

Judge Ungaro-Benages severely criticized government agents:

Mr. Matthews has been really used by the United States govern-ment...periodically Mr. Matthews would get busted and periodically the Government, with a wink and a nod, ...would say, okay, Rodney, well, if you'll just fly a few more loads for us, we'll forget about it....The govern-ment's very ugly underbelly ... sick, symbiotic, manipulative, exploitive relationship with Matthews that culminated in a trial that pitted the United States government versus the United States government....[The government's conduct was] an embarrassment, and the United States gov-ernment in many respects should be ashamed of itself....Mr. Matthews has been really used by the United States government.

The prosecutor had based much of his case against Matthews on the argument that Matthews bribed Nestoroff and Cardwell, and this argument probably resulted in the guilty verdict. Now, without the jury being present to hear the judge's rebuke of that position, the judge revealed the absence of any support for the prosecutor's argument. The judge had allowed this false argument to influence the jury and then compounded the outrage by inflicting a greater sentence than required upon Matthews. She was aiding and abetting each of the outrages and corrupt acts perpetrated by the DOJ prosecutor.

Naive Jury Believed the Prosecutor's Argument

Despite the many government agents who risked their careers to testify on Matthews' behalf, the jury, ignorant of the widespread government miscon-duct, partly of their own choosing, held Matthews guilty. They knew that he would probably be imprisoned for the remainder of his life. They share guilt for making possible the continuation of the corruption so prevalent in the most corrupt and most dangerous of all government agencies: the U.S. Department of Justice!

Judge Orders Three Life-In-Prison Sentences

In February 1994, Judge Ungaro-Benages sentenced Matthews to life im-prisonment on a Continuing Criminal Enterprise (CCE) conviction, on the pretense that Matthews had transported into the United States 50,000 kilos of cocaine. This was the cocaine that the DOJ witnesses smuggled into the United States, and which Matthews knew nothing about! This was bizarre! First she criticizes government agents for misusing Matthews, and then she sentences Matthews to life in prison!

$169 Million Judgment Based On Terrorist's Perjured Testimony

Further rubber-stamping the Justice Department prosecutor's fraudulent charges, Judge Ungaro-Benages held that Matthews had made more than $169 million profit on the 50 flights—made by Escobar's aide—Jimmy Ellard, and Emmons. The judge used figures based on Ellard's perjured testimony. If any profit were made, they would be made by Ellard, his partner—Pablo Esco-bar—and Emmons. And much of this profit would shortly be made available to Ellard as the DOJ prosecutor moved to have Ellard released, placed in the witness protection program, and allowed to keep millions of otherwise forfeit-able assets.

Explaining the $169.2 Million Profit

Matthews explained how the DOJ prosecutor made the profit argument to the jury:

There was no evidence whatsoever that I made $169.2 million profit. Even Ellard claimed he only made $20 million. The $169.2 million was based solely on prosecutor Thompson's arithmetic that 50 loads (flown by Ellard' pilots) equaled $500 million in profit and my profit out of that was $169.2 million. That was the craziest thing I've ever seen in a U.S. court. The government charged me with Ellard's and Escobar's drug flights.

My indictment included a long list of expensive race horses and other properties I have never ever heard of. All of Ellard's planes and everybody else's planes were listed on my indictment. I had put away less than one million for emergencies which the attorneys took in short order. I worked in Unicor prison Industries for over two years making about 75 cents an hour trying to help with expenses while the government was charging me with making a profit of $169.2 million. This is strictly toothfairy tales and the judge knew it was a sham to whitewash the first sham conviction.

In addition, Customs personnel seized Matthews' Fort Lauderdale residence that had been in the family name for years, and the family heirlooms that had no relationship to any possible drug offense. After seizing the home, Miami Customs agents used it for their personal residence, destroying the family heirlooms that had been in the family for centuries.

Government's Refusal to Pay Its Debts to Matthews

Matthews was arrested in June 1992, at which time the government owed him $240,000 for the last five flights that he had flown. Four of these flights were simply providing transportation, hauling drugs from Colombia to destinations in the United States at the direction of Customs and DEA agents. The other flight was flying two fugitive drug traffickers to the United States. The government never denied owing him the money; they simply refused to pay. During Matthews' trial, government agents testified that the government owed him the money. But to now pay would undermine the prosecutor's charge that Matthews had no authority to work for the government. It would also reveal the shipment of drugs ordered by government agents.

Going after Government Agents who Testified Truthfully

Justice Department's prosecutors retaliated against many of the people who testified for Matthews, including DEA agents Jerry Garner, J.D. Morman, and Mike McDaniels; Customs agents Tony Singleton and John Farley, and Texas DPS agent Robert Nestoroff. The Justice Department went after a businessman and friend of Matthews who testified at the trial, Tony Dinorcia. As a result of the government's retaliation, Dinorcia lost his business, Marble Edge, a factory and installation business that employed about 75 people in Palm Beach, Florida.

Seeking To Bring About Matthews' Death in Prison

Justice Department personnel didn't give up on Matthews after bringing about his life-in-prison sentence. With control of the federal prisons, they could inflict further harm upon him. Many murders occur in prisons that often eliminate inmates who have highly sensitive information against government officials. In late 1993, Justice Department personnel transferred Matthews from the Metropolitan Correctional Center in Miami to the North Dade Detention Center, placing Matthews in a small 18-man cell-block for about three weeks with a witness who would be testifying against Matthews, Frank McGuire. This could be expected to result in a violent and possible fatal confrontation. When this failed to produce a confrontation, Matthews was placed for several weeks in a cell block with a Cuban national, Carlos Duque, and eight of his Cuban friends. Matthews' previous testimony resulted in Duque receiving a 40-year prison sentence. This was a volatile and life-and-death situation that resulted in Matthews receiving several serious beatings.

Request That Court Punish AUSA Thompson

After Matthews was sentenced, former AUSA Peter Aiken filed an 18-page motion with U.S. District Judge Jose Gonzalez, requesting that AUSA Terrence Thompson be punished for withholding key data from the defense. Aiken referred to two tape recordings sent from a Texas prison by Jimmy Ellard to his wife, advising her that AUSA Thompson agreed to reward Ellard for testifying the way the prosecutor wanted him to testify. Also, that Ellard's wife would not be prosecuted, that Ellard's prison sentence would be immediately reduced, that he would be released after a brief period, that he would be placed in the witness protection program, and he would be allowed to keep his drug-acquired assets. This was a clear case of purchased testimony, barred by statute.

DOJ Paying Ellard $2000 While in Prison

Aiken discovered these tapes during the final stages of another and subsequent trial in which he defended a Fort Lauderdale aircraft broker, William Safarie, who was acquitted on December 8, 1994. Aiken learned that the DEA gave Ellard $2,000 while Ellard was in prison, and that government agents had evidence showing Ellard's wife to be actively involved in money laundering. Under federal rules, such exculpatory evidence must be turned over to the defense before the start of the trial. It had been known for years that prosecutors routinely violate this rule, allowing thousands of defendants to receive long prison terms, while the prosecutor escapes any consequences for his or her corrupt actions.

Justice Department Payoff to Terrorist and Escobar Associate

Waiting several months after the Matthews trial ended, AUSA Terrence Thompson quietly filed a motion with Judge William Zloch to carry out his end of the deal: release Ellard from prison and into the general population. Ellard's past was not unknown to the judge.

Objection Letter from Former U.S. Attorney Protesting
Release of Airplane Bomber and Major Drug Trafficker

In response to the Justice Department's motion to release Ellard from prison, attorney Peter Aiken wrote to Judge Zloch stating that the purpose of the letter was to "bring to your attention certain facts and circumstances surrounding a defendant who has a pending motion for a sentence reduction before you." Aiken wrote,

As a former agent, former Assistant United States Attorney, member of the

Bar and citizen of this country, I was shocked at what I perceived to be the unconscionable deal given to Jimmy Norjay Ellard by Assistant United States Attorney Terry Thompson.

In the Safarie case, Ellard admitted to importing into the United States of America in excess of $1 billion in cocaine. He admitted to being a former law enforcement officer, who as a fugitive on drug charges, imported into this country in excess of fifty thousand kilograms of cocaine. He admitted to being Pablo Escobar's partner, and further, admitted being the only gringo who could sit with all four Colombian cartels. He admitted to meeting with Pablo Escobar and providing Pablo Escobar with technical expertise as to how to construct bombs with plastic explosives and radio activated detonators for the purpose of blowing up airplanes.

It is true that he testified that it was his understanding that the bombs would only be used to kill their own drug pilots, if it appeared apprehension was imminent. However, Pablo Escobar then used Jimmy Ellard's plans to bomb the Avianca Airline and kill in excess of one hundred ten people. Jimmy Ellard testified that he was present with Pablo Escobar when they passed around photographs of three informants who had been skinned alive.

Jimmy Ellard testified that he was aware that his partner, Pablo Escobar, had assassinated the vice-presidential candidate of the country of Colombia. What was even more shocking was the fact that Jimmy Ellard admitted and testified in my trial that he was in the process of setting up a cocaine network to infiltrate the Communist world with cocaine, with Pablo Escobar as his partner.

I was further distressed to learn that when Pablo Escobar declared war on the people of Colombia, it was Jimmy Ellard who made a phone call to arrange for the purchase of Stinger missiles and guns for Pablo Escobar. ... As Judge Ungaro-Benages said in her comments, there can't possibly be a more evil man than Jimmy Norjay Ellard.

Jimmy Norjay Ellard has in fact already beaten the system. He testified in the proceeding in front of Judge Gonzalez that as a former law enforcement officer, he knew how to plea bargain and that it was "the American Way." He testified in my trial that he knew at the time he made the decision to become a smuggler that if he was apprehended, he would be able to trade that information for light treatment. He has in fact successfully used his knowledge as a law enforcement officer to substantially beat the system.

In this transcript, he describes and predicts how he is going to manipulate the government. I learned of this transcript, not as a result of its voluntary production by Mr. Thompson, but as a result of successfully prevailing on a motion to compel favorable evidence. I urge the court to read this transcript because it will provide to the court a very clear picture of one of the most evil, manipulative, vile defendants to ever appear before a court.

I recognize that Mr. Terry Thompson has filed a motion to further reduce Mr. Ellard's sentence. I urge this court not to do so. ... If there were *true justice, Jimmy Norjay Ellard would be extradited by the country of Colombia, prosecuted there, and shot before a firing squad. He is responsible for the deaths of one hundred ten human beings. He is responsible for $1 billion in drugs within this country. The fifteen-year sentence meted out by this court is a fraction of what he truly deserves. ... In these times, where street-level drug dealers routinely receive fifteen and twenty-year sentences for two or three ounces of crack cocaine, it is an absolute miscarriage of justice to let someone like Jimmy Norjay Ellard escape with a similar sentence.*

Aiken brought out the fact that the Justice Department had allowed Ellard to keep most of his many millions of dollars of drug-related assets.

DOJ Benevolence for Murderer and Drug
Kingpin not Available to Individual Americans

Judge Zloch released Ellard, despite Ellard's threat to the public as shown by his prior murderous conduct. Possibly the thousands of people whose husbands, wives, mothers, sons, or daughters are in prison with long sentences for minor drug offenses—anything is minor compared to Ellard—deserve to have similar benevolence given in their cases!

Ellard Again Arrested for Drug Smuggling Offenses,
And Again Protected by Department of Justice Attorneys

Ellard voluntarily entered the federal witness protection program, which enabled him to return to smuggling drugs into the United States, as the Justice Department group surely recognized. And as expected, he returned to his drug smuggling activities. He was arrested in September 1998 by federal authorities in New York.

Despite his arrest on charges of bringing large quantities of drugs into the United States, DOJ personnel arranged for his release. *Pittsburgh Post-Gazette* investigative journalist Bill Moushey wrote to Matthews (March 23, 1999) explaining what he heard about Ellard:

I have just heard that charges were dropped against Jimmy Ellard because he produced taped recordings that contradicted the New York feds who said Ellard had no authority to do the [drug] deal in question. I understand that he got into the deal because the feds were going to allow him to make $40 million from a large cocaine deal.

Ellard and Escobar Cartel Protected by the CIA

Repeatedly, the large drug traffickers—those reportedly tied in with CIA drug trafficking—either don't get charged, go free, receive light sentences, or are released from prison with no publicity. If the information that I have received from my CIA and other deep-cover contacts for the past ten-plus years is correct, that the CIA has close ties with some of the drug cartels, it would explain why Escobar and Ellard were protected by DOJ personnel. It would also explain why Matthews may have been targeted because he threatened to inflict serious damage upon the CIA-connected drug organizations.

DOJ Again Protecting the CIA-Drug Cartel Coalition

When this conduct is compared to the many reports that I have received over the years from CIA and other insiders who reported CIA drug trafficking with drug cartels and organized crime, the most logical conclusion is that the

Escobar cartel was supplying drugs to the CIA and Matthews was interfering with this arrangement.

Matthews' Appellate Remedies Sabotaged

Under law, Matthews had various legal remedies available to overturn the injustices inflicted upon him by Justice Department attorneys, the judge, and even the jury. Matthews' appeal (Appeal case 94-4480) was heard in Miami by three judges in the Eleventh Circuit Court of Appeals. The court granted Matthews' attorneys the right to present oral argument, but retracted this authority after the government packed the courtroom with government officials. The three judges were intimidated by the large block of government personnel in the courtroom. Instead of correcting the violations of Matthews' civil and constitutionally-protected rights, the three-judge panel approved the violations and denied the appeal.

Matthews' Attorney Scared by the Block of Government Officials

Matthews explained how scared his appellate attorney was during the appeal appearance:

Customs officials packed the Miami courtroom for the appeals hearing, attempting to give the appearance they were there in the interest of justice while they were actually there in the interest of a high-level coverup. The corrupt officials were effective, for the appeal court judges declined to hear oral arguments they had previously scheduled. [That is the reason for calendaring a hearing in a court of appeals: present oral arguments. The written briefs have been filed prior to that time.] *My appeals attorney, Thomas Dawson, was still shaking at our meeting the next day from the subtle but effective intimidation. Dawson said he felt fortunate he made it out of the courtroom and out of Miami without incident or accident. Dawson was thoroughly shaken. He never filed another motion in my case even though he was paid and I had requested he appeal to the Supreme Court* [Petition for writ of certiorari].

Prosecutor Prosecuting Agents who gave Truthful Testimony

In October 1994, after Nestoroff and Cardwell gave favorable testimony in Matthews' trial, Justice Department prosecutors obtained indictments from a grand jury against them. The Department of Justice charged them with conspiring to help Matthews evade arrest, to avoid drug charges, giving perjured testimony during Matthews' trial, and giving Matthews AWACS schedules—all based upon the statements of their star witness—Ellard!

The same Justice Department employees who had just used government power to pay for suborned and perjured testimony from a major drug trafficker were now charging government agents with perjury and obstruction of justice for testifying truthfully!

Government Agents Fearful of Giving Honest Testimony

During Matthews' trial, F. Lee Bailey said to Matthews, "Both men expressed fear of retaliation for testifying against the government. Mr. Nestoroff was very much concerned that there would be retribution. He was afraid if he testified truthfully he'd be indicted."

DOJ's prosecutor Thompson filed charges in Miami against Nestoroff and Cardwell, where he had more control over the grand jury and the prosecution process. But defense attorneys for Nestoroff and Cardwell moved to have the case transferred to Houston, which was then ordered by Judge Jose A. Gonzalez.

In another abuse-of power retaliation, Thompson threatened former state prosecutor Ralph Gonzalez who had testified favorably for Matthews, on the basis of Gonzalez's handling of a government-sanctioned marijuana case in Richmond, Texas.

Threatening or Retaliating Against A Witness is A Federal Crime

It is a federal crime to threaten a witness or to retaliate against a witness for having given testimony. [34] But who is there to prosecute the Justice Department employees perpetrating this offense when the same government employees are authorized to initiate such prosecution?

Finally, Street-Smart Texas Jurors

The Justice Department prosecution of Nestoroff and Cardwell occurred in Texas, and the jurors were not rubber-stamping the prosecutor's charges. The jurors in the Nestoroff-Cardwell trial took less than two hours to find Nestoroff and Cardwell not guilty of the charges. One of them, Howard Weaver, said afterwards, "Frankly, we pretty much thought this case was a joke. This case should never have been brought to trial. We all thought the prosecutor appeared to have a vendetta against the two." The jurors felt that the charges against Nestoroff and Cardwell were retaliation for testifying in defense of Matthews in the Florida trial. The Texas media gave a great deal of publicity to the charges against Nestoroff and Cardwell. A *Dallas Morning News* article stated in part,

Supporters say [that Nestoroff and Cardwell] are victims of a vindictive U.S. prosecutor who obtained conspiracy indictments against them in the wake of a state-federal drug investigation turned sour. As described in interviews with attorneys and state and federal drug agents, the charges against the two lawmen grew out of a multi-agency drug sting in Texas marked by miscommunication and foul-ups.

Customs officials refused to discuss the case against Agent Cardwell, but DPS Director Col. James Wilson said Sgt. Nestoroff is a scapegoat whose reputation in a distinguished career, has been trashed. At the heart of the issue, DPS official say, was testimony in Miami by the two lawmen at the 1993 federal trial of Texas drug pilot Rodney Matthews, who was convicted and sentenced to life imprisonment. Those statements angered the prosecution and led to the indictments, the DPS officials say. Col. Wil-

---

[34] Title 18 U.S.C. § 1512. Tampering with a witness, victim, or an informant –
(b) Whoever knowingly uses intimidation or physical force, or threatens another person, or attempts to do so, or engages in misleading conduct toward another person, with intent to –
    (1) influence, delay or prevent the testimony of any person in an official proceeding:
shall be fined ... or imprisoned ... or both. [1988 amended reading]"
Title 18 U.S.C. § 1513. Retaliating against a witness, victim, or an informant. (a) Whoever knowingly engages in any conduct and thereby causes bodily injury to another person or damages the tangible property of another person, or threatens to do so, with intent to retaliate against any person for – (1) the attendance of a witness or party at an official proceeding, or any testimony given or any record, document, or other object produced by a witness in an official proceeding; or (2) any information relating to the commission or possible commission of a Federal offense ..."

*son said, Bob (Nestoroff) went in and told the truth, and there's clear in-
dications it angered the prosecutor. The prosecutor has certainly implied
we were obstructing his efforts. And that is a blatant lie.*

So convinced were Texas officials of Nestoroff's innocence that they kept him
on the payroll during the charges and the trial.

Personal Tragedies Narrowly Averted

Nestoroff and Cardwell could be locked in prison today, with a life-in-
prison sentence, if those jurors had been the typical naive, illiterate about government misconduct, rubber-stamp jurors that are responsible for destroying
the lives of so many innocent people. That's how close these two agents came
for having the backbone and character to testify honesty. This is a rare commodity in today's government and society. Another plus that saved them was
the courage of some Texas papers that printed the truth rather than the usual
coverup and protection of government corruption.

Media Coverage Favorable to Defendants

A *Dallas Morning News* (January 29, 1995) article stated:

*The Feds said to Matthews: "Do whatever you need to do." The phrase
'carte blanche' was used time and again. According to a DPS official who
was briefed on the meeting. "As state officers, we can't authorize breaking the law to make a case. The feds, however, can. Justice Department
officials confirmed that federal law, under strict limits, allows undercover
operatives to set up drug deliveries to help make cases."*

*DPS and federal agents familiar with the task force investigation, who
spoke on condition of anonymity, outlined the following scenario: On
Christmas Eve 1988, Mr. Matthews phoned Sgt. Nestoroff, telling him,
"It's gonna be a white Christmas," that is, he would fly in a load of cocaine the next day. Sgt. Nestoroff alerted a Customs supervisor and was
told the information would be passed on. Mr. Matthews landed in Florida
on Christmas Day with 1,400 pounds of cocaine.*

*Instead of following orders to notify authorities immediately, he
loaded the cocaine onto a truck and drove to California. DPS, officials
said. There, DEA agents, unaware of the Texas-based investigation, seized
the drugs. The charges were dropped after task force officials intervened.
The resulting DEA protests created bad feelings within the task force
agencies, a DPS agent close to the task force said. "Suddenly, it became
clear that Customs didn't have it together on this investigation," he said.*

*Mr. Matthews resumed his undercover role. A few days later, he phoned
Sgt. Nestoroff that he'd bring in another drug flight New Year's day. Sgt.
Nestoroff passed the word to Customs officials, who again said they would
pass on the information.*

*Apparently, not everyone got the message. Mr. Matthews plane was
targeted by Customs radar as a possible smuggler as he flew into Florida
from Colombia. Mr. Matthews, with radar-detection equipment aboard,
changed course for Texas. Landing at his private strip in Fort Bend
County, he unloaded the cocaine onto a truck, DPS officials said. Meanwhile, Customs officers in Houston, apparently unaware that the flight
might be government-sanctioned, surrounded the landing field. Agent*

Cardwell was part of that team.

When officers stopped Mr. Matthews as he drove away, he told them he worked for the government and asked them to phone Sgt. Nestoroff. Sgt. Nestoroff told authorities to contact the Justice Department officials heading the task force, DPS officials said. Again, no charges were filed. The relationship between DPS narcotics and Customs had now become strained.

"This whole thing was instigated by the federal government. But when it blew up, they blamed everyone else," a longtime DPS agent said. "Later, there were some backdoor apologies. But nothing official."

Sgt Nestoroff's supervisors advised him to tape any phone calls from federal authorities about the Matthews case. "We were learning the hard way that we had to watch our backs all the time," the longtime DPS agent said.

Customs Retaliated Against Cardwell for Truthful Testimony

Houston attorney Mike Ramsey, defending Cardwell, said his client had received no official support from U.S. Customs but was supported by state and federal drug agents across the state. "Here's a guy with a good reputation, a background free of taint. A lot of folks in Customs and other agencies are ready to testify for him. They feel the government's gone after a good guy for no reason." Internal pressures finally forced Cardwell to leave government service.

In a July 8, 1996, letter to attorney Daniel Cogdell of Houston, Matthews explained Jimmy Ellard's involvement with placing bombs on airliners and other airplanes:

Jimmy Ellard attempted to contact me to activate a remote controlled explosive device that would be concealed on Ellard's own drug planes in the event they were interdicted and followed while approaching the U.S. Ellard suggested I activate the bomb from an observation plane. Ellard's plan was to kill the drug pilots he had hired before they were captured by U.S. authorities, to prevent them from identifying him. Ellard may be hesitant to deny this on the stand, having since learned of my collection of tape recordings.

Mr. Ellard solicited Mr. Escobar's help in accomplishing this murderous plot while at the same time attempting to gain Escobar's confidence by a demonstration of evil deeds, comparable to Escobar's. Mr. Escobar embraced Ellard's idea on the surface and used a modified version of Ellard's plan to bomb the Avianca airliner, killing persons that threatened his security.

Escobar's concern was losing a load of cocaine and his own security; he had no concern that Ellard might be exposed or that he himself would be exposed as a drug trafficker which was already a well known fact. Without Ellard's knowledge, Escobar sent two of his sicarios to see me in Florida. They relayed Escobar's modified plan to shoot down the U.S. interdiction plane instead of the drug plane. His plan was to shoot down the interdiction plane from a specified point on the ground with rifle fire. After reaching the U.S. coast line the interdiction plane would be following close behind the drug plane, also at low altitude.

In successfully neutralizing Ellard's murderous plot to kill his own drug pilots, and Escobar's modification of the plan to shoot down the interdiction plane, I explained the following logistics to Escobar's sicarios: The chase plane will sometimes be at a higher altitude, or maybe there will be more than one chase plane, one at a much higher altitude and it would be impossible to bring it down with rifle fire from the ground. I convinced them the only sure way the U.S. Customs chase plane could be brought down was with a faster jet fighter type plane equipped with at minimum, 50 caliber machine guns.

Escobar's men believed I was furnishing AWACS schedules that facilitated many of their drug flights. They had been fortified with cash and were under instructions from Escobar to give me anything I needed in assistance. To console Escobar and his men, I agreed to purchase a surplus military jet fighter and reinstall the 50 caliber machine guns, all at their expense. This is where the HA-200 surplus military jet fighter/trainer came into the picture. It was agreed that Ellard would not be told of the plan. Apparently Escobar did not want Ellard to know his people were in contact with me.

There was never any real intention on my part to reinstall the 50 calibers. I knew I could delay the proposed machine gun installation for a year or two or until the objectives were accomplished. Escobar's men gave me the money to purchase and refurbish the HA-200. After the purchase, I showed them the machine gun ports and the lead weights in the nose compartment that kept the plane in balance while the machine guns were removed.

The main point of all this goes to the credibility of government witness Jimmy Ellard. While it may be true that Ellard did not intend to kill those particular people on that Avianca Airlines flight, he intended to kill other people on other airplanes to save his own hide. Had I not neutralized both those plans, at the risk of being prosecuted, Nash and McGuire and a few U.S. Customs pilots would be in the beyond with the Avianca passengers on that ill fated flight.

That same letter referred to Matthews' attempt to placate Escobar a year later when questioned about why the machine guns had not been installed.

After about a year, Escobar's henchmen surprised me at my Ft. Lauderdale hangar, wanting to see the 50 calibers, while brandishing their own machine pistols. They insisted on meeting the aircraft mechanic who was to be paid $200 thousand for installing the 50 caliber machine guns. To make the ruse work and in an effort to satisfy Escobar's men, I drove them to Ft. Lauderdale Executive Jet Service, at that time called Don Haines Aviation. It was located on the opposite side of the airport and had performed most of the maintenance on the HA-200. I explained I would have to take the money in and pay the mechanic as he refused to make the deal known to anyone else if he was to do the work. [Don Haynes Aviation was later renamed F.X.E. Jet Center when Dan E. Karns took over from Don Haines]

Escobar's men waited and watched while parked outside in front of the office as I carried their $200 thousand in to pay the mechanic. I was on the spot in reference to what to do with the $200 thousand. The owners, Don Haynes and Dan E. Karns. had previously complained to me about financial problems related to the IRS locking their doors. This was a perfect opportunity to offer them assistance in the form of a cash loan. They gladly accepted the loan, and it was put on their company books and my company books as a consulting fee to be paid back to Rod Aero Aircraft Brokerage in installments to be worked out with my accountant, Ronald Briggs and his CPA accounting firm. Should Mr. Briggs testify again, he would surely testify truthfully to this, as he was unaware of any wrongdoing. However, he was aware that Rod Aero and myself provided covert type flying services for the U.S. government and were paid in the form of cash, checks, and airplanes.

The letter went into how Matthews discovered Ellard's role in the bombing of the Avianca Airliner:

I did not learn of Escobar's and Ellard's involvement in the Avianca flight bombing until Ellard bragged to me that "We took out some snitches on that Avianca flight; we snuffed the son-of-a-bitches," referring to himself and his alleged partner Pablo Escobar. In talking about it, Ellard swelled with pride. I asked Ellard if he knew how many of the people on board were targets. He answered evasively, saying "We got all of them." Ellard went into detail about the explosion and the mangled bodies strewn all over the place, while bursting into an excited hideous laughter.

No End to Misuse of Federal Power by DOJ Employees

To insure that Matthews' life was as miserable as possible, AUSA Terrence Thompson told the prison that Matthews was an extreme escape risk, and that he was planning to escape using hostages. Matthews wrote, "I suppose the objective is to keep the pressure up on me, it just seems kind of absurd since I was never in prison before, much less attempted escape." Matthews, a non-violent person, would be one of the least likely inmates that would try something as foolish as escaping from the maximum-security prison at Leavenworth.

Tactics to Keep the Media from Matthews

Not content with having destroyed Matthews' family and with sentencing him to life in prison, Justice Department attorneys, through their prison administrators, put Matthews into solitary confinement on April 30, 1998. A little-known fact of prison life is that many prisoners commit suicide in solitary confinement. Another interesting DOJ retaliation is to place a deranged prisoner—one who may have already murdered—in with a prisoner they wish to target. The murdered troublemaker is no longer a problem.

This transfer out of the prison population followed the threat by Assistant Executive Warden Bob Bennett that if Matthews went ahead with an ABC Television Primetime interview, he would end up in the "hole." And that is what happened. Prison authorities tried to justify their actions on the position that Matthews' sister, Wanda, reimbursed someone outside the prison $25 for the stamps they used on behalf of Matthews.

Still not satisfied with what they did to Matthews, the DOJ prison officials transferred Matthews in November 1998 to worse conditions. They placed him in a cage-like environment which the prisoners call the "Dog House," where he remained confined 24 hours a day in a small cell, in a 100-year-old building with inadequate heating in the winter, and inadequate cooling in the summer.

America's Devil Island

Matthews wrote about his living conditions:

They finally moved me to the infamous Dog House, a 100-year-old disciplinary unit without adequate heating or cooling. Windows are broken out and birds fly in and out at will. Two men are stuffed into a 4 ½ x 9' cell locked-down 24 hours a day without enough room to walk. Prisoners are not usually provided warm clothing, consequently you must stay under the covers in the bunk to keep from freezing.

The tiny open bar-faced cells are stacked five levels high with surrounding catwalks. The noise is deafening at times, especially when prisoners on a regular basis mimic the living conditions by barking and howling like dogs. Thus the name "Dog House."

This place is seldom without the screaming and murmurings of the paranoid schizophrenics who are housed here. Violent or tough guys are broken easily and quickly by four-pointing them until they become submissive (i.e. strapping them to a concrete bunk at all four limbs). After a few days of urinating and defecating on themselves and eating like a dog on its back, they quickly realize it's not at all like the movies.

To break the more sophisticated, they are placed in special cells that aren't talked about, with the small window painted over, little or no ventilation, poor heating or cooling. They will then deliberately place one certified-nut after the other in your cell, the worst psychotics they can muster, guilty of the most heinous murders you can imagine.

Matthews' January 1, 1999 letter stated:

It is below freezing in my cell here in Dog House unit and I have no warm clothes. This makes it difficult to write as my fingers become stiff from the cold. I must get back under the covers to warm up. The ice forming on the toilet water is my thermometer.

On January 5, 1999, I wrote a letter to Warden J.W. Booker demanding to know why he had put Matthews into this crowded cage-like unit. He replied with a letter for me to get Washington authorization to allow prison officials to release information to me. It was a typical bureaucratic run-around.

I contacted *Primetime* producer Jude Dratt concerning the inhumane and retaliatory treatment Matthews received as a result of granting the ABC show an interview. She said prison authorities gave her the run-around also. I was disappointed that *Primetime* could not have aired a show dealing with retaliation against people who expose government corruption.

Customs Agent Reveals Customs Coverups and Lying

The ABC documentary aired on July 8, 1998, toned down the gravity of government misconduct, but was still strong when compared with the usual coverup by the mainstream media. Mark Conrad, a Customs veteran and chief of Customs Internal Affairs division in Houston, appeared on the show and showed extraordinary courage. Conrad said on the ABC News documentary, "It is a coverup that continues today."

Asked by DOJ to Commit Perjury

Conrad retired in December 1998, and in a January 1999 letter to me he provided further information about the problems in Customs and the Justice Department. He stated *very* strongly he did not trust AUSA Terry Thompson. Another former AUSA I talked to, Ronald Tonkin, had even stronger words for Terrence Thompson.

Prosecutor Asking Government Official to Commit Perjury

Conrad said he was "asked to lie by the DOJ prosecutor during a court trial in Fort Lauderdale, to ignore blatantly false representations to a federal judge in San Diego, to lie in an internal investigation." This is the type of conduct that sends people like Matthews to prison with a life-in-prison sentence.

Criminal Charges Against Former AUSA Rozan

In 1994, U.S. Attorney Jim Seykora in Montana filed criminal charges against former Assistant U.S. Attorney Steven Rozan, charging him with mail fraud and money laundering. These charges related to the Montana ranch that was placed in his control by Matthews, and which Rozan conveyed to his law partner, as if it was his own. (District of Montana, Missoula Division CR-95-30-M-CCL-01; CR-94-39-M-CCL-01) Because of Matthews' peripheral involvement with Rozan, Matthews was called to testify. Tape-recorded evidence that was subpoenaed in Miami was used in the Montana prosecution.

One Justice Department Attorney Protecting Another

For various complex reasons, U.S. Attorney Terrence Thompson came to Rozan's rescue, producing a bogus document to undermine the Montana prosecutor's charges against Rozan. Rozan had previously cooperated with Thompson in withholding evidence in the Matthews' trial and now Thompson, in exchange, returned the debt to Rozan by giving false testimony and producing a forged document into the Montana trial that undermined the prosecutor's case. (Compartmentalization exists in every government agency.)

During one of several meetings in 1993 and 1994, before his transfer to Leavenworth and while Matthews was in prison at Allenwood, Pennsylvania, Customs agent David Smith from the Great Falls, Montana office, and AUSA Jim Seycora from the Helena, Montana office, visited Matthews in prison. The purpose of the visit was purportedly seeking information for their prosecution of Rozan and his law partner Sid Berger. During these conversations, Seycora and Smith brought up the subject of Nestoroff and Cardwell, which was rather strange since they had no role in the Montana case. Matthews responded that Nestoroff and Cardwell were being falsely accused by DOJ prosecutor Terrence Thompson and that they were innocent of the charges that Matthews paid them $5 million for AWACS schedules.

A significant part of the Montana prosecutor's case against Rozan relied upon Matthews telling the truth. During Rozan's trial, Thompson testified in Rozan's defense and produced an unsigned memorandum allegedly prepared by Customs agent Smith which said that Matthews told Smith that he had paid Customs agent Richard Cardwell $5 million for AWACS schedules and bribes to Nestoroff. That statement was untrue, and Matthews had stated the very opposite to Smith. That unsigned document was provided to Rozan's defense attorneys by AUSA Thompson, who then used it to undermine Matthews' credibility.

DOJ Power To Suborn Perjured Testimony and Forged Documents

Although Seycora had initiated the prosecution of Rozan and Berger before Thompson got into the picture, he was nowhere to be seen during the trial. He avoided showing his face in a prosecution initiated by his office that the DOJ was now trying to undermine. The highly sensitive trial was conducted by a young assistant, AUSA Chris McLean. The probability is that Justice Department officials in Washington wanted the prosecution halted.

Customs Agent Smith's Evasive Answer

During recess, after the unsigned document was presented by Rozan's defense attorney, Smith and AUSA McLean came to Matthews in his holding cell (during the trial), during which time Smith stated the document "was a misstatement." He later told Matthews' brother, Lester, in Texas, that Matthews "did not make that statement."

Customs Agent Smith's Peculiar Response

In December 1998, I sent a letter to Smith in Montana, who was then retired from government service. I requested that he tell me whether he actually prepared and signed that document and whether it reflected what Matthews had actually said to him. Smith answered through a Great Falls, Montana law firm:

> *Mr. Smith denies any wrongdoing regarding the Rozen and Berger prosecution. He had no control over what a defense attorney did with Jencks Act material.*

The problem with that non-responsive reply was that Smith did not confirm or deny that he prepared and signed the false document. If he *had* prepared it, there would be no reason to deny it. If he had *not* prepared it, it would be understandable, despite its cowardice, not to be responsive. By the wording of that response, a person could deduce that Smith was saying he was not responsible for what was said in that memorandum that was used to sabotage the Montana prosecutor's case. A person could argue that Smith aided and abetted the presentation of a false or forged document to a federal court, and aided and abetted obstruction of justice. These are federal crimes.

Matthews feels that the unsigned Smith document was falsified and presented to the grand jury in the Nestoroff-Cardwell prosecution by AUSA Thompson, and then used to exonerate former AUSA Rozan in the Montana trial. Matthews believes that the Seycora-Smith visit to his prison cell was intended to provide the basis for the falsified Smith memorandum to placate Thompson, which backfired on the Montana prosecutor.

Same DOJ Tactics Used to Silence other Whistleblowers

In my many years of investigative experience and contacts with dozens of government personnel and government whistleblowers, I find that the tactics used against them by Justice Department personnel and by federal judges are similar. False charges, prosecutor lying, judges who subvert defendants' rights, and jurors who are too dumb to learn the facts of life.

Media Exposure of DOJ Human Rights Violations

The *Pittsburgh Post Gazette* published a series of ten highly detailed articles in November and December 1998, following two years of investigations, giving dozens of examples of people whose lives were destroyed by the corrupt actions of Justice Department prosecutors. The articles went into great detail showing how Congress and federal judges have given prosecutors more power, and more immunity, to where virtually any form of prosecutorial fraud is perpetrated with immunity to the perpetrator, while the defendant victims suffer agonizing personal and financial disasters. These articles are described in the chapter devoted to Justice Department misconduct.

Major Threat to the People of the United States

What has been done to the Matthews family has been done to thousands of others who were innocent. Little does the public realize the major threat and the harm being inflicted upon families throughout America by the personnel in the U.S. Department of Justice.

As this book is written, Matthews has been in prison for seven years. His family is destroyed. His wife and seven-year-old son fled to Latin America to escape Justice Department retaliation. Major drug traffickers who had shipped tons of cocaine into the United States were released from prison for providing perjured testimony against Matthews.

Motion for A New Trial

In 1998, Matthews' Boulder, Colorado, attorney, Clifford Barnard, filed a motion for a new trial based upon discovery of an 18-page document prepared by U.S. Customs in San Antonio on February 15, 1989. This document directly concerned Matthews and could have been used in his defense to demonstrate a coverup, but DOJ prosecutors had not made it available for Matthews' defense, as required by law. That document surfaced during another trial several years after the Matthews trial. By omitting key facts, the document came to a false conclusion.

Based upon that document, Barnard filed a motion for a new trial, raising several arguments, including:

- Customs agents and supervisors who testified at Matthews' trial for the prosecutor had covered up for the authority that they had given Matthews to fly the holiday drug loads.
- The falsified document came to a false conclusion by omitting from it the authority given to Matthews to fly the drug loads and the immunity for earlier drug loads not authorized by government agents, reflecting a pattern of lying. Under federal law, omitting key information from a document that changes the conclusion constitutes fraud.
- That Customs agents and supervisors lied during Matthews' trial to support the conclusion reached in that document.
- The falsified document's conclusion showed a proclivity to lying, including during trial.
- The memorandum was itself evidence of a Customs cover-up of the authority that Customs and the Department of Justice had given to Matthews.

Withholding from Matthews' Defense Evidence Included in 1553-page House Report on Customs Mismanagement and Corruption

As I accumulate evidence for the preparation of my various books, and in Matthews' case, this book, I feel he has several other strong issues to justify vacating the sentence. Another document withheld from Matthews was the evidence included in the 1553-page House report that revealed an epidemic pattern of mismanagement and various forms of corruption in the southwest region of U.S. Customs, as detailed elsewhere within these pages in the section specifically dealing with U.S. Customs.

Seeking to File an Amicus Curiae Brief on Matthews' Behalf

On February 12, 1999, I submitted a motion to the court requesting approval to file an amicus curiae brief and affidavit that addressed other issues not addressed by the trial court or the appellate court, and not known to Matthews' present attorney. In the motion, I stated that I was a former federal investigator, the head of a coalition of several dozen present and former government agents and whistleblowers, and had accumulated considerable evidence that would show Matthews to be innocent of the charges. I stated that I wanted to include an affidavit that would prove Matthews' innocence. Further, I stated that I would be presenting information on federal crimes perpetrated by federal personnel and that the report would meet the mandatory requirements of Title 18 USC § 4, which required anyone knowing of a federal crime to report it to a federal judge (or other federal officer).

Judge Ursula Ungaro-Benages responded on April 15, 1999: "Ordered and adjudged that Rodney Stich's motion/request to file Amicus Brief and Affidavit is denied." That denial not only prevented information from being inserted into Matthews' motion, but also blocked my reporting of federal crimes under the federal crimes reporting statute, continuing the years of judicial coverups that are documented in my various books.

Continued DOJ Retaliation

In one of Matthews's letters he said:

I sat through my 1993 trial in bewilderment, wondering how the government could authorize something on one hand and prosecute it with the other hand. I couldn't believe I could be convicted. It was especially troubling subsequent to the "Clean Slate" meeting in 1990 and in light of all the successful missions I had flown for the government since then. The first few years in prison, every time I heard the phone ring, "I would wait with anxious anticipation" for someone to come to my cell to release me and tell me that it was all a big foul-up that had been cleared up. It took me years in prison to finally figure out that the government knew exactly what they were doing because they have been doing this for more than 30 years to hundreds of pilots.

A Mother's Tearful Request for Help

Answering my phone on February 23, 1999, a crying mother asked, "What can I do to help my son?" She had called once before asking if it would help if she went to Washington seeking help. I felt that members of Congress would ignore her as being simply another mother seeking help for a son properly convicted and sentenced to the long prison term that they had legislated.

I told her that as soon as the manuscript that I was working on was published, estimating manuscript completion in a few months, with the book in hand, she then had something concrete to use to seek help for her son.

Seeking Help from Israeli Involved in the Iraqi Pilot Defection

I asked Matthews if, after he was arrested, he contacted Abe, who assisted in the Iraqi pilot defection, in the possibility some help could be coming from that direction. Matthews said, "My ex-wife, Judith, got in touch with Colonel E.G. who had moved up in rank. He told Judith that my prosecution was political and anything the prosecution learned would only be used against me." I didn't accept that assessment, but it is obvious that help must come from another source. Possibly this book will help him and many others in somewhat similar positions.

Matthews Replaced by Another Contract Agent,
Who Encountered the Same DOJ and Judicial Sabotage

After Matthews was arrested, another contract pilot filled in, working for Customs in the same southwest region and in Texas. He suffered a similar fate when he was about to bring about the arrest of major Colombian drug lords and after he discovered other high-level corruption among U.S. personnel. Details are shown in the next chapter.

****

Released Big-Time Drug Smuggler Ellard Again Arrested

Before we leave this convoluted saga, let's see how Jimmy Ellard was doing. After the Department of Justice's persistence resulted in Pablo Escobar's top aide, Jimmy Ellard, being released from prison, Ellard resumed smuggling drugs for himself—and the government—through DEA agents in the New York area.

This drug trafficking led to the arrest of Ellard and his son William in September 1998 by Florida agents. They were charged with hauling 187 pounds of marijuana. Upon being arrested, Ellard told the Florida agents he was working for DEA agents. This arrest, reported in the media, *forced* U.S. Attorney Terry Thompson to charge Ellard with a drug-smuggling offense.

Using the Defense "Government Authority"

Ellard's long-time attorney, William Norris of Coral Gables, Florida, raised the defense of "government authority." A trial date was set to try Ellard on the drug smuggling charge. Shortly before the trial was to start, Ellard's attorney produced a 21-minute tape of a telephone conversation between Ellard and DEA Special Agent Eldo Rocco, showing DEA involvement in drug smuggling and DEA knowledge of Ellard's drug activities.

DOJ Dropping Charges Against Major Drug Trafficker

Possibly wishing to avoid adverse publicity—including for himself—Department of Justice prosecutor Terrence Thompson dropped charges against Ellard and his son for the drug smuggling charge.

If the charges had not been dropped, Ellard and his son faced over 25 years in prison, and the drug smuggling activities of government agents and agencies would become known to the small segment of the public reading the Miami Herald newspaper. (Despite the gravity of this arrest, no known newspaper or news service outside of the Miami area carried the story, another example of the media's withholding of the government's role in drug trafficking.)

Imprisoned Men and Women & Their Families Should Be Outraged!

The thousands of people in prison on minor drug offenses should be more than outraged that they have not been given the same "understanding" as the DOJ prosecutor gave to Ellard and his son.

Judge Zloch was not so Benevolent

Although the Department of Justice dropped charges against Ellard and his son, District Judge William J. Zloch, on April 30, 1999, sentenced Ellard to five years in prison for violating his probation. (The son went free, all charges dropped.) Ellard was still under Judge Zloch's supervision on the basis of Ellard's 1990 parole arising out of a cocaine smuggling operation at Fort Lauderdale Executive Airport. Upon hearing of Ellard's arrest for drug smuggling and subsequent dropping of charges by the Department of Justice, the judge ordered Ellard arrested on the basis of violating parole.

The judge said, "I don't care if the President of the United States came down from Washington and recruited Mr. Ellard, I want to see any piece of paper signed by this court authorizing him to work under cover for the DEA." (In 1997, federal prosecutors in New York asked Judge Zloch to transfer Ellard's probation to New York. Zloch refused the request in a confidential sealed ruling.)

The judge's involvement caused a federal investigation to be conducted, which would not have happened otherwise. The judge demanded to know who defied his order that barred the government from using Ellard for smuggling drugs. Ellard told Customs agent Paul Hilson that he was working with the DEA agents on a drug smuggling operation with three major Mexican drug cartels and Mexican politicians, but that at the last minute they were required to run a smaller test run.

Major Drug Trafficker and Murderer Working for Government

Ellard started hauling drugs for himself, and also for the DEA. Ellard worked closely with DEA Special Agents Sam Trotman of Camden, New Jersey and Aldo Rocco of New York. These government agents knew, directed, and/or authorized Ellard to smuggle large quantities of drugs into the United States in the 1990s, until the day of Ellard's arrest. The first reaction of the government and the DEA agents was to deny Ellard was working for them. At least initially.

DEA Agent Complaining Of DOJ Prosecutor's
Responsibility for Drugs Entering the United States

Ellard tape recorded some of his conversations with DEA agents showing government agents authorizing him to fly drugs into the United States from Mexico and other locations. On the tape, DEA agent Rocco complained to Ellard that U.S. Attorney Thompson was allowing tons of cocaine to enter the United States. (He also made this possible by blocking Matthews' undercover operation against the Pablo Escobar organization.) In one section of the tape Rocco said:

It's criminal. It really is. I mean, Thompson's no different than a cartel attorney. The bottom line is he's making it easier for stuff, not only coming to this country, but to get distributed.

DEA Agent Knew Ellard was Smuggling Drugs for Himself

DEA Agent Rocco said to Ellard, "I'm not going to lie to you, if I was in your position, I wouldn't do it," referring to his knowing Ellard was smuggling drugs into the United States. Knowing of a felony and not reporting it is a crime, and in this case, the federal agent's crime is far worse than those of many incarcerated people.

During the 20-minute-long taped telephone conversation, Ellard and the DEA agent discussed the various ways to bring cocaine from Mexico. Ellard described air routes from Mexico through other countries that would disguise Mexico as being the source of the drugs. Jamaica was stated as one of the "friendly" countries to use. In another part of the tape the DEA agent was urging Ellard to consummate a 26,000-pound cocaine deal with Mexican drug traffickers.

DEA Disguising Employing Major Drug Kingpin and Murderer

DEA agents sought to disguise employing Ellard, a major drug trafficker and murderer, and disguise violating Judge Zloch's order, by registering Ellard's brother as a confidential informant and using the brother as a conduit to Jimmy Ellard. The recorded telephone conversation showed that this was a ruse and that Ellard was in fact working directly for the DEA agents.

Using "Stand-In" Common to Evade Lawful Prohibition

It is common for U.S. agents to evade the spirit and the clear intent of U.S. law by using stand-in non-U.S. citizens to conduct undercover operations in foreign countries—when such actions on the part of U.S. agents would be prohibited. It is similar to the long-standing disavow practice by the CIA and other government agencies to deny responsibility for their covert and usually illegal operations. A lie.

Avoiding an International Incident with Mexico

It was explained on the tape by Rocco that the Mexican origin of the drugs had to be hidden to avoid any further strain between Mexico and the United States after a major 1998 operation by the United States against Mexican banks and bankers. It was also brought out that any undercover operation involving Mexico had to be made known to Mexican military, police and politicians, and this would make any such operation worthless.

CHAPTER TEN

MONTANA DRUG GATEWAY

There is a good possibility there was more to the Top Gun Ranch than Matthews realized. The ranch had been owned by a major drug trafficker and aide to drug kingpin Pablo Escobar. It was in an isolated area close to the Canadian border with an equally isolated area in Canada. Further, Canada has a less hostile attitude toward drugs than exists in the United States.

The mainstream media has given virtually no publicity to the drugs coming from Canada into the Montana area. This silence exists despite many reports of these activities and the duplicity of local and state law-enforcement and political figures—and especially the usual coverups by U.S. agencies, especially Department of Justice personnel.

Montana had been the home of several well-known crime figures. For instance, Alfred J. Luciano, Sr., a nephew to crime-figure "Lucky" Luciano, had a home in Montana, as did Joseph Bonano. It would be unusual if they did not use the unique opportunities provided by the remoteness of Montana for shipping drugs into the United States.

Canadian Border Problems

Surveillance by U.S. agencies along the Canadian border is a fraction of what exists along the southern borders. Less than 300 Border Patrol agents are assigned to the Canadian border which is over 3,000 miles long. In contrast, the United States reportedly has over 7,000 agents assigned to the U.S.-Mexico border (*Seattle Times* March 18, 1999). Deputy Chief Border Patrol Agent Eugene David, testifying in March 1999 before a House Subcommittee on Immigration, stated that "Over the last 10 years, we have experienced large increases in organized crime along the border." (The Border Patrol is a division of the Immigration and Naturalization Service which is under the Department of Justice.)

Montana's Version of Arkansas

In the 1980s, hundreds of reports were made by local residents about drug trafficking at Mena Airport in Arkansas, followed by state and federal "law enforcement" coverups. The same conditions exist in Montana. Many non-government investigative reports have been made about the drug trafficking from Canada into Montana, the criminal involvement of local and state law enforcement personnel and politicians, and the coverups by state and federal officials. This chapter focuses briefly on these matters in Montana.

The greatest number of reports of Montana drug trafficking came from an area known as the Hi-Line where the Burlington Northern Railroad runs parallel to the Montana-Canadian border. People reported planes landing at small airstrips, drugs being off-loaded, and the involvement of government personnel in the criminal activities.

People who made reports of drug trafficking activities to county, state, or federal law enforcement offices found their reports were either ignored, or, *they* became the subjects of government retaliation. As in Arkansas, many people who sought to expose the political involvement in drugs ended up dead—their deaths often falsely reported by county personnel as suicides.

Carry Drugs for County Attorney or Suffer the Consequences

During an interview by private investigator Darby Hinz with Clinton Mullen, owner of Mullen Trucking Company, Mullen stated that County Attorney Phillip Carter in Sidney, Montana wanted to use his trucking company to haul drugs. When Mullen refused, the local bank, First United Bank, withdrew funding for his operation, and his credit rating in town deteriorated.

A Few Courageous People Spoke Out

Several courageous people attempted to expose the involvement of Montana personnel in the drug trafficking. One was James Douglas Alexander, a respected Montana attorney. Alexander graduated from Western State University in San Diego; he helped found the Rutherford Institute of Montana; he was active in Republican politics; he was Pat Buchanan's 1992-campaign chairman in Montana.

Alexander started discovering drug trafficking connected to local and state personnel in 1989 while defending another attorney from Sidney, Thomas Halvorson. Halvorson had been accused of wiretapping the county attorney's office—during which time he recorded telephone conversations showing drug trafficking activities involving county and police personnel. After the wiretaps were discovered, the Commission on Legal Practices sought to revoke Halvorson's license to practice law in Montana.

While defending Halvorson, Alexander discovered additional evidence that the deputy county attorney in Sidney and a police detective were involved in drug trafficking. In the August 1996 edition of *Strategic Investment* Jack Wheeler, it's co-editor, wrote:

Mena in Montana? The Republicans may have their own drug smuggling scandal, similar to Bill Clinton's in Mena, Arkansas. Due to all the bad publicity, the drug cartels moving coke from Mexico through Mena may have relocated a substantial part of their operation to Montana, bringing the stuff in from Canada. Corruption among state officials is reported to be widespread, reaching right into the governor's office. DEA sources have hinted that Governor Marc Racicot or some of his top aides might be indicted. Trouble for the Republicans is that Racicot is one of them.

Co-editor with Wheeler was former CIA Director William Colby, who drowned under mysterious circumstances in the spring of 1996.

Infamous Barry Seal Operating In Montana

Information obtained by Alexander and other investigators indicated that Barry Seal—famous for his Arkansas drug trafficking as part of covert government operations—was setting up a drug smuggling operation from Canada into Montana. One reason for this was that Arkansas and other areas along the southern coast of the United States were becoming so highly patrolled that it was difficult to bring drugs into the United States. Information obtained by Alexander, investigator Don Hopsicker and others indicates that Seal was flying drugs into Montana from Canada in 1985. One of Seal's government handlers was reportedly DEA agent Ernst Jacobson.

Alexander wrote that it is believed former U.S. Attorney Pete Dunbar was involved with the government-associated drug trafficking that included Barry Seal. (Dunbar now has a private investigation firm in Billings, Montana.) Alexander said that while he was providing information to the FBI about the county prosecutor Phillip Carter, Carter was fraudulently stating to Alexander's law clients that Alexander was a convicted felon.

Journalist Describing His Findings of Montana Drug Trafficking

Adding to Alexander's knowledge of drug trafficking and political involvement was journalist Mike Perry of Chinook who started telling Alexander in 1992 of the political involvement in drug trafficking that he had uncovered. Perry told Alexander of drug aircraft landing at Montana airstrips near Havre, Chinook, and Glasgow, which Alexander explained:

I began communicating with a journalist in Chinook named Mike Perry. Perry gave a whole litany of similar, parallel events that were occurring: airplanes coming in, people unloading cocaine from airplanes, people getting beat up or killed. It always led back to members of law enforcement. In Chinook, four police officers had lost their jobs because they had tracked airplanes coming into the airport, or other drug-related corruption involving the county attorney and other individuals in Chinook. I began to work with Mike Perry at that point and we've worked together, with other journalists, to this day.

Mike Roe, a high-profile investigator, started working with us. He is a private investigator from Phoenix with a good reputation. He was very well known high-profile investigator. We felt like it was better to bring in someone from out-of-state to help us. We hoped, through his contacts with the FBI in Salt Lake City and with other federal agencies in Phoenix, we could get something done. By the time he came in, in 1992, we began to realize that the drugs were a very large-scale operation. Roe began to get in contact with residents in Chinook and Sidney, and there was a whole flood of people coming forward, asking for something to be done, begging us to look into the drugs and murders that appeared to trail back, again, to law enforcement personnel.

Pressure and threats from local police and sheriff department personnel, and political pressures, forced Perry to leave Montana in December 1998.

A written report dated February 2, 1994, was prepared by private investigator Michael W. Roe of Roe Investigations in Phoenix, Arizona (and a copy sent to the Great Falls FBI office). Roe's 12-page report identified people and places involved in Montana drug trafficking, the many murders of people threatening to expose the relationship between drug crimes and city and county personnel, including law-enforcement people, and the names of the many witnesses providing key information.

Under "general allegations," the Roe report stated:

- Bill Larson, president of the Chinook Branch of the Bank of Montana, was allegedly involved in laundering of drug money through that branch of the Bank of Montana; that he was involved in the transportation of narcotics; that he was involved in a conspiracy relating to the murder of two people in Chinook (Richard Cowen and Bernadette Doiron, on or about January 21, 1987) for which two people were convicted: Lloyd James Wilson and Robert Henry Bone.
- Don Ranstrom, Blaine County Attorney, was reportedly involved in the importation, use and sale of narcotics, in the murders of Cowen and Doiron, and there is a belief that he ordered the murders.
- The firing of Chinook police chief Bernie Brost by the mayor after Brost started investigating alleged drug activities by Bank of Montana banker Bill Larson, Blaine County Attorney Dan Ranstrom, Chinook police officer Alan Delk, and others.
- Former county attorney and now city attorney Phillip Carter was involved in drug trafficking, threats against people who would not cooperate in hauling drugs, including trucking firm owner Clint Mullen. After Mullen refused Carter's reported request to haul drugs, Mullen started receiving retaliation from law enforcement personnel, and the local bank—whose attorney was Carter—suddenly disrupted Mullen's financial activities, and he was physically beaten by friends of the city attorney. The Roe report of February 1994 supplemented Roe's earlier report which was allegedly "lost" by Great Falls FBI agents.

Destroying Anyone Who Exposes Their Corruption

The Roe report referred to former Circle city attorney Arnie Hove who sought to expose the political involvement in drug trafficking and then was subjected to political harassment and physical violence. The report said, "Mr. Hove became very concerned for his personal safety and feared for his and his children's lives. Mr. Hove expressed growing fear for his safety."

Hove was at the time attorney for the city of Circle, Montana, served as appeals court judge at the Fort Peck Reservation, and was prosecutor for McCone County. He was a rising player in Republican politics in Eastern Montana. But when he started exposing political involvement in drug trafficking, state and federal retaliation followed. Alexander described what Hove went through in retaliation for exposing the FBI involvement in Montana drug matters:

Hove came under heavy attack during this period of time—from the fall of 1996 to early 1999. Law enforcement was everywhere investigating Hove for all kinds of criminal activity. It was horrible how they did him, but it was also similar to what they did to me [as a standard practice done to many other government personnel, including me]. Only Hinz has videotapes of witnesses who were offered money to testify falsely against

Hove!

Charges were filed against Hove, and he underwent a period of intense harassment. In a not uncommon tactic to discredit anyone exposing government misconduct, the charges were followed by an order committing him to Warm Springs State Hospital. He was forcibly injected with drugs which caused substantial physical damage. This effectively silenced another of the very few people with sufficient backbone and character to speak out when outrage is required.

Convenient Death of Key Witnesses

The Roe report, and information obtained from Alexander, described the "convenient" deaths of key people. These included banker Bob Kropp of Farmer's State Bank in Conrad, who was killed (March 31, 1983) shortly before he was to testify about bribery at drug money laundering. The vice president of Whitefish Mountain Bank at Whitefish, John Ochenrider, died March 31, 1983, two weeks before he was to testify in a money laundering trial with codefendant Alfred Luciano.

Ochenrider's death was reportedly due to a fall suffered while mountain climbing—an activity that the banker had never done before. Montana Highway Patrolman Michael Remz was killed as he started investigating aircraft landing on small airstrips near the towns of Libby and Eureka. A journalist who was investigating Luciano's drug smuggling activities died in a fire in Eureka in late 1997. Many others were killed who had given information about the drug trafficking. Mike Wolf and Bruce Madsen were killed outside Sidney (December 1993) after Wolf wrote his mother that he was about to be murdered. Jerry Herdt died under mysterious circumstances near Glendive after he told acquaintances he was providing information to the FBI about a Sidney prosecutor that Herdt believed was dealing in drugs.

Whitefish Mountain Bank Drug-Money Laundering

The Mountain Bank of Whitefish, in Whitefish, Montana, close to the Top Gun Ranch, was reportedly involved in money laundering. One of its directors, Alfred Luciano, a nephew of Lucky Luciano, was indicted in 1993 at Missoula, Montana, for money laundering, along with his son, Frank. Charges were dropped against Al Luciano, and his son Frank fled the United States while waiting for trial and is reportedly living in the Caribbean area. After Al Luciano complained of being under 24-hour surveillance by the FBI, he was killed in a suspicious car crash.

The Whitefish Mountain Bank had been a money-laundering center for the drug operation. Its former president, Werner Schreiber, was sent to prison along with four other bank officers. Alexander confirmed this to *Chinook Opinions* editor Mike Perry. Whitefish Bank was a money-laundering center for Iran-Contra folks. Schreiber was an attorney and friend of Marc Racicot, the governor.

Before indictments were handed down, grand jury members heard testimony from a FINCEN audit specialist "that $150 million had been laundered through the tiny bank." Band president Schreiber and five other bank officers were charged with embezzling over $6 million from the bank (which was actually their fee for laundering the drug money). Schreiber later complained from federal prison that he had been forced to "take a fall" for big folks who were never indicted.

Pleading Guilty to Bank Fraud under Suspicious Conditions

In December 1989, John Earl Petersen pled guilty to bank fraud, money laundering and conspiracy charges stemming from the financial collapse of Whitefish Mountain Bank. District Judge Fred Van Sickle sentenced Peterson to 12 years in federal prison. Federal prosecutors were suspiciously protective of Peterson, going overboard in referring to Peterson's cooperation (no other charges were filed, and no other resulting cooperation could be seen). AUSA John Griffith of Washington, D.C. said a motion would be shortly filed to reduce Petersen's sentence. This sequence suggested that Petersen pled guilty to keep sensitive information from leaking out, and was told that he would be released after attention was diverted from his case; a "normal" practice.

Report Government Corruption—Suffer the Consequences

In a series of interviews by Wesley Phelan of *Washington Weekly* in 1998, numerous witnesses confirmed that nearly everyone who came forward with information on drug trafficking experienced harassment from police or other government agencies. Alexander said prosecutor Phillip Carter began intimidating and threatening some of the witnesses. These threats against witnesses were federal crimes for which the FBI has responsibility to prosecute.

Explaining the Latest Drug Routes into the United States

Chip Tatum, formerly undercover government operative involved in the Montana operations, explained the flight plan for drugs going from Colombia into Montana via Canada:

> *An aircraft departs Colombia, flies to the Bahamas to rest and refuel, and then, when a weather window opens, continues the flight to Nova Scotia or Quebec. Again, rest and refuel. Then continue to a US-Canadian border landing strip. An associate of Huxtable owned a ranch south of Wayburn, Canada, which provided a perfect landing zone. From Wayburn, the cocaine could easily be flown into Montana or North Dakota via small aircraft.*

Tatum further explained the involvement of FBI Special Agent Terry Nelson and U.S.-Canadian contract undercover operative Mike Huxtable:

> *Nelson not only recruits the law enforcement officials and politicians he needs, he can also supply data from the law enforcement arena such as the DEA NADDIS computer, Customs TECS II, EPIC, FBI, and others involved in ongoing investigations. Nelson then provides this intelligence to his drug contacts. This helps obstruct any investigation and diffuse potential problems. Terry Nelson, a senior agent for the Federal Bureau of Investigation, continues to provide his valuable services to drug cartels and others who will pay his fee, out of his FBI office in southern Florida.*
> [Tatum said that Huxtable was a Canadian smuggler who did undercover work for U.S. and Canadian agencies and organized crime groups.]

Tatum said that the same far off-shore northern route along the east coast of the United States to Canada is also done along the west coast of the United States, entering Canada in British Columbia. He also advised that drug-laden planes from Canada were also landing in North Dakota and Wyoming.

Colombian Radar Warns Drug Pilots of Plane Intercepts

Tatum described how Colombian drug cartels installed radar on Swan Island in the Caribbean that monitors aircraft movements to avoid interdiction of their aircraft heading for the United States. He gave an example: A drug pilot flying drugs for the cartels is monitored on radar controlled by the drug cartels as it proceeds from Colombia northward. If radar shows their plane was being followed, the pilot is advised by radio to immediately return, thereby avoiding interdiction by U.S. aircraft.

Obstruction of Justice by Montana Crime Agency and Governor

In 1991, Sidney City Councilman Richard Hobbs said that he and a group of other concerned people provided the Montana Crime Investigation Bureau (MCIB) with several dozen witness statements showing local official involvement in drug trafficking. These statements included witnesses seeing planes landing and drugs being unloaded. Other witnesses also reported drug planes landing at small airstrips at the Glasgow Air Force Base and on the Fort Peck and Fort Belknap Indian reservations. Despite this evidence, the state agency—under control of then attorney general and future governor Marc Racicot, said they could find no evidence of criminal conduct.

Pattern of FBI Obstruction of Justice Throughout United States

After city, county and state personnel covered up for the drug trafficking reports, Alexander and others reported these to the FBI. They encountered the same Justice Department coverup as repeatedly encountered by others described within these pages, including the Arkansas coverups, the coverup when FBI Special Agent Richard Taus made such reports, reports by INS agent Joseph Occhipinti, and others. The coverups and obstruction of justice—with great harm to the United States—included the United States Attorney General. During the Clinton administration, this was Janet Reno.

FBI Avoiding Evidence from Witnesses

Despite the fact that Alexander and others provided the FBI with dozens of witness statements showing government involvement in drug trafficking, none of the witnesses were contacted by the FBI to determine the accuracy of their information. Alexander explained that he obtained over 70 witness statements in the Sidney, Montana, area from 1990 to 1995 from people who had observed the drugs being unloaded from aircraft and who observed or knew about the political involvement of city, county and state personnel in the drug trafficking.

Justice Department Obstruction of Justice Tactics

Alexander explained that by 1993-1994, the FBI had shifted the investigation to its Glasgow, Montana office and assigned it to FBI Special Agent Scott Cruse. He said: "Cruse apparently did almost no investigation at all. Certainly he did not talk to anyone in Chinook. There were bank employees in Chinook who were ready to come forward and provide documentation and testimony about money laundering there, and other things related to the drug operation. These witnesses were ignored." At the same time, FBI Special Agent Scott Cruse began to investigate wire fraud allegations against Alexander.

FBI Offering Favors to Witnesses

Circle City attorney Arnie Hove found himself targeted in a series of heavy-handed "investigations." At one point prior to the November 1998 elections as Hove campaigned for McCone County Attorney, he was prosecuted on allegations of sexual misconduct with a client. It was during this time that Hove's defense attorney Mark Parker of Billings exposed the blatant prosecutorial misconduct against Hove by the U.S. Department of Justice. An article in the Billings Outpost (July 29, 1998) was titled, "FBI Accused of Offering Favors to Witnesses." The article stated in part:

> In one instance, Mr. Parker said after the arraignment, a juvenile has given a videotaped statement that he was offered his release from jail and his GED if he would testify against Mr. Hove. Hove was acquitted after a jury trial, but the harassment continued until Hove was forced to temporarily close his law office.

Justice Department Tactics to Silence Alexander

Alexander explained how Justice Department prosecutors sought to silence him, using his humanitarian efforts relating to adoption of war orphans to retaliate and halt his exposure of government-involved drug trafficking. He explained:

> I went to Europe in January of 1990 with a former AP writer from Helena, Garry Moes. I went over there and began to do some of the first adoptions in Romania by U.S. Citizens. I also helped coordinate humanitarian efforts over there. I became good friends with members of the new leadership that emerged after the revolution. I began to do business over there, and had a very successful international adoption practice. I did the first Romanian adoptions after the revolution. I helped a state senator in Romania to establish the Romanian adoption laws. I worked with the leadership of the state government there. What we did was transfer the approval from Bucharest to the state governments in Transylvania and to the other state governments so they could approve adoptions.
>
> I was charged with wire fraud related to some adoptions which I later did in Macedonia. The family back in the states was denied an adoption there because they had falsified their mental health records. They had a history of mental illness. They got over there and disclosed that, and they were rejected. They came back to the United States and said adoptions could not be done in Macedonia.
>
> By that time, the political forces in Montana zeroed in on me and used these false allegations to take my license. They have continued to use this to discredit me, and have brought federal felony charges against me. They are claiming that adoptions were not allowed in Macedonia. But we have reports from the State Department showing that there were 12 adoptions that year, and we were the first to attempt to do it. Obviously the state has no case, and as this thing unwinds, I think the answers to why I was targeted and this was done to me, and why Arnie Hove was arrested, are going to become quite apparent.

Alexander explained how he learned about Montana drug trafficking and heavy involvement of local, state, and federal personnel. In a March 13, 1999, letter Alexander wrote:

> We began to gather reports involving drug smuggling into Sidney-

Chinook-Havre in the early '90s. We had more than 70 statements in-
volving witnesses to local law enforcement and prosecutors being in-
volved in drug dealings. There are dozens and dozens and dozens of affi-
davits! When I came out publicly against the drugs, the attacks on me be-
gan in earnest. I was driven out of the practice of law and Montana. After
I left the state, I was contacted by Orlin Grabbe, then others who I've
since been advised were linked to NSA and others.

Mike Roe met with FBI agents in Great Falls for seven hours at one
time. I was interviewed in Helena in 1994 for four hours. Neither meeting
resulted in 302's [FBI report of witness statements]. The agent who was
assigned to my case, Scott Cruse, also was assigned to investigate the
drug allegations. Chip Tatum identified Cruse as one of the Montana FBI
agents involved in drug trafficking with the Nelson operation. Cruse later
gave false testimony to the Great Falls grand jury to get me indicted on
the wire fraud charges. By amazing coincidence, another investigator,
Walter Hammermeister was on the grand jury and was able to confront
Cruse. He was then booted off the grand jury! The attorney prosecuting
the case was Carl Rostad.

[Reported Canadian Indictment of FBI Agent]

FBI Agent Terry Nelson was indicted in Regina, Saskatchewan Pro-
vincial Court. Blain County Sheriff Pete Paulsen; journalist Paul
Richardson, then of Indian County Today, and myself, confirmed this from
the RCMP in Regina. The investigator I spoke to there was Detective
Leach. Tatum released more details of the flights and identified the pilots,
the articles were later published under pseudonyms "Spook Houses in
Glasgow," and "Donna Does Glasgow," by Hi-Line Mary. The investi-
gator also identified Mike Huxtable, a Canadian National, as one of the
persons indicted.

[U.S. Pressuring Canadians to Cover up Drug Smuggling]

The U.S. government pressured the Canadians to seal the file and it is
sealed at present. Nelson is a dual citizen: Canadian-US and has a fancy
home in Montreal. The smuggling operation also involved Chapeau Air-
strip in Quebec.

Further explaining political involvement in drugs, Alexander wrote in an
April 1, 1999, letter:

I came to realize that Sidney attorney, Phillip Carter, was involved in
drug trafficking while acting as an investigator for Maurice Colbey, an
investigator for the Montana Commission On Practice appointed in the
Halvorson matter. I came upon documents indicating that then Montana
Attorney General Marc Racicot and FBI Special Agent Scott Cruse were
actively deflecting drug allegations against Philip Carter. Sidney attorney
Tom Halvorson had allegedly wire tapped the Richland County Attorney's
office and had obtained tape recordings of drug conversations involving
then Deputy County Attorney Carter and a police detective, David Schet-
ting discussing a large scale drug operation.

I was approached by Maurice Colbey to obtain affidavits from wit-
nesses and did do so. The affidavits of Jeff Curry confirmed that Halvor-

son had solicited him to use a parabolic microphone to obtain tape-recorded conversations from the office of Phillip Carter. The FBI via agent Cruse immediately focused on Halvorson. I still have the letter from Carter to Scott Cruse, which stated that Marc Racicot approved of the investigation! Halvorson was sanctioned by the Montana Supreme Court, but the complaint regarding the wire-taping allegation was dropped. Arnie Hove testified against attorney Halvorson in that proceeding, saying that Halvorson was making statements concerning Carter dealing drugs! Years later, Hove himself was targeted for saying the same thing.

[Drug money from Drug Lord to Montana Governor?]

It was only later—after I was forced out of Montana—that I found [Montana Governor] Marc Racicot was involved in the drug scheme. There are wire-fund-transfers from Banque Suisse to the Norwest Bank of Helena branch accounts directly to Marc Racicot, his family, and assistants. Those funds came from the Fabio Ochoa operation! Darby Hinz had confirmed from an independent source flights into Montana for the Fabio Ochoa organization.

Substituting One Sham Charge for Another Sham Charge

Charges arising out of Alexander's adoption activities were dropped, and then other sham charges were filed against him on August 25, 1998, by U.S. Attorney Carl Rostad in Great Falls, Montana. Rostad fraudulently charged Alexander with obstruction of justice and interstate communication of threats or violence. Walter Hammermeister, a grand jury member, charged that Rostad and FBI Special Agent Cruse gave perjured testimony to the grand jury in order to obtain the indictment. Not tolerating anyone they could not control on the grand jury, the DOJ prosecutor arranged to have Hammermeister removed as a juror.

Alexander had raised as one of his defenses that the charges filed against him were retaliation for reporting state and local government involvement in drug trafficking crimes. Alexander said Mark Werner, who was his court-appointed attorney, was protective of government personnel involved in drug trafficking, and had stated to a federal grand jury that "Mr. Alexander was delusional based on Mr. Alexander's concerns expressed to him regarding the allegations of drug trafficking." This indicated Werner was not only sabotaging his client, but obstructing justice before the grand jury that would aid and abet the prosecutor's actions to cover up for the drug-related crimes. (My 30 years of dealing with attorneys makes this arrogant misconduct no surprise.)

Nothing is too bizarre for attorneys holding the power of the Justice Department prosecutor's office, The U.S. Attorney twisted this testimony by Alexander's attorney to be obstruction of justice!

Alexander repeatedly tried to dismiss Werner, whose conduct was aiding and abetting the drug traffickers and undermining his client's defenses, but ran into resistance from the judge and the prosecutor.

The Department of Justice filed an *in Limine* motion on February 22, 1999, seeking a court order barring Alexander from raising that defense, which would keep any information concerning the Montana drug trafficking and government involvement out of the record. The Justice Department's motion stated in part:

> *For example, the obstruction count of the indictment itself is predicated on evidence that proves the defendant attempted to have his then counsel, Mark Werner, pursue an unsubstantiated claim that his prosecution was politically motivated and retaliatory to his efforts to reveal drug trafficking in the Sidney, Montana area.*

DOJ Charging Alexander with Obstruction of Justice for Reporting Government Involvement In Drug Crimes

This was bizarre! Department of Justice attorneys were calling Alexander's attempts to report the drug trafficking an obstruction of justice! Something like this was done to me by U.S. Attorney David Levi in Sacramento, California, when I sought to report high-level criminal activities. Levi and federal judges held me in criminal contempt of court for trying to report to a federal judge (under Title 18 USC Section 4) the criminal misconduct that I and several government agents and deep-cover agents discovered. It was one of hundreds of examples of DOJ attorneys covering up and obstructing justice while simultaneously filing sham charges against those courageous individuals who sought to report the criminal activities! (Further details are found in the third editions of *Unfriendly Skies* and *Defrauding America*.)

Charging U.S. Attorney Seycora with Criminal Acts

A September 18, 1997, letter by private investigator Darby Hinz to Mark Werner accused AUSA Jim Seykora with making serious false statements and omissions in Seykora's September 15, 1997, internal memorandum to Judge Shanstrom. The Hinz letter indirectly linked Seykora with "a sophisticated attempt to suppress witnesses in Sidney and Chinook who may have information related to official misconduct." The Hinz letter referred to an investigation which began in the spring of 1991. It referred to an alleged request by County Attorney Phillip Carter to Mullin, requesting him to haul drugs from Canada into Montana and other points in the United States, and the misuse of prosecutor power to retaliate against Mullin when he refused to engage in the criminal activities

Private Investigator Reveals Official Involvement in Drugs

In an April 18, 1999, motion titled "Ex Parte Motion To File Under Seal," Alexander filed a motion with an attached affidavit by private investigator Darby Hinz. The affidavit was filed under Title 18 USC Section 4, and addressed the matters of "drug corruption in eastern Montana." That motion and affidavit stated in part that U.S. Attorney Carl Rostad gave false testimony to a federal grand jury; that Rostad continued to seek an indictment against Alexander after receiving uncontroverted information indicating his innocence; that FBI agents gave false testimony, and refused to contact witnesses willing to give evidence of official involvement in drug trafficking.

The Hinz affidavit stated FBI Agent Scott Cruse was under Department of Justice investigation for drug related misconduct; that the investigation targeted Scott Cruse in a Canada to Montana smuggling operation involving Mike Huxtable of Canada and Miami, Florida FBI Agent Terry Nelson.

Drug Money to Montana Governor Racicot?

In another section of the affidavit, it stated that "funds were paid into an account at a financial institution in Switzerland, Banque Suisse, by the conspirators to current Montana Governor, Marc Racicot. The payments were made to allow the drug shipments through Montana."

Referring to FBI attempts to have witnesses give perjured testimony, the affidavit stated:

Although not presented at trial, three video tape statements from witnesses who claim that FBI agents solicited them to give false information ... the solicitation of witnesses to give false testimony by FBI agents is part of a scheme to harass or discredit attorney Arnie Hove. The harassment may be directly linked to Mr. Hove's cooperation with the internal investigation conducted by the Department of Justice referenced herein.

Controlling the Grand Jury

The affidavit referred to the request of AUSA Carl Rostad to the judge for removal from the grand jury of a juror who was aware of the Justice Department misconduct. (Removal of non-cooperating jurors is another tactic used by Justice Department attorneys to make grand juries rubber-stamps for DOJ indictments.) The affidavit said that attorney Phillip N. Carter of Sidney, Montana, and Donald Ranstrom of Chinook, Montana, were also implicated in the investigation of the smuggling operation.

Hinz ended the motion and affidavit stating: "Based on information and belief, I allege that sealed criminal indictments may now exist in Regina, Saskatchewan Provincial Courts as to individuals Terry Nelson and Mike Huxtable. Such indictments have been confirmed to Montana law enforcement personnel as well as journalists who inquired with the RCMP [Royal Canadian Mounted Police] in Regina [Canada]."

Explaining the Sudden Disappearance of Chip Tatum

In other pages, and in my third edition of *Defrauding America*, I describe Chip Tatum's government-related drug smuggling activities and his sudden disappearance. Alexander explained in an April 3, 1999 letter that in one of the last of over 150 telephone conversations with Tatum, he learned why Tatum was no longer available:

During the last months before Tatum left the United States, he was approached by [FBI Special Agent] Terry Nelson and offered $750,000 to back off the story. Eventually Tatum reached a settlement with the "government" and an agreement to clear up his record. The person who approached Tatum with the $750,000 offer was Nelson's brother-in-law, Mr. Olson.

Large Numbers of State and Federal Officials Implicated

Montana will surely be more in the news as this drug-smuggling frontier is addressed by more of the media that is willing to report these matters. The heavy involvement of state and federal personnel in obstructing justice in drug-related matters in Montana is one more example of these criminal and subversive activities. Of some interest, George Bush was in the loop with drug smuggling during the Iran-Contra affair, and Bush's son George Bush, Jr., is politically aligned with Marc Racicot.

***Washington Weekly* Exposure of Montana Drug Activities**

Wesley Phelan's articles in the *Washington Weekly* documented inter-

views with numerous people who reported the Canada-to-Montana drug trafficking and the involvement of key politicians and law enforcement personnel.
Phelan interviewed over 20 people who had information about the Canadian-
Montana drug operation. In a March 2, 1998, article, Phelan described his
contacts with Ron Gold, a former special agent for Army Intelligence, who did
numerous interviews confirming what Phelan wrote in his earlier article. Phelan also reported what he learned from other investigators.

In his March 2nd article, Phelan described his interview with Legal Advocate Melissa Buckles for the Assiniboine-Sioux tribe on the Fort Peck Indian
Reservation in Montana. During this interview, she described the many drug
airplanes and helicopters landing at night at the remote Indian reservation, the
many drug-related killings occurring on the reservation, and her charge that
FBI agents in the Glasgow, Montana office were involved with protecting the
drug operations. She described the coverups by the Billings Bureau of Indian
Affairs office, and similar drug activities at other Montana Indian reservations
including Fort Belknap. She described a letter Gold sent to FBI Director Louis
Freeh on December 15, 1997, and never answered. That letter stated in part:

> *1. South Florida FBI Agent Terry Nelson is a target of an internal
> agency investigation....The drug smuggling
> operation occurred in flight routes to Nova Scotia and Chapeau Airfield
> in Quebec; then over to Weyburn, Saskatchewan and down into North Da-
> kota and Montana. The major shipping zones in Montana were Sidney,
> Chinook, Havre and clandestine airstrips on the Fort Peck Tribal Lands.
> Alternative routes into Eureka, Libby, Whitefish, and Shelby may also
> have been used.*

> *3. Corrupt Montana authorities in Chinook, Sidney and the Fort Peck
> tribal lands coordinated protection of the smuggling operations. A promi-
> nent Montana state official received payments into accounts in the Helena
> Norwest Bank branch in conjunction with the multi-ton shipments of Co-
> lombian Cali-cartel heroin and cocaine.*

> *6. FBI agents operating out of the Glasgow office assisted the Nelson
> smuggling operations and involved Fort Peck tribal police as well as
> other tribal members in illicit activities.*

> *10. Two Glasgow FBI agents involved in the drug operation likely
> compromised dozens of investigations on the Fort Peck and Fort Belknap
> tribal lands. Witnesses are available and have information directly linking
> the Glasgow FBI agents and other officials to drug related activities and
> violent civil rights abuses.*

In other parts of her letter, she described the many murders of people exposing
the drug-related activities, including forty people murdered on one reservation
alone. She added, "There are people in Montana who are clearly scared and
are begging for help." Freeh never responded to her letter and none of the witnesses were contacted.

FBI Director Coverup: What Else Is Not New!

Buckles wrote a letter to U.S. Attorney General Janet Reno, making reference to Gold's letter to Freeh, the failure of the FBI Director to respond, and
then gave details of the serious drug smuggling problems and the involvement

of Montana and FBI agents in the trafficking. She never received a response.

Coast Guard Intelligence Officer Supported the Findings

Another person interviewed by *Washington Weekly* investigator Phelan was David Hume, a former police officer and former intelligence officer with the U.S. Coast Guard from 1978 to 1991. Hume confirmed the southbound flow of drugs from Canada into Montana, adding, the drugs from Colombia "go out as far east as Bermuda and then go up to Nova Scotia. Then they would come south and be able to off-load their drugs." Hume talked about the minimal or lack of radar coverage that permits aircraft to fly undetected from Canada into Montana. He confirmed Weyburn, Saskatchewan, as being a key drug transshipment point. He wrote:

> *My sources all agree that many state and local officials in Montana, and many agents of the federal government, are involved in one way or another with smuggling drugs into the state. These claims are not new, nor are my sources the only ones making them.*

Further provocative information is provided by the following letter:

DARBY HEINZ
PRIVATE INVESTIGATOR

NORWEST BANK OF HELENA   04-12-99
Dennis Hansen
350 N. Last Chance Gulch
Helene, MT 59601
    Phone (406) 447-2000 ext. 2026   <u>Sent via US Mail</u>
    Re: Wire Transfer Funds/Norwest Bank of Helena
Dear Mr. Hansen:

    I have received information concerning the electronic transfer of funds to the Norwest Bank of Helena from offshore accounts. The funds originate in the Swiss financial institution Banque Swisse and are traced to your branch. My information indicates that the fund may be linked to international drug smuggling and laundering from Canada by a Colombian group linked to Cali/Medellin cartel member Fabio Ochoa. Additionally, the funds may have been illegally in Swiss account/accounts without proper declaration and identification for U.S. tax purposes.

    My major source is concerned because of the sensitivity of the matter, and the safety of several of the witnesses could be jeopardized and requests that the matter be referred to federal authorities or investigators outside the State of Montana. My source is prepared to co-operate with the authorities and co-ordinate efforts with other witnesses, provided that they are recognized and protected according to law. It is my understanding that wire fraud transfer records exist which substantiate these claims.

    I am prepared to meet with investigators or the appropriate federal agency immediately in regards to the above.

Very Truly yours,

Darby Hinz

CHAPTER ELEVEN

AIRLINE PILOT TO UNDERCOVER AGENT

Richard Pitt filled the void left by Matthews' departure. He left the good life as a pilot for United Airlines, looking for adventure and excitement, which he definitely found; far more than he expected: Danger-filled drug flights, gun fights at remote jungle strips, tortured and imprisoned in Mexico, and more. In the end, he was sabotaged, like Matthews, by government agents when he learned too much about government involvement in drugs and as he was about to inflict serious harm upon a major drug cartel.

First, a little history. Pitt was born on an Indian reservation in Sundance, Wyoming on March 31, 1949, not far from his Sioux Indian heritage. He was adopted by his aunt and uncle at six months of age and raised in Thermopolis, Wyoming. It was a hard life. He developed a strong interest in aviation at an early age and learned to fly at local airports. He joined the Air Force and became a C-130 pilot and flight instructor. Upon leaving the military, he was employed as a pilot for United Airlines from 1977 to 1986. Because of his Air Force instructor experience teaching aircraft systems, United Airlines used him as a DC-8 flight instructor.

United Airlines Tragedy-Associated Corruption Changed My Life
Ironically, in 1962 I had completed my pilot training at the same United Airlines DC-8 ground and flight training center while I was an inspector for the Federal Aviation Administration. Inspecting the safety of that DC-8 and other United Airlines' programs then became my primary responsibility. Although the initial training program, Pitt's area of flight activities, was excellent, the annual training and competency checks conducted by United's Flight Standards was tragically corrupt. The great number of crashes and deaths resulting from this misconduct were evidence of that fact. (This area is detailed in the third edition of *Unfriendly Skies*.)

It was this corruption at United Airlines, and that which I discovered in the Federal Aviation Administration, that caused me to become a crusader for the next 30 years. It was my assignment to United's crash-plagued program that *started* years of grief for me. For Pitt, his grief began after *leaving* the UAL DC-8 assignment. In a peculiar way, United Airlines played a part in both of our stories.

After Pitt read *Unfriendly Skies*, he wrote that some of the events described in the book brought back memories of events he had almost forgotten: "Your book tells me a lot about what was going on around me that I saw and heard."

From Airline Pilot to Meeting America's Craving for Drugs

Wanting excitement and adventure, Pitt took a leave of absence from his job as an airline pilot and flight instructor and began transporting marijuana from Mexico into the United States. This role required living in run-down border towns such as Ciudad Juarez, Nuevo Laredo and Matamoros. He met smalltime Mexican marijuana traffickers, some of whom are heads of major drug cartels today.

After discovering that Jamaica had better and cheaper marijuana, Pitt shifted his operations away from Mexico. He was successful and, in time, his success at transporting drugs caught the eyes of top Colombian drug lords, who asked Pitt to fly loads of cocaine for them, which he did.

Huge Profits In Meeting the Demand

Pitt said there were huge profits in transporting drugs into the United States from Central and South America in the early 1980s. The standard fee paid to pilots was $4000 per kilo and he would sometimes gross over $2 million for 16 to 20 hours' work transporting from 300 to 600 kilos (660 to 1320 pounds) of cocaine. It was great; he was well paid and he was meeting the demands of U.S. drug consumers. Is it any wonder that pilots took the risks associated with transporting drugs? But Pitt said it wasn't the money that attracted him to this high-risk activity; it was the excitement. He spent or gave the money away as fast as it came in.

Pitt told how he and his wife Patti traveled to South America, Europe, Hawaii, Cabo San Lucas, Acapulco, and other places, and took entire families with them on completely paid-for vacations, traveling first class. He described how he lavishly gave money to others. Whoever had the biggest sob story. If someone couldn't make their house payment, he would pay off the mortgage. If someone had trouble making a car payment, he would pay off the car loan. His wife Patti, a beautiful model and singer who married Pitt in November 1979 while he was working at United Airlines, was furious at him for his money habits. She could not understand giving money to friends to pay off their cars or home mortgages, especially when they still had a mortgage on their own relatively modest house in Denver.

Patti frequently shouted, "Richard, can't you see these people are just using you?" Pitt said, "Sometimes she would take a swing at me over it. I'd duck, and she would miss. Other times she'd connect, and the shock of that hit at the end of her little fist would seem to vibrate through her arm, down her body, and then resonate in her high heels. She'd then turn and walk off all huffy."

Patti went into the bedroom one day and saw what a million dollars looked like. Their baby, Kailie, had crawled under the bed and pulled out a box containing the money. She playfully spread it all over the bedroom floor.

America's Drug Consumers Fueling U.S. Commerce

Pitt described how America's drug users funded vast industries throughout South and Central America and the United States. He told how the drug consumers fuel Miami's economy, including real estate agents, jewelry stores, banks, aircraft dealers, night clubs. All receive a share of the narco dollars. Pitt told of the $22,000-a-night parties in Miami, more than he ever spent during his years in Wyoming's sheepherder country where he grew up. Pitt said he was on a first-name basis with almost all the major jewelry stores in Miami and Fort Lauderdale. There was a standing joke among his friends that if a girl in Miami wore a $10,000 Rolex watch, she must be one of Richard's girlfriends.

Pitt discovered how America's drug users fund bribes to government personnel throughout Central and South America, Mexico, and the United States. The money funds the drug cartels, the drug transporters, and all types of violent and non-violent criminal activities. Surely some type of monument should be erected to America's drug users!

Dangerous Flying Conditions

The huge income from transporting drugs for America's drug users was partly offset by the hazards. Pitt experienced crashes as he flew heavily loaded aircraft into and out of short airstrips, crashes due to fuel being water-contaminated, and crashes due to soft ground that hindered the aircraft's acceleration to flying speed. In addition to the plane crashes, he encountered gun battles with machine-gun wielding bandits at remote landing strips, danger associated with flying long distances at night barely ten feet over the water so as to avoid detection by radar, and other problems.

Two of his contacts in Colombia, Alonzo Cardenas and a guy named Carlos, told Pitt about an American pilot who was killed a few days earlier in Colombia. A few men from a small village seventy miles south of Cartagena, on the west side of the 1000-mile-long Magdalena River, had come across an airstrip cut out of the jungle. When a Beech Queenair aircraft arrived, the group killed the pilot and all but one of the loading crew. They then burned the plane, and became the owners of 300 kilos of cocaine. Pitt explained:

Meanwhile, the one living member of the Ochoa's ground loading crew made it back to Medellin, half alive, and reported the deed that had befallen them. The Ochoas, along with a younger, soon-to-be Senator Pablo Escobar, and an entourage of pistoleres, headed for the strip. A trail of plainly visible hoof prints from horses and mules led directly to the small village some fifteen miles further south.

According to Alonzo, who was also there, questions were asked of the first two villagers the cartel came upon. Their legs were shot out from under them, and then they were asked if they knew anything about a burned airplane and missing cocaine. Needless to say, they did. The whole town was rounded up, some two hundred people. I don't know if that included children or their mothers; but I do know from what Carlos and Alonzo told me, all the men were shot after confessing, as an example to future enthusiastic entrepreneurs. The rest of the people were told politely to pack up and resettle their town much further down the road, which they did.

The army in Colombia was another problem. Through a simple mix-up with the Colombian army in 1981 at Aracataco, a contingent of Colombian soldiers descended upon the landing strip where Pitt had landed a short time earlier and began shooting. Pitt jumped into a ditch for cover, not knowing that the soldiers were shooting above his head. They then seized the drugs and personal possessions located in the aircraft-—and also took the prized elephant-skin cowboy boots he was wearing. Eventually the Army commander, who was on the drug lords' payroll, heard about the attack and ordered the soldiers to return the things they had taken—including Pitt's boots.

In one incident, while flying a Cessna 404 Titan, Pitt got caught in a major thunderstorm over the interior of Colombia and had to divert from his planned landing at a remote airstrip to a combination civilian-military field at Tenerife. On the west end of the field was a crop duster operation and at the other end a military detachment. After landing, with the engines shut down and the aircraft lights off, he tried unsuccessfully to call Alonzo Cardenas who was waiting for him at the destination airstrip. The mountain range separating Pitt from Cardenas caused the high frequency 7270 kilocycle signal to skip over the location where Cardenas was waiting. Pitt then called home in Coral Gables, Florida, where his brother Tony was supposed to be waiting for a radio call in the event any problems arose.

His wife, Patti, answered. "Hi, honey, what are you doing and where are you?" She didn't know Pitt was out of town, let alone out of the country on a remote airstrip a thousand miles from home. Pitt instructed Patti to call Cardenas on the same frequency, advising Cardenas to switch to another frequency which would enable them to communicate with each other. This was done, and Pitt told Cardenas that he was down safe and that he would go to the intended landing strip at sunup.

"Please Come Again"

Pitt took off the next morning before sunrise, proceeding to the intended landing airstrip. Cardenas, not knowing that Pitt had already taken off, and worried that the military might arrest Pitt, rushed to the airport to pay off the right people. Cardenas paid $10,000 to the puzzled commander of the small garrison to forget the matter. The officer did not even know Pitt had been there. With the commander and a few of his soldiers in tow, Cardenas then went to the crop-duster operation where Pitt spent the night, paying them $10,000. They all responded that it would be fine for the American plane to stay overnight anytime.

Government personnel throughout Central and South America demanded and received bribes to protect drug traffickers, funded by the "Yankee" drug dollars. These people received money beyond their fondest dreams by allowing drugs to flow through their countries, and this especially included Mexico. It is easy to understand how people throughout the world have their lives and entire economies of some countries funded by America's drug users.

Pitt's Luck Runs Out; Mexico's Biggest Drug Bust At That Time

Pitt's luck ran out in September 1982. While his plane was being refueled at a Mexican airstrip, Palenque Chiapas, near the archeological ruins at Palenque National Lagunas de Montebello, and while paying off a local Mexican army captain as he had done in the past, along came another army detachment, headed by a major who was not on Pitt's list of bribed officials. The major wanted to look at the aircraft, and when he did, he discovered the 600 kilos (1320-pound) cocaine load from the Pablo Escobar and Ochoa families that Pitt was transporting from Colombia to the United States. Pitt, and four people with him, including Mike Culler, were then arrested. It was ironic for anyone to be arrested for transporting drugs in a country that is awash with drug activity today. But Pitt was not a Mexican; he was a "gringo" from the United States. The Mexican newspapers at the time reported the arrest as the largest cocaine smuggling arrest in Mexican history. Pitt explained:

I was arrested an hour later when he [Mexican Major] saw what was on the plane. Trying to protect the lower level Mexican captain, I told him that the captain had no idea what was in the plane. The Americans arrested with me were Scott James, Gayla Steffin, Mike Culler, and Alfonso Santana, a Mexican national educated at Berkeley, and who spoke English better than you and I.

We had been using the Mexican army and some of Mexico's remote strips in the Yucatan Peninsula to refuel, so as to carry larger [drug] loads. I had recruited a Mexican army captain and his squad of ten men to help us by providing protection in Tulum. For a year and a half everything went fine. Finally, he was transferred to the ruins (Mayan) at Palenque Chiapas.

We moved there with him on our next run, and upon landing, I lost the right brake in my Cessna 404 Titan, almost running off the end of the short paved runway. We were all gathered around the plane trying to fix it, when a convoy of another group of soldiers led by a Major out of Villahermosa Tabasco passed by. Due to the activity at the far end of the field, he turned onto the airport, down the runway, and stopped to check it out. He outranked the captain.

Mexican Police Brutality

Mexican police tied Pitt with rope, placed a bag over his head, and drove him to a Mexican prison, keeping Pitt in a hog-tied position for the next 24 hours. During the night he heard the other captives moaning with pain. Pitt was developing "charlie-horses" in his shoulders that were knotting up periodically with excruciating pain. As one of the Mexican guards entered the room, Mike Culler yelled out, "Chinga tu madre pendejo Puto," a very derogatory term. This caused the guard to hit Mike in the head with a rifle butt, putting him into even worse pain. Pitt said that he believes Mexican police torture all prisoners to "set the atmosphere as to who is boss." Mexican police inflicted six days of electric shock and other torture tactics upon Pitt and his group.

Mexican Police and Officials Wanted Part of the Action

They questioned Pitt on where he had gotten the drugs and from whom. They weren't interested in where the drugs were going. He later learned that the head of the federal police in Mexico City, Florentina Ventura, wanted to sell government protection for drug loads going through Mexico, something that Pitt said that Ventura and other Mexican government personnel subsequently did on a regular basis. Pitt said:

I had no idea at the time that's what he wanted. If I would have known, I'd quickly have given the names and addresses along with phone numbers so he could call the Ochoa's and Alonzo Cardenas. Remember, at that time [1980-1982] I was probably the very first drug smuggler to be routing (staging) through Mexico. He was crooked, but unfortunately for me, inexperienced with the cocaine and the Colombians. He was not up on how to directly come out and ask for direct involvement in this business. There were over 20 agents in the room including the Mayor of Mexico City. It was the largest bust of cocaine in Mexican history at that time. It was 600 kilos, but only 343 were reported. The rest was stolen by the authorities.

Life in A Mexican Prison

Pitt, who had earlier enjoyed all types of luxuries, received a 12-year prison sentence and was placed in one of Mexico's worst prisons: Cerro Hueco prison in Tuxtla Gutierrez Chiapas. Pitt said the prison did not furnish prisoners with food, clothes, housing, or medical aid. Prisoners were placed in a large prison yard, surrounded by a 12-foot stone wall, and expected to make their own shelter, relying upon outside friends and relatives for food and other necessities.

Mexican Prisons Resemble A Zoo

Pitt said Mexican prisons are like a zoo. The "zoo keepers" or guards stay on the outside and the prisoners stay on the inside. Under these conditions, thievery and violence are rampant among the prisoners. "The tremendous psychological impact and trauma I suffered with that one singular solitary event," said Pitt, "is almost impossible to put into words."

Planning for Spectacular Aviation Stunt

While Pitt and Culler were in the Mexican prison, Culler told Pitt about the spectacular beauty of Angel Falls in Venezuela, a drop of over 3,000 feet. Both Culler and Pitt were world-class skydivers at the time, and both had run skydiving clubs. Other people had sought government permission to make parachute jumps off the falls but government officials refused all requests. Having worked with government officials in Colombia and Mexico, Pitt felt that he could get clearance in Venezuela by simply paying off the right people. Pitt decided that when he was free he would try it.

Escape Plans

Pitt and Culler came up with various escape plans. One night, one of the Mexican prisoners, Amilicar Constantino, came running to Pitt's prison cubicle, shouting in rapid Spanish, which Pitt could not understand. The big Mexican literally pulled Pitt outside, and standing there in the rain, drunk, was Mike Culler, with a long length of one-inch galvanized pipe trying to vault over the prison wall. Two guards were on the wall with their guns leveled at Culler. To save Culler from being shot, Pitt tackled him to the ground. The next day, after Culler recovered, a more sensible escape plan was decided upon.

Escape From Prison

On December 12, 1982, during the biggest fiesta in all of Mexico called Mother of Guadalupe, Pitt and Culler escaped while the guards were drunk. Pitt explained, "Mexicans have a party for everything, including holidays, and even one called the Day-of-the-Prisoner." Pitt managed to get all the guards drunk by using his last $360 to buy liquor for them. After the drinking had gone on for some time and the guards inebriated, Pitt shorted out the prison's primitive electrical system. Pitt and Culler then went over the wall using two hammocks tied together and fastened to a hook that was caught on the top of the 12-foot wall.

For the next week they hiked 70 miles through the jungle of Chiapas to Villahermosa, Tobasco. One morning, Pitt and Culler swam a river flowing from the Sumadaro Canyon, not knowing it was infested with crocodiles. Making his way back to Denver, Pitt returned to the drug transportation business that had been interrupted during his short three-month stay in the Mexican prison.

Expanding into Other Businesses

During the time Pitt was in the drug hauling business he found the time, and he had the money, for other business ventures. As his business grew, he added more planes and pilots. At one time in 1983, he had eleven aircraft and two helicopters, including a DC-3. Five of these planes were used for drug transportation. The planes included a Cessna 404 Titan, Cessna 421, Piper Aztec, Aero Commander 500, and Aero Commander 690 turboprop. The helicopters included a Bell Jet Ranger 206B and a Hughes 500D.

Putting Together A Team of Top Skydivers

Pitt purchased the DC-3 in Oshkosh, Wisconsin, from Bassler Flight Service. He obtained an FAA type rating to fly it, and then put together a team of top skydivers, including Mike Schultz, Jerry Bird, Ron Eurton, and Don Caltweet. Schultz, six foot three, had attended Georgetown University and has several degrees behind him. He had made over 8000 parachute jumps and taught in the Delta Force compound in North Carolina, teaching parachute jumps from high altitude with low altitude parachute opening. Bird, an ex-Green Beret, did work for the SAS in England. Pitt used the DC-3 extensively for hauling sky-divers from 1983 to 1986 throughout the eastern United States. Pitt explained the sky-diving activities never made any money, but he did it in appreciation for the help that the skydiving community provided him as he was learning to fly over-grossed planes off short dirt strips and building up his flight hours.

Making Films For Commercials

He owned Mark III Studios in North Miami, Florida that had over $3 million in equipment. The studio made films for commercials such as Water Bed City, "See Miami Now" for the Florida Tourist Bureau, cruise ship commercials, various rock group videos, Miami Zoo commercials, Sea World on Key Biscayne, and many others. Pitt said that this studio was the first to start the NFL football recruiting videos for prospective draftees into pro-football.

Producing Movies and Writing Lyrics

Pitt was the founder of First American Entertaining in Fort Lauderdale, producing movies, the first one called "Master Blasters," for which he wrote the lyrics for the musical score. Pitt wrote the lyrics for the song, "It's a Dirty Job," and others. He wrote "Love Song" for his daughter, Kailie, who was five years old at the time. He wrote his own lyrics along with Alain Salvati, who worked for Pitt at that time. Pitt said Alain was a pro in the recording studio business and had done recordings and music arrangements for the Bee Gees, Julio Iglesias, and had the number-one hit in France a few years ago.

Pitt owned "Awesome Force" in London, England, and made a movie called "Black Panther," with Ian Merrick. The company did Englebert Humperdinck concerts at the Royal Albert Hall in London in 1985. Pitt did skydiving stunts for "Master Blasters," and set up a DC-3 to be cartwheeled for the movie, "Good Morning Vietnam," obtaining FAA approval from the Miami FAA Flight Standards District Office in March 1985.

Drug Trafficker Helping Fund Nancy Reagan's Anti-Drug Concert

Pitt gave money to old folks' homes around Miami and Fort Lauderdale. He took boxes of five and ten-dollar bills that none of the drug traffickers wanted and threw them out the car window while driving at night through Miami's skid-row district. Once, in 1985, through one of his attorneys, Anthony Storn, he gave a $50,000 check to help finance the Nancy Reagan anti-drug concert at the Kennedy Center in Washington, D.C.

Carrying Out His Plan to Parachute off Angel Falls

Pitt was now ready to carry out his plan to jump off Angel Falls. With the team and equipment assembled, Pitt headed to Angel Falls via Caracas, Venezuela and to Canaima, where Angel Falls is located. In Venezuela, Pitt hired several local skydivers, one whose father was head of Venezuela's secret police. Pitt chartered a Hughes 500D helicopter in Caracas and flew it to Angel Falls. A jungle camp was set up by a German named "Jungle Rudy." Putting this plan together cost Pitt over $40,000. This included paying Jungle Rudy for a week's room and board, airline tickets for everyone, renting a helicopter, paying for five other Venezuelans and their girlfriends to come along, party supplies, Indian guides who worked for Rudy, canoes to move supplies up the river from the main camp to the base camp at the foot of the falls, and the entourage of cameramen and equipment that were brought from Miami. Almost six hours of film was taken, which was cut down to three minutes for television viewing.

Into The Guinness Book of World Records

Pitt explained that the jungle was three-layers thick and inside you could hardly see daylight. This is the area that had to be cleared for the helicopter to land. Mike Schultz suggested that two of Jungle Rudy's Indian guides be lowered from a rope off the side of the helicopter. Schultz, standing on the skids outside the door-less Hughes helicopter, yelled for the Indians to come out and slide down the rope. The Indians, who had never been in a helicopter before and who had been anxious for a ride, suddenly lost their eagerness once the helicopter was over the drop zone. They took one look at the distance from the helicopter to the ground, saw the wildly gyrating rope that they had to slide down, and refused to go. Schultz took their machetes away from them and threw them into the jungle trees below. He gave the Indians the choice of going with the rope or without one. They went down the rope. Four hours later, the landing zone was cleared. A base camp was set up at the bottom of the 3,000-foot falls. The jump was filmed the next day, with Pitt making the first jump. The film was later shown on "That's Incredible," and Ripley's "Believe It or Not," and the event was placed into the 1985 Guinness Book of World Records.

Richard Pitt

Becoming Friends and Guest of Major Colombian Drug Lords

Pitt's reputation as a transporter of drugs propelled him into the higher echelons of the drug trade. Pitt had several key Colombian friends who also facilitated Pitt's entry into the drug cartels. One was Jorge Ortiz Restrepo, the nephew of a wealthy Colombian, with whom Pitt was in the Mexican prison. Another was Alonzo Cardenas, a young Colombian pilot whose wife, Angelina, was one of Ochoa's daughters. Pitt gave Alonzo advanced training in flying helicopters and fixed-wing aircraft, including auto-rotations in Alonzo's Hughes 500 helicopters, of which his family had seven.

Pitt and Alonzo frequently flew to various locations in Colombia, including Leticia where many drug labs were located. Pitt said that Alonzo Cardenas was the real brains behind the Ochoa and Pablo Escobar families. Pitt was a month-long houseguest of Alonzo and Angelina Cardenas Ochoa in Medellin, Colombia and at their house on the coast.

U.S. Military Flying Drugs from Secret Colombian Airstrips Owned by Ochoa-Escobar Families

Alonzo told Pitt about U.S. military planes flying drug loads from Central and South America into the United States. For years, many of my CIA, FBI, DEA and other sources described U.S. military drug smuggling. Pitt had trouble accepting this as true until he landed several weeks later at one of the ranches owned by the Ochoa-Escobar families on the north coast of Colombia about 70 air miles south of Cartagena. Just prior to touchdown on this dirt airstrip used by drug-laden airplanes, Pitt passed close to a cargo C-123 aircraft with U.S. military markings and could clearly see the crew in military uniforms. "It blew my mind," he said.

Kidnapping Ochoa's Sister

Pitt frequently took Angelina Cardenas Ochoa and her children on flights if the destination was the Ochoa ranch south of Cartagena. Another sister, Leona Ochoa, was kidnapped in the early 1980s by Colombia's M-19 guerrillas. I asked Pitt if he knew of Leona's kidnapping, which I described in the third edition of *Defrauding America*. Pitt said, "I remember it because Carlos, my middleman in Miami from 1979 to 1982, commented on it. At the time, Carlos had told him, 'Boy, the M-19 group has sure pissed-off the Ochoas.'" Pitt went into more detail:

> One story was how they all had a meeting at the Intercontinental Hotel, and also, at the restaurant, just above the Intercontinental Hotel called Carlos. It was and probably still is, a really nice place, with good food; a plush eating place. I've only eaten there twice, both times were back in the early eighties. It was due to this kidnapping of Leona Ochoa by the M-19 guerrilla group, that the seven or so main families (running 95 percent of all the cocaine at that time into the United States), decided to sit down and have a pow-wow. They were getting bigger and richer. Colombians, since no one knows when, have been kidnapping one another to put food on the table through ransom money.
>
> My good friend, Alonzo Cardenas, Angelina's husband, was at that meeting. I never really paid that much attention to it, it wasn't important to me at the time. So consequently, I only heard and remember parts of it

through idle talk. The families decided to work together in a cartel that would share information, some loads, but most of all, protection.

The government of Colombia, the military, had been after the M-19 group for years, plus a few other groups depending on what part of the country you lived in. All these years the government had not been able to stamp out the various guerrilla groups. The cartels in a few weeks, with all their resources, almost accomplished this goal, until the M-19 yelled "uncle."

The big mistake for the M-19, according to Alonzo and Carlos, was the day they decided to snatch Leona. What the military couldn't do, the newly formed Medellin Cartel did. M-19 got its slate cleaned once the Cartel went after it. A lot of people got killed, and according to Carlos, M-19 handed Leona back to the Ochoas and the Medellin Cartel, along with the necessary apologies. It wouldn't surprise me that the CIA had something in some way to do with it all. It's just that this is the story and the way Leona's brother-in-law told it to me backed up by Carlos here in Florida at that time.

Ten years earlier CIA operative Gunther Russbacher told me about the CIA's role in arranging this meeting and about the kidnapping, which is described in more detail in the third edition of *Defrauding America*. Another one of my sources who I described in earlier pages, Russell Bowen, flew the CIA-provided DC-3 that transported Leona to a remote location where she was held until her release.

Working with Four Major Colombian Drug Cartels

Pitt worked with the four major Colombian drug organizations: the Cali Cartel (headed by the Orejuela brothers); the Medellin Cartel (headed by the Ochoa Family, Juan, Jorge, Angelina and Fabio); the Bogota Cartel (headed by the Moncadas family), and the Cartagena Cartel (headed by Don Edwardo). Pitt said the Orejuela brothers took control after Escobar went on the run in 1989. Pitt explained that most of the cartels avoided the publicity that focused on Pablo Escobar and Carlos Lehder and which led to their demise. Don Arnulfo worked directly for Angela Ochoa, who ran the family drug business out of Medellin while her brothers were in a Bogota prison. Don Arcesio handled some of the drug shipments for the drug producers operating out of Cali, Colombia.

Florida Indictment for Pitt

While Pitt was flying into and out of the United States, with his wife Patti living in Denver, two of Pitt's former drug trafficking associates, Mike Culler from Spokane, Washington, and Chuck Greenfield from Miami, made an unscheduled landing near Daytona Beach while hauling drugs. The electrical system on the Cessna 404 Titan failed after the plane was struck by lightning. If they had read the flight manual, they would have realized that they could have restored the electrical power by turning the master switch off and then on. They called Pitt at his Miami residence for the loan of his car, which was then used to carry the drugs from the plane to their intended Miami destination. Pitt didn't play any role in the drug shipment except to loan a car to a friend. Under law, that made him a part of the conspiracy to haul drugs, and subject to whatever length of imprisonment was provided by the amount of the drugs that the drug traffickers were hauling.

That load got through, but they were later arrested in the Bahamas and extradited to Miami. In an attempt to have the charges dropped, Culler and Greenfield named over a hundred people they claimed were in the drug business. Pitt was among the ones they named, based upon the car that they borrowed from him a year earlier. Florida obtained an arrest warrant for Pitt.

"Don't Hurt My Mommie!"

The warrant was carried out at Pitt's home in Denver while Pitt's wife Patti and their daughter were home alone. In typical thug-like fashion, a multi-agency paramilitary force seeking Pitt broke down the door, stormed into the hose, and threw Pitt's wife, Patti, onto the floor. Her little three-year old daughter cried, "Don't hurt my mommie!" Pitt wasn't there, so no arrest was made, and the extradition warrant from Florida was forgotten.

First American Extradited to Mexico

On the basis of an extradition request from Mexico, another arrest was attempted and this time Pitt was arrested in Denver (July 22, 1985). The Mexican extradition request was based upon his prior escape from the Mexican prison. Pitt said at that time there hadn't been any Americans extradited to Mexico from the United States and that the extradition treaty between Mexico and the United States had just recently been signed. He said that Secretary of State George Schultz personally signed the papers extraditing him to Mexico. Pitt said Denver's U.S. District Judge Schuster hesitated to order Pitt extradited because of the documented torture inflicted upon prisoners in Mexican prisons and the fact Pitt had previously been tortured there.

The U.S. government wanted him extradited to Mexico in a prisoner exchange for Rafael Caro Quintero, a big-time Guadalajara drug trafficker who had recently killed U.S. DEA agent Kiki Camarena in January 1985. The DEA went all out to show the world that no one kills an American agent and gets away with it.

Pitt learned from several sources, including United Airlines pilot Jamie Lindsey, and from a Congressman in Washington who spoke with his attorney, Norm Pacheco, that U.S. officials approached Mexico and said, "We give you an American and you give us a Mexican, preferably Caro Quintero." The Mexicans outsmarted the United States: Mexico got Pitt, but the United States got no one. Quintero did end up in Reclusorio Oriente Prison in Mexico City and Pitt felt Quintero would stay in prison a long time because he knew too much about high-level government involvement in drug trafficking. Pitt said:

Even Ventura Fonseca's son, who escorted me back to Mexico City from Denver on December 5, 1986, told me, "The United States does not tell us what to do. They will never get Quintero." He meant that, I knew, as he looked me square in the eyes. So, even though I had escaped from a Mexican prison on the night of December 12, 1982, I never would have been caught up in this international playing of pawns and exchanging of citizens if it had not been for Kiki Camarena playing Rambo in a country that did not, and still does not, want to be messed with, as far as drugs are concerned.

Attorney Problems

Pitt had hired Denver attorney Norm Pacheco to block the extradition, but the attorney was not competent to handle the matter, knowing nothing about extradition, and only wanting money. Pitt said that when friends gave the attorney $12,000 to send to Pitt in the Mexican prison, the attorney kept the money for himself.

Pitt explained that the first one and a half years in the Mexican prison were very rough because he was kept in solitary for this entire period. It was considered one of Mexico's worst prisons. As punishment for having escaped in 1982, prison authorities put Pitt into the "hole, which was infested with rats as big as a small cat. An open sewer system with an incredibly bad odor flowed through the cell. There were no electrical light sockets or bulbs, and only a short section of electrical wire where a ceiling bulb and fixture had once been located.

Reducing the Rat Population

To reduce the number of rats entering his cell, Pitt improvised a method to electrocute them. At night, he pulled the electrical wire out of the wall and ran it over to the metal cell door. He splashed water on the bottom of the door, which caused the rats coming in under the door to be electrocuted. This worked fine until one morning Pitt forgot to disconnect the wire from the door. As one of the guards checked on him during prisoner count and grabbed the bars on the door to look into the cell, the electrical shock caused him to yell with a high-pitched scream. That was the end of Pitt's anti-rat prevention device. The electrical wire was removed from the cell.

During his isolation in the "hole" Pitt came out only every three months when people from the U.S. Embassy in Mexico City made their periodic visits. After Pitt was released from solitary and entered the prison population, he had to build his own shelter out of scrap wood and boxes.

The prison population consisted of over 1000 Mexican prisoners, mostly Mayan and Aztec Indians. Absence of food during Pitt's initial imprisonment caused his weight to drop from 205 down to 156 pounds.

Fight To the Death

Pitt lost the use of his left thumb after a mentally impaired prisoner attempted to kill him. Pitt explained, "His kick in life was to sneak up on people while they were sleeping and slit their throat, just to watch them bleed." This prisoner stuck a knife in Pitt's back, but a leather weight-lifting belt under his shirt prevented the knife from penetrating. Feeling the knife's pressure, Pitt woke up and fought him off. The Mexican dropped the knife and began chasing Pitt with a crowbar. Pitt grabbed a three-foot-long pipe and subsequently killed his attacker.

Living Like A King in Prison

Somewhat of an exaggeration, Pitt said he lived like a king in prison, compared to the other inmates. Pitt's brother, Tony, brought money to Pitt every few months, enabling him to buy "luxuries" other prisoners could not afford. Tony brought him weight-lifting books from which Pitt duplicated several Nautilus machines using a welder that he obtained from outside the prison. He made a complete gym that became the center of attraction at the prison.

Strangers from nearby Tuxtla came just to talk to Pitt—the gringo—and to look at the gym equipment Pitt had built, something that was superior to what most of them had or that was available in any gym in the city. Dave Guinn, the retired United Airlines pilot with an orphanage west of Tuxtla, wanted a set for his kids. Even Mexican drug smugglers visited Pitt, seeking information on how they could sell drugs in the United States. To broaden his interest, Pitt started painting the prison. He painted his "cell" inside and out, and then started painting the prison entrance. He was asked to paint the inside of the adjacent women's prison, and spent more time there than in the regular prison area.

One Thing Favorable about Mexican Prisons

Pitt explained there were some benefits a Mexican prison has over prisons in the United States. Wives, children, or girlfriends can come to the prison and stay overnight. If the family could not afford a place in town, they could stay with the prisoner. In time, Pitt became friends with a 24-year-old woman named Beatrice who worked as a prison psychologist. Eventually she quit her job and moved in with him. In 1998 she lived in Miami with a son from that relationship, working on a Ph.D. in psychology. He thought she was one of the most intelligent, fun loving women he had ever met.

"Doctor Pitt"

There were virtually no medical facilities at the prison, motivating Pitt to became the de facto "doctor." This included sewing up prisoners who were cut in fights. Mexican prisoners were free to possess knives for cutting the meat brought to them by friends or families outside, and machetes to cut the lawn. Fights would occasionally erupt and these knives were used. Pitt said fights would start from a bad call in a soccer game or when inmates started drinking their homemade brew called "la chiche" made from pineapples.

Final Release from Mexican Custody

Pitt's original 12-year prison sentence was reduced on appeal, and on February 28, 1992, he was released. The order for Pitt's release was dated November 22, 1991, but the Mexican authorities never got to Pitt until three months later, at which time they transported him to the airport for return to the United States.

Before Pitt was released he had been contacted by DEA agent Jack Bax from Reno, Nevada, seeking Pitt's help in making contacts with DEA targets in Mexico. Because of Pitt's contacts in Central and South America, Bax told Pitt the DEA would like Pitt to be a "confidential informant" (CI) and sell chemicals for processing heroin and cocaine to drug smugglers in Mexico, Guatemala, and Belize. This operation was eventually canceled, as drug processors were able to get an unlimited amount of chemicals from Europe, primarily Germany.

Watching the Evolution of the Drug Business

Pitt said he had seen the drug business change from a relatively violence-free environment in the United States to one of great violence, and wanted nothing more to do with it. His plan was to not return to drug trafficking. Events changed, and he did return, but this time working for the U.S. government to bring about the arrest of those engaging in drug trafficking. He filled the void left by Matthews.

Debriefed By U.S. Attorney

Upon return to the United States, Pitt was debriefed by Assistant U.S. Attorney Gail Connely from Tampa, Florida, a normal practice when Americans imprisoned in a foreign country return to the United States. After the debriefing, Florida Department of Law Enforcement (FDLE) agents offered Pitt an opportunity to work as a contract undercover agent, which Pitt did for a short time. Because state agents were not authorized to handle international operations for which Pitt was most useful, he was reassigned to the Fort Lauderdale DEA office. Pitt said he found the office manager, Cindy Schultz, difficult to work for, adding she was "The only agent I ever met that should never have been allowed to have a badge, let alone a driver's license." (Politically-correct hiring?)

Directions and Authority, But No Funding

Pitt was penniless after his release from the Mexican prison. Pitt had become friends with Dr. Barry Becker and his wife Pat who owned a string of dental offices in Florida, and who had a strong interest in combating the drug problem. They, along with a wealthy individual in Mt. Vernon, Indiana, named Jim Poshard, funded several of Pitt's early government-authorized undercover operations. Pitt paid them back upon receiving government checks.

Working Full Time for U.S. Customs

In the fall of 1992, Pitt started working primarily for the Beaumont, Texas, office of U.S. Customs under Special Agent in Charge Roger Bowers and his assistant Chuck Mohle. Customs offered Pitt a lucrative contract to work for them as an undercover contract agent. Pitt said, "I immediately accepted. I never even thought about dickering with them for a higher price." Pitt used attorney Al Nygaard of Vermillion, South Dakota, to handle financial arrangements with the government, submitting compensation requests and receiving government checks for operations Pitt carried out.

Paid Handsomely During These Undercover Operations

Pitt's compensation during these undercover operations was as much as *one million dollars* for a single operation. Deducted from this amount were expenses, investment in expensive aircraft, maintenance, upkeep, and paying bribes along the way. Pitt kept precise records of his expenses during these undercover operations, sometimes putting them on his credit card, for government scrutiny.

Forming His Own Undercover Group

Operating like a well-oiled business, Pitt hired other undercover people to work with him, who were then approved by Customs agents Bowers and Mohle. These people were usually ex-drug smugglers who knew how to infiltrate drug organizations. They would usually report to him, but sometimes, when Pitt was too busy doing something else, they reported directly to Bowers or Mohle. A key member of his team was Roy Segers who had many contacts in Europe, Mexico and the United States.

"Keep records of all expenses over $200,000"

Bower and Mohle instructed Pitt to keep records of his travel and other expenses that exceeded $200,000 so as to justify the compensation that the government would pay for any particular operation. Pitt's word would be taken for expenses less than $200,000. Pitt kept records of all expenses, including those below $200,000, because he was dealing with different drug groups and the expenses incurred to bring down any one group could therefore be accurately allocated.

Serious Threat Not Recognized

Pitt faced, as did Matthews, a threat that neither one of them knew about; the corruption in Customs Service, the lying, the deception, that would eventually have an effect upon Pitt as it had on Matthews. The culture in the Customs Service, as in other similar government agencies, did not permit reliance upon verbal authority to carry out undercover drug operations.

Acting as Drug Trafficker to Catch Drug Traffickers

Pitt knew the art of acting and speaking like a drug trafficker to infiltrate targeted drug operations. This required Pitt, as was the case with Matthews, to transport drugs as part of complex undercover operations. His bragging about prior drug smuggling operations to drug traffickers would be used at a later date when the targeted drug traffickers were arrested and offered to trade testimony about Pitt's "drug trafficking" statements for their freedom. The pattern is the same over and over again.

Using Local "Law-Enforcement" Personnel

In 1993, Pitt's Customs handlers introduced Pitt to a sheriff in Texas by the name, "Buddy," who was the head of the task force in the Eastern District of Nacogdoches County. The Customs agents instructed Pitt to notify the sheriff ahead of time when he was flying a load of drugs into Nacogdoches Airport so the sheriff could advise Customs and DEA that it was a government-authorized operation and for them not to get involved.

Establishing A Bad Rap Sheet

Pitt told how government agencies entered into government databases an arrest record that would make him look like he had a criminal record and thereby be more readily acceptable to targeted drug organizations if they penetrated the government's computer system. Years ago, CIA operative Gunther Russbacher told me about this practice. He explained that some criminal elements had access to such government records, and by showing multiple violations, it improved his image in the eyes of criminal organizations being infiltrated.

However, times have changed. The drug bosses now realize that many people with prior drug-related arrests that result in long prison sentences— who are not in prison—are probably working as government informants and are not to be trusted.

Recruiting Foreign Nationals

To assist in infiltrating foreign drug organizations, Pitt recruited foreign nationals into his undercover operations. This practice also allowed Pitt to circumvent government regulations requiring that American agents obtain in-country clearance from foreign governments before carrying out an undercover action against a drug trafficker in that country. In most countries where drug production or trafficking is widespread, government personnel (including the military, the police, the politicians), either protect drug traffickers or are themselves involved in the business. Requesting from these same people authority to conduct an in-country undercover operation would at best, fail, or worst, get the undercover person killed.

Customs agents in Beaumont approved Pitt's use of Colombian and Mexican nationals for undercover operations, and documented them as undercover agents. One was Esteban Borges Figeroa from Tuxtla Gutierrez Chiapas, Mexico. Esteban helped Pitt infiltrate high echelons of the Mexican government, including the office of President Carlos Salinas de Gortari, through his brother Raul.

The other was a Colombian national, Jorge Ortiz Restrepo, who Pitt described as a young Colombian from Pereira, Colombia, with whom Pitt had been in the Mexican prison. Pitt saved his life a couple of times when Mexicans showed their contempt for non-Mexican inmates. The nephew of a wealthy Colombian, Restrepo had a large number of contacts, making him especially valuable because he had been a middle-man for the drug cartels and had been to the United States setting up cells or distribution points. The Colombian drug bosses kept the cells isolated so that if one cell got busted, the others remained intact, and they could easily relocate.

Beaumont Customs agents promised both of these foreign nationals help in immigrating to the United States with their families. That promise would end tragically as Justice Department prosecutors sabotaged them and made possible their demise. More about this later.

Mexicans Ripping Off Colombians

Colombian drug traffickers started doing business with Mexicans in the early 1990s, but soon learned that the Mexicans were ripping them off. Pitt said that when the Colombians decided they had to stop doing business with the Mexicans, high-level Mexican officials heard about this and sent representatives to Cali to try to correct the problem. It was agreed that if the Colombians gave Mexican officials the names of any Mexican ripping them off, the Mexicans would be promptly dealt with.

Dealing with Drug Lords was the Easy Part

Pitt explained that dealing with the drug lords was the easy part. The difficult part was dealing with bureaucrats in the various U.S. agencies such as the DEA, Customs, and the Florida Department of Law Enforcement (FDLE). He said that the squabbling, bickering and inter-agency hostility were so overwhelming that many potential drug busts collapsed. Pitt told about the tremendous rivalry between the various agencies, and even in different offices of the same agency. Agents and agencies want to keep the publicity of a big bust for themselves, including the financial benefits that went with it. They all wanted the credit of drug busts but not the blame that goes with unsuccessful operations.

Bowers told Pitt that he often had to drive from Beaumont to Houston to discuss sensitive matters with his supervisor (who Pitt knew as Guinn) so as to avoid the often-monitored phone conversations and to avoid interference from local supervisors. (I experienced similar problems while I was an FAA inspector, having to huddle in a corner or go outside to discuss serious problems with other FAA inspectors concerning United Airlines. Some inspectors interested in gaining stature with the airline, and maybe employment, would repeat what inspectors were discovering about unsafe or illegal operations.)

One Agency or Division Not Talking to Another

Customs agent Bobby Rutherford told Pitt in 1994 that the DEA in Jamaica refused to cooperate with the DEA in Miami; they were hardly talking to each other, and that there was rivalry between the divisions (and between agencies). Rutherford said:

Customs would have a hard time working with DEA out of Jamaica because DEA would want credit for seizing the load. Furthermore, the Jamaican police would want to bust half the load right there on the strip in order to get credit and look good in the eyes of the media. They need to show that they're doing something too. So, by the time you get the rest of the load back to the States, maybe half, someone from Jamaica is bound to have already called ahead of you and warned off the folks on this end. They're going to be pissed at you and probably want to shoot someone. You sure you want anything to do with Jamaica, Richard?

Referring to problems with local law enforcement personnel, Rutherford explained "The Jamaicans don't look for drugs down there, Rich, they let us find it for them and then expect half the bust. It's all politics at its best. The whole process stinks, doesn't it?"

Bureaucratic Naïveté

Pitt explained how complex schemes to entrap drug traffickers could not be comprehended by bureaucrats in the DEA and Customs and therefore not approved. Government regulations also interfered with carrying out drug busts of high-level drug traffickers. Some government personnel, looking for the rewards accompanying drug busts, would allow contract agents to circumvent these restrictions. But then, when one of the operations backfired, the contract agent was hung out to dry. Customs agents Roger Bowers and Chuck Mohle frequently stated to Pitt: "Don't tell us how you are doing it, just do it!"

Wires Crossed Between Agencies

Government agents from one agency, seeking to ensnare drug traffickers, sometimes run into a sting operation run by another agency, or even another office of the same agency. Something like this happened to Pitt several times, including once while he was conducting a sting operation in Florida for the Beaumont Customs office.

In that incident, Tampa FDLE (Florida Department of Law Enforcement) agent Billy Wolfe had set up a sting operation against the same target that Pitt and Esteban were targeting. Pitt and Esteban met the supposed drug traffickers in a hotel room near the Tampa Airport and noticed a standard government-used camera lamp in the room, indicating they were dead center into a sting operation conducted by another agency. After leaving the hotel, Pitt called Customs agent Mohle and described what they discovered. Mohle then checked with the DEA, FBI, Customs, and FDLE offices to determine if they had a sting operation going. They all denied it, even though Billy Wolfe set up the hidden equipment.

Despite denying that he had a sting operation going, Wolfe complained to Pitt that he should have notified FDLE of the meeting before it occurred. As Pitt said, how was he to know it was a state sting operation when the facts implied that it was an international operation. Wolfe then tried to have Pitt arrested, which was blocked by higher authority. Pitt described Wolfe as "an obnoxious government agent built like an old bulldog, with a potbellied frame and bowed legs that caused him to wobble like a duck with a corn cob stuck up its ass."

Drug Seizures Blocked by Washington

Upon returning from a Customs-approved trip to Cali, Colombia, Pitt reported to Customs agent Rutherford that there was a stash of over 20 thousand kilos of cocaine sitting in Haiti and the Dominican Republic that the Colombians wanted to get removed before there would be a blockade around the island. This blockade did subsequently occur. Pitt offered to work with the Colombians to get the drugs into position so that U.S. agencies could seize the load. Approval was denied by U.S. officials on the basis that Washington determined that Haiti and the Dominican Republic were fully cooperating in the war on drugs. The evidence was overwhelming that these countries were *not* cooperating in the war on drugs and were shipping large quantities of drugs to the United States. The Haitian and Dominican Republic military later helped ship the drugs to the United States and Europe.

Illegal Government-Directed Kidnapping

In another operation, Agent Billy Wolfe from the Florida Department of Law Enforcement (FDLE), asked Pitt to go to Governor's Harbour in the Bahamas and kidnap a Bahamian national, B.J. Johnson, and bring him to Florida. Johnson was accused of being a co-conspirator in the killing of a state trooper during an attempted drug bust. Before carrying out the kidnapping, Pitt checked with his attorney, Al Nygaard, with Customs agent Roger Bowers, and people from the U.S. Department of State. They all approved the plan, but warned Pitt that the Bahamian government would probably issue an international warrant for Pitt's arrest and that an extradition warrant would be honored by most countries and Pitt would be arrested and extradited. Pitt decided he would not go ahead with Wolfe's request. Several years later, Wolfe retaliated, by filing charges against Pitt which resulted in several years of incarceration in a Florida state prison, ending in 1999.

DEA Said No Drug Trafficking at Cartagena, Colombia!

Pitt was directed by Customs agents to fly to Cartagena, Colombia, and pick up a 700-kilo cocaine load from Mexican drug trafficker Julio Martinez, which would be turned into an arrest when the drugs were picked up in the United States. After getting Customs approval, Pitt checked with the DEA liaison officer at the U.S. Embassy in Bogota and was told that there was no drug smuggling going on at Cartagena International Airport and that no undercover operation would be permitted. Cartagena was the home of one of Colombia's four major drug organizations, and to say no drugs were going through its airport would be somewhat preposterous. This was another example of the DEA and State Department protecting the cartels.

Pitt had already agreed with Martinez that he would pick up the drugs. To get out of that drug pickup, Customs agents suggested that Pitt fake his own death in an airplane crash in order to get Julio off his back. Because of the impracticality of that bureaucratic suggestion, Pitt talked Customs into faking a drug-flight intercept and to arrest him for three days in Cuba at the Guantanamo Naval Base. This permitted Pitt to remain in good graces with Julio Martinez and his Mexican smuggling group.

To avoid another drug pickup requested by Martinez, Pitt took off from Florida's Lantana Airport while a lookout for Martinez named Pancho watched to make certain that the flight departed. Pancho reported to Martinez that Pitt's plane had just departed and headed southeast over the ocean. But Pitt did not carry out that assignment. He flew on that heading for about 20 miles and then made a right turn, flying to Opa Locka Airport, where he was met by his girlfriend, Teresa.

They spent the next three days at Orlando's Disney World. Martinez had advanced $200,000 to buy the plane and twice lost $300,000 protection money for the Cartagena Airport pickup. Pitt did call Martinez and said that he had been forced down at the Guantanamo Bay Naval Air Station and had been arrested. This sequence of events resulted from the bureaucratic bungling and the coverup by the DEA in Colombia.

Guatemala's "Cooperation" in the Drug War

It was the White House's policy that Guatemala, a major drug transshipment point for drugs going to the United States, was fully cooperating in the war on drugs. Therefore, the United States would not permit any undercover operation to be conducted in that country. In 1992, Pitt received a call from Esteban in Mexico, advising him that the ex-secretary of agriculture in Guatemala City, Ivan Farfan, offered to sell him drugs. After notifying Customs agent Bowers, Pitt flew the following day to Guatemala City on American Airlines with another undercover agent, Roy Segers, to check on the offer.

After meeting with Farfan, Pitt and Segers discussed what they had learned. Pitt said, "Ivan had drug smuggling in that country completely under his control. From the president on down to and through the army, air force, and police, every avenue was protected. Pay your money to him and he would distribute it through the police to the right people."

Farfan owned one of the largest cattle ranches in Guatemala, called "El Pensumiento." Farfan and his son were educated in animal husbandry at Austin, Texas, and spoke fluent Spanish and English. Pitt said Farfan offered Colombian drug cartels any airport in Guatemala as a midpoint between South America and the United States, acting something like a truck stop for drug-carrying aircraft: fuel, restaurant, sleep facilities, and small store.

Farfan had developed lifelong friends with people who headed Guatemala's military, secret police, and even the office of the president. Pitt learned that Guatemalan police had confiscated a load of Colombian drugs from a drug trafficker who tried to pass through Guatemala without paying "protection" money. It was this load of drugs that Farfan and a general known as General Sanchez wanted to sell, and they wanted Pitt and Segers to find buyers in the United States.

Drug Smuggler's Dream

Pitt considered Guatemala to be a drug smuggler's dream; generals, the president, the police, the military, providing protection, tipping off the drug smugglers when U.S. DEA agents launch their interdiction airplanes. Farfan repeatedly referred to the "stupid DEA" during their conversations. When Pitt asked why he belittled the DEA, Farfan explained:

Richard, a good friend of mine is the liaison officer between my country and yours to the DEA. They have to report all their movements in my country to him, and he in turn reports it to me. Anytime a DEA plane is launched to somewhere in my country, a man in the control tower radios to us exactly where that helicopter or plane is going. The Americans come here and boss us around and we submit, they think; how stupid they are.

Pitt reported these events to Bowers, who suggested getting these comments on tape. Pitt and Segers returned to Guatemala City, meeting with Farfan, and taping the conversation. Pitt invited Farfan to Beaumont, Texas to meet with Pitt's alleged drug-bosses. Farfan agreed, stating that he had to go to Austin, Texas, where he owned some fine breeding bulls that had to be shipped to Guatemala. Before Pitt and Segers left, Farfan introduced them to several high government officials and military generals.

Segers picked up Farfan at the Houston International Airport and drove him to Beaumont, taking him to the hotel room in which Pitt was staying and which had been wired for sound and video. Farfan repeated his prior statements promising assistance and protection for transporting drugs through Guatemala, naming generals and politicians who would cooperate, and implied that the president of Guatemala would also help if needed. Pitt asked:

What if we were working with some army general down there, and some third party person, jealous of our position, went to the president's office to squeal on us? What if he said to the president, "Listen Mr. President, Ivan and Richard, two low life drug smugglers are using our country as a launching platform for drugs to the United States. What can we do to stop them?"

Farfan said that the president would do something like this: "He would tell this man that he would look into it. The president would then let it be known to us, that in five days time he would send in the country's narc police to investigate. We would of course have already moved the operation and when the police got there, they would find nothing." These tapes were given to Beaumont Customs agent Roger Bowers, who in turn sent them to Customs in Washington. That was the end of that; Pitt never heard any more about the matter.

Impatience by General Sanchez

Several times Guatemalan General Sanchez pressured Segers and Pitt to take his 300-kilo load of confiscated cocaine into the United States. He didn't trust the Mexicans and couldn't figure out why Pitt and Segers couldn't just go and fly the drugs into the United States. Pitt and Segers could not function because the White House declared that Guatemala (and Mexico) was fully cooperating in the war on drugs.

Cancun Meeting

At the end of 1993, Farfan called Pitt and asked for a meeting in Cancun, Mexico, which was held the next day. It had been over ten years since Pitt had been in Cancun. At that time, in 1981, Pitt's smuggling group had a large condominium in Cancun which they used while they smuggled drugs out of Tulum, 50 miles south of Cancun. Upon arriving at Cancun Airport and passing through Customs into the large lobby, Pitt found himself being followed by Mexican federal police. They quickly turned away when Pitt was met by two well-dressed Latins: Farfan and another person who was the head of the federal police for that area of Mexico.

The federal police commander told Pitt that he wanted to charter a private jet that was one step up from Pitt's Aero Commander Prop Jet. The commander wanted cocaine hauled from Cancun to the United States and also from Cancun to Mexicali on the border with California. He said federal police transport drugs from Cancun to Mexicali and Tijuana by planes and 18-wheeler trucks.

The drugs came from Colombia to Cancun via long canoes powered by twin outboard motors, a spectacular feat considering the long passage from Cartagena, across the open stretch of water. These wooden canoes were over 30 feet long and handled by two seamen, and usually carried about 1500 kilos of cocaine. The drug load was covered with tarpaulin for protection against sun and rain.

Conducting A Concert in Guatemala City

At another time, Ian Merrick, one of Pitt's friends from London, arrived in Miami and asked Pitt if he had any connections in Guatemala who could help set up a concert in that country. Merrick and Pitt had put on the Englebert Humperdinck television show from the Royal Albert Hall in London in May of 1985. Merrick needed someone to cut through the red tape in foreign countries such as Guatemala. Pitt, thinking of Farfan, told Merrick that he had just the man.

Pitt called Farfan in Guatemala, who said his aunt had assisted the last concert in Guatemala. What luck! Farfan said he, his wife Linda, and son Salvador, were flying into Miami the next day to buy medicines and things for his race horses and they could talk about it then.

The next day, Pitt and Segers drove Farfan and Merrick around Miami and Fort Lauderdale to the different feed and seed stores, while Pitt's girlfriend, Teresa, took Linda Farfan shopping at the different malls. Teresa's ability to speak five different languages fluently made her valuable in these matters. The next day Farfan, Merrick, and Segers left for Guatemala City. Farfan called one night and asked Pitt to have Teresa come to Guatemala and help set up the concert, which she did, accompanied by Pitt who concentrated on finalizing the drug operation for Customs. Teresa sped from one social function to another, going to meetings, getting commitments and promises of support.

Farfan laughed and made a joke about how he couldn't get an appointment that day with one of the generals because he was meeting with some beautiful French woman, and then finding out later that it was Teresa. Farfan joked about asking her to start introducing him around his own country. Guatemalan officials were flying her around Guatemala in a twin-engine jet helicopter. Later, the concert went off without a hitch.

Another Example of Mexican Police Involvement in Drugs

In one undercover operation, Pitt located 14,000 pounds of amphetamine-processing chemicals in Mexico City. A Mexican federal police captain showed Pitt the stash of chemicals stored at the captain's house as he tried to sell it to Pitt. That same Mexican federal police captain was responsible for security at Mexico City's D.F. Airport. Pitt said the captain was one of the tallest and largest Mexicans he had ever seen.

Drug Arrest Canceled Because of Mexico's Drug "Cooperation"

In another operation arranged by Pitt's Esteban Borges Figeroa, Pitt was to land at Vera Cruz, Mexico, and pick up a load of heroin. But this operation had to be canceled because the U.S. State Department declared that Mexico was cooperating in the drug war and he therefore could not get an in-country clearance.

Lose A Drug Load and Die

Drug lords deal harshly with anyone who loses drug loads. A Guatemalan Pitt knew as Sergio worked with one of the Colombian groups out of Cali that had opened shop in Guatemala City. Farfan and Sergio were constantly competing to represent the Colombians and in seeking cooperation from Guatemalan generals who would safeguard the loads. Sergio, working with a representative of one of the Colombian groups named Jamie, sought to avoid paying the Guatemalan military commander. This resulted in the commander seizing a million-dollar Aero Commander 840 Turbo Prop airplane and its drug cargo. The Colombian boss in Cali lost his plane and the drug shipment that had been seized. He called Jamie back to Colombia, where Jamie was then killed.

Drug Lord's Missing Cocaine

Colombian drug trafficker Don Eduardo from Cartagena asked Pitt to find out what happened to a 4000 kilo cocaine shipment that got lost and possibly confiscated in Miami. It was the practice among Colombian drug organizations that if a shipment was lost or stolen, whoever was responsible for the shipment must pay for its loss, unless it was seized by government agents. In this case, the recipient of the container shipment arriving by ship was never notified that the container had arrived, and therefore its status was not known. The person responsible for the shipment was concerned. Pitt gave the following explanation:

> As Jorge relayed the story to me, it came out something like this. Eduardo, about twenty-nine years old, and his partner had sent a shipping container full of cocaine to the United States. His partner was responsible for acquiring the cocaine and Eduardo was responsible for transportation. However you want to look at it, the two of them together were in real deep water if they couldn't find the load of coke soon. The rules in the drug trade are fairly clear-cut. If you lose a load to the cops, no problem. The slate is wiped clean. That's the cost of doing business. But if you lose the load to stupidity or theft, that's a whole other set of unwritten rules. Basically on the second set of rules, about the only thing you can really count

on is the choice of death.

Jorge said that Eduardo sent the load to Venezuela. There it was put on a container ship along with about thirty other containers, and sent on to Miami. The name of the ship and its description were then forwarded on to the receiver, a woman named Sofia, in Kendall, a Colombian-populated suburb of Miami.

On the day of the planned arrival, a lookout was sitting in place with a clear view of the shipping channel. He watched the harbor tug boat guide the ship slowly down the center of the inlet to its assigned dockage. Task completed; he went home to await the phone call to come pick up his load of cocaine. The phone call never came.

What the drug agencies sometimes do, to cause internal conflicts that lead to drug organizations shooting one another is this: when they really don't have a lot of evidence on the players, they confiscate the load and let it sit. They don't report it to the newspapers or TV folks. This drives the Colombian partners and all their workers right up the walls. They start false accusations against one another, bad mouthing the next guy down the totem pole of authority, and sometimes taking guns and filling each other with holes, which was exactly what the agencies want them to do.

Pitt said he then called Customs Agent Mohle, who called Customs Agent Rutherford in Miami. It was learned that the drug container was discovered during a chance inspection and then seized. Rutherford gave Pitt the Customs seizure documents the next day. This information was then given to Eduardo and relayed back to the drug cartel, relieving Eduardo and his partner of responsibility. Pitt added:

The one thing that was becoming clear was longshoremen at the port of Miami were in up to their thick necks in the drug unloading business. Containers wound up bypassing Customs and then moved right on out of the cargo area. It cost the Colombians a lot but it was a sure way to get a big drug shipment into the United States. The longshoremen are a close-knit group. It was harder than hell for Customs and DEA to penetrate these guys. It's like uncles, cousins, sons, and long-time friends are the only ones hired in. Everyone else is an outsider.

Moles in U.S. Customs

A confidential U.S. Customs document was faxed to Pitt by one of the drug bosses and Pitt showed it to Rutherford in the Miami Customs office. Rutherford studied it for a few seconds and then got his supervisor. They were very disturbed to find that one of their most confidential documents had been faxed to Pitt by a Colombian drug trafficker. The supervisor pulled out a thick secure file and found the original of the faxed form. This discovery was frightening to Pitt because an insider in Customs could be leaking his identity to the drug cartels that Pitt was infiltrating.

Mexican Operation

During one operation, conducted in Mexico, the target was a Mexican citizen well connected in the PRI (Institutional Revolutionary Party), Jesus (Jessie) Macias. He was wanted by the DEA in El Paso and was in charge of aircraft activity at Ciudad Juarez, including drug-loaded aircraft coming from

Guatemala, Panama, and Colombia. Macias took Pitt to a PRI rally at their convention center when President Carlos Salinas de Gortari flew in from Mexico City. The place was crawling with federal police, a group Pitt detested as being corrupt, violent, and unsavory. (They had tortured Pitt for six days back in 1982 as they tried to extract information from him.)

Macias noticed Pitt's attitude. He walked to the head of the president's security detail, spoke a few words, and both returned to Pitt. Introducing Pitt to the general, Macias explained Pitt had been a guest of their country for over five years in a Tuxtla prison. The head of security laughed, "That had to be the worst place in all of Mexico to go to prison in; it's so backwards down there."

Asking Pitt if He Ate Rats

In a joking manner, he asked if Pitt ate rats while there. Pitt said, "No, but I killed enough of them." Pitt then got into Macias' red Corvette and drove to the airport south of Ciudad Juarez. Pitt said, "At the airport he showed me the hangar that I should taxi into with drugs on future flights from Guatemala. He also told me about a dirt airstrip southeast of Juarez about 30 miles away. He said large airplanes landed here." Pitt wanted to ask questions of Macias but realized it was not healthy to ask.

Macias gave Pitt $20,000 to make a down payment on a Beech Queenair he wanted to buy. Pitt could not carry out any undercover operations against Macias because the White House held that Mexico was fully cooperating in the war on drugs. The truth was, of course, Mexico's entire government structure was geared to facilitate the flow of drugs into the United States. Pitt said the same applied to intelligence that he brought to government agents over a three-year period concerning drug trafficking from Jamaica, Guatemala, and Mexico. State Department personnel blocked any undercover operations involving these countries on the argument that they were fully cooperating in the war on drugs.

Mexican Drug Smugglers Accessing Confidential Data Banks

Pitt told how Macias once asked him for his social security number, explaining that he had access to the highly confidential DEA NADDIS data bank at El Paso to determine what government agents were doing in Mexico on any particular day, what operation they had going with a particular undercover agent, and who the government was seeking to arrest. Drug traffickers with connections could then learn the identity of undercover agents. Hearing this, Pitt feared that his undercover role could be discovered; a path to torture and eventual death.

Pitt immediately called Rose Pinada with the Florida FDLE and Customs agent Chuck Mohle, asking them to check the NADDIS data base to find out what was being said about him. A few days later, an El Paso rogue officer, using his own social security number to gain access to the data base, called up Pitt's record. Pitt's name in the database had a Flash Notice Lock on it, which automatically requested the identity of anyone looking for information.

Discovering Stolen Bearer Bonds

By acting like criminals, Pitt and Segers discovered criminal activities other than drug related but which fell within the jurisdiction of a government agency for which they had undercover contract relationships. In 1992, while conducting an investigation in England, Pitt and Segers came across $1.6 billion worth of bearer bonds stolen from a major bank in England. These original bonds had been stolen by employees of the British bank who lifted them out of the bank vaults and replaced them with phony computer-generated laser-printed bonds for the purpose of bank audits. (Bearer bonds do not have the owner's name on them and can be conveyed or used almost like cash by whoever has them in their possession.)

In response to my question about how he learned the original bearer bonds were replaced with forged duplicates, Pitt replied: "By and through a Brit [British citizen] named Allen and his son who brought the bearer bonds to Roy Segers while I was still in prison in Mexico." Pitt added:

This was told to us [Pitt and Roy Segers] by Allen who gave Roy two of the bonds. One was picked up by the FBI through Roy and the other, we gave a copy to Roger Bowers at Customs in Beaumont, who in turn sent it to the U.S. British Embassy liaison officer [U.S. Customs] who in turn gave it to Scotland Yard in the summer of 1993. Its value alone was three million dollars, a small bond compared to the rest.

Insolvency of A Major British Bank?

Strangely, Scotland Yard showed no interest. Even the bank which suffered the loss wouldn't act on the information. England had just gone through two major bank scandals and no one wanted another one to be publicized. It was felt that if it became known that such a large amount of bank assets were worthless forgeries that the bank might have been declared bankrupt. Seeking more information on the matter, I contacted Roy Segers in late 1998 in South Africa where he was pilot for a corporation. I asked him about the bearer-bond switch. He replied:

A quick overview. Someone was approached one day and asked if there was a secure way to market or sell a "bearer bond." An affirmative answer was given, along with a "commission rate" for the sale. A few weeks later, a bearer bond showed up in the amount of English Pounds, $13.5MM. Certain people were contacted and the bond was placed into the system for collection.

A copy of the bond was kept by someone, and certain persons within the Law Enforcement System were notified. At first, no one believed that the bond was legit, but after a few days the report came back, it was legit, and was NOT listed as stolen, but belonged to a large insurance company in the U.K. (at least "believed" to belong to this company), which had it listed (as a public company) as part of their asset base. Discreet inquiries were made and it was found that the supposed owners, in fact, believed it to be in their possession. Of course, it wasn't; so an "estoppel" action was placed on the money that was issued (on the sale). The money was "confiscated" along with the "bond" and quietly, a certain person was asked to check things out--as to HOW this bond got into the hands of others than the rightful owner.

Turns out, in the vaults of a major bank in the U.K., this insurance company held billions of pounds worth of stocks and bonds. The "word" was, certain persons who had access to the vaults, would, on occasion, pull a bond, it would be replicated as best as possible (done quite well we hear), the "false" one put back into the vault—and the real one quietly disposed of. This had been going on for years.

When Scotland Yard and the Metro Police became involved--there was at first much interest. However, as a certain "Lord" was identified as being involved, along with the realization that LARGE amounts of these bonds had been copied, and the real ones were nowhere to be found. Several scandals had already taken place and it was felt that this insurance company would "go under" and that "royalty" was involved--the investigation was dropped. End of story. No other conspiracy or anything else involved, just rotten royalty, rotten politicians, police who did, will turn their heads, and criminals who do well. If you can tell this story without naming names, so be it. You don't want to get explicit, believe me.

Stolen Bearer Bonds: A Favorite CIA Trick

Stolen or forged bearer bonds placed with lending institutions as collateral was a frequent trick that former CIA agent Gunther Russbacher told me about years ago, including those that *he* stole under CIA orders. I had wondered why this information was not publicized. The reason given by Pitt and Segers made sense. It is frightening to think that vast amounts of assets in financial institutions may be valueless, with banks and governments keeping the lid on the problem.

Billions in Bogus U.S. Currency

While in Europe, Segers discovered a $500 million stash of counterfeit U.S. currency and reported this discovery to the U.S. Secret Service in Miami. Pitt explained the subsequent meeting at the Secret Service office:

Myself, Roy [Segers], my girlfriend Teresa from France who happened to accompany us to this meeting, and Roy's girlfriend Naomi from Guatemala, were all present at the meeting in Miami's Secret Service office in 1993. None of us could believe all of this. They were briefing us on this because Roy [Segers], by accident had stumbled upon a 30-ton press in England that was used to print money and was for sale on the black market. In the process of trying to film it (which he did), and selling it under approval of Scotland Yard, he was busted by another group of agents and thrown into Brixton Prison in London. Pat Becker, plus Scotland Yard, and U.S. Customs, were finally able to get him out after a couple of weeks, but not before a hit to kill him was put out by Allen (who I later was able to convince in Guatemala, that Roy was not a cop or working for them). Allen wanted to kill him just to make sure he hadn't made an error in judgment on his part. But Allen finally called off the hit. If he hadn't, I would have killed Allen and his son in Guatemala City in 1993.

Allen traveled under various names and at least three passports that I know of and saw over the years. I knew him personally. He never told me his real name, but he is 6 feet, blond hair, 50 years old and looks a lot like Gene Wilder in appearance. Roy got wind of the press for phony money in England. When we reported it to the U.S. Secret Service in Miami, that was when and why they began to tell us about the 500 million-plus, and gave all four of us a short course on how to I.D. bogus bills. Teresa thought it was neat and wanted to keep one of them.

Naomi really didn't care and Roy and I, as I said already, were dumb-founded at what was going on. The Secret Service considered the two girls as part of our [government undercover] operation. They knew that I had a group and the women were out-of-this-world beautiful. So that's why they were so open at the meetings, plus we had come recommended by the FBI, Customs and the FDLE.

The U.S. Secret Service in Miami briefed us that they had found over 500 million counterfeit dollars in the U.S. Federal Reserve Banks here in the United States and had been totally unaware of it. Segers and I were briefed about this due to the fact the Secret Service wanted to find out who was giving the treasury changes on 100s, and 50s, to the Iraqis and Iranians so that each month they could make the new [plate] changes. We did not know.

Mossad's Arming Cuba

In early 1993, Pitt and Segers discovered a gun-smuggling operation conducted by Israel's Mossad in Guatemala. Guns shipped by boat from Israel to Guatemala were being flown once a week to Cuba on a Boeing 737 of Guatemala's airline, Aviateca. Pitt and Segers discovered this through Segers' girl friend, Naomi, who was a flight attendant for the airline. They could hardly believe that Israel, an ally to the United States, would be smuggling large quantities of guns into Cuba. This information was given to DEA agent Jack Bax in San Diego with whom Pitt had previous contacts. Bax gave this information to a CIA representative in El Paso, Texas. This was followed by a U.S. government coverup which made possible the continued gun shipments. Pitt wrote:

Roy and I moved out of the Camino Real Hotel to a very plush apartment building the next street over behind Camino Real. Roy's girlfriend, Naomi was a flight attendant for Aviateca Airlines (Guatemala's National Airlines). "By chance," one day, she tells Roy about a weekly Wednesday night flight in a 737 from Guatemala City to Havana by the same crew of two pilots, no flight attendants. And on board are arms. Almost all the employees at the operations base in Guatemala knew about this and it was no big deal as far as she saw. Roy's and my ears picked up on it right away. Arms from Guatemala to the regime of Fidel Castro, we could not believe it.

A week or so later, Naomi and Roy are coming into our security-conscious apartment building when a tall, well-dressed, good-looking gentleman walks out. Naomi recognizes him as the man that is always hanging around operations, especially on Wednesday nights.

Roy, a few days later, strikes up a conversation with the guy because he lives in the apartment three floors below us. We were on the top floor with a beautiful view of the city. It turns out that this tall very distinguished looking gentleman is from Israel. Head of Mossad in Guatemala? We didn't know for sure.

Roy spends a few different nights drinking and shooting the breeze with the guy and can find no discernible reason why this guy is hanging out in a backward country like Guatemala. Naomi is now checking around and talking to other airline employees at the request of Roy to find out what is going on at Aviateca Airlines on Wednesday nights. Roy jaunts on over there on this particular evening and witnesses a cargo load being put on a 737, and sure enough, there is the Israeli hanging out. The plane leaves and the Israeli leaves for the apartment.

Naomi talks to the pilots the next evening and sure enough, they had flown to Havana the night before. Roy keeps striking up conversations with his new Israeli friend, who constantly keeps trying to pick Roy's brain to see why he's in Guatemala City. Roy plays the same stupid act. Meanwhile, I'm traveling between Colombia, the United States, and Guatemala.

Both of our girls had the ability, with their good looks, to get the Pope to talk about smoking in the "John" if they set out to do so. Both were beautiful and smart. At one time, when we were in Guatemala (and to produce a reason why we were there), we started putting on concerts. Of course you needed the approval of everyone from the president to the Army General, who felt the auditorium was his. I made the mistake of siccing Teresa on them, and by the end of the week, she had almost taken over the country. It seemed as if the general of the Army was being led around his country on a leash. She had his helicopter for the running around and when other country ministers couldn't even get an appointment with the general, she would walk them into his office. Ivan Farfan, the minister of agriculture was the one who Teresa took to see the General of Guatemala on a moment's notice. I believe the General had visions of getting into Miss T's pants. We all called Teresa Miss T. (She was a French gal with the most incredible body you ever saw in your life, with dark hair that hung all the way down past her butt.)

Roy and I contacted the CIA through Jack Bax (RAC in San Diego, California, for U.S. Customs). He internally set it up with the CIA out of El Paso, Texas, where the joint drug war's main processing and clearing house was run at that time. (Probably still is.)

After a month, Jack told us that they didn't want to know any more about it. It was U.S. arms shipped to Israel, then resold or/and shipped to Guatemala where it was flown on to Cuba.

We had stumbled right into the middle of the whole CIA operation jointly run by Israel and Guatemala. Later, I got to meet the man and then one afternoon, while flying in from Miami, I happened to run into the guy walking through security (by flipping some type of an ID) with several other well-dressed Israelis and a couple of Americans. They didn't look like Russians and they sure as hell were not Latins.

Selling Cocaine to Mexicans: Double Sting Operation

Pitt gave an account of the cocaine shortage in the United States in 1994 after the May 24, 1994, murder of Roman Catholic Cardinal Juan Jesus Posadas Ocampo at the Guadalajara Airport. The shortage was due to the great amount of police activity in Mexico that interrupted normal drug transporting activities. Established drug traffickers were running short of cocaine to supply their customers in the United States. Pitt took advantage of this to engineer a double-sting operation in which cocaine that had been seized earlier by the DEA would be offered for sale to Mexican drug dealers. Pitt said:

*God, you would not have believed all the agencies involved on that one. All of them standing around smiling, looking cool and tough when it was over with. But in the beginning, no one would believe Bowers, Mohle, and I, that Mexicans wanted to buy dope on **this** side of the border in that much of a quantity.*

Pitt proposed a number of drug sting operations targeting Mexican drug traffickers to Bowers, who ran it by his boss in Houston. The plans were rejected on the basis that it was the official U.S. policy that Mexico was fully cooperating in the war on drugs.

Drug Traffickers Evolving into Cartels and Corporations

Pitt said years ago the drug traffickers were usually small mom-and-pop operations but that the business had become so large and lucrative that it developed into cartels, and then into corporations. Pitt described the violent confrontations that once existed between the four major Colombian drug organizations and how they had joined forces:

The cartels used to be just independent cartels in different Colombian cities. But today they have all merged into mostly one large cartel or corporation run by a few select top Colombians. They work closely with the Bolivians, Mexicans and other countries, mostly the governments, to supply our drugs. It's no longer, as I've said before, mom and pop operations. The terms corporation, or one big super cartel, is not my title. It belongs to the DEA and the State Department. They coined it about two or three years ago. I had seen it developing in 1992 to 1994 while in Mexico and Colombia. Cali guys were working side by side with men from Medellin and Bogota. Unheard of before. In the past they would have killed one another.

Corporations is how the DEA, CIA and the Colombians refer to the cartels now. They, the big ones, have all joined together into one big corporation with the common goal of sharing intelligence, routes, expertise, and anything else they've got. All this in order to move their drugs into the United States unchecked and unabridged. Scary, huh?

NAFTA, A Bonanza for Drug Cartels

Pitt explained how the logistics of drug smuggling into the United States changed over the years. At one time, most drugs arrived by aircraft, but the North American Free Trade Agreement (NAFTA) opened up the Mexican and Canadian borders to massive drug shipments via ships, trucks, and trains with relatively little risk of detection. These new transportation methods overwhelm the drug-detection facilities. Pitt told how Colombian and Mexican drug traffickers were investing heavily along the Mexican-U.S. border in businesses—even *before* NAFTA took effect—using these facilities to ship tons of drugs into the United States. Pitt, referring to a major Mexican drug trafficker, said:

Jesus (Jessie) Macias almost would get a hard-on talking about it when I was with him in Ciudad Juarez in 1993. All the Mexicans, he said, that had any money to invest in warehouse or businesses along the frontier, were doing so because of the openness and easy access to the United States. Even the Colombians were putting up money to help them get into business, a legal front, where drugs would be placed along the back wall of the United States. From there, a hundred ideas could be thought up in order to get them across. This has been done in the last five years as you can see from the low price of cocaine.

Pitt told how Macias controlled the milk distribution in Ciudad Juarez and throughout that Mexican State, and how his activities were protected by the ruling PRI political party. Macias had a fleet of trucks along the main drag in Juarez that paralleled the border. Jessie bragged how his trucks hauled more than just milk. Pitt said, "The trucks 'mooed' the sound of corruption as they rumbled down the streets and across Northern Mexico."

Becoming Concerned about Verbal Authority to Carry Drugs

Pitt's undercover operations for the government required him to act and talk like a drug trafficker. This included hauling drugs trying to get evidence on drug organizations. Because authority to carry drugs was given to Pitt by local government agents, Pitt was becoming concerned that he might be charged with criminal acts by other government agents who would not know—or would not recognize—the verbal authority under which he was acting. In 1994, at the suggestion of a CIA case officer in Miami, Pitt started to tape record his conversations with government agents, some of which I heard, along with transcripts of such recordings. There was not the slightest doubt that government agents were giving Pitt authorization to carry out his undercover activities, which included flying drugs into the United States.

Don't Tell Us, Just Do It!

A typical statement recorded during these telephone conversations with Customs agents Bowers and Mohle was, "Don't tell us, just do it!" While this may be an efficient way to conduct complex and ever-changing undercover operations, government agencies and agents were disorganized and the authority given by an agent in one office or agency was often not honored by other agents or agencies. Pitt did not know this about this problem, but he would soon learn. Typical of several of the tapes that I listened to was a recorded July 5, 1994, telephone conversation during which Bowers told Pitt:

You and I have an understanding how things are done.... My supervisors in Houston are knowledgeable of this.... If you need to perform any tests for the Colombians, we do not want to know about them, or the deal, or the Colombians, till the case is well developed and on its way to fruition. Then fill us in completely. What may appear bad can always be lost in the paperwork. People do not look at the bad part of a successful drug bust.... Let's get this thing done!

Exact Words Used by Customs Agents with Matthews

Many of these instructions given to Pitt by Customs agents in Beaumont were given earlier to Rodney Matthews by Customs agents in the San Antonio office, authorizing drugs to be flown for undercover operations authorized by government agents, or simply transporting drugs requested by these agents.

Paper Trail Shows Government Knowledge of Pitt's Activities

Typical of the many government forms and letters showing Pitt's undercover status was a report dated November 23, 1993, titled, "Claim For and Award Of Compensation For Original Information" which was filed by Pitt's attorney Al Nygaard. This form was routinely filed under title 19 USC Sections 1619, 161-11, 161.15, C.R. to provide expenses and compensation for undercover agents who do work for the government. That form was followed by a January 13, 1994, letter from Nygaard to INS agent Stuart Seidel. Nygaard, referring to the urgency in receiving payment for Pitt's last undercover operation:

> The claimant [Pitt] is actively engaged in further cooperation with the USCS under the guidance of Agent Roger Bowers. These are significant matters drawing attention at the highest levels of the USCS. Currently, cooperation in the enforcement efforts of the USCS is the claimant's sole occupation, and he is virtually without funds both to support himself and to pay for those things that are necessary to establish and maintain the confidence of investigative targets. However, the claimant remains committed to do everything within his power to aid the USCS in its mission. It is in the interest of the USCS to provide expedited treatment of this claim because a speedy award will allow the claimant to better pursue pending and future operations with the USCS.
>
> For these reasons, this letter is to request expedited review of the pending claim. We greatly appreciate the prompt response of various offices of the USCS thus far; and we look forward to a similarly prompt response from International Trade Compliance in the Office of Regulations and Rulings. Please call or fax me if you anticipate any delays or problems in the review of this claim. I would be pleased to provide further information you may need, and I am prepared to visit with you at your office on very short notice if that would be helpful to you. Under the authority of 19 C.F.R. Section 103.12(g)(4), (5), and (6), the claimant requests that this letter be exempt and withheld from disclosure from the Freedom of Information Act (FOIA). Such a disclosure would cause foreseeable harm within the meaning of the Attorney General's recent memorandum on FOIA, and it could reasonably be expected to disclose the identity of a confidential source, would disclose investigation techniques, and could reasonably be expected to endanger the life or physical safety of the claimant or the Beckers.

A March 30, 1994, letter from Nygaard to Pitt was an accounting of $250,000 received by Nygaard from the government on Pitt's behalf for services involving a recent operation. Further support was shown by a letter written by Nygaard to John Jumper, District Director for Port Arthur, Texas, through Customs agent Roger Bowers, with a copy to Stu Siedel, Director of the Office of Regulations and Rulings, United States Customs Service. That letter accompanied Customs Form 4623, a power of attorney for Nygaard to act on Pitt's behalf with the government. Also enclosed were copies of an agreement between Pitt (who was identified as SA-73-PU) and the United States Customs Service, referring to seizure number 93-2101-00023 and expenses incurred by

Pitt. Attached to that letter was a claim for compensation from the federal government, based on assets that were identified, seized, and forfeited as a result of information or activities provided by Pitt. The memorandum stated in part:

> That SA-73-PU [Pitt] had been working as a CI for the USCS for over one and one half years. A major portion of the monies spent would not be acceptable expenses under the CI agreement with the USCS, nor is the Claimant seeking reimbursement pursuant to the agreement. The point I am making is that to appear to be a "successful drug smuggler" and to gain the confidence of people such as the three indicted in PU02CR3PU004 the Claimant had to spend money which he did not have. In seeking the maximum reward of $250,000 pursuant to section 161.13 under 19 U.S.C. 1619, the Claimant will be able to reimburse hard working citizens who have been trying to help fight the war on drugs. Your prompt attention to this Claim For Reward would be greatly appreciated as the Claimant continues to be significantly involved in similar actions with USCS under the guidance of Agent Roger Bowers.

Another letter dated February 22, 1994 from U.S. Customs in Washington to Nygaard stated in part:

> You are hereby referred to the Special Agent in Charge, Houston, Texas, for payment of Award of Compensation No. 19007, in the amount of $250,000, to your client (claimant SA-73-PU), as authorized by Title 19, United States Code, Section 1619. The award is for original information furnished concerning violations of the Customs or navigation laws, or certain other laws enforced by the Customs Service, as covered by Port Arthur District Case No. 93-2101-00023 and Port Arthur Office of Enforcement No. PU02CRPU004.

> Sincerely,

> Stuart P. Seidel
> Director, International
> Trade Compliance Division

That notice was followed by a memorandum from United States Customs, Acting Chief, Penalties Branch, to the Resident Agent in Charge, Beaumont, Texas 77701, subject matter being Award of Compensation to SA-73-PU. That memorandum, signed by Charles Ressin, stated:

> This is to advise you that an award of compensation in the amount of $250,000 will be made to SA-73-PU through the office of the Special Agent in Charge, Houston, Texas. Attached is a copy of the award letter sent to the SAC in Houston.

These notices were then followed by a March 30, 1994, letter to Pitt at his Florida address, Penthouse 110, 43 N. Federal Highway, Pompano Beach, Florida 33062, and referenced to "Accounting for Reward Monies," in which

Nygaard described the distribution of the $250,000 received from the government.

Planning one of the Biggest Drug Busts in History

Pitt had penetrated some of the largest drug cartels in the Western Hemisphere and came up with a plan that would have inflicted major harm on their distribution cells in the United States. The plan was to use a large boat capable of hauling many tons of Colombian cocaine and delivering the product to their distribution cells in the United States. Pitt proposed the plan to Customs agents Bowers and Mohle, and they authorized him to proceed. If the plan succeeded, the Customs agents would have their careers enhanced as never before. They felt the use of the boat eliminated the need for Customs to coordinate with the DEA or other government agencies, thereby eliminating the chaos that often arises when more than one agency becomes involved in a single operation.

Selling Top Colombian Drug Cartels on the Plan

Pitt proposed his plan to one of his Colombian contacts, Don Arcesio Abrehales, in November 1993. Arcesio was a middle man for the Orejuela Brothers' Cali cartel in Colombia. Arcesio made his money by arranging deals, bringing people together, developing new contacts, and developing new ways to get the drugs transported to distributors in the United States and Europe. Arcesio thought it was a good idea, and arranged a meeting with other cartel members, including Marian and Don Rodrigo of the Cali cartel; Don Edgar and Don Arnulfo of the Medellin Cartel (an old friend and business associate of Pablo Escobar and the Ochoa families), and Don Edwardo of the Cartagena Cartel. (It was the lost 4000 kilo load of cocaine, belonging to Don Edwardo, that Pitt discovered through Miami Customs agent Bobby Rutherford, which raised Pitt's status in his eyes.) Arnulfo worked directly for Angela Ochoa who ran the Medellin cartel's business while her brothers were in prison. Don Arcesio took care of the loads for the Cali cartel.

Bringing in A Member of the Pagans Biker Group

In planning the boat operation, Pitt needed someone experienced in handling a large boat. He had met Michael Strube a year and a half earlier and learned that Strube had the experience needed. Strube and his father had years of experience raising sunken ships in the United States, Mexico, the Dominican Republic, and elsewhere, and many successful searches for sunken treasure. Their activities as treasure hunters were featured in a 1979 *National Geographic Magazine* front-cover story entitled "Quick Silver Galleons." Strube and his father owned one of the largest inventories of aircraft instruments and spare parts in the world, located in four cities under the business name of William P. Strube, Inc. They also did considerable work for the defense industry.

Strube was a pilot, and the family business owned jets and piston-powered aircraft. At the age of 29, Strube had acquired a 100-ton captain's license and had over 15 years experience moving hundreds of multi-million-dollar yachts in and out of the United States. Pitt described the operation to Strube, that he was working for U.S. Customs, and that Strube could receive considerable money when the operation was completed. Strube accepted the offer on condition that his only role would be piloting the boat and that he would never be asked to testify against anyone. The next task was finding a suitable boat.

Strube was national secretary-treasurer of the Pagan Biker Club in Pennsylvania, members of which the FBI had been trying for years to take out of circulation. The Beaumont Customs agents approved Strube's role in the plan.

Increasing Cartel's Confidence in Pitt and Strube

Pitt and Strube flew to Colombia with Strube's wife and mother in January 1994, staying as houseguests with several top Colombian drug traffickers. Many of the Colombians were avid Harley Davidson bike riders and upon learning that Strube was a charter member of the Pagans Biker Club and a racing expert they gave him preferential treatment. Strube tuned up several of their motorbikes and taught them various racing tricks. The Colombian drug organizations invited them back to Colombia for a Harley Davidson rally and race scheduled in April of 1994. Many pictures were taken of Pitt and Strube with high-ranking members of the Cali, Medellin, and Bogota drug cartels. All of these pictures were turned over to U.S. Customs in Beaumont, Texas.

Cali Cartel Banquet with Don Arcesio (arms up)

The Ridgely Warfield

Pitt and Strube had looked at several boats before deciding to buy the Ridgely Warfield. It was built by the Bethlehem Steel Company for Johns Hopkins University, and used in oceanographic research. It was a 110-foot-long aluminum catamaran, 38-feet wide, weighing 260 tons. It had four large Cummins diesel engines and two large electrical generators that could supply enough electrical power for a small city. It had a 21,000-gallon fuel capacity, large fresh-water tanks and could support 20 people for a month at sea. On the back was a 22-ton A-frame and a 15,000-pound crane on the aft deck which would facilitate the transfer of drugs from and to the ship.

Fabulously Profitable—If It Succeeded

The plan would be immensely profitable for Pitt if it could be carried off. Pitt would be paid by the Colombians $3000 per kilo, or $48 million for the entire 16,000-kilo load. The U.S. government would pay Pitt the maximum of $1 million per target, and since there were three different groups putting their loads on the boat, Ridgely Warfield, Pitt would receive $3 million from the government plus expenses.

Suitcases Filled With Cash

On January 16, 1994, Pitt showed an advertisement and picture of a boat offered for sale, the Ridgely Warfield, to one of the Cali cartel members, Rodrigo Lauriano, at his Tosty's Chicken restaurant in Pereira, Colombia. He appeared very interested and Pitt left his phone number in the event he cared to contribute money for its purchase. On January 31, 1994, Pitt received a call on his cellular phone to meet a Hispanic individual identifying himself as "Cus" at the Burger King on Biscayne and Ives Dary Road in North Miami. When Pitt arrived, Cus gave him a suitcase containing $169,875 in cash to help buy the Ridgely Warfield.

Reporting Source of Funds: Cali Drug Cartel

Pitt called Customs agent Bowers with this information and Bowers had Pitt contact IRS agent Ted Hinkel in Fort Worth, Texas. Pitt's attorney went with Pitt on February 2, 1994, to Citibank Federal Savings Bank in Deerfield Beach, Florida to assist in making the deposit and making out the various government forms for receipt of the money and the deposit. These forms must be filled out when cash received exceeds $10,000 or is of suspicious circumstances. Pitt inserted the following information in a February 2, 1994 form titled "Currency Transaction Report" (IRS form 4789):

- Where the transaction took place: Burger King, Biscayne and Ives Dary Road, North Miami, Florida.
- Where the money was deposited: Citibank Federal Savings Bank, Deerfield Beach, Florida.
- The person paying the money: Rodrigo Aristizaba Lauriano.
- Whether the person paying the money was an individual or corporation: Organization.
- Form of that person's business: Cali Drug Cartel.
- Business of person providing the money: Drug smuggling.

Pitt obviously wasn't hiding the source of drug-money from the government. Nor did these responses cause any reaction from the IRS or Justice Department, something that would have been quick in coming if the government did not know and had not authorized what he was doing.

Pitt filed on February 2, 1994 an IRS 8300 form entitled, "Report of Cash Payments Over $10,000 Received in a Trade or Business." The various boxes that were marked or filled in included the following:

- The person providing the suspicious money: Rodrigo Lauriano.
- Residence: Pereira, Colombia.
- Name of business providing funds: Cali Cartel, Colombia.
- Description of property purchased: 106' x 33' x 8' draft, all-aluminum catamaran oceanographic research vessel, Ridgely Warfield, Seafood, NY.
- Total price: $310,000.
- Amount of U.S. currency received: $192,000.
- Name of business reporting the transaction: Rapid Air Transport Services, Inc., Lantana Airport, Lantana, Florida.
- Description of business in Part 45: Drug smuggling.
- Who provided the money, in Part II, 22: Member of the Cali drug cartel.
- Describe their business, section 25: Drug smuggling.

Declaration

Attached to these forms was a declaration by Pitt:

I am a C.I. with United States Customs out of Beaumont, TX. I am signed up with agent Roger Bowers. I was in Pereira, Colombia on Sunday, January 16-17, 1994. I met with Rodrigo Lauriano at his Tosty's chicken restaurant. I showed him a advertisement for the sale of a oceanographic research vessel. He said he would like to invest in the purchase of it. Lauriano is a member of the Cali Cartel. I gave him my mobile number here in Florida and he said he might contact me. I was called on 1/31/94 and told to meet a man named Cus at the Burger King on Biscayne and Ives Dary Rd, North Miami. It took me 30 minutes to get there.

I met a Hispanic individual who identified himself as Cus. He spoke fluent English and was about 25 years old, thin build, sandy blond hair, and about 5'8" tall.

Late on 2/1/94 I again received the same call on my mobile phone. I met at the same spot and received $169,875.00 .

This person is a Cartel member and is interested in supplying drugs to Europe. For identity, contact Roger Bowers, Resident Agent in Charge in Beaumont, Tx. At 409-839-2401. This individual listed on Form 8300 served time in the United States prison system (federal). He has a twin brother named Aurelaene Audio Laureno. When I was in Colombia, I took photos of the two brothers and gave them to Roger Bowers. The photos were taken in their place of business in Pereira, Colombia. Please contact agent Rose Pinada at F.D.L.E. at 305-942-2460 as the funds have been used to purchase a vessel that will be based out of Florida.

Richard Pitt
President
Rapid Air Transport Services

Government Instructions to Hide Boat Ownership

As revealed by the recorded telephone conversations, Bowers instructed Pitt on how to establish a company to hold ownership of the boat and other assets so that it would hide any connection between the boat and Bowers' undercover agent should the plan backfire. Pitt incorporated a shell company called Rapid Air Transport Services (RATS), which was also intended to provide a cover against drug cartel snooping.

Purchasing the Ridgely Warfield

The present owner, Brian Degulas, had the boat listed at $499,000, but after negotiations the price was lowered to $320,000 if it was purchased within ten days. Strube gave a $10,000 deposit, Pitt used the $189,000 given to him by the Colombian drug trafficker, and Strube's mother provided them with a $130,000 loan. The sale was completed.

At the time of purchase, the boat was moored at Montauk Point at the eastern tip of Long Island, and the changing weather threatened to prevent moving the boat until spring. Strube quickly got a crew together and headed the boat for Miami. Storms unexpectedly moved into the area, causing swells 20 feet high, making the trip miserable. All types of problems occurred, including bad fuel, engine breakdowns, and generator failures, extending the trip several weeks. During this time, Strube and Pitt kept Bowers and Mohle advised of the boat's progress.

Miami Customs Agent Inspecting the Ridgely Warfield

Once the boat reached Miami and moored at the Merrill Stevens Boat yard on the Miami River, it was inspected by Miami Customs agent Bob Rutherford, who was so enthused about the boat and the plan that he came back with his supervisor the next day. Bowers told Pitt that his regional bosses in Houston approved the plan. Other government offices contacted Pitt seeking to have the Ridgely Warfield used in other undercover drug operations. Strube took pictures of the Customs agents inspecting the boat.

Seeking Future Publicity for the Planned Drug Bust

Pitt didn't intend to have the drug bust go unnoticed. He advised television producer Randy Grinter of the planned drug bust and suggested he take television footage of the boat. Grinter helped place hidden television cameras and microphones in key positions on the boat to record the entire operation which could be used for subsequent drug prosecutions. He also notified Douglas Waller and Melinda Liu of *Time* magazine.

San Andres Island—Major Drug Gateway

The plan was to take the Ridgely Warfield from Miami to a point 22 miles offshore from Colombia's San Andreas Island on the 300 degree radial from the island's radio beacon, the accuracy of the rendezvous point provided by Global Positioning System (GPS) equipment. The cocaine would be brought from the island by boat at night and transferred to the Ridgely Warfield.

San Andres Island is a major drug transporting location, and immensely profitable for the military and civilian government personnel extracting fees from those using the island for shipping drugs. Pitt explained that various drug lords and drug traffickers store drugs in a facility under the control of the island military commander, and upon instructions, he releases a certain amount of the drugs to designated parties to be taken either to an airplane or boat.

The plan was to have Customs agents on the Ridgely Warfield to witness the operation and for a U.S. Coast Guard cutter standing by over the horizon in the event of trouble. It was planned that three drug loads would be placed on board the boat on three successive nights, and after each load, the Ridgely Warfield would rendezvous with the Coast Guard cutter and transfer the loads. The Ridgely Warfield would then return to its rendezvous point for loading the drugs from each of the two subsequent shipments. After the three loads were delivered to the boat, the Ridgely Warfield would go to Key West, where the drugs would be transferred to a Coast Guard C-130 aircraft. This aircraft would then fly the drugs to various destinations for final delivery by Pitt and Jorge Restrepo to the recipients in New York, Houston, and Miami. The deliveries would be monitored at every step by government agents and at the opportune time, drug arrests would be made that would destroy a major Colombian drug distribution network. If it succeeded, it would inflict enormous damage on Colombian drug distributors.

An Unanticipated Danger to Pitt's Plan

As described in the third edition of *Defrauding America*, the CIA has been secretly—at least as far as the American public is concerned—engaging in drug trafficking for decades with drug cartels and organized crime families. Assuming that this scenario is correct, and I and many others know it to be so, then Pitt's plans to inflict major harm on three of Colombia's major drug cartels, and their vast distribution networks in the United States, would threaten CIA operations. Obviously, Pitt's plans would have to be sabotaged somewhere along the way. Many times in the past, when government agents discovered this relationship, Justice Department prosecutors would enter the picture and file false charges against the individual, insuring that the information would not reach the public.

Sudden Change in Plans

Although the cartel members approved the plan, one of them demanded that Pitt and Strube first prove their trustworthiness. In June 1994, while waiting for the go-ahead from the cartels, Don Arcesio told Pitt that the cartels had one remaining reservation to be resolved: Pitt had to transport three loads of drugs already in the United States from Los Angeles to New York. Pitt then contacted Customs agents Bowers and Mohle, and Bowers approved the test runs, with the usual self-protective comment, "Don't give me the details, just do it."

Test Run Problems

When the Colombians set up the first test run on July 13, 1994, Pitt was unable to carry it out because he was a primary witness for the government in a criminal trial at Beaumont, Texas. He asked Strube to take a commercial flight to Los Angeles and baby-sit the Colombians until he got there. But the Colombians pressured Strube to take the load even though Pitt was not there. Rather than risk losing the cartel's confidence, Strube drove the load to Las Vegas, where another member of Pitt's team, Wallace Pitt, drove it to New York. As instructed by Don Arcesio, three different cells in New York received the cocaine: 15 kilograms were delivered to a trafficker named Roberto, 35 kilos were to be delivered to Gloria Ramirez and her partner, Hugo Medina, and 100 kilos went to an unknown third party.

Pitt finished his testimony and Customs provided him a plane ticket on American Airlines to Los Angeles; they knew he was carrying out one of the test runs. Ordinarily, Pitt would have flown these test runs with his airplane, but it was out of service for repairs, forcing Pitt to use a van. During the second test run in July of 1994 from Los Angeles to New York, Pitt stopped overnight at Strube's home in Columbia, Pennsylvania, and the next morning continued on to New York City.

Big Trouble on the Third Test Run

On August 20, 1994, the third and final test run of 186 kilos of cocaine was picked up by Pitt, his brother Tony, and Duane Honaker, a pilot for the U.S. Department of Agriculture who was working in Mexico. Unknown to them, a State of California drug task force had intercepted a telephone message by Colombians referring to the drug shipment Pitt was to pick up.

The message contained a code, 24-150-900. The 24 referred to a particular member of the drug organization, the 150 meant 150 kilos of cocaine, and the 900 referred to a particular location. Elsewhere, agents were carrying out a surveillance of a house at 6112 Indian Terrace in Pasadena, California, being used by the drug group. As a pickup truck-camper left the house, agents followed it and eventually saw the drugs transferred to Pitt's van. The van was followed eastbound out of Los Angeles until it passed the small town of Victorville, where the California Highway Patrol stopped the vehicle and arrested the occupants.

Calling Customs Immediately Upon Being Arrested

Immediately upon being arrested, Pitt called Customs agent Bowers, explaining the problem. Bowers then called California authorities, advising them that Pitt was a documented undercover agent. After several months, California

Attorney General Dan Lungren dropped state charges against all three of them. Tony Pitt and Honaker were released. Charges filed by the Florida Department of Law Enforcement (FDLE) for a matter occurring nine years earlier delayed Pitt's release.

Florida FDLE agent Billy Wolfe in the Tampa office, with whom Pitt had once worked, was angry that Pitt left them to work undercover for Beaumont Customs and had filed charges against Pitt based on a conspiracy charge. This charge arose from Pitt loaning his van to two former drug-trafficking friends, Mike Culler and Chuck Greenfield. They had used Pitt's vehicle to move drugs when their airplane made an unplanned emergency landing on May 25, 1985, close to Daytona Beach. The far-reaching conspiracy statute came into play.

Continuing the Planned Sting Operation while Incarcerated

While Pitt was in jail, Customs agents came into the West Valley Detention Center in San Bernardino, California, to help record phone calls Pitt made to the Colombians, including Don Arcesio. Arcesio told Pitt he had obtained additional drugs to put on the Ridgely Warfield, raising the amount from the previous 16,000 kilos to 21,000 kilos. That would have been the biggest drug bust in U.S. history, and would have inflicted great harm upon three of the key Colombian drug kingpins, and decimated the Colombian's distribution centers in the United States, if nothing stopped the plan.

Who's On First?

While putting distance between themselves and Pitt, Bowers and Mohle insisted that Strube continue with the Ridgely Warfield drug pickup plan. During the weeks and months following Pitt's arrest, and while he was still incarcerated, Strube made many three-way telephone calls between Pitt and the Colombian traffickers, between Pitt and his undercover group, and with Customs agents Bowers and Mohle.

Feared He Also would be Sabotaged by DOJ Prosecutors

Strube feared that he could be suddenly abandoned and subsequently charged with a drug-related offense, and began recording phone calls. He was also concerned for his physical safety. The Colombians had already invested over a quarter of a million dollars in the Ridgely Warfield and considered themselves partners with Pitt and Strube. Members of the Colombian cartels had even visited his home.

Customs agents Bowers and Mohle wanted Strube to carry on without Pitt, playing the active undercover role formerly played by Pitt. Strube protested because he did not have the Colombian contacts that Pitt had, and he didn't speak Spanish.

Mexican Standoff Between Customs and DOJ

Customs asked Strube to obtain evidence against a local Pennsylvania drug trafficker, George Morales. But more bizarre events were unfolding. While Strube sought to obtain evidence against Morales for the U.S. Customs, Justice Department prosecutors were offering to drop charges against Morales on condition that he testify against Strube. It was like a Mexican standoff, spy against spy, except that the major drug trafficker, Morales, had the power of the U.S. Department of Justice behind him.

Customs Fiefdom Versus Justice Department Fiefdom

For two years after Pitt's August 20,1994 arrest, Beaumont Customs agents communicated with Strube, encouraging him to continue with the Ridgely Warfield plan and also to obtain information about Morales. Unknown to Strube and Pitt, Customs agents were *now* working with Justice Department prosecutors to charge Strube and Pitt with drug-related offenses related to the three test runs that were part of the Customs-approved undercover operation involving the Ridgely Warfield. These charges could result in life-imprisonment for each of them.

Before this change occurred between Customs and Strube, Mohle confided to Strube that he himself was being investigated by the FBI for his role in the three test runs. Mohle would have to either admit the test runs were part of the authorized undercover operation—and face charges by a career-happy prosecutor, or disclaim any knowledge of the operation.

DOJ Sabotaging the Greatest Drug Bust In U.S. History

For months, while Justice Department agents prepared a case against Strube, they knew Strube was a documented undercover agent for U.S. Customs in Beaumont. They knew Strube and Pitt were in the midst of inflicting great damage upon three Colombian drug cartels and many of their distribution cells in the United States. Justice Department personnel, up to and including Attorney General Janet Reno, knew that the greatest harm ever inflicted upon the Colombian drug cartels and their distribution centers in the United States was about to occur—unless Pitt and Strube were stopped.

Typical Justice Department Fraud to Obtain Search Warrant

Based upon fabricated statements obtained from imprisoned drug trafficker Morales, DOJ prosecutors obtained a search warrant for Strube's home from U.S. Magistrate Arnold C. Rappoport. (Magistrates are often part-time federal employees, who often have a private law practice, and are retained only as long as they please Justice Department prosecutors.) Morales gave an affidavit stating that he had seen a one-pound block of methamphetamine in Strube's home. It was actually a salt-block commonly found on farms for cattle and deer. Morales sought a get-out-of-prison reward for testifying as DOJ prosecutors wanted him to testify.

Paramilitary Attack on Strube's Home

Over 150 government agents stormed Strube's home, ransacking it for two days (August 20 and 21, 1994), seizing several dozen tape recordings that Pitt and Strube had made of conversations with Customs agents Bowers and Mohle. They seized pictures of Customs agents on the Ridgely Warfield, and seized Pitt's two diaries, all of which were crucial to their defenses against the charges about to be made against them by the Department of Justice.

A Federal Law That Puts Many Innocent People in Prison

A federal law not known to many people states that anyone convicted of a felony, which can be any one of thousands of minor technical offenses, cannot possess or have available to him or her, firearms. Possibly not knowing this, Strube's wife, Star, engaged in firearm sales as a federally licensed dealer and kept an inventory of various rifles and pistols in the home. Federal prosecutors than charged Strube with felony possession of firearms and charged his wife with aiding and abetting this offense.

Aiding and Abetting Major Colombian Drug Cartels

Justice Department prosecutors charged Pitt and Strube with cocaine possession, conspiracy, and money laundering, based upon the three test runs. Pitt and Strube admitted doing the acts that the DOJ prosecutor charged them with doing, but argued that these acts were part of a government agent approved plan to bring about a major drug bust.

Using Drug Traffickers to Imprison Government Contract Agents

Incredibly, the Department of Justice charges against Pitt and Strube were based upon the testimony of convicted drug traffickers already in prison or facing prison, including Morales, Gloria Ramirez and her drug partner Hugo Medina. These were the same people who would be charged with drug offenses by U.S. Customs based upon the testimony by Pitt and Strube.

More Suitable For A Movie or Book Satire

The Department of Justice's conduct was unreal, more suitable for a satirical novel. But for Pitt and Strube, it was real. DOJ prosecutors were using the fabricated testimony of known drug dealers to undermine two undercover agents who at great personal risk sought to bring about the biggest drug bust in U.S. history. If the contract agents succeeded, great harm would occur to several of the Colombians' biggest drug organizations and their distribution centers in the United States. Coincidentally, these same major drug organizations had long ties with elements within the CIA!

Strube Had Virtually No Role in Any Part of the Operation

Strube had virtually no part in those test runs. The three individuals who played a major part in the test runs were already released and not charged with any crime. Even the venue was wrong for filing the charges, suggesting that DOJ prosecutors were shopping for a judge who would assist in the sham cases against Pitt and Strube. The cases were filed in the Eastern District of Pennsylvania at Harrisburg, while Strube lived in the Middle District, and drug activities occurred in other court jurisdictions.

Court-Appointed Attorneys

On May 4, 1997, the court appointed attorney Bryan Walk of Harrisburg, Pennsylvania, to defend Pitt. Walk had never handled a federal criminal trial before, and was not familiar with or authorized to handle classified documents under the Classified Information Procedural Act (COPI). The attorney was overwhelmed by prosecutorial tactics, and failed to obtain depositions or testimony from important witnesses.

Weak and Amateurish Defense Attorney Opening Statement

The trial transcripts showed the opening statements of Pitt's attorney as the worst I had ever seen. Instead of outlining the issues, he discussed trivial facts that had no place in an opening statement where issues are in order. He rambled on until the judge had to order the attorney to conclude his speech.

Strube Did Even Worse With His Court-Appointed Attorney

Strube probably did even worse with his attorneys. Strube hired and paid in advance attorneys Carman Hasuti and Jeff Miller of the Philadelphia law firm of Hasuti and Miller, paying a substantial sum of money up front. After a meeting with FBI agents Dan P. Harelson and Scott Dimmick, the attorneys refused to provide any defense, and refused to return the money that had been put aside for defending the Strubes. This was their first encounter with the culture in the legal fraternity that I have been documenting for the past 30 years.

Strube's mother provided $58,000 and the Pagans Biker Club put up $10,000 to hire Harrisburg attorney Mark Lancaster. According to Pitt and Strube, hiring Lancaster was really a disaster. Lancaster had major personal problems with his wife who was planning a divorce. Instead of preparing for trial which included subpoenaing witnesses, obtaining discovery material, and taking depositions, he went on a one month vacation in the British Virgin Islands, coming back just six days before the start of trial. Boxes of exhibits had to be analyzed and a defense prepared. When he did return, Strube had difficulty contacting him, and when he did make contact, it was for minutes at a time, instead of the hours and even days of close contact required for a proper defense and to justify the large retainer that he was given.

Strube stated that the defense was chaotic and at best, incompetent. During the trial, Lancaster took long out-of-town trips instead of preparing for the next court date. During the trial, attorney Lancaster had to leave town to pick up his son who had run away from home. They said Lancaster had romantic problems involving his wife and an office secretary.

Lancaster bragged in court at the defense table about getting into her pants the night before. This was hardly the kind of research needed to prepare for the next day's trial! Pitt complained to Strube, "What he found in her pants is sure something he would have liked to know that pertained to our case!"

Another Major Attorney Mistake

Strube's attorney did not allow Strube to testify during the trial, causing the jurors to think that he must be guilty. And the prosecutor made this inference during his closing argument. Strube's attorney would have had to take time to prepare if Strube was to testify, but he was too busy with personal matters and his sexual activities.

The Pagan biker group had been targeted by local and federal officials for years, and was the recipient of harsh media reporting. Some members of motorcycle groups who joined the Pagans, did engage in drugs and other crimes. Strube was an officer in the mother club in Pennsylvania, responsible for security and setting up meetings, often held in various parts of Pennsylvania. During trial, regardless of his innocence, the jury would be prone to believe the worst of him, especially since the jurors came from the area where the Pagans were greatly disliked.

Pitt's Test Runs Had Direct and Implied Government Authority

The prosecutor argued during trial that Pitt and Strube were not authorized to fly the three test runs. Even if, for argument, Customs agents did not know and did not authorize the three test runs, a recognized doctrine of law, "implied authority," gave them authority to carry out the test runs as part of the overall authority given to obtain evidence on drug traffickers. Government agents instructed Pitt not to be concerned with giving them all the details of how he was going to carry out the operation. Further, if for argument, Pitt and Strube had misunderstood the extent of their authority, the fact that they did these acts as part of an approved government undercover operation did not justify the punishment the Department of Justice was seeking.

Denying Possession of Tapes That Receipts Showed They Had

During discovery, before the start of trial, Pitt's attorneys requested return of the tapes, pictures, and diaries that had been seized during the search of Strube's home. Prosecutor Eric Pfisterer repeatedly refused to return them. Finally, under pressure, Pfisterer released a few of the less-incriminating tapes the day after the trial started, but refused to return about 25 others. The evidence withheld would have provided still further proof that Pitt and Strube were acting under authority and knowledge of government agents.

Prosecutor Falsely Denies Having Important Exculpatory Evidence

During trial, defense attorneys again requested return of the seized tapes. Judge Sylvia Rambo called the attorneys to the bench, during which time the prosecutor said he had no other tapes and the judge accepted this denial. But the tapes were listed on the seizure list by federal agents and their existence could not be denied. The recorded tapes and pictures would show, for example:

- Florida agents instructing Pitt to kidnap a defendant from the Bahamas and bring him into the United States to be arrested.
- Customs agent instructing Pitt how to conduct sting operations in a foreign country without obtaining an in-country clearance.
- Customs agent instructing Pitt how to handle and hide money received from targeted drug traffickers.
- Customs agent instructing Pitt how to hide the ownership of the Ridgely Warfield.
- Customs agent instructing Pitt how to get around government regulations or policies prohibiting certain types of operations, instructions to hire foreign nationals in order to circumvent rules pertaining to U.S. citizens and agents.
- Customs agent instructing Pitt to contact a Texas sheriff when bringing a load of drugs into the United States; how to set up a corporation to hide the true ownership of aircraft and a boat used in a government-authorized operation, and instructions not to give them details of the test runs.
- Pictures of Customs agents on the Ridgely Warfield, which would impeach their testimony that they knew nothing about the boat or the operation.
- Tax records provided to the prosecutor at a "proffer" hearing showing the government's knowledge of drug money given to Pitt, its source, the purpose for the money: to purchase the Ridgely Warfield, and to show that the government knew almost every step of the operation.
- Pitt's diaries that recorded the day-to-day conversations with government agents.

Finally Releasing Some of What They Said They Didn't Have

The prosecutor finally returned one of Pitt's diaries but kept the one with the most sensitive information. He returned the photo album seized from Strube's home that originally had pictures of Customs agents on board the Ridgely Warfield—without the pictures that they had removed from the plastic pocket folders that had held them.

Prosecutorial Fraud During Trial

Prosecutor Eric Pfisterer initiated his deception during his opening statement:

> *Good morning. My name is Eric Pfisterer, and I represent the United States of America in this case. This case is about drugs as the judge has told you, specifically about cocaine, a lot of it; 486 kilos, roughly something over a thousand pounds. Cocaine distributed by these men, or intended to be distributed by them. The government will prove that Richard Lyman Pitt and William Michael Strube are drug dealers that conspired with others to distribute and intended to distribute that amount of drugs, and that they laundered approximately a million dollars in proceeds from the sale of those drugs.*

While making these statements, Pfisterer had in his arsenal of tricks perjured testimony from major drug traffickers. He withheld evidence showing the defendant's innocence that by law he was required to provide to them. He covered up for government authority that Pitt and Strube relied upon as they carried out their dangerous mission. If this Department of Justice attorney had a non-government position with a corporation or as a defense attorney, these same acts would result in a felony charge against him.

Judge Aiding Fraudulent Justice Department Charges

Chief Judge Sylvia H. Rambo conducted the trial at Harrisburg in the Eastern District of Pennsylvania. She committed a series of judicial abuses that insured Pitt and Strube would not receive a fair trial. She repeatedly:

- Protected the prosecutor's misconduct.
- Refused to allow the jury to hear the results of a lie-detector test that showed Pitt was telling the truth about being authorized to make the three test runs; that showed Pitt was telling the truth about Customs agents authorizing the operation and Customs agents being on the Ridgely Warfield, which Customs agents denied even knowing about.
- Allowed inflammatory statements by the prosecutor that had no basis in acts and which constituted grounds for a mistrial.
- Refused to require the prosecutor to return the audio tapes, picture and diary in pre-trial discovery and during the trial.
- Rushed the defense attorneys to finish the case, stating she had another trial coming up.
- Refused to allow the jury to hear significant segments of the few tapes that *were* introduced by the defendants that would have impeached the prosecutor's witnesses. Judge Rambo refused to allow the jurors to see any of the tape transcripts and limited the playing of the tapes to a few minor statements, avoiding hearing enough so that they could understand the nature of the authority given to Pitt.

Judge's Reported Prior Association With Drug Traffickers

A friend of mine, Darlene Novinger, who I wrote about in the third edition of *Defrauding America*, was a confidential informant working in Pennsylvania, and helped develop evidence that brought about the conviction of several Pennsylvania state prosecutors. Novinger told me that years earlier she learned about Judge Rambo's social and other contacts with drug users and dealers.

Government Employees' Coordinated Pattern of Lying

The testimony by the prosecutor's government witnesses was that the three test runs were not known by government agents, that the test runs were not authorized, and that the government agents had no knowledge of the Ridgely Warfield or its planned operation. They lied. At that time the prosecutor and his witnesses *did not know* that Pitt and Strube had other tape recordings that Pitt had left in attorney Al Nygaard's possession. The testimony by government agents then changed to the usual, "I don't recall," a diversionary practice made famous by the President Bill Clinton administration that sidesteps the need to lie.

Roger Bowers, Resident Agent in Charge (RAC) of the Beaumont office, testified falsely during the trial. He testified that he did not know about the three test runs, that he did not know about the Ridgely Warfield, that he did not authorize the Ridgely Warfield operation, and had never made any of the other statements that tape records showed *he did make*.

After several prosecution witnesses testified that they knew nothing about the test runs or the Ridgely Warfield, Pitt's attorney introduced transcripts and tapes of telephone conversations that had been made between Pitt and Customs agents Bowers and Mohle. Here are a few of the key statements Judge Rambo prevented the jury from hearing:

A December 23, 1993 tape shows Customs Agent Bowers stating to Pitt: *You report to me what you want to report to me .... I don't know about it. I don't know about it. I don't know about it. I don't know any other way to put it any clearer than that...The big boss in Houston signed off on the deal.....And so, as I was telling you earlier, however you want to handle that is the best way to handle it....*

A December 27, 1993 tape shows Customs Agent Bowers stating to Pitt: *I don't know, I don't know. How can I make it any clearer than that? My supervisors in Houston are knowledgeable of this. You and I have an understanding how things are done.*

A January 5, 1994 tape shows Bowers instructing Pitt how to hide the ownership of the boat and how to circumvent government regulations: *The original purchaser needs not to be you. I'm an agent of the government. I can't do certain things but my boat can get around these rules if it's in a corporation. It can go to Colombia. You know what I'm saying.*

A February 3, 1994 tape between Pitt, Bowers, and Mohle reveals Customs agent Bowers saying he doesn't want details concerning how the test runs were being carried out and if such details were about to be given to him, he would stop the conversation: *If I don't need to know about it, I'll stop you and tell you that I don't really need the details....All I need is the generalities....I don't really need the details....I think you and I have a understanding about how we do things....If the bad boys want to help pay their way into prison, I don't have a problem with that....We had an allowance for that.... My supervisors and I have discussed these issues before....You report to me what you want to report to me...* [Bowers tells Pitt how to sneak money out of

Mexico to launder it; discusses the crewing of the Ridgely Warfield; instruction for Pitt to keep a diary; instruction not to discuss anything with other Customs offices, or with Florida FDLE Agent Rose Pinada, or the IRS].

These are only a fraction of the tapes and revealing statements that were known to Justice Department personnel and which Judge Rambo barred from being heard. Throughout the recorded tape conversations, Bowers and Mohle are shown telling Pitt and Strube not to give them details of the operations, including the three test runs. They authorized the test runs but didn't want the details. As government agents, they gave Pitt and Strube implied authority to carry out the mission.

Overwhelming Evidence of Pitt and Strube's Innocence

Attorney Al Nygaard testified that Pitt made out IRS and other government forms showing in great detail his undercover drug operations and receipt of drug money from drug lords. Nygaard testified that Pitt kept his government handlers aware of every step of the operation.

Nygaard testified about the government checks paid to Pitt for his undercover drug operations, and presented a copy of one check for $250,000. FBI agent Harelson testified, referring to a FBI 302 form that he had made out, showing that Customs agent Roger Bowers did not want to be kept abreast of the details in Pitt's undercover operations.

Dropping Charges Arising From the Third Test Run

The dropping of charges by the State of California relating to the third test run after Customs intervened was further indication that the test runs were authorized. Otherwise, why would the charges have been dropped?

Warned About DOJ Perjured Testimony

During an interview in state prison, Customs Agent Joe Wolfe from the Harrisburg office, with IRS agent Frank Monaghan present, warned Pitt (October 31, 1996) that Customs agent Rutherford was going to give perjured testimony. After discovering that Rutherford's voice was on some of the tapes showing that he knew of the approved operation, the prosecutor canceled Rutherford's planned appearance. A Justice Department employee, and prosecutor Eric Pfisterer's boss, close to the case, told a newsman that "He's deeply disturbed and embarrassed with what U.S. Customs agents said and did in this case."

Documents Confirming Sanctioned Undercover Work

Nygaard testified to Pitt's undercover activities and the attorney's function to coordinate claims for reimbursement of expenses and compensation with the government. Among the documents Nygaard presented into the trial was a November 23, 1993, application to the government for reimbursement and compensation as an undercover agent, Nygaard filled out the claim form. Under "circumstances." Nygaard wrote:

The Claimant, SA-73-PU, entered into an agreement with the United States Customs Service concerning a case involving Enrique Cedeno Acereto et al (PU02CR3PU004) on June 6, 1993. Pursuant to that Agreement, Claimant provided the USCS with the original information that led to the forfeiture of $1,190,260.00 USD in cash in connection with viola-

tions of the Customs laws relating to controlled substances. Per paragraph 15 of the Agreement between the Source and the USCS (see attached copy of the Agreement), the Source was allowed to keep $100,000 of the monies given to him by the violators. This amount is not included in the $1,190,260.00 which was seized and forfeited by the USCS. Paragraph 2 of the Agreement allows for reimbursement of expenses incurred in this investigation if approved by the USCS; the Source has not sought reimbursement of expenses nor has he been paid any for this investigation. The source has received no amount in advance for a claim of compensation or reward for original information under 19 U.S.C. 1619.

Under the Agreement, SA-73-PU arranged for the sale of cocaine to the violators. This sale is known as a "reverse" The violators payed $1,290,260.00 to SA-73-PU as an illegal payment in connection with the purchase or attempted purchase of cocaine. SA-73-PU turned $1,290,260.00 over to the USCS and this led to the above seizure of funds received by the Source. In fact, SA-73-PU delivered the money from McAllen, Texas to Beaumont, Texas in his own aircraft. As a result of the information and cooperation of the Source, it led to the arrest of Enrique Cedeno Acereto, Oscar Gil Urena, and Lyle Kenneth Stelter for violations of the controlled substances laws: 18 USC 981, 21 USC 841, and 21 USC 846.

Government Agencies Repeatedly Rely Upon Polygraph Tests

The CIA, the FBI, and other government agencies rely upon the results of lie detector tests. And when the tests can prove a person's innocence, and protect against a life-in-prison sentence, it is outrageous to block their use. Strube also took a lie detector test after the trial in April 1998, and the results also showed that he was acting upon the understanding that the test runs were government-authorized. In this trial, there was such a conflict between testimony given by Pitt and government agents that, in the interest of justice, the results of Pitt's lie detector tests were absolutely proper.

The contract agent agreement between Pitt and U.S. Customs called for periodic lie detector tests. The last one that Pitt took was on June 3, 1995, which he passed with no problems.

Judge's Prejudicial Jury Instructions

Before the jury started deliberation, Judge Rambo read jury instructions to them, omitting key defenses Pitt and Strube relied upon and to which they were entitled under law. The judge told the jury that government agents lacked authority to authorize Pitt to transport drugs in a undercover operation. That was stated despite the fact that government agents routinely engage in such activities.

Supreme Court: Government Drug Transportation Permissible

Further contradicting Judge Rambo's statement to the jury, a U.S. Supreme Court decision held that it was a permissible practice. In *United States v. Russell*, 411 U.S. 423, 432 (1973), the Supreme Court upheld the general rule that "criminal prohibitions do not generally apply to reasonable enforcement actions by officers of the law." It was saying that the government's limited undercover participation in an unlawful operation is "a recognized and permissible means of investigation."

Guilty Said the Naive Jurors!

On September 2, 1997, the jurors rendered a decision, holding Pitt and Strube guilty. Despite all the evidence showing the innocence of Pitt and Strube, the jurors, possibly thinking the government surely would not charge a person with a criminal offense if the person was not guilty, took the easy way out and held both of them guilty. In this way, the jurors aided and abetted the crimes by the prosecutor, enabled drug traffickers to go free, caused two contract agents involved in very dangerous activities to go to prison—for life, and destroy their families.

The illiteracy of the average person to the corruption in government certainly plays a role in the tragic decisions many jurors render. Probably the worst type of juror for aiding and abetting prosecutorial misconduct is the middle-class person—too lazy to get informed, who is smug in thinking himself honest, and who makes possible some of the worst government outrages ever committed in the history of the United States.

Conservative and Ignorant About Corruption in Government

During trial, U.S. Marshals who transported Pitt and Strube to and from the court room explained that the Harrisburg jury was a very conservative group, typical middle-class who remain ignorant of government corruption, and will believe virtually anything the government claims.

Sorry Form of Legal Counsel

After the jury decision, instead of speaking favorably of his client when asked by reporters, Lancaster said, "Let the indictment speak for itself." Lancaster was implying that the jury's decision was justified. How stupid of this incompetent attorney whose miserable performance and conduct enabled his client to receive a life-in-prison sentence!

Judge Compounds Prosecutorial Corruption

Strube and Pitt were sentenced on different dates. For living in the same house as his wife who conducted a gun business, Chief U.S. District Judge Edward N. Cahn, in Allentown, Pennsylvania, sentenced Michael Strube (June 16, 1998) to a six-and-half-year prison sentence and ordered him to pay $50,000. No evidence was presented that he ever handled any of the firearms.

Strube was sentenced in Harrisburg (July 9, 1998) to three prison sentences by Chief U.S. District Judge Sylvia H. Rambo: 30 years, 30 years, and 20 years. Strube's only role in the test runs was to operate the Ridgely Warfield. He played a minor role in transporting the first test run from Los Angeles to Las Vegas when Pitt was unavailable so that the planned operation did not get sidetracked.

Star Strube, who had no role whatsoever in the government-authorized test runs, was sentenced (August 3, 1998) by Chief U.S. District Judge Edward N. Cahn in Allentown, Pennsylvania, to five years probation with the first year confined to home. She was licensed by the federal government as an arms dealer and had a right to engage in this occupation. But because her husband had *access* to the guns, the Justice Department prosecutors charged her with *conspiracy*, a convenient catchall charge that can make most Americans unindicted felons.

Pitt was sentenced (June 18, 1998) by Judge Rambo to three life-in-prison terms for the test runs and 20 years in prison for money laundering associated with the tests. She also ordered Pitt and Strube to forfeit over $1 million in drug profits they allegedly made during the test runs, when there was no evidence that they made any money on the runs. But the money judgment made it possible to seize all the assets belonging to Strube and Pitt, which had been in the family for years and were not in any way related to any drug profit.

Received Additional Tapes Showing Their Innocence

After the trial, Justice Department employees returned to Strube a truck-load of personal items that they seized during the pre-trial raid (December 1998), and accidentally included many of the revealing audio tapes that had been withheld during the trial. Strube's attorney, Bill Tunkey, who was preparing Strube's appeal, had them transcribed. Throughout the tapes were statements by Customs agents Bowers and Mohle authorizing the Ridgely Warfield operation and directing Pitt on how to hide ownership of the boat and the government forms that should be made out. The following are a few of the statements made by Bowers and Mohle showing that they lied under oath during trial:

Bowers: Let me know when the big boat arrives. I may fly down there and take a look at it myself.

Mohle: I can make a phone call and probably get you free security for it [Ridgely Warfield] down at Palm Beach [referring to the West Palm Beach Customs officer].

Bowers: As far as I'm concerned, you know, these people over in Colombia have entered into a half-boat deal with you, which in itself is not illegal. But until such time as they engage in any kind of illegal activity, I have really no interest in that, nor should anyone else with Customs as far as you're concerned. I certainly wouldn't wave it in front of Rose [Rose Pinada of Florida FDLE] or anyone else's face either. As far as the actual transaction and that sort of thing, you be very careful who you confide in there. If I don't need to know about it, I'll stop you and tell you that I don't really need the details. All I need is the generalities. But you know, I think you and I have a understanding about how we do this. And they have an overall objective to them.

Bowers: Richard, I've tried every way I can to get this done through the proper channels. You know what's gotta be done, I can't tell you any more. We discussed this on several occasions this problem. Let's get it done. OK!

Plea by Friend of Attorney General Janet Reno

A former friend and attorney-associate of U.S. Attorney General Janet Reno was so outraged by the miscarriage of justice in the Pitt-Strube cases that Miami attorney William R. Tunkey wrote a letter to Reno (April 28, 1998) stating in part:

A tragic miscarriage of justice is slowly unfolding in Harrisburg and Philadelphia, Pennsylvania. The complexity of the issues implicated in these cases warrant my humble request for your personal attention to the task of righting this wrong. You know me well and long enough that I would not make such a plea lightly or in the absence of just cause.

Mr. Strube ... may soon be sentenced to life in prison ... arises from his whole-hearted, well-intentioned effort....Mr. Strube's Harrisburg, Pennsylvania, convictions for conspiracy to distribute and distribution of cocaine, and money laundering devolve from his sincerely well-intentioned and government-sanctioned efforts to strike a major blow against the Cali drug cartel: the seizure of approximately 16,000 kilograms of cocaine and untold millions of dollars in drug cash, the identification and arrest of dozens of drug traffickers, the destruction and decimation of four United States-based cells of the cartel and the seizure of vehicles and properties owned by drug traffickers.

Mr. Strube has risked his life (and his incarceration exposes him to that same threat) as well as the lives of his family, in service to his country. Please review this, then give me an opportunity to meet and discuss the steps that I believe should be taken to redress the injustice of Mr. Strube's incarceration.

Reno never acted on this letter. Pitt and I exchanged many letters and he provided me a great amount of facts and documentation. In one letter he wrote:

Never in my 49 years have I heard of nor seen an attorney sabotage a case as I did Mark Lancaster of Mike's (Strube). He was totally incompetent, lied to Mike and I about his past experience in federal court. After the trial, he absolutely abandoned Mike, making Mike whole-heartedly believe that he was going to do the post-trial motion, doing them, and that everything was going along on schedule. He lied to Mike, outright lied to him. The deadline came and went to submit the motions, and not a word from Lancaster. When Judge Rambo indicated she would grant more time, Mark left the impression with Star, Mike and Bill Tunkey that he was going to go ahead and file the briefs for Mike. He didn't, and Mike lost all those chances.

Referring to his trial lawyer, Bryan Walk, Pitt said:

Bryan Walk was not that competent in this type of a trial. It was the first federal case he had ever tried. And he was always telling me about his fear of working again in federal court, and how he didn't want to piss anyone off. As far as classified material was concerned, Bryan had no idea how to ask for it, let alone even how to subpoena Bowers and Mohle, plus the files they had on me.

Turning Families Against Each Other

A standard prosecutorial practice is to file, or threaten to file, sham charges against other members of a family including a wife, mother, or aged parents. The defendants are then given the choice of having the charges against the innocent family members dropped if they plead guilty to charges that they may not be guilty of, or to greatly exaggerated charges. Or members of the family may be pressured to give testimony to avoid being charged. Pitt said:

What hurt so bad during the trial is that my brother Tony Pitt caved into the copious coercive verbiage Pfisterer and Customs agent Wolfe threw

*at him. I thought he had more balls than that. It's not that Tony's testi-
mony was anything less than veracious, he told the truth as much as I
could tell and remember. We did what we were told to do by Customs, but
for my own brother to jump to the side of the prosecution was too much.
I noticed that during the whole trial while my brother was on the stand,
he could not look at me or Mike. It's a shame when a prosecutor can
cower a family into turning against one another.*

Pitt thought back to better times when he and his brother were close friends:
*All the things my brother and I have been through together since we first
met in 1978, the drug runs, the escape out of Mexico in 1982 (he helped).
Sometimes he came to bring me my monthly care packages after I was extradited back to Mexico in 1986 through 1992. I could not believe he
dropped his tail between his legs and crawled into the courtroom at the
beckoning of the prosecutor's office. All I can say is that he's a gutless
bastard.*

DOJ-Arranged Assassination of Undercover Agents

When Justice Department prosecutors sabotaged Pitt's undercover activities and conducted a trial in open court, they knowingly revealed the identities
of foreign nationals working as documented undercover agents in Mexico and
Colombia. It was obvious that they would be killed as soon as their role became known to the drug cartels.

In early 1998, Pitt wrote that he expected Esteban Borges Figeroa, a
Mexican living in Tuxtla Gutierrez Chiapas, Mexico, and Jorge Ortiz Restrepo, a Colombian living in Pereira, Colombia, to be assassinated before
long. Both were undercover agents approved by Customs agents Bowers and
Mohle and had been recruited by Pitt. Despite the need to keep their identity
secret, Justice Department prosecutors revealed their names during the trial.
Both had been promised by Beaumont Customs agents assistance in obtaining
permanent visas to bring their families into the United States. Instead, they
were betrayed.

Pitt's Prophetic Forecast of Assassinations

In a prophetic June 12, 1998 letter, Pitt wrote:
*He [Jorge Ortiz] was talked about in trial and indicted along with the rest
of us. If he's not dead yet, he soon will be. He's a good kid. He does not
deserve this. I believe, and have believed since the first day Mike and I
were in court, that Jorge is a dead man, his days are numbered in his
country. I would not be surprised to have someone tell me soon that Jorge
is dead in Colombia. Colombians kill their own, without prejudice, for
simply messing up a drug shipment. They take great pleasure and spend
many hours, or days, toying with a traitor (one of their own), while skin-
ning him alive.*

The First to Be Assassinated

Esteban was the first to be assassinated. He was gunned down in Mexico
on July 26, 1998, as Pitt predicted and Justice Department personnel expected.
His dream, and that of his family, of immigrating to the United States, was not
to be. His widow conveyed her fears to Pat Becker in Florida that she too may
be assassinated. Jorge would be next.

The Next to Be Assassinated

On October 26, 1998, Jorge was gunned down in Brazil. Neither he, nor his family, would experience the dream of immigrating to the United States. His death was also made possible by the corruption in the U.S. Department of Justice.

Ortiz Restrepo—Richard Pitt--Arcessio Esteban

Government check for Pitt: $250,000

A Depressed Richard Pitt

These deaths affected Pitt very hard. He had recruited, trained, and worked with the victims for several years. Especially hard to take was Jorge's assassination. Pitt's October 31, 1998, letter stated:

That happy, handsome young Colombian, who I spent five years in a Mexican prison with, who fought along with me back to back holding off the Mexicans at times, due to the fact we were the foreigners in their country. The kid I lifted weights with and bought him 2000 dollar suits in order for him to look good in front of the cartel big wigs—is dead. He had nowhere to run, nowhere to go and a corporation looking for him. It's no longer single cartels. They're now called a corporation with some of the longest tentacles in the world for feeling out their enemies. We must have done a very very good job of penetrating them as deeply as we did in order for them to hunt down Jorge and Esteban—to kill.

Today I sat alone on the bleacher here on the recreation field. No one else was around. It's Saturday and was early, and I had went out to do my running as soon as the doors opened. While sitting there, I turned to the empty seats and asked Jorge and Esteban if they were there. Of course I got no reply, didn't expect one, because I haven't went off the deep-end yet. Anyway, I went on to explain to them that they get the easy way out. I get to rot away alive in a prison instead of in the ground, as it should be.

Notice Of Another Assassination Tied in With DOJ Misconduct

I received notice of Esteban's death in a Mexican newspaper clipping that was sent to me by one of my other sources who is named in these pages; Rumaldo Solis. He was a veteran agent of the U.S. Immigration and Naturalization Service who was fraudulently prosecuted by Justice Department prosecutors after he reported and persisted in following up on a DEA drug trafficking operation in Mexico. The details are in other pages. When a Mexican journalist tried to investigate Solis' charges, which threatened to expose the DEA's involvement in Mexican drug trafficking, the journalist was killed. His death was reported in the same article that reported Esteban's murder. Here was *another* case in which Justice Department officials played a role. If they had not engaged in covering up criminal acts on the part of DEA agents operating a clandestine Mexican drug smuggling operation, and had not retaliated against Solis, that reporter probably would not have been killed.

Ugly Culture in DOJ Spreads its Human Tragedies

The deaths, the life-in-prison sentences, the destruction of families, brought about by the corrupt acts of Justice Department personnel resulted in benefits to all but the innocent. Justice Department prosecutors received outstanding personnel reports and bonuses. The large-scale heroin traffickers who gave the perjured testimony were released from prison. The Colombian drug cartels were saved from a devastating seizure of drugs and distribution centers. Again and again, this is the culture in government, which trickles down into the culture on a national and local level.

Appellate Briefs

On January 18, 1999, legal briefs were filed on behalf of Pitt and Strube. Strube's Miami attorneys, Benjamin Waxman and William Tunkey, filed an excellent brief that should, if the law was followed, vacate the judgment and sentence. Pitt's trial attorney improved on his dismal performance at trial and filed a more professional brief, which may have been prepared by another attorney.

The briefs, referring to Pitt and Strube as appellants, filed by the attorneys for Strube and Pitt, raised many defenses, including:

- Government authority defense. Government agents authorized Appellants to carry out the complex undercover operation. The judge committed reversible error when she refused to instruct the jury on the defense of "public authority." There was evidence entered into the trial showing that government agents possessed authority to authorize the undercover operations and that such operations were routine
- Outrageous government misconduct defense.
- Excluded exculpatory evidence. Refused to allow the jury to hear sufficient amount of the recorded telephone conversations between Appellants and the Customs agents. The judge abused her discretion when she improperly refused the request of the defense to play recorded conversations between government agents and the Appellants in support of their defenses.
- The DOJ failure to rebut the evidence that Appellants relied upon the representations of the government agents that they had authority to carry out the mission to bring about the arrest of the drug traffickers. The Appellants provided sufficient evidence that they were entrapped. It is the burden of the government to rebut the defense by proof beyond a reasonable doubt [which was not done].
- The DOJ violated mandatory rules of disclosure when it failed to provide the defense with discovery of the files and any documents relative to administrative sanction against the Customs agents involved.
- Absence of venue. The DOJ failed to provide any evidence that the crimes committed occurred within the Middle District of Pennsylvania. Therefore, venue did not rest within the trial court.

Filing A Motion to Submit an Amicus Brief

On February 12, 1999, I submitted a motion to the court of appeals seeking approval to file an amicus brief and affidavit, as provided by Federal Rules of Appellate Procedure Rule 29. In this request I stated that I had information pertinent to the case, that I would file an affidavit in support of my evidence, and that I would file a copy of this chapter, or of the completed book, along with the amicus brief.

Normally, a motion is acted upon within a short period of time, and in this case time was critical. When I did not hear any word on my motion I sent a March 29, 1999, letter to the court inquiring about its status. I included in my letter the comments:

The value that I can provide to the court would be via an affidavit and exhibits....will help fulfill obligations to report a pattern of criminal activities under federal law to a federal judge, as required to be reported by Title 18 USC Section 4.

Federal judges are required by law (Title 18 USC Section 4) to receive evidence of criminal activities offered to them. The court refused to receive my evidence that was attached to my motion to file an amicus brief. In a March 31, 1999, order, the court refused my motion and my offer to present evidence of criminal activities.

Other Harm Arising From DOJ Corruption

There was considerable fallout from Justice Department corruption upon which an entire book could easily be written. The misconduct by Justice Department personnel in this case brought about, for instance:

- Blocking the great harm that was about to be inflicted on several major Colombian drug organizations and their vast distribution network in the United States.
- Bringing about the deaths of two documented undercover agents and related grief to their families.
- Sentencing two government contract agents working highly dangerous undercover operations for the government to life in prison.
- Depriving Star Strube of her husband and eventual forfeiture of their home.
- Contributing to the spreading of moral decay, the corruption throughout government and society, causing other government agents to recognize the futility of honest conduct and the rewards for dishonest performance.
- Protecting and rewarding major drug traffickers who received suspended sentences or had charges dropped for providing perjured and suborned testimony requested by Justice Department prosecutors.
- Encouraging government agents to lie, to commit perjury, to further the DOJ's corrupting influence in government and throughout society.

Colombian Drug Lords Got the Last Laugh on Americans

Those who got the last laugh in this tragic drama of Justice Department corruption surely would include the Colombian drug lords who were targeted by Pitt and Strube and who were instead protected by DOJ personnel.

Covert Operations with Key Drug Lords Were Threatened

The largest drug bust in U.S. history was about to occur, inflicting enormous damage to three of the major drug cartels in Colombia and shutting down hundreds of distributors throughout the United States. Years of information from my many deep cover sources leaves no doubt in my mind that the CIA has close ties with major drug cartels, and that Pitt's operation threatened to inflict serious harm upon this relationship.

In addition, Pitt and Segers had uncovered other high-level criminal activities, providing still another reason to eliminate him. Strube's close relationship with Pitt required that he also be taken down.

DEPARTMENT OF THE TREASURY
U.S. CUSTOMS SERVICE
WASHINGTON, D.C.

ENF 2-02 CO:R:IT:P
631013 ST

Eldon Nygaard, Attorney
c/o Special Agent in Charge
4141 North Sam Houston Parkway, East
Houston, Texas 77032-3839

Dear Sir:

You are hereby referred to the Special Agent in Charge, Houston, Texas, for payment of Award of Compensation No. 19007, in the amount of $250,000, to your client (claimant SA-73-PU), as authorized by title 19, United States Code, section 1619. The award is for original information furnished concerning violations of the Customs or navigation laws, or certain other laws enforced by the Customs Service, as covered by Port Arthur District Case No. 93-2101-00023 and Port Arthur Office of Enforcement Case No. PU02CRPU004.

Sincerely,

(signed) Stuart P. Seidel

Stuart P. Seidel
Director, International
Trade Compliance Division

Customs Letter Awarding Pitt $250,000

Form 8300

Report of Cash Payments Over $10,000 Received in a Trade or Business

(Rev. February 1992)

Department of the Treasury
Internal Revenue Service

Failure to file this form or filing a false form may result in imprisonment.

► See Instructions.
Please type or print.

OMB No. 1545-0892
Expires 09-30-94

Check appropriate boxes if: a ☐ amends prior report; b ☒ suspicious transaction.

Part I Identity of Individual From Whom the Cash Was Received

2 If more than one individual is involved, see instructions and check here . . . . ► ☒

3 Last name	4 First name	5 Middle initial	6 Social security number
Lauriano	Rodrigo	Kristizabe	un Known

7 Address (number, street, and apt. or suite no.)		8 Occupation, profession, or business
Testys Tele 34552 Pereira Colombia		Fast Food Restaurants Colombia

9 City	10 State	11 ZIP code	12 Country (if not U.S.)	13 Date of birth (see instructions)
Pereira	Columbia		Colombia	estimated 35 yrs old

14 Method used to verify identity: N/A a Describe identification ► See attached sheet b Issued by c Number

Part II Person (See Definitions) on Whose Behalf This Transaction Was Conducted

15 If this transaction was conducted on behalf of more than one person, see instructions and check here . . . . . ► ☒

16 This person is an: ☒ individual or ☒ organization 17 If funded by another party, see instructions and check here . ► ☐

18 Individual's last name or Organization's name	19 First name	20 Middle initial	21 Social security number
Lauriano	Rodrigo	Kristizabel	unknown

22 Doing business as (DBA) name (see instructions)		Employer identification number
Calli Cartel Colombia		unknown

23 Alien identification: a Describe identification ► See Report b Issued by c Number · unknown

24 Address (number, street, and apt. or suite no.) 25 Occupation, profession, or business

26 City 27 State 28 ZIP code 29 Country (if not U.S.) 30 Date of birth (see instructions)

Part III Description of Transaction and Method of Payment

31a ☐ personal property purchased d ☐ business services provided g ☐ exchange of cash
b ☐ real property purchased e ☐ intangible property purchased h ☐ escrow or trust funds
c ☐ personal services provided f ☐ debt obligations paid i ☒ other (specify) ► See attached

32 Specific description of property or service purchased. Give serial or registration number of car, airplane, etc., address of real estate, etc.
116' x 33 x 8' draft all aluminum Caterman oceanographic Research vessel; "Ridgley Warfield" Seaford n.y. (see attached Report)

33 Total price $ 20,000 .00 34 Amount of U.S. currency received $ 192,000 .00 35 Amount in $100 bills or larger $ 59,600 .00

36a Amount of cash received in other than U.S. currency (see instructions) . . . . $ None .00
b Specific description of cash received in other than U.S. currency See attached copy of $54,000 in bills plus a photo of all cash, plus deposit slips.

37 If part of an installment sale, give information below and check box . . . ► ☐ 38 Date of transaction
a Number of payments _____ b Amount of each payment $ _____ .00
c Frequency: ☐ monthly ☐ other (describe) d Balloon payment (amount) $ _____ .00

Part IV Business Reporting This Transaction

39 Name of reporting business	40 Employer identification number
Read air Transportation Services, Inc.	

41 Street address (number and street) where transaction occurred	Social security number
Ives Dairy Rd. / USS	

42 City	43 State	44 ZIP code	45 Nature of your business
North Miami	FL		Drug Smuggling

46 Under penalties of perjury, I declare that to the best of my knowledge the information I have furnished above is true, correct, and complete.

Sign Here

Authorized signature–See instructions)
(Type or print signer's name below)

(Title) President (Date signed) 2/2/54 (Telephone number of business) (305) 646-6228

Cat. No. 621338 Form **8300** (Rev. 2-88)

Pitt's Report of Drug Money Received

CHAPTER TWELVE

MEXICO'S ROLE IN
DRUGGING AMERICA

Mexico's widespread, endemically corrupt, government institutions constitute one of the greatest threats to the United States as they relate to the drug crisis. Collectively, Mexico is not only *not* cooperating in blocking the flow of drugs into the United States, it is actively *encouraging* other countries to ship their drugs to America via Mexico.

Who is to Blame for America's Drug Crisis?

Before looking at Mexico's role in America's drug crisis, attention must focus on where the crisis starts: and that is with America's drug users who lack the character and responsibility to alter their behavior. *They* are the ones who fund every aspect of drug-related crimes, murders, bulging prison populations and other tragedies associated with their gluttonous demand for drugs. Having said that, let's look at the problems in Mexico related to drugs.

Mexico's Drug Trafficking Poses Great Threat to U.S.

DEA chief Thomas A. Constantine warned (February 24, 1999) the Senate Caucus On International Narcotics Control that Mexican drug traffickers posed the worst criminal threat to the United States that he had seen in 40 years of law enforcement. Constantine went into details of the utter corruption in Mexico and how its military and its politicians are directly involved in moving drugs to the United States. He said in part:

Unlike the American organized crime leaders, organized crime figures in Mexico have at their disposal an army of personnel, an arsenal of weapons and the finest technology that money can buy. They literally run transportation and financial empires, and an insight into how they conduct their day-to-day business leads even the casual observer to the conclusion that the United States is facing a threat of unprecedented proportions and gravity.

Without the *direct actions* of many Mexican politicians, its presidents, its military, and its state and federal police, hundreds of tons of drugs flowing into the United States yearly would not be possible.

Relying on A Country Riddled with Corruption

The corrupt acts described in this chapter are but the tip of the iceberg, and for every reference given, there are thousands of similar occurrences. There are, of course, exceptions. Many brave Mexican people have spoken out, including journalists, police, politicians, and others, and many of them have suffered threats, torture, and death. Much of Mexico's population is hostage to these acts and seemingly powerless to halt the corruption that feeds down from corrupt government people—as in the United States.

Teaching Mexico's Police the Finer Points of Bribing and Stealing

The Mexican magazine, *Nexos*, published a report (early 1998) describing the culture in Mexico's police force. The report said police academy instructors taught the trainees the finer points of taking bribes and how to rob professionally. The report also described the practice of hiring admitted murderers as police and the utter corruption in the police force.

President's Brother Amassed A Fortune Providing Government Protection To Mexican and Colombian Drug Traffickers

From 1988 to 1994, while his brother Carlos Salinas was president of Mexico, Raul Salinas received vast sums of money for providing police, military and political protection for drugs shipped through Mexico to the United States.

Cartel's Nickname For the President's Brother—"Blood Sucker"

Not too pleased with the high drug protection money demanded by the president's brother, Colombians often referred to Raul Salinas by the nickname, "Chupa Sangre"—Blood Sucker. Salinas demanded an ever-increasing price for providing government protection to drug traffickers.

A 1998 *Washington Post* article said Swiss investigators discovered Raul Salinas received over $500 million in payoffs from drug dealers, including Cali and Medellin drug cartels, and that Swiss authorities seized $114 million of that money located in Swiss banks. The report was based upon examining over 30,000 documents and questioning over 70 witnesses. The Swiss report stated that Miguel Rodriguez Orejuela of the Cali cartel and Jose Gonzalo Rodriguez Gacha of the Medellin cartel gave tens of millions of dollars to Raul Salinas and that Salinas "took control of practically all drug shipments transiting Mexico" after his brother became president.

Secret Agreement Between Two Mexican Presidents

Bordering On Chaos, written by *Miami Herald* reporter Andres Oppenheimer, described Mexico's social and government sectors as a mass of corruption and injustice. The book claims that a 1995 agreement between President Carlos Salinas and Ernesto Zedillo assured the outgoing President Salinas that he would not be prosecuted for any crimes by the incoming presidency. The book explains the hodgepodge of cliques, political and business, and overlapping interests, in the ruling Institutional Revolutionary Party (PRI).

Hand-Picked Presidential Candidate Threatening the Dynasty

In Mexico, the outgoing president usually picks the candidate for the ruling Institutional Revolutionary Party, and in 1994, President Salinas picked Luis Donaldo Colosio to be the PRI's candidate. During his campaign, Colosio criticized the excessive power held by the office of the president and he vowed to change that. These were words the power base and political dynasty did not want to hear; such changes would drastically alter their control in Mexico.

Political Assassination of Colosio

During a campaign rally in Tijuana (March 23, 1994), a gunman killed Colosio. The gunman was seen on video tapes communicating with several members of the police services shortly before the murder—the same police hired to protect Colosio. The killer, Mario Aburto Martinez, was quickly caught.

Another Political Assassination

Several months later, another political assassination occurred (September 28, 1994). Shortly before President Ernesto Zedillo took office, Jose "Pepe" Francisco Ruiz Massieu was killed. He had been the general secretary of the ruling PRI party and was to become majority leader of Congress on December 1, 1994. Ruiz Massieu also favored changes from the former political system, which made him a threat to the ruling elite and to Carlos Salinas' behind-the-scene power base which he had intended to maintain after leaving office.

The gunman, Daniel Aguilar, promptly confessed, naming a half dozen accomplices, including Fernando Rodriguez, a top aide to PRI Congressman Manuel Munoz Rocha. Fernando then confessed, stating that he hired the gunman on orders of Congressman Munoz Rocha, who in turn got his orders from a group of PRI hard-liners who didn't want the changes that Ruiz Massieu had proposed.

Ruling PRI Party Protecting Politicians Charged with Murder

All of the named accomplices in Francisco Ruiz Massieu's murder were arrested and told the same story. They admitted they were working for a high-level political group in the PRI party that they said included PRI Congressman El Meme Garza and PRI Senator Enrique Cardenas from Tamaulipas. They also confirmed that Congressman Munoz Rocha knew the identity of the top people in the PRI hierarchy. When police went looking for Rocha, they found he had disappeared.

Despite the testimony of the people charged with the murder, including the two PRI politicians, the PRI leadership refused to remove legislative immunity from any of the congressmen, including the fugitive, Munoz Rocha. Instead, the PRI leadership granted the fugitive and suspects in the murder leaves of absence.

More Never-Ending Political Intrigue in Mexican Politics

President Salinas ordered Deputy Attorney General Mario Ruiz Massieu to lead the investigation into his brother's death. The General Mexico's top narcotics enforcement official, controlling Mexico's very corrupt Federal Judicial Police and its entire counter-narcotics program.

Initially, it appeared he was making great strides, interviewing many witnesses. Suddenly and somewhat inexplicably, in November 1994, shortly before President Salinas' presidency would end on December 1, 1994, Mario Ruiz announced that politicians allied with drug traffickers had ordered his brother's murder and were blocking the investigation. He used this excuse to resign.

Discovery That President's Brother Ordered Political Assassination

New prosecutors in President Ernest Zedillo's administration discovered that Mario Ruiz distorted the reports of witnesses so as to cover up for the role played by former president Salinas' brother in the assassination of Francisco Ruiz.

Deputy Attorney General Working with Top Drug Traffickers

It was *also* discovered by the incoming administration that while Mario Ruiz Massieu was Deputy Attorney General he provided legal protection to drug smugglers, including the Juan Garcia Abrego group, which is believed to have smuggled over 200,000 pounds of cocaine into the United States during the past 15 years.

Mario Ruiz's top aide and a former judge, Jorge Stergios, made over two dozen trips to Houston in 1994 with suitcases full of $20 and $50 U.S. bills, totaling over $9 million, which he deposited into Texas Commerce Bank. (These funds were subsequently seized by U.S. authorities in March 1995 after Mario Ruiz Massieu became the target of a criminal investigation in Mexico.)

Drug Money Paid To Prior Deputy Attorney General

Testimony from drug traffickers revealed that duffle bags of money were also delivered to Mario Ruiz's predecessor as part of the continuing culture of bribery between Mexican politicians and drug traffickers.

Chief Investigator Flees Mexico

On March 2, 1994, Mexican prosecutors in the new administration questioned Mario Ruiz concerning his ties to drug traffickers and his investigation into his brother's killing. Within a few days the newspaper headlines read, "Mario Ruiz Massieu Flees Mexico, Arrested In Newark." The reason for the arrest at Newark Airport was Mario Ruiz's failure to declare $40,000 cash in his briefcase.

The newspaper article said Mario Ruiz had covered up for the involvement of Raul Salinas in Francisco Ruiz Massieu's murder and that he had over $7 million in unexplained funds on deposit at the Houston branch of the Texas Commerce Bank. Also, that nearly $100,000 in cash was found in his houses in Cuernavaca and Acapulco. The deposits had been made within a nine month period in 1994 while his government salary was less than $80,000 per year.

Jorge Stergios, the former Mexican judge who assisted in the money laundering, also fled Mexico.

Decision To Kill Francisco Massieu Made During Salinas Gathering

Information surfaced indicating that the decision to kill Francisco Ruiz Massieu was made in 1993 at a Salinas family gathering—while President Salinas was present—along with Munoz Rocha. The reason given for the planned murder was that Massieu wanted to modernize the country, which would destroy the power wielded by the Salinas family. It was also reported that the funds to kill Francisco Massieu came from President Salinas' office via Salinas' private secretary, Justo Ceja.

Mexico sent an extradition warrant to the United States seeking Mario Ruiz's return to Mexico, but the United States refused to act on it. While waiting for a decision on deportation charges, Ruiz's incarceration was changed to house arrest in 1998. He was also providing testimony for the U.S.

Department of Justice in several criminal cases as part of a reported agreement to avoid extradition to Mexico. Ruiz revealed many secrets about high-level Mexican involvement in drug smuggling to a Houston federal grand jury (July 1998).

President Carlos Salinas' Brother Charged with Drug Offenses

Shortly after President Carlos Salinas left office, the protection he provided his older brother Raul ceased to exist. Raul was charged with involvement in the murder of Jose Francisco Ruiz Massieu and with drug trafficking offenses. The highly sensitive arrest of the former president's brother was approved by President Zedillo.

Small Style Military Battle Between Competing Mexican Police

In carrying out the arrest of Raul Salinas, two armed convoys proceeded to the Mexico City home of former president Salinas' sister Adriana (February 28, 1995), where Raul Salinas was staying. The group was composed of Federal Judicial Police, members of the Presidential Guard, and local police. (The presidential guard is responsible for protecting present and former presidents of Mexico.) At the same time, another section of the presidential guard, protecting the brother of the former president—was heading to the same location with bullet-proof vehicles, ready to do battle to prevent Raul Salinas from being arrested. This was about to be truly a Mexican standoff.

A U.S. Parallel: The FBI Having A Shoot-Out with ATF Agents

The two groups were rushing to where Raul Salinas was staying, and were within a few minutes of engaging in a fierce gun battle against each other. Suddenly, a stern radio command from General Roberto Miranda, chief of the Presidential Guard came across the radio: "Stop that action; it's an order!" This last minute command stopped a bloody confrontation that surely would have made international headlines. It also reflected the fragmented nature of Mexico's various police and military units, with one ready to battle the other at a moment's notice. Compare this to the FBI engaging in a gun battle with ATF agents in the heart of Washington, D.C.!

President of Mexico and NAFTA

During Carlos Salinas de Gortari's term as president from 1988 to 1994, the North American Free Trade Agreement (NAFTA) was signed between the United States and Mexico. This agreement—as expected—would greatly facilitate the shipment of drugs into the United States and increase the amount of bribe or protection money for the many fragmented segments of Mexico's local and federal police, military forces, and politicians.

Former President Fleeing the Country to Avoid Arrest

The arrest of his brother alarmed former president Carlos Salinas. Fearful of also being charged and arrested, the former president fled Mexico in March 1995, a week after his brother Raul was arrested on charges relating to the disappearance of Francisco Ruiz Massieu. The former president selected a country that had no extradition agreement with Mexico: Ireland. A parallel to this scenario would be former president Bill Clinton fleeing the United States to avoid arrest and his brother being charged with murder and drug-related offenses.

Drug-Related Millions in Enrique Salinas' Bank Accounts

Investigations following the start of the Zedillo presidency discovered that another Salinas brother, Enrique Salinas, had deposited tens of millions of dollars into overseas bank accounts. A Zurich attorney, Ulrich Kohli, said that he moved from $10 to $40 million for Enrique Salinas between banks.

Finding The Missing Congressman: Buried on Raul Salinas' Ranch?

Investigators excavating an area on Raul Salinas' ranch in the Mexico City district of Cuajimalpa discovered human remains (October 1996) they believed to be those of Manuel Munoz Rocha, the missing congressman from the ruling PRI party. It was believed that Munoz helped kill and dispose of Jose Francisco Ruiz Massieu's body and that Raul Salinas killed Munoz to eliminate a witness. Munoz Rocha disappeared the day after the September 28, 1994, assassination of Jose Francisco Ruiz Massieu.

Also arrested, on a related charge of coverup was Lt. Colonel Antonio Chavez, Raul Salinas' chief bodyguard. According to statements made by Mexican Attorney General Antonio Lozano and an article in the Mexican magazine *Proceso*, Antonio told prosecutors he assisted Raul Salinas in hiding the car driven by Munoz.

But Wait—There is More!

No soap opera could have dreamed up what was going on in Mexico. A New York Times article (February 24, 1999) told how the body found on Raul Salinas' ranch was not the missing Manuel Munoz Rocha, or Jose Francisco Ruiz Massieu, but of someone else, who had been buried there to frame Raul Salinas for a murder:

> *The police are hunting for Pablo Chapa Bezanilla, who until December was Mexico's highest prosecutor, chosen by the President to try to solve several political killings that mesmerized the nation. The former special prosecutor, whose zealous investigations led to the imprisonment on murder charges of Raul Salinas de Gortari... is now wanted himself. Mr. Chapa failed to respond to a police summons on February 3 and vanished. He is accused of taking part in a conspiracy to plant a body on a ranch belonging to Raul Salinas to frame him in a 1994 assassination that Mr. Chapa was investigating.*
>
> *Mr. Chapa was dismissed by President Ernesto Zedillo on December 2 ...Mr. Chapa brought his superior, former Attorney General Antonio Lozano Gracia, down with him. The manhunt for Mr. Chapa and the ongoing investigations to determine whether Mr. Lozano was also involved in planting the body are another aspect of the turmoil that has left Mexico's justice system close to breakdown.*
>
> *"This is a soap opera that is very badly written," said German Dehesa, a social critic and newspaper columnist. "It just makes Mexico look ridiculous and backwards to foreigners, particularly Americans."*

President's Brother Sentenced to Prison

Raul Salinas was sentenced to 50 years in prison, without the possibility of parole, for his role in providing government protection to drug traffickers and money laundering and his role in the assassination of Jose Francisco Ruiz Massieu (Associated Press, May 13, 1999).

Personal Accountant of President's Brother Arrested

In Ciudad Juarez, Mexican federal prosecutors arrested (July 1998) Juan Manuel Gomez Gutierrez, the personal accountant of Raul Salinas. He was charged with unaccountable accumulation of money (i.e., drug money). Salinas had hidden some of his assets by placing them in the name of his accountant, who was charged with helping Salinas hide the drug-related money.

Raul Salinas' Secretary Arrested

The attorney general arrested Ofelia Calvo, a former secretary of Raul Salinas, for giving false testimony.

Raul Salinas' Wife Arrested by Swiss Authorities

While in prison, Raul Salinas sent his wife, Paulina Castanon, to Switzerland to withdraw $84 million he had hidden in Swiss banks. Swiss police arrested her (November 15, 1995) when she and her brother tried to withdraw funds using false identification.

Paulina Castanon had also been charged by Mexican authorities with witness-tampering charges. In 1997, she was sentenced to three years in prison for seeking to have a witness change his testimony in the murder case against her husband and for lying to a judge about this attempt. On May 11, 1999, she settled the case by paying a fine (Associated Press, May 13, 1999).

President's Secretary Charged with Unaccountable Millions

In July 1998, a Mexican arrest warrant was issued for President Carlos Salinas' personal secretary, Justo Ceja Martinez, in connection with the unaccountable accumulation of millions of dollars found in several bank accounts. From 1988 to 1994, while making less than $3000 per month, he accumulated over $3 million. The Mexican newspaper, *El Universal*, reported Ceja had a close relationship to Adrian Carrera Fuentes, the former head of the Mexican national police who collected millions from drug traffickers for protecting their drug shipments going to the United States.

Drug Money to Ruling Political Party (PRI)

Joining the many Mexicans fleeing Mexico after Carlos Salinas left office was banker Carlos Cabal Peniche. Mexico's attorney general's office charged the banker with providing drug money to a PRI fund controlled by the governor of Tabasco State. (*Wall Street Journal*, June 10, 1996). An investigation showed Governor Roberto Madrazo Pintado received over $70 million in cash for his November 1994 election as the PRI candidate. A sizable part of this cash came from Cabal through an entity called Sociedad Lomas Mill SA, directed by Paul Karam Kassab, allegedly associated with drug trafficking.

$10 Billion A Year Income for One Mexican Drug Lord

Amado Carrillo Fuentes, a major drug kingpin, whose house in Juarez could be seen from the El Paso side of the border, was another example of how America's drug users enrich foreign drug lords. Carrillo convened meetings in 1994 attended by many of Mexico's drug lords, stating he would import the drugs and wholesale them to anyone who would transport them from Mexico into the United States. He helped organize many individual drug traffickers into one cohesive group.

The Lord of the Skies

He was known in Mexico for his drug shipments using Boeing 727s, earning him the nickname El Senor de los Cielos, "The Lord of the Skies." In earlier pages, CIA and DEA contract agent Bo Abbott described helping unload drugs from 727s landing on flat desert land in Mexico less than 100 miles from the Texas border.

Despite his reputation for being one of Mexico's top drug traffickers, he was never arrested even though he made many public appearances. He had key Mexican local, state and federal police on his payroll, and they were frequent guests at his many parties. Federal police were hired to be his bodyguards.

Carrillo was Mexico's most powerful drug trafficker until his reported death in January 1998, following extensive facial surgery seeking to change his appearance.

Life and Death Sensitive Information Given by U.S. Officials To Cartels Via Head Of Mexico's Drug Enforcement Office

In January 1997, Army General Jesus Gutierrez Rebollo, who was also the commissioner of the National Institute to Combat drugs, visited the United States, at which time U.S. drug czar Barry McCaffrey gave him highly sensitive information on undercover activities and undercover agents in Mexico. In the wrong hands, this information, especially the names of undercover agents, could result in their torture and death at the hands of powerful drug lords.

Publicly Lauding Protector of Major Mexican Drug Cartel

The see-no-evil White House's drug czar publicly lauded General Gutierrez Rebollo's integrity and patriotism. Several days after U.S. personnel gave this information to Mexico's drug czar, a special Mexican task force arrested the General (February 6,1997), charging him with drug money laundering and protecting powerful Mexican drug traffickers, including Amado Carrillo Fuentes. Gutierrez was sentenced to 30 years in a Mexican prison.

Very Sensitive Information Revealed by U.S. To Gutierrez

Also giving the General highly sensitive information on undercover drug activities was the outgoing head of Mexico's anti-narcotics unit, Francisco Molina, including documents dealing with undercover operations, wiretaps, and a great amount of information on the drug trafficker who Gutierrez was protecting: Amado Carrillo Fuentes.

Molina lost his job when his job as head of the National Institute to Combat Drugs when his boss, Attorney General Antonio Lozano, was fired by Zedillo for failing to resolve two high-profile murders: Colosio and Massieu.

Selective Toughness on Drug Traffickers

General Enrique Cervantes, Mexico's Defense Minister, who arrested General Jesus Gutierrez Rebollo, had personally recommended Gutierrez for the job, to which he was appointed on December 6, 1996 by incoming President Ernesto Zedillo. Gutierrez's selection was reportedly based upon his toughness on drug traffickers. But, as in the United States, the toughness was selective. In Gutierrez's case, his toughness eliminated competition to a drug trafficker protected by the general: Amado Carrillo Fuentes.

The incoming Zedillo administration soon learned what was known for years, that Gutierrez had been protecting the Amado Carrillo Fuentes drug cartel for years and receiving protection money throughout this period. The rental on Gutierrez' Mexico City apartment cost more than his government salary provided. No problem, the rent was paid by drug trafficker Carrillo Fuentes. And this was no secret to the Salinas administration.

Gutierrez spent seven years as commander of the Fifth Military Region in Guadalajara, during which time he worked closely with the U.S. Drug Enforcement Administration, learning more about U.S. drug operations.

Drug Czar Ordered Torture of Former United Airlines Pilot

Some years earlier, as described in previous pages, Gutierrez ordered the torture of former United Airlines pilot Richard Pitt as Gutierrez sought to get information about Colombian drug lords for the purpose of doing business with them. This was before Mexico starting soliciting drug business from Colombian drug traffickers, and which now is in a greatly expanded stage, reportedly responsible for over half the drugs smuggled into the United States.

Former Head of Drug Institute Charged with Torture

The former head of the National Institute for the Combat Of Drugs, Ignacio Weber Rodriguez, was charged (September 1997) with kidnapping and torturing a member of the Tijuana drug cartel for the purpose of extracting information to give to another drug cartel.

Culture Of Drug Corruption in Mexico Culture

Mario Ruiz Massieu—who would later flee Mexico—became the head of Mexico's Attorney General office during Carlos Salinas' presidency and was also put in charge of Mexico's drug enforcement program. This was an odd choice (or maybe it wasn't). It was customary for the Attorney General to select the commanders of the different Mexican states, and the commanders paid back to the Attorney General a part of the drug protection money received from drugs shipped through their state. The states with the greatest amount of drug trafficking would generate the greatest amount of drug-protection money and this in turn resulted in a greater drug-money kickback to the Attorney General. It's a well-oiled system.

Angry Because He Wasn't Receiving His Share Of the Drug Money

Mario Ruiz discovered that his immediate subordinate in the Attorney General's office, Adrian Carrera Fuentes, was becoming wealthy from protection money paid by drug traffickers, which angered him because he wasn't receiving a sufficient share. Under pressure, Carrera gave Ruiz six payments of $300,000 each from November 1993 to August 1994.

Carrera said he received cash from two federal police commanders in Mexico's provinces, who in turn were being paid for providing government protection to large drug traffickers. One of these commanders, David Grajeda Lara, had seized 16,000 pounds of cocaine that had been flown into a remote airstrip in northern Mexico (August 1993). Grajeda then sold the cocaine back to the traffickers. What a system!

As with many other Mexican politicians and military officers, Mario Ruiz used American banks to bank the proceeds of his drug activities, depositing over $8 million in Texas banks, which was later seized by the United States.

Former Head of Mexico's National Police: A Drug Trafficker

Another head of Mexico's National Police, Adrian Carrera Fuentes, was arrested in March 1998 by the newly formed Organized Crime Unit of the federal police force that he had earlier led. Confronted with overwhelming evidence, he chose to become a cooperating witness. Mexico allowed him to travel to the United States and testify before a federal grand jury in Houston. He testified that while he was the director of the federal police force (1993 and 1994) he collected and distributed over $2 million in drug money and turned it over to a colleague, Mario Ruiz Massieu.

Drug Trafficker Requesting Protection from National Police Head

Earlier, while Carrera served as warden in a Mexico City prison, before he became head of the federal police force, he made contact with several drug traffickers who were inmates at the prison, including Amado Carrillo Fuentes. Upon being released, Carrillo met with Carrera, who at that time had become commander of the Federal Judicial Police. According to an article in the Mexico City newspaper *Reforma*, Carrillo asked Carrera if Carrera would give his drug trafficking activities protection for a part of the action.

Price for Federal Police Protection: $1,500 Per Kilo

It was agreed that Carrillo would give Carrera $1,500 for every kilo of cocaine that Carrillo shipped from Mexico to the United States, and reports showed that Carrera took bribes from Carrillo and other drug traffickers for protecting their drug shipments. In addition, Carrera appointed Federal Judicial Police commandantes who worked with the drug lords.

Key Police Commander Blows the Whistle and Flees for His Life

Guillermo Gonzalez Calderoni joined the federal Judicial Police in 1983, and in 1988 he became a senior commander. He held the position of national director of drug interdiction and reported to Mexico's drug czar. That position was similar to the senior FBI official responsible for drug matters. Gonzalez started revealing innermost secrets of corruption in Mexico's political, military and police entities in 1996. This had adverse consequences.

Gonzalez said charges and threats were made against him after he reported government corruption to Mexican and U.S. officials, forcing him to flee to the United States in 1993. After his arrival in the U.S., Gonzalez described to law enforcement personnel what he learned about drug crimes during ten years in key undercover positions. The FBI and DEA gave him written commendations for his disclosures.

Revealing Drug-Protection Payoffs to President's Brother

Gonzalez told of a Mexican drug trafficker making large cash protection payments to Raul Salinas while Raul's brother was president of Mexico. Gonzalez said he relayed this information to President Salinas and to U.S. authorities in 1992, but neither responded. He said this was the time when Mexican and U.S. officials wanted NAFTA passed and neither side wanted the American people to know about the Mexican government's widespread drug activities that would surely escalate with the passage of NAFTA.

Recertification and Selective Drug Prosecutions

Gonzalez told how Mexico's Attorney General Coello Trejo ordered him to arrest a major drug trafficker, Miguel Angel Felix Gallardo, who had been protected by the system for years. When Gonzalez asked why now, Coello replied, "The certification is coming." The Bush Administration—itself heavily involved in drug trafficking during the Contra affair—then praised Mexico for having arrested Felix.

Mexican Election Fraud

Gonzalez related that in the beginning of Mexico's 1988 presidential campaign he carried out a request by Raul Salinas to bug the telephones of the challenger to Carlos Salinas, Cuantemoc Cardenas.

Gonzalez told how Deputy Attorney General Coello Trejo ordered him to torture a politician opponent, Hernandez, to sign a false admission to stockpiling arms, which Hernandez did after a 14-hour torture session. Hernandez received a 35-year prison sentence.

Gonzalez said that the drug trafficker in control of the cocaine shipments through Mexico's Gulf coast, Luis Medrano, said he paid Raul Salinas for help in trying to buy the state-owned businesses that administer the ports of Salina Cruz on the Pacific coast and Coatzacoalcos on the Gulf coast. These payments were made in 1991, but Raul Salinas' months of efforts were unsuccessful.

Cables from the American Embassy in Mexico to Washington reveal these actions were known by U.S. officials. Director of the Drug Enforcement Administration's intelligence center at El Paso said, "I can tell you that much of what he says fits with the intelligence we had."

"It could bring down your government"

U.S. Ambassador James Jones, during a meeting in 1994 with President Salinas, after Mexico requested Gonzalez's extradition, described to Salinas the charges against his brother. Jones said, "Gonzalez Calderoni has so much bad stuff on your administration that it could bring down your government." Jones said Salinas showed no reaction. (In 1998, a U.S. judge refused to extradite Gonzalez, stating Mexican officials had fabricated evidence against Gonzalez.)

NAFTA and Its Expected Surge in Drug Shipments from Mexico

With the passage of the North American Free Trade Agreement (NAFTA), the smuggling of tons of drugs into the United States escalated—as expected by members of Congress, President Clinton, drug traffickers, and the Mexican government. Since it passed, it has become practically impossible to interdict any but a minute percentage of the tons of cocaine and heroin crossing the border from Mexico. Drugs are hidden in tons of produce and other products, in fuel tanks, in axles, in tires, and hundreds of other inaccessible places. Over one million trucks a year pass through the three bridges from Mexico to the United States at Laredo, Texas. And that is only one of many border crossings.

The logistics of drug smuggling have changed radically for the big-time drug traffickers. Years ago, aircraft were the primary means of bringing drugs into the United States (and still are for small-time smugglers). But NAFTA changed that, at least in the west and southwestern part of the United States.

The border between the United States and Mexico is over 2,000 miles long, with smaller drug loads crossing in rural areas. In 1997, for instance,

Customs seized over 46,000 pounds of cocaine and over 600,000 pounds of marijuana, and Customs estimates that over 90 percent of drugs shipped across the border escapes their detection. If that figure is correct, over 460,000 pounds of cocaine enter the United States from Mexico every year, in addition to all the other entry points.

Drug Traffickers Buying Factories for NAFTA Trade

A *Wall Street Journal* article (February 11, 1998) told of a confidential report titled "Drug Trafficking, Commercial Trade and NAFTA," prepared by a task force of law-enforcement officials along the border. The report said that evidence showed drug traffickers were buying factories, warehouses and trucking companies to use in transporting drugs into the United States. The report followed a two-year research by Operation Alliance, an El Paso group of local, state, and federal police along the border. (Several of my inside sources, including those described within these pages, told me earlier about this practice.)

An article in the *Wall Street Journal* (December 23, 1998) said drug traffickers had shifted much of their drug trafficking to containerized shipping as a result of NAFTA:

> *Colombian drug traffickers had been flying huge loads of cocaine into Mexico on stripped-down passenger jets, easily outrunning Mexican police aircraft. But drug flights into Mexico have stopped as the traffickers have shifted to maritime shipments through the Gulf of Mexico, into the Yucatan Peninsula and up the Pacific coast, and to overland transportation, mainly by truck.*

Three Tons of Cocaine in Railroad Tank Cars

Director Lori Wallach of Global Trade Watch, a division of Public Citizen, founded by Ralph Nader, said, "This new report is basically documenting from ground zero what we predicted and what only the administration NAFTA-boosters continue to lie about." The group found that drug traffickers were buying into Mexican transportation companies, adding that one major Mexican drug trafficker was using "railroad tank cars with false compartments on either end capable of carrying some three tons of cocaine."

Drug traffickers were hiring shipping consultants to determine what type of merchandise moved quickest across the border under NAFTA. The report said Colombian drug traffickers "routinely attend conferences and courses to learn about trade issues" and determine what type of products are best to camouflage the shipment of drugs. Before NAFTA went into effect, drug kingpin Juan Garcia Abrego was found with documents relating to upgrades in highways and ports that would facilitate drug shipments. The report said "The NAFTA trade agreement will prevent the U.S. from putting on political pressure to clean up the corruption in Mexico."

Mexico's Cartels Protected at Every Level of Government

A *Washington Post* article (December 14, 1998) described other aspects of the Mexican drug culture:

> *"Quintana Roo has become the first narco-state in Mexico," said a U.S. official familiar with both U.S. and Mexican anti-drug investigations in the state. The Yucatan peninsula is one of the biggest drug-trafficking*

gateways to the United States, with Mexico's most powerful drug Mafia, the Juarez cartel, recently establishing a huge base of operations in Quintano Roo.

At least four Mexican anti-drug agencies and the DEA have investigated charges that the Juarez cartel receives protection at every level of government in the state, including the local police, the Mexican military force assigned to the region, and Governor Villanueva. U.S. and Mexican officials said state police as well as military troops assigned to Quintana Roo routinely permit passage of drug shipments that arrive on the beaches by boat, at clandestine airstrips and overland, through neighboring Belize and Guatemala. U.S. authorities, particularly anti-narcotics officials involved in making recommendations on the drug certification of Mexico, say they are dismayed by the impunity with which the cartel and its leaders operate in the Cancun area.

The article stated the governor of the Yucatan State, which includes the Cancun resort area, was in the pay of powerful drug traffickers who then received government protection. These traffickers included Ramon Alcides Magana, also known as El Metro, the most powerful drug trafficker on the Yucatan peninsula. The article described the increasing frustration of investigators in Mexico and the United States who complained that their investigations were blocked by many of Mexico's highest-ranking elected officials.

These facts may be sobering to American tourists lying on the beach or touring the countryside at Cancun, knowing that their country is being undermined by nearby government officials and drug kingpins.

Mexican Railroad Carrying Drugs into United States

A secret 1997 report by the CIA landed in the State Department's Bureau of International Narcotics and Law Enforcement Affairs (INL), showing concern about the Mexican railroad line, Transportacion Maritima Mexicana SA (TMM) its chairman, Jose Serrano, and the planned merger with Kansas City Southern Industries, Inc. The Mexican railroad ran several trains a day from Mexico into Texas. The report revealed that Mexican counter-narcotics experts suspected Serrano was laundering money for the key Juarez drug cartel headed by Amado Carrillo Fuentes.

The report revealed Serrano had prior drug confiscations, automatic-weapons shipments, and a joint venture with a Colombian shipper whose ships were frequently carrying drugs, and close business ties with known Mexican drug traffickers. Despite all this, Kansas City Southern Industries and its chairman, Landon Rowland, entered into a partnership. The merger changed the name of the operation to Transportacion Ferroviaria Mexicana (TFM).

Kansas City Southern--A CIA Front?

A long-time CIA contact, Gunther Russbacher, had operated secret CIA financial operations in Missouri. Based on his activities in the Midwest, I asked him (March 1999) if he knew anything about the railroad. He told me Kansas City Southern was a CIA asset and that he worked with them while he was active with the CIA in the 1980s.

Narcotics Trade Run by Top Politicians and Businessmen

A *Wall Street Journal* article (June 8, 1998) described a "Top Secret"

Mexican CIAN report (Mexican equivalent of CIA). Titled, "Purported Mexican Official Report Alleges Top-Level Drug Conspiracy." It stated in part:

A purported Mexican intelligence document is making the rounds alleging that the narcotics trade here is run by a dense conspiracy of top politicians and businessmen. The document, marked "Secret" and bearing the seal of the Mexican military's Center for Anti-Narcotics Intelligence, suggests that Mexico's establishment may be even more steeped in the narcotics trade than Colombia's. "In Colombia, the [drug] cartels use public officials to carry out their illicit activities. In Mexico, the cartels are used by the Narco Power, comprised of people of national renown," says the lengthy analysis, which is dated September 1995. [The report] was produced by the Mexican intelligence agency, which goes by its Spanish initials CIAN. CIAN is known to be a liaison with the U.S. Central Intelligence Agency. And in fact language and allegations in the report appear to have found their way into a January 1997 CIA analysis of Mexican drug trafficking and money laundering. The analysis also displays an interpretation of U.S. antidrug efforts.

State Department Coverup of Drug Smuggling Problems

Jonathan Winer, deputy assistant Secretary of State, had been investigating international conspiracies for years, including the Bank of Credit and Commerce International and others. Winer ran into obstacles which could be expected in light of the State Department's prior drug smuggling coverups. The State Department's Bureau of Inter-American Affairs blocked Winer from getting his report to Secretary of State Madeleine Albright. (His confidence in Albright acting on his report was surely misplaced!) Albright, a protégé of President Clinton, stated to the media (February 27, 1998), "The Colombian National Police and counter-narcotics forces have conducted an effective eradication and interdiction effort." (*Sun-Sentinel*, South Florida). The lies come out like diarrhea of the mouth!

More Of the Same "Honesty" From the Clinton Group

Speaking for President Clinton's drug czar, General Barry McCaffery, Robert Weiner said, "We have seen no evidence of additional drugs coming in because of NAFTA." There was so much evidence of this that no one in his position could be *that* dumb.

Clinton Promoting Drug Trafficker for World Trade Organization

As President Carlos Salinas' term was ending in 1994, President Clinton recommended his candidacy to head the World Trade Organization. Fortunately, his recommendation was ignored. Shortly after Clinton made that recommendation, Salinas fled Mexico and went into self-imposed exile in Ireland.

OTHER EXAMPLES OF MEXICO'S CRIME CULTURE

The drugging of America from Mexico is not the doings of a few rogues in the Mexican government. It comes about as a result of a culture that is rampant with corruption, unlike anything normally found in western European countries. A brief description of this culture will help understand the problems coming from Mexico and the improbability of any changes for many years to come.

Kidnappings Out of Control in Mexico

In Mexico City, kidnappings are out of control, and often committed by Mexico's police. President Zedillo appointed General Enrique Salgado Cordero as Mexico City's police chief to control these crimes. One problem: The General was responsible for the paramilitary squads that committed thousands of atrocities against Argentineans, including killing street children. He wasted no time using similar methods in Mexico.

One night, Mexico City police kidnapped and killed six children whose bodies were found the next morning, riddled with large-caliber bullet holes. Normally, police killings are ignored, but the media publicity and subsequent public outrage caused military prosecutors to charge and arrest the police who murdered the youths. Three high-ranking military officers were arrested for covering up for the guilty. When military personnel went to arrest the police who committed the murders, the police from that unit barricaded themselves inside their barracks and blocked the arrest of fellow policemen.

Police Kill the Father Seeking Son's Release

In one case, the father of a kidnapped boy was killed while trying to pay ransom for his son's release. It was reported that the kidnapers from the office of the attorney general recognized the undercover police accompanying the father and fired upon them.

Mexican Anti-Kidnap Officials Protecting Kidnapping Rings

Mexico's attorney general's office received evidence that the head of the state police's anti-kidnapping unit, Alberto Pliego Fuentes, accepted $11,200 to protect the Arizmendi gang, which was famous for cutting off the ears of their victims and sending them to relatives to speed up payment. Another anti-kidnapping chief in the state of Morelos, Armando Martinez Salgado, and Federal police officer Jose Domingo Tassinari, were arrested for ties to Daniel Arizmendi Lopez and his gang. (*Reforma*, July 1998)

Mexico Approaching Colombia in Kidnapping Epidemic

Insiders believe that over 2,000 kidnappings a year occur in Mexico— with police involved in many of the kidnappings. Former FBI agent Paul Magallanes was one of many former FBI agents working in Mexico and intervening in kidnapping cases. As he and many others have found, Mexican police were often the ones perpetrating the kidnapping. A *Knight Ridder Newspapers* article (August 13, 1998) said:

Many Mexicans believe police frequently are involved in crimes, so most victims shun authorities and deal directly with kidnappers. Recently, federal officials arrested the chief of an elite anti-kidnapping unit in Morelos State on suspicion of working with kidnappers. Carmen Genis Sanchez believed the problem of police involvement was so severe, she started an organization called the Citizen's House in Cuautla to speak out against it.

"But soon we saw members of the organization being kidnapped," Genis Sanchez said, "and then the arrival of protection rackets: gangsters demanding payments from families to avoid kidnappings."

Between January and June of this year, according to a government report obtained by a Mexican magazine, 170 kidnappings were reported throughout the country; 12 of the victims were murdered, even after ran-

soms were delivered.

Another newspaper article titled, "Kidnapping In Mexico: Brutal acts and Bribes," described the Arizmendi kidnapping gang:

"The key to Mr. Arizmendi's confidence has been a wall of official protection cemented together with bribes to municipal, state and federal police officers and prosecutors," senior Mexican officials said in interviews. A federal official who helped arrest the family of Mr. Arizmendi said that one of his most important protectors had been the chief of the Morelos State police anti-kidnapping unit, who was arrested in January as he dumped in a neighboring state the body of a prisoner he has been accused of torturing to death. Aides to Mexico's Attorney General, Jorge Madrazo, have also arrested a Federal Police agent and a federal prosecutor and charged them with racketeering for protecting Mr. Arizmendi, officials said.

Mexico City Police Officers Arrested for Murders and Rapes

Mexico City's new police chief, Alejandro Gertz Manero, ordered the arrest of 44 Mexico City policemen (November 1998), some of whom had warrants issued as long as six years earlier for major crimes but had never been served. Over 200 other policemen were listed in other arrest warrants for crimes ranging from murders, rapes, and extortions. The police chief explained that the escalating violent crimes were caused by Mafia leaders defying attempts to end police corruption. Mexico City District Attorney Samuel del Villar said the roundup was "an unprecedented effort to impose the rule of law." So complete was police corruption that the arresting detectives wore masks to avoid being recognized by the police they were arresting as protection against retaliation.

Mexicans Fearful of Crime and Mexican Police

A *Christian Science Monitor* article (October 6, 1997) stated, "Ask most Mexicans, and they'll tell you the only thing they fear more than the criminals running amuck in many neighborhoods are the crime fighters themselves."

Mexican Government Threats and Contempt for United States

A *Wall Street Journal* article (June 17, 1998) described death threats made by Governor Mario Villanueva of the Mexican State of Quintana Roo against U.S. Consul David Van Valkenburg at Merida, Mexico:

Last June, a U.S. diplomat was driven to the airport here in an armored Jeep Cherokee, flanked by two gun-toting bodyguards after receiving death threats. The diplomat had been pressing for a Mexican investigation into the accidental deaths of several U.S. citizens in the resort of Cancun. Mr. Van Valkenburg told his staff that the threats came from Mario Villanueva, the governor of neighboring Quintana Roo State...the case demonstrates how difficult it remains for the U.S. and Mexico to cooperate on seemingly simple law-enforcement matters.

In the case of the threatened consul, U.S. and Mexican officials have worked to keep the matter off the public radar screen. Valkenburg's trouble with the governor began when he started investigating Mr. Gutenkauf's death, which occurred in February 1997. According to unclassified dispatches cabled by Mr. Van Valkenburg, Mr. Gutenkauf was killed by a speeding police car, reportedly without headlights, as he crossed Cancun's main street shortly after midnight. A police commander riding in the car left the scene, the cables say. Two other policeman prevented the first arriving ambulance from taking the fatally wounded Mr. Gutenkauf to the hospital.

Afterward, police officials pressured witnesses, according to the consul's cables. Gov. Villanueva promised Mr. Van Valkenburg a speedy investigation and said one policeman would be charged with negligent homicide. Mr. Van Valkenburg did meet with a state deputy attorney general, Humberto Guevara, the governor's point man on the Gutenkauf affair. He told Mr. Van Valkenburg the initial investigation had been thrown out and the police officer involved would be charged with simply a traffic violation. Mr. Van Valkenburg protested. Mr. Guevara answered Mr. Van Valkenburg with something diplomats say the consul took as a threat: "Drive very carefully. Not only tourists die in car accidents."

Mexico's Coalition of Drug Producers and Traffickers, Operating Like A Well-Run Business Operation

Like an efficient business expanding to meet Customer demands, Mexican drug cartels have expanded their merchandise base and started producing a fine grade of heroin. In the past, Mexico's production of heroin was cheap, low-grade heroin, sometimes called "black tar," which was 7 to 20 percent pure. Cambodian and Thai heroin experts taught Colombian and Mexican drug traffickers how to refine opium latex into heroin and increase the percentage of heroin content. Some of it reaches 90 percent purity. As a result, Colombian and Mexican suppliers have surpassed Asian suppliers as the primary source of heroin for U.S. drug users.

Mexican Drugs Decreasing U.S. Population Density

The unexpected greater potency is affecting the number of drug-related deaths in the United States; the increased purity and potency—which is not stated on the package—brought about the deaths of 14 young people in the Dallas area in 1996. With no way of knowing the potency of injected drugs, users play "Russian Roulette," and sometimes they die!

This higher purity and potency of the Mexican heroin does not have to be injected into the blood stream to get the expected result as with the low-purity product; it can be smoked or inhaled like cocaine.

U.S. Media's Praise of Mexico's Drug Operation

Trendsetters in the U.S. media praised President Carlos Salinas during his presidency. The *Economist* called Salinas "One of the great men of the 20th century." Kissinger wrote, "Salinas quelled corruption and brought into office an extraordinary group of highly trained technocrats. I know of no government anywhere that is more competent." One media source that disagreed was GQ magazine (April 1997):

President Clinton eulogized Zedillo as a reformer—as other Mexican presidents were called by U.S. presidents. Beginning in 1993, and allegedly at the direction of President Carlos Salinas, fifty secret bank accounts were set up around Mexico. The accounts were slush funds for the candidates of the ruling party. The fifty secret bank accounts were nour-

ished by drug cartels in Colombia and Mexico, and when the election "folderol" ended in late August 1994, as much as three-quarters of a billion dollars had cascaded through these slush funds. In early 1996, Alvaro Cepeda Neri, a Mexican lawyer and human-rights advocate published an account of the buying of the elections. In May of that year, he was severely beaten and hospitalized.

President's Brother Assumed Control of All Drug Shipments

In the 1990s, Swiss authorities conducted an extensive investigation into the source of Raul Salinas' money deposited in Swiss banks, obtaining statements and testimony from over 70 witnesses and examining over 30,000 pages of documents. Included in their final report of 369 pages was the statement, "When Carlos Salinas de Gortari became president of Mexico in 1988, Raul Salinas de Gortari assumed control over practically all drug shipments through Mexico."

Mexican Army and Police Protected Drug Trafficking

A *New York Times* article, making reference to the Swiss report, stated, "Through his [Raul Salinas] influence and bribes paid with drug money, officials of the army and the police supported and protected the flourishing drug business." The report described "green light days" during which government trucks and railroad cars were used to transport cocaine loads through Mexico without fear the army, the police, or the military would intervene.

U.S. Department of Justice Ignored Drug
Money Laundering by Key Mexican Officials

Very little is said about the involvement of U.S. banks in drug-money laundering, even though it exists. As a result of the large scale investigation by Swiss banks, information surfaced about American Express and Citibank's dealings with drug traffickers. These exposures *forced* the DOJ to "investigate," and file charges against a low-level scapegoat.

Despite the fact that American Express had alerted DOJ personnel to what could have been drug money—and which DOJ personnel covered up by doing nothing—in the middle 1990s DOJ prosecutors charged an American Express banker with laundering large amounts of drug money. The money was being deposited by Mario Ruiz Massieu, Mexico's deputy attorney general in charge of, would you believe, drug investigation. Ruiz deposited over $9 million in small bills—a clear signal the money came from drug activities.

American Express banker Antonio Giraldi had filed dozens of government-required reports showing large amounts of cash being deposited for the Mexican government official—who Justice Department officials knew was connected with drug trafficking. Giraldi even made telephone calls to government personnel about the large cash deposits that far exceeded the amount he could be obtaining from his government employment.

None of the DOJ or other government personnel receiving the reports took any action—as if they were protecting the Mexican official. Too bad the same "understanding" wasn't shown to the tens of thousands of American men and women sent to prison on real and bogus drug charges filed by the same DOJ.

DOJ Witness Testified Against Giraldi while Guilty of Far Worse

During the trial against Giraldi, Citibank's Amy Grovas Elliott testified in detail the steps taken by Citibank to avoid violating money-laundering laws. The very steps she outlined were the same steps she and Citibank were violating at that very same time as they accepted over $100 million in obvious drug-related money from Raul Salinas between 1992 and 1995. Her testimony as to Citibank's policies—not her conduct—caused the jury to be more critical of what Giraldi did at American Express even though he did far more than Elliott to report the drug money to federal authorities. The jury convicted Giraldi of money laundering (June 2, 1994).

Citibank: Drug Trafficker's Bank

At Citibank, Amy Elliott handled the $100 million-plus money from Raul Salinas—often in small bills—in a manner typical of a deliberate money laundering operation. The bank did not simply wire the money to the destination Swiss banks as would be expected. Instead, on its own initiative, Citibank took a circuitous route, transferring the money through several offshore banks, which made it far more difficult to trace the money. There was no reason to do this unless Citibank wanted to disguise the source of the funds. This was money laundering!

Amy Elliott had on-the-job training at Citibank, and it is probable that senior bank officials taught her the tricks of the trade. Since she had earlier testified against Antonio Giraldi, a former Citibank banker who was then with American Express, she was doubly aware of the nature of the Citibank circuitous money transfers. Despite all the publicity in banking circles on the American Express matter, and knowledge that the money was undoubtedly drug money, Citibank and Amy Elliott accepted hundreds of millions in cash from Raul Salinas—giving the bank a tidy commission.

Maybe Salinas Was Little Orphan Annie's Daddy Warbucks!

In a later deposition concerning the hundreds of millions of cash deposits given to her by Salinas, Elliott testified that she felt Salinas had legitimate reasons for wanting to move large sums secretly. Referring to her deposition, the *Wall Street Journal* (January 27, 1999) said:

> We roll our eyes at her deposition, in which she said Raul Salinas was like a 'Rockefeller,' somebody whom everyone understood to be wealthy and well connected and to have legitimate reasons for wanting to move large sums around discreetly.

Believe it or not, this was the same Amy Elliott who testified several years earlier against the American Express banker.

Citibank's Aggressive Role to Hide the Drug Money

Swiss investigators learned from testimony given by Salinas (December 1995) that Citibank officials in New York "came up with the whole strategy" to shift money around via different banks. This strategy used untraceable Cayman Islands shell corporations and European bank accounts so that the money would end up in the relative safety of a Swiss bank account.

Citibank undoubtedly knew the money was from illegal activities; they were not innocent lambs in this area. Raul Salinas' income as a government official was $3,000 a month, not quite enough to amass over $500 million. He had no other known source of income. The funds were generated in an area known for heavy drug activities and from government personnel known to receive huge sums of money for protecting drug shipments. Citibank wasn't born yesterday! Citibank did not alert government regulators to the suspicious nature of the huge deposits, as did Giraldi. According to several of my sources, Citibank had CIA contacts, and if this is true, they would have CIA protection.

Surely A Mexican Official Would not Launder Drug Money!

Testifying to Congress about why the many red flags that were clear indications of drug money did not alert government officials, Stanley Morris, the head of the Treasury Department financial crimes task force, said that no flags went up when the Mexican official was depositing millions in cash because Massieu was a "well-known Mexican official." The endemic drug-related corruption among Mexican politician and military figures was known throughout government, and millions in small bills would look innocent only to a complete moron. Or liar.

Drug Cartels Paying $80 Million to Mexican Politicians
For Assistance in Shipping Drugs to United States

Testifying in Switzerland, Guillermo Pallomari, a former key accountant for the Cali cartel, testified that the cartel paid $80 million to politicians in Mexico during a three year period from 1990 to 1993, and that most of that money went directly to Raul Salinas. Cartel ledgers supported this testimony. Pallomari was a key personal assistant from 1990 to 1994 to Miguel Rodriguez Orejuela, one of the four Cali cartel chiefs. Pallomari testified that the cartel paid the money to Salinas through Amado Carrillo Fuentes, the head of Mexico's largest cocaine cartel. Pallomari testified that the help expected from Raul Salinas for the millions in bribe money was to protect and facilitate drug flights through Mexico to the United States and release any drugs accidentally seized in Mexico.

U.S. Department Of Justice Already Knew About
Mexico's Shipment of Drugs into the United States

Media reports said that evidence obtained by Swiss authorities about Colombian cartels paying Raul Salinas money to protect drugs transitioning into the United States were already known by DOJ personnel. This knowledge was obtained from testimony and evidence generated in prior criminal cases in the United States, which was kept under wraps, and which protected top people in the drug business.

Why did President Clinton Withhold this Information?

The question arises, Why did DOJ personnel ignore evidence that Mexican politicians and military were responsible for the massive shipment of drugs into the United States while President Clinton was certifying Mexico as cooperating in the war on drugs? Why did he deceive the American people by stating Mexico was cooperating in the war on drugs when just the opposite was true? And why did he continue sending billions of taxpayer dollars to Mexico as part of this deception?

Seizing Funds from Carrillo in U.S. Banks

U.S. authorities moved to seize funds in four U.S. financial institutions belonging to deceased Mexican drug lord Amado Carrillo Fuentes (July 1998). The institutions included an Antigua affiliate of Stanford Group Co., a Houston stockbroker, Republic National Bank of Miami, Nations Bank Corp, and Bear Stearns. The investigation leading up to the seizures showed how Mexican drug traffickers used U.S. financial institutions to launder their cash. The organization, headed by Carrillo, had purchased an interest in the bank holding company called Grupo Financiero Anahuac. The investigation revealed over $100 million went through three Anahuac accounts in November 1996. Anahuac accounts controlled by Carrillo Fuentes' organization sent over $30 million to Miami accounts controlled by Juan Alberto Zepeda Mendez and Jorge Bastida Gallardo, front men for Carrillo Fuentes.

Operation Casablanca

In the late 1990s the United States conducted an undercover operation dubbed "Operation Casablanca" with the intent to discover the complex methods used by foreign banks to launder drug money. Following the secret three-year investigation by U.S. Customs agents conducted in Mexico without the knowledge of Mexican officials, a federal grand jury in Los Angeles handed down (May 1998) indictments, including three Mexican banks and 26 Mexican bankers, charging them with laundering millions of dollars in drug money. It was considered the largest drug-money-laundering case in U.S. history and the first time Mexican banks and bank officials were officially charged with laundering drug proceeds for the Cali and Juarez cartels.

Over 100 people were arrested. Some arrests occurred at the Casablanca Casino Resort near Las Vegas at Mesquite, Nevada, and in San Diego. Simultaneously, Mexican authorities were asked to arrest over two dozen other bankers and operatives, a request that was mostly ignored.

Money laundering charges were filed against several Mexican banks including Grupo Financiero Bancomer, Banca Confia, and Grupo Financiero Serfin SA, Mexico's second and third largest banks. A total of 14 Mexican and Venezuelan banks were charged with money laundering. Banca Confia was owned by the Mexican government at the time charges were filed, and many of its assets were purchased by Citibank. Operation Casablanca revealed that drug money laundering by the Mexican banking system existed without doubt. The investigation was kept secret from Mexican authorities to prevent its disclosure to those being investigated.

Mexican Defense Minister Among Many
Politicians Involved with Drug Traffickers

Many revealing recorded conversations occurred between undercover Customs agents and Mexicans who were later arrested in the United States. During one telephone conversation, managers from Mexico's second largest bank told the undercover agents that part of the money being laundered belonged to Defense Minister General Cervantes. This conversation had been set up to discuss laundering over $1.5 *billion* in cash consisting of $500 million from New York, a similar amount in the Netherlands, and $150 million in Mexico City. For political reasons, the defense minister was not charged. (Remember, President Clinton said Mexico was cooperating in the war on drugs!)

Money-Laundering Legislation Threat to the Mexican Banks

If any of the banks pled guilty, or were found guilty, legislation passed by

Congress known as the Annunzio-Wylie Anti-Money Laundering Act of 1992 required the Federal Reserve to revoke their charter to operate in the United States. This legislation came about as a result of the BCCI scandal and provided that the Federal Reserve must initiate license-revocation hearings against foreign banks guilty of money laundering. If this were to happen, it would create major financial and political problems for Mexico's already precarious banking system.

Arrests Loudly Proclaimed as Success in War on Drugs—Initially

With the announcement of the arrests, U.S. authorities proclaimed a successful undercover operation in the war on drugs. At least, initially. A *Wall Street Journal* editorial (May 22, 1998) questioned whether the greatly ballyhooed operation was really as significant as U.S. government officials claimed.

> *The banks are nearly all mid-level functionaries, and the amount involved, perhaps $72 million over three years, pales against a multi-billion drug market. So what exactly has been proven? Treasury Secretary Rubin claimed that "we have hurt the drug cartels where it hurts most, in their pocketbooks." But surely this amount is a routine business cost in what by its nature is a high-risks business. It would be nice, though, just once to see Treasury or the Justice Department indict and convict some prominent American lawyers, accountants, bankers, banking institutions, federal bureaucrats or even politicians who are serving as enablers of the drug trade in the United States. We'd call that significant.*

The *Wall Street Journal* was being very polite in addressing the dynamite nature of political corruption relating to drugs in the United States. In other editorials and articles in the *Journal*, reference was made to infamous Mena, Arkansas, a major CIA drug operation that was known and protected by Governor Bill Clinton, the U.S. Attorney, the DEA, the Department of Justice, U.S. Attorney General, and other government agencies.

Outrage from the Bowels of Mexico's Drug-Related Politicians

Operation Casablanca activities brought about outrage from Mexican officials who claimed—rightfully—violation of its national sovereignty as U.S. Customs agents conducted undercover operations in Mexico. Mexico's ambassador in Washington, Jesus Reyes Heroles, called the undercover operation "an act of a criminal nature similar to the crimes it was supposed to uncover." In his May 29, 1998, letter, the ambassador defended Mexico's anti-drug record.

President Zedillo Took Objections to the United Nations

President Ernesto Zedillo stated in a speech (May 1998) that the undercover operation in Mexico was "inadmissible because it tramples on our laws" and demanded the extradition for criminal prosecution of the U.S. Customs agents who conducted the operation in Mexico. Zedillo brought the matter to a General Assembly session at the United Nations on drug trafficking (June 8, 1998):

> *We all must respect the sovereignty of each nation so that no one becomes a judge of others, so that no one feels entitled to violate other countries' laws for the sake of enforcing its own.*

Zedillo properly objected to the U.S. undercover operation, just as America would object to an undercover operation in the United States by another country such as China, Russia, or Cuba. However, this argument does not exonerate Mexico for its aggressive conspiracy with drug traffickers to smuggle drugs into the United States and thereby violate its sovereignty.

Zedillo Says U.S. Should Pay Mexico for Drug Damage

During a news conference in Guadalajara (October 21, 1997) President Ernesto Zedillo placed the blame for drug-related crimes in Mexico upon U.S. drug users:

The United States want to certify us. They should reimburse us for the mess they have left us. Mexico is squeezed between U.S. consumer demand for drugs and narcotics production by poor South American countries. That's the cruelty of this phenomenon. They make a sandwich for us. Fortunately we are not consumers of drugs.

President Clinton Apologizes to Mexico While
Covering Up for Mexico's Key Role in Drugging America

President Clinton called Mexico's President Ernesto Zedillo (May 25, 1998) and apologized for not informing Mexican authorities about the American undercover money-laundering operation being conducted partly in Mexico. However, if Mexican government officials *had* been notified, the close-knit relationship between Mexican government officials and the drug traffickers would have scuttled the operation.

Omitting Reference to Worse High-Level Mexican Involvement

The backlash from Mexico caused reference to Mexico's Defense Minister, General Cervantes and other Mexican personnel—who had been involved in the drug money laundering—to be omitted from charges filed by the U.S. Department of Justice. U.S. authorities remained silent about even more explosive evidence concerning government and military drug trafficking to keep the matter from further exploding.

Mexico's Attorney General, Jorge Madrazo Cuellar, issued a statement denying that senior commanders of the Army and officials of the Mexican government were involved in any form of drug trafficking or drug money laundering. Really!

Removing U.S. Agents from Mexico for Their Protection

Threats from Mexican sources after Operation Casablanca caused the DEA to pull its agents out of parts of Mexico (June 1998) and the Justice Department warned U.S. personnel on both sides of the border about Mexican retaliation. A *Washington Times* article (June 8, 1998) said:

The new threat they face isn't violence from narcotics traffickers, but hostility from their law-enforcement counterparts in the Mexican federal judicial police. An urgent warning was sent on June 2 to all U.S. law-enforcement agencies with officers working along the border or in Mexico to stay alert for "retaliation" from the Mexican police as a consequence of the sting, known as Operation Casablanca.

As a precaution, the DEA has withdrawn all agents from a joint U.S.-Mexico task force in Tijuana, the home city of the Arellano Felix brothers, who control Mexico's second-largest drug cartel. The alert was issued when the El Paso Intelligence Center, the federal law-enforcement intelligence clearing house, noticed an abrupt rise in reports from various federal agents of hostility from their Mexican counterparts. The federal Bureau of Alcohol, Tobacco and Firearms (ATF) later verified the danger.

The Danger to U.S. Agents was Real

In 1996, a DEA agent shared the names of some of its informants with Mexican authorities and the list was promptly given to Mexican drug trafficker Amado Carrillo Fuentes. Included in the list was Rocio Aguero Miranda, whose dismembered body was found shortly thereafter in a barrel, blood oozing from her rectum where a rod had been stuck deep inside and twisted—a favorite Mexican torture trick.

U.S. Version of Mexican Brutality

This type of brutality also occurs in the United States by government employees paid and entrusted to protect the people. On August 9, 1997, three police officers held down a suspect in a Brooklyn police station while another officer shoved a long jagged stick into the person's rectum, ripping apart his rectum and bladder and causing serious bleeding into the abdominal cavity. The police officer then shoved the feces-covered stick into the victim's mouth.

The officer committing this atrocity bragged to other members of the police department about what he had done, showing them the feces-stained stick and having them smell it. None of the officers who knew of the brutality spoke out until months later when the media gave the matter heavy publicity. If a federal prosecutor had not entered the case and filed criminal charges against "New York's Finest," the brutality would have been unknown as in many other instances.

Many other examples of police brutality occur on a routine basis, including the shooting and killing of innocent people. In many ways, the same conditions existing in Mexico also exist in the United States. The only difference appears that government corruption in the United States is more "sophisticated" and kept under wraps by government authorities and most of the media.

Mexican Banks Plead Guilty

"Two Mexican Banks to Plead Guilty in Laundering Case," was the title to a *New York Times* article (March 30, 1999):

Two of Mexico's biggest banks have agreed to plead guilty to criminal charges of money laundering, officials said today, bringing a swift end to the most important legal cases stemming from a major investigation into the movement of illegal drug profits. Officials said the banks, Grupo Financiero Bancomer S.S. and Grupo Financiero Serfin S.A., will forfeit millions of dollars seized by the Government and pay fines of $500,000 each....the United States Customs Service resisted strong pressure from both the Mexican Government and the banks to have the criminal charges dropped. One official of the United States Attorney's office here said, "And there was a great deal of pressure."

[Attempted Coverup by Department of Justice]

The guilty pleas also raise questions about what many officials described as the reluctant handling of the case by some of the federal prosecutors in Los Angeles, and about the consideration that was given by some in the Clinton Administration to scaling back charges against the banks to avoid further strain on relations with Mexico.

Several officials said federal prosecutors who included the principal Assistant United States Attorney on the case, Duane R. Lyons, argued that the banks should not be indicted on criminal charges because it was not clear they had benefitted from the actions of the bankers who were ultimately charged with helping drug traffickers to launder millions of dollars in illicit earnings.

The prosecutors had initially planned to file criminal money laundering charges against at least four more banks whose employees were implicated in the case.

[Protecting American Bank Interests]

The prosecutors did retreat on one of the three indictments they brought last year against Mexican banks, agreeing not to pursue criminal charges against Banca Confia, a smaller Mexican bank that was subsequently bought by Citigroup.

Mexicans Torturing and Killing DEA Agent

Mexican drug traffickers, with the aid of Mexican police, brutally tortured and killed DEA agent Enrique Camarena in 1985. Reportedly aiding in the brutality were several people, including Doctor Humberto Alvarez Machain and Mexican businessman Ruben Zuno Arce, a brother-in-law of former Mexican President Luis Escheverria. U.S. agents sneaked into Mexico in 1990 and seized Zuno, and brought him to the United States where he stood trial for the torture murder of Camarena.

A U.S. jury held Zuno guilty (1992) and a judge sentenced him to life in prison. The key witness against him was Hector Cervantes Santos, a Mexican policeman who worked for Mexican drug lords before becoming a paid DEA informant. Six years later, in 1998, Cervantes recanted his testimony, stating that DOJ prosecutors urged him to testify falsely against Zuno, two co-defendants, and key Mexican officials. Zuno was later freed by a U.S. courts on the basis the U.S. agents violated the sovereignty of Mexico.

Savage Drug-Related Killings Everywhere Throughout Mexico

Attorneys, journalists, priests, and judges, among others, are randomly killed when they speak out against drug trafficking. A September 24, 1997 newspaper article stated that nearly two dozen Mexican journalists had been killed and countless others kidnapped and attacked for reporting drug trafficking matters. These attacks had been virtually ignored by the Mexican government, itself at risk from meddling reporters who report government involvement in drug trafficking. In Ensenada 19 people, including children and babies, were pulled from their home, huddled together, and gunned to death, because of problems between drug traffickers (September 1998). Almost 500 people were killed during 1998 in the relatively low-populated area of Baja California.

Recertification: Another Hoax on Gullible Americans

Every year the president of the United States must render a decision as to whether certain nations are cooperating in the war on drugs. With the day approaching when President Clinton would have to certify Mexico as fully cooperating in the war on drugs, Mexico announced a "total war on narcotics" (February 4, 1999). Four key Mexican security officials held a news conference to show America Mexico's dedication to the war on drugs: Interior Secretary Francisco Labastida Ochoa, the Secretaries of Defense and Navy, and the Attorney General. The crux of the conference was that Mexico would spend more money (surely U.S. money!) on planes and radar. To avoid embarrassing matters, reporters were not allowed to ask any questions.

Mexico Announces Total War On Drugs: Don't Believe It!

A *New York Times* article (February 5, 1999) had the title: "Mexico Announces 'Total War' on Narcotics." Anyone making such a statement had to assume that the listener was totally ignorant about these matters, and that they could get away with such a statement to the American people. It was surely said with "tongue-in-check." Anyone who believed that statement would be a candidate to buy the Brooklyn Bridge. The article stated:

Mexico's four top security officials jointly announced today what they called a new anti-narcotic strategy, based largely on the introduction of radar and other technology. Interior Secretary Francisco Labastida Ochoa, who made the announcement with the Secretaries of Defense and Navy and the Attorney General, said Mexico would spend $400 million to $500 million over three years to buy new planes, ships, radar and other military and law enforcement equipment.

In addition to the new spending, the strategy involves pledges to coordinate Mexico's law enforcement agencies and combat corruption more efficiently. Mr. Labastida called it "a total war against drug trafficking." The rare joint public appearance by the four officials in an auditorium at the Interior Ministry and their somewhat extravagant description of the initiative suggested it might have been timed to influence United States officials three weeks before the Clinton Administration must certify whether Mexico is a reliable partner in the narcotics war. Reporters were not allowed to ask questions after the officials' speeches.

Coming Back to Reality

Another *New York Times* article (February 14, 1999) referred to realities:
Drug seizures by the Mexican police have fallen significantly. Nearly all of the most important Mexican narcotics traffickers identified last year remain at large. The promised extraditions of some Mexican drug suspects to the United States have not materialized, and drug enforcement programs have been rocked by a series of public conflicts between the two governments.

Drug investigations that have touched on several well known Mexican politicians and at least a dozen high-ranking military officers have not yet led to any arrests, despite what American officials describe as strong evidence that some of the politicians and officers have sought to protect traffickers in return for large bribes.

American intelligence and law-enforcement officials have provided their Mexican counterparts with information on the whereabouts of powerful drug traffickers, only to have Mexican agents mishandle the intelli-

gence or wait for hours before carrying out raids. "We give them houses, we give them phone numbers, and nothing happens. Cases go nowhere."

In one debacle last spring, American officials said, officers of the military intelligence unit recognized two of the most important traffickers in the Cancun organization, Ramon Alcides Magana and Allbino Quintero Meraz, but made no attempt to capture them. On other occasions, American intelligence officials gave officers of the military unit home addresses and telephone numbers for each of the two traffickers. But again, officials said, opportunities to arrest the pair were lost.

Last October, the unit appeared to get an important break when it captured Gilberto Garza Garcia, the trafficker who oversaw the Mafia's movement of cocaine shipments from Cancun up the gulf coast to McAllen, Texas. But United States and Mexican officials said that after negotiating with the general who headed the military unit and promising to help him trap Mr. Magna, Mr. Garza Garcia was placed in the custody of two detectives from whom he escaped the next day.

Sacrificing an Occasional Drug Trafficker for Recertification

When Mexico releases a drug trafficker to the United States, it is for public relations, to gain accreditation each year by the president of the United States. Together they play a hoax on the American people by claiming Mexico is doing what it definitely is not—helping to fight the war on drugs. Juan Garcia Abrego, the head of the Gulf cartel, was one example when in 1996 Mexico turned him over to the United States for drug-related prosecution. He was expendable and others would soon take his place.

Annual Exercise in Hypocrisy and Duping the American People

A *New York Times* editorial (February 15, 1999) said of the annual ritual of certifying Mexico's "cooperation" in the war on drugs:

Mexican officials recently unveiled a $400 million high-tech anti-narcotics strategy billed as a "total war" on drug trafficking. Grandiose plans for stopping the flow of cocaine and lavish praise from Washington for Mexico's anti-drug efforts have become annual February events. The process has become an annual exercise in hypocrisy and should be stopped, in part because the use of illegal drugs in the United States fuels the problem.

The State Department said last week that the Government of President Ernesto Zedillo is "strongly committed" to fighting drug trafficking. Drug trafficking, which makes accomplices out of the very agencies designed to combat trafficking, has stymied governments worldwide.

Mexican Staging of Events for Favorable Publicity

An example of the way Mexican politicians orchestrate an arrest for favorable media coverage was shown in a *New York Times* article (April 15, 1998):

First, the authorities announced his arrest in advance, inviting reporters to film him as policemen escorted him handcuffed out of the hotel. Then the hotel manager said that the room in which Mr. Munoz was arrested had been rented not by Mr. Munoz, but by the police a week earlier.

"This was one of those deals that appeared to be prearranged," said a Texas lawyer involved in related proceedings who spoke on the condition of anonymity. "There was pressure on the Mexican government to do something, and so they did something. Why arrest him in a hotel? It smacked that he made an appointment with the authorities so they wouldn't arrest him in front of his children."

Later, more disturbing information emerged. Two Mexican officials involved in the arrest and trial of Mr. Munoz were accused in American court testimony of receiving huge bribes from his drug organization.

The police officer who orchestrated Mr. Munoz's arrest and assembled the initial evidence was Elias Ramirez Ruiz, the powerful Federal Police commander in Chihuahua, the state in which Ciudad Juarez is situated. Javier Coello Trejo was the Mexican Deputy Attorney General, based in Mexico City, who channeled evidence received from American officials to Mexican prosecutors in Ciudad Juarez and supervised the Munoz case.

Late in 1990, even before Mr. Munoz's first trial ended, Mr. Ramirez and Mr. Coello were driven from office by a barrage of corruption charges. Since the resignation of Mr. Coello, several witnesses in at least three federal trials in Texas have detailed how he received suitcases of cash from the Ciudad Juarez and other drug cartels.

Mexican press reports accused Mr. Ramirez of staging several phony cocaine seizures as window dressing for Mexico's antidrug effort. And two years later, Mr. Ramirez was charged with narcotics smuggling and racketeering. Federal prosecutors sought his arrest, but he obtained an amparo from a judge and has never been detained. [Amparo is an order from a judge barring the person from being arrested.]

Rafael Munoz was linked to a large drug seizure at a warehouse in the Los Angeles community of Sylmar, where over 40,000 pounds of cocaine was stored. Records showed that billions of dollars of cocaine passed through the warehouse. Mexicans at the warehouse said the drugs belonged to a Mexican drug trafficker, Rafael Munoz Talavera who lived in Juarez and had a multi-million-dollar house in El Paso. (Richard Pitt remembered him well from the early days of drug trafficking.)

Mexico's Cooperation Is "Absolutely Superlative," Said White House Drug Czar Barry McCaffrey

Possibly the Clinton "disease" afflicted U.S. drug czar Barry McCaffrey who fatuously claimed that Mexico's cooperation was "absolutely superlative." At the same time the drug czar was making that statement, a DEA confidential report prepared by a Tim Golden concluded that "the government of Mexico has not accomplished its counter-narcotics goals or succeeded in co-operation with the United States government." The report added, Mexican drug trafficking had increased and the corruption of its enforcement agencies "continues unabated."

The See-Nothing Team Supports Clinton's Certification

Media articles (March 28, 1999) referred to the "assurances" given to the American public by President Clinton's loyalists Madeleine Albright, Attorney General Janet Reno, and drug czar Barry McCaffrey:

> Last month, President Clinton certified Mexico as an ally in the international fights against drugs. We believe that this decision was correct and that Mexico's senior leadership is strongly cooperating with the United States in this fight. We believe Mexico has made significant progress in recent years and meets the standard under the law. Mexican officials at all levels work closely with their U.S. counterparts across a full spectrum of counter-drug activities.

Newspaper comments appearing in the same article said:

> Sixty percent of the cocaine sold on American streets comes through Mexico, even while Mexico's cocaine seizures sharply declined last year. Despite the Mexican government's having entered numerous orders of extradition, Mexican courts have prevented the extradition of any Mexican nationals on major drug-trafficking charges.

**Basing Its Evaluation of Mexico's Drug Cooperation
On Statements of Mexicans Involved in Drug Trafficking**

The Clinton Administration based much of its Mexican drug strategy *rhetoric* on assurances given by one of Mexico's top officials involved in promoting drug trafficking: General Cervantes. The Clinton Administration spin doctors—with their well-worn straight faces—said they were confident that Cervantes was above reproach. While putting many of its citizens in prison, sometimes for life, the Clinton Justice Department was cooperating with and protecting one of the biggest drug traffickers in Mexico. The *New York Times* article continued:

> But a detailed account of the case, based on confidential Government documents, court records and dozens of interviews, suggests that United States officials have been haunted by the spectacle of Mexican officials' being linked to illicit activities soon after they are embraced in Washington. And just weeks before the Customs investigation, known as Operation Casablanca, ended last year, Administration officials received intelligence reports indicating that the Mexican military's ties to the drug trade were more serious than had previously been thought.

President Clinton Lauds Mexico's Cooperation in War on Drugs

"Clinton Lauds Mexico regime as drug ally," was the euphemistic headline in a *Chicago Tribune* article (February 16, 1999). Clinton had access to evidence proving the endemic corruption in the Mexico government and the involvement of all levels of government with drug traffickers that encouraged drugs to be shipped into the United States through Mexico. Clinton certified, as fully cooperating, 22 of the 30 major drug producing and drug transition countries, including Mexico, Haiti, Dominican Republic, and others. Colombia was not certified, but received a special waiver. Almost all the countries certified produce or transship tons of cocaine into the United States every year, and most all receive U.S. taxpayer money. The only people being fooled by Clinton's statements are the American people, and they seem to approve.

Clinton Administration Provided Further Protection
To Mexican Drug Trafficking and Money Laundering Operations

Early in 1998, the Clinton Administration ordered an end to a major Mexican money laundering investigation that was about to end with a $1.15 *billion* drug money bust. Evidence reportedly linked Mexican politicians with a huge money laundering operation. One of the Mexicans involved was reported to be Mexico's Defense Minister, General Enrique Cervantes.

Senior Customs agent William F. Gately, now retired, headed a U.S. Customs undercover investigation of an operation that had already helped Colombian drug traffickers launder over $60 million as part of a bigger operation. If that operation had not been canceled, it would have revealed far worse involvement by the Mexican government in sending drugs to the United States.

Gately wrote the 1994 book, *"Dead Ringer,"* describing the ties between the Italian Mafia and Colombian drug cartels. Gately's group used insiders to carry out the drug money laundering, thereby discovering how it was done. They learned drug traffickers were depositing money with Mexican bankers who handled the money in such a way that the funds were returned through cashier checks drawn on U.S. accounts that the Mexican banks used for doing business in the United States.

Justice Department Protecting Major Drug-Money Launderers

During the investigation, agents posing as money launderers operating from a front company, Emerald Empire Corporation, began collecting money from various drug cells and laundering them through Mexican banks. One Customs undercover agent, using the alias, Javier Ramirez, infiltrated the powerful Mexican drug cartel headed by Amado Carrillo Fuentes. Gately said his investigative team ran into administration obstacles almost from "Day-One" as Justice Department personnel sought to block the investigation. Since U.S. Customs was a division of the Treasury Department and not under the direct control of the Justice Department, Gately was able to continue the investigation. Gately had also been involved in Operation Casablanca.

Clinton Administration Protecting Major Mexican Drug Operation

As the Clinton administration shut down the operation, Gately asked, "Why are we sitting on this kind of information. It's either because we're lazy, we're stupid or the political will doesn't exist to engage in the kind of investigation where our law enforcement efforts might damage our foreign policy." (Being compartmentalized, Gately may not have been aware of the endemic corruption in the Department of Justice.) A *New York Times* article (March 16, 1999) referred to the high administration coverup:

> *Senior Administration officials denied that foreign policy had influenced their decision to end the operation, saying they had been moved primarily by concerns for its security.* (The undercover agents weren't concerned with their security!)

Mexican Judicial System—Massive Corruption

Reports over the years clearly show Mexico's criminal justice system is chaotic and corrupt. The U.S. General Accounting Office (GAO) told a congressional committee (March 1998) that a Mexican police unit fighting organized crime trusts only one of Mexico's 500 federal judges and magistrates to authorize wiretaps without tipping off the suspects. They reported that thousands of fugitives avoid arrest by paying judges to issue an amparo (writ that bars arrests or further detention). They stated that corrupt officials and accused criminals can easily buy an amparo by paying the going price to a local judge.

Although given virtually no publicity, this also occurs in the United States to a limited extent. Chicago was famous for that, as are many state courts in the south. For years, my sources told me about paying off governors to get sentences commuted or pardoned, including sources I had in Arkansas, and sources who described money going to Governor Bill Clinton for pardons. On the federal level, compromising federal judges is usually done in a different and more sophisticated manner, as described in *Defrauding America*, and usually involves protecting high-level government personnel or corrupt operations.

Mexican Judges Protecting Government Drug Trafficking

Mexican judges ordered the Mexican attorney general's office to rehire over 400 police who had been fired for drug-related offenses (July 1998) Attorney General Jorge Madrazo criticized the ruling and stated he would appeal it. Many of the dismissed police were on the payrolls of drug traffickers and kidnappers, and charged with murders and rapes. Mexican policemen, fired by one law enforcement agency for corrupt activities, are frequently hired by another "law enforcement" agency.

A 1996 United Nations survey asked Mexicans what they thought of their criminal justice system. Typical of the response was the statement: "We have a justice system immersed in the routine violation of every basic principle," said law professor Eduardo Lopez Betancourt of the national university. He added, "Nothing is respected. Prosecutors rig evidence and judges sell verdicts according to the highest bidder, without delay, favoring every kind of criminal from drug traffickers to car thieves." Most Mexicans consider every element in the criminal justice system to be corrupt, including the police, the prosecutors, the judges, and the jailers

Mexican Culture Eulogizing the Corrupt

Mexico's problems with corruption are deep, and events don't indicate any improvements, including Mexico's youth, whose morals are often affected or determined by lyrics. A *New York Times* article (February 19, 1999) wrote about one of Mexico's most popular troubadors who eulogized drugs, crimes, and murders in his songs, and the audiences who applaud the lyrics. Instead of making ball players into heroes, as is done in the United States, the article described how drug traffickers are made into heroes by troubadors such as Quintero. The article described how Quintero composed many corridos about killings perpetrated by the Arellano Felix brothers who control the drug trade in northwestern Mexico, and that the Mexican bands follow a similar theme.

As Mario Quintero steps to the microphone, strums his guitar and begins singing about the pleasures of snorting cocaine after a few drinks, scores of teen-age girls crowd the outdoor stage screaming, "I love you, Mario!" Mr. Quintero and his wildly popular band, the Tucanes de Tijuana, or Toucans of Tijuana, follow with a song about a smuggler's love for his rooster, parrot and goat, underworld symbols for marijuana, cocaine and heroin.

"I live off my three fine animals," Mr. Quintero sings to roars of approval from thousands of cowboy-hatted fans packed into an outdoor concert grounds here. His next ballad is "Most Wanted Men," in which he assumes the voice of a powerful trafficker who boasts about bribing politicians and the police "to control whole countries."

The Tucanes are one of the most successful of hundreds of Mexican country bands whose lyrics chronicle traffickers' daily lives and violent routines. The extraordinary popularity of their music here and in the United States underscores the profound roots the drug industry has sunk into North American popular culture, suggesting that millions of fans quietly admire the smugglers' fabled wealth, anti-establishment bravura and bold entrepreneurial skills.

"The drug trade has permeated our social fabric," said Manuel Valenzuela, a professor at a research institute in Tijuana who studies the drug ballads, known in Spanish as narco-corridos. "The political elite, the army, the church and the banks have all been corrupted, and in this context many young people see in narcotics their route to early wealth, even if they fear dying before they're 25. The corridos just reflect this evolution."

A Corrupt System Can't be Reformed from the Inside

The U.S. State Department in May 1998 issued warning that the crime rate in Mexico City "had reached critical levels. In several cases, tourists report that uniformed police are the crime perpetrators, stopping vehicles and demanding money, or assaulting and robbing tourists walking late at night." Shakedowns, corruption, bribes, are the most notable traits of Mexican politicians, police, and military. And it always has been. I remember my trips into Mexico in the early 1950s as an airline pilot, with the obvious police corruption at that time. It is much worse now due to the immense profits made possible by America's drug users. The same applies to the United States, as every government check and balance is implicated.

Compare Mexico's Corruption to That in the United States

Almost every form of Mexican corruption can be found in the U.S. government and in some cases even worse, as documented in the third edition of *Defrauding America*, and revealed by several dozen government insiders. For instance:

- U.S. government personnel and agencies involved in drug smuggling into the United States. People in control of the *CIA have been smuggling drugs into the United States* for the past half-century. (During the Iran-Contra affair of the 1980s, drugs were being flown into the United States by contract agents for the CIA and DEA, and military aircraft, as part of the arms-shipment logistics to Central America, the returning aircraft carrying drugs.) In Mexico, the government units and personnel are not known to be inflicting the drug scourge upon their own people as occurs in the United States.

- Coverup, aiding and abetting, of these drug crimes by people in control of key government offices. Coverup by divisions of the Department of Justice (FBI, U.S. Attorneys, DEA, Washington headquarters). In the United States, most of the broadcast and print media assists in the coverups, disinformation, discrediting of those people who courageously reveal the drug related corruption by government personnel.
- President's involvement in drugs. During the Contra operations in the 1980s, the drug smuggling into the United States involved the White House (George Bush), National Security Council (Oliver North), and Governor Bill Clinton who protected the CIA's drug activities at Mena, Arkansas.
- Encouraging—protecting—other countries who ship drugs into the United States, made worse by the CIA liaison working closely with major drug cartels in Colombia and elsewhere.
- Justice Department personnel blocking investigations and prosecution of major drug organizations.
- Governors of different states collecting protection money for drug shipments through their areas of jurisdiction. Several books have been written on this matter.
- Laws seizing property for virtually every offense, and laws permitting the seizure of property from innocent people, unable to regain the properties corruptly seized.
- Key government officials, including the vice-president, U.S. Attorney General, U.S. Attorneys, the federal drug czar, FBI director and various FBI offices, all involved in protecting drug trafficking.
- U.S. Navy, U.S. Army, and U.S. Air Force used to smuggle drugs.
- FBI and CIA agents engaging in actions to silence government agents and others who expose these crimes, misusing government offices and power to financially destroy those people who expose government involvement in drugs.
- Judges blocking the exposure of government-related drug trafficking.
- Judges sentencing whistleblowers to prison.
- Most members of Congress legislating laws resulting in placement of large numbers of their constituents in prison for many years. Worse than in Mexico, these people have brought about the greatest number of citizens of any country who are and who will be in prison.
- FBI, CIA, and other law enforcement agents engaged in murders and other crimes. Crime and corruption by police are rampant throughout the United States, something that I first saw while growing up in the Jersey City area with its corrupt Democratic machine, similar to that of Chicago and New York. Things haven't changed for the better since those early years of mine in the 1920s and 1930s. A May 1999 television documentary *(Discovery)* showed the endemic corruption in the New Orleans police force, police extracting protection money from merchants, engaging in widespread drug trafficking, killing of witnesses, killing of fellow police-officers, very similar to the worst in Mexico. Most U.S. print and broadcast media—aware of these high-level government crimes—became ac-

complices through disinformation, contradictory articles, or silence. Members of Congress engaged in a conspiracy of silence and coverup that prevented the American people from obtaining relief against the government drug trafficking and government protection of other drug traffickers. Invading foreign countries on simplistic excuses and then using the war's logistics to smuggle large quantities of drugs into the United States.

- Subverting foreign governments throughout the world.
- Openly engaging in planned assassination of foreign leaders.
- Government personnel engaging in a continuous pattern of corruption against its own people. These include duping the public into funding and approving wars upon Korea, Indochina, Nicaragua, Panama, Yugoslavia, undermining foreign countries, and such domestic corruption as October Surprise, CIA looting of the HUD and savings and loan programs, Iran-Contra Affair, government corruption in the bankruptcy courts, and much more. (See *Defrauding America* and *Unfriendly Skies*.)

Mexico Reminds the U.S. of America's Corruption

Mexico's foreign ministry's undersecretary Juan Rebolledo reminded the United States of its role in the drug problems:

You read a lot about how drugs make it from South America, through Mexico and to the border, but the same sources are not telling the public how it is that these same drugs make it from the border to Chicago. They don't just magically make it there overnight. Drug dealers spread their money all along the trail from source to consumption, so it's naive to think that it is not spread north of the border as well.

CHAPTER THIRTEEN

EVERYONE DESERVES
A FAIR TRIAL

E veryone deserves a fair trial, and certainly someone charged with a non-violent offense. Anyone charged with an offense also deserves to have an attorney who is not involved in a conspiracy with the prosecutor to undermine the defendant's lawful defenses. That was not the case with Claude DuBoc, a French-Canadian, who was arrested in Hong Kong in 1994 on an international arrest warrant issued by U.S. Attorney Michael Patterson in Gainesville, Florida. The warrant falsely charged that DuBoc headed an organization transporting marijuana into Florida.

DuBoc had never been in Florida and his drug transporting activities never touched the state. There were several reasons for seeking to trap DuBoc into committing an offense that he had no intention of doing. The informants sought to have charges dropped against them by giving perjured testimony about DuBoc that was requested by the prosecutor. The prosecutor wanted to bolster his record of convictions and seizure of forfeitures. And DuBoc had over $100 million in assets that would be fabulous trophies for anyone who brought about a conviction.

The informants concocted a scheme seeking to induce DuBoc to ship marijuana into Florida, when DuBoc had no interest in doing it—and never did. The government informants tried several times to get DuBoc to agree to their plan, and he repeatedly rejected their attempts.

Regardless of DuBoc's refusal to become involved in a drug operation concocted by the prosecutor and government informants, DOJ prosecutors obtained an indictment against DuBoc from a grand jury in Gainesville, Florida, on the basis of perjured testimony.

Supplier of Marijuana, But not in Florida or the United States

For 15 years, until his arrest on March 23, 1994, DuBoc controlled companies that transported marijuana, supplying the burgeoning demand for that product. These companies operated primarily into Canada, but not into Florida where the indictment was obtained. The proceeds from their operations were controlled by off-shore Hong Kong companies, and their attorneys and accountants resided in Switzerland and Luxembourg. Justice Department prosecutors did not seek to indict these other sources, possibly because sham charges against them would not succeed.

Imposing U.S. Fiat Upon the World

Under law or by practice, a country can legalize the production, use, or transportation of drugs. The legalization or decriminalization of drugs had been considered and recommended by many people in the United States. I don't recommend that this be done, but if the United States can consider legalizing drugs, there is nothing that keeps another country from doing the same, either by law or by accepted practice.

In California, for instance, the state's primary cash crop is said to be marijuana, and many law enforcement personnel look the other way, allowing this practice to continue. In 1998, various communities in California enacted laws legalizing "medicinal" use of marijuana, including Oakland and San Francisco.

DuBoc's companies conducted much of their marijuana transportation from Hong Kong. Arguably, United States authorities in Florida, 8000 miles away, should not have any jurisdiction to indict someone in Hong Kong and extradite him to stand trial in Florida for activities occurring in countries outside the United States.

DOJ Purchase of Perjured Testimony

The charges against DuBoc were based upon the statements of drug traffickers seeking to have the Justice Department drop charges against them. It has become common practice for prosecutors to reward people charged with criminal offenses or those already in prison, for testimony against a defendant. Oftentimes the testimony is knowingly false, or the false statements are given to the informant by the prosecutor for use during grand jury or trial proceedings.

Getting on the Conspiracy-To-Foster-A-Crime Bandwagon

Justice Department prosecutors in Gainesville, Florida, encouraged Sonia Vacca and attorney Matthew Martenyi to induce DuBoc to ship drugs into Florida. Also attempting to get criminal charges dropped was Clifton Brown, a fugitive from prosecution in Gainesville, Florida, who was wanted on a drug smuggling charge. He heard about the scheme to get DuBoc arrested and recognized an opportunity to give false testimony and get charges dropped by joining Vacca and Martenyi in trying to get DuBoc to commit a federal drug offense. Government agents were seeking to bring about a criminal act where none would otherwise occur without their connivance.

Despite repeated efforts, including meetings with DuBoc in Los Angeles and San Francisco, DuBoc rejected their overtures. This rejection was known to Justice Department attorneys and revealed by testimony given in a criminal trial several months earlier. (*U.S. V. Nicholas Grenhagen, Matthew Martenyi and Sonia Vacca*, 1:93:CR. 01043) During the trial, Vacca and Martenyi described their attempts to induce DuBoc to ship drugs into Florida and his refusal to do so. In that trial, the jury refused to convict the defendants.

Fabricating Criminal Charges

Despite DuBoc's refusal to ship marijuana, Justice Department prosecutors used false statements from government informants to obtain an indictment from a federal grand jury at Gainesville, Florida (March 10, 1994). The indictment charged DuBoc with possession of marijuana with intent to distribute, conspiracy to import marijuana into Florida, and conspiracy to transport funds relating to the marijuana. (The case number in U.S. District Court at Gainesville was Case Nr. 94-CR-01009.) For jurisdiction to exist in Florida, it was necessary that some part of the criminal activities be accomplished in that state.

Despite the absence of jurisdiction and absence of an offense, DOJ prosecutors sent an extradition warrant to Hong Kong for DuBoc's arrest. The Justice Department arranged with a U.S. Customs informant to induce DuBoc to attend a meeting in Hong Kong at which there was to be a transfer of assets owned by DuBoc. When DuBoc appeared, he was arrested on the basis of the Florida extradition papers.

DuBoc's First Mistake: Relying on and Trusting Attorneys

Shortly after being arrested in Hong Kong, DuBoc sought legal advice from attorney Henry J. Uscinski of the Coudert Brothers law firm that had offices in the United States and overseas. Uscinski said he was an expert in extradition. After being hired—and without making an adequate check into DuBoc's defenses. Uscinski urged him to waive extradition. This was *very* bad advice.

Under international law, DuBoc had the right to challenge the evidence upon which the U.S. extradition was based. For instance, U.S. law relating to extradition requests from other countries is stated in Title 18 USC Section 3184:

> *[The accused and subject of the extradition shall] be brought before [the judge] to the end that the evidence of criminality may be heard and considered. If, on such hearing, he deems the evidence sufficient to sustain the charge under the provisions of the proper treaty or convention, he shall certify the same, together with a copy of all the testimony taken before him, to the Secretary of State, that a warrant may issue upon the requisition of the proper authorities of such foreign government, for the surrender of such person, according to the stipulations of the treaty or convention; and he shall issue his warrant for the commitment of the person so charged to the proper jail, there to remain until such surrender shall be made.*

Insuring Windfall Legal Fees

The Coudert Brothers law firm could have filed an objection to the extradition and within a matter of days determined through investigation that the charges against DuBoc were without foundation. But by encouraging DuBoc to waive extradition, they could expect sizable legal fees from defending him in the United States that could not have been obtained by simply defending against extradition. (Also, as described in greater detail in *Defrauding America*, many law firms are covert fronts for the CIA and Justice Department and could be expected to provide advice beneficial to their hidden government ties and adverse to their clients.)

Attorneys Surely Knew of DOJ Fraud and Perjured Testimony

The Coudert law firm surely knew that once DuBoc waived his extradition defenses that he would be virtually powerless to defend himself against the misuse of power by federal prosecutors. It was known throughout the legal system that Justice Department prosecutors routinely hide exculpatory evidence, repeatedly fabricate evidence and pay witnesses to lie. Also known throughout the legal fraternity, DOJ prosecutors would seek a court order blocking DuBoc from using his own assets to hire his own attorneys on the argument that the assets were obtained from criminal activities and thereby forfeitable. One exemption from denial of funds for legal counsel is when the attorneys make a secret deal with the prosecutor to sacrifice their client for prosecutors' approval to use seized assets for legal fees.

Without access to his own funds, DuBoc would have to rely upon court-appointed attorneys. And these court-appointed attorneys usually provide dismal defenses and often protect their relationship with government attorneys.

Second Mistake: Hiring Media-Dubbed Dream Team of Lawyers

Foolishly waiving extradition, DuBoc arrived in California in chains. Instead of hiring the Coudert Brothers law firm, DuBoc hired Robert Shapiro to be his legal counsel. Shapiro was based in Los Angeles and DuBoc's criminal trial was in Florida, making Shapiro an unsuitable legal counsel.

Shapiro then hired as co-counsel, who would do most of the work, Florida-based F. Lee Bailey, who was a partner in a Miami law firm that was closer to the trial location. Bailey was best known for such high-profile clients as Patty Hearst, the Boston Strangler, Dr. Sam Shepard, the air traffic controllers union, and being part of the media's so-called "dream team" representing the killer of two innocent people, O.J. Simpson.

DuBoc Trusting Bailey with Millions: Another Mistake

Bailey demanded DuBoc pay a huge up-front retainer fee. DuBoc transferred to Bailey, for safekeeping and security for fees, 602,000 shares of pharmaceutical stock in a Canadian growth company, BioChem Pharma, Inc. At that time, the stock was worth over $6 million, and expected to greatly increase in value after the FDA approved an AIDS drug that the company had developed. Its value would then increase to over $26 million.

Bailey became lead counsel and brought into the case another attorney, Ed Shohat of the Miami law firm of Bierman, Shohat, Loewy, Perry & Klein. DuBoc now had Ed Shapiro, Francis Lee Bailey, and Ed Shohat technically defending him, which should have been a fabulous defense team. Looks are often deceiving.

Defense Evidence was Readily Available, and Ignored

Even the most basic defense investigation required that DuBoc's attorneys examine the transcript of the Grenhagen trial where the charges against DuBoc were allegedly raised, contact the attorneys involved in that trial, and those witnesses who testified. This was not done. (In the Grenhagen case, Lloyd Vipperman was Grenhagen's counsel, and the law firm of Wachtel and Weinberg were the attorneys for Vacca and Martenyi.)

Sabotage Against DuBoc Started Early

Bailey met with Justice Department attorneys before he met DuBoc, and the conversations between Bailey and the prosecutor bode very poorly for Bailey's client. None of the usual investigations were conducted by Bailey, which would have shown that the prosecutor's case against DuBoc was riddled with holes. Bailey relied almost completely—or solely—on what the prosecutor stated to him.

Sabotage your Client—Or You Don't get Paid!

The prosecutor told Bailey that the fees and assets DuBoc had turned over to him were forfeitable assets and that he would have to turn them over to the government. *However*, the prosecutor said, if Bailey could get DuBoc to plead guilty to every charge made against him and conveyed to the government all of DuBoc's worldwide assets, Justice Department prosecutors would allow Bailey and his attorney associates to keep up to $3 million of DuBoc's assets. DuBoc's assets totaled over $100 million. Not a bad deal for sabotaging a client! (I encountered the same sabotage with a Las Vegas attorney, Joshua Landish, who conspired with government attorneys to corruptly strip me of the $10 million in assets that funded my exposure activities against the government. (See the third editions of *Unfriendly Skies* and *Defrauding America*.)

DuBoc's Attorney Became A Secret Agent for the DOJ Prosecutor

Bailey agreed to do as the prosecutor demanded. He secretly become an agent for the prosecutor, undermining his own client, with the expected result that DuBoc would spend the remainder of his life in prison. This secret agreement was a contingency agreement with the prosecutor. Bailey's goal would be to convince his client to abandon all defenses available under the laws and Constitution of the United States, forfeit his worldwide assets, and agree to go to prison for the remainder of his life—so that Bailey could get a $3 million windfall.

If Bailey did *not* convince DuBoc to plead guilty, Bailey would lose the prosecutor's assistance in getting a fee, and Bailey would have to rely upon the normal legal process to collect fees from his client. This required more effort than was required by sabotaging his client.

Pressuring DuBoc to Plead Guilty

Within days of DuBoc's arrival in Florida, and without performing the most elementary check of DuBoc's defenses, Bailey told DuBoc that the evidence against him was overwhelming. This, of course, was not true. DuBoc was pressured by Bailey to plead guilty to all charges and to transfer his worldwide assets to the U.S. government.

At that time, DuBoc didn't know the particulars relating to the charges, and assumed that Bailey and the other attorneys he hired were performing the normally required defense investigations. He had no awareness of the culpability in the legal fraternity, the Justice Department, or as he would soon learn, by federal judges.

On April 13, 1994, DuBoc appeared for arraignment in the U.S. District Court at Gainesville, Florida, and by that time Bailey had sabotaged his client. DuBoc's goose was cooked!

Prosecutor Violated Legal Duty to Turn over Exculpatory Evidence

Under law, it is the prosecutor's responsibility to turn over to the defense any exculpatory evidence that they have which would support the defendant's innocence. The requirement to turn exculpatory evidence over to the defendant is often referred to as the Brady rule.[35] This duty was violated in DuBoc's case. This responsibility is openly and repeatedly violated by prosecutors, causing many men and women to be sentenced to prison, sometimes for life. Rarely, if ever, are prosecutors punished for corrupting the legal process in this matter. The system protects them.

American Bar Association Defense Requirements

Under the ABA's Defense Requirement criteria (4-4.1), a defense attorney is required to perform an examination of the government's charging documents, conduct an examination of the evidence, interview the accused, interview potential witnesses, and interview the prosecutors, among other defense responsibilities. The guidelines required by the National Legal Aid and Defender Association for Criminal Defense Representation (12-1994) state that legal counsel cannot effectively advise their client as to the optimal course of action without knowing all the facts. None of DuBoc's first group of attorneys performed these basic requirements.

Dining With Co-Conspirators

On April 19, 1994, Bailey and Shapiro had dinner with Assistant U.S. Attorneys Greg Miller, Tom Kirwin, Roy Atchison, and DEA Agent Carl Lilley. During the dinner meeting, the previous attorney fee agreement was again confirmed, that Bailey would sabotage his client by having DuBoc plead guilty to all charges and transfer all assets to the U.S. government. The conversation focused almost entirely on the $3 million that Bailey would receive.

Judge Secretly Approved the Scheme

The secret contractual agreement between the Justice Department and DuBoc's attorney needed the approval of U.S. District Judge Maurice Paul. Prior to the judge granting his approval, DEA agents had warned Judge Paul of the corrupt nature of the secret agreement and its violation of federal due process protections. Judge Paul, a former Justice Department prosecutor, conducted a hearing in his chambers (May 17, 1994), during which the details were again given to him. Despite the corrupt nature of the arrangement between DuBoc's attorneys and DOJ prosecutors and the criminal nature of the conspiracy, Judge Paul approved the plot against DuBoc. There was no court reporter present and no records were kept, which eliminated any record of the corrupt arrangement.

That agreement, with judicial approval, required that Bailey totally abandon all of DuBoc's safeguards provided by statutes, decisional law, and the Constitution. With Judge Paul's approval, the secret agreement:

- Violated federal law requiring judges to insure that defendant's legal counsel did not have any interest that conflicted with their client.

---

[35] *Brady v. Maryland*, 373 U.S. 83, 82 S. Ct. 1194, 10 L. Ed.2d 215 (1963) A prosecutor may not refuse a request by the defendant for evidence which is favorable to him and is material either to guilt or to punishment. Suppression of such exculpatory evidence which helps the defendant, even as a mistake, is basis for reversal.

- Violated criminal law against conspiracies,[36] and the agreement between the prosecutor and DuBoc's attorneys constituted a conspiracy.
- Violated criminal law relating to fraud.
- Violated DuBoc's legal and constitutional rights to have competent and honest legal counsel, as defined in part by the Sixth Amendment to the U.S. Constitution; Federal rule of civil procedure 44;[37] title 18 USC Section 3006(A)(b).
- Violated Florida Bar Rules of Professional Conduct prohibiting attorneys from entering any business transaction adverse to their client.

"It is troubling..."

Loyola School of Law professor and former federal prosecutor Laurie Levenson later said that forfeiture agreements are in writing, almost never verbal, especially when such a large amount is involved. Putting it extremely mildly, Levenson said that the unwritten deal in the judge's chamber makes federal prosecutors and Bailey look bad.

It strikes me as unusual for the U.S. Attorney's office to appoint Bailey as stock advisor for DuBoc's assets. It is troubling to say the least. It raises questions about whether Bailey is representing DuBoc or representing the government. And the problem with lack of procedures is that there is lack of accountability. Then people become suspicious of each other.

Another indication that the secret hearing took place, in Judge Paul's chambers, was a January 4, 1996, letter Bailey sent to Judge Paul. That letter reminded the judge of the May 17, 1994, hearing at which it was agreed between Assistant U.S. Attorney (AUSA) David McGee and the judge that Bailey would receive $3 million for inducing DuBoc to plead guilty to all charges and forfeit his worldwide assets.

Relying Upon Good Faith of Justice Department Prosecutors!

During a discussion between Bailey, Shohat, and Shapiro, Bailey stated he was going to recommend that DuBoc plead guilty. Bailey told DuBoc that his case was untriable, and that "We would rely on the good faith of the government to do that in a fair manner and that the onus to perform was on DuBoc." Nobody in their right mind, who is privy to the culture in the Justice Department, would associate "good faith" with Justice Department conduct. Shapiro, refusing to sabotage DuBoc, spoke out and said, "If we don't have an agreement, we're going to trial!" Apparently Shapiro didn't know about the secret agreement between Bailey and the prosecutors. Also, he didn't persist with sufficient aggressiveness to protect the client who initially put his trust in Shapiro's hands.

Legal Requirements Before the Judge Can Accept A Guilty Plea

On May 17, 1994, DuBoc changed his plea from not guilty to guilty. That was probably the worst mistake DuBoc had ever made in his life. Court records show that the plea agreement provided that DuBoc's drug-related assets

---

[36] Conspiracy: An agreement between two or more persons to accomplish together a criminal or unlawful act or to achieve by criminal or unlawful means an act not in itself criminal or unlawful. 16 Am J2d Consp Sections 2, 3. Conspiracy is also a wrong which will constitute a cause for a civil action.

[37] Under Rule 44(c), the court is to take appropriate measures to protect each defendant's right to counsel unless it appears "there is good cause to believe no conflict of interest is likely to arise" as a consequence of the continuation of such joint representation.

would be forfeited *at the time of his sentencing*, pursuant to Title 21 USC Section 853. To insure defendants are not deprived of their legal protections, federal law requires that the decision to plead guilty must be made knowingly and voluntarily, which means the defendant must know all the facts relating to his case, including what the charges are based upon, and what defense evidence exists. Obviously, a conspiracy between the defendant's attorney, the prosecutor—and even the judge—did not meet these protections.

A federal publication, referring to Federal Rule of Criminal Procedure rule 44(c), described its intent:

It is contemplated that under rule 44(c) the court will make appropriate inquiry of the defendants and of counsel regarding the possibility of a conflict of interest developing. Whenever it is necessary to make a more particularized inquiry into the nature of the contemplated defense, the court should "pursue the inquiry with defendants and their counsel on the record but in chambers so as to avoid the possibility of prejudicial disclosures to the prosecution." In United States v. Foster, it was emphasized that each defendant be "fully advised of the facts underlying the potential conflict and is given an opportunity to express his or her views." United States v Alberti, 470 F.2d 878 (2d Cir. 1973). The rule particularly requires that the court personally advise each defendant of his right to effective assistance of counsel, including separate representation.

Rule 11 Protection

Another protection provided by Federal Rules of Criminal Procedure rule 11 requires that if a defendant pleads guilty, the judge must address the defendant in open court and inform him of certain legal protections. The judge must ask if the offense to which the defendant pleads guilty was not the result of force, threats or of promises apart from the plea agreement. When a prosecutor assures a defendant that if he or she pleads guilty, he or she would only get a light or suspended sentence, the defendant can't admit this to the judge. The defendant has to say "no," when in fact the truth is "yes," he *was* promised something in return for having pled guilty. The judge knows this; in most cases, he was a prosecutor or attorney.

In DuBoc's case, Judge Paul *knew* DuBoc did not know about the secret agreement between DuBoc's attorney and the prosecutor—which Judge Paul approved, and that he himself was sabotaging the defendant appearing before him.

One of many Supreme Court decisions addressing conflict of interest was *Faretta v. California*, 422 U.S. 806 (1975):

When a trial court finds an actual conflict of interest which impairs the ability of a criminal defendant's chosen counsel to conform with the ABA Code of Professional Responsibility, the court should not be required to tolerate an inadequate representation of a defendant. Such representation not only constitutes a breach of professional ethics and invites disrespect for the integrity of the court, but it is also detrimental to the independent interest of the trial judge to be free from future attacks over the adequacy of the waiver or the fairness of the proceedings in his own court and the subtle problems implicating the defendant's comprehension of the waiver.

Under such circumstances, the court can elect to exercise its supervisory authority over members of the bar to enforce the ethical standard requiring an attorney to decline multiple representation.

DuBoc Starts to Recognize Attorney Misconduct

When DuBoc placed his BioChem Pharma stock with Bailey for safe keeping, DuBoc told Bailey that none of the stock was to be sold. In December 1995, DuBoc discovered Bailey *had sold* some of the stock. Feeling betrayed, DuBoc filed a motion with the court (December 22, 1995) for substitution of legal counsel, replacing Bailey with Henry Uscenski and Mark Lebow of the Coudert Brothers law firm. This substitution was approved on January 11, 1996.

Change of Attorneys Continued the Sabotage

If DuBoc thought changing legal counsel would improve the quality and integrity of legal representation, he would soon find out otherwise. It was the Coudert Brothers that encouraged DuBoc to waive extradition when there was sufficient evidence to oppose being extradited. Upon replacing Bailey, the Coudert Brothers simply continued the secret agreement Bailey had with the prosecutor, and made no meaningful investigation of DuBoc's defenses. The Coudert Brothers *had* to continue the secret agreement, or their legal fees would not be assured; they would have to work for them. Court filings showed that by their own admission, the Coudert attorneys failed to review any of the records of evidence in the case, that they continued the course set by Bailey, and entered into the identical fee agreement as existed between Bailey and the prosecutor.

Thank You Letter for Sabotaging Client's Legal Rights

A "thank-you" letter for sabotaging their client was sent (February 14, 1997) by Justice Department attorney Linda M. Samuel to attorney Henry Uscinski of Coudert Brothers. Samuel wrote that she appreciated the "assistance that your firm has rendered to date." None in this legal fraternity showed any concern for the sordid treatment of a client!

The assistance she was referring to was the law firm sabotaging DuBoc's legal defenses. Samuel was special counsel to the Department of Justice asset forfeiture and money laundering section. DuBoc could not be expected to feel the same appreciation!

On August 11, 1997, the Coudert Brothers filed a motion for interim payment of fees and expenses, despite the fact that instead of providing DuBoc a defense, they sabotaged him. The fees were approved by the "system:" the DOJ prosecutor and Judge Paul.

Substitution of Attorneys Meant Big Problems for Bailey

The substitution of attorneys meant big problems for Bailey. The substitution prompted Justice Department prosecutors to set an emergency hearing for April 24, 1996, seeking a court order requiring Bailey to turn over to the government DuBoc's stock which had been left with Bailey for safekeeping. The seizure was sought under Title 21 U.S.C. Section 853.[38] Under the guilty plea that DuBoc foolishly signed, there would be no forfeiture until the court sen-

---

[38] Title 21 Section 853. Criminal forfeiture. (a) Property subject to criminal forfeiture.

tenced him, and he had not yet been sentenced. There should not have been any forfeiture motion or hearing. No problem; just ignore the rules!

Without DuBoc's permission and contrary to DuBoc's instructions, Bailey sold 200,000 shares of the original 602,000 shares of BioChem Pharma stock for $3 million. Bailey then borrowed another $2 million from the Swiss bank, Credit Suisse, using the remaining 402,000 shares as collateral for the loan. He now had $5 million of DuBoc's money and for it the only thing he had done was sabotage his client.

DuBoc didn't want the stock sold, as the president of BioChem was a good friend and the sudden sale of a large block of stock would adversely affect the value of the remaining stock and the company. Since DuBoc placed his stock in Bailey's control, it had risen in value to almost $30 million.

With this cash windfall, Bailey purchased two airplanes, a 76-foot yacht, put a $200,000 down payment on a house in Florida, paid for extravagant personal expenses, and funded his many trips to Los Angeles as part of the O.J. Simpson trial. Like a little boy who didn't want to give up his toys, Bailey said after court: "They gave me the stock! They said you can do whatever you want with it! Nobody ever made a claim on it! There are no documents!"

Judge Paul ordered Bailey to turn over to the government the remaining 402,000 shares of the BioChem stock and return the money Bailey had received from the sale of the other 200,000 shares. The Justice Department argued that Bailey was authorized by the government to use the proceeds from the sale of the stock only to cover his expenses in selling DuBoc's European real estate. Justice Department prosecutors claimed Bailey used the proceeds from the sale of the stock for personal expenses rather than for the expenses associated with the sale of DuBoc's properties, spending an additional $3 million for personal and professional expenses unrelated to this function. Justice Department attorneys accused Bailey of milking DuBoc. But what the prosecutors meant was that it was *they* who wanted to "milk" DuBoc's assets. Judge Paul said:

From the evidence presented to this court, it would not be an overstatement to say that Mr. Bailey, from May 1994 until the present time, has lived and financed his businesses almost exclusively from the funds generated by sale or loans secured by the BioChem Pharma stocks.

Further Legal Sabotage

During the forfeiture hearing, two attorneys from Coudert Brothers were listed as attorneys of record. But neither attorney made an appearance on DuBoc's behalf. If they had made an appearance, and had objected to the seizure of DuBoc's stock, they would have put themselves in violation of the secret agreement that they had with the prosecutors. And this meant they would not get any fees from the assets the government was seizing from DuBoc. DuBoc was forced to appear without an attorney and without advice of legal counsel as he waived his rights to the stock.

Pay or Go to Jail

During the January 25th hearing, Judge Paul gave Bailey until February 29th to surrender the BioChem Pharma stock and provide financial records pertaining to the 602,000 shares he had initially received. He must also pay to the court the $3 million he had withdrawn from a Swiss account and which he used for personal expenses. The next hearing was set for February 3, 1996.

More Legal Chicanery

An article in the *Florida Star-Banner* (February 3, 1996) said:

AUSA David McGee further struck at Bailey, asking if he knew that his attorney [Zuckerman] had just the day before told the Swiss authorities in a letter that the stock was from drug money. The Swiss government then froze the stock, after the U.S. court had already ordered that Bailey produce the stock.

Trying to avoid appearing at the February 3, 1996, hearing, Bailey asked a New York judge to set a hearing on another case for the same Friday. Bailey then sought to use that conflict in court appearances as an excuse for not appearing in the Ocala, Florida court. The plan didn't work.

During the February 3rd court appearance, Bailey told the court he did not remember how he spent the proceeds from selling $3 million in stock. (Friend of Bill Clinton?) He testified that he did not report it as income because he was advised by his attorney and accountants that he didn't have to. A $3 million windfall and he didn't have to report it as income!

A Liar, A Cheat, and Unethical

Prosecutor McGee accused Bailey in court of being a liar, a cheat and unethical. "He has defied the order of this court. I suggest, your honor, that you put Mr. F. Lee Bailey in jail in this district until he produces to this court the money he has stolen from the people of the United States." (People of the United States? These European assets were stolen from DuBoc under corrupt conditions by government employees; the people of the United States had no right to them!)

McGee continued, "You sold Mr. DuBoc down the river for a little money—I should say, a lot of money—didn't you, Mr. Bailey?" This was something like the "pot calling the kettle black." Later, McGee accused Bailey of cheating on his income tax return and failing to show the money that was generated from the sale of the stock. No charges for income tax evasion were filed against Bailey. The threat by the Justice Department to charge Bailey with faillure to report the income could easily cause the prosecutor to pressure Bailey to sabotage another client—or be charged with a felony.

The Media's Dream-Team in Action: Not Seen on TV

During this hearing, two of the nation's most publicized attorneys faced each other in U.S. District Court at Ocala, Florida. Members of the media-drubbed "dream team," F. Lee Bailey and Robert Shapiro, were in court as the government sought to wrest control of DuBoc's stock from Bailey. Shapiro testified about the ownership of the stock, stating that everyone familiar with the deal knew Bailey was not supposed to keep the stock or any money he received from the sale of it. Bailey called Shapiro's testimony "an absolute fabrication."

Bailey-Shohat Partnership Exploded

Another attorney at odds with Bailey was Ed Shohat of the Miami law firm of Bierman, Shohat, Loewy, Perry & Klein, who Bailey had hired to help with the DuBoc case. But this partnership soured real fast. Shohat sued Bailey in 1996. According to court records, Bailey said Shohat "was a liar, could not conduct himself with honesty and fidelity, was guilty of misconduct, was guilty of a felony, would conspire to kidnap a criminal defendant's child, and could not be trusted to conduct himself honorably in or out of court." Bailey accusing someone else of character flaws?

Revealing Legal Fraternity Culture in Pattern of Deception

Possibly the reason for Bailey's remarks about Shohat was that Shohat was a witness whose testimony was unfavorable to Bailey as the government sought to have Bailey turn DuBoc's assets over to the court. Bailey had accused Shohat of plotting deals to help DuBoc win favor with federal officials. "It's really sad that it has come to this," said Mark Lebow of the Coudert law firm, which at that time was representing DuBoc. For DuBoc, this could have been viewed as an incredible comedy of legal fraternity deception if it didn't have such terrible consequences for him.

Further Confirmation of Secret Agreement to Sabotage Client

During Bailey's contempt of court hearing on (February 2 and 3, 1996), attorney Lebow—allegedly defending DuBoc—testified, "Your honor, we have a duty to cooperate with the government [Justice Department]." In the contempt proceedings against Bailey, prosecutor David McGee stated:

Mr. Bailey took the money, put it in his own pocket and made up an absurd and unbelievable lie to bring this court when caught red-handed doing it. He has acted in complete and total derogation of his obligations to the people of the United States, in complete and total derogation of his obligations to his profession, and in complete and total derogation of his obligations to his client. He did it for the oldest, the more tiresome and the least excusable reason—to put money in his own pocket. For that, he gives up ethics, he lies, and he cheats.

Judge Paul rendered an order: "If Mr. Bailey fails to purge himself of this contempt by the times outlined in this order, he shall surrender himself to the United States Marshal in Gainesville, Florida, on March 1, 1996, to commence serving his sentence of contempt."

"Clutching, Clawing and Scraping"

Bailey filed a notice of appeal to vacate Judge Paul's order. In his appeal, Bailey argued that he had made a good-faith effort to comply with the judge's order to turn over the stock but that he had not yet succeeded. Bailey argued that Justice Department prosecutors, with the verbal approval of Judge Paul, agreed that Bailey could keep the stock on condition that DuBoc pled guilty to all charges and conveyed his worldwide assets to the government. Bailey said that this agreement allowed him to profit on the increased value of the stock. On March 1, 1997, Court of Appeals Judge Ed Carnes turned down Bailey's appeal and said Bailey had been "clutching, clawing and scraping" to keep the assets.

Jail For Bailey

Bailey surrendered to the U.S. Marshall in Gainesville, Florida, on March 1, 1996. From jail, Bailey was able to borrow money to cause release of the stock. In April, Bailey entered into an agreement, turning over to the court the remaining BioChem Pharma stock, a 74-foot yacht purchased with the proceeds of an earlier stock sale, and other assets. Bailey's time in jail gave him a small taste of what his client, Claude DuBoc, would be facing for the remainder of DuBoc's life—thanks in major part to Bailey's sabotage of his client.

Bailey was released from jail, but Bailey's attorney, Roger Zuckerman, said Bailey would try to reclaim the shares through "a more appropriate form" like the Court of Claims. This was stated despite the fact that Bailey signed an agreement with the court that prohibited him from pursuing any claim "now or in the future, not only in this forum but in any other."

In October 1996, Bailey sued the federal government in the Court of Claims for $10 million, arguing that DuBoc's stock, taken from him by Judge Paul, rightfully belonged to him. Or at least, that the increase in the stock's value should belong to him.

During a hearing in the Court of Claims on the Justice Department's motion to dismiss the complaint, Bailey's attorney, Roger Zuckerman, argued that prosecutors failed to document the agreement reached in Judge Paul's chambers in May 1994 that Bailey was to keep the stock. (No one asked DuBoc under what conditions he placed the stock in Bailey's hands.)

DOJ Admitting to the Secret Agreement Against DuBoc

In the Court of Claims, AUSA Patterson acknowledged *prosecutors did have an agreement with Bailey*, but that it was an oral agreement. After admitting to such an agreement, Patterson then argued his prosecutors did not have the authority to enter into such agreement between DuBoc's attorneys and the Justice Department. The Court of Claims denied the Justice Department's motion to dismiss Bailey's complaint:

Although (the defendant [US] vociferously asserts that none of the agents of the U.S. who were involved in this case had authority to bind the government to the contract alleged by the plaintiff, it has proffered little evidence to refute the repeated allegations in the plaintiffs complaint that a contract was formed between himself and the government agents who had authority to bind the US. The defendant's own statement suggests that under the appropriate circumstances, a contract could have been formed

At a later court hearing, attorney Edward Shohat said, "Mr. Bailey told me he had a *secret deal* with the government that he couldn't tell me or Mr. DuBoc about." Shohat told the court he was uncomfortable with not having an accounting of the funds. Attorney Shapiro, who had selected Bailey as co-counsel, stated to the court that Bailey had not given him an accounting of DuBoc's funds.

Dangerous to Have Bailey as Legal Counsel?

Watching this spectacle surely was ironic for DuBoc. He trusted attorneys who promptly sabotaged him and may be the cause of him being in prison for the remainder of his life. Unfortunately, he wasn't the only client who suffered by having Bailey as legal counsel. The air traffic controllers had Bailey as their legal counsel in 1981 when they conducted an illegal strike, causing most of them to be fired. Patty Hearst, who hired Bailey for her defense, later said that Bailey spent very little time defending her because he was busy writing a book.

Public name-recognition, and the media's dream-team label given to Bailey and other members of the O.J. Simpson defense team possibly made DuBoc consider Bailey to be competent and responsible. Hoot Gibson, a former TWA airline pilot and friend, stated to me that he frequently appeared as a witness for Bailey, and Bailey was often inebriated and obnoxious. Another pilot friend who appeared several times for Bailey, Gerald Loeb, said that Bailey often displayed the "shakes" experienced by heavy drinkers.

Like A Pack Of Wolves Fighting For The Carcass

The atrocious legal advice and client-sabotage created chaos for DuBoc, and major rifts among government agencies as agents fought over the spoils. A rift arose between federal prosecutors and investigators over who should get the money from DuBoc's assets. U.S. Customs Service officials requested Judge Paul to appoint a special prosecutor to investigate the unwritten deal between the U.S. Attorney and Bailey—unaware that the last thing Judge Paul wanted was his role in the sordid conspiracy to be publicized any more than it already had been. This was the sixth complaint from Customs officials who accused Patterson and his staff of leading an 18-month-long campaign to discredit Customs agents, and thereby cut them off from DuBoc's forfeitable assets.

Customs agents and informants sought at least five times to have the Justice Department's Office of Professional Responsibility (OPR) investigate the U.S. attorney, and each time the request was either denied, or never received a response. Anyone familiar with that division of the Justice Department should have known that instead of ferreting out corruption, the OPR is most famous for covering it up. A summary of Customs' complaints:

- On March 21, 1995, U.S. Customs attaché Paul Beaulieu asked the Office of Professional Responsibility to investigate Patterson's office, that Patterson was conducting a witch-hunt with the grand jury to discredit Customs agents and their informants. True to form, the Justice Department's OPR found nothing wrong as it continued its years of coverups.
- Dennis Cameron, another attorney representing an informant, wrote a March 26, 1995, letter asking the Justice Department's Office of Professional Responsibility to investigate the "unprofessional conduct" of the prosecutor.
- On August 3, 1995, Beaulieu requested Attorney General Janet Reno to "address this intolerable conduct by the U.S. attorney in Tallahassee," stating that Patterson's office was seeking revenge because he tried to protect the identity of confidential informants.
- On October 26, 1995, Washington attorney Herbert Miller, representing informant Stephen Swanson, requested the Justice Department to review the matter.

The request by Customs to Judge Paul for a special prosecutor accused U.S. Attorney Patterson of violating policy by entering into the verbal deal with Bailey.

DOJ Using Grand Juries and IRS to Discredit Customs Agents

Customs said that Patterson's office was using federal grand juries and IRS investigations to discredit Customs agents and informants who built the case against DuBoc. Customs also said federal prosecutors knew Bailey was transferring money from DuBoc's Swiss bank account into his own personal account but did nothing about it until DuBoc reported it to Judge Paul.

Under federal law, government agencies and their informants are entitled to a share of assets that are seized in which they provide *original* information leading to arrests and seizures. It was therefore important to determine who *first* provided the information that brought about the arrest. If DuBoc was actually guilty and the court actually had jurisdiction over him, the assets exceeding $100 million would be a windfall for whoever first provided the information that brought about his arrest.

DOJ Exposing Government Agents to Danger

Customs accused Justice Department prosecutors of divulging the identity of two of their confidential informants, putting them in danger of their lives. Customs attaché in Paris, Paul Beaulieu, accused the U.S. Attorney's office in a March 1995 letter of leading an investigation to "systematically destroy the reputation of several Customs agents and their confidential resources." In this letter, Beaulieu stated that U.S. Attorney Patterson impaneled a federal grand jury in Tallahassee to take testimony to investigate whether Beaulieu and other agents and informants in the DuBoc case were conspiring to defraud the government of DuBoc's assets.

In opposing the complaints, Justice Department prosecutors claimed the original information relating to DuBoc came from the Drug Enforcement Administration, and only then did the information go to Customs officials in France—or so says DOJ personnel. And surely they would not lie! Patterson's office challenged the "originality" of the information received from the Paris Customs office and their informant. Patterson claimed that the information was already known by his office. Beaulieu claimed that DuBoc would never have been arrested, and his assets never forfeited to the government, but for the work of Stephen Swanson and his operative.

The information Swanson provided enabled Customs working closely with DEA in Gainesville and the U.S. Attorney's office in Tallahassee to locate and arrest DuBoc in Hong Kong in March 1994. In my opinion, this investigation is based on the U.S. Attorney's office and DEA's almost obsessive desire to take all the credit for the case and be able to claim all the seized assets.

Customs agents and informants claim they built the case against DuBoc and repeatedly complained that U.S. Attorney Michael Patterson and his Tallahassee staff abused the power of the grand jury to keep the drug assets for themselves.

Another slant to the bizarre case. Attorney Dennis Cameron, representing another informant in the case looking to share in the assets, wrote to a Justice Department official (February 21, 1996) about an ongoing RICO investigation (Racketeering Influenced and Corrupt Organizations Act) of his client. He claimed U.S. Attorney Patterson was seeking to discredit his client so as to eliminate any need to share forfeited assets with him.

Judge Condemns Rewards to Customs Agents

An Associated Press article (June 18, 1998) showed objection to the practice of rewarding Customs agents for seizures when such work was part of their duties for which they were paid. The practice likened government agents to bounty hunters. The article said in part:

A federal judge says the Customs Service's policy of rewarding some inspectors who make drug seizures is wrong and potentially dangerous....
"Such a program creates perverse law enforcement incentives that have an unduly dangerous propensity to encourage unreasonable searches and detentions."

Five Years in Prison Without A Decision

In 1999, DuBoc had been in prison five years without being sentenced. He had provided valuable assistance in several major drug cases and had voluntarily forfeited to the United States over $100 million in assets. He had expected to be released. Instead, he faces life in prison.

New Legal Counsel Discovered Lack of Evidence

After being imprisoned for five years, having been subjected to incredible and scandalous sabotage of his legal rights by government agents conspiring with his own attorneys, DuBoc again changed legal counsel, hiring Tallahassee attorney William E. Bubsey. Bubsey did what the first group of attorneys never did; he investigated the evidence upon which the Justice Department predicated their charges. He quickly discovered evidence contradicting the prosecutor's charges, revealing DuBoc's innocence. Bubsey obtained an affidavit from Matthew Martenyi stating that the group met twice with DuBoc in Long Beach and once in San Francisco and that DuBoc refused to ship the marijuana that DOJ prosecutors claimed he agreed to do.

DuBoc's Many Legal Defenses

Considerable evidence and government misconduct strongly calls for DuBoc's release:

- Absence of evidence showing DuBoc shipped marijuana into the State of Florida.
- Conspiracy between DuBoc's attorneys, the Department of Justice prosecutors, and the judge, constituting criminal acts and sabotage of rights and protections under the laws and Constitution of the United States.
- Judge's misconduct, secretly assisting in the sabotage of DuBoc's defenses by approving the secret agreement between DuBoc's legal counsel and the Justice Department prosecutor.
- Withholding exculpatory evidence, a violation of the Brady rule.
- Statutory defense against paying witnesses for testimony. Title 18 USC Section 201(c)(2)[39] clearly prohibits the payment of any money or other compensation to obtain a person's testimony. The wording is very clear. DOJ prosecutors constantly violate it, and in that way send innocent people to prison—sometimes for life.

---

[39] **Title 18 USC Section 201. Bribery of public officials and witnesses.**
(c) Whoever–(2) Directly or indirectly, gives, offers or promises anything of value to any person, for or because of the testimony under oath or affirmation given or to be given by such person as a witness upon a trial, hearing, or other proceeding, before any court, any committee of either House or both Houses of Congress, or any agency, commission, or officer authorized by the laws of the United States to hear evidence or take testimony, or for or because of such person's absence therefrom; shall be fined under this title or imprisoned for not more than two years, or both.

- Violated federal case law protecting a defendant's right to a conflict-free legal counsel. In *Lopez v. Sculley*, 58 F.3d 38 (2nd Cir. 1995), the court held that a defendant was entitled to a conflict-free counsel prior to and including sentencing. Justice Department attorneys entered into a secret contractual agreement with DuBoc's legal counsels and threatened them with loss of all fees if they did not cause their client to plead guilty—regardless of guilt or innocence. This is undoubtedly one of the most gregarious examples of attorney fraud, attorney misconduct, attorney malpractice, and obviously, not conflict-free.
- Ineffective legal representation.
- Fraudulent legal representation.
- Corrupt violation of DuBoc's legal and constitutional rights.
- Absence of venue.

Motion to Withdraw Guilty Plea

Bubsey filed a motion (April 8, 1998) to withdraw DuBoc's guilty plea, as provided in federal law.[40] His brief was well done but omitted any reference to one of DuBoc's key defenses: the conspiracy agreement between the Department of Justice, DuBoc's initial attorneys, and the judge's involvement in it. If Bubsey had raised that point, federal judges would thereafter retaliate against him, rendering unfavorable decisions against his clients and adversely affect Bubsey's livelihood. Bubsey stated in his motion:

To the extent that there was a money laundering charge, there is absolutely no nexus or evidence to support jurisdiction and venue in the Northern District of Florida. (Thereby requiring dismissal of the charges See, United States v. Kramer, 73 F.3d 1067, 1072 (11th Cir. 1996)). DuBoc's change of plea [to guilty] was not knowing and voluntary, as he relied upon the fraudulent representation of his attorney, F. Lee Bailey, who had a secret contract with the prosecutor to violate DuBoc's civil and constitutional rights. Federal Rules of Criminal Procedure Rule 32(e) Plea Withdrawal states:

If a motion to withdraw a plea of guilty or nolo contendere is made before sentence is imposed, the court may permit the plea to be withdrawn if the defendant shows any fair and just reason. At any later time, a plea may be set aside only on direct appeal or by motion under 28 USC Section 2255.

The record of evidence in this case amply supports the proposition Bailey was grossly ineffective in his representation of DuBoc and clearly labored under the most severe conflict of interest. The Court will recall that the United States vehemently argued that Bailey sold his client out for his own interests.

Absence of Venue

Federal Rules of Criminal Procedure rule 58(c)(2) requires that the venue be proper, that a criminal complaint be filed where some part of the alleged offense occurred. This did not exist in DuBoc's case because there was no

---

[40] Federal Rules of Criminal Procedure rule 32(e) Plea Withdrawal. If a motion to withdraw a plea of guilty or nolo contendere is made before sentence is imposed, the court may permit the plea to be withdrawn if the defendant shows any fair and just reason.

evidence of any federal offenses occurring in Florida. That rule states in part: "A defendant who is arrested, held, or present in a district other than that in which the indictment [or] information is pending against that defendant may state in writing a wish to waive venue and trial in the district in which the proceeding is pending." DuBoc never waived venue in writing.

Motion To Vacate Forfeitures

Bubsey simultaneously filed a motion to vacate the forfeitures, stating in part:

> *Mr. DuBoc's attorneys, in essence conspiring with the federal government, have manipulated the government and more importantly, the defendant, into unwittingly turning over the majority of his assets without regard to whether the assets were tainted, untainted, or drug-related, directly or indirectly. Once the transfer was completed, the defendant was again double crossed by the government, in the form of the government's initiation of forfeiture actions, completely inconsistent with the terms and spirit of the Plea Agreement, and inconsistent with the understanding of the parties.*
>
> *The United States Department of Justice has essentially agreed with Bailey's position that the U.S. Attorney for the Northern District of Florida did, in fact, enter into an agreement to employ Bailey, but that the local office did not have the requisite authority to enter into or bind the United States to the agreement.*

Judicial Complicity Insured Rejection

Bubsey's motions to vacate the forfeitures and withdraw the guilty plea were bound to fail, regardless of their merit. The motions had to be acted upon by Judge Maurice Paul—who was a key party to the highly explosive conspiracy and secret agreement. To now allow DuBoc to withdraw his guilty plea, and to reverse the forfeitures, would expose the judge's misconduct, that of the Justice Department, reveal corruption in the judicial system, and play havoc with the $100 million in worldwide assets that were taken from DuBoc. The motions were denied.

Compounding Judicial Arrogance

In a further act of judicial arrogance, Judge Paul granted the Justice Department's motion holding that DuBoc did not cooperate and thereby he was not to be shown any favorable consideration in sentencing. That meant life in prison!

DuBoc had pleaded guilty to charges that the facts showed he was not guilty of. He acted as witness in many drug cases that brought about the arrest of many high-level drug traffickers. He conveyed over $100 million of worldwide assets to the United States to which they were not entitled.

Seeking Perjured Testimony from Prisoners

DuBoc's brother-in-law, Joe Shelesky, told me in January 1999, that prisoners incarcerated with DuBoc at the Federal Correctional Center in Tallahassee were being prompted by the prosecutors to provide perjured testimony against DuBoc. Shelesky stated they were offered release from prison and other benefits if they testified that DuBoc and his Tallahassee attorney, Penelope E. Shelfer, planned to offer Judge Paul a $1 million bribe if he ordered DuBoc released.

One thing was surely obvious to DuBoc; Judge Paul was so deeply implicated in the conspiracy with Justice Department prosecutors that the last thing the judge would do is take a bribe. The judicial and Justice Department misconduct in DuBoc's case added to the massive amount of evidence showing this misconduct to be the culture in these government offices. It was necessary for the Justice Department and the judge to divert attention from their actions by fabricating charges against DuBoc.

For Those Having no Sympathy for A Marijuana Supplier

For those who have no sympathy for DuBoc because of having transported marijuana in other parts of the world, consider the following:

- If it wasn't for the insatiable demands of U.S. drug users, there would be no need for people to transport drugs, and there would be no money to pay for such practices.
- More guilty of any federal offenses would be those people in government, especially the CIA, who have—while holding positions of trust—played a direct or indirect role in smuggling drugs into the United States.
- Close behind, we have those who aid and abet the drug trafficking, including Justice Department personnel and other government agencies who knew about the government-related drug trafficking and covered up for it. Those involved in the complicity of coverup would also include members of Congress, federal judges, and much of the broadcast and print media.
- Just because it may be illegal in the United States to engage in transportation of drugs, that doesn't make it illegal, either by law or practice in some other country. Many people in the United States have sought to legalize drug use and transportation. If the United States has the right to legalize drug use, why doesn't another country have the same right, either as shown by their laws, or their tacit approval of such activities.
- Like any other person, DuBoc was entitled to the substantive and procedural protection of the laws and Constitution of the United States. If someone such as O.J. Simpson can go scot-free for the brutal murder of two defenseless people, DuBoc certainly doesn't deserve life in prison.

CHAPTER FOURTEEN

GREATEST THREAT
TO INDIVIDUAL AMERICANS

The greatest threat to the people of the United States is the culture and the group in control of the United States Department of Justice (DOJ). Thirty years of investigations, evidence gathering, and exposure to the various divisions of the U.S. Department of Justice leaves no doubt that the mindset in that government entity—composed mostly of attorneys and their culture—makes it dangerous beyond almost anyone's comprehension. The people in control of the DOJ are a greater threat to men, women, and their families than any other government group.

Organized Crime in the U.S. Justice Department

"Organized Crime in the U.S. Justice Dept" was the heading in the Forum section of the *Sacramento Bee (October 27, 1991)* accurately reflecting the decades of criminality in the most misnamed agency of the federal government: "*Indications...point to a widespread conspiracy implicating government officials in the theft of Inslaw's technology.*" *I*nslaw, bad as it was, constituted only the tip of the iceberg. Inslaw is described in detail in *Defrauding America*, and consisted of Justice Department attorneys forcing a company into bankruptcy so they could steal its computer software called PROMIS. The attorneys had an interest in a company which would be bidding on a lucrative government contract worth a half-billion dollars to install a computer program in Department of Justice offices.

DOJ Blocked Every Effort to Halt
Crash-Related Corruption in the Aviation Field

For 30 years, Justice Department attorneys blocked every attempt I and other government agents made to report high-level government corruption that we discovered as part of our official duties. If my reports, or those by other government agents, of criminal activities had received the reaction required by law, there would not have been the extent of government corruption that now exists (and which is largely unknown to the majority of the public).

Responsibilities of Justice Department Employees

Under federal law, the responsibility for ensuring that the laws of the

United States are properly enforced belongs to the United States Department of Justice, which is under the control of the U.S. Attorney General, and in turn, the President of the United States. In practice, the politically-appointed Attorney General routinely has used the Justice Department to cover up corrupt and criminal acts involving high-level government personnel or corrupt covert activities of the CIA and other covert agencies—including CIA drug trafficking. These problems occurred during the Reagan and Bush administrations and were especially prominent during the Clinton presidency, as Attorney General Janet Reno protected him and the Democratic Party. Occasionally the checks and balances work as intended, and the person in that position of trust goes to prison. Attorney General John Mitchell, for instance, went to prison, as did Webster Hubbell and other attorney generals. Subsequent attorney generals have committed federal offenses involving far more serious crimes, and were never prosecuted or called to task by the poorly-functioning checks and balances in government and the media.

Responsible for Protecting the Civil Rights of American Citizens

Within the U.S. Department of Justice are numerous divisions, each of which has similar cultures and standards as the politically-appointed Attorney General. These include the Federal Bureau of Investigation (FBI), responsible for investigating crimes; the Criminal Division, responsible for prosecuting federal crimes; the U.S. Trustee, responsible for preventing fraud in the bankruptcy courts, and the Drug Enforcement Administration (DEA), responsible for drug-related matters.

Purpose of This Chapter and How it can Protect You

The purpose of this chapter is to give examples of how the Department of Justice culture has escalated the incarceration of thousands of men and women—like yourself—many of whom were guilty of nothing, or guilty of far lesser offenses than charged. This chapter will show how the same can happen to you and anyone you know. There are thousands of government agents and government informants who must justify their jobs and their compensation by finding technical violations, or fabricating violations, that can bring about the long-time imprisonment of you, your wife or husband, your son or daughter, or your parents. If you think this is an exaggeration, read on, and you will find how easily it is being done to thousands every year.

Forget everything you were taught or felt about integrity, honesty, guilt or innocence. You will discover the sordid depths of raw government power routinely used against good people. Forget everything you may have heard about people sentenced to prison deserving what they got. Their integrity may be equal to or better than yours. Some were simply targeted or in the wrong place at the wrong time and got drawn into a sham DOJ dragnet.

Growth Industry: Putting Americans in Prison

The putting-people-in-prison phenomenon has resulted in many growth industries, all of which *require* an increasing number of people to be incarcerated. These growth industries include, for instance:

- Massive increase in the number of government agents and government informants. They need to justify their pay and position, and are looking for technical violations to put people in prison, or setting up criminal operations to bring in victims or people against whom they can make false accusations.

- Building of prisons, including private prisons, that will need an increasing number of inmates to pay expenses and the mortgage.
- Managing and staffing prisons.
- Prison industries, such as the federal UNICOR program, that pay prisoners from 20 cents to a dollar an hour to produce goods that are sold to other government agencies and the private sector.
- Attorneys and law firms supported by the ever revolving mass of humanity seeking defense against charges that are often sham or greatly exaggerated.

Feel-Good, Self-Serving Legislation That Incarcerates Americans in Wholesale Numbers

The start of the population transfer into prisons came when members of congress, seeking to gain political advantage at the polls, legislated draconian prison sentences for anyone even remotely involved with drugs—or not involved at all. By legislating laws on the pretense of fighting the so-called war-on-drugs and other crimes, they argue that they are tough on crime. Contradicting their tough-on-crime rhetoric is the fact that *they* have covered up crimes far more serious involving misconduct by government personnel, including the decades of CIA drug trafficking into the United States.

The tactic of gaining votes through appearing tough on crime is nothing new. A similar demagoguery was used with the race card and continues to be used, long after its justification was gone, and despite the fact that it generates hostility between the races that would not otherwise exist. President Clinton was especially adapt at this, focusing special benefits on special groups to gain their votes, and at the same time gain their support when his dirty linen surfaced.

Politicians Charging Each Other With Softness on Crime

In the 1984 elections, Republican politicians accused Democratic politicians of being soft on crime, gaining an advantage. In 1986, Democrats got back by suddenly pushing through draconian legislation that has inflicted incalculable human suffering on many of the same people they claimed to be protecting. Massachusetts Representative Tip O'Neill pushed through a bill that became known as the Mandatory Minimum Sentencing Law that required federal judges to sentence defendants to the term specified by a guideline, leaving the judge virtually no discretion for mitigating circumstances.

Following the summer recess, O'Neill and fellow Democrats rushed the legislation through so as to get credit during the November elections for being tough on crime. There were virtually no hearings and no experts called. In less than a month after O'Neill conceived the vote-getting idea, the committees wrote the legislation, without any significant input from law enforcement people, the Bureau of Prisons, or civil rights groups. The bill passed both houses in time for the politicians to take credit for their tough-on-crime legislation to profit at the November elections.

As it turned out, most major drug kingpins and major drug traffickers have remained free—especially those with CIA connections—while the average

"Joe" or "Jane" has been sent to prison for years, decades, or life, with a relatively small amount of drugs. Or no drugs!

Federalization of Criminal Offenses

In a pattern of constant demagoguery, members of Congress passed legislation making state offenses—often relatively minor ones—into federal crimes. This legislation makes members of Congress look—to the naive public—tough on crime, while simultaneously contributing to one of America's fastest growth industries--putting unprecedented numbers of men and women in prison.

What makes this preposterous to anyone close to the scene is that members of Congress have a long record of criminal coverups of many corrupt high-level government personnel and corrupt covert activities, as described in each of my books. Speaking about this federalization of state offenses, Supreme Court Chief Justice William Rehnquist said (January 7, 1999) the "pressure in Congress is to appear responsive to every highly publicized societal ill," and that "Federal courts were not created to adjudicate local crimes that can and should be handled by state courts."

Draconian Prison Sentences Mandated by Members of Congress

Let's look at the prison sentences imposed by members of Congress for possession of drugs. The length of prison sentence is based upon the amount of drugs *stated in the charges filed by the prosecutor*. For one gram of LSD, the mandatory minimum sentence is five years without possibility of parole. What is one gram? A gram is about the weight of one M&M candy. Five years in prison, a family put into poverty, a family destroyed—for that!

Drug Type	Five-Year Sentence	Ten-Year Sentence
LSD	1 gram (1 M&M)	10 grams
Marijuana	100 plants/100 kilos	1000 plants/1000 kilos
Crack cocaine	5 grams	50 grams
Powder cocaine	500 grams	5 kilos
Heroin	100 grams	1 kilo
Methamphetamine	10 grams	100 grams
PCP	10 grams	100 grams

Tons of Cocaine—Go Free: But M&M Quantity—Years in Prison

Consider this contradiction: Tons of cocaine were brought into the United States by and with the knowledge of government personnel as part of the Nicaraguan operation, and no one was charged with drug offenses. But for plain Joe or Jane, with an M&M size quantity, years in prison. This surely must be another version of affirmative action!

Criticized By Knowledgeable Experts

Despite being criticized by experts in this area, despite the great injustices, despite the family tragedies arising from the legislation that they enacted, members of Congress refuse to change. The U.S. Sentencing Commission, responsible for making recommendations relating to the mandatory minimum sentencing law, has repeatedly since the early 1990s criticized the draconian sentences required by this legislation. Judges, attorneys, and even many prosecutors have criticized the harshness of the legislation. But members of Congress receive praise from the ill-informed public for feel-good legislation touted as being tough on crime.

Determining Length of Prison Removed from Judges to Prosecutors

As a result of the Mandatory Minimum Sentencing Act, judges lost their authority to determine the length of sentence, which is now determined by the imagination used by the prosecutor in filing charges. Even though the minimum sentencing law determines the minimum prison sentence for each offense, the prosecutor, by using his fertile imagination—and a rubber-stamp jury—can determine how long the person will be in prison.

Federal Judge Declares Unconstitutional Feel-Good Legislation

U.S. District Judge Robert Sweet in New York declared the Mandatory Sentencing Law unconstitutional in a 1988 case. But the ruling was overturned by the 2nd Circuit Court of Appeals. Judge Sweet described his anguish at having to sentence a 17-year-old, who had virtually no involvement with drugs, to a ten-year prison sentence. Sweet felt that dealing with the drug problem in a criminal way is wrong, adding that if it is treated in that way, at least it should be fair.

Quitting the Bench Because of the the Law's Inhumanity

Sweet lamented how some judges had simply quit the bench, refusing to be a part of the inhumanity. He described how he frequently wrote to the Senate and House judiciary committees describing the inhumane result of the mandatory minimum sentencing and conspiracy laws, without any reaction. He explained that the judge is limited to trying to have trial procedures handled fairly, and very few judges have the integrity to insure that occurs. Most are former Justice Department attorneys and protective of Justice Department culture.

Crying When They Carry Out Congressional Sentences

Instances have occurred when judges, disturbed by the draconian sentences legislated by members of Congress, must sentence often-innocent people or those with minor drug offenses, to long prison sentences. One judge cried and said, "I don't want to do that. I didn't want to give this young man 30 years, but I have no choice, this is the law." Most judge don't care.

To make a successful prosecution more attractive for the prosecutor's career, he or she will have the paid witness increase the amount of drugs that he falsely states he saw in your possession, or which he claims you had told him. If the witness simply testifies that he saw drugs in your possession, the prison sentence may only be five or ten years. But if the witness testifies that he saw, or you said, a kilo of cocaine or crack cocaine, or ten kilos, whatever, your sentence will be increased. The only difference between a defendant (and this could be you), receiving five years in prison or a life sentence, is how much the government-paid witness will exaggerate his testimony.

Outrageous Prison Sentences and World's Greatest Incarceration

America reportedly has the greatest percentage of its population in prison of any country in the world. This record has been brought about by legislation passed by members of congress, seeking votes through feel-good legislation approved by a primarily naive public.

Vicious criminals, killers, such as the darling of America's sport fanatics, O.J. Simpson, go free, while honest people go to prison for decades, or even life. Talk about a sick society!

"The Greatest Tragedy of My Professional Life."

Former counsel to the House committee on the Judiciary, Eric E. Sterling, played a role in the passage of the mandatory minimum sentencing laws. As president of the Criminal Justice Policy Foundation in Washington, DC and co-chairman of the American Bar Association, Committee on Criminal Justice, he stated:

The work that I was involved in, in enacting these mandatory sentences, is probably the greatest tragedy of my professional life. There have been literally thousands of instances of injustice where minor co-conspirators in cases have been given the sentences that Congress intended for the highest kingpins. None of us envisioned that the Justice Department would so profoundly misuse this statute. Families are wrecked, children are orphaned, and the taxpayers are paying a fortune for excessive punishment. It is such a waste of human life. It's awful.

Political Chicanery for Political Self-Gain

Sterling described the political benefits discussed behind the scenes that led to the massive human tragedies that have occurred following the drug legislation. In describing how these laws came about, Sterling said:

These laws came about in an incredible conjunction between politics and hysteria. It was 1986, Tip O'Neill comes back from the July 4th district recess and everybody's talking about the death of the Boston Celtics pick, Len Bias [who drugged himself to death]. That's all his constituents are talking to him about. And he has the insight, "Drugs, it's drugs. I can take this issue into the election." He calls the Democratic leadership together in the House of Representatives and says, "I want a drug bill, I want it in four weeks." And it set off kind of a stampede.

Everybody started trying to get out front on the drug issue. ... I mean, every committee...not just the Judiciary Committee—Foreign Affairs, Ways and Means, Agriculture, Armed Services. Everybody's got a piece of this out there, fighting to get their face on television, talking about the drug problem. And these mandatories came in the last couple days before the Congressional recess, before they were all going to race out of town and tell the voters about what they're doing to fight the war on drugs. No hearings, no consideration by the federal judges, no input from the Bureau of Prisons.

Even the DEA didn't testify. The whole thing is kind of cobbled together with chewing gum and baling wire. Numbers are picked out of air. And we see what these consequences are of that kind of legislating. Ten-year mandatory minimum, routine sentences are 15, 20, 30 years, without parole. Then you have conspiracy, and suddenly, you have people facing 50 years, people facing either life in virtual terms or as a real sentence. That's what's happening. Fifteen thousand federal drug cases a year. Bulk of them mandatory minimum cases. Most of them minor offenders. Only ten percent of all the federal drug cases are high level traffickers.

You wonder, who's asleep at the switch at the Justice Department? What you have is conviction on the basis of [perjured] testimony. You have drugless drug cases. You don't need powder, all you need is the witness to say, "I saw a kilo." People are amazed. "Well, aren't there drugs?" There don't have to be drugs. All there have to be are witnesses who say, "I saw the drugs," or, "He said there were drugs." That's what you need.

When asked, "Couldn't you guess this would happen?" he responded:

I don't think any of us fully anticipated what these numbers would generate. DEA agents and assistant U.S. attorneys are misusing this statute, with the complicity of their managers in the Department of Justice, to engage in what now has really become a pattern and practice of racial discrimination in almost overwhelmingly prosecuting people of color for tiny amounts of drugs and sending them away for kingpin sentences.

Why are they doing it?

They're doing it because it's easy. These cases are the easiest cases to prosecute. They're cut and dried. The lawyers are public defenders. There's not any kind of real defense....These are little cases. However, it's good training for young ambitious attorneys who want to acquire jury experience. For DEA agents, this is safe. I mean when DEA agents go to Colombia or Mexico, their life is in danger. Going after some poor schnook who's the corner crack dealer, that doesn't threaten their lives. The statistics look good.

Referring to the mandatory minimum legislation, Sterling said:

No one ever thought at all about what the implications were of applying conspiracy. No one envisioned that by applying the statute to anyone in a conspiracy, no matter how low they were in the conspiratorial chain, that they would get the maximum that could be imposed for the kingpin. Nobody figured that out as we were working on it in 1988. It was a total oversight. Now, of course, you can't change it, because that's soft on drugs.

Sterling continued:

The current sentencing situation is a sort of witch's brew of three poisons put together making an abominable poison: mandatory minimums designed for kingpins with very long sentences; conspiracy bringing in the lowest level offenders who become eligible for those; and substantial assistance policies...that means telling a wild story to avoid spending almost life in prison without parole; there are many people who will do that. The incentive is, "I'll tell any story I can." They are people who are often very desperate. They realize, "If I can get five years instead of 30 years, if I tell a story against that other guy, tell me what I have to say, I'll say it."

Referring to the fact that DOJ induced perjury is rampant, Sterling said:

The entire criminal justice system knows that perjury is the coin of the realm. In New York City, police officers call it "testalying." In Los Angeles they call it "the liar's club." Everybody knows that lying takes place. The prosecutors don't feel bad about it, this is simply part of the system. Police officers conform their testimony to what they know the courts expect to hear in order to get the results that they want, not on the basis of what the facts are.

Referring to the meaningless instruction by the judge to tell the truth, Sterling said:

When a judge tells a witness, "Let me remind you, you're under oath and if you lie under oath, you'll be prosecuted for perjury," this is a disclaimer. The judge in effect is washing his hands or her hands of any responsibility for the lie which is forthcoming. This is part of the ritual; it's a ritual statement, it's not a real statement. It's like when you ask a defendant who's pleading guilty if they understand what they are doing. They always say, yes. They're supposed to. They often don't have a clue what they're doing.

Surely the DOJ Would Not Be Prosecuting an Innocent Person!

Referring to the naiveté—or ignorance—of the average juror, Sterling said the average juror thinks, "If the government is trying to convict this dope dealer, well, this person is probably guilty, or why else would we be here?" He continued:

We believe in the presumption of innocence as a society. Once you get in the courtroom, that presumption is very, very thin. It's not a whole lot of protection. And when you have a witness who says, "Yes, I am getting a deal, but I was there and this is what the defendant did," jurors will say, "Even if I don't believe all that he's saying, I believe enough of it and that enough is proof beyond a reasonable doubt for me."

Sterling added:

The war on drugs is one of the great evils of our times. We have federal judges who have resigned, federal judges who have wept on the bench. Senior federal judges who say, "We refuse as a matter of conscience any longer to take these kinds of cases." Those are people at least who have the opportunity to step out. I had the opportunity to step out by leaving my job in the government and am now working to help expose what I think are these problems. When I meet with the family members of people serving these sentences, it is very hard. At times I am moved to tears when I sit across from someone whose loved one is serving a 30-year sentence for something that I played a role in getting enacted. It's an awful feeling.

Prosecutors Prefer Dumber and More Naive Jurors

It is generally realized that prosecutors don't want informed people on the jury. The dumber they are, the less likely they will question the government's prosecutor. Informed people can't be manipulated as easily.

"The Public Doesn't Know What the Laws Are"

Responding to a question of whether the public understands what is going on, Sterling replied:

The ignorance about what's going on exists on a bunch of different levels. Number one, the offenders themselves are ignorant of what the penalties are that they could incur. Congress says, "We're going to pass these tough laws to send a message to the criminals to stop." But there's a complete disconnection between what Congress hopes and what criminals actually understand. They don't watch C-SPAN, they don't read "Congressional Record." They simply don't know. They're astonished when they get punished. Congressmen also don't know what the laws are. Many of them don't even know that parole [in drug cases] was abolished. The public doesn't know what the laws are. The public still believes that people are getting slapped on the wrist. These are examples which then allow a member of Congress to say with a straight face, "We need to get tougher."

Alien to What Was Once the American Way of Life

Sterling, addressing the harm members of Congress and DOJ Attorneys have brought down upon the people, said:

The implications of the war on drugs, the sense of how alien it is to American values, the use of informants, paying informants....We have hundreds of thousands of informants. Informants can make a living professionally in their role as informants. This is simply an anathema to the way in which we think a free society ought to operate. The role of wiretapping, of monitoring telephone conversations, of taping conversations. Defense lawyers now are afraid that their clients may be trying to entrap them. The government has said, "We believe we have the power to go to a man represented by an attorney and unbeknownst to that attorney, try to get that man to incriminate the attorney." To think that we would undermine our legal system in this way is reminiscent of the Soviet Union.

A Hateful Society Spurned By Culture in Congress and DOJ

Sterling said:

If we look at the way in which so much of our society functions today, it looks like the kind of highly regimented Soviet system that we were repulsed by in the early 1950s. Informants in the work place. Fear of having conversations with people. Fear of our children informing against us. Not knowing what the charges might be. Offenses for which bail is no longer available.

Army of Informants Looking For Victims—Another Growth Industry

Government agencies, and especially the various divisions of the Department of Justice, have thousands of agents and informants who must find offenses committed by people. They search public and financial records looking for technical errors that they can charge as federal crimes—and the list is endless, including matters committed by almost any adult.

They set up elaborate pseudo criminal enterprises and look for people they can entice into them in such a way that criminal charges can be filed. The coalition of government agents, informants, and prosecutors are quite imaginative. Anyone trapped into one of them doesn't stand much of a chance against this coalition with unlimited funds and juries that will believe virtually anything the "government" charges.

One example: a government informant may induce a "patsy" to assist him in undercover work, falsely encouraging him to assist in bringing about the arrest of alleged drug traffickers. The patsy is told to contact certain people—who are actually undercover government agents—and to gain their confidence by bragging about past drug trafficking activities. The patsy doing the bragging may never have been near drugs or involved in any drug offense, but he is told it is a chance to work for the government and be well paid. Unknown to the patsy, he is telling these tall tales to government undercover agents who arrest him after his fabricated drug-trafficking statements are recorded. Based simply upon these statements—no drugs are involved—the patsy who is no match for this government conspiracy, is charged, tried, and then naive jurors find him guilty. Chalk up another "win" for the public and Congress' tough-on-crime stance. The jurors have a "feel-good" attitude, and government agents receive bonuses. Oh yes, the patsy may get life in prison with no chance of parole.

Agents Transferred to Undesirable Locations if No Arrests

During an April 1999 phone call with a former ATF and DEA agent, Michael Don Stewart, he described the quota-system that requires ATF agents to fabricate cases against innocent people. "If you go two months without making an arrest, a search warrant, a seizure, or open or close an investigation, you are transferred to some place where they need you, and you don't want to go, such as Detroit, East LA, little Cuba—Miami."

I responded, "This practice encourages agents to file sham charges, doesn't it." Stewart replied, "You are exactly right; most people aren't aware of that." He said that agents, to avoid being transferred, look for technical paper violations to justify opening an investigation. The agents go to pawn shops, gun shops, and other places looking at records and seeking some technical mistake—no matter how innocent or minor—which permits them to conduct an investigation and make sham charges against the person.

Searching Records for Targets to Destroy

A practice similar to that had been described to me many years ago by CIA asset Gunther Russbacher. CIA and other government personnel examine financial records, looking for people and companies that can be forced into involuntary bankruptcy, where the rampant corruption in bankruptcy courts then seize and loot the assets. (See *Defrauding America.*)

Adding Conspiracy Laws to Feel-Good
Tough-On-Crime Self-Serving Legislation

Not to be outdone by the other political party, politicians pushed through—just before election time—*another* law showing them as being tough on crime: the drug conspiracy statute. The conspiracy statute greatly expanded the number of people ensnared by the draconian minimum sentencing law. Now, almost anyone can be sentenced to a long prison term—or even life without parole—no drugs even need be present to convict as a major drug kingpin.

In real life, as applied by Department of Justice prosecutors, men and women have been sent to prison with long prison sentences—even life in prison—who were guilty of no crime, and who are in prison because of the imaginative fertile imagination of career-obsessed attorneys in the United States Department of Justice. This law, as members of Congress knew, targets innocent people who have no connection to drugs, who had never entertained any drug-related thoughts, and to this day can't understand why they are in prison.

American men and women in prison now exceed the combined population of Alaska and Wyoming. In 1998, for instance, a dozen European countries making up the European Union, whose population exceeds the United States' by over 100 million, had only one third as many people in prison (*San Francisco Examiner*, May 10, 1999).

What This Country Needs is A Go-To-Prison Form of Monopoly

What this country needs is a game, something like "Monopoly," showing all the ways that Congress and the Department of Justice employees can cause *you* to join the hundreds of thousands of others in prison in one of America's great growth industries. It would be not only informative, but a teaching tool for how to stay out of prison!

The Catch-All Conspiracy Charge That can Put YOU in Prison

Congress' drug conspiracy laws have put more people in prison than any other statute. A man or woman doesn't even need to possess drugs, handled any drugs, or played any role in any drug transaction. For the prosecutor and informant, the "beauty" of it is that they can send someone to prison for years or for life who doesn't even know what he had done! The convicted and imprisoned defendant is often guilty of nothing except the fertile imagination of a Department of Justice prosecutor working with an informant who will fabricate whatever testimony is requested by the prosecutor.

A "Dry" Conspiracy

A "dry" conspiracy is the name given to a conspiracy where there is no evidence of any drugs. All it requires for conviction is a government-paid witness testifying to something that he claims you said. You might have even been bragging, without ever having done anything you claim, but you end up with a long prison sentence.

How DOJ Attorneys Improve Their Performance Record

The conspiracy legislation permits a prosecutor to sit behind his desk and let his imagination wonder. With a little mental calculation, he can concoct the type of conspiracy to charge against our Joe or Jane target, which needs no relationship to reality; great for attorneys! Almost any businessperson or someone active in the business world can be charged with some type of conspiracy. Anyone can be approached by a government informant and sucked into a conspiracy scheme concocted by your friendly government agents. No evidence is needed!

A Conspiracy of One—Another DOJ Trick to Imprison People

Attorneys in the Department of Justice have even expanded on the conspiracy statute. A conspiracy requires two or more persons. No problem; Justice Department prosecutors now charge single persons with a conspiracy when there is no other person involved.

Very Few Countries Have Conspiracy Laws

Former counsel to the U.S. House committee on the Judiciary, Eric E. Sterling, said that very few countries have conspiracy laws as exist in the United States because "they can be so badly abused." He added:

Our conspiracy law is such that long after you've dropped out of the conspiracy, you're still responsible for things that you may have done way in the past. The criminal organization marches forward. You've gone straight. But when the chain gets connected all the way to the back, you can still be held liable for things that you had no responsibility for and you could not foresee. It's a terrible problem, the way in which conspiracy is being used in these cases.

Another Growth Industry—DOJ's Paid Perjurers

Perjury-for-sale is the type of growth industry that an insider could associate with the culture in the Department of Justice. This practice greatly increases the number of people sent to fill new prisons or crowd into old ones. DOJ prosecutors routinely compensate witnesses to testify before grand juries and trial juries as they want the witness to testify.

Some of them are paid on an occurrence basis. Others are on a monthly salary. Some are in prison, willing to say anything to bring about their release. Others may be charged with a criminal offense and are offered to have charges dropped for parroting what the prosecutor wants said. And they have another advantage: they have the Department of Justice protecting them against being charged for criminal perjury, regardless of the extent of their lying under oath.

The Liars Club

Another name for this group is "Liars Club." Some are professional perjurers who travel around the country testifying for DOJ prosecutors. The Liars Club includes prisoners, some with life sentences, who read newspapers to learn or fabricate facts about people recently arrested, most of whom they had never seen, heard of, or dealt with. Their expertise at fabricating testimony to use before grand juries and during trial is their greatest value.

"Jumping On the Bus"

A term defining the process is "jumping on the bus." Prisoners obtain information from other prisoners—even buy the information—and then contact DOJ prosecutors and offer their services to testify against a person prosecutors want arrested, or who had just been arrested and is waiting for trial.

The best liars for DOJ prosecutors are prisoners and people charged with criminal offenses. The longer their sentences, the more willing they are to fabricate testimony exactly as requested by the DOJ attorneys. They also know the lingo and the ropes.

A release-from-prison promise in exchange for perjured testimony does not take into account the crime for which the person is in prison. He may be a brutal murderer, a major drug kingpin, and someone who will return to his prior crimes once he is released.

And even more bizarre—and there is no limit to the bizarre angles involved—the target against whom testimony is being "paid" may be guilty of a very low offense, or even no offense. One answer is that the new conviction increases the prosecutor's conviction record; the hell with justice!

Working the System

The real hard-core incarcerated drug trafficker works the system. He thinks to himself, "What do I have to do to get out of prison?" He asks the prosecutor, "What do I have to say? Who do I have to testify against? How much drugs do I have to say that he discussed?" With the government backing the liar, most naive jurors believe the witness called by the government. The liar is sitting with the government at his side. The government presents the liar in the court. Is the average juror going to doubt the integrity of the United States? [Forget Clinton for the moment!] Surely you can believe your own government! [Forget again the history of government lying for the past 50 years.]

Major Drug Kingpins Get Released Through Fabricated Testimony

Often, a high-level drug kingpin will give testimony against a low-level participant in a drug operation—or someone totally innocent—and the drug kingpin gets released from prison. "Big fish" are given their freedom to provide testimony against minor offenders. It's like the food chain; major drug dealers snitch on low level dealers and go free, while innocent or low-level people end up with long prison sentences.

Like Crooked Cops Holding the People Hostage

Other criminal statutes are often simultaneously violated when this crime occurs, including falsely accusing a person of a crime, conspiracy, obstruction of justice, among others. But who is going to prosecute the prosecutor? It's like having a department of crooked cops holding the citizens hostage.

Worse Than Hitler's Gestapo

When I was growing up in the late 1930s, as Hitler came to power, I remember the many media articles decrying the culture of informants or neighborhood spies which Adolph Hitler's Gestapo used to get neighbors to spy on neighbors. The United States, through its Congress and Department of Justice, has gone far beyond what Hitler initiated. Now, family members testify against each other, children testify against their brothers or sisters, children testify against parents. This is what the attorneys in the Department of Justice have brought upon America as their slime permeates throughout government, industry, and society.

Encouraging Someone To Give False Testimony Is A Crime

Under federal criminal statutes, the prosecutor is guilty of a crime if he procures another person to commit perjury. When a law-enforcement officer commits this crime, it is far worse than when done by someone else. The law says:

> Title 18 U.S.C. § 1622. Subornation of perjury. Whoever procures another to commit any perjury is guilty of subornation of perjury, and shall be fined ... or imprisoned ...

The evidence is overwhelming that the very same Justice Department attorneys responsible for prosecuting people guilty of subornation of perjury have been routinely perpetrating this crime, with tragic human consequences, for years, and getting away with it! They hold themselves above the law, with one standard for the people, and another for themselves.

Compensation for Testimony is A Federal Offense

Under federal criminal statute, Title 18 USC Section 201, it is a criminal offense for *anyone* to give any form of compensation to a person providing testimony, whether it is before the fact or after the fact. Title 18 USC § 201(c)(2) says:

> *Whoever...directly or indirectly, gives, offers or promises anything of value to any person, for or because of the testimony under oath or affirmation given or to be given by such person as a witness upon a trial, hearing, or other proceeding, before any court...authorized by the laws of the United States to hear evidence or take testimony...shall be fined under this title or imprisoned for not more than two years, or both.*

That statute does not require that the testimony be proven false; only that some type of compensation be promised for a witness's testimony.

Section 201(b)(3) of the same Title addresses the matter of compensation given to *influence* the testimony. DOJ prosecutors have been violating both of these statutes for years and continue to do so.

American Bar Association Rules of Professional Conduct (Section 3.4(b) says: A lawyer shall not (b) ... offer an inducement to a witness that is prohibited by law. The theory against paying for testimony was reflected in a Florida case (*The Florida Bar v. Jackson*, 490 So.2d 935 Fla. 1986):

> *The very heart of the judicial system lies in the integrity of the participants.....Justice must not be bought or sold. Attorneys have a solemn responsibility to assure that not even the taint of impropriety exists as to the procurement of testimony before courts of Justice. It is clear that the actions of the respondent in attempting to obtain compensation for the testimony of his clients...violates the very essence of the integrity of the judicial system and the disciplinary rule and the code of professional responsibility, the integration rules of the Florida Bar and the oath of his office.*

In another example, the lawyer who paid $50 for a police officer to testify truthfully for his client was suspended from practice for 18 months. (*In re Kien*, 372 N.E.2nd 376 (111.1977))

Legal Challenge to DOJ Compensated Testimony

During a 1998 trial in Denver, DOJ prosecutors charged Sonya Singleton and Napoleon Douglas with money laundering and conspiracy offenses. Before trial, DOJ prosecutors offered to drop charges against Douglas if he testified against Singleton as they wanted him to testify. This offer was made despite the statute barring payment for testimony. With this compensation and freedom against perjury, Douglas accepted the prosecutor's offer. Singleton was convicted on the basis of this compensated testimony.

It is possible neither one was guilty of the charges. But for one of them to be assured freedom from prison, maybe from a life-in-prison sentence, it paid Douglas to fabricate lies, especially when the prosecutor protected him against criminal perjury charges. It was another "he-said she-said" type of trial, with Douglas having the benefit of the government of the United States alongside him. The naive jurors received the impression that he was probably telling the truth, despite the fact that DOJ prosecutors routinely solicit and pay for perjured testimony.

Denver attorney John "Val" Wachtel appealed Singleton's conviction based upon the fact that the sole witness against Singleton was paid to testify, and that this violated the clear wording of the federal statute. Three judges[41] in the Court of Appeals Panel at Denver heard the appeal.

OK For DOJ Attorneys but not Defendants' Attorneys

Justice Department attorneys argued that it was legal for them to pay or compensate people for testimony during grand jury and trial jury proceedings even though it was not legal for defense attorneys to do so. The prosecutor has the advantage of being able to free a prisoner or drop charges; the defense attorney of course cannot do that. The DOJ attorneys argued that Title 18 USC § 3553(e) permitted them to request a reduction of sentence or dropping of charges for those who provide testimony that prosecutors wanted. That section says:

> *Upon motion of the Government, the court shall have the authority to impose a sentence below a level established by statute as a minimum sentence so as to reflect a defendant's substantial assistance in the investigation or prosecution of another person who has committed an offense. Further, USSG § 5K1.1 provides for reduction of sentence.*

They also sought support in Federal Rule of Criminal Procedure Rule 35(b):

> *The court, on motion of the Government made within one year after the imposition of the sentence, may reduce a sentence to reflect a defendant's subsequent, substantial assistance in the investigation or prosecution of another person who has committed an offense...*

The three-judge Court of Appeals decision denied the government's position, holding that *assistance* did not include *purchasing* testimony. They held that reduction in sentence could be provided for *information*, but not for *sworn testimony*:

> *Each of these provisions of law authorizes only that substantial assistance can be rewarded after it is rendered; none authorized the government to make a deal for testimony before it is given, as the government did with Mr. Douglas. [The paid witness against Singleton.] However § 201(c)(2) prohibits even the rewarding of testimony after it is given; it prohibits anything of value to be given, offered or promised because of "testimony" given. 18 U.S.C. § 201(c)(2). The sentencing provisions may thus appear to conflict by authorizing something of value (a motion for and grant of sentence reduction) to be given because of testimony rendered. We believe the statutes can be read together in this way: in light of § 201(c)(2), "substantial assistance" does not include testimony. Congress enacted the sentencing provisions against the backdrop of its general prohibition against giving anything of value for or because of testimony... Our reading of the statutes will not impair the substantial assistance provisions, because a defendant can substantially assist an investigation or prosecution in myriad ways other than by testifying .... In the circumstances before us, the appropriate remedy for the testimony obtained in violation of § 201(c)(2) is suppression of its use in Ms. Singleton's trial.*

---

[41]   Judges Paul J. Kelly, David M. Ebel, and Chief Judge Stephanie K. Seymour.

The appeal panel held that the statute's plain words barring any type of compensation for testimony meant what it said, and applied both to government agents and the public. The Court of Appeals decision reversed the conviction of Singleton, requiring the prosecutor to retry the case without using compensation-tainted testimony. (*U.S. v. Singleton*, 144 F.3d 1343 (1998)) The decision made sense.

A similar district court decision was made in Miami on August 4, 1998 by U.S. District Judge William J. Zloch in the case of *U.S. v. Lowery*. In that decision, Judge Zloch held that the deal for a co-defendant's testimony gave him "every reason to fabricate, falsify or exaggerate his testimony in an attempt to curry favor."

Motion For *EnBanc* Rehearing by All 12 Judges

After the three-judge Court of Appeals panel overturned the Singleton dismissal, Department of Justice attorneys filed a motion for the entire 12-judge Court of Appeals to hear the matter *en banc*, which it did. On January 8, 1999, the 10th circuit Court of Appeals rendered a decision overturning its three-judge panel, holding that the word, "Whoever," in Title 18 USC § 210 applied only to the public and did not apply to DOJ prosecutors!

Therefore, DOJ prosecutors could continue paying compensation to their witnesses, even though the statute clearly prohibited it. Defense attorneys were barred from doing the same, and innocent people could continue to be imprisoned in this manner. (Many of the Court of Appeals judges were former Department of Justice attorneys.)

Forfeiture Laws, Another Feel-Good Self-Serving
Tough-On-Crime Legislation That Boomeranged On the Public

Another feel-good legislation passed by self-serving members of Congress that boomeranged back on the public was the forfeiture statutes that are being constantly expanded as the other "tough-on-crime" legislation. Members of Congress passed forfeiture statutes in the 1970s to make themselves look tough on crime. As attorneys, they certainly could see how the seizure laws would inflict serious financial losses upon people that were often totally out-of-proportion to the real or imaginary offense. The seizure of assets has been expanded to include those who have never been charged with any offense and who don't get the property back. Rather clever, don't you think!

Property that had been loaned, or rented to someone else, may be seized for an offense that the owner could not foresee or have any control over. For some people, the loss of the asset may be that person's primary asset. The property may have been accidentally seized, or seized without justification. The value of the property seized could be totally out of proportion to the offense. A million dollar or more plane can be seized and forfeited if a few marijuana seeds are found—or planted by government agents or informants.

A couple of drinks before or with a meal may have raised your blood alcohol level to the legal level of as low as .08. In some jurisdictions, this relatively low blood-alcohol level results in seizure of your car. For some people barely surviving financially, this seizure can be catastrophic.

Many asset seizures can occur from even minor technical violations, and the list of offenses is growing as government personnel continue to take away rights that had existed for the first 200 years of this country's existence. A passive public makes this possible.

License To Steal Approved by Supreme Court Justices

"License to Steal" was the heading on an article in San Francisco's legal newspaper, *Daily Journal* (March 18, 1996). The subtitle said, "In Supreme Court Ruling, Rights of the Innocent Are Forfeited." The article made reference to the Supreme Court's March 1996 decision upholding the right of government agencies seizing property from innocent people. The article stated in part:

> *The U.S. Supreme Court has given its stamp of approval to states that steal property from innocent people. Such a forfeiture doesn't violate the constitutional protections of due process, the high court said... Chief Justice William Rehnquist...writes opinions as if he were writing algebraic formulas—they make no reference to the lives they affect...The high court just issued Michigan and other states a license for theft...Justice Ruth Bader Ginsburg wrote a concurring opinion that in effect apologizes for the decision—yet supports it.*

A *Wall Street Journal* article (December 29, 1997) was titled, "The Dangerous Expansion of Forfeiture Laws," stating in part:

> *Asset forfeiture laws have been spreading like a computer virus through the nation's statute books .... more than 100 federal laws authorize federal agents to confiscate private property allegedly involved in violations of statutes on wildlife, gambling, narcotics, immigration, money laundering, etc. The vast expansion of government's forfeiture power epitomizes the demise of property rights in modern America.*
>
> *Federal agents can confiscate private property with no court order and no proof of legal violations. Law-enforcement officials love forfeiture laws because a hefty percentage of the takings often go directly to their coffers.*
>
> *A federal appeals court complained in 1992: "We continue to be enormously troubled by the government's increasing and virtually unchecked use of the civil forfeiture statutes and the disregard for due process that is buried in those statutes."*
>
> *A September 1992 Justice Department newsletter noted: "Like children in a candy shop, the law enforcement community chose all manner and method of seizing and forfeiting property, gorging ourselves in an effort which soon came to resemble one designed to raise revenues."*

Innocence is Irrelevant in Forfeiture Of Property

> *In many forgfeiture cases, innocence is irrelevant. The Supreme Court further tilted the legal playing field against ordinary people last year in a decisison in a case involving the innocent co-owner of confiscated property. John Bennis stopped on his way home from work to dally with a prostitute in his Plymouth; Detroit police descended on the scene and seized the car, whose co-owner was Mr. Bennis's wife, Tina. The court ruled 5-4 that the seizure did not violate the wife's constitutional rights even through she clearly was not complicit in her husband's illicit behavior.*

Chief Justice William Rehnquist wrote: "The government may not be required to compensate an owner for property which it has already lawfully acquired under the exercise of government authority." By asserting that the government had already "lawfully acquired" the Bennises' car simply because it had a law authorizing seizure of the car, Justice Rehnquist basically granted government unlimited power to steal: If it wants to "lawfully acquire" private property without compensation, all it needs to do is write more confiscatory laws.

The article, written by James Bovard, author of *Lost Rights: The Destruction of American Liberty*, described how Justice Department employees strip a defendant of the funds needed to defend herself or herself. Referring to a bill pushed by Representative Henry Hyde, chairman of the House Judiciary Committee,

The new bill greatly expands the power of the prosecutor to seize people's assets before trial (thereby potentially crippling a person's ability to hire defense counsel), makes it much more difficult for citizens to get summary judgments against wrongful seizures, and greatly increases the number of crimes for which government can seize a person's or a corporation's assets.... "Virtually any business that has any substantive inventory and is extensively regulated by the government is in danger of having its goods seized—even for non-criminal regulatory infractions."

Your Property Is Seized, Now What?

After seizure, government employees don't have to tell you how to get it back. And major steps must be taken to even *try* to get it back. The time limit for taking these steps is usually very short, sometimes only ten days after seizure, before the average person even recognizes what happened. Then, the person must find an attorney to take the case, have the money to pay the attorney, and post a bond. Many people cannot meet these requirements.

Who Benefits by Seizing Your Property?

In many cases, property seized by a government agency remains the property of that agency. Homes that are seized are sometimes occupied by government agents. Cars or airplanes that are seized are often used by the seizing agency. Or the proceeds from the sale of the assets go to the seizing agency. Where government informants are involved, they get a percentage of the asset value. The more assets that a person has, the greater the incentive for government agents and government informants to file sham charges and seize the assets. Even though innocent, failure or inability to promptly take the necessary legal steps means the assets are lost.

A SAMPLING OF GOVERNMENT FRAUDS
PERPETRATED UPON INNOCENT PEOPLE

The following cases are examples of people who suffered the consequences of the tough-on-crime legislation that can happen to almost any man or women in the United States, including you.

Make A Casual Drug-Related Remark—Go to Prison!

Someone in your group says, maybe in jest, "Let's get some cocaine and sell it; we'll make a lot of money." Nothing else may ever be said or done. But by being present when that statement was made, criminal charges can be filed against you or anyone else who was present. The person being charged may not have done a thing after that statement was made. The charge is conspiracy to engage in drug trafficking. Your length of imprisonment depends upon how boastful the drug statement was.

The person making that casual statement may be a government informant and looking for a target—it could be you. The next step, a paramilitary group breaks down the door to your home several days later, with guns drawn, hollering obscenities, slams you and your wife to the floor, holds a large-caliber gun to your heads that could at any moment accidentally—or purposely—discharge. After you are arrested, your assets are seized. If you have a business, that is shut down. If you have a job, you lose it. If your wife is also charged, your children may end up in foster homes. Surprise; this is part of Congress' tough-on-crime laws that the public was demanding.

Your assets are seized, so you have to rely upon a government-provided attorney—who doesn't want to offend the government people who hired him—and he raises a lackluster defense; or is incompetent. A naive jury believes the prosecutor and believes the "government" would not make these charges against you if they were not true. It finds you guilty.

The jurors usually have no idea what their guilty decision means for the defendant in length of imprisonment. Maybe you are lucky, and it may only be ten or twenty years. Your children are placed in foster homes. Think it can't happen to you? Think again; many others felt the same way. You become another victim who ignored warnings about government corruption. You are partly to blame for what has happened to you and your family!

Offer Merchandise for Sale—Go to Prison

How many people would suspect that offering merchandise—a car or real estate—for instance, can result in a long prison term? Tens of thousands of government agents and informants are looking for victims to carry out this next trick. Let's look at a few examples. Understanding how this is done can save you from a prison sentence

In 1989, German citizen Helmut Groebe, wanted for crimes in four countries, was hired by Department of Justice personnel as an informant. At that time, he had defrauded his new wife, defrauded several other women, and even defrauded his daughter and her husband by stripping their company of its assets. Just the type of person compatible with DOJ culture!

Because of his criminal convictions in other countries, Groebe was not eligible for citizenship in the United States. DOJ personnel offered him citizenship in the United States and then set him loose to prey upon individual Americans. DOJ personnel eventually paid him over $600,000 for perjured testimony that was used against the Groebe-DOJ victims.

Wolfgang von Schlieffen—one of the victims of this DOJ-inspired conspiracy—told me what happened during a 1996 correspondence while he was in prison. Groebe, looking for his next victim or prey, contacted Von Schlieffen, who owned a car dealership in Miami. Grobe, knowing that Wolgang had a Rolls Royce car and a condominium for sale, falsely told Wolfgang that he had two friends interested in buying in his automobile showroom the condominium that Wolfgang had for sale. This was a Justice Department-approved lie.

During a meeting to close the deal, Wolfgang concentrated on describing the car. The pseudo buyers periodically interjected that they were drug dealers. Not being familiar with this Justice Department scam, Wolfgang didn't know he was being set up for prison.

A tape of the conversation showed Wolfgang telling them he had no interest in drugs and what they were doing was wrong, that this meeting concerned a car deal. Caught off-guard and not familiar with this common Justice Department entrapment scam, Wolfgang didn't know he was in a trap. The government agents put $10,000 on the table as a down payment, and when Wolfgang picked it up, government agents pulled out their guns and arrested him.

DOJ prosecutors charged Wolfgang with conspiracy to launder drug money through the sale of the car and the condominium. He was guilty of nothing except being the prey in another Justice Department scam, far worse than a financial scam that merely strips a victim of money.

During the subsequent trial, the unsophisticated jurors believed the charges by the prosecutor and the perjured testimony of the professional con artist, finding Wolfgang guilty. The years of work acquiring a business were all lost. Groebe, who had a history of swindling innocent people, was paid a tidy sum by the Department of Justice for carrying out this fraud.

"How Could Something Like This Occur in America?"

From prison, after losing his business, his assets, his freedom, and his good name, Wolfgang wrote, "How could something like this occur in America?" He didn't know the America that *once* existed is now in an advanced stage of corruption, with the DOJ culture spreading like a cancer through government and society.

Groebe and DOJ Preying on A Lonesome Widow

During the trial against Wolfgang, DOJ prosecutors withheld from the defense several important facts about Groebe's background. In one case, Groebe defrauded a woman, Elena Abuawad, who he had promised to marry. After defrauding her, he set her up for prison as part of a DOJ scheme by promising to repay her in cash. She was trying to sell a condominium, and Groebe said he had someone who would buy it, and the purchase price would be paid in cash.

DEA Special Agent Lucas, along with several other DEA agents, all part of the scheme against this lady—unsophisticated in the undercover tricks of the Department of Justice—then arrived to pay her cash. Lucas casually told her the money came from drug deals; the legal implications of that statement were far beyond her understanding—as it would be to 99 percent of the public. That statement didn't mean anything to her. She knew nothing about drugs, and was simply trying to sell a piece of real estate.

Within minutes, the DEA agents arrested her, handcuffed her, and put her in a jail cell. DOJ prosecutors then charged this twice-defrauded woman with a drug-related conspiracy, using the con artist that defrauded her earlier to carry out the scam! She had no criminal record and probably never would have thought of doing anything illegal. The only participants were government agents and the professional con-artist hired and paid by the government agents who set up and carried out the scheme.

Would you, your wife, or your parents, have been sophisticated enough and quick-witted enough to have known what to do if such a statement was casually made out of the blue?

Again, a dim-witted jury held her guilty while approving the conduct of the Justice Department-con artist conspiracy.

"I was in love," the Victimized Widow Later Said

The woman later said: "I was in love. I wanted to get married, and I wanted to have a home again. If he asked me to do something, I was going to do it because I didn't want to lose him." The woman's attorney later filed an appeal, stating in it:

> It is difficult to imagine misconduct more egregious, more immoral, more unfair or more improper than that of the government using and paying an informant to falsely profess his love to a woman with no prior criminal record, to violate her person by making love to her, under the pretense that he has romantic feelings for her to become involved in a criminal offense by playing on and with her emotions and taking advantage of her psychological vulnerability.

America's Gun Owners Beware—Prison May Be Your Next Stop

Millions of gun owners who purchased guns that were legal at the time of purchase can end up in prison and be financially destroyed, solely at the whim of a bureaucrat from the ATF or Justice Department. I first heard from W.J. Chip Stewart in 1997, whose home was Springdale, Arkansas, after he had been charged with a federal offense by the ATF for having in his possession two semi-automatic handguns. They were legal to own when he purchased them, a small 22 caliber and a 45 caliber semi-automatic pistol made by the Holmes Firearms Company, similar to those owned by millions of other people. ATF bureaucrats decided, after many of these guns were sold, that the widely-sold semi-automatic guns could be converted by a gunsmith to become an automatic weapon and were therefore illegal.

Government agents had gotten Stewart's name from the gun manufacturers' registration records. ATF agents notified Stewart that the (legally purchased) guns were now unlawful. After ATF notified Stewart that his two pistols were put onto the banned list, Stewart voluntarily turned the guns over to them. Eight months later, Justice Department prosecutors obtained a grand jury indictment against him.

Stewart, who owned an auto wrecking business and was a relatively permanent member of the community, could have been served peacefully with the warrant for his arrest. Instead, sixteen heavily armed ATF and FBI agents and local sheriff's department personnel converged upon his home, breaking down the door. Fortunately for Stewart, he wasn't home. Otherwise, he could have met the deadly fate of Scott, the Weavers, the Branch Davidians, or the many others who were killed by the brave men of ATF and FBI.

ATF and Justice Department attorneys, assisted by the typical naive jurors, unsophisticated to the corrupt culture in the Department of Justice, caused Stewart to be sentenced to federal prison for twenty-seven months. As a result of his imprisonment, Stewart lost his business, his wife (who didn't wish to be inconvenienced by his imprisonment), his credit worthiness, and his money.

Imprisoning A Doctor on Perjured Testimony

In 1997 I started receiving information from a physician who had been targeted in a similar gun-charge. Dr. Jed Cserna was an MD with a private practice in Ely, Nevada, and a Lt. Colonel in the Idaho National Guard, with 16 years of military service behind him. His problems started in Ely, Nevada, where he was a physician. Cserna told me how it appeared to start. While he was treating a patient, Doris Gratzer, she told him, "If I'm ever shot, Steve [her husband] did it." Dr. Cserna told this to the hospital staff and they said that she always had problems, and this occasion was no different than others. A week later, she was found dead, killed by a bullet wound to the head.

Cserna said her husband, Steve Gratzer, was influential in the town, especially with the sheriff, who was responsible for conducting an investigation into his wife's killing. Cserna was now a danger to Gratzer. According to Cserna, false statements were made by a government informant, seeking to justify his position and pay, that resulted in a raid by ATF agent Doreen on his doctor's office. His home was broken into and possessions disappeared. Participating in the ATF raid was the sheriff who he referred to as Burnie (Ronero), who would soon participate in sham charges filed against the doctor.

Government agents arrested Cserna a short time later and charged him with possession of a machine gun and a short-barreled rifle. The guns in question were an AR-15 that was not an automatic, and a Uzi 9mm that had been sold to him with a folding stock and various barrels. He had used both guns two and three times a week at the local police firing range and was never questioned about their legality.

Inflammatory Statement by DOJ Prosecutor

Witnesses testified that the guns were legal and in common use by gun hobbyists. By misrepresenting the facts, the prosecutor convinced a jury that the doctor did in fact commit a federal offense and that it was their duty to find him guilty. Inflaming the jury in his closing argument, the prosecutor said, just before the jurors recessed, "Either this gun nut will take his machine gun and kill you and your kids or he'll sell it to someone who will."

The jury came back in 21 minutes with a guilty verdict. With that verdict, Dr. Cserna, an MD who spent nearly ten years to get his license and who had devoted long hours to his medical practice in a small town, lost his right to practice medicine in the United States.

DOJ Retaliation Because of Refusing Ruby Ridge Participation?

Cserna told me about an event that happened in Idaho while he was the physician assigned to the Idaho National Guard air wing. During the Ruby Ridge attack that killed Mrs. Weaver and her son, ATF agents had gone to the Idaho National Guard base and told the Commander of the helicopter division, "We are ordering you to activate your choppers to go north and strafe Ruby Ridge." The Colonel refused, stating, "This is against the law, the constitution, and finally, Randy Weaver is an Idaho Citizen, Either you get out or I'll have you thrown out."

According to Cserna, the ATF wanted to take out their frustration on *any* high-ranking Idaho Guard member. Everyone of rank who lived in Idaho was fairly well secure in the state, but he, a Lt. Colonel with the Idaho National Guard, lived in Nevada, and didn't have the long-standing connections the other officers had. Cserna thought this could have played a role in why the ATF then went after him. The charges against Cserna were similar to what I learned over the years from other gun owners who were also falsely charged under similar circumstances. Cserna's evidence relating to Doris Gratzer's murder was blocked by filing false charges against him.

"I Was Guilty Of Believing In the United States"

Upon release from prison in 1998, Cserna left the United States and settled in Switzerland. In one of his letters he wrote, "I was guilty, not of the charges, but instead, of believing in the United States." Decades earlier I first learned the frustration of the corroding of quality of life in California by the legal and judicial fraternity, and how I thought about what a group, in control, can do to corrupt an area. The same legal and judicial fraternities are now corrupting life on a national scale. Over the years a number of my sources have left the United States because of this same pattern of corruption by people who have taken over key offices in the U.S.

Tsunami Expert Set Up As Patsy: Goes to Prison

George Pararas-Carayannis was known for his expertise on major tidal waves known as tsunami that are triggered by earthquakes. He was director of the Tsunami Information Center in Hawaii. He also had a small jewelry store as a side business to his government job. He would shortly be one of the thousands of victims of Department of Justice fraud who was put in prison without having committed any offense except to fall victim to a DOJ-con artist conspiracy.

Federal agents had earlier arrested a Canadian, Lauri McEwen, in Honolulu on drug charges, and offered to drop charges if she could get evidence against Pararas. McEwen carried out the fraudulent sting operation by becoming friendly with Pararas, falsely representing herself as an interior decorator and head of an escort service.

The young and attractive McEwen, wearing stunning clothes, feigned a love interest in Pararas. After getting into his confidence, she asked Pararas to run credit card charges from her "escort" business through his credit card machine at the jewelry store. He made no money out of it and was simply doing a favor for someone he thought was his girl friend. He promptly turned the money over to her after it was credited to his account.

Federal prosecutors then accused Pararas of money laundering resulting from processing money from a prostitution ring through his merchant credit card account. When Carayannis next saw his lady friend, she no longer had the low-cut dresses and loving smile.

Federal prosecutors offered to reduce the charges if he pled guilty to one of them. He refused. He wasn't guilty of anything. Fighting the power of the government with its unlimited funds and ability to intimidate jurors, Carayannis lost everything after a jury decided he was guilty and the judge sentenced him to three years in prison. As a result of the false charges, he was fired from his government job in 1995. He later said, "I had faith in this system. I thought with this kind of evidence and due process, I would be acquitted." Having already suffered several heart attacks, prison was difficult for him.

Apply for Loan--Be Charged with Drug Money Laundering

Beryle Johnston, from Papillion, Nebraska, was offered a deal by undercover government agents to refinance his farm. They instructed him to meet the lenders in Florida to complete the transaction. During the discussion, government informant Jerry Woody told Johnston that the people putting up the money for the loan were members of the Cali Cartel. That did it. Johnson, like most people, didn't know the significance of that DOJ statement, that it was a standard trick used by Department of Justice attorneys to destroy another victim. He did not know the legal ramifications. What came next? You guessed it; DOJ prosecutors charged him with drug money laundering.

During the trial, FBI agents perjured themselves, falsely stating that Woody owned a bank and had handled billions of dollars. The truth was, Woody didn't have any bank. He didn't have any money. He was living off his girlfriend's credit cards. The government agents knew this. Based upon this DOJ fraud and perjury, a jury convicted Johnston. Woody later admitted his testimony was perjured. But it was too late to save Johnston or the farm the government seized. And the legal and judicial system has made government agents immune from suit to where neither they—nor the government—could be sued for their criminal misconduct.

Hire A Lobbyist—Go to Prison

Lobbyists and bribery go hand in hand when dealing with members of Congress. But it is a different scenario for non-government small fry, even when they are innocent. For example, William Moore's company developed an optical scanning device that he tried to sell to the U.S. Postal Service. He publicly criticized the postal service for sticking to an inferior product. A government undercover agent advised Moore to seek a lobbyist to promote his device with the postal service. He did. He hired lobbyist John R. Gnau, Jr., who, unknown to him, had been passing bribes with William Spartin to a member of the Postal Service's board of governors, Peter E. Voss. All three of them were being investigated by the DOJ. All of this was unknown to Moore.

Tearing Up Immunity Agreement for Refusing to Lie

DOJ employees had made a written agreement with Spartin that if he cooperated in the prosecution of Gnau and Moore he would not be prosecuted. Spartin was willing to testify about Gnau's bribing, but said that Moore knew nothing about it. For refusing to commit the requested crime of perjury, the DOJ prosecutor tore up the immunity agreement and said he would prosecute Spartin.

Spartin's attorney then asked the prosecutor for another chance, after which Spartin "refreshed" his memory and stated that Moore did know about the bribes, which everyone knew was a lie. The prosecutor then marched Spartin into the grand jury room and asked Spartin if he had told postal inspectors that Moore knew about the bribes. Spartin replied in the affirmative. The corrupt prosecutor never told the jurors that Spartin had said over a dozen times in earlier questioning that Moore did *not* know.

DOJ Requesting Others to Commit Perjury

That was not the end of the prosecutor's misuse of prosecutorial power. He prepared a statement for one of Moore's employees, Frank Bray, to sign, stating that Moore knew about the bribes. When the employee refused to sign, the DOJ prosecutor threatened to charge him with perjury.

Moore, one of America's naive public, said: "I did not believe this could happen to somebody like me in America. I'm a patriot, businessman. I got to the pinnacle of my success and these guys used criminal statutes to bring me down when I hadn't done anything." Moore lost his company and was put into a state of poverty.

True to form, the DOJ Office of Professional Responsibility held that the prosecutor's conduct was acceptable. Robert Bennett, one of Moore's attorneys (who later represented President Bill Clinton) called the DOJ conduct "an outrageous and shameful exercise of prosecutorial power, frighteningly abused."

Moore's Attorney Sued the Government

Moore was fortunate in finding a law firm that was willing to sue the government on a contingency fee basis. The Cleveland firm of Jones, Day, Reavis and Pogue agreed to file suit on a contingency basis, filing the case in a Texas court seeking $30 million in damages. The lawsuit charged that the DOJ prosecutor Valder brought the suit because Moore had criticized the government. The lawsuit charged that the DOJ prosecutor and postal inspectors with multiple offenses: pressured witnesses to give perjured testimony; withheld evidence showing Moore's innocence; provided false, misleading, or incomplete evidence to the grand jury, and concealed or destroyed exculpatory evidence. The lawsuit charged that the federal prosecutor told postal inspectors he didn't care if Moore was guilty or not, and wanted to obtain a high-profile indictment to further his own career.

In response, the DOJ argued that the government was absolutely immune for its conduct, no matter how illegal or corrupt. This argument was upheld by the judge protecting the system, who probably also wanted to protect the concurrent judicial immunity that was part of the government-immunity doctrine.

I think back to how I offended powerful people in government. First, as an FAA inspector I tried to expose a pattern of criminal misconduct at United Airlines and within the FAA related to a series of fatal airline crashes. Later, as I sought to expose other criminality documented in my other books. Raw government power was criminally misused against me to silence me and to retaliate against me for exposing the crud.

Preying On Financially Strapped DeLorean

DOJ personnel use these corrupt schemes to prey on those vulnerable due to severe financial problems. They did this with financially ailing carmaker, John DeLorean. DeLorean had no interest in drugs, but government agents set up a scheme and then induced or pressured him to cooperate.

DOJ: Cooperate or your daughter's head will be in a paper bag!

At one point, when DeLorean did not want to go along with the government's scheme, one of the Justice Department's agents seeking to induce him to continue, said, "John, I want you to understand something. If you don't cooperate, your daughter's head will be brought to you in a paper bag!" (Attorneys in the Department of Justice were never known to have any recognizable finesse.)

Fortunately for DeLorean during the 1986 trial, the jury recognized the scheme and acquitted him on the basis that he would not have considered committing a drug offense if government agents had not induced him into it. The jury felt that government agents went after a desperate man to commit an act that he would not otherwise have committed. Bravo for a rare intelligent jury!

Introduce Two People to Each Other—Go to Prison

For arranging a meeting between a drug supplier and a drug dealer, Clarence Aaron was arrested and sentenced to three consecutive life-in-prison sentences. Aaron had no drugs. He had no money. He simply arranged a meeting. For giving testimony against Aaron, DOJ prosecutors dropped charges against the people actually dealing in drugs. If DOJ prosecutors had filed charges against the actual drug traffickers and none testified for the government, they might have been acquitted. But by having the real drug traffickers testify against an innocent person, at least the Justice Department can get a guilty verdict from the jury in most cases.

Watch Your Friends

A drug sting instigated by a friend who faced federal prosecution for another drug offense caused an 18-year-old boy, Joey Settembrino—who had never committed an offense—to be sentenced to ten years in prison without parole. His friend had been arrested earlier, and the DOJ prosecutor offered reduction in charges if he would implicate others. Settembrino became the target. The friend asked Settembrino to get him LSD, which was done, and a DEA agent was waiting to arrest him. The joint conspiracy using the DEA agent worked: Settembrino went to prison, the DEA agent got his reward, and the friend who was into drugs had charges dropped.

DOJ Paying Witnesses to Engage in A Conspiracy and Lie

DOJ agents paid former lobbyist Ron Cobb, who had been arrested on drug charges in 1989, $4000 a month and a $150,000 bonus if he could assist in targeting state legislators in South Carolina. Cobb then lied in an effort to bring about the conviction of several targeted legislators. Cobb lied to a federal grand jury with full knowledge of Justice Department prosecutors. U.S. District judge Falcon Hawkins dismissed the charges in 1997, stating:

The breadth and scope of the government's misconduct and the involvement of the FBI during this entire incident was and is shocking. Most offensive to this court is that the government sat silent when it knew that its silence would not only fail the efforts of the defendants to fully develop defenses to which they were entitled, but would misrepresent facts to both the grand jury and the trial court, and mislead the court to such an extent as to affect its rulings. This silence is subornation of perjury.

Violate A Technical Business Requirement—Go to Prison

A check is placed in the mail and this invokes the mail fraud statute if any of the thousands of government technical requirements are violated. Eugene Kent learned about this the hard way. Mail fraud charges were filed against him for co-mingling money in a self-insurance fund his insurance company had set up for a number of South Dakota banks. No money was lost or misplaced; it was *technical violation*. Kent hadn't done anything vicious or with the intent to defraud. Company funds were casually placed in the same account as the reserve funds. The jurors acquitted Kent of all charges except the mail fraud, and this opened the door for a prison sentence.

He might not have been indicted except for the fact that during grand jury testimony a government agent gave perjured testimony. The lying government agent did not suffer any consequences. When Kent later discovered this fact and filed a motion for a new trial, the judge refused to grant it, stating that the information withheld from him by the DOJ should have been raised during the trial. Kent went to prison, and this was followed by the usual financial and personal tragedies, including family breakup.

Employee Charged for Crimes Committed by Boss

Another way that your world can come tumbling down is to be an employee in a business where, unknown to you, there is drug activity. The boss is arrested and given a chance to implicate others, thereby giving the prosecutor a witness to back up the charges. Suddenly, *you* are charged with being a drug kingpin based upon the perjured testimony of the *real* drug kingpin!

Here is another example. Norberto Guerra and Ramon Jimenez worked on a boat that brought drugs into the United States. They suspected something like that was going on but had no role in it. DOJ prosecutors first charged their bosses—who were bringing in the drugs—with drug-related offenses. When the evidence against the real drug traffickers was difficult to track down, DOJ prosecutors made the real drug traffickers a deal. Justice Department prosecutors used the known perjured testimony of the actual drug traffickers—Raul Sanchez who brought tons of cocaine into the United States and also confessed to two murders, and convicted murderer, Leonardo Alvarez—against the two employees. They were charged with being the kingpins responsible for bringing almost four tons of cocaine into the United States.

DOJ Fraudulently Withholding Exculpatory Evidence

Despite repeated requests by defense attorneys to turn over information about their witnesses, the requests were improperly refused. DOJ attorneys fraudulently stated they had no information. Sanchez failed a lie-detector test, which was withheld from defense attorneys. It was later learned that DOJ agents and prosecutors had destroyed hundreds of pages relating to interviews and data on their key witness, Sanchez. During trial, Sanchez falsely stated that he had not received any promise of leniency in return for his testimony. That was perjury, and the DOJ personnel hearing it aided and abetted it by remaining silent.

Don't Anger Department of Justice Employees

Lawyer Patrick Duffy said, as he defended archaeologist Peter Larson in South Dakota, "Don't anger the Department of Justice." Larson had obtained authorization from a property owner to search for what he found, the skeleton of a fossil. He had paid the ranch owner for the find and then *donated* it to the Black Hills Institute of Geological Research. DOJ prosecutors then stepped in, claiming the person who gave Duffy permission to search for fossils had placed his property in trust with the federal government and the government agents now claimed the fossil belonged to the government. That fossil would never have been found except for the diggings by Duffy. Duffy appealed this claim to federal courts, without success. For having fought the matter in court—which Duffy warned could result in DOJ retaliation—DOJ prosecutors charged Larson with a federal offense which ended up with a two-year prison sentence. For a fossil!

Escort Service Owner Refuses to Conspire With DEA—Goes to Prison for Ten Years

Robin Marie Head ran an "escort service" in Austin and Houston, Texas, the type found in large cities throughout the United States, which most police departments ignore. She was approached by ATF, DEA and FBI agents seeking to have her become an informant and give them the names of her clients. They wanted to blackmail political figures and judges, influence elections and court cases, and engage in extortion. The agents were particularly interested in obtaining information on critics of President Bill Clinton. Further, they wanted to become co-owners with her in her business.

Head told them the only way she could reveal the names would be through a court order. Angered at this defiance, federal agents started harassing her, making threatening phone calls, and finally after a year of this, federal agents charged her with operating an organized criminal activity (i.e., running an "escort service").

Head said that they went after her son, and made life miserable for him. After she was sent to prison, her phone lines were taken over by government agents who lured her former customers to another escort service controlled by covert government agents.

Several of my deep-cover sources have told me over the years that many escort services (and adult movie or porn shops) are fronts for the CIA and other government agencies, and they particularly described their contacts with escort services in the San Francisco area and adult movie operations in San Diego.

Head described how undercover agencies "lure young naive females into doing overseas drug smuggling in order to bust them, thereby holding these young ladies under submission."

She said one of the ATF agents, Mike Taylor, who was involved in the attack upon the Waco Davidian group, threatened her. She said her court-appointed attorney sabotaged her defense, warning her that he would file habitual criminal charges against her if she did not plead guilty. She said that her attorney repeatedly said, "I will see that you get the life sentence that you deserve." She explained:

> This is a very tight organization of old time good-old-boys. It is very elite and includes all the heavies and power people. They want more power; i.e. election fraud, more judicial control, etc. This clique is greedy and vile to the core. They will kill, or pay to have someone killed. This elite gang also includes attorney Richard Racehorse Haynes and the like. They are the backbone of Texas, true power, and they want more.

In describing the arrogance of the ATF agents, she described an incident in which they shot the owner of a topless club because he demanded they pay the $5 cover charge, and then put the owner in jail, which was followed by getting the IRS after him.

Government-Entrapped Victim Received Greater Sentence Than Murderer Who Killed His Wife on Their Honeymoon

Out of a job, a government informant named Scott had been busted on drug charges. DOJ prosecutors offered him a reduction in sentence if he could find someone else to charge. Scott then pressured a friend, Staufer, to find LSD for him, something that Staufer had not done before. Staufer had no money to finance such a transaction, but government agents took care of that. At first, Staufer could not get enough LSD to satisfy the prosecutor who was seeking to send him to prison for a much longer term. The informant kept pressuring Staufer until he was able to find a supplier who would sell him the larger amount on consignment. Staufer was then arrested by the government agents who developed, funded, and coordinated the entire conspiracy.

A Los Angeles judge sentenced Michael Staufer to the mandatory 12-year prison sentence. The judge lamented that the Court of Appeals had just over-turned a life sentence that he gave to a man who killed his wife by throwing her overboard on a honeymoon ship cruise. He was now required, by law passed by Congress, to give the 21-year old Staufer a longer sentence than the murderer received.

Casual Statement to FBI Agent on Beach—Go to Prison

U.S. Attorney Joseph Russoniello at San Francisco charged U.S. District Judge Robert P. Aguilar (June 1989) with misusing his judicial position in a racketeering enterprise (RICO) and obstructing justice. What were the charges based upon?

- He allegedly made false statements to an FBI agent while Aguilar was sitting on the beach in his swimsuit at Waikiki during a Hawaiian vacation.
- He gave legal advice to an attorney friend to use in defending Aguilar's brother-in-law.
- He told his brother-in-law not to call him because the brother-in-law's phone might be tapped.

The *real* reason for prosecuting Aguilar for these relatively minor matters was that Aguilar often disagreed with the Justice Department prosecutors in judicial proceedings. Aguilar halted the deportation of refugees that Justice Department attorneys wanted deported. He also once engaged in a heated argument with U.S. Attorney Russoniello in open court, threatening Russoniello with contempt of court. No one was harmed by Aguilar's acts and he made no money or profited in any way.

Accountant Makes an Error on *Your* Tax Form: *You* Go to Prison

Another judge targeted by Justice Department prosecutors (1986) was U.S. District Judge Harry Claiborne in Las Vegas. Prosecutors charged Claiborne with bribery and other offenses related to failure to properly show expenses on his income tax statement. Claiborne's accountant had failed to list the profit made on one of several real estate transactions on Claiborne's income tax report. Claiborne had rendered decisions unfavorable to the Justice Department in the past. This retaliatory prosecution removed Claiborne from a position where he could oppose DOJ prosecutors. It also sent a warning to other judges who might not be sufficiently cooperative with DOJ prosecutors.

Justice Department prosecutors used Nevada brothel owner Joseph Conforte, who had been sentenced to prison, to testify against Claiborne. In return, DOJ prosecutors promised Conforte that charges would be dropped against him. Conforte had been sentenced for income tax evasion, compounded with bail-jumping charges for fleeing to Brazil where he was presently located. By giving false testimony, Conforte would have his prison sentence dropped, would retain his otherwise forfeitable assets, and be granted immunity for perjury.

DOJ Threat Against Members of Congress

The mere investigation by the FBI, DEA or any other division of the Department of Justice can cause a member of the U.S. Senate or House to lose an election. Justice Department employees can easily fabricate charges, especially conspiracy charges, which can be almost fabricated out of thin air, and your career is destroyed.

Possibly the fear of what Justice Department employees can do was one of the reasons every member of Congress to whom I brought evidence of government corruption during the past 30 years refused to respond. But this was no excuse for aiding and abetting the criminal activities. They had a duty under federal criminal statutes and by their position to perform their congressional oversight duties or responsibilities. When they accepted their position, they assumed the responsibilities that went with the pay, the perks, and the prestige. If they were too cowardly to perform, they should have resigned. Dream on!

Dangerous For Defense Attorneys to Vigorously Defend Clients Against the Justice Department

In the San Francisco area, Justice Department prosecutor Anthony White, displeased with attorney Clarence Hallinan's vigorous defense of his clients against Justice Department charges, used one of Hallinan's clients, Ciro Wayne Mancuso, to make false charges against the attorney. Mancuso had been convicted earlier of income tax fraud and fled to South America. Justice Department prosecutors offered Mancuso a deal: release from the prison sentence, dropping of forfeiture actions against $600,000 in a Swiss bank account, and Mancuso could keep over $4 million in property that would otherwise have been seized. In exchange, Mancuso would have to testify as DOJ prosecutors wanted him to testify, against Hallinan. An additional plus for Mancuso: DOJ would immunize him against the perjured testimony. He couldn't lose.

Jurors with Greater "Street Smarts" Than Most

Fortunately, the jury in Reno had more street smarts than most jurors, especially middle class jurors who shield themselves from unpleasant realities. They didn't believe the DOJ prosecutor, and they didn't believe the DOJ's paid witness. The jury found Hallinan not guilty (*United States v. Hallinan*, CRN-39-HDM Nevada). In 1996, Mancuso's lawyers appealed his sentence claiming that DOJ's prosecutor White had promised that he would not get any prison time if he testified against Hallinan.

Apply For Loan, Embellish Details—Go to Prison

Here is a trick by which Justice Department employees can prey on almost any adult and put almost *anyone* in prison. You submit a loan application and somewhere in the many details you exaggerate your income, your length of employment, your assets, or some other information. People are prosecuted and sentenced to prison on this minor matter all the time.

It doesn't matter that you have made your payments on time, that no one suffers any loss, that the lender is happy, or even that the loan has already been paid off. Thousands of government agents and informants comb through records in financial institutions, in pawn shops, in gun shops, looking for technical violations with which they can charge some luckless man or woman with a federal crime. Any ambitious prosecutor, government agent, or informant, can go over old loan records and find where you or your wife, or anyone who co-signs with you, even your aged parents, exaggerated some part of your application, and charge all of you with offenses that can send each of you to prison. I've met people who suffered like that for the last 12 years.

Let's add a little more reality to the above scenario. You've already committed this "crime," maybe 20 years ago. During the night, a paramilitary force breaks down the door to your home, the thugs terrorize your family, ransack your home, destroy furniture. If you happen to suspect they are criminals and appear with a gun, you may be shot dead. You are hauled off in chains, and your neighbors think you are guilty of some major crime; they think, *surely* the government wouldn't do something like this if you weren't guilty of a heinous offense! This is not far-fetched; I've met people who were sent to prison under these same conditions.

Threatening an Aged Parent or Wife to Obtain Confession

This culture preys on everyone. If you refuse to plead guilty, they have another trick to play on you. Your wife, mother, or some other member of your family is threatened with criminal charges if you don't plead guilty. It doesn't matter that you are innocent; that's the last thought that would enter the minds of the Department of Justice gang. The "government" that you previously thought would *never* do such things has been doing them for years. Wake up; it happens all the time. And it happens because the uninformed and apathetic Americans let it happen.

Refuse to Lie for the Department Of Justice—Go to Prison!

A federal judge sentenced a young lady to federal prison (1989) for failure to remember details of stock transactions that happened several years earlier while she was a stock broker for Drexel Burnham Lambert (which incidentally had and maybe still does have, CIA connections). Lisa Jones, a 24-year-old dropout and runaway who became financially successful at the Wall Street investment firm of Drexel, was one of the first witnesses called by Justice Department attorneys investigating insider trading and other security violations at Drexel. Her sense of honesty and integrity prevented her from fabricating the testimony requested by Justice Department attorneys. And for refusing to lie, she paid a heavy price.

In retaliation for refusing to lie, Justice Department attorneys charged her with perjury and obstruction of justice, resulting in an eighteen-month prison sentence. She was paraded in chains from prison to prison, a standard humiliation inflicted by arrogant government personnel misusing the raw power of government. Prison transportation for a woman is especially hard, traveling in chains and the subject of leers and snide remarks by male inmates.

After all this, Drexel's attorneys sued the young lady for payment of legal fees that Drexel had agreed to pay. In response to Drexel's claim that they would sue Ms. Jones for the amount of money that they had advanced, San Francisco attorney Daniel Bookin stated: "It is inconceivable to me that Drexel would sue Lisa after all that she's gone through, and in view of her serious psychological problems. All issues of compassion and decency aside, however, one simple fact seems certain: Lisa has virtually no assets; she could not even begin to repay the cost of her legal representation."

Sacramento Real Estate Developer Refused to Lie: Goes To Prison

Another example in the same judicial district: Justice Department prosecutors charged a Sacramento area real estate developer, Marcel Cordi, with a federal crime for refusing to falsely testify against a bank officer whom Justice Department prosecutors wanted to convict. Sacramento U.S. Attorney David Levi wanted Marcel to testify against a bank official and alter the facts in his testimony. Marcel was willing to testify, but would not lie to enable Justice Department prosecutors to falsely convict the person. In retaliation for refusing to commit perjury, U.S. Attorney Levi charged Marcel with fraud based upon an incorrect statement on a prior loan application relating to his length of employment.

Contempt Of Court for Reporting Government Corruption
That Included Justice Department and Judicial Coverups

Levi charged me with contempt of court in 1987, retaliating against me for filing an action in the U.S. District Court at Sacramento seeking to report to a federal judge serious criminal activities that I and several of my CIA assets had discovered. This report to a federal judge (or other federal officer) is mandatory under the clearly worded requirements of federal criminal statute, Title 18 USC Section 4. Levi and Judge Milton Schwartz refused to receive our evidence. In retaliation for seeking to make such reports, they charged me and prosecuted me for criminal contempt of court for seeking to present such evidence, based upon an earlier order that barred me from federal court for the remainder of my life: an obviously unlawful and unconstitutional order. In the process, they also violated the constitutional right to a jury trial which ended up in a Kangaroo Court trial and sentence. Details on this matter can be found in the third editions of *Unfriendly Skies* and *Defrauding America*.

Levi's conduct may have played a role in his appointment in 1992 to a federal judgeship, where he is now a U.S. District Judge in Sacramento. It is standard practice to appoint Justice Department officials who "cooperate" to the federal bench, increasing the probability of Justice Department prosecutors prevailing in court.

Aircraft Broker Sells Airplane, Refused To Lie—Goes to Prison

A Memphis aircraft broker sold an aircraft to a customer who later used it to fly drugs. The aircraft broker had no way of knowing the background of the buyer or how the plane was to be used—nor was he required to become an investigator. Later, when federal authorities arrested drug traffickers and were building a case against the suspects, they requested the aircraft broker to fabricate testimony to assist in obtaining convictions. The broker was willing to testify, but had enough integrity that he wasn't going to lie. Justice Department attorneys retaliated, charging him with misprision of a felony (Title 18 USC Section 4) on the basis that he failed to report to federal authorities the aircraft was to be used in unlawful activities. (Strange, I was charged with contempt of court for reporting high-level government corruption which I sought to report under the same statute!)

The aircraft broker was subsequently put on trial with 32 other defendants, some of whom *were* guilty of drug-related offenses. Without competent legal counsel to provide an adequate defense, and unsophisticated, lazy, or naive jurors who accepted the "government's" charges as true, the aircraft broker was held guilty under the conspiracy statute and sentenced to five years in federal prison. He never committed a crime.

He, and the others listed here, and the thousands of others not listed here who were innocent, provided figures showing the "success" of the Congressional legislation and the public's "feel-good" response to crime.

Suicide Induced By Federal Tactics

There are other unfortunate consequences to these "feel-good" practices. When that broker was in a county jail near Memphis waiting for trial, he witnessed the fatal consequences of these outrages. His cellmate, Mike Scarlett from Texas, had been enticed by federal agents into making the controlled substance "speed." Knowing that Scarlett was having serious financial problems supporting his family, he was excellent prey. Federal agents encouraged him to produce the drug, taught him how to produce it, financed the operation, and set him up with the equipment and a location.

On the first day Scarlett started to make it, federal agents arrested him, charging him with manufacturing amphetamines that they had induced him to make—and which he would not have made without their coaxing, pressure, assistance, and equipment. He would never have committed the offense if it hadn't been set up for him by these government leeches.

While in prison, Scarlett discovered that his wife was sleeping with one of the federal agents who set him up. The aircraft broker told me that Scarlett was very distraught-looking after phoning his wife. He described how the inmate wrote what was later discovered to be a suicide note. Scarlett hung a bed sheet over the prison bars, as if he wanted privacy for sleeping. Behind the sheet, Scarlett stepped onto the rim of the toilet and tied a strip torn from a bed sheet to a grill near the ceiling. Scarlett then stepped off of the toilet and hung himself.

Forcing Wife into Sex To Avoid Federal Charges

A DEA agent in Northern California reportedly forced a wife to have sex with him and then testify against her husband, according to an action filed in the U.S. District Court at San Francisco by attorney J. Tony Serra who specializes in cases involving the underdog. John Dalton was indicted in 1996 for involvement in a marijuana-related conspiracy in the heavy marijuana growing area of Northern California. Testifying against him was his wife, who reportedly had sex with DEA agent Mark Nelson. The DEA agent reportedly encouraged her to tape record her husband's comments about marijuana while they were in bed together. The DEA agent reportedly threatened the woman with money laundering charges if she did not cooperate.

Killing A Nearly Blind Rancher: Another "Success" In the Drug War

A screaming paramilitary force burst into the home of a wealthy and nearly blind rancher, Donald Scott, near Malibu, California (October 2, 1992). Federal personnel had tried to buy the ranch to expand the adjacent Santa Monica Mountains National Recreation Area but Scott, a recluse, partially blinded by recent cataract surgery, didn't want to sell. The multi-agency drug task force of over two dozen heavily armed California and federal agents[42] mounted a military-type assault upon Scott's home late at night. They used the excuse that an informant said there was a field of marijuana spotted from a plane flying over the 200-acre property in the hills above Malibu called Trail's End.

Instead of going to the ranch in a peaceful manner with a search warrant, they conducted a commando-type raid, breaking into Scott's home while he was sleeping, and killed him as he came out of his bedroom. No marijuana plants or drugs were found on his property. There was no reason for this commando-type raid, as there was no need for the element of surprise. If Scott had actually been growing fields of marijuana, he could not suddenly dump it down the toilet. The peaceful serving of a search warrant was all that was necessary.

Investigation showed that the real motive was not a search for drugs, but a desire to seize Scott's ranch under federal forfeiture laws. Scott's wife had been a former drug user and if the slightest speck of drugs could be found on the property, the five million-dollar ranch could be seized under the draconian federal forfeiture laws.

Subsequent investigation revealed that federal agents had obtained a property appraisal before invading Scott's home, showing the value of adjoining property and indicating the desire to seize the property. Federal personnel in charge of the raid advised the attacking agents to look for evidence of drugs so as to justify seizing the property. None of the killers were ever punished.

Multiple Life Sentences for Someone who never saw any Drugs

Peter Hidalgo escaped from Cuba to the United States in the late 1960s and become a boat builder and racer. He, his wife, and small daughter lived in a modest cottage and felt they were in paradise compared to what they left. But that would change in late 1992 as they joined the endless list of victims of Congress' feel-good legislation and DOJ fraud.

Hidalgo had not been part of any drug operation. He had no involvement with drugs. He knew nothing about them. Taped conversations showed his name never appeared in any government surveillance. Drug traffickers, who had already been arrested, were offered release if they implicated someone else. Through fabricated testimony, they testified that Hidalgo was the drug kingpin. Now, Justice Department prosecutors had people willing to testify, so

---

[42] The invaders were from the Los Angeles County sheriff's department, the Los Angeles Police Department, the U.S. Drug Enforcement Administration, National Park Service and California National Guard.

a conviction was more certain and easier to obtain. The people used by DOJ prosecutors to testify against Hidalgo were major drug traffickers and killers. Hidalgo lived a modest life style raising a family.

The Department of Justice reportedly paid one witness $500,000 to testify as the prosecutor wanted him to testify. Another witness against Hidalgo bragged to his cellmates that he had received a substantial reduction in his prison sentence in exchange for lying during trial. One witness, not happy with lying, told his sister he feared for his safety for not being willing to lie. He was found dead shortly thereafter, probably murdered to keep the DOJ scheme from being exposed.

False Confidence in Jurors

Hidalgo felt confident that he would be found innocent. His name never appeared in any of many taped telephone conversations, suggesting his innocence. But Hidalgo didn't realize that it didn't matter that DOJ prosecutors knew he was innocent; they would prosecute anyone to show another conviction on their record. In 1999, in Leavenworth federal prison, Hidalgo was reported to have said, "These people have broke me financially; they broke up my family. The only thing they won't be able to break is my dignity and my principle. If they get me a new trial, I'm gonna show what the government has done, that it's out of control." Lots of luck, Hidalgo, you'll need it!

Sending A Senior Citizen to Prison: $4 Million in Taxes not Enough

Justice Department prosecutors charged Leona Helmsley with evading income taxes and sentenced the 72-year-old woman to four years in federal prison, leaving behind her 81-year-old husband who, at his age, could be dead before her release date. Helmsley's accountants had claimed as business expenses, charges that Justice Department attorneys considered not business related. Helmsley paid over $4 million federal income taxes in the disputed tax year, and the amount owed by the disputed charges was a very small percentage of that amount. Much of the media—who were simultaneously covering up for much of the corruption in government—jeered this lady.

Seeking Incarceration for Playing Chess

Justice Department prosecutors found time in December 1992 to investigate and indict[43] Bobby Fischer for playing a chess game in Yugoslavia, charging him with violating a presidential order barring business relations with communist countries. At the same time, government agents were engaging in all types of criminal activities: gun smuggling, undermining governments, smuggling drugs into the United States, and much more.

Mother of Two Infants: Ten Years for Telephone Conversation

On December 7, 1990, Judge Samuel Conti sentenced a young black girl from Oakland, California—the mother of two infants—to ten years in prison on a drug-related conspiracy charge. The young girl had a telephone conversation with another person concerning the sale of drugs. The conversation never went any further, but federal agents, monitoring the phone call, charged the girl with conspiracy to traffic in drugs. She was in tears when U.S. Marshals

---

[43] Fisher violated a June, 1992 executive order by President George Bush restricting commercial relations with Yugoslavia. The indictment subjected Fisher to ten years in prison and a fine of as much as $250,000. Is it any wonder the United States has the highest percentage of its citizens in prison?

drove her back from the federal court house in San Francisco to the Dublin Federal Detention Center after Judge Conti sentenced her to ten years in a high security prison. As described in the latest edition of *Defrauding America*, this same judge played a major role in blocking my exposure of CIA drug trafficking and other criminal activities.

Pushed Into Government Conspiracy—Go to Prison

In one case, government agents pressured Lorenzo Naranjo for months to purchase cocaine that he would never have done. Naranjo finally succumbed to the pressure and obtained a small quantity. Because the DEA agent wanted the target to be charged with a greater offense, he pressured Naranjo to accept a gun in exchange for the cocaine. The law reads that if a gun is available during a drug offense, the penalty is doubled.

The gun was not used in carrying out the offense, and would not have been there except for the action by the conspiring undercover agents. DOJ employees brought about the crime, provided the gun, and arguably, should have been charged with conspiracy, drug offenses, and the gun offense. Naranjo was charged and a jury convicted him. The DEA agent looked good. The prosecutor chalked up one more conviction. But for Naranjo, his wife, and children, the personal and financial tragedies destroyed the family and inflicted harm from which it will never recover.

Guilty Of Nothing—Ten Years in Prison for Mother Of Five

A mother of five children in Texas drove her boyfriend's van into Mexico and upon returning to the United States she was arrested at the border. Her boyfriend had hidden cocaine in her van without her knowledge. The jury, assuming that Justice Department officials would not prosecute an innocent woman, rendered a decision holding her guilty, causing her to receive a 10-year mandatory minimum sentence. She knew nothing about being used as a "mule."

Force Companies into Bankruptcy—Seize and Loot the Properties

Brief reference is made here to a practice described in the third editions of *Defrauding America* and *Unfriendly Skies*. That is the practice of forcing companies and people with lots of assets into involuntary bankruptcy and then looting everything. The practice of targeting people and companies for the purpose of seizing their assets, by forcing them into bankruptcy, is widely used by CIA operatives who operate jointly with the corrupt attorneys, law firms, Justice Department trustees, and judges, and is rampant throughout the United States.

Government Agents Report Government Corruption—Go to Prison

All three of my books describe government agents who reported high-level government corruption and are then fraudulently charged with criminal offenses. These victims included agents of the FBI, CIA, DEA, INS, Customs, FAA, among others. The felonious retaliation carried out by Department of Justice attorneys against government inspectors and covert agents constitutes obstruction of justice, retaliation against witnesses, and other criminal offenses.

DOJ Lying to Have Sister Testify Against Brother

DOJ prosecutors charged James Rounsavall and his sister, Mary Ann

Rounsavall, with drug-related offenses in 1994. DOJ prosecutor Bruce Gillen tried to get Mary Rounsavall to testify against her brother. When she wouldn't, the prosecutor told her that her brother was dying and that he would be dead within a short time, so she might as well testify against him. Further, she would be recommended for a sentence reduction. Reluctantly, based upon her brother's imminent death, she testified, using testimony given to her by the prosecutor. Her brother was then sentenced to life in prison, their assets seized, and the sentence reduction that she had been promised never came. She was sentenced to 20 years in prison. She later learned that her brother was *not* dying.

Rancher Fills In Mosquito-Breeding Hole—Goes to Prison

Justice Department prosecutors sent Allen Kafkaesque to prison for filling in a mosquito-breeding low spot on his 103-acre ranch. He allowed two loads of dirt to be dumped in the spot as a base for a shed. Federal officials then charged him with filling in "wetlands," which has been made a crime by members of Congress seeking the votes from far-out environmentalists (probably trying to save from extinction some type of cockroach!). DOJ prosecutors sought to have him imprisoned for 27 to 33 months. When the judge reduced the sentence to six months, Justice Department prosecutors appealed, seeking to have Kafkaesque imprisoned for almost three years!

Farmer Files A Crop-Loss Claim—Goes to Prison

A farmer in Illinois, James Catton, filed a crop insurance claim following a very dry year in which his crops suffered heavy damage. This claim was allowed by the insurance provisions. A DOJ prosecutor charged Catton with fraud and at trial a government employee testified that the claim was fraudulent. After the trial, and after the jury convicted Catton, he learned that the government "expert" had never seen his farm—or the adjacent one which suffered the same damage and for which a similar claim had been paid during the same period. This critical information was withheld from the defense and from the jurors. The fraudulent prosecution caused Catton to lose his farm in bankruptcy.

Another Conspiracy Sham—Dentist Ends Up In Prison

In 1980, Dr. John W. Newton, a dentist, was arrested in front of his patients and charged with drug conspiracy. I received a call from a mother who told me how her dentist son was targeted by a DOJ informant. She explained that he had never been anywhere near drugs. Fortunately for him, the jurors were not rubber stamps for the prosecutor and handed down a not-guilty verdict. However, the dental board revoked his license, solely on the word of a government-paid informant in collusion with a DOJ prosecutor. For the next 15 years Newton worked at odd jobs to support his family, which went through terrible financial problems.

In 1996, he managed to get his dental certification back. It was his mother, Margaret Newton, living in Apex, North Carolina, a feisty lady in her eighties who tried to wake up people to the threat posed by government agents, especially in the Department of Justice. She wrote to me stating "Americans are too indifferent and too lazy to be concerned." She was active in promoting the information written in *Defrauding America*. At 80 years of age, she had more courage and character than most people in the United States. A few people like her gave me the inspiration to continue the almost hopeless task of waking up even a small percentage of the American people.

Government Targets Wife of CIA Asset Gunther Russbacher

Rayelan Russbacher, while she was the wife of one of my key CIA sources, Gunther Russbacher, described how she was targeted in a drug-sting operation that would probably have succeeded if she hadn't been far more sophisticated and aware of the Department of Justice fraud than most people.

She had been very vocal as a speaker in helping to expose several major government scandals that are described in *Defrauding America*, starting with her exposure of the October Surprise scandal. She explained how the scam was carried out. Rayelan was called on the phone and asked to meet certain people at a nearby Denny's restaurant who told her they had information about government misconduct that she would want.

She met two men who, during the conversation offered to help her financially if she would sell something for them. She immediately sensed they were talking drugs. Outraged, she got up and with outrage said, "If you want me to sell drugs I'll have nothing to do with it!" She got up from the booth and left the restaurant. If she had stayed, even out of politeness, and allowed the talk to go into drugs, she would probably have been arrested before leaving Denny's on a drug conspiracy charge. It is *that* easy to prey on innocent people and put someone in prison in these United States!

Consequences of Abolishing Paid Testimony

Justice Department prosecutors argued that barring the payment of compensation for testimony would hamper their attacks upon crime. Fewer people will be arrested and incarcerated. "Justification" for the billions of dollars spent in the war-on-drugs will be missing. Bulging government agencies such as the DEA and DOJ would not be justified. Paid informants could not be justified. Surely we can't let that happen!

Innocence Or Guilt Is Of No Concern—The Goal Is Convictions

People not willing to give perjured testimony requested by Justice Department prosecutors often pay the consequences. In some cases the prosecutors have retaliated by using the perjured testimony of the original target against the person refusing to give perjured testimony. Innocence or guilt is of no concern; the prosecutor wants a record of convictions. Perjury is the driving force in many DOJ prosecutions.

Jurors Often Don't Know the Consequences of Their Decisions

Another problem area is the jurors' lack of understanding of the punishment a judge can, or must, hand down after the jury makes a guilty decision. If the jury holds the defendant innocent of all charges except conspiracy that makes possible, or requires, a prison term equal to all charges. Because of their ignorance, laziness, or naiveté, thousands of people go to prison for years or for life. Jurors often express surprise when they hear their guilty verdict resulted in a life-in-prison sentence.

Juries of People with Inadequate Knowledge and Comprehension

Federal grand juries usually consist of 23 people, often people with no understanding of what really goes on in the Justice Department and the criminal justice system. (The same applies to trial juries.) Their low level of understanding legal and criminal matters forces them to rubber-stamp whatever the prosecutor wants, and makes for the reputation that "a grand jury would indict a ham sandwich if requested by the prosecutor." With one or more shills on the jury, the prosecutor can manipulate the jurors to do whatever the prosecutor wants. It takes only a simple majority to bring about an indictment against the person the U.S. attorney seeks to prosecute. Federal prosecutors have great power and can act irresponsibly knowing that they will not suffer any retaliation, as would be suffered by a citizen.

Deputy Attorney General Arnold I. Burns, during President Reagan's tenure, said, "The federal grand jury is no longer a protection of the person who is suspected of crime, it is a vicious tool. The grand jury process today is as far afield from what it was intended to be as it could possibly be."

Congress and DOJ Making Prisons into Future Burial Places

Thousands of people—given life-in-prison sentences—compliments of Congress' feel-good prison sentences and DOJ's put-anyone-in-prison culture, will die in prison. This includes many people who never committed the crimes fabricated against them by DOJ attorneys. They don't realize they are considered prey by DOJ and similar agencies.

Judges Protecting DOJ Corruption

Former New York State prosecutor Bennett Gershman, who taught law at Pace University in New York, wrote the 1997 book, "Prosecutorial Misconduct." He wrote that federal judges had done nothing about the prosecutorial misconduct that continues to inflict such grave harm on people in all walks of life. "They are now simply a rubber stamp," he said, asserting that federal prosecutors know that no matter how bad their misconduct, it is almost impossible for a criminal defendant to sue a federal officer or prosecutor, and this came about due to judicial decisions that subvert civil rights statutes. He said judges know what is going on and excuse their conduct by saying it was the jury's decision, not the judge's.

Occasional Judicial Protest Against Prosecutorial Misconduct

Occasionally, a judge will express concern about the abuses with DOJ use of purchased testimony. In one Ninth Circuit Court of Appeals case at San Francisco, the three-judge panel said in their opinion:

What we find most troubling about this case is not the assistant U.S. Attorney's initial transgression, but that he seemed to be totally unaware he'd done anything at all wrong, and that there was no one in the United States Attorney's office to set him straight. [Could it be that they were all corrupt!] *Nor does the government's considered response, filed after we pointed out the problem, inspire our confidence that this kind of thing won't happen again. How can it be that a serious claim of prosecutorial misconduct remains unresolved--even unaddressed—until oral argument in the Ninth U.S. Court of Appeals? Surely, when such a claim is raised, we can expect that someone in the United States Attorney's office will take an independent, objective look at the issue. Yet, the United States attorney allowed the filing of a brief in our court that did not own up to the problem, a brief that itself skated perilously close to misrepresentation.*

Prosecutor's Immunity From Civil Rights and Criminal Violations

Federal judges—many of them former DOJ prosecutors—have rendered decisions holding that federal prosecutors are immune from the consequences of their acts. This is not what the civil rights statutes say, which have priority over case law, but it is what federal judges have done to protect the system. The San Francisco area legal newspaper, *Daily Journal*, carried an article (September 22, 1994) stating in part:

> *Prosecutorial misconduct is encouraged—if not indirectly condoned—by pervasive judicial abstention and "buck passing." Although appellate courts sometimes threaten to dismiss a case based on prosecutorial misconduct, they rarely do so, either finding the wrongdoing "harmless" or suggesting alternative remedies such as contempt.*
>
> *It is well-documented that in reality there often is no effective sanction for prosecutors who engage in unethical conduct .... This misconduct included violation of grand jury rules, violation of defendants' Fifth and Sixth Amendment rights, knowing presentation of false information to the grand jury, and mistreatment of witnesses. The report documents the fact that the Justice Department effectively ignored the courts' findings of governmental abuse, and that not one of the individuals involved was sanctioned, thereby raising "serious questions regarding what the Department considers "prosecutorial misconduct."*
>
> *There is virtually nothing that an aggrieved party [defendant] can do when a court declines to sanction unethical government conduct, because prosecutors are absolutely immune from suit. In Imbler v. Pactman, 424 U.S. 409, 431 (1976), the Supreme Court ruled that a Los Angeles deputy district attorney who intentionally suborns perjury cannot be sued by the defendant who is wrongfully convicted ... leaves the genuinely wronged defendant without civil redress against a prosecutor whose malicious or dishonest action deprives him of liberty, the Supreme Court, quoting an earlier case, decided that it is "better to leave unredressed wrongs done by dishonest officers than to subject those who try to do their duty to the constant dread of retaliation."*

Similar reasoning is used by judges to hold *themselves* immune from their wrongful and sometimes criminal acts. They argue that to hold judges liable for unlawful acts would dampen the judicial spirit. Federal statutes have priority over judge-made case law, and give citizens the right to sue *anyone* who violates their civil or constitutional rights. And in the English language, that includes judges.

DOJ Prosecutors Grinding Up People

Former U.S. Attorney General Ramsey Clark said that the impact of prosecutors withholding exculpatory evidence is especially bad because it impacts defendants who can't pay for high priced lawyers to uncover withheld evidence. Both Gershman and Clark said that this prosecutorial misconduct has gotten worse over the years, which parallels the worsening government corruption that I have documented for the past 30 years. Clark said, "It is really tragic how we grind up poor people in these situations."

Misnamed Division—DOJ Office of Professional Responsibility

Another misnamed government office, a division of the Department of Justice, is its Office of Professional Responsibility (OPR), which has the responsibility of investigating misconduct in the Department of Justice. Instead of meeting the trust, it has functioned to *cover up* such misconduct, aiding and abetting it, and in some cases, it constitutes obstruction of justice. In any event, innocent people are continuing to be prey for corrupt Justice Department prosecutors.

Extension of Legal Fraternity Culture into Prosecutor Role

Decades of experience working with attorneys, in and out of government, part of it detailed and documented in my other books, makes if easy to understand how the sleaze in the legal fraternity surfaces in the prosecutor's office. With an almost unlimited power to inflict harm upon people, the prosecutor's position provides the power to satisfy the mentality of many attorneys.

Among the Congressmen Openly Approving These Outrages

Almost all members of Congress openly or tacitly approve the outrages described in this and my other books. Congressman Bill McCollum (R-Fl) said as he approved of these outrages: "I am much more concerned about the loss of life to drugs and to the crime that's going on out there and the need to stop it and protect our innocents and our citizens than I am about anybody's concern over [the abuses arising from] informants." McCollum was one of the members of Congress covering up for the CIA drug trafficking and other high-level government crimes.

I have no problem with the judicial system in regard to what we're doing. We're trying to lock up people, most of them very bad people who are causing a problem. Ninety-three percent of those who are in our state prisons for drug dealing are there because of violent offenses or they're there for multiple offenses, and almost all of the people who are there in the system for cocaine trafficking are there for large quantities. So I think we're doing the right thing by what we're doing in our federal law enforcement system.

There are very few people in jails today in the United States who didn't deal in large quantities of the drugs. Occasionally you'll run into somebody that's in there on a conspiracy charge because that's the easiest way to get them convicted, but that doesn't mean they haven't committed multiple offenses. They're violent offenders with a long track record—look at their histories. There are very few people in there who did not have substantial drug trafficking histories before they were ever put away, and for those that are there, they're there usually because the prosecutor has tried to get them to cooperate and they've refused to squeal on somebody who is higher up.

Senator Jeff Sessions (R-Ala), former U.S. Attorney, said of the drug laws, and with a straight face: "I think what we tried to do is give the taxpayers the best return on their dollar. The prosecutors do a good job."

In response to the question, "Isn't it a problem that conspiracy law allows innocent people to be convicted on testimony alone?"

That's a theoretical problem; that's not reality. People do not testify against innocent people; they only testify against guilty people. I have not found that to be a problem. Innocent people are not getting convicted under this on any kind of routine basis.

Double Standard Between the Public and Those In Power

One of Senator Richard Shelby's constituents, Jerry Lundy, wrote a letter to the senator asking for his help on behalf of Lundy's son who was sentenced to 30 years in prison on drug charges when the son never had any drugs, never was near any drugs, and sentenced solely on the purchased testimony coerced by DOJ prosecutors. That witness later recanted his testimony and made out an affidavit describing how he was coerced and threatened by DOJ prosecutors to provide the perjured testimony. The father was seeking the senator's help. Senator Shelby responded:

We must take a strong stand against drugs, and I support strict punishment for individuals involved in the possession or distribution of illegal drugs. I believe that our nation's drug problem is serious enough to warrant harsh sentences.

But when it came to his own son, his position took a complete reversal. The senator's son, Claude Shelby, was arrested upon arriving by plane at Atlanta's Hartfield Airport with 13.8 grams of hashish. Shelby applied the proper pressure in the right places and instead of a long prison sentence, the charges were reduced to a simple misdemeanor and an order to pay a $500 administrative fine. Without the senator's involvement, his son would probably be a prison inmate with a long prison sentence.

Series of Pittsburgh Post-Gazette Investigative Articles

The *Pittsburgh Post-Gazette* ran a ten-part series of articles written by investigative journalist Bill Moushey in November and December 1998 titled, "Win At All Costs—Government Misconduct in the Name of Expedient Justice." The titles on these articles tell much about what was found during the two-year investigation. The paper wrote a synopsis of what was discovered during the past year and printed in the articles:

About this series: Hundreds of times during the past 10 years, federal agents and prosecutors have pursued justice by breaking the law. They lied, hid evidence, distorted facts, engaged in coverups, paid for perjury and set up innocent people in a relentless effort to win indictments, guilty pleas and convictions, a two-year Post-Gazette investigation found.

Rarely were these federal officials punished for their misconduct. New laws and court rulings encourage federal law enforcement officers to press the boundaries of their power while providing few safeguards against abuse. Victims of this misconduct sometimes lost their jobs, assets and even families. Some remain in prison because prosecutors withheld favorable evidence or allowed fabricated testimony. Some criminals walk free as a reward for conspiring with the government in its effort to deny others their rights.

Air Force Veteran Discovered America's Domestic Enemies

In the first article, Moushey describes the plight of Air Force veteran, Loren Pogue, who was sentenced to 22 years in prison on a drug conspiracy and money laundering charge. Pogue had never used drugs. He was never near them. He did not buy or sell them. It was another setup preying on people unaware of the scheming tactics by Justice Department attorneys.

Pogue had sold land to a government informant who later testified that Pogue knew he was a drug smuggler, which was a lie. DOJ prosecutors then used the drug smuggler's testimony to charge Pogue under the catchall feel-good drug conspiracy and drug money laundering statutes. A jury found him guilty. But he was guilty of nothing! The government agents involved in the conspiracy—and a conspiracy is a federal crime—escaped punishment and received bonuses for their corrupt activities. Pogue, sentenced to prison at the age of 65, will probably die in prison, never again to see any of his 15 adopted children. Pogue is baffled that the government for whom he served in the military for 30 years would betray him like that.

It is time—long overdue—for millions of American vets to wake up to the threat from within that is inflicting *more harm* on people in the United States than any foreign country has ever done. It is time for them to start doing something helpful for the country rather than parading around in military gatherings or having reunions!

Apply For Government Contract—Go to Prison

In one of the cases described in the *Pittsburgh Post Gazette* series, FBI agent John Clifford, using the alias of Hal Francis, approached Dale Brown, a small manufacturer offering products for sale to the government in the space industry. The FBI agent told Brown that he had developed a product that NASA might want to buy which he described as an ultrasound device.

The FBI's scheme was to trap small business people seeking to sell products to the government space program. The FBI agent told Brown and several other manufacturers that the product was proven reliable and provided pictures and documents to support that statement. Everything looked professional and on the up-and-up.

When Brown and several others entered into an agreement with the undercover FBI agent to promote the device, FBI agents filed charges against them for trying to sell a known phony device to the government. After indictments were handed down by the grand jury against the 15 defendants, FBI agents pressured all but two to plead guilty, warning them that if they tried to fight the charge they would end up with long prison terms, large fines, property seizures, and family humiliation.

FBI Agent Francis testified that Brown (and the other defendant who fought the charge) knew that the device he was trying to sell to the government was phony and this amounted to fraud against NASA for trying to win contracts for a bogus product. The undercover agent paid Brown $500 for expenses to promote the product and then fraudulently claimed this was bribe money which Brown accepted.

Serious Physical Consequences of False DOJ Charges

In fighting the charges, Brown suffered a massive heart attack requiring complex surgery, and was on life-support system the day he was indicted by DOJ agents. Brown said, "I lost my fiancee, my health, my cars, my house, was forced into bankruptcy and underwent two open-heart surgeries, intestinal surgery and brain surgery because of a massive stroke due to the stress." Quite a change from a former skydiver and athletic person. Brown explained, "The government agents intentionally and methodically drove our companies and personal bank accounts to zero and drove our reputation to ruin."

Brown filed a lawsuit against the government, which a federal judge promptly dismissed, claiming federal "law enforcement" officers are immune from civil lawsuits, despite the gravity or illegality of the actions perpetrated by the federal employees.

DOJ Prosecutors Providing Perjured Testimony to Mob Figure

The *Pittsburgh Post-Dispatch* described the case of crime figure John Pree who admitted that "FBI agents approached him and asked him to lie to help win indictments against more than a dozen reputed Detroit-area gangsters." Pree described how government agents provided him information concerning several crimes and the murder of a Detroit gangster so that he could plead guilty to being part of them, bring about the conviction of others, and then he would quietly be released from prison shortly thereafter. Pree said government agents promised him a new identity, monthly compensations, and cash. He admitted he had never met some of the people with whom he was to have committed the crimes and against whom he would be testifying. Pree failed several polygraph tests given to him by DOJ employees before the trial, but they used him anyhow. During the trial, he failed to identify one of the defendants with whom he allegedly committed some of the crimes.

DOJ Generating Crimes Where None Would Otherwise Exist

The *1998 Pittsburgh Post Gazette* articles described how government agents set up crime scenes that generate "crimes" when they otherwise would not exist. Government agents—under control of DOJ personnel—brought sham charges against innocent people and exaggerated charges against others. The series said, "Time after time, former criminals, con artists, dope smugglers, perjurers, and killers were employed to help catch suspects in exchange for reduced sentences or even six figure payoffs. With straight faces, prosecutors insist in court that none of these witnesses have an incentive to lie."

Human Tragedies from Lying Government Informants

Paramilitary forces break into homes based upon false information given by government informants who must justify their compensation. This happened to Don Carlson (1992) as a military-like force invaded his San Diego-area home after an informant, being paid $2000 a month, made up a story about drugs. When the agents stormed Carlson's home in the middle of the night, he shot through the door, thinking they were criminals. The government agents shot back, shooting him in the back.

The *Pittsburgh Post-Gazette* article described what happened:

That arrangement [between confidential informants] can prove slippery. This investigation found dozens of cases where agents became so close to their informers that they crossed the line—sometimes assisting them in their criminal activities or protecting them, or even joining them and sharing in the profits of their crimes.

Released Murderers and Drug Traffickers Returning To Old Habits

The one-year investigation by the *Pittsburgh Post Gazette* revealed criminals released from prison under the Witness Security Program have gone on to commit hundreds of crimes, many of them violent, and over 20 murders. The study showed that most criminals released from prison under this program revert to their old habits. And this includes murder.

PBS Series Documented the Personal Tragedies

In the latter part of 1998, PBS ran a television documentary entitled "Snitch," describing the conspiracy between government agents and government informants. The human tragedies followed along the line exposed in the *Pittsburgh Post-Gazette* series.

District Attorneys Lie and Conceal Evidence to Win Cases

A January 11, 1999, article in the *Chicago Tribune* was titled, "Study: DA's Lie, Conceal Evidence to Win Cases" and stated in part:

Of 381 verdicts overturned, 67 defendants had faced execution. With impunity, prosecutors across the country have violated their oaths and the law, committing the worst kinds of deception in the most serious of cases. They have prosecuted black men, hiding evidence the real killers were white. They have prosecuted a wife, hiding evidence her husband committed suicide. They have prosecuted parents, hiding evidence their daughter was killed by wild dogs. They do it to win. They do it because they won't get punished. They have done it to defendants who came within hours of being executed, only to be exonerated. In the first study of its kind, a Chicago Tribune analysis of thousands of court records, appellate rulings and lawyer disciplinary records from across the United States has found repeated instances of prosecutors hiding evidence showing the defendant was innocent, allowing them to receive long prison sentences or even death sentences.

National Law Journal Investigation

An investigation continuing for almost a year, and reported in the *National Law Journal* (NLJ), stated in part:

Abuses by informants and law enforcement threaten the rights and the safety of innocent people, as well as the integrity of the courts. The war on drugs is the engine driving this development. New forfeiture laws have made drug busts a law enforcement prize, generating lots of cash both to pay informants and to increase their own operating budget. Mandatory sentencing laws and crushing prison terms adopted in the 1980s have created powerful incentives for criminals to go to any lengths to avoid jail.

The NLJ study showed the federal government paid over $100 million a year to informants, making this a cottage industry exceeding the outrages inflicted by Adolf Hitler's SS Guards. It was rare that Hitler's informants were motivated by profit and lying, as exists in America today.

Judicial Warning About DOJ Witnesses

Judge Stephen S. Trott, a judge on the Ninth Circuit Court of Appeals in San Francisco, said during a lecture to federal prosecutors:

Criminals are likely to say and do almost anything to get what they want, especially when what they want is to get out of trouble with the law. This willingness to do anything includes not only truthfully spilling the beans on friends and relatives, but also lying, committing perjury, manufacturing evidence, soliciting others to corroborate their lies with more lies and double-crossing anyone with whom they come into contact....Career criminals acting as informants are remarkably manipulative and skillfully devious, playing on the investigators' inexperience, laziness or unchecked ambition to generate cases that will get them off the hook.

U.S. District Judge Marvin Shoob in Atlanta said, "Informants are sometimes worse criminals than the defendants on trial."

Former veteran DEA agent Celerino Castillo said:

Informers are running today's drug investigations; not the agents. They are paid two or three times as much as the agents, and agents have become so dependent on informers that the agents are at their mercy....All of the federal law agencies, and DEA in particular, have been hiring agents out of college with no previous investigative experience. These are people who have never been street-trained on how to deal with informants. That's where the problem is coming from. The federal agents have allowed the informants to take over investigations, and the agents don't make a move without getting approval from their informants. Our rights as citizens and the United States Constitution are now in the hands of a group of about 15,000 wild out-of-control informants. If you get in their way, they will take you down, and the agents are ignorant enough or lazy enough to let them do it.

Frontline Interviews

The television program *Frontline* questioned U.S. Attorney J. Don Foster in the Southern District of Alabama, concerning the use of paid informants. Without batting an eye, the Justice Department prosecutor said he would continue to use purchased testimony as long as it was truthful. But prosecutors don't care if the testimony is truthful. On the contrary, DOJ prosecutors often coach witnesses on what to say, making it clear that if they don't make those statements under oath, they will not receive any compensation.

When asked, "How do you know that they are testifying truthfully," the prosecutor replied with a straight face: "We try to evaluate based on experience and based on careful examination, based on corroboration." When asked, "Does the jury know that they are benefiting from their testimony," the prosecutor answered, with tongue in cheek no doubt: "It's hard to make up a story that fools twelve people."

As to the practice of allowing witnesses to share the same prison cell prior to testifying, so as to compare notes and synchronize their stories, the prosecutor responded: "If the judge tells them not to talk and they talk, they're in violation of the judge's order, and the judge does tell them not to talk with each other, does tell them not to tell each other what they have testified to." Either Foster had been living on another planet since birth, or he is a gifted liar. My belief is the latter.

Prisoners Seeking Release On Perjured Testimony Are Honest?

When the questioner asked in disbelief, "You count on this admonition," Foster replied: "I think that's a very important admonition. I think federal judges make an impact on witnesses. And witnesses try to do the right thing. And they try to obey the judge's orders, I believe."

A particular case was mentioned, in which a person received a life sentence based solely on the uncorroborated testimony of a paid witness. The witness stated that he delivered nine kilograms of cocaine, with no evidence other than that. Based on this type of "evidence," anyone in the United States can be imprisoned for life, on perjured and purchased testimony. It happens all the time!

Informant Admits What Everyone Knows—They Lie for DOJ

Appearing on a *Frontline* documentary was an informant using the alias, Tony, with his faced blacked out. He admitted lying to get out of prison. He admitted the Department of Justice prosecutor told him the testimony he would have to give against the defendant. He stated that when he initially refused to give the false testimony, the Justice Department arrested his mother and brother. After this was done, he then gave the perjured testimony that the prosecutor wanted him to give. Tony admitted the people he testified against were absolutely innocent. But he said, given the alternative of 30 years to life in prison, he was forced to do this, another crime that would not have been perpetrated if Department of Justice attorneys had not brought it about.

Which of Two Defendants Will Lie To Avoid Life in Prison?

Another informant, Ronald Rankins, appeared on the show, describing how DOJ prosecutor Donna Barrows pressured him to give false testimony. He and his co-defendant, Algernon Lundy, were drug users, not dealers. During the part of the taping that was aired, Rankins said prosecutor Donna Barrows told him:

One of you is going to receive a life sentence, Mr. Rankins. Now, it don't matter to me which one of you receives a life sentence. I can assure you the federal government have a 98.6 conviction rate, and if I tell you you're going to receive a life sentence, you can call your family and tell them to break you plate because you won't be coming home again.

Rankins asked, "Let me ask you a question. If you were faced with a life sentence right now, and they tell you, 'Well, Miss Oprah, if you don't testify on this guy, your next-door neighbor, that you saw him selling drugs, we're going to make you part of this conspiracy, and give you a life sentence,' what are you going to do? You going to take that life sentence?"

Rankins gave false testimony against Lundy to avoid life in prison. Later, he wrote letters, claiming his testimony was coerced, to Attorney General Janet Reno, President Clinton, *Oprah Winfrey, 60-Minutes, Hard Copy, New York Times, Mobile Press*, and many others. None responded.

Recanting Doesn't Help

Where informants have admitted, years later that they lied to bring about the imprisonment of someone still in prison, and who will remain there until he dies, judges and lawyers say, "Are you lying now, or did you lie then? Are you trying to help somebody get out of jail or help somebody with their appeals?" Recanting seldom helps the victim of earlier perjured testimony.

Over $1 Million for Testimony

A *New York Times* article (March 8, 1995) stated the FBI paid $1,056,000 to Emad Salem for his testimony against Sheik Omar Abdel who was charged with others in planning to bomb the Holland and Lincoln tunnels under the

Hudson River between New York and New Jersey and the United Nations building. (In other pages it is shown how Justice Department coverup led to the bombing of the World Trade Center building.)

Routine DOJ Practice of Releasing into Society Dangerous Killers

DOJ personnel frequently release dangerous killers into society, regardless of the threat they pose to people who may be their next victim. A *Sacramento Bee* article (April 17, 1999) reported an El Dorado County grand jury near Sacramento indicting a former member of the federal witness protection program who had been living in Cameron Park under the name of Robert Rameses. The article said: "Rozier, an admitted seven-time murderer, was living under the name of Robert Rameses, the identity given him under the federal witness program."

19 Murders: DOJ Arranges Freedom and $8 Million Compensation

In the Gotti case, Salvatore Gravano, guilty of over 19 cowardly murders, was given his freedom for providing testimony against John Gotti and allowed to keep over $8 million in illegally gained assets and government compensation. This tradeoff was a distorted use of the federal Witness Security Program, sometimes called the witness protection program. Wherever Gravano or many others like him live today, his neighbors—and he could be your neighbor—do not know about his past or when he will kill again.

Releasing Mass Murderer to Incarcerate Government Agent

In other pages I describe the Justice Department's actions that brought about the release from prison of Jimmy Ellard, a partner with infamous Colombian drug lord Pablo Escobar. Ellard played a key figure in the placement of a bomb on a Colombian airliner that killed 110 people and had admitted bringing tons of cocaine into the United States. His release was based on testifying against Rodney Matthews, an undercover contract agent for U.S. Customs who had learned too much about the government's involvement in drug trafficking and the diversion of drug money to a political party. Ellard became a darling to DOJ prosecutors and was paid for giving perjured testimony that blocked the exposure of high-level government corruption.

Public Obsessed with Released "Child Abuse"
Offenders and Indifferent to Murderers in Their Midst

The public is obsessed with people released into their neighborhood who were once convicted of "child abuse," which could be simply touching someone in the wrong place. The same people who are terrified of that person are oblivious to the murderers released into their midst under the government informant program.

Blackmail Members of Congress to Block Corrective Actions

It is well known that FBI Director J. Edgar Hoover was skilled at obtaining incriminating and embarrassing information on political figures, and had a file on almost every member of Congress. In *From the Secret Files Of J. Edgar Hoover*, author Athan Theoharis describes Hoover's interest and ability in gathering scandalous information about prominent political figures. The CIA and other government agencies have similar activities to exert control over key politicians, media personnel, and publishers.

Good People, Remaining Ignorant, Allow These Tragedies to Happen

You say this can't happen in the United States? Good people, remaining ignorant or too cowardly to speak out, allow—or cause—these tragedies to happen. Wake up; things have changed in America. It *is* happening, and it *is* getting worse. And it is getting worse because good people are not getting informed and not exercising a little courage. Good people, failing to speak out, made Adolf Hitler's rise to power possible, and the horror that followed. Some form of that tragedy can and probably will happen to America, because of the endemic corruption, the endemic coverups, and the endemic indifference by the public.

Another Consequence of Corruption, Fraud, and Public Indifference

Another of the thousands who were either set up, or who played a minor peripheral role in drugs, was David Correa. He was the fall guy in the usual Justice Department trade of using testimony from major drug pushers for the easy prosecution of a peripheral one-time player.

Correa's parents fled Cuba when Fidel Castro came to power. He obtained a Bachelor of Science degree from the New Jersey Institute of Technology and was an engineer for the National Aeronautics and Space Administration (NASA). He was a pilot for Eastern Airlines until the day of his arrest. (Remember Eastern Airlines top management who knew their airline was being used for drug trafficking and who never were presecuted by federal prosecutors.)

Correa told me he was set up by the Rickabough family from Altoona, Pennsylvania, who were reportedly involved in gambling, prostitution, drug trafficking, and stolen motorcycles. Correa said the group gave testimony against him in exchange for charges being dropped against them. They had a long criminal record and Correa had none. They went free and Correa received a life-in-prison sentence with no chance of parole.

Wanting To Die

Correa wrote in an April 25, 1999, letter that he wanted to die—now! He said:

It looks like I will die in prison. I and many like me, including people who are older than me who are also first time, non-violent drug violators with draconian sentences, would rather that the government kill us and get it over with, rather than endure all the mental cruelty of watching our families suffer. Allow us to die. We are not suicidal, but people like me are very tired of this way of being and if we are condemned to die in priison for no just reasons, then we choose to die now. We want to be able to choose our own method of expiration because we do not want to have to suffer any further! Its been ten years in prison and I am just tired of this way of being with no hope of ever going home.

This is the type of agony that many non-violent people, some guilty of the perjured self-serving imagination of another, or the record-setting goal of an arrogant prosecutor, Combined with this, Congress' self-interest in appearing tough on crime and the public's indifference to real injustices.

CHAPTER FIFTEEN

CRIMES OF COVERUP

Ｎone of the corrupt practices described within these pages—or in any of my other books—could occur without the complicity of certain government and non-government checks and balances. Most all of them engaged in coverups, disinformation, obstruction of justice, AND retaliation against those few who sought to expose the serious problems.

I have documented for 30 years the people and entities that made possible the continuation of these outrages. The most prominent include, for instance, the Department of Justice, which was directly involved in the corruption its employees were paid and entrusted to prevent and correct. Members of Congress. Most of the broadcast and print media. These are the leaders that the public had an expectation would perform their duties, and who did not.

A tremendous amount of evidence was obtained of the corruption. I wrote the books for the primary purpose of informing those people who are capable of understanding these matters and have the character to show outrage and help correct the tragedy-related consequences.

The corruption described in these pages includes that of which I have direct knowledge, either as a federal inspector, or as a private investigator obtaining information and documentation from many present and former government agents and other people directly involved in the criminal activities. These areas of serious criminal activities that had a national impact included, for instance:

- Pattern of deliberate air safety and criminal violations directly involved in a continuing pattern of fatal airline crashes, especially the corruption at the management level at United Airlines and the Federal Aviation Administration. The details of this area are found in the third edition of *Unfriendly Skies*.
- Retaliation by United Airlines and the Federal Aviation Administration against federal air safety inspectors who sought to carry out their federal responsibilities and who were threatened and who suffered serious retalia-

tion—at the cost of many air disasters and many lives.

- Drug smuggling into the United States by people in control of the Central Intelligence Agency (CIA), among others. Evidence that I acquired came from what I discovered as an airline pilot in worldwide operations, and my years of investigations including the dozens of insiders. These insiders included the heads of secret CIA airlines and CIA financial operations, pilots who flew the drugs for the CIA and DEA, major drug traffickers, and Mafia family members.
- Rampant looting of people's assets in the bankruptcy courts, involving corruption among federal trustees, including those from the Department of Justice, attorneys and law firms, CIA personnel who often forced people and companies into involuntary bankruptcy, and federal judges.
- A string of other scandals, including CIA involvement in the HUD and savings and loan looting, October Surprise, Iran-Contra affair and especially the drug smuggling in the Contra affair that involved the National Security Council, the White House, the Justice Department and others; fraudulent U.S. funding in arming Iraq prior to its invasion of Kuwait, and more, as described in *Defrauding America*.

Concentration of Media Control in A Few Conglomerates

With the concentration of the media in fewer large conglomerates, making it easier to control the news, some of the greatest threats to the nation, and to individuals, are increasing.

No Lack of Investigative Expertise or Financial Resources

Many newspapers, such as the *Wall Street Journal*, have excellent investigative staffs and print excellent articles, but refuse to publish any articles on hard-core government corruption, the type documented in my books.

Over the years, many reporters told me that they prepared well-researched and documented articles about some form of government corruption and had their articles rejected because the publisher wanted to cover up for the scandal.

Some of the reasons for the coverups would include:

- Desire to maintain harmony and access to government handouts, which would be adversely affected if they printed articles adverse to the government personnel who provide them with the "news."
- Diverse interests that profit from the government-related or protected corruption. This would include, for instance, the savings and loan fraud that profited many people in industry; the drug trafficking that fuels many non-government and government interests, law firms and attorneys who are either fronts for such government agencies as the CIA and FBI or receive lucrative government contracts.
- Cowardice, especially by smaller media outlets, fearing ridicule from the large media. Examples of this include the attacks upon the *San Jose Mercury* when it published a series of articles on CIA drug trafficking and was then ridiculed by The *New York Times*, *Los Angeles Times*, and *Washington Post*. Other examples include the ridicule following the exposure by *CNN-Time* of the killing of American POWs, or the scandals described in *Defrauding America,* which include October Surprise.

- Control exerted by covert CIA personnel in these organizations who receive pay from the agency, and are there to block any adverse story, discredit any that do appear, and attack those who are courageous enough to come forward.

Government Coverups Revealed by Government Insiders

Hundreds of government insiders, FBI agents, CIA operatives, agents from other government agencies, have for years brought evidence of government corruption to the media and Congress that met the criteria for credibility.

The Public Pays the Consequences

The public pays the consequences of the coverups and obstruction of justice by the media (and Congress). Millions of people have been adversely affected by the criminal activities and the coverups. Drugging America is only one of these criminal activities inflicting great harm upon the people.

Coverup in the Chappaquiddick Death Related to Senator Kennedy

During an appearance on Larry King's television program on June 28, 1989, Leo Demoore, the author of *Senatorial Privilege*, told of the coverup he witnessed as a reporter covering Kennedy's Chappaquiddick accident. He discussed the coverup by the press of the more sensitive and sordid parts of the scandal, claiming that although public attention forced news coverage, most if not all the papers omitted extremely serious misconduct by Kennedy and those who covered up for him. They distorted the facts. He said that the press protected Kennedy as much as possible. The press didn't want to hear anything that might blemish Kennedy's image. Demoore made it clear that both the press and the publishing houses wanted the matter kept as quiet as possible.

Book Contracts Canceled by Publishers

Demoore had a firm contract with Random House to publish *Senatorial Privilege*, which had already been accepted in 1985. Suddenly, Random House refused to go to print, claiming they were dissatisfied with the contents, even though they had already expressed complimentary approval of the first half. Demoore felt that unknown people pressured Random House not to publish the book. Random House was also one of the publishers that had tentatively agreed to publish my first printing of *Unfriendly Skies*, and then suddenly refused to do so.

The Mafia, CIA, and George Bush

Another of many similar examples happened to journalist Peter Brewton, who had a firm contract with Doubleday to publish *The Mafia, CIA, and George Bush*. Despite assurances that the book would be published by the summer of 1992, before the presidential elections, Doubleday stalled and then refused to proceed with publication. Brewton then had his book published by SPI Books, a division of Shapolsky Publishers.

Blocking Publication of Book on Lockerbie Bombing

Donald Goddard and Lester Coleman authored the book, *The Trail Of The Octopus*, revealing what really happened in the bombing of Pan Am Flight 103 over Lockerbie. After the initial publication in London, the book was withdrawn from the market. Attempts to get it published in the United States repeatedly failed, despite the highly detailed account of what really happened, including the CIA-DEA drug pipeline using Pan Am aircraft. Coleman, a friend of mine, provided me with the manuscript and inside information that he learned while working undercover in the Middle East for the Defense Intelligence Agency (DIA).

DOJ prosecutors sought to silence Coleman by filing sham charges against him, charging him with providing a perjured declaration to Pan Am's law firms describing what he knew about the Lockerbie bombing and charging him with a passport violation. It is standard procedure for people working under cover for a government agency to use a bogus passport provided by the government, and this DIA-provided passport was then used as the basis for the false charges against Coleman.

Blocking Airing of Television Documentary on Lockerbie Bombing

Allan Francovich, with whom I had been in frequent contact until his mysterious death, produced several television documentaries widely broadcast in Europe, including one on the Lockerbie disaster, the *Maltese Doublecross.* His attempts to have the film shown in the United States were repeatedly blocked, despite strong interest in the Pan Am disaster.

Investigative Reporters Silenced by Their Editors

Investigative reporter Peter Brewton of the *Houston Post*, author of *The Mafia, CIA, and George Bush*, wrote about the block put on many of his stories associating the looting of the savings and loans with the CIA and powerful politicians. These included former Texas Senator Lloyd Bentsen (subsequently appointed to President William Clinton's cabinet). This coverup enabled the public to be saddled with debts that will go far into the 21st Century and contribute to possible financial collapse of other government programs.

In *The CIA and the Cult Of Intelligence*, the authors describe the pressure and threats upon newspapers and book publishers not to publish matters adversely reflecting upon the CIA or other government agencies. The book tells of the planting of CIA moles in the news media, including radio and television networks, and the pressure not to report government misconduct.

Dangerous For Congresspersons to Expose Government Corruption

Author Ralph McGehee states in *Deadly Deceits: My 25 years in the CIA*, "There's a little bit of fear that if you go after the intelligence community, your career is threatened." Several CIA operatives have told me that the CIA had blackmailed Senator Boren, Chairman of the CIA Senate Oversight Committee, warning him that they would release pictures of alleged homosexual and pedophile activities if he didn't cease his opposition to the nomination of Robert Gates as Director of the CIA in 1992.

Buying Media Coverup

A *Harper's* magazine article (July 1989) stated how politicians leak the "news" to favored reporters, who then reciprocate by rarely reporting unfavorable articles about those who give them the "news." The article described the government oligarchy in which power vests in a few persons doling out government press releases:

> *By their subjugation of the press, the political powers in America have conferred on themselves the greatest of political blessings—Gyges' ring of invisibility.*

Spoon-Feeding the White House Press Corps

A January 15, 1990, *Newsweek* article described the role of the media in prolonging the savings and loan debacle:

While the White House press corps waited to be spoon-fed instructions, scandals in housing programs and savings and loan regulation went unreported. No administration really wants reporters snooping through the Agriculture Department or other places they can break new ground; better to have them hanging around the White House briefing room, waiting for handouts. It's this system, rather than any particular handler or press secretary, that conditions and corrodes Washington coverage. That's why it's up to reporters to redefine the concept of news so that it relies more on what they find, and less on what the president—or his press secretary—would have them believe.

Occasionally, the media will focus on an issue that targets on a particular individual rather than on a large-scale area of corruption, as it did against President Nixon in what became known as Watergate. For its own reasons, the *Washington Post* flamed the relatively minor two-bit burglary, while simultaneously continuing the pattern of coverups on large-scale criminal activities such as CIA drug trafficking and other very serious matters described in my various books.

Ethics—Or the Lack of Them—and the Press

In an in-depth investigative report that is as true today as the day it was published (July 25, 1967), the *Wall Street Journal* identified the news distortion and coverup: "Ethics & the Press, Conflicts of Interest, Pressures Still Distort Some Papers' Coverage." The in-depth article told how "Advertisers and outside work of newsmen color stories," thereby halting investigations:

In Boston and Chicago, newspaper investigations into suspected hanky-panky suddenly are aborted. In one case, a subject of inquiry turns out to be a stockholder of the paper and friend of the publisher. In the other, the investigation threatens to embarrass a politician who could help the paper in a building project.

In Denver, the advertising staff of a big daily wrestles with an arithmetic problem. A big advertiser has been promised news stories and pictures amounting to 25 percent of the ad space it buys; the paper already has run hundreds of column inches of glowing prose but is still not close to the promised allotment of "news" and now is running out of nice things to say.

Victimized Readers

All this hardly enhances the image of objectivity and fierce independence the U.S. press tries so hard to project. Yet talks with scores of reporters, editors, publishers, public relations men and others reveal that practices endangering--and often subverting—newspaper integrity are more common than the man on the street might dream. Result: The buyer who expects a dime's worth of truth every time he picks up his paper often is short-changed.

All newspapers, including this one, must cope with the blandishments and pressures of special interests who seek distortion or omission of the truth.

On some papers the trouble starts at the top; it is the publisher himself who lays down news policies designed to aid one group or attack another.

It is plain, however, that a sizable minority [or is it majority] of newspapers still are putty in the hands of their advertisers, that they allow personal as well as business considerations to favor the news to a marked degree, ... that they tolerate staff practices hardly conducive to editorial independence and objectivity....blackouts of news involving newspapers are quite common; hardly a working journalist could deny that one of the gravest weaknesses in coverage exhibited by the American press is its coverage of itself....another grave fault of a good many papers: Favoritism toward business in general and advertisers in particular....the paper itself, by actual policy or common practice, distorts the news to suit advertisers or literally hands over news space to them....Everyone in newspapering pays lip service to the ideal that a paper's news columns should not be for sale,...a staffer is "on the take"...

Wall Street Journal Coverups

The *Wall Street Journal* article described the news distortion of virtually every media in the United States caused by pressures from vested-interest groups and from financial benefits. The Federal Communications Commission charged NBC-TV with falsely presenting the facts associated with general aviation and airline problems in midair collisions. The FAA ordered NBC to take "appropriate steps to achieve fairness" and stop distorting the facts.

Selected Exposures by *Wall Street Journal*

The morals of the *Wall Street Journal* are two-sided. Since the 1960s, when I was an FAA investigator seeking to address the air safety and criminal activities involved in a continuing series of airline crashes, I reported these crimes to the *Wall Street Journal*. I expected the newspaper would exercise its media responsibility and report these charges by an FAA insider in their columns. They never did, making possible the continuing related tragedies.

Publishing A Newspaper Is A Sacred Trust, Said the Journal

The *Journal* wrote in a January 12, 1993, issue:

This progress report carries forward a custom begun 16 years ago. It reflects our belief that publishing a newspaper is a public trust for which we are accountable first of all to you, our readers.

Their responsibility to the public was correctly stated, but the Wall Street Journal's reporting of government corruption was controlled, as during the Iran-Contra affair when they were protective of the Republican White House drug trafficking. However, they have to be given credit for revealing part of the truth about the endless number of scandals surrounding Governor and then President Bill Clinton when most of the media was covering up for his more serious misconduct.

Former *New York Times* Chief Of Staff Admits Press Coverup

Giving a toast in 1953 before the New York Press Club, the former Chief of Staff of the *New York Times*, John Swinton, stated:

There is no such thing, at this date of the world's history, in America, as an independent press. You know it and I know it ... The business of the journalist is to destroy truth; To lie outright; To pervert; To vilify;

To fawn at the feet of mammon, and to sell his country and his race for his daily bread. You know it and I know it, and what folly is this toasting an independent press? ... Our talents, our possibilities and our lives, are all the property of other men. We are intellectual prostitutes.

San Francisco Chronicle Coverup

In February 1988, I gave two reporters from the *San Francisco Chronicle,* Jeff Paline and Bill Wallace, details and documentation of the corruption that I had uncovered which fell within areas of state and national interests. These reporters contacted a friend of mine, falsely stating that they did not write an article on the matters I brought to their attention because I refused to give them supporting material. That was a lie. I had supplied them with a great deal of written material and withheld nothing. I described to them the corruption I discovered in the aviation area, in Chapter 11 courts, and the persecution judicially inflicted upon me to block my exposure activities. I referred them to specific federal filings at San Francisco and Sacramento that enlarged upon the corruption that I had found, and which were now of judicial record. Instead of reporting these charges, they kept the lid on the scandal.

Report U.S. Related Atrocities and Pay The Consequences

"The Complicity of Silence" was the heading on an article in *Lies of Our Times* (June 1993), as it related to the media coverup of the U.S. directed assassinations occurring in Central America and particularly the El Mozote massacre in El Salvador (December 1981). The article told how *Time* magazine reporter Raymond Bonner sent an article to the home office describing the brutal murders at El Mozote, primarily of women and children, by the U.S.-trained Atlaeatl Battalion. Bonner was at the assassination site and personally interviewed the handful of survivors. He then became the target of a media smear campaign to discredit him and to remove him from his reporting activities.

The editors of *Time* then transferred Bonner out of the Central America assignment to quiet him. On March 15, 1993, the U.N.-sponsored Truth Commission on El Salvador released its report on the El Mozote massacre, proving that the massacre had occurred, that it was directed by the CIA, which the media had known and covered up for years.

Time reacted in similar fashion, firing several of its investigative reporters, after they prepared a documentary on the killing of U.S. servicemen in Indochina, a practice for which I provided documentary evidence in the third edition of *Defrauding America.*

Wall Street Journal editor Robert Bartley, protecting the Republican Administration, savagely attacked Bonner and his reports and especially the one on February 19, 1982 about the massacre. The *Wall Street Journal's* attack upon Bonner caused other newspapers and magazines to instruct their reporters to keep the lid on the massacre, ensuring that the massacre of other civilians would continue. The *Wall Street Journal* editorial caused one major newspaper to send copies of that editorial to its correspondents in Central America warning them: "Let's not let this happen to us."

Pressure On Advertisers to Remain Silent

Following a series of Delta Air Line near-crashes in mid-1987, Delta put financial pressure on the media to stop reporting them. An *Associated Press* article (August 13, 1987) described Delta's threats to cancel large blocks of advertising with the print and broadcast media that were making these reports. Delta responded to media criticism of this policy, stating there was a "misunderstanding." What else could they say?

An *Air Transport World* article (March 1970) described the value of airline advertising: "Airlines are a major source of ad revenue." Airlines such as Delta run full-page ads in the *Wall Street Journal*, which rarely runs articles detrimental to the airlines' interests.

Yearly advertising budgets for a major airline easily exceed one hundred million dollars, ensuring that any newspaper, radio station or network will withhold any unfavorable information about such a valuable advertiser. Federal Express dropped its ads on ABC Primetime television network after a critical report on ABC's 20/20. The program reported Federal Express mishandled government and military documents and packages, and that drug activities were rampant at the airline. (*New York Times*, October 18, 1989, report of the July 7, 1989, show)

$40 To $100 Million Lost Revenue from One Account

Federal Express' President Frederick Smith wrote (July 14, 1989) that the company was canceling its prime-time advertising, with the exception of commercials scheduled for the ABC telecast of the World Series and Monday Night Football. Federal Express spent over $40 million a year on advertising, according to the Standard Directory of Advertisers, an industry publication. In another letter, President Smith wrote that this cancellation would cost ABC "in excess of $100 million." It's easy to understand how the news media hesitates to print anything that would dissatisfy a valuable customer.

Media and Congress Covering Up for History of Fraud and Other Problems at United Airlines Involving Crashes and Near-Crashes

The criminal acts at United Airlines that are documented in FAA records, and described in the third edition of *Unfriendly Skies*, have been repeatedly covered up by the media, Congress, and the National Transportation Safety Board. And the coverups made possible subsequent crashes and near-crashes.

Example of Many Near-Crashes Covered Up

In late 1998, the nation's worst air disaster was missed by only 100 feet separation as a United Airlines Boeing 747 was mishandled by the pilots and nearly crashed into Mount Bruno after takeoff from San Francisco International Airport. The FAA kept the lid on the scandal, as did almost all of the media. It wasn't until the *Wall Street Journal* published (March 19, 1999) a long article on the near-disaster that hardly anyone even knew about it. A few key sections of the *Wall Street Journal* article follows:

Because of poor flying techniques, the co-pilot who was at the controls slowed and nearly stalled and crashed the plane. "Push [the nose] down" to pick up speed, shouted two extra pilots sitting in the rear of the cockpit. The co-pilot did, but now the jet was off course and heading toward San Bruno Mountain northwest of the airport. The jet's ground-proximity warning sounded, and the extra pilots shouted, "Pull up, pull up!" Carrying 307 passengers and crew, the plane cleared the hill by only 100 feet. The jet also barely missed apartments and houses with hundreds of sleeping residents. A crash of the jet which was heavily loaded with fuel would have been one of the worst aviation accidents in history, The incident— just now being publicly disclosed—has rocked the world's biggest airline and spurred the Federal Aviation Administration to force changes in United's pilot-training techniques. United ... acknowledged the incident and says that it has spurred the carrier to take a series of steps, ranging from a safety audit of all its 9,500 pilots to a major shakeup in its pilot training. The agency is now pushing United hard to improve skills of its pilots, especially its 747-400 copilots, or to ground some of them.

Additional United close calls in recent months—also never publicly disclosed—have broadened the concern beyond the 747-400 crews. "In the past months, we have had several operational incidents," airline jargon for close calls, W.J. Carter, chief of United's Honolulu-based pilots, wrote in a Feb.23 internal memo to his flight crews. Major accidents historically are preceded by a series of these seemingly unrelated incidents. This disturbing trend is cause for concern," the memo continued.

More of the same, and the people who weren't as lucky as on that San Francisco flight, can be found in the third edition of *Unfriendly Skies.*

Report Citizen Complaints and Suffer Financial Retaliation

Boston radio station WHDH experienced the consequences of offending Procter & Gamble. The station had broadcast the activities of a local citizen group that was critical of one of the company's products. Procter & Gamble then pulled local ads for all of its products from the station, resulting in the loss of $1 million of advertising revenue. Procter & Gamble reportedly warned that it would pull commercials from any station broadcasting the announcement from the citizen group (*San Francisco Daily Journal*, April 1, 1991). The newspaper article stated: "P&G's message reinforced what station managers already believed: don't criticize business, and stay away from controversial topics, or it will cost the station business. Actions such as Procter & Gamble's don't have to happen often before media outlets become self-censoring."

Report Car Defects and Suffer Economic Retaliation

Carmakers retaliate against magazines printing articles reporting weaknesses or defects in their products. General Motors, for instance, withdrew advertising for three months after a magazine's editor, David E. Davis, delivered a speech against the automaker concerning the closure of twenty-one plants, eliminating 74,000 jobs. Toyota Motor Corporation withdrew ads after its models did not make *Road and Track*'s 1991 "10 Best List." The loss of this type of advertising can make the difference between profit and loss, or even survival.

Selective Exposure of Government Corruption

The *Wall Street Journal* publishes many detailed and well-researched articles on government corruption; but is very "selective." In matters relating to the crimes of Governor and then President Bill Clinton the *Journal* reported the corruption as the media is expected to do. But in crimes that heavily implicated the Republicans, the *Journal* covered up: October Surprise; Iran-Contra drug smuggling involving The National Security Council, Oliver North, President George Bush, and other crimes.

Selective Opposition to Government Corruption

In all fairness, selective outrage or selective reporting of government misconduct is widespread. Even on talk shows that allow guests to speak out against the government, the hosts and the stations will usually limit their subjects to far-out issues that will never threaten the corruption in government. Examples are talk show hosts who spend considerable time on such matters as UFOs, extra-terrestrial aliens, and the unconstitutionality of the income tax. This types of subject doesn't threaten the corruption in government, thus relieving the host and the station of government retaliation. Covert government forces could even arrange to have such shows on the air so as to divert attention from matters of hard core government corruption. When an insider does appear on a show, his reporting of true corruption either goes unnoticed, or he is labeled with guests talking about far-out matters. Many shows and hosts will not allow a guest to appear who has evidence of high-level corruption, such as CIA drug trafficking. Talkshow hosts have even admitted this to me.

My Personal Experiences

Although I have appeared as guest and expert on over 3,000 radio and television shows since 1978 in the United States, Canada, and Europe, there are some stations that will not allow me to appear. I can think of at least four times in the last two years when a major network scheduled me to appear and then at the last moment cancel me out. In the San Francisco area I had repeatedly appeared on radio and television shows in the 1980s when my subject was air safety. But once I started talking about my book, *Defrauding America* (and also the third edition of *Unfriendly Skies*), which detailed and documented high-level government corruption, especially in the California area involving both the federal government and California judges, that was the end of my appearances. Many listeners called into the stations asking that I be called to appear, but not once was I called. I was simultaneously appearing on radio shows throughout the United States. I even had German and Dutch television stations send crews to the United States for the sole purpose of interviewing me.

Reporter's Disclosure of Killed Stories on Government Corruption

For years, reporters have stated to me that they have written stories on various government scandals and that the stories were killed, despite the gravity of the corruption, the ample supporting evidence, and the consequences of coverup. Their experiences coincided with the media coverup that I encountered during the past 30 years of attempting to expose corruption. Nearly a half page was devoted by the *Wall Street Journal* (January 6, 1997) to the matter of media coverup relating to major government misconduct:

> One of the striking things about press coverage of Whitewater is the number of star reporters who, for one reason or another, are no longer on the beat. Investigative reporter Douglas Frantz quit the Los Angeles Times over its handling of a December 1993 Troopergate story that he co-authored with Bill Rempel. ABC's Jim Wooten took himself off the scandal

beat after the network killed a Troopergate-related story, Mr. William Powers reported. Washington Post reporter Michael Isikoff left the paper after a bitter internal dispute over the Paula Jones story...the tabloid New York Post let reporter Christopher Ruddy go...

Survivors on the Whitewater beat report, both on and off the record, that life is uncomfortable. [Referring to the pressure from "cooperating" journalists], *in what Mr. Powers called a chilling "divide-and-conquer approach," whispering campaigns about allegedly shoddy work are launched in an effort to convince reporters to ignore the work of their colleagues...*

[In referring to the death of Kevin Ives and Don Henry, related to the Arkansas CIA drug trafficking that also implicated then-Governor Bill Clinton, and the killing of that story by CBS and "60 Minutes"], *reporters view [these] attacks as a kind of drip-drip water torture to try to undermine the credibility of journalists working the story.*

In 1994, when the [ABC] network was set to run a story including Gov. Clinton's use of state troopers to procure women, Mr. Clinton's private attorney, David Kendall flew to New York to lobby against the piece (and applied pressure to kill the story). In June, the White House launched a furious blitz at ABC executives to block former FBI agent Gary Aldrich from appearing on "This week with David Brinkley" to discuss his book on White House mores...NBC's "Dateline" and CNN's "Larry King Live" canceled plans to interview Mr. Aldrich. "We killed it," Mr. Stephanopoulos later boasted.

[In another similar case] *White House spokesman Mike McCurry was furious and ... complained to network executives, and in an angry call to* [ABC investigative producer] *Chris Viasto, he screamed: "You're never going to work in this town again."*

New York Daily News reporter David Eisenstadt was fired Nov. 11 after filing a story linking top Clinton fund-raiser Terry McAuliffe to Asian fund-raising and Mr. Huang. Mr. Eisenstadt's attorney sent the Daily News a letter saying he would file a lawsuit because the paper had "improperly thwarted the truth and succumbed to political pressure" in terminating the reporter .. James Ledbetter of the Village Voice reported that Mr. Eisenstadt was fired "after the Clinton campaign reportedly complained to News co-publisher Mort Zuckerman," a frequent White House guest.

Covering Up for A Federal Crime is Itself A Federal Crime

As previously stated, a person has committed a felony if he or she knows of a federal crime and does not promptly report it to a federal judge or other federal tribunal (Title 18 USC Section 4). Most of the mainstream media, members of Congress, many lazy or cowardly citizens, are certainly guilty of this crime. Those in the broadcast and print media who refused to report the charges of government crimes, or knowledge of the crimes, are morally and criminally guilty. Those who engaged in deliberate misinformation to cover up for these crimes were guilty of even worse crimes.

A Few Courageous Newspapers

Several of the alternative newspapers have courageously sought to expose the corruption in government. In some cases they exposed criminality by federal personnel that the mass media later was forced to report—at least part of the scandal, as in the Iran-Contra affair. An isolated number of the mainstream press did print articles on government corruption. For instance, the *Arkansas Democrat* exposed for several years the vast arms and drug trafficking at Mena Airport in Arkansas; the *Houston Post* reported the CIA involvement in looting the savings and loans until pressure caused them to drop the series, and *Playboy* wrote articles on the CIA and October Surprise.

Public Relation Firms and the CIA

The CIA uses public relations firms to perform domestic activities that the CIA is barred by law from doing. Washington-based Hill & Knowlton, for instance, acted as a conduit for propaganda news releases to the media. The firm had numerous CIA and other intelligence agency personnel on its board of directors. Robert Gray, who created and operated Hill and Knowlton since 1961 had numerous contacts with the CIA and other intelligence groups and with such CIA personnel as William Casey, Edwin Wilson, Oliver North, and Robert Owen. Gray also formed his own company with CIA contacts and was on the Board of Directors of several covert CIA companies that fronted for Task Force 157, an Office of Naval Intelligence operation.

Covert Action, in its Spring 1993 issue, told how U.S. intelligence agencies use public relation firms, journalists, and authors to print what they want the American public to hear. The article reported that "In a typical issue of the *Wall Street Journal*, more than half the news stories were based solely on [government-provided] press releases." The article continued: "Reporters were paid by the CIA, sometimes without their media employer's knowledge, to get the material in print or on the air." They reported that news organizations ordered their writers to repeat what was fed to them by the CIA.

A former CIA employee, Robert T. Crowley, whose job was to act as liaison with corporations, admitted that public relations firms are continuously used by the CIA "to put out press releases and make media contacts." The CIA's use of U.S. media has been well detailed in publications related to the intelligence agencies. Much of what is stated as "news" by the media is really press releases from CIA-connected public relation firms. Author Susan Trento wrote:

> *Reporters were paid by the CIA, sometimes without their media employers' knowledge Reporters were paid by the CIA, sometimes without their media employers' knowledge, to get the material in print or on the air. But other news organizations ordered their employees to cooperate with the CIA, including the San Diego-based Copley News Service. But Copley was not alone, and the CIA had "tamed" reporters and editors in scores of newspaper and broadcast outlets across the country. To avoid direct relationships with the media, the CIA recruited individuals in public relations firms like H&K to act as middlemen for what the CIA wanted to distrib-*

ute.[44]

The Spring 1993 issue of *Covert Action* described the misleading news given to the American public:

> *In a typical issue of the Wall Street Journal, more than half the news stories were based solely on press releases [from government personnel]. Hill and Knowlton...were perfect "cover" for the ever-expanding CIA. The CIA...used its H&K connections to put out press releases and make media contacts to further its positions. H&K employees at the small Washington office and elsewhere, distributed this material through CIA assets working in the United States news media. Since the CIA is prohibited from disseminating propaganda inside the U.S., this type of "blowback"—which former CIA officer John Stockwell and other researchers have often traced to the Agency—is illegal. While the use of U.S. media by the CIA has a long and well-documented history, the covert involvement of PR firms may be news to many.*

Who Rules America?

Covert Action described how reporters depend upon the close intelligence community for much of their "news," and how the media protects these sources. An article written by the research staff of *National Vanguard Books* described the slanted news by the press and entertainment media: *Who Rules America?*

> *Their power...reaches into every home in America, and it works its will during nearly every waking hour. It is the power which shapes and molds the mind of virtually every citizen, young or old, rich or poor, simple or sophisticated. The mass media form for us our image of the world and then tell us what to think about that image. Essentially everything we know—or think we know—about events outside our own neighborhood or circle of acquaintances comes to us via our daily newspaper, our weekly news magazine, our radio, or our television.*
>
> *Employing carefully developed psychological techniques, they guide our thought and opinion...Most Americans fail to realize that they are being manipulated. Even the citizen who complains about "managed news" falls into the trap of thinking that because he is presented with an apparent spectrum of opinion he can escape the thought controllers' influence by believing the editor or commentator of his choice. Every point on the permissible spectrum of public opinion is acceptable to the media master, and no impermissible fact or viewpoint is allowed any exposure at all, if they can prevent it.*

Media Circus

In the book, *Media Circus*, written by *Washington Post* media critic, the author ridicules the lack of investigative reporting, absence of penetrating insight, or newsworthy news that exists in America's newspapers:

> *The nation's watchdogs have become lap-dogs, and groveling spineless mutts at that. And nobody, the American public especially, appears to give a thinker's damn.*

---

[44] Interview with John Stockwell, *Propaganda Review*, No. 6, Winter 1990, p. 14.

Costly Scandal after Scandal Covered Up by the Media

The book reveals the failure of the media to acknowledge the savings and loan and HUD scandal, to which must be added October Surprise, Iran-Contra's drug trafficking, the involvement of CIA and other government officials in the drug trafficking causing great instability in the United States, and much more. Worse, the media has engaged in disinformation and misinformation. He explains that reporters are too dependent upon government sources for "news" to risk offending government officials.

American Press and the Public Richly Deserve One Another!

The book states, "Under-reporting of unpleasant [news] wouldn't occur so easily or often if such practices hadn't already become a well-worn habit encouraged by a public that doesn't want to know the truth if it undermines their collective confidence." The book stated, "The American press and their public richly deserve one another." Of course, the public is paying a very heavy price for its absence of citizen responsibilities.

Some of the most well-known media personnel are those who have placated government officials by repeating their lines—and lies—and became favored recipients of government disinformation handouts. Most well-known Washington reporters profit by playing this deception, receiving large sums through salaries and compensation from CIA and other government agencies.

Media Admission of Being CIA Fronts

It is well known in the intelligence community that the intelligence community has many media personnel and corporations on their payroll, insuring that the public is denied knowledge of the true facts and the long list of costly corrupt activities described in these pages. Many articles have been written about this fact of life. For instance, the *Washington Post* (February 16, 1996) described the CIA's use of American journalists and news organizations during "the past 19 years," and even using them as cutouts or fronts for CIA activities.

Using Covert Media Sources Continues as CIA Policy

The article made reference to earlier discoveries "that the CIA had clandestine agents posing as American journalists for decades." Executive editor of the *Washington Post*, Leonard Downie, Jr., stated that "It's disturbing to hear that the CIA has either used the cover of legitimate journalistic organizations without their knowledge, or somebody working for them has been recruited by the CIA." CIA spokesman Mark Mansfield said the use of the media is permitted by a regulation "waived by the agency's director...and has been and continues to be the CIA's policy."

Over 800 News and Public Information Sources and Individuals

A December 1977 article in the *New York Times* reported that in the mid 1960s the CIA "owned, subsidized or otherwise influenced...more than 800 news and public information organizations and individuals."

JUDICIAL COVERUP

The years of documentation that I have acquired, and describe in my books, clearly document the felony coverups, obstruction of justice, and retaliation, by federal judges, up to and including the justices of the U.S. Supreme Court. Under federal criminal statutes federal judges have a responsibility to receive information about any federal crimes, including corruption by federal personnel. The clear wording in one statute shows their responsibility to receive reports of federal crimes: Title 18 USC Section 4:

> Whoever, having knowledge of the actual commission of a felony cognizable by a court of the United States, conceals and does not as soon as possible make known the same to some judge (or other person in civil or military authority under the United States), shall be fined...or imprisoned not more than three years, or both.

The First Attempt To Comply with Federal Crime-Reporting Statute

Seeking to report the crash-related criminal activities that I and other FAA inspectors discovered, I sought to report the activities through a federal filing[45]in the U.S. District Court at San Francisco. The federal district judge sympathized with my position, but dismissed my attempt to make such report when the Department of Justice filed an objection to my reports. The Justice Department was acting to void the statutory requirement to report federal crimes—protecting high-level people in the FAA and at United Airlines—while they were simultaneously filing criminal charges against ordinary citizens for failing to report federal crimes, that did not implicate federal officials.

I then appealed the refusal of the court to receive this evidence. During oral arguments before the Ninth Circuit Court of Appeals in San Francisco, the three-judge panel argued that this was a matter for Congress and not the courts. I argued otherwise, stating that under Title 18 USC Section 4 any federal judge had the statutory responsibility to receive evidence of a federal crime that was presented to them. Also, that a federal judge had the responsibility[46] to order a federal agency to halt unlawful actions. Again the action was dismissed, and again, the dismissal caused the deeply entrenched problems to continue, as well as the resulting crashes and deaths.

The Second Filing Related to World's Worst Air Disaster

I filed a similar action following the 1978 PSA San Diego crash, which was at that time the world's worst air disaster, taking the title away from the New York City crash that occurred on the program for which I had air safety responsibilities (United Airlines DC-8 crash into Brooklyn). In the PSA crash, the NTSB falsified the official accident report by covering up for the all-night partying and drinking by the airline crew. The hangover effects of this partying resulted early the next morning in a horrible tragedy in a residential area of San Diego.

Following a long-established pattern, the NTSB covered up for the underlying cause of the crash. I then petitioned the NTSB to receive my evidence relating to the all-night partying, which they wrongfully refused to receive. I then filed an action with the district court at San Francisco (*Stich v. National Transportation Safety Board*, 685 F.2d 446 (9th Cir. 1982) seeking to have the

---

[45] *Stich v. United States, et al.*, 554 F.2d 1070 (9th Cir.) (table), *cert. denied*, 434 U.S. 920 (1977)(addressed hard-core air safety misconduct, violations of federal air safety laws, threats against government inspectors not to report safety violations and misconduct);

[46] **Title 28 U.S.C. § 1361. Action to compel an officer of the United States to perform his duty.** The district courts shall have original jurisdiction of any action in the nature of mandamus to compel an officer or employee of the United States or any agency thereof to perform a duty owed to the plaintiff.

court order the NTSB to receive my evidence and that of a witness who could testify to the partying.

Shortly after I filed the action, Assistant U.S. Attorney George Stoll called and stated to me over the phone that he was supporting my position and was recommending to his superiors in Washington that this be done. That relatively new AUSA with the Justice Department was unaware of the prior Justice Department involvement and coverups. He did not realize that supporting my position could expose the air safety and Justice Department scandal that already existed. The AUSA then filed a motion to have my action dismissed, which the judge (and former Justice Department attorney) did.

I made other attempts to report evidence of the CIA drug trafficking and some of the other high-level criminal activities described in my books and each time Justice Department attorneys and federal judges—acting in unison—blocked my efforts. To the best of my knowledge, no one had ever sought to use the federal crime-reporting statute to report criminal activities by government officials to a federal judge. If this right and responsibility were to be allowed to occur, all government corruption, of which there has been a great amount, would be threatened by use of this statutory and judicial remedy. Obviously, I had to be stopped.

Complicity of Supreme Court Justices in the Underlying Crimes

Several times I took the matter all the way to the U.S. Supreme Court, and ran into another judicial block, in which the Justices of the U.S. Supreme Court were clearly shown as becoming criminally involved through coverups. And this is another very serious side to the corruption I describe in my various books. They too blocked every attempt to report the government-related crimes.

DOJ Attorneys Given Immunity for Subornation of Perjury Crimes

Subornation of perjury is a crime. But Justice Department attorneys, responsible for prosecuting these offenses, routinely commit the crime, and never pay the consequences. In real life, it is only members of the public who pay the consequences of crimes that DOJ personnel routinely commit. Witnesses who lie for the DOJ also receive immunity not available to the public, or the defense.

Vicarious Criminal Liability

Under law, the head of an organization is financially and criminally responsible for the actions of those over whom he has supervisory responsibilities. This liability increases if he or she knows of the criminal acts and allows them to continue, and if he fails to report the acts to proper authorities.

The Justices are the heads of the federal judiciary, responsible for the misconduct of federal judges, and responsible to act when judges over whom they have supervisory responsibilities engage in felony coverups, obstruction of justice, and retaliation against those seeking to report the crimes. They have a fiduciary duty to protect the public against corrupt actions of federal judges, Justice Department attorneys, and any other unlawful or improper activity occurring in federal courts.

Failure to Act Is A Crime

Under universally applicable conspiracy laws, co-conspirators are criminally responsible not only for their own criminal acts, but also for the actions of their co-conspirators performed within the scope of the conspiracy, and in furtherance of the conspiracy. A 1994 article in the San Francisco legal newspaper, *Daily Journal*, described the criminal acts under state and federal law perpetrated by those officials in the federal and state government who have a duty to act and who fail to perform that duty. The article described the law in detail, and explained how the "law of negative acts" or "omissions" are another form of criminal activity. The article explained that "in certain circumstances the failure to act (the omission) satisfies the requirement of criminal law." Referring to the law book, *R. Perkins & R. Boyace, Criminal Law* 66467 (3d ed. 1982), the article explained that there are several situations in which the omission to perform a duty is criminally culpable and satisfies the *actus reus.*

Supreme Court Justices Engaged in Repeated Criminal Acts

The Justices, in effect, aided and abetted the crimes which I and other government insiders sought to expose. If ever such criminal activities as the CIA's involvement in drugging America is addressed, the role of those who aided in the coverups and obstruction of justice—including the Justices of the U.S. Supreme Court—must also be addressed because of the criminal nature of such acts.

Refusal To Perform A Fiduciary Duty

In the event of a fatal airline crash, a government official, such as an FAA official, or one with the National Transportation Safety Board, would be guilty of a crime if that official knew of unsafe or criminal acts relating to air safety, and if that person then covered up for it. Making matters worse would be if the crashes resulted in deaths. That certainly happened in many of the crashes I describe in the book, *Unfriendly Skies.*

Culpability of Supreme Court Justices

The same laws that made members of Congress and the media liable and culpable under federal statutes applied to the Justices of the United States Supreme Court. The Justices had covered up the pattern of criminal behavior by federal judges over whom the Justices had supervisory responsibilities.[47] Like a police chief protecting rampant criminal behavior of their police officers, the Supreme Court Justices protected the criminal behavior of those over whom *they* had supervisory responsibilities. Because of their positions of trust, the Justices were more guilty of criminal acts for such crimes as misprision of felonies, coverup, accessory after the fact, conspiracy, obstruction of justice, and others.

Unprecedented Federal Action Against Supreme Court Justices

Since the Supreme Court justices had covered up for the criminal activities that I described and documented in my various books, and on the basis that I suffered the consequences (along with many others) I filed a lawsuit against them[48] in the U.S. District Court in the District of Columbia.[49] The complaint

---

[47] Rule 17.1(a) of the U.S. Supreme Court. Responsibility to intervene exists when a lower court "has so far departed from the accepted and usual course of judicial proceedings, or so far sanctioned such a departure by a lower court, as to call for an exercise of this Court's power of supervision."

[48] William Rehnquist; Antonin Scalia; Sandra O'Connor; Anthony Kennedy; Thurgood Marshall;

was factual, precise, and permitted under federal law. It was unprecedented and unique.

This was probably the first time in history that Supreme Court Justices were sued for civil, constitutional, and RICO violations. The facts raised in the complaint were correct and very serious. But it was bizarre that *anyone* would be forced to resort to suing the Justices of the nation's highest court to report federal crimes.

The truthfulness of the serious allegations made in the complaint could be easily verified by the media. Every major news service monitors the filing of complaints in federal courts. But again, the media kept the lid on this unusual filing and the gravity of the charges made in the complaint.

DOJ Admitted the Justices Knew of the Charges

Justice Department attorneys filed a motion to dismiss my complaint (August 17, 1989), admitting that the Justices *knew* of my allegations and that they failed to act. Their response did not deny the truthfulness of the charges or the resulting harm, and under federal law allegations made in a complaint must be accepted as true at that stage of the proceedings. The primary defense raised in the motion was that the Justices of the U.S. Supreme Court "enjoy absolute immunity from plaintiff's claims."

Supreme Court Justices Motion to Dismiss Riddled with Falsehoods

The motion to dismiss the defendant Supreme Court Justices was riddled with false statements of facts and law, and with trivial matters. The Justices argued that the complaint should be dismissed because "Rule 8 (a)...requires that a complaint be a short and plain statement." After arguing that the complaint was too long (there is no page limit in federal complaints), the justices then argued that the allegations were not specific enough! The justices argued that the complaint did not "state facts with particularity in his complaint that demonstrate who did what to whom and why." The complaint stated very clearly what the Supreme Court justices had done. A complaint does not have to *prove* the allegations, but make reference to them so the defendants know the nature of the alleged wrongful acts. As was a standard pattern by federal judges refusing to allow me to have my day in court, never did they address the issues that I raised.

Unbelievable Allegations Said the Justices of the U.S. Supreme Court

The justices argued that the complaint stated "unbelievable allegations." The charges were certainly unusual, but not unusual to anyone who knows of the covert activities of the Justice Department and the CIA. They would possibly be "unbelievable" to a sequestered nun!

As said before, under federal law the allegations made in a complaint must be recognized as true for the purpose of preventing dismissal of the action. Many of the facts stated in the complaint were supported by taking judicial notice of legal proceedings in the California courts, in federal courts. The justices argued that the statute of limitations prevented lawsuits against them, but never stated how the *ongoing* wrongful acts could have imposed a statute of limitations defense.

William Brennan; John Stevens; Byron White; Henry Blackmun.

[49] Filed February 17, 1989, No. 89-0470 SS; amended complaint filed March 14, 1989.

Allegations Already Adjudicated?

The justices then argued that the allegations were already adjudicated and dismissed by other federal courts. Not one of the federal actions had ever been heard on the merits, and never once did I have my day in court. Nothing had ever been adjudicated. Further, the justices were never named in any lawsuit, so obviously the matters could not have been adjudicated. The Supreme Court justices argued:

The nine justices of the Supreme Court are entitled to absolute judicial immunity from plaintiff's claims. A judge will not be deprived of immunity because the action he took was...done maliciously, or was in excess of his authority.

The criminal statutes, such as misprision of a felony and civil rights statutes, do not state a judge is immune when he violates criminal statutes.

Former CIA Legal Counsel Dismissed the Action Without A Hearing

District of Columbia Judge Stanley Sporkin came to the Justices' rescue. He rendered a *sua sponte* dismissal (January 17, 1990), violating federal law barring dismissal of a lawsuit that stated federal causes of action. Sporkin, a former CIA legal counsel, could also have been motivated by a desire to cover up for the dirty linen in which he himself might have been implicated while employed by the CIA and knowledgeable about CIA drug trafficking.

Further Complicity of Supreme Court Justices

On August 12, 1997, I filed a petition for writ of certiorari with the U.S. Supreme Court. That petition was *very* sensitive, and its filing would have made a Supreme Court record of the criminal activities described within these pages, including the extensive involvement of federal judges. The petition was timely submitted for filing in response to the dismissal of an appeal by the Court of Appeals in the District of Columbia (97-5007), and was authorized under Title 28 USC Section 1254 and Supreme Court Rule 13.

If that petition had been *filed*—as the law required—it would have made a record in the Supreme Court, putting the Justices of the United States Supreme Court on record of knowing of the criminal and subversive activities described in the petition for writ of certiorari.

Justices Had Right Not to Hear, But no Right to Reject Filing

The Supreme Court Justices had the prerogative of not granting a hearing on the petition for writ of certiorari. They did *not* have the authority to deny its filing. Normally, the Justices hear only a small fraction of the petitions that are filed. But in this case, the mere act of filing the petition put the justices on notice of very serious criminal and subversive activities. This was a very sensitive matter with enormous implications.

Filing Requires Copies Sent to Major Law Libraries Throughout US

Automatic exposure to the legal fraternity of petitions to the Supreme Court occurs by the procedures in place. A person filing a petition for writ of certiorari with the U.S. Supreme Court must file an original and 40 copies in booklet form, many of which are then sent to law libraries throughout the United States. These petitions are then read by media sources who report on the contents of significant filings even if the Justices do not choose to hear the matter. The highly sensitive nature of the charges in the petition could cause unknown consequences, and in any case, show the Supreme Court Justices had been made aware of the charges and the supporting documentation referred to in the petition.

Justices' Deception to Keep the Charges From the Public

The Justices addressed this serious problem by refusing to file the petition, which they could not do under law. The Justices had the clerk fraudulently write that the filing was not timely, when the petition was filed several weeks *before* the 90-day jurisdictional period had expired.

I responded in an August 23, 1997, letter to Supreme Court clerk William K. Sutter, precisely showing the fraudulent nature of the denial, sending copies of that letter, and a copy of the petition to each of the Justices, insuring that they were on notice and could not at some future date claim ignorance of the issues and facts stated in the petition. For years Supreme Court Justices have been made aware of my charges, and where evidence supporting them could be found.

Gravity of Supreme Court Justices' Coverup

Obviously, the coverup by Justices of the Supreme Court of such serious crimes against the United States constitutes impeachable and criminal offenses. This was definitely not the first time the Justices blocked my filing, or refused to address the issues after being filed. In an earlier case, the expensively-prepared booklet-form of petitions were rejected on the phony excuse that the space between the lines did not meet Supreme Court requirements. The spacing met the requirements.

Implying the Seriousness of My Charges

Only once did a Justice of the Supreme Court make any type of response, and that was highly unusual and significant. A Justice simply does not write personal letters to a litigant, especially a *pro se* litigant. In response to my petition addressed to Justice Byron White, which he refused to grant, he stated in an October 28, 1991, letter:

As a single Justice I can be of no help to you.

I am returning your petition.

My charges were specific and of serious national importance. If any one of them was true, a serious undermining of the United States was under way. I was a former federal investigator holding authority under law to make such determinations. A check of prior federal actions would have supported certain of my charges. I offered government documents to support some of my charges.

CRIMES OF CONGRESSIONAL COVERUPS

During the last few decades, hundreds of government insiders testified to members of Congress—in closed-door hearings—about CIA drug trafficking, CIA working with organized crime in drug-related activities, and much more. Hundreds of letters have been sent to members of Congress by government and other insiders describing the specifics of the drug trafficking and the involvement of people in control of the federal government. Every major area of criminality touching upon high-level corruption has been covered up, as I've documented in my various books.

Initial Expert on CIA Drug Trafficking

Alfred McCoy, who published two early books[50] on the CIA's involvement in drug trafficking, testified in 1972 to congressional committees about the CIA role in the developing global narcotic trade. He described members of Congress enthusiastically accepting the CIA's denial of any role in drug trafficking, despite the overwhelming evidence of its existence. Two decades later, despite many closed-door hearings receiving testimony from hundreds of insiders providing further evidence of this relationship, members of Congress continue the coverup and obstruction of justice with catastrophic consequences for many innocent people.

CIA asset Richard Brenneke testified to Congress, presented hard evidence of his role in the CIA, drug sales by the CIA to the Gotti crime family, CIA drug-money laundering for the crime organization. Brenneke was never prosecuted for perjury. His testimony was true. I have seen the confidential transcripts of that testimony, which was given in 1989. A decade later, with dozens if not hundreds of other insiders testifying to similar criminal activities by the CIA, the public is still being victimized by the congressional coverups.

Testimony of Ramon Milian Rodriguez

Hundreds of people directly involved in drug trafficking and drug-money laundering have testified in closed-door congressional hearings about the CIA, DEA, and Customs involvement in these activities. This revealing testimony rarely gets into the hearing records available to the public. Many of these witnesses sought to give evidence to various U.S. agencies about the drug trafficking and drug-money laundering, and were blocked.

On February 11, 1988, Ramon Milian Rodriguez, a major drug-money launderer, testified in Congressional hearings[51] that he had tried to blow the whistle years earlier on the CIA drug trafficking and drug money laundering. Rodriguez testified that he also contacted members of Vice President George Bush's South Florida Task Force in 1983, including people that he knew as Sathos and Summerall, and was likewise rebuffed.

Government Insiders Providing Data To Drug Traffickers

Rodriguez testified, as did others, that insiders in government provided the Medellin and Cali cartels with information about the names and identification of DEA agents, the radio frequencies and the schedules of Coast Guard and Navy interdiction aircraft.

Rodriguez described the huge amount of drug money shipped from the United States, and the logistic problems associated with moving large pallets of money out of the United States. He described the drug traffickers' use of Eastern and Braniff Airlines for shipment of drug-money from the United States to Central and South America. (In earlier pages, Eastern Airlines Captain Gerald Loeb reported similar activities to Congress.) The shipments were in containers or on pallets, and often loaded without any cargo manifest. In Panama and other Central and South American countries, the aircraft would

---

[50] *The Politics of Heroin–CIA Complicity In The Global Drug Trade* and the earlier *The Politics of Heroin in Southeast Asia.*

[51] Hearings before the Subcommittee on Terrorism, Narcotics and International Communications, February 11, 1988.

be met by armed guards, the drug-money unloaded, and then taken to banks, such as Banco Nacional de Panama. Station agents and other airline employees working for Braniff or Eastern would be in the pay of the drug cartels or other drug traffickers.

Rodriguez elaborated upon the complexities and sophistication involved in drug-money laundering, requiring expertise in accounting, banking, logistics, security, bank secrecy laws, and the mechanics of incorporating. Dummy corporations would be set up, and the money transferred from one corporation to another to mask the money path. Cutouts would be used to separate high-level personnel from the source of the drugs or drug money.

A series of accounts would be set up with dummy corporations through which the drug money would be processed. These dummy corporations would be filed with the Secretary of State of various states in the United States, especially Florida, California and New York. Some legitimate businesses were used to front for the drug-money laundering. Dummy corporations were also set up in the country where the destination banks were located. A Panamanian corporation could be used as a cutout for a Swiss, Liechtenstein, Luxembourg, or Hong Kong company. Another tactic was to make a Panamanian company a stockholder of a Netherlands Antilles company.

Rodriguez testified that his money laundering out of the United States amounted to approximately $200 million per month, or over two billion dollars a year. This huge amount was just for his operation, and primarily for drug activities in New York and Chicago. Rodriguez also testified that he had as many as fifty aircraft flying the money out of the United States, including Boeing 727s. Rodriguez was on the board of directors of several banks, including Ponce de Leon Savings and Loan in Miami. He identified some of the countries favored for money laundering as Switzerland, Hong Kong, Panama, Curacao, Cayman Islands, and the Bahamas. Asked what happens to the drug money laundered from the United States into foreign banks, Rodriguez replied that it would be invested in real estate, stocks, bonds, CD's, and other financial investments within the United States.

Cooperation of U.S. Bankers in Drug-Money Laundering

Rodriguez testified that many U.S. banks cooperated in his money laundering, and that they often had a special representative who dealt with drug-money launderers. He identified the banks routinely and knowingly dealing in drug-money as "Citibank, Citicorp, Bank of America, and First National Bank of Boston." He testified that there was competition among U.S. banks to receive the drug-money.

Describing the power of the drug cartels in Colombia, Rodriguez testified that the cartels owned airlines, soccer teams, radio and TV stations, newspapers, and "politicians." Rodriguez described how Colombia's M-19 kidnapped "one of the Ochoa women [Leona]," how the individual drug traffickers merged into a group, and formed its own army of 2,000 people. This testimony coincided with what other CIA assets had stated to me, including Gunther Russbacher, Trenton Parker, Russell Bowen, and others.

Rodriguez testified that drug proceeds were used to fund the Contra fighting, and that in turn provided the logistics for massive drug shipments into the

United States, facts that are well known to everyone except the American public.

Companies Used in Drug-Related Crimes

Rodriguez described some of the companies used in drug-related activities. One was Frigerificos de Puntarennas, a shrimp warehouse used as a CIA front with a chain of interlocking companies, including Ocean Hunter. Ocean Hunter imported shrimp into the United States and hid drugs inside the shipments. The company was also used to launder money to the Contras. Despite the drug-related activities of Frigerificos, the Reagan-Bush administration awarded lucrative contracts to that company to provide "humanitarian assistance funds from the State Department" (i.e., guns on the way south, and drugs on the return trips).

Senator John Kerry's Protection of Involved CIA And Politicians

Rodriguez testified that the CIA was involved in the weapon shipments and drug-money laundering with his various companies. Senator John F. Kerry (D. Mass.) made reference to the repeated denials by White House and National Security Council officials about U.S. arms shipments to Iran and the Contras, while the arms shipments were continuing to occur. During testimony by various witnesses, whenever a witness was about to name a U.S. politician or the CIA involvement in the drug trafficking, Kerry interrupted the witness and said this would be discussed in executive or closed-door session. The American public never heard of the criminal activities by high-level government officials and various government agencies.

Obstruction Of Justice by Congress

The May and June 1989 edition of *Freedom* magazine said, "Two congressional subcommittees and the U.S. Customs Service are investigating secret activities around the quiet mountain town of Mena, Arkansas, including alleged drug running and arms smuggling." Congressional testimony proving the existence of government-related drug trafficking is routinely kept from the American people. Over the years thousands of documents showed the drug smuggling by the CIA, including that at Mena, Arkansas. No one could be so stupid or naive as to doubt that this practice existed.

Usual Coverups by Independent Prosecutors

In 1991, Arkansas Attorney General Winston Bryant gave independent prosecutor Lawrence E. Walsh boxes of evidence showing the CIA's role in Arkansas drug trafficking. This evidence consisted of depositions, Arkansas State Police reports, investigative files, sworn statements, FBI reports, and court documents, proving the existence of drug-related activities in the Iran-Contra operation involving the CIA, the National Security Council, the Mossad, and other government officials.

Walsh covered up for it, even though this was the most important part of the Iran-Contra affair that he was charged to investigate. Walsh's coverup was a crime far worse that what he was reporting. The corruption that he covered up had done and continued to do great harm, along with the continuation of the drug trafficking that his coverup made possible.

Walsh's investigation—including his coverup—cost the American people over forty million dollars. I also presented Walsh with evidence concerning criminal activities, and encountered the same coverup. It is important to keep in mind that these coverups by people employed by the federal government are far greater crimes than the offenses that have sent thousands of people to federal prison.

Unbelievable Coverup Said Congressman Alexander

In talking to the press, Congressman Alexander said: "I've never seen a white-wash job as good as has been executed in this case. It is unbelievable to me that such crimes can be gotten away with in this country."

FAA Coverup of Drug Trafficking

The number of concerned government employees exposing the coverup and obstruction of justice by federal personnel escalated as my activities became known. Shortly after Christmas 1994, several present and former FAA investigators revealed to me the obstacles they faced from FAA management in retaliation for reporting drug activity involving aircraft, that they discovered during their official duties.

FAA Inspector Fired for Reporting Drug-Related Stolen Aircraft

One of them, David Jennings, told me how he was fired by FAA management for continuing to make such reports. He and other FAA inspectors assigned to the security and drug divisions revealed numerous instances of FAA management interference with this division's drug responsibilities. Their statements showed that the same problems I found as a federal investigator for the FAA have not changed, and if anything, worsened.

CIA Drug Trafficking is Unknown
Only to the Victimized American Public

One of the many bizarre aspects of this massive drug trafficking, involving key government agencies and branches of government, including the White House, is the illiteracy and indifference of the American public when so many highly documented books have been written about the activities.

Hundreds of witnesses have testified before Congress[52] about their direct knowledge and/or participation in this drug trafficking. Many television shows have addressed this fact, with witnesses who were part of it. The criminal elements are aware of it. Those connected with the intelligence agencies are aware of it. What is the public's problem?

---

[52] Senator John Kerry's office released on October 14, 1986 a classified report describing the testimony of over four dozen witnesses before the committee that he headed. This report described the drug trafficking into the United States by persons associated with the CIA and other government agencies. Thirteen of the government people identified in the drug trafficking were among the defendants in the Christic Institute's lawsuit. No actions were taken by any law enforcement agency against these government employees.

CHAPTER SIXTEEN

WHAT DO WE DO NOW?

Can Any, Most, Or All Of This Be True?

I know for a fact that most of what is stated here—and in my other books seeking to inform people about high-level government corruption—is true. I base this determination upon, for instance:

- What I have actually seen, experienced, and documented as a federal investigator.
- What I discovered and documented for the last 30 years as a private investigator and confidant to several dozen present and former government agents and operatives.
- What was discovered by people—who have confided in me for years—who were part of the activities I write about, or discovered the activities as part of their government duties. These include personnel from such agencies as the CIA, ONI, DIA, DEA, INS, Customs, FBI, FAA, Secret Service and others. They also include former drug traffickers, Mafia family members, and officers from various police departments. My person-to-person contacts covered a period of years of information gathering, often during deposition-like questioning, and exchange of probing questions and answers. Some have even provided me with sworn affidavits, some of which I have entered into federal court proceedings.
- As a former Navy and airline pilot, I was able to more easily gain the confidence of these sources, especially after I became friends with a few deep-cover insiders. These contacts permitted me to tap into the experiences of unusual people whose combined deep-cover experiences easily surpass 200 years. To most of them I was a friend, and they were willing to divulge much to me.
- Knowledge gained as head of a coalition of present and former government whistleblowers. Many of these people are ready to testify at a meaningful hearing.
- What I learned as a victim, as powerful forces in control of federal agencies attempted to silence me.
- Copies of secret transcripts of testimony given in closed-door congressional hearings.
- Copies of hundreds of classified documents provided to me over the years

by deep-cover sources.
- Many highly detailed investigative articles written in newspapers and magazines, and exposé books written by insiders.
- Over 30 years of constant almost daily exposure to some segment of the matters detailed and documented in my books—plus the considerable other information on government corruption that has never been put into book form.

The Specific Problems Associated With the Drug Crisis

A few of the more prominent problems associated with the multiple tentacles of the drug crisis would include:

- The *drug users* in the United States, who fund the long chain of drug-related crimes. Without those people there would be *no* drug problem as we know it today.
- People in control of the government agencies and covert operations that have been smuggling drugs into the United States for the past 50 years, starting with the CIA and primarily involving that agency. Without them, it is very probable that the drug crisis would be only a small part of what it is today.
- People in control of key government offices who have covered up for the CIA and other drug trafficking for years. They include for instance the Department of Justice, the State Department, National Security Council, the U.S. military, the White House, federal judges, members of Congress, and others.
- Members of Congress who compounded their coverups by legislating draconian prison sentences to enhance their standing with their constituencies while knowingly inflicting great harm upon them through a back-door approach, and who consistently refuse to correct their wrongful acts.
- That segment of the broadcast and print media that covered up for the corrupt activities that I document in my various books. Their coverups, disinformation, ridiculing of those courageous people who speak out, have played a key role in the tragedies inflicted upon the public and the country.
- Those arrogant government employees in the Department of Justice who file sham charges against innocent people for their own self interests, who engage in corrupt acts, lying, perjury, and set the culture in and out of government that is corrupting all aspects of life in the United States.

Recognize That It Can Happen To *You* and *Your* Family

People must recognize any of these tragedies can happen to them. Many people come to me after they have been victimized. They also were among those who refused to become informed and refused to speak out. They, with the remainder of the public, are partly responsible for what happened to them by remaining ignorant and indifferent.

Comparison of Roles and Offenses Between Drug Users, Drug Traffickers, and Corrupt Government Personnel

To help better understand the drug crisis and how we got to this stage, let's compare the blame of the men and women charged with drug-related offenses with those who legislated and who carry out the draconian prison sentences:

Those Responsible for Drugs in America

- *Government personnel involved in drug trafficking.* People in control of various factions in the Central Intelligence Agency and those CIA officials responsible for a half century of drug trafficking. This would include people in other government departments, including the DEA and the U.S. military, who engaged in drug trafficking after the CIA first initiated it. Also involved in drug trafficking during the Iran-Contra affair, were the National Security Council (Oliver North), the White House (Vice President George Bush), military, DEA, State Department, and Justice Department. The nature of these actions—perpetrated by high-level government personnel—cause them to be criminal and subversive, and of far greater severity and harm to the United States than any drug user or small-time drug trafficker.
- *Government personnel involved in coverup of government drug trafficking.* People holding federal office who cover up for government drug trafficking, which include the Department of Justice and its various divisions, including the FBI, U.S. Attorneys, and DEA, the State Department, and other offices.
- *Members of Congress*, who have known for decades about CIA and other covert agency drug trafficking into the United States.
- *Federal judges* who have known about the drug trafficking for years, and who have not only aided and abetted these activities through coverups, but have aided in the retaliation against government agents who seek to report these crimes. Reference is also made to federal judges blocking people from reporting these federal crimes to them, including the retaliation against me for using this statute to report such crimes.
- *People in the broadcast and print media* who knew of these corrupt and subversive activities for decades, and who covered up for them, thereby becoming part of a criminal conspiracy obstructing justice.
- *State and local government personnel* who often help carry out these corrupt activities.
- *The thousands of city, county and state law-enforcement personnel* who have themselves engaged in drug trafficking and who have escaped punishment.

Recognize What This Corruption is Doing To America

Besides inflicting horrendous personal and financial harm upon hundreds of thousands of individuals, everyone involved in any way with this corruption is helping to destroy our form of government and destroy or corrupt its institutions.

Recognize What Won't Work

It is important to recognize what won't work in the present drug crisis. For instance:

- Spending billions of dollars a year to stop the growing of drugs in other countries cannot possibly work. There are too many people and places willing to grow and produce drugs when such growth and production is halted elsewhere. (And it never is halted, despite the claims of U.S. leaders.) At a June 8, 1998 General Assembly session of the United Nations on drug trafficking, Britain's Deputy Prime Minister, John Prescott, speaking on behalf of the European Union, said: "It is no use stopping opium cultivation in one place just to see more grown elsewhere. We gain nothing by closing one trafficking route to see another opened." Politicians, police, the military, and the economy in many countries, depend on the Yankee drug dollars. They are not going to give up these benefits. The drug problem is an internal problem in the United States, brought about by the breakdown in character and culture.

- Hiring more government agents will not work. With the passage of NAFTA and the thousands of railroad cars and 18-wheeler trucks entering the United States every month, there is no way that any but a small percentage of drugs can be detected. It is estimated that over 60 percent of drugs consumed by U.S. drug users enter via Mexico.
- Rescinding NAFTA to reduce the great amount of traffic between Mexico and the United States is not feasible; billions of dollars have been invested in Mexico by U.S. corporations as a result of NAFTA. Further, Mexico's economy would be adversely affected, creating another crisis. Jack A. Bloom who worked with the Senate Judiciary Committee on various congressional investigations in the past, said Mexico's drug economy far exceeds $30 billion a year. If this amount was suddenly cut off, major economic chaos would occur in Mexico. Over ten percent, and probably much more, of Mexico's economy is fueled by dollars from U.S. drug users. A cutoff of this windfall would inflict great economic harm throughout the Mexican economy and to those who live off America's drug users.
- Continuing to put hundreds of thousands of non-violent men and women in prison will further destroy the United States.

Constitutional Failures

The Constitution has serious deficiencies, possibly due to the inability of the framers of this document to comprehend the extent of corruption in government offices as now exists. Changes are needed to the Constitution. Federal judges and government prosecutors, among other government employees, must be subject to civil and criminal damages when they engage in corruption that inflicts harm upon innocent people. The offices of the Attorney General and the Department of Justice must be removed from the control of the President of the United States, and no longer protect presidential misconduct.

An Ombudsman Agency Is Badly Needed

An "ombudsman" agency is badly needed, that is totally separate from any other government agency or official, and staffed in such a way that it would be very difficult to cover up.

Patriots and "Heroes" Needed To Correct These Outrages

The meaning of "heroes" does not apply to the media's portrayal of the word, which is applied to ball players and others—that make a mockery of the term. Never has America needed real heroes more than now. Never has there been such a low percentage of them in the general population. Americans don't seem to know the meaning of the word. A comparable devaluing of the "hero" meaning was by a local newspaper in my area, *Contra Costa Times*. In 1999 it had a daily listing called "Local Hero," listing people who had certainly not done anything heroic.

Our form of government *requires* its citizens to be patriots. The true patriots are those few people who had the courage to fight the epidemic corruption and the overwhelming odds. True and honest democracy does not come cheap.

Suggestions to Consider in Addressing the Drug Problems

The following are steps that should be considered and which have merit: For various reasons, we simply cannot incarcerate for years at a time all of the people using drugs and those who are fulfilling the demands of U.S. drug users. The users must on their own show some sense of character and responsibility, recognize that it is they who are funding every segment of the violence, the killings, the bribery, the corruption, associated with drugs.

But focusing on these noble principles won't do the entire job. Here is one suggestion for addressing the drug problem to reduce people's demands and consumption of illicit drugs:

- *Appeal to the need to build character and integrity—totally foreign to the use of drugs.* This must be continuously stressed and attention paid to trying to get back to some degree of national integrity that once existed, years before most people now living were born. And things weren't like this at that time. One large drawback is the pattern of corruption and violence in the movies, what is called music, and other forms of entertainment. The effect upon young people, upon people of all ages, to the constant barrage of violence in what is called entertainment, has been known for years to be establishing a culture of violence among the people, and especially the young people. But the financial interests in continuing the status quo will outlast any temporary and soon-forgotten event such as school violence, including that which occurred in Littleton, Colorado in April 1999. Instead of facing the obvious problem, guns are blamed rather than the culture.

Possible Replacement for Barbarous Congressional "Remedies"

- Promptly replace the minimum sentencing statute, with heavy consideration for an entirely different approach to the drug problems.
- *Probation for first two drug offenses.* For the first two "detentions," place the drug user on probation (possibly for one year after the latest detention; require that the user promptly enter a drug treatment plan in a low security environment. Require an understanding instead of a hostile attitude by the people carrying out the programs.
- *Periodic drug tests.* Require that anyone charged with drug use undergo periodic drug tests to be sure they have not gone back on drugs. The frequency of drug tests would be determined after studies with experts. Possibly every two weeks, with the person being tested required to pay for the test, or a lien filed under their name with the country recorder. If they fail a drug test, back to a low-security environment for possibly another two or three months. The testing requirements might continue, for instance, for one year after a drug conviction.
- *Nominal confinement in low-security, non-hostile redemption environment.* After two probation periods, if the person tests positive for drug use during the testing period, have the person confined to a low-security and

non-hostile environment for a short period, such as one or two months. (Violent people, those who exhibit any type of violent behavior, would instead go to a jail situation.)

- *The costs.* The cost of these procedures could be taken from the billions of dollars used to carry out the draconian methods now in place and probably have 90 percent of the funds left over for useful purposes.

What to Do About the Drug Trafficker?

More difficult to address is the penalty against those who transport and sell drugs. When these are non-violent offenses, thought must be given to the fact that it is the users who are responsible for the drug crisis, with those who fulfill the demand further down the responsibility chain. There should be penalties, harsh financial penalties, but the incarceration should be far less severe than called for by the present legislation.

Relief for Those Imprisoned on Drug Charges

Not to be forgotten are those victims of sham criminal charges, or overblown charges, or those recipients of outrageous prison sentences, who were sentenced to long prison terms, even life. A panel should be appointed with the power to promptly release most of those people charged with conspiracy offenses and where the evidence came from paid informants. Blanket immediate releases could be ordered for certain offenses, and releases ordered for many others within a reasonable time whose sentences were obviously far in excess of the severity of their offense. No one charged with a non-violent drug offense should have a life-in-prison sentence, and definitely far less than presently existing!

Recognize Those with A Vested Interest in Continuing the Status Quo

For various reasons—some of them obvious—certain groups will block any effort to change the present system.

- Corporations who have invested heavily, and plan to continue such investments, in the growth businesses associated with incarcerating large numbers of men and women. The growth industries associated with U.S. drug consumption include prison construction, prison management, prison suppliers.
- Thousands of government agents and informants, who depend upon incarcerating large numbers of people to justify their jobs, salaries, forfeitures, and bonuses.
- Members of Congress who do not want to lose the demagoguery associated with feel-good, tough-on-crime, legislation and rhetoric.
- People in control of the Department of Justice and its various divisions and the head of it, the Attorney General.
- Federal and state prosecutors will go after key people in any movement to expose government corruption.
- Attorneys and law firms—although they won't admit it—as they earn huge legal fees from the status quo.
- Those profiting from the huge consumption of drugs, including whatever agenda the CIA has had for its drugging of America.

Will the Public Ever Meet Its Responsibilities?

Most of the public remains unaware and indifferent to the harm made possible by their being uninformed and their indifference about government corruption. I witnessed this apathy for the past 20 years as I appeared as guest and expert on over 3000 radio and television shows, seeking to inform the American people of the great harm being inflicted upon them and motivate them to show some civil responsibility.

Many listeners expressed concern—and then did nothing. Even relatives of people killed in fraud-related air disasters that I had exposed did nothing, and none offered to help me expose this corruption. Their only interest appeared to be rushing to a law firm for financial enrichment. Those who say the public will *never* wake up and respond may be right. The same goes for people who read the books and do nothing to focus attention on the problem.

The Ugly American

A little self-evaluation might also help in understanding America's deteriorated morals, culture, and character. Many years ago authors William J. Lederer and Eugene Burdick wrote a novel based on conduct by Americans in Southeast Asia: *The Ugly American*. The book's introduction says:

The Ugly American is about men and women in Southeast Asia-people making mistakes, people being a little corrupt, people trapped by the beauty of a land or of a woman, people being bought cheap with champagne and caviar.

This unflattering conduct has certainly escalated to an unprecedented degree today. The conduct of people in control of key government offices today, and of many Americans, more than ever supports that title. Because the United States is a government structure of, by, and for the people, that means the people approved of the conduct of its government. Let's look at some of the conduct that the American public, as a whole, approved, which surely justifies a modern version of *The Ugly American*:

- Inflicting war upon the people of Indochina, killing hundreds of thousands of plain simple people defending their country, including women and children as in the Mai Lai massacre, torturing and killing over 40,000 Vietnamese in the CIA's Operation Phoenix. The excuse for this CIA operation? The United States could not allow the poor people of this third world country to decide who their leaders would be, and the simplistic "domino theory."
- Undermining the duly elected governments throughout the world, including Nicaragua, again repeating simplistic excuses that only a dumbed-down public could swallow.
- Invading Panama and killing hundreds of people while trying to capture the head of Panama on a charge that he was trafficking in drugs (while the CIA, the National Security Council, the President and Vice President, were doing the same, often using Panama).
- Invading Granada and killing defenders on the excuse that an airstrip was being enlarged to accommodate Russian bombers. That airstrip today is enlarged, and used for the original purpose: tourist flights.
- CIA teaching, funding, and arming torture squads throughout Central and South America, resulting in tens of thousands of tortured and killed innocent people.

- Undermining governments throughout Central and South America, providing arms and money, which resulted in many governments being toppled, and many people killed.

- Sending missiles into foreign countries, such as in Sudan where the United States blew up a pharmaceutical plant on the flimsy—and thoroughly discredited claim—that it was producing terrorist chemicals, blowing apart a residence of the Libyan head of state and killing his child on the unproven claim that Libya was responsible for a bombing in Europe, blowing apart the Chinese Embassy in Belgrade, and much more. Any single one of these acts could have resulted in hundreds of missiles blowing apartment U.S. cities, something that is sure to come. The United States has made enemies of large segments of Moslem countries, China, Russia, and many other countries, any of which will surely applaude when the United States gets what it inflicted upon people of other nations.

- CIA involvement in killings, including the involvement by presidents of the United States in planning the murders of foreign leaders, including Fidel Castro.

- Large numbers of Americans funding all forms of drug-related corruption, crimes, and murders—made possible by their drug dollars.

"If you don't like what is going on in the United States, leave!"

Some like the country as it is, as shown by talk show host Larry King, who stated during one of his shows, "If you don't like what is going on in the United States, leave!" With that type of mentality, is it any wonder the United States is in such a state of decline? Americans have the right to expect honest government, and the alternative is not for honest Americans to leave the country.

Can America Survive These Deteriorated Values?

Those of us who fought in World War II and saw what America was like in the mid-1900s, have seen the deterioration of constitutional rights, the arrogance of government, the deterioration of morals and culture—and the congressional and public approval of massive incarceration of its people.

Even children are taught violence and contempt for others as they watch violent movies, violent television programs, listen to violent noise they consider "music." Years ago the movies and the music had an uplifting quality. The vulgarity and violence in movies and "music" today have the opposite effect. The April 1999 murder of 13 students by two school students who later committed suicide shows the effect of this profitable violence-prone entertainment that goes on year after year with the American public unable to understand why their children have violent thoughts! Rather than face the real problem, and face a formidable foe who has lots of money at stake continuing the status quo, the public goes after the gun manufacturers who cannot be expected to mount a formidable defense!

Fools and Their Freedom are Soon Parted

Fools and their freedom are soon parted was stated two centuries ago and the statement is probably truer today than it was then. The following warning message is reportedly attributed to Cicero, 42 B.C.:

A nation can survive its fools and even the ambitious. But it cannot survive treason from within. An enemy at the gates is less formidable, for he is known and he carries his banners openly. But the traitor moves among those within the gates freely, his sly whispers rustling through all the alleys, heard in the very halls of government itself. For the traitor appears not traitor: He speaks in the accents familiar to his victims and he wears their face and their garments and he appeals to the baseness that lies deep in the hearts of all men. He rots the soul of a nation. He works secretly and unknown in the night to undermine the pillars of a city; he infects the body politic so that it can no longer resist. A murderer is less to be feared.

Quotations as Applicable Today as When First Written

In a quotation attributable to Martin Niemoeller:

In Germany they came first for the Communist, and I didn't speak up, because I wasn't a Communist. Then they came for the Jews, and I didn't speak up, because I wasn't a Jew. Then they came for the trade unionists, and I didn't speak up, because I wasn't a trade unionist. Then they came for the Catholics and I didn't speak up, because I was a Protestant. Then they came for me, and by that time no one was left to speak out.

A public illiterate about government corruption. A public that idolizes public figures, ball players, entertainment figures who portray corruption. A public too lazy to exercise its civic responsibilities. Are there enough people to save this mess before it goes the way of ancient Rome?

The Public's Record For Integrity and Courage Isn't Encouraging

The American public has tacitly approved the infliction of grave harm throughout the world—while simultaneously boasting about its human rights stands. The public has a responsibility under our form of government to stay informed; instead, they have remained ignorant about important matters. Public morals, government morals, have gone deeper and deeper into the gutter, and only a few voices are heard in protest.

We have a generation of people who don't know what constitutional rights existed before they were born—and which no longer exists. Who don't know how the murder rate was kept very low—by prompt payment with their lives. We have become a vulgar, corrupt, and violent society, and the harm we inflicted throughout the world will probably be returned within their lifetime with much of the world turned against the United States.

There is hope. But only if enough people become informed and aggressively speak out. At the very least, this book and my others will help the reader avoid becoming the prey of those in control of powerful government offices such as the various divisions of the Department of Justice and other government agencies.

Public's Record for Courage Is Not Encouraging

It takes courage to speak out and do something about corruption in government, or to come to the aid of a victim. For years, newspapers have been reporting the spectre of people watching and doing nothing to help someone being beat up. Typical is the headline in the San Francisco Examiner (July 16, 1998), "Bystanders Watch Woman's Beating." The paper reported, "150 people watched and did nothing" as a young woman was being beaten in the heart of San Francisco. Similar headlines have appeared over the years in newspapers in Massachusetts, New York, New Orleans, and other places, showing the cowadice is rampant. (One problem with fosterring cowardice is the refusal of some states or counties refusing to issue gun permits to law abiding people.)

It takes courage to tackle government corruption, and the dismal lack of courage on the part of almost the entire nation is all too obvious. Making the problem even more dismal is the approval by the public of government misconduct.

The nation tackles school shootings not by addressing the teaching of violence through movies, songs, and videos—where resistance would be encountered, but by going after the gun manufacturers: an easy target that won't fight back. The problems with the unpredcedented numbers of brutal murders are addressed by giving the perpetrators free room and board instead of the prompt execution of death sentences—making possible the increasing number of such vicious crimes.

What Can *You* Do About Other Forms of Government Corruption?

- First and foremost, realize that you and others like you are prey to those acting under color of state and federal law, using the awesome powers available to them, knowing they will be protected by the system. Remember, you and other men and women, of all ages, are the prey!
- Discover the facts by extensive reading of factual material concerning these matters that are written by insiders and knowledgeable people. Reading a daily newspaper is only a start—and far from adequate.
- Inform others of hard-core corruption that you learn about.
- Make repeated phone calls to radio and television shows describing what you have learned, and encourage them to have the authors of exposé-type books appear as guests. Remember, however, that many hosts will not want to address these highly sensitive issues.
- Recommend that others read this and other books, and encourage them to get involved.
- Make repeated reference to this and related books on the Internet in as many places as possible, and encourage discussion of the charges made in the book. But be aware of those on the Internet whose function is to discredit those who seek to expose the truth.
- Keep away from screwball or highly subjective issues that take attention away from hard-core government corruption, and that will only discredit you by touching on these matters.
- Demand—don't ask—your members of Congress to investigate. Don't accept their off-the-shelf evasive responses. Send certified letters to each of your U.S. senators and representatives, demanding that they immediately take the following actions, reminding them of their responsibilities, but realizing that their answers will in most cases be off-the-shelf meaningless responses. Stay on it to insure that members of Congress promptly conduct non-coverup hearing into these charges. Have insiders, such as my group of government insiders, appear and present testimony at open

hearings. These hearings should be into every area of corruption that I detail and often document in my books. Keep in mind that most prior congressional hearings are coverups. Insure that the hearings are open and not secret behind closed doors. Keep the pressure on, even after hearings start. It is standard practice in congressional hearings to address a small and remote part of a scandal while covering up for the serious parts. Iran-Contra investigations were a good example, with the CIA drug trafficking well hidden while addressing minor issues.

- Pressure Congress to provide legislation and ample funding for an ombudsmen division in government that is staffed by people totally isolated from political influence and with the power to fully investigate and recommend prosecution.
- Pressure Congress to pass legislation eliminating the immunity of government prosecutors, federal (and state) judges, and other government employees whose actions are obviously illegal, unconstitutional, and/or retaliatory. This legislation should cover the Civil Rights Act, Federal Tort Claims Act, and provide authority on its own for people who have been harmed to sue in federal court, with a jury. *Anyone* who acts under color of state or federal law, acting in violation of settled law and constitutional protections, inflicting harm upon any person, should be capable of being sued for damages.
- Pressure Congress to pass legislation subjecting members of Congress and state and federal judges to investigation and punishment by a body not subject to political influence when they commit crimes for which a citizen would be subject to prosecution and imprisonment. This would include misprision of a felony, meaning having knowledge of a federal crime and not promptly reporting it to a federal tribunal that is not itself involved in the crime or its coverup.
- Start becoming informed by reading the information made available by courageous insiders, and show some form of reaction and responsibility.
- Provide constitutional changes to eliminate the president from appointing or controlling the attorney general and the selection of U.S. attorneys.
- Pass legislation to force federal judges to comply with the clear intent of the crime-reporting statute, Title 18 USC Section 4, making it a felony for any judge to refuse to receive evidence of criminal activities (that is already clearly stated). This is a very important statute for anyone to report a federal crime when Justice Department employees are covering up, such as for any of the crimes detailed in my books, including CIA drug trafficking that government agents have known about for decades. If federal judges had not blocked the reporting of these crimes under Title 18 USC Section 4, the advanced stage of high level corruption could not exist. Also make clear that it is a federal crime for anyone, including media personnel, who knows of a federal crime and who does not report it promptly to a federal judge or other federal official.
- Pass legislation requiring that all criminal proceedings, regardless of the length of possible imprisonment, require a jury. (Although this is required by the U.S. Constitution, federal judges have openly violated it, holding

that a prison sentence of six months or less does not require a jury trial.)

- Pass legislation circumventing judicial rulings, that permits a private party to sue a federal judge or prosecutor if either of them violates clearly stated statutory or constitutional law, and the right to a jury trial in these cases. This protection exists already, but judges have held themselves immune. Statutes specifically making judges liable will address this issue.
- Pass legislation permitting people whose assets have been corruptly taken from them in Chapter 11 courts to sue the government and the Judges, Trustees and law firms, in jury trials. Have the statute of limitations start to run from the day the legislation is passed, and have an adequate period of time to file administrative claims under the Federal Tort Claims Act and time to initiate RICO or civil rights violation actions.
- Pass legislation barring seizure of assets on the pretense that the person violated some particular law.
- Pass legislation or make constitutional changes eliminating life tenure for federal judges.

You Can Either Help—Or Do Nothing—And Be Part Of the Problem!

Everyone has a responsibility under our form of government to stay intelligently informed about government misconduct and react within his ability to do whatever is needed. Most of the harm inflicted upon people described in my books continues to occur for various reasons, one of which is the continued ignorance of future victims.

Many of the victims described within these pages helped bring about their own fate by remaining ignorant and indifferent. In the area of aviation corruption, the resulting crashes and deaths are identified in *Unfriendly Skies*, and give a clue of what you can expect in the future. In *Defrauding America*, many of the other schemes that devastated and continue to devastate thousands of people every year are identified. And in *Drugging America*, the corrupt practices that have already affected hundreds of thousands are identified. You or your family could be among the thousands of yearly victims

APPLICABLE FEDERAL LAW

Many of the actions and inactions described in these pages are criminal acts under federal law, and are poorly understood by the general public. The following brief description of selected criminal statutes will help to understand this association.

Accessory Before and After the Fact

An accessory is a person who in some manner is connected with a crime, either before or after its perpetration, but who is not present when the crime is committed. (21 Am J2d Crim L § 115.) Title 18 U.S.C. § 3. An accessory *before* the fact is a person who contributes to a felony committed by another, but is too far away to aid in the felonious act. In some jurisdictions the accessory before the fact is also charged with the crime of those committing the actual act. An accessory *after* the fact is a person who knows a felony has been committed and who *comforts or assists the felon in any manner to avoid prosecution.* (21 Am J2d Crim L § 126)

An attorney in the Justice Department, a judge, a member of Congress, someone in the print or broadcast media, who knows of a crime and has the duty to expose it, but doesn't, would be guilty of this criminal offense. As will be seen, the list of groups and individuals guilty of this crime is endless.

Accomplice

An accomplice is a person who knowingly, voluntarily, and with a common interest with others participates in the commission of a crime as a principal, as an accessory, or aider and abettor. That would include a government official who refuses to perform a duty to prosecute someone guilty of a federal crime.

Aiding and Abetting

Any person who "commits an offense against the United States or aids, abets, counsels, commands, induces or procures its commission, is punishable as a principal." Any person who joins any conspiracy, even if they are unaware of the actual act committed by others, or why, become equally liable with the others. Title 18 U.S.C. § 3. This is another crime that has been and is being perpetrated by officials in all levels of government.

Conspiracy

Conspiracy is an agreement between two or more persons to accomplish an unlawful act. Conspiracy is a separate offense over and above whatever other acts the parties conspired to accomplish. The existence of a conspiracy is usually determined from *circumstantial evidence*, looked at collectively. This is usually the only means of determining a conspiracy,[53] and is generally established by a *number of indefinite acts, each of which, standing alone, might have little weight. But taken collectively, they point unerringly to the existence of a conspiracy.*[54] The existence of a conspiracy may be proven by *inference from conduct, statements, documents, and facts and circumstances* which disclose a common design on the part of the accused persons and others to act together in pursuance of a common criminal purpose. This offense is rampant throughout these pages. It is a common tactic to ridicule anyone claiming a conspiracy exists, even though conspiracies are possibly the most common offense committed, being simply an agreement between two or more people to commit some act.

Corruption

The term corruption covers a multitude of official wrongdoings, and especially anything which adversely affects the administration of justice; or subverts the instrumentalities of government; or impedes justice and the administration of justice. (*United States v Polakoff*, 121 F2d 333)

Corruption applies to many of those involved in the activities described earlier and those activities yet to be described.

Fraud

Fraud is deceit, deception, or trickery operating prejudicially to the rights of another, and so intended by inducing him to surrender some legal right. It is anything calculated to deceive another to that person's prejudice. It is an act, a word, silence, the suppression of the truth, or any other device contrary to the plain rules of common honesty. (23 Am J2d Fraud § 2)

Misprision of A Felony

Misprision of a felony is a criminal offense and arises from failure to inform a federal court or other federal authority of a federal offense that has been witnessed or that has come to the person's knowledge. It is also the failure to prevent a felony from being committed. (21 Am J2d Crim L § 7.) It is also the failure to disclose a felony coupled with some positive act of concealment, such as suppression of evidence, harboring of criminal, intimidation of witnesses, or other positive act designed to conceal from the authorities the fact that a crime has been committed. (Title 18 U.S.C. § 4)

Obstruction Of Justice

Obstruction of justice is the criminal offense of knowing of a crime and interfering with the administration and due course of justice. This statute was repeatedly violated by corrupt federal judges and Justice Department attorneys.

Mail and Wire Fraud

Under Title 18 U.S.C. §§ 1341 and 1343, mail and wire fraud is any scheme to harm another by false or fraudulent pretenses, dishonest methods,

---

[53] *United States v. Calaway* (9th Cir. 524 F.2d 609).
[54] *State v. Horton*, 275 NC 651, 170 SE2d 466.

tricks, deceit, chicane, overreaching, or other wrongful acts, using the mail or wire. DOJ prosecutors filing false charges against people would be included here.

Malfeasance

Malfeasance is the doing of an act which is positively unlawful or wrong, and which causes injury to another person or property. It is the performance by a public official of an act in an official capacity that is wholly illegal and wrongful.

Misfeasance

Misfeasance is the improper doing of an act which a person can lawfully do, but done in an unlawful and injurious exercise of lawful authority. This would include a federal judge or Justice Department official who prosecutes informants in retaliation for reporting federal crimes.

Nonfeasance

Nonfeasance is the failure to act where duty requires, such as when a public officer neglects or refuses, without sufficient excuse, to do that which it is the officer's legal duty to do, whether willfully or through malice or ignorance.

Perjury

Perjury is making false statements under oath. Anyone who subscribes or signs any material matter which he does not believe to be true is guilty of perjury.

Treason

Treason is that act committed by a citizen who gives aid and comfort to the enemy; who betrays a trust or a confidence; who commits a breach of faith; who betrays his or her country.[55] Within these pages this offense will arguably apply to various CIA activities yet to be described and to others.

Vicarious Liability

Vicarious civil or criminal liability exists when a person performs a wrongful act, or refuses to perform a duty, such as an employer or management. Where an employee is the proximate cause of the harm, his or her superior is liable on the theory of vicarious liability.

Where an employer, or the government, exercises control over an employee, that employer or government agency has vicarious liability. Where an employer gives a federal employee substantial or complete control over certain acts, an agency relationship exists. As it relates to federal judges, for instance, the federal government pays the salaries of the judges, provides the courts, provides instructions for administrative duties. The same principle applies to Justice Department attorneys and other government checks and balances.[56]

Federal Sentencing Guidelines

A minimum prescribed prison term for a particular offense. A longer prison term is prescribed for government officials who betray their trust as

---

[55] *United States v. Wiltsberger* (US 5 Wheat 76, 5 L Ed 37. A criminal attempt to destroy the existence of the government. *Republica v Chapman* (Pa) 1 Dall 53, 1 L Ed 33. Breaching an allegiance to one's country. Also shown under Article III, § 3 of the U.S. Constitution.

[56] Cases relating to vicarious liability includes *Crinkley v. Holiday Inns, Inc.*, 844 F.2d 156 (4th Cir. 1988); *Cislaw v. 7-Eleven, Inc.*, 92 Daily Journal D.A.R. 4136 (March 30, 1992); *Beck v. Arthur Murray, Inc.*, 245 Cal.App.2d 976 (1966); *Nichols v. Arthur Murray, Inc.*, 248 Cal.App.2d 610 (1967); *Porter v. Arthur Murray, Inc.*, 149 Cal.App.2d 410 (1967); *Wickham v. Southland Corp.*, 168 Cal.App.3d 49 (1985).

they commit offenses under civil rights and criminal statutes.

FEDERAL STATUTES

Title 18 U.S.C. § 2 provides that any one becomes a principal to a criminal act who in any way aids or covers up for an offense. This could include federal judges, Justice Department attorneys, members of Congress, and the media.

Title 18 U.S.C. § 3. Accessory after the fact.[57] It is a felony for any person, who knows that an offense against the United States has been committed, to obstruct justice by assisting the perpetrators through blocking the reporting of the crimes by an informant or victim. This felony would include federal judges and Justice Department attorneys, members of Congress, media personnel, who knew about the criminal activities described within these pages and either refused to make the crimes known, or worse, who engaged in a coverup.

Title 18 U.S.C. § 4 (misprision of felony).[58] It becomes a felony if any person who knows of a federal crime does not promptly report it to a federal judge or other federal officer.

Title 18 U.S.C. § 35. Imparting or conveying false information.[59]

Title 18 U.S.C. § 153. Embezzlement by trustee or officer.[60] This felony is rampant in federal Chapter 11, 12, 13 courts, with the knowledge of federal judges, Justice Department officials, and many others.

Title 18 U.S.C. § 241. Conspiracy against rights of citizens.[61] This felony applies to anyone, including judges and Justice Department attorneys, who intimidate, threaten, or inflict harm upon any person in retaliation for exercising federal defenses against acts taken to silence him or block him from defending himself.

Title 18 U.S.C. § 371 Conspiracy to commit offense or to defraud United States.[62] There are many ways to commit an offense against, or to de-

---

[57] **Title 18 U.S.C. § 3. Accessory after the fact.** Whoever, knowing that an offense against the United States had been committed, receives, relieves, comforts or assists the offender in order to hinder or prevent his apprehension, trial or punishment, is an accessory after the fact.

[58] **Title 18 U.S.C. § 4. Misprision of felony.** Whoever, having knowledge of the actual commission of a felony cognizable by a court of the United States, conceals and does not as soon as possible make known the same to some judge or other person in civil or military authority under the United States, shall be fined not more than $500 or imprisoned not more than three years, or both.

[59] **Title 18 U.S.C. § 35. Importing or conveying false information.** (a) Whoever imparts or conveys or causes to be imparted or conveyed false information, knowing the information to be false...
(b) or with reckless disregard for the safety of human life, imparts or conveys or causes to be imparted or conveyed, false information, knowing the information to be false...shall be subject to a civil penalty...or imprisonment....

[60] **Title 18 U.S.C. § 153. Embezzlement by trustee or officer.** Whoever knowingly and fraudulently appropriates to his own use, embezzles, spends, or transfers any property or secretes or destroys any document belonging to the estate of a debtor which came into his charge as trustee, custodian, marshal, or other officer of the court, shall be fined not more than $5,000 or imprisoned not more than five years, or both.

[61] **Title 18 U.S.C. § 241. Conspiracy against rights of citizens.** If two or more persons conspire to injure, oppress, threaten, or intimidate any citizen in the free exercise or enjoyment of any right or privilege secured to him by the Constitution or laws of the United States, or because of his having so exercised the same;...They shall be fined...or imprisoned...or both;

[62] **Title 18 U.S.C. § 371.** If two or more persons conspire either to commit any offense against the United States, or to defraud the United States, or any agency thereof in any manner or for any purpose, and one or more of such persons do any act to effect the object of the conspiracy, each shall be fined not more than $10,000 or imprisoned not more than five years, or both.

fraud the United States. As a matter of law, the word "defraud" is broadly used to include obstructing the lawful operation of any government agency by any "deceit, craft or trickery, or at least by means that are dishonest." To convict someone, including a federal official, under Title 18 U.S.C. § 371, it is only necessary to show that the person (1) entered into an agreement (2) to obstruct a lawful function of the government (3) by deceitful or dishonest means and (4) had committed at least one overt act in furtherance of the conspiracy. Obstructing the lawful functions of the federal courts, or the Justice Department, would also cause violation of this statute. Prosecuting a citizen seeking to report government corruption would be a crime.

Title 18 U.S.C. § 1001. Statements or entries generally. It is a federal crime for **anyone** within the jurisdiction of any department or agency of the United States to knowingly and willfully falsify, conceal or cover up by any trick or scheme a material fact or to make any false, fictitious or fraudulent statement or representation.

Title 18 U.S.C. § 1341. Frauds and Swindles. This statute relates to using the mail to defraud another person or the United States.

Title 18 U.S.C. § 1343. Wire fraud. This section applies to anyone who defrauds another while using the telephone or other communications.

Title 28 U.S.C. § 1361. Action to compel an officer of the United States to perform his duty. This statute permits any citizens to invoke federal court jurisdiction to report government misconduct and to obtain a court order compelling a government official to halt the wrongful acts or to perform a lawful duty. A federal judge lacks jurisdiction to void, or to punish a citizen, for exercising this right.

Title 18 U.S.C. § 1505. Obstruction of proceedings before departments, agencies, and committees[63] This criminal statute was repeatedly violated by government personnel, primarily Justice Department attorneys and federal judges, who obstructed justice by blocking the reporting of federal crimes.

Title 18 U.S.C. § 1512. Tampering with a witness, victim, or an informant.[64] It is a crime to interfere or retaliate against a person seeking to report

---

[63] Title 18 U.S.C. § 1505. Obstruction of proceedings before departments, agencies, and committees. Whoever corruptly...influences, obstructs, or impedes or endeavors to influence, obstruct, or impede the due the proper administration of the law under which any pending proceeding is being had before any department or agency of the United States...shall be fined not more than $5,000 or imprisoned not more than five years, or both.

[64] Title 18 U.S.C. § 1512. Tampering with a witness, victim, or an informant.
(a) Whoever...prevents the attendance or testimony of any person in an official proceeding;
(b) prevents the production of a record...in an official proceeding;
(c) prevents the communication by any person to a law enforcement officer or judge of the United States, of information relating to the commission or possible commission of a federal offense...(2)(b) Whoever knowingly uses intimidation...or threatens another person, or attempts to do so, or engages in misleading conduct toward another person, with intent to (1) influence, delay or prevent the testimony of any person in an official proceeding; (2) cause or induce any person to (A) Withhold testimony, or withhold a record, document, or other object, from an official proceeding; (3) hinder, delay, or prevent the communication to a law enforcement officer or judge of the United States of information relating to the commission or possible commission of a federal offense...(c) Whoever intentionally harasses another person and thereby hinders, delays, prevents, or dissuades any person from (1) attending or testifying in an official proceeding; (2) reporting to a law enforcement officer or judge of the United States the commission or possible commission of a federal offense...(3) arresting or seeking the arrest of another person in connection with a federal

a crime. This would apply especially to Justice Department employees or judges.

Title 18 U.S.C. § 1513. Retaliating against a witness, victim, or an informant.[65] This criminal statute applies to anyone, including judges and Justice Department officials, who retaliate against anyone for reporting federal crimes.

Title 18 U.S.C. § 1515 (a)(3)(A). Misleading conduct means knowingly making false statements.[66] This criminal statute was violated by government personnel in the criminal activities described throughout these pages.

Title 18 U.S.C. § 1515 (a)(3)(B); Intentionally omitting information from a statement and thereby causing a portion of such statement to be misleading, or intentionally concealing a material fact.[67]

Title 18 U.S.C. § 1515 (a)(3)(C). With intent to mislead, knowingly submitting or inviting reliance on a writing that is false or otherwise lacking in authenticity.[68] Same as other section 1515 violations. Title 18 U.S.C. § 1515 (a)(3)(D). With intent to mislead, knowingly submitting...material that is misleading in a material aspect.[69]

Title 18 U.S.C. § 1515 (a)(3)(E). Knowingly using a trick or scheme to mislead. Misleading statements made by government personnel throughout these pages were violations of this statute.

Title 18 U.S.C. § 1621. Perjury generally.[70]

Title 18 U.S.C. § 1622. Subornation of perjury.[71] This felony was re-

---

offense; or (4) causing a criminal prosecution...to be sought or instituted, or assisting in such prosecution or proceeding...shall be fined...or imprisoned..

[65] **Title 18 U.S.C. § 1513. Retaliating against a witness, victim, or an informant.** (a) Whoever knowingly engages in any conduct and thereby causes...injury to another person...or threatens to do so, with intent to retaliate against any person for (1) the attendance of a witness or party at an official proceeding, or any testimony given or any record, document, or other object produced by a witness in an official proceeding; or (2) any information relating to the commission or possible commission of a federal offense...shall be...fined or...imprisoned...

[66] **Title 18 U.S.C. § 1515. Definitions of terms in criminal statutes (as used in sections 1512 and 1513).** (a)(2) the term "physical force" means physical action against another and includes confinement; [including prison.] (a)(3) the term "misleading conduct" means − (A) knowingly making a false statement; (B) **intentionally omitting information from a statement** and thereby causing a portion of such statement to be misleading, or intentionally concealing a material fact, and thereby creating a false impression by such statement; (C) with intent to mislead, knowingly submitting or inviting reliance on a writing or recording that is false...or otherwise lacking in authenticity; (D) with intent to mislead, knowingly submitting or inviting reliance on a ... object that is misleading in a material respect; or (E) knowingly using a trick, scheme, or device with intent to mislead; (4) the term "law enforcement officer" means an officer or employee of the Federal Government, or a person authorized to act for or on behalf of the Federal Government or serving the Federal Government as an adviser or consultant − (A) authorized under law to engage in or supervise the prevention, detection, investigation, or prosecution of an offense; (5) the term "bodily injury" means − (E) any other injury to the body, no matter how temporary. (a)(1) the term "official proceeding" means...(C) a proceeding before a Federal Government agency which is authorized by law. [FAA included.]"

[67] Title 18 U.S.C. § 1515 (a)(3)(B); Intentionally omitting information from a statement and thereby causing a portion of such statement to be misleading, or intentionally concealing a material fact.

[68] **Title 18 U.S.C. § 1515 (a)(3)(C).** With intent to mislead, knowingly submitting or inviting reliance on a writing that is false or otherwise lacking in authenticity.

[69] Title 18 U.S.C. § 1515 (a)(3)(D). With intent to mislead, knowingly submitting ... material that is misleading in a material aspect.

[70] **Title 18 U.S.C. § 1621. Perjury generally.** Whoever (1) having taken an oath before a competent tribunal...willfully and contrary to such oath states...any material matter which he does not believe to be true, he shall be fined...or imprisoned..

peatedly perpetrated by FAA management during the FAA Denver hearing.

Title 18 U.S.C. § 1623. False declarations before grand jury or court.[72] **Title 18 U.S.C. § 2071. Concealment, removal, or mutilation generally.**[73] This criminal statute was violated by the FAA and NTSB in covering up for behind the scene facts in several air disasters described in detail in *Unfriendly Skies*.

Title 18 U.S.C. § 2075. Officer failing to make reports; felony omission of a duty to act.[74] This criminal statute was repeatedly violated by federal employees and officials, federal judges, members of Congress, and particularly Department of Justice employees

Fraud arising in misleading government reports. It is a federal offense to prepare a report that omits material information that as a result of the omission results in a different inference. This offense is described in many federal decisions, including *Branch v. Tunnel*, 937 F.2d 1382 (9th Cir. 1991) and *Orson v. Tyler*, 771 F.2d 277, 281 (7th Cir. 1985). In these cases the courts held that deception exists when material omission in a writing exists, wherein less than the total story is described, and where a different inference is drawn.

---

[71] **Title 18 U.S.C. § 1622. Subornation of perjury.** Whoever procures another to commit any perjury is guilty of subornation of perjury, and shall be fined...or imprisoned...

[72] **Title 18 U.S.C. § 1623. False declarations before grand jury or court.** (a) Whoever under oath ... or statement under penalty of perjury...before or ancillary to any court or grand jury of the United States knowingly makes any false material declaration, or makes or uses any other information...knowing the same to contain any false material declaration, shall be fined...or imprisoned...

[73] **Title 18 U.S.C. § 2071. Concealment, removal, or mutilation generally.** (a) Whoever willfully and unlawfully conceals, removes, mutilates, obliterates, or destroys, or attempts to do so, or, with intent to do so takes and carries away any record, proceeding, map, book, paper, document, or other thing, filed or deposited with any clerk or officer of any court of the United States, or in any public office, or with any judicial or public officer of the United States, shall be fined not more than $2,000 or imprisoned not more than three years, or both.

[74] **Title 18 U.S.C. § 2075. Officer failing to make returns or reports.** Every officer who neglects or refuses to make any return or report which he is required to make at state times by any Act of Congress or regulation of the Department of the Treasury, other than his accounts, within the time prescribed by such Act or regulation, shall be fined not more than $1,000.

The following books may be of interest:

- *Defrauding America* (3rd edition) Rodney Stich, Diablo Western Press.
- *Unfriendly Skies, Saga of Corruption.* (3rd edition) Rodney Stich. Diablo Western Press. 1990.
- *A Very Thin Line, the Iran-Contra Affairs.* Theodore Draper, Simon & Schuster. 1991.
- *Blond Ghost*, Ted Shackley and the CIA's Crusades. David Corn. 1994.
- *Bluegrass Conspiracy.* Sally Denton. Avon Books. 1990.
- *Called To Serve.* Col. James Gritz. Lazarus. 1991.
- *Casey, The Lives and Secrets of William J. Casey.* Joseph Persico. Penguin, 1991.
- *CIA and Cult of Intelligence.* Victor Marchetti and John Marks. Knopf. 1964.
- *Cocaine Politics, Drugs, Armies, and the CIA in Central America.* Peter Dale Scott and Jonathan Marshall. University of California Press. 1991.
- *Compromised, Clinton, Bush and the CIA.* Terry Reed & John Cummings. SPI. 1994.
- *Den of Thieves.* James Stewart. Simon and Schuster. 1991.
- *Disavow, A CIA Saga of Betrayal.* Rodney Stich and T. Conan Russell. Hallmark. 1996.
- *Disposal Patriot, Revelations of a Soldier in America's Secret Wars.* Jack Terrell with Ron Martz. National Press Books. 1992.
- *Dope, Inc.* By the editors of Executive Intelligence Review. 1992.
- *Everybody Has His Own Gringo.* Glenn Garvin. 1992.
- *Inside the CIA.* Revealing the Secrets of the World's Most Powerful Spy Agency. Ronald Kessler. Pocket Books. 1992.
- *Invisible Government.* David Wise and Thomas Ross. Random House. 1964.
- *Iran-Contra, the Final Report.* Times Books. 1994.
- *Kings of Cocaine,* Guy Gugliotta and Jeff Leen. Harper. 1989.
- *My Turn To Speak*, Bank-Sadr. Brassey's. 1991.
- *October Surprise,* America's Hostages in Iran and the Election of Ronald Reagan. Gary Sick. Times Books. 1991.
- *October Surprise.* Barbara Honegger. Tudor. 1989.
- *Our Man in Panama.* The Shrewd Rise and Brutal Fall of Manual Noriega. John Dinges. Times Books. 1991.
- *Out of Control.* Leslie Cockburn. Atlantic Monthly Press. 1987.
- *Powderburns, Cocaine, Contras & and Drug War.* Celerino Castillo III and Dave Harmon. Mosaic Press. 1994.
- *Profits of War,* Inside the Secret U.S.-Israeli Arms Network. Ari Ben-Menashe. Sheridan Square Press. 1992.
- *Secret Team.* L. Fletcher Prouty. Institute for Historical Review. 1973.
- *Sellout,* Aldrich Ames and the Corruption of the CIA. James Adams. Viking. 1995.
- *The Big White Lie*, the CIA and the Cocaine/Crack Epidemic. Michael

Levine. Thunder's Mouth Press. 1993.
- *The CIA and the Cult of Intelligence.* Victor Marchetti and John D. Marks. Knopf. 1974.
- *The Cocaine Wars.* Paul Eddy with Hugo Sabogal and Sara Walden. Norton. 1988.
- *The Mafia, CIA and George Bush.* Corruption, Greed, and Abuse of Power in the Nation's Highest Office. Pete Brewton. SPI. 1992.
- *The Politics of Heroin,* CIA Complicity in the Global Drug Trade. Alfred W. McCoy. Lawrence Hill Books. 1991.
- *Whiteout—The CIA, Drugs and the Press.* Alexander Cockburn and Jeffrey St. Clair.
- *Drug Crazy,* Mike Gray.
- *Above the Law—Secret Deals, Political Fixes, and Other Misadventures of the U.S. Department of Justice,* David Burnham.